Netherlands

Ryan Ver Berkmoes
Jeremy Gray

LONELY PLANET PUBLICATIONS
Melbourne • Oakland • London • Paris

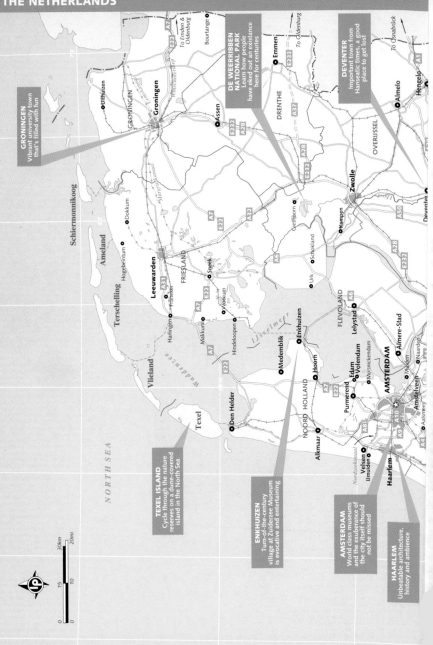

GRONINGEN
Vibrant university town that's filled with fun

DE WEERRIBBEN NATIONAL PARK
Learn how people have eked out an existance here for centuries

DEVENTER
Important town from Hanseatic times, a good place to get lost

TEXEL ISLAND
Cycle through the nature reserves on a dune-covered island in the North Sea

ENKHUIZEN
Turn-of-the-century village at Zuiderzee Museum is evocative and entertaining

AMSTERDAM
World class museums and the exuberance of the city itself should not be missed

HAARLEM
Unbeatable architecture, history and ambience

NORTH SEA

Contents – Maps

CYCLING IN THE NETHERLANDS

Cycling Routes 104
Baronie Route 105
Mantelingen Route 106
Amstel Route 107
Paterwoldsemeer Route 108

NOORD HOLLAND & FLEVOLAND

Noord Holland & Flevoland 164
Edam 169
Alkmaar 177
Texel 180
Haarlem 184

UTRECHT

Utrecht 198
Utrecht City 199

ZUID HOLLAND & ZEELAND

Zuid Holland & Zeeland 208
Leiden 212
Den Haag (The Hague)
Centre 219
Den Haag (The Hague)
Area 222
Gouda 228
Delft 231
Rotterdam 237
Dordrecht 248
Middelburg 253

FRIESLAND

Friesland 261
Leeuwarden 262
Frisian Islands 270

GRONINGEN & DRENTHE

Groningen & Drenthe 275
Groningen City 277

OVERIJSSEL & GELDERLAND

Overijssel & Gelderland 287
Deventer 288
Nijmegen 294
De Hoge Veluwe 299

NOORD BRABANT & LIMBURG

Noord Brabant & Limburg ..303
Den Bosch 305
Maastricht 308

COLOUR MAPS
end of book

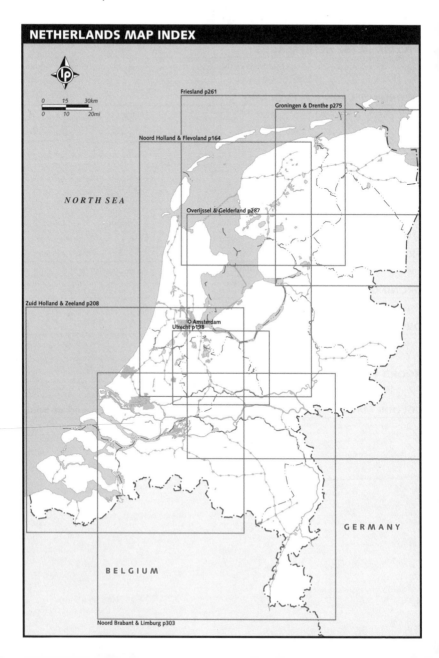

The Authors

Ryan Ver Berkmoes

Ryan grew up in Santa Cruz, California, which he left at age 17 for college in the Midwest because he was too young and naive to realise what a beautiful place it is. His first job was in Chicago at a small muckraking publication where he had the impressive title of managing editor because he was second on a two-person editorial staff and the first person was called editor. After a year of 60-hour weeks, Ryan took his first trip to Europe which lasted for seven months and confirmed his long-suspected wanderlust. Since then his byline has appeared in scores of publications and he has covered everything from wars to bars. He definitely prefers the latter. Among his work for Lonely Planet, he is the author of *Chicago* and *Moscow*, co-wrote *Texas*, *Canada* and *Western Europe*, co-ordinated *Russia*, *Ukraine & Belarus*, *Great Lakes*, *Out to Eat London*, *Britain* and *England*. In the future, Ryan hopes to add more warm weather destinations to the list above, although he found that relaxing in a warm Dutch brown cafe with people who could pronounce his surname had its pleasures as well. He and his journalist wife Sara Marley reside in London near the point of inspiration for noted musician Nigel Tufnel.

Jeremy Gray

A Louisiana native, Jeremy studied literature and business in the wilds of Texas before taking a university scholarship to Germany in 1984. Infatuated with Europe, he chucked his MBA plans and embarked on a glittering career as an English teacher and clerk for the US Air Force in Wiesbaden (speciality: plumbing translations).

Next came a master's degree in politics at Canterbury and a string of jobs in the rough-and-tumble of financial journalism – in Woking, Surrey, and in equally lovely Frankfurt. While freelancing for the *Financial Times* in Holland he tumbled into Lonely Planet, and has since worked on titles including *Germany*, *France* and LP's city guides to *Munich* and *Montreal*. Jeremy lives canalside in the Oostelijke Eilanden district of Amsterdam.

FROM THE AUTHORS

Ryan Ver Berkmoes Working on this book was a pleasure thanks to the help, inspiration and friendship of many people. They include: the fabulous Marlien Meijer in the London NBT office, Marin Geurts and Wilma Wilma Lankhorst in Nijmegen, the van Essen family in Giethoorn, Jeremy Bangs and Bart in 't Veld in Leiden, Marianne van der Zalm-Waterreus in the Hague, Olga Coolen in Utrecht, the amazing Gert-Jan Jacobs in Deventer, Irene van Oort, Elain de Vries, Athal Wynhoven, Pepÿn Wÿnhoven and the delightful Wim Gloudemans in Maastricht, Miranda van der

Heul and Debbie Prade in Rotterdam, Janet Gervedink Nijhuis in Groningen, the fascinating Guus de la Bije in Leeuwarden, Trees de Jong in Utrecht and Rodney Maton at Holland Rail. There are countless more, but I'll have to stop with special thanks to the guy with a cat on his shoulder who leaned out of his window as I examined the Hof in Dordrecht one rainy night and told me its entire history. The Dutch are a remarkably open and generous people.

At LP, Chris Wyness and Lisa Borg were delights as always and thanks to Rob van Driesum for first talking to me about the book over countless glasses of port. Jeremy Gray, who has been around long before my life at LP, was a sterling partner. Who would have thought it would come to this?

Finally, thanks to my grandfather Peter Ver Berkmoes, who taught me to love cheese at an early age. And the biggest thanks of all to Sara Marley, love of my life.

Jeremy Gray Those deserving gratitude include Rob van Driesum and Nikki Hall, authors of Lonely Planet's Amsterdam city guide, for allowing me to use their excellent material, and all the editors and cartographers in Melbourne who helped make this book a reality. Thanks are also due to the Amsterdam Tourist Board and VVV tourist offices in North Holland and Flevoland for their generous support. Last but not least, I send a *hartelijk bedankt* to co-author Ryan Ver Berkmoes for his expert blurring of the line between work and fun.

This Book

From the Publisher

This is the 1st edition of *Netherlands*. Coordinating author Ryan Ver Berkmoes wrote the introductory chapters as well as the regional chapters of Utrecht, Zuid Holland & Zeeland, Friesland, Groningen & Drenthe, Overijssel & Gelderland and Noord Brabant & Limburg. Jeremy Gray was responsible for the Amsterdam chapter, which drew on the *Amsterdam* city guide written by Rob van Driesum and Nicki Hall, as well as the Noord Holland & Flevoland and Cycling in the Netherlands chapters.

Production of this edition of Netherlands was coordinated by Birgit Jordan (mapping and design) and Darren O'Connell (editorial). Shelley Muir and Yvonne Byron assisted with editing and proofing. Ray Thomson, Adrian Persoglia, Mark Germanchis and Paul Dawson assisted with mapping. Cris Gibcus assisted with local knowledge. Quentin Frayne prepared the Language section and the cover was designed by Simon Bracken. New illustrations were supplied by Mick Weldon and Kelli Hamblet.

Foreword

ABOUT LONELY PLANET GUIDEBOOKS

The story begins with a classic travel adventure: Tony and Maureen Wheeler's 1972 journey across Europe and Asia to Australia. Useful information about the overland trail did not exist at that time, so Tony and Maureen published the first Lonely Planet guidebook to meet a growing need.

From a kitchen table, then from a tiny office in Melbourne (Australia), Lonely Planet has become the largest independent travel publisher in the world, an international company with offices in Melbourne, Oakland (USA), London (UK) and Paris (France).

Today Lonely Planet guidebooks cover the globe. There is an ever-growing list of books and there's information in a variety of forms and media. Some things haven't changed. The main aim is still to help make it possible for adventurous travellers to get out there – to explore and better understand the world.

At Lonely Planet we believe travellers can make a positive contribution to the countries they visit – if they respect their host communities and spend their money wisely. Since 1986 a percentage of the income from each book has been donated to aid projects and human rights campaigns.

Updates Lonely Planet thoroughly updates each guidebook as often as possible. This usually means there are around two years between editions, although for more unusual or more stable destinations the gap can be longer. Check the imprint page (following the colour map at the beginning of the book) for publication dates.

Between editions up-to-date information is available in two free newsletters – the paper *Planet Talk* and email *Comet* (to subscribe, contact any Lonely Planet office) – and on our Web site at www.lonelyplanet.com. The *Upgrades* section of the Web site covers a number of important and volatile destinations and is regularly updated by Lonely Planet authors. *Scoop* covers news and current affairs relevant to travellers. And, lastly, the *Thorn Tree* bulletin board and *Postcards* section of the site carry unverified, but fascinating, reports from travellers.

Correspondence The process of creating new editions begins with the letters, postcards and emails received from travellers. This correspondence often includes suggestions, criticisms and comments about the current editions. Interesting excerpts are immediately passed on via newsletters and the Web site, and everything goes to our authors to be verified when they're researching on the road. We're keen to get more feedback from organisations or individuals who represent communities visited by travellers.

Lonely Planet gathers information for everyone who's curious about the planet – and especially for those who explore it first-hand. Through guidebooks, phrasebooks, activity guides, maps, literature, newsletters, image library, TV series and Web site we act as an information exchange for a worldwide community of travellers.

Research Authors aim to gather sufficient practical information to enable travellers to make informed choices and to make the mechanics of a journey run smoothly. They also research historical and cultural background to help enrich the travel experience and allow travellers to understand and respond appropriately to cultural and environmental issues.

Authors don't stay in every hotel because that would mean spending a couple of months in each medium-sized city and, no, they don't eat at every restaurant because that would mean stretching belts beyond capacity. They do visit hotels and restaurants to check standards and prices, but feedback based on readers' direct experiences can be very helpful.

Many of our authors work undercover, others aren't so secretive. None of them accept freebies in exchange for positive write-ups. And none of our guidebooks contain any advertising.

Production Authors submit their raw manuscripts and maps to offices in Australia, USA, UK or France. Editors and cartographers – all experienced travellers themselves – then begin the process of assembling the pieces. When the book finally hits the shops, some things are already out of date, we start getting feedback from readers and the process begins again ...

WARNING & REQUEST

Things change – prices go up, schedules change, good places go bad and bad places go bankrupt – nothing stays the same. So, if you find things better or worse, recently opened or long since closed, please tell us and help make the next edition even more accurate and useful. We genuinely value all the feedback we receive. Julie Young coordinates a well travelled team that reads and acknowledges every letter, postcard and email and ensures that every morsel of information finds its way to the appropriate authors, editors and cartographers for verification.

Everyone who writes to us will find their name in the next edition of the appropriate guidebook. They will also receive the latest issue of *Planet Talk*, our quarterly printed newsletter, or *Comet*, our monthly email newsletter. Subscriptions to both newsletters are free. The very best contributions will be rewarded with a free guidebook.

Excerpts from your correspondence may appear in new editions of Lonely Planet guidebooks, the Lonely Planet Web site, *Planet Talk* or *Comet*, so please let us know if you *don't* want your letter published or your name acknowledged.

Send all correspondence to the Lonely Planet office closest to you:

Australia: Locked Bag 1, Footscray, Victoria 3011
USA: 150 Linden St, Oakland, CA 94607
UK: 10A Spring Place, London NW5 3BH
France: 1 rue du Dahomey, 75011 Paris

Or email us at: talk2us@lonelyplanet.com.au

For news, views and updates see our Web site: www.lonelyplanet.com

HOW TO USE A LONELY PLANET GUIDEBOOK

The best way to use a Lonely Planet guidebook is any way you choose. At Lonely Planet we believe the most memorable travel experiences are often those that are unexpected, and the finest discoveries are those you make yourself. Guidebooks are not intended to be used as if they provide a detailed set of infallible instructions!

Contents All Lonely Planet guidebooks follow roughly the same format. The Facts about the Destination chapters or sections give background information ranging from history to weather. Facts for the Visitor gives practical information on issues like visas and health. Getting There & Away gives a brief starting point for researching travel to and from the destination. Getting Around gives an overview of the transport options when you arrive.

The peculiar demands of each destination determine how subsequent chapters are broken up, but some things remain constant. We always start with background, then proceed to sights, places to stay, places to eat, entertainment, getting there and away, and getting around information – in that order.

Heading Hierarchy Lonely Planet headings are used in a strict hierarchical structure that can be visualised as a set of Russian dolls. Each heading (and its following text) is encompassed by any preceding heading that is higher on the hierarchical ladder.

Entry Points We do not assume guidebooks will be read from beginning to end, but that people will dip into them. The traditional entry points are the list of contents and the index. In addition, however, some books have a complete list of maps and an index map illustrating map coverage.

There may also be a colour map that shows highlights. These highlights are dealt with in greater detail in the Facts for the Visitor chapter, along with planning questions and suggested itineraries. Each chapter covering a geographical region usually begins with a locator map and another list of highlights. Once you find something of interest in a list of highlights, turn to the index.

Maps Maps play a crucial role in Lonely Planet guidebooks and include a huge amount of information. A legend is printed on the back page. We seek to have complete consistency between maps and text, and to have every important place in the text captured on a map. Map key numbers usually start in the top left corner.

Although inclusion in a guidebook usually implies a recommendation we cannot list every good place. Exclusion does not necessarily imply criticism. In fact there are a number of reasons why we might exclude a place – sometimes it is simply inappropriate to encourage an influx of travellers.

Introduction

It's not just Amsterdam which provides a good reason for a trip to the Netherlands. The capital city's cafes, canals and churches are definitely dynamite reason enough to visit, but you'd only be scratching the surface of what this country has to offer.

Contrary to popular belief, Holland constitutes just two of the 12 Dutch provinces. In Holland you'll find deeply historic cities such as Haarlem, Leiden and Delft and the vibrant city of Rotterdam.

Along the northern coast are five islands with shimmering golden sand and vast natural expanses. The north also has the surprising city of Groningen and the pleasurable lakes and canals of Friesland.

In the heart of the country, Deventer is one of many ancient Dutch towns that grew wealthy as part of the Hanseatic League in the 12th century. You can go even further back in history to the Roman era at Nijmegen and down south at Maastricht. The latter was the spot where the European Union was born, a fitting honour as Maastricht is the most international of cities. Also in the south are the fascinating sea defences and dikes of Zeeland.

And that's just a start. Great Dutch artists have spanned the centuries and at the great museums of Amsterdam and Den Haag, you can see the masterpieces of Rembrandt and his contemporaries. Near Arnhem, you can see one of the world's finest collections of Van Gogh at a museum in the middle of a delightful national park.

Amsterdam's phenomenal and diverse nightlife is world-famous but it's not unique. The wonderful Dutch brown cafes, where you can pass hours in the mellow companionship of friends new and old, can be found in every town. You'll discover that cliches such as tulips and windmills have their joys too. Ribbons of flowers swathe the fields in colour for as far as the eye can see every spring near Leiden. Elsewhere it will seem like a tulip or daffodil is growing in every empty pot and plot in the country. And

being in a working windmill is fascinating; it's like stepping aboard a creaking old sailing ship.

Seeing the countryside is another treat. The Dutch live on bicycles and you can too. Almost every train station has a shop to rent a bike and soon you're off on the ubiquitous bike paths blazing your own trail. The trains linking the stations are a delight as well. The service is fast and frequent and you can get from one end of the Netherlands to the other in under three hours.

Finally there's the Dutch themselves, warm, friendly and funny. You'll have a hard time being alone in a cafe as someone will soon strike up a conversation, and usually in English. In researching this book, time after time we were struck by the generosity of the Dutch, who wanted us to enjoy their country as well as understand it.

So prepare yourself for a great trip. Enjoy Amsterdam, don't miss Maastricht or Rotterdam and pick a bunch of small towns to add contrast. It's a very big small country.

11

Facts about the Netherlands

HISTORY

Between waves of invaders and invading waves, the Netherlands has a turbulent past that is not immediately apparent to a visitor. But with a little background knowledge, the evidence of the Dutch people's colourful past becomes readily apparent. One important point to remember is that the Netherlands only came into existence in 1579. Before that, the entire region of the Low Countries – today's Netherlands as well as Belgium and Luxembourg – was intertwined politically and culturally.

The confirmed evidence of human habitation in the Netherlands dates back 250,000 years at a quarry near Maastricht. These earliest inhabitants were literally cave men and women who were drawn to the natural shelter provided by the scores of caves in the local soft limestone.

Although hard evidence is scant, it is thought that roving bands of hunters and gatherers could be found throughout the Netherlands from that time until modern history began. The first large-scale evidence of past inhabitants is just that: large. Called *hunebedden*, the long burial monuments built from huge stones are primarily found in the province of Drenthe. As is the case with the Druids at Stonehenge, nobody knows much about the builders, except that around 3000 BC they showed a remarkable aptitude for moving huge rocks into carefully planned patterns that are thought to be burial chambers.

The next significant evidence of the Netherlands' ancient past can be found near Drenthe in the province of Friesland. Here, over a period of a few centuries roughly 2000 years ago, the local people built enormous mounds out of the local mud to give them a place to live above the frequent sea-driven floods. Today over 1000 of these *terpen* can still be found dotting the otherwise pancake-flat landscape. It's amazing to ponder the amount of manual labour that must have been necessary to build these hills.

The first known invaders were the Romans, who, under Julius Caesar, waged a seven-year conquest of the region from 59 to 52 BC. The Romans settled a wide area along the various branches of the Rhine River (which then flowed farther north than they do today) and counted a variety of Celtic and Germanic tribes among their subjects. Over the next three centuries, the Romans built their famous roads and towns and organised large farms. However, they never bothered to dirty their feet, so to speak, in the muddy regions to the north, such as terp-covered Friesland.

The Roman era lasted until the 3rd century. Even during this time, the Franks, an aggressive German tribe to the east, had been sniffing around the region. Between the 7th and 8th centuries, the Franks finished their conquest of the Low Countries and concentrated on converting the local populace to Christianity, using force whenever necessary. Charlemagne became king in 768 and he built a palace at Nijmegen on the Waal River. After his death in 814, the empire fell apart and power passed on to a whole plethora of local fiefdoms and lords.

Growth of Towns

The next people to pose a threat were the Vikings during the 9th and 10th centuries. Sailing up the multitude of rivers, the ill-tempered Scandinavians engaged in your basic looting and pillaging at every opportunity. This caused the various local rulers to develop their own defences, even though they had nominal allegiance to the Holy Roman Empire. The many fortified towns grew quickly and instituted their own forms of government and laws.

Conflict soon arose between the increasingly affluent merchants and artists in the towns and the lords, who still dominated the countryside. The townspeople would back their local lord when he wanted to muscle into someone else's territory, but in return they would demand various freedoms.

Beginning in the 12th century, these relationships were codified through charters, documents which not only spelled out the limits of the lord's power, but also detailed a range of other legal and bureaucratic matters, not the least of which was taxation.

Many Dutch towns, especially those like Deventer and Zwolle which were on the IJssel River, joined the Hanseatic League. This mostly German federation of towns and cities grew wealthy through its single-minded development of laws, regulations and other policies that promoted trade. In many ways it was a very early forerunner of the European Union.

Meanwhile the many little lords met their match in the dukes of Burgundy, who gradually took over the Low Countries. Duke Philip the Good, who ruled from 1419 to 1467, showed the towns of the Low Countries who was boss by essentially telling them to stuff their charters. Although this limited the towns' freedoms, it also brought to the region a degree of stability that had been missing during the era of quibbling lords.

The 15th century was a period of great prosperity for the Low Countries. The Dutch became adept at shipbuilding in support of their Hanseatic trade. Merchants grew wealthy selling pricey luxury items such as tapestries, fashionable clothing, paintings, jewellery and pottery. However, the Dutch also made money from more mundane commodities, especially salted herring and beer. The former capitalised on the vast North Sea fisheries. With beer, the Dutch produced a superior product that was popular for its clean and crisp taste. This was at a time when most European beer was as dubious as the murky water from which it was brewed.

With their relative wealth easily tapped through taxes, the Low Countries were coveted by a succession of rulers. In 1482, Mary of Burgundy, Philip's granddaughter, passed on the Low Countries to her pleasantly named son, Philip the Fair. There followed a period of intrigue worthy of a costume drama: Philip married Joanna, the daughter of King Ferdinand and Queen Isabella of Spain. He then bequeathed the

Low Countries to his son Charles in 1506. A member of the Spanish branch of the house of Habsburg, Charles V was crowned Holy Roman Emperor in 1530. He was a fairly benevolent ruler and the Low Countries' wealth continued to grow. However, this changed dramatically when Charles handed over Spain and the Low Countries to his son Philip II in 1555.

The Fight for Independence

Philip II had no love for the Low Countries. He was both fiercely Catholic and fiercely Spanish. Conflict was inevitable, especially as the religious reform movement swept the Low Countries. Lutherans had some influence, but most colourful were the Anabaptists, who were polygamists, communists and also promoted nudity as a means of equality among the masses (obviously this was a seasonal aspect). However, it was Calvinism which eventually came to be the main challenge not only to the Roman Catholic Church in the Low Countries, but to Philip's rule as well.

A big believer in the Inquisition, Philip went after the Protestants with a vengeance. Matters came to a head in 1566 when the puritanical Calvinists went on a rampage through Catholic churches destroying art and other treasures. Evidence of this is still readily apparent in the barren interiors of surviving Dutch churches today.

Religion was not the only issue causing strife between the Dutch and Philip. High taxes (a perennial revolution starter) and restrictions on trade had stirred dissent among the merchants. Finally deciding that enough was enough, Philip sent one of his cronies, the Duke of Alba to the Netherlands along with an army of 10,000. The duke was not one to take prisoners and his forces slaughtered thousands. It was the beginning of the Dutch war of independence which was to last from 1568 to 1648.

The Prince of Orange, William the Silent, so called for his refusal to argue over religious issues, became the leader of the Dutch revolt against Spanish rule and was summarily outlawed by Philip. William, who had been Philip's lieutenant in Holland, Zeeland

and Utrecht, began to rely on the Dutch Calvinists for his chief support. William championed the principle of toleration and this philosophy became part of the foundation of an independent Dutch state. The rebels' cause, however, was hampered by lack of money and patchy support from towns.

In 1572 the war took a turn for the better for the Dutch as for once help – rather than harm – came from the sea. William hired a bunch of English pirates to fight for his cause. Known as the Watergeuzen, or Sea Beggars, they sailed up the myriad of Dutch rivers and seized town after town from the surprised and land-bound Spanish forces. By the end of the year William controlled every city except Amsterdam.

The Spanish responded by sacking the Duke of Alba and sending in a new commander, Alessandro Farnese, who was a more able leader. Much of the 1570s saw a constant shift of power as one side or the other gained temporary supremacy.

In 1579 the Low Countries split for good, when the more Protestant and more rebellious northern provinces formed the Union of Utrecht, an explicitly anti-Spanish alliance that became known as the United Provinces. This formed the basis for the Netherlands as we know it today. The southern portions of the Low Countries had always remained Catholic and were much more open to compromise with Spain. They eventually became Belgium.

Although the United Provinces had declared their independence from Spain, the war dragged on. In 1584, they suffered a major blow when William was assassinated in Delft. The English (this time the government, as opposed to pirates) assisted the Dutch cause from 1585 to 1587 and the Spanish were weakened further by the English victory over the Armada in 1588. The Dutch, in a series of brilliant military campaigns, drove the Spanish out of the United Provinces by 1600 and in 1609 a truce was declared. Trouble with Spain was far from over, however, and fighting resumed in 1621 as part of the larger Thirty Years' War throughout Europe. In 1648 the Treaty of Westphalia, which ended the Thirty Years'

War, included the proviso that Spain recognise the independence of the United Provinces, ending the 80-year conflict between the Netherlands and Spain.

The Golden Age

The 17th century is the period of Dutch history known as the 'Golden Age', a time of great economic prosperity and cultural importance. Building upon the economic success of the 15th and early 16th centuries, the United Provinces became the foremost commercial and maritime power of the Continent, with Amsterdam the financial centre of Europe. Dutch vessels transported most of Europe's cargo. Even at the peak of the rebellion, the Spanish had no alternative but to use Dutch boats for transporting their grain. The Dutch then used this revenue to help fund the revolution.

The sciences and the arts flourished in the robust political and economic climate. The Dutch infatuation with tulips began to sprout during the Golden Age, with the mid-1630s representing the zenith of the tulip market.

The Dutch East India Company was formed in 1602 and quickly became the world's first multinational corporation. The company quickly grew to monopolise shipping and trade routes east of Africa's Cape of Good Hope and west of the Strait of Magellan, making it the largest trading company of the 17th century. The Dutch East India Company imported costly spices and Asian luxury items such as Chinese porcelain. The company was almost a sovereign state as it was permitted to raise its own armed forces and to establish colonies. It even had its own navy.

The Dutch West India Company, founded in 1621, traded with Africa and the Americas. It enjoyed the same freedoms and monopoly power as the Dutch East India Company and it was at the centre of the American slave trade. Explorers working for both companies discovered or conquered countries including New Zealand, Malaysia, Sri Lanka and Mauritius. Working for the Dutch East India Company, Henry Hudson stumbled upon the island of

Manhattan in 1609 as he searched for a Northwest Passage, and the Dutch soon settled there, naming it New Amsterdam.

The Union of Utrecht promised religious tolerance and this led to a surprising amount of religious diversity, a rare situation in Europe at the time. Calvinism was the official religion of the government, but various other Protestants, Jews and Catholics were allowed to practise their faith. However, in a legacy from the troubles with Spain, Catholics had to worship in private, which led to the creation of clandestine churches.

Culturally, the United Provinces flourished. The wealth of the merchant class supported scores of artists. Among the most renowned were Jan Vermeer (1631–75), Jan Steen (1626–79) and Frans Hals (1580–1666), with the most illustrious being Rembrandt van Rijn (1606–69). See the Arts section later in this chapter. The sciences and scholarship also thrived. Dutch physicist and astronomer Christiaan Huygens discovered Saturn's rings in 1655 and invented the pendulum clock two years later. Celebrated rationalist philosopher and religious thinker Benedict de Spinoza wrote *Ethics Demonstrated with Geometrical Order* whose thesis was that the universe is identical with God. Frenchman Rene Descartes, known for his philosophy, 'I think, therefore I am', found an intellectual freedom to be himself in the Netherlands and stayed for two decades during this time.

Politically, after the Dutch Republic prevailed in its conflicts with Spain it faced internal governmental struggles. Following the Peace of Westphalia in 1648, the House of Orange-Nassau battled the republicans over control of the country. The princes favoured centralising power under the Prince of Orange, who would be chief magistrate, or stadholder, while the republicans, or states' rights party, believed the cities and provinces should retain the power to run their own affairs. Prince William II acted swiftly to contain the dispute and was victorious. But then he died suddenly three months later, one week before his infant son was born. The leaders of the States of Holland exploited this power vacuum by calling a special assembly that abolished the stadholder and authority was decentralised. The dominant political figure for the republicans was Johann de Witt, who later became council pensionary to the States of Holland and acted as virtual prime minister.

Perhaps it was inevitable, given their competing interests around the world, but in 1652 England and the United Provinces went to war. One of the main issues was the English attempts to muscle in on the Dutch East India Company's monopoly. However, most of the issues were far from clear-cut and in an era marked by political intrigue the period was really one great diplomatic soap opera. The English and the Dutch went from enemies to allies to enemies again repeatedly. This hotchpotch of alliances variously included Spain, France, Sweden and other European states as each of the powers tried to gain supremacy. The navies, which fought most of the battles, often had no idea if ships encountered from another country were to be considered friends or foe. During one round of treaties resulting from the conflicts, the Dutch agreed to give New Amsterdam to the English (who promptly renamed it New York) in return for Surinam in South America.

In 1672 King Louis XIV's army marched across the Netherlands. Unfortunately for the Dutch, the country had devoted most of its resources to its navy, instead of its army, leaving the country nearly helpless against the French invasion. De Witt was blamed for the troubles and the country again turned to the House of Orange. William III of Orange was appointed captain general and admiral general, in addition to being named stadholder of Holland and Zeeland. Later that year, de Witt was murdered by an angry mob loyal to William.

In 1677 William sought to improve relations with the English through rather unconventional means: he married his cousin Mary, daughter of the English king James II. Opponents of the king feared that the Roman Catholic Church would be restored in England, so they secretly invited William to invade the country in 1688. Perhaps sensing he was no longer welcome in England,

Mad about Tulips

During a period of a few months in late 1636 and early 1637, a mania for tulips swept the Netherlands – speculative buying and selling that saw the price of bulbs increase more than 10-fold to the point where some examples cost more than an Amsterdam house. Driven by alcohol-fuelled traders, the market went wild as even ordinary people sank all of their savings – however meagre – in a few bulbs. Needless to say, it didn't last.

Tulips had originated as wild flowers in Central Asia and were first cultivated by the Turks, who filled their courts with these beautiful spring blossoms ('tulip' is Turkish for turban). In the mid-1500s, the Habsburg ambassador to Istanbul brought some bulbs back to Vienna where the imperial botanist, Carolus Clusius, learned how to propagate them. In 1590, Clusius became director of the Hortus Botanicus in Leiden – Europe's oldest botanical garden – and had great success growing and cross-breeding tulips in Holland's cool, damp climate and fertile delta soil.

The exotic flowers with their frilly petals and 'flamed' streaks of colour attracted the attention of wealthy merchants, who put them in their living rooms and hallways to impress visitors. As wealth and savings spread downwards through society so too did the taste for exotic products, and tulips were no exception. Growers rose to service the demand.

Ironically, the frilly petals and colour streaks were symptoms of an infection by the mosaic virus transmitted by a louse that thrived on peaches and potatoes – healthy tulips are solid, smooth and monotone. Turks already knew that the most beautiful tulips grew under fruit trees but the virus itself wasn't discovered until the 20th century.

The most beautiful tulips in 17th-century Holland were also the weakest due to heavy cross-breeding and grafting, which made them even more susceptible to the virus no-one knew about. They were notoriously difficult to cultivate and their blossoms unpredictable. A speculative frenzy ensued, and people paid top florin for the finest bulbs that would change hands many times before they sprouted. Vast profits were made and everyone joined in. Speculators fell over themselves to out-bid each other. The fact that such bidding often took place in taverns and was fuelled by alcohol no doubt added to the enthusiasm.

James fled to France, and William and Mary were named king and queen of England in 1689. Using his strong diplomatic skills, William created the Grand Alliance that joined England, the United Provinces, Spain, Sweden and several German states to fight the expansionist ambitions of France's Louis XIV.

The Grand Alliance successfully defeated the French several times and in 1697 Louis XIV agreed to give up most of the territory France had conquered since 1678. As if to drive the point home, the Dutch again joined the English to fight the French in the War of Spanish Succession, ending with the Treaty of Utrecht in 1713. However, the wars had exhausted the Dutch both politically and economically, and the treaty marked the beginning of the country's decline as an economic and political power.

Dutch Decline and French Rule

Weakened by the ongoing wars with France, the United Provinces pursued a policy of peace at any cost in the 18th century. The maritime fleet was clapped out after the wars and this allowed the French and the British to move in on the trade routes the Dutch had once dominated. Domestically, the population was decreasing and even worse, the dikes were also clapped out. There was no money to repair them and widespread floods swept across the country in 1713. Commercially, merchants were

Mad about Tulips

At the height of the Tulipmania in January 1637, a single bulb of the legendary *Semper augustus* fetched the equivalent of more than 10 years' wages for the average worker, who was lucky to make 300 florins a year. One unfortunate foreign sailor made himself rather unpopular with his employer by slicing up what he thought was an onion in order to garnish his herring. An English amateur botanist was intrigued by an unknown bulb lying in his host's conservatory, proceeded to bisect it, and was put in jail until he could raise 4000 florins.

The craze for tulips extended beyond drunken speculators in pubs, too. An Amsterdam doctor, Claes Pietersz changed his surname to Tulp (Dutch for tulip) because of his love for the flower. He was later immortalised in the Rembrandt painting *The Anatomy Lesson of Dr Tulp* which now resides in the Mauritshuis in Den Haag.

Of course the bonanza couldn't last, and when several bulb traders in Haarlem failed to fetch their expected prices in February 1637, the bottom fell out of the market. Within weeks many of the country's wealthiest merchants went bankrupt and many more people of humbler origin lost everything they thought they had acquired. Speculators who were stuck with unsold bulbs, or with bulbs that had been reserved but not yet paid for (the concept of options was invented during the Tulipmania), appealed for government action but the authorities refused to become involved in what they considered to be gambling.

The speculation and mania disappeared, but love of the surprising tulip endured and it remained an expensive flower. Cool-headed growers perfected their craft. To this day, the Dutch continue to be the world leaders in tulip cultivation and supply most of the bulbs planted in Europe and North America. They also excel in other bulbs such as daffodils, hyacinths and crocuses.

So what happened to the flamed, frilly tulips of the past? They've mostly vanished, as the underlying disease which caused the wild colours has been all but eliminated. A few are grown by British bulb collectors and others are healthy replica bulbs created by cross-breeding.

'Tulipmania' continues to resonate not only for its insight into human preoccupations but for its cogent example of the perils of investment frenzy. Search the Internet for the word and you'll get a rash of hits for articles about the South Sea Bubble of 1720, the boom preceding the Great Crash of 1929 and – showing that we are all doomed to relive history – the wild overvaluation of Internet stocks.

more likely to spend their profits on luxuries rather than sensible investment in their businesses. This contributed to the overall Dutch decline economically.

A series of political struggles between the House of Orange and its opposition known as the Patriots, which favoured democratic reforms, led to a civil war in 1785, which was settled three years later when the stadholderate agreed to limit its powers. The many Dutch who were eager for constitutional reform, including members of the Patriot Party, welcomed the arrival of French revolutionary forces in the mid-1790s. The United Provinces collapsed and the area was renamed the Batavian Republic, which survived only until 1806 when Napoleon named it the Kingdom of Holland, installing his brother Louis Bonaparte as king. But Louis proved to be not quite the kind of king (or maybe even brother) Napoleon would have liked. He actually seemed to like his subjects and often favoured them over France. His position became completely untenable after he decided to send less Dutch money back home and in 1810 Napoleon booted Louis out of office.

With Napoleon's attention increasingly elsewhere, the House of Orange supporters invited Prince William VI back. He landed at Scheveningen in 1813 and was named prince sovereign of the Netherlands. The next year he was crowned King William I, and ruled until 1840.

Independent kingdom

The independence of the Netherlands was restored at the Congress of Vienna in 1815; the Netherlands in the north and Belgium in the south were joined into a United Kingdom of the Netherlands, with William as king.

The marriage was doomed from the start. The partners had little in common, including their dominant religions (Calvinist and Catholic), languages (Dutch and French) and favoured way of making money (trade and manufacturing). Matters weren't helped by William, who generally sided with his fellow northerners.

In 1830 the southern states revolted and in 1839 the other European powers forced William to let the south go. In a nice historical twist, William abdicated one year later so he could marry – surprise! – a Belgian Catholic. It's not known if he ever spoke French at home.

His son, King William II, granted a new and more liberal constitution to the people of the Netherlands in 1848 which included a number of democratic ideals and even made the monarchy the servant of the elected government. This constitution remains the foundation of the Dutch government. Its role on the world stage long over, the Netherlands maintained a policy of strict neutrality from 1815 to 1939 and consequently played only a small role in European affairs.

During WWI, the Netherlands remained neutral despite the fact that its shipping industry was damaged by both the Allies and the Germans. The Allied forces mounted a blockade that prevented goods from being

Dutch Jews

The Nazis brought about the almost complete annihilation of the Dutch Jewish community. Before WWII there were about 140,000 Jews in the Netherlands of whom about 90,000 lived in Amsterdam, where they formed 13% of the population. (Before the 1930s this proportion was about 10% but it increased with Jews fleeing the Nazi regime in Germany.) Only about 25,000 Dutch Jews survived the war. About 6000 returned from the camps while the rest managed to stay hidden.

They played an important role in the city over the centuries. In medieval times few Jews lived here but their expulsion from Spain and Portugal in the 1580s brought a flood of Sephardic refugees. More arrived when the Spaniards retook Antwerp in 1585. They settled on the newly reclaimed islands in Amsterdam's Nieuwmarkt neighbourhood, one of the few places they could afford land.

The monopolistic guilds kept most trades firmly closed to these newcomers but some of the Sephardim were diamond-cutters, for which there was no guild. Other Sephardic Jews introduced printing and tobacco processing, or worked in similarly unrestricted trades such as retail on the streets, banking and medicine. The majority, however, eked out a meagre living as labourers and small-time traders on the margins of society, and lived in houses they could afford in the Nieuwmarkt area, which developed into the Jewish quarter. Still, they weren't confined to a ghetto and, with some restrictions, could buy property and exercise their religion – freedoms unheard of elsewhere in Europe.

The 17th century saw another influx of Jewish refugees, this time Ashkenazim fleeing pogroms in Central and Eastern Europe. Thus the two wings of the Diaspora were reunited in Amsterdam but they didn't always get on well. Sephardim resented the increased competition posed by Ashkenazic newcomers, who soon outnumbered them and were generally much poorer, and the two groups established separate synagogues. Perhaps because of this antagonism, Amsterdam became a major Jewish centre in Europe.

The guilds and all remaining restrictions on Jews were abolished during the French occupation, and the Jewish community thrived in the 19th century. There was still considerable poverty and the Jewish quarter included some of the worst slums in the city; but the economic, social and political emancipation of the Jews helped their burgeoning middle class, who moved out into the Plantage area and later into the suburbs south of the city.

shipped into the Netherlands for fear the goods would reach Germany, while the Germans' indiscriminate submarine warfare claimed many Dutch ships.

Following WWI, the Netherlands embarked on many innovative social programs that targeted poverty, the rights of women and children, and education. Industrially, the coal mines of south Limburg were exploited to great success, Rotterdam became one of Europe's most important ports and the scheme to reclaim the Zuiderzee was launched in 1932.

WWII

The Dutch wished to continue their neutrality during WWII but the Germans had other ideas. The German army flooded over the borders during May 1940 and the totally inadequate Dutch army could do little to stop it. In an incident that continues to rankle the Dutch, the Germans levelled much of Rotterdam in a raid designed to encourage the Dutch to surrender. They did. Queen Wilhelmina and her family escaped to England where they made many encouraging broadcasts to the folks back home over the BBC. Germany put Dutch industry and farms to work on its war needs and there was much deprivation. Thousands of Dutch men were taken to Germany and forced to work in German factories. A far worse fate awaited the country's Jews. See the boxed text 'Dutch Jews'.

During the five years of German occupation, Dutch resistance was primarily passive. Any open dissent often resulted in execution on the spot, especially later when the war

Dutch Jews

The Holocaust left Amsterdam's Jewish quarter empty, a sinister reminder of its once bustling life. Many of the houses, looted by Germans and local collaborators and deprived of their wooden fixtures for fuel in the final, desperate months of the war, stood derelict until they were demolished in the 1970s.

Throughout the Netherlands there are pre-war synagogues with haunting memorials to entire congregations who were taken away. There are many individual stories of great courage on the part of everyday Dutch citizens who risked death by hiding Jews for the duration of the war. Indeed, one of the greatest fears for Jews in hiding and those who hid them were not the Nazis but Dutch citizens who would turn them in. This was how Anne Frank and her family were finally found.

One Dutch effort at sheltering Jews stands out. The tiny village of Nieuwlande in Drenthe made the decision to shelter as many Jews as possible. Led by Arnold Douwes, the son of a pastor, Johannes Post, a farmer and town counsellor, the 119 townsfolk protected more than 50 Jews who had been ordered to report to the Westerbork deportation camp some 18km to the north (see the Groningen & Drenthe chapter for details). Today, the camp stands as a memorial to those who died and a museum of the Holocaust. Because the entire town was involved, there was little chance anyone would rat.

But for many Dutch, their largely passive role in the holocaust remains a deeply disturbing one. The National War and Resistance Museum in Overloon in Limburg has an unvarnished look at the holocaust and the Dutch (see the Noord Brabant & Limburg chapter for details). Amsterdam's Museum of Jewish History also has excellent displays.

Some estimates put the current Jewish population of Amsterdam at 30,000 (out of possibly 40,000 in the entire country), but many are so integrated into Dutch society that they don't consider themselves distinctly Jewish. Amsterdam slang incorporates many terms of Hebrew or Yiddish origin, such as the alternative name for Amsterdam, Mokum (from *makom aleph*, the best city of all); the cheery goodbye, *de mazzel* (good luck); *joetje* (f10, from the 10th letter of the Hebrew alphabet); *gabber* (friend, mate) from the Yiddisch *chawwer*, companion; and the ultimate put-down, *kapsones maken* (to make unnecessary fuss) from *kapsjones* (self-importance).

was going badly for the Germans. However, many Dutch profited from the German occupation and some actively collaborated. Although many Dutch risked all to save Jews, others cheerfully accepted bounties for revealing Jewish hiding places. Some even did it for free, which is what sealed the fate of Anne Frank in Amsterdam.

The worst part of the war for the Dutch was the so-called 'Winter of Hunger' of 1944–45. The British-led Operation Market Garden through the heart of the Netherlands in the autumn of 1944 had been a huge disaster (see the boxed text 'Operation Market Garden' in the Overijssel & Gelderland chapter) and the Allies abandoned all efforts to liberate the Dutch. The Germans stripped the country of much of its food and wealth and there was mass starvation. Many people were reduced to trying to subsist on tulip bulbs.

The Netherlands was not liberated until just a few days before the end of the war in Europe in May 1945.

Postwar Reconstruction

The Netherlands faced major concerns in the postwar years both at home and abroad. Domestically, it had to restore trade and industry while rebuilding the battered country. Wisely, it concentrated on its old speciality: trade. The Dutch shipping industry and the Port of Rotterdam expanded their role in transporting goods. The discovery of large natural gas fields in the North Sea off the Dutch coast brought new wealth, while Dutch farmers became among the most productive in Europe. As the economy grew, social programs were expanded by the fairly liberal governments. Retirement ages were lowered, benefits increased and health care improved.

Overseas, the colonies began to clamour for independence. The Dutch East Indies, occupied by the Japanese during the war, declared itself independent in 1945. After four years of fighting and negotiations, the independence of Indonesia was recognised at the end of 1949. Surinam became independent in 1975, and the Netherlands Antilles decided to remain part of the Kingdom of the Netherlands while retaining autonomous control of its government.

The same social upheavals that swept the world in the 1960s were also felt in the Netherlands. Students, labour groups, hippies and more took to the streets in protest. Among the more colourful were a group that came to be known as The Provos. See the boxed text 'Provos' for details.

The marriage of Princess Beatrix (now Queen) to Claus von Amsberg provoked a huge outcry from some Dutch not just because of the cost, but also because he was a German. A huge squatting movement sprung up in Amsterdam in the 1960s and lasted for more than two decades. Homeless groups took over empty buildings – many of which had once belonged to Jews – and refused to leave.

The Dutch's tolerant attitude toward drugs and homosexuals, in particular, also evolved in the 1960s and 1970s. The country's drug policy grew out of practical considerations of the time, when a flood of young people populated Amsterdam and made the policing of drug laws impracticable. Official government policy became supportive of homosexuals, who are able to live openly in Dutch cities.

Queen Beatrix ascended the throne in 1980 after her mother, Juliana, abdicated (as did her mother, Queen Wilhelmina, before her).

All governments since 1945 have been coalitions, with parties differing mainly over economic policies. However, coalitions shift constantly based on the political winds. The most recent election in May 1998 saw the Labour Party making strong gains, with Wim Kok continuing as prime minister. Kok, who in 2002 will be up for re-election, is a popular leader, eschewing the trappings of power for simple things of life, even riding his bicycle to important government meetings.

The Netherlands and 10 other European countries voted in May 1998 to adopt the euro as the new single European currency. This continued Dutch policies that have been consistently in favour of European unification.

Provos

The Provos awoke Dutch society from its slumber in the 1960s. Their core consisted of a small group of anarchic individuals, successors to the beatniks, who staged street 'happenings', or creative, playful provocations (hence the name). Misguided and disproportionately harsh police reprisals made the general public uneasy about the established order.

In 1962, an Amsterdam window cleaner and self-professed sorcerer, Robert Jasper Grootveld, began to deface cigarette billboards with a huge letter 'K' (for *kanker,* cancer) in order to expose the role of advertising in addictive consumerism by the *klootjesvolk* (narrow-minded populace). He held get-togethers in his garage – dressed as a medicine man and chanting antismoking mantras under the influence of pot – which attracted other bizarre types, such as the poet Johnny van Doorn, a.k.a. Johnny the Selfkicker, who bombarded his audience with frenzied, stream-of-consciousness recitals; Bart Huges, who drilled a hole in his forehead – a so-called 'third eye' – to relieve pressure on his brain and attain permanently expanded consciousness; and Rob Stolk, a rebellious, working-class printer, whose streetwise tactics came to the fore when the get-togethers moved to the streets.

In the summer of 1965 the venue of choice was the rather appropriate *Lieverdje* ('Little Darling') on Amsterdam's Spui square, the endearing statuette of a local street-brat donated to the city by a cigarette company. The police, unsure of how to deal with 'public obstructions' by excited youngsters chanting unintelligible (and indeed often meaningless) slogans around 'medicine man' Grootveld, responded the only way they knew: with the baton and arbitrary arrests.

The pub terraces lining the square were a favourite haunt of journalists, resulting in eyewitness accounts of mindless police brutality against kids having mindless fun. Soon it seemed the whole country was engaged in heated debate for and against the authorities. The generation gap was only part of it: many of the older generation, uneasy about how little had changed after the war, came out in favour of the Provos and could not understand why the authorities had so completely lost the plot.

Throughout 1965 and 1966 the Provos maintained the initiative with a series of White Plans to protect the environment, including the famous White Bicycle Plan to tackle the city's traffic congestion with a fleet of free white bicycles. They symbolically donated a white bicycle that was promptly confiscated by the police.

The Provos won a seat in the municipal elections of 1966, much to the horror of some of the true anarchists at the heart of the movement. The movement split and dissolved during the more cynical 1970s. However, it did have one lasting effect on Dutch society; the squatting movement saw scores of people occupy uninhabited in buildings in Amsterdam, Rotterdam, Leiden and elsewhere. Eventually, this forced governments to adopt measures that would prevent the non-rich from being priced out of city centres.

The Lieverdje (Little Darling) on Amsterdams Spui Square, an appropriate focus for campains by the Provos

GEOGRAPHY

Bordered by the North Sea, Belgium and Germany, the Netherlands is largely artificial, its lands reclaimed from the sea over many centuries and the drained polders protected by dikes. Some 24% of the country's 40,000 sq km lie below sea level. Much more of the land is at or just above sea level with the consequence that there are 2400km of dikes to keep the waters out. Some are more than 25m high. See the boxed text 'The Delta Project' in the Zuid Holland & Zeeland chapter for some of the watery details.

Completed in 1932 as part of the Zuiderzee project, the 30km-long Afsluitdijk turned the sea into the freshwater IJsselmeer and in the intervening years vast areas amounting to 1700 sq km have been drained to create the polder province of Flevoland.

The only area that even qualifies as hilly is in the south-east Limburg province. The highest point in the Netherlands, Vaalserberg, bumps above the rolling countryside at an elevation of 321m.

The south-west province of Zeeland is the combined delta area of the Scheldt, Meuse (Maas in Dutch), Lek and Waal Rivers; the Lek and Waal are branches of the Rhine, carrying most of its water to the sea. The mighty Rhine itself peters out in a pathetic little stream (the Oude Rijn, or Old Rhine) at the coast near Katwijk.

Although slightly larger than Belgium – a point the Dutch are quietly happy about – the Netherlands is twice the size of Israel, twice the size of the US state of New Jersey and about 60% of the size of the Australian island-state Tasmania.

CLIMATE

The Netherlands has a temperate maritime climate with cool winters and mild summers. The sea and the Gulf Stream moderate the weather to a great extent so that it never gets as cold as the country's northern situation would suggest (although those same waters provide the seemingly never-ending sea breezes).

The weather is often blustery and changing and there are only an average of 25 completely sunny days a year. This helps explain why on a per capita basis the Dutch are some of the most avid travellers in the world, eagerly journeying to sunnier climes on the Mediterranean and beyond.

Precipitation, which averages 79cm annually is spread rather evenly over the year. It often seems to be falling in a never-ending drizzle, though in the spring months of March to May it tends to fall in short, sharp bursts. May is a pleasant time to visit: the elms along the canals are in bloom and everything is nice and fresh.

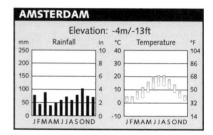

The sunniest months are May to August and the warmest are June to September. Summer can be humid and uncomfortable for some people, but more often it is colder than tourist brochures showing sunny beaches would suggest. Indian summers are common in September and into early October, which is usually an excellent time to visit. Blustery autumn storms occur in October and November.

December to February are the coldest months with occasional slushy snow and temperatures around the freezing point. Frosts usually aren't severe enough to allow skating on the canals, but when they are, the city comes alive with colourfully clad skaters. When snow adds a serene white setting, you really couldn't wish for better photo material.

ECOLOGY & ENVIRONMENT

The Dutch environment is one that has been heavily exploited. Agriculture uses 27% of the land, while much of the rest is heavily developed for industry and urban uses. With so much of the nation consisting of land that has been drained of water through pumps, dikes, fill etc, the ecology of the Netherlands has not been mostly natural in two millennia.

During the second half of the 20th century, the Dutch showed the same increasing awareness of the environment that was experienced elsewhere. However, unlike many nations they have been fairly successful at following up their words with actions. The Dutch enthusiastically sort their rubbish and they have been enthusiastic supporters of various pro-bicycle and anti-car initiatives. These measures have included reductions in city-centre parking spaces, speed bumps and other impediments on city streets and even the relining of country roads to emphasise bike lanes at the cost of room for cars.

Billions of guilders spent on water treatment mean that even Amsterdam's once notorious canals are fairly clean – although you probably wouldn't want to take a sip. Agriculture and industry have been presented with 'voluntary' goals to reduce runoff and pollution. The goals become mandatory if they are not met in an agreed period of time.

Still, water pollution remains a problem. The Rhine, Maas and the Scheldt Rivers enter the Netherlands bearing pollutants from less fastidious nations upstream. Major problems include heavy metals, organic compounds, nitrates and phosphates.

FLORA & FAUNA

The extensive impact of humans on the Netherlands means that there are few areas that remain truly natural or wild.

Flora

Mention plant-life in the Netherlands and most people think of tulips. Indeed these cultivated bulbs are in many ways representative of much of country's flora in that they were imported from elsewhere (in this case Asia) and then commercially exploited. A range of fruits, vegetables and other flowers fit this profile.

Much of the nondeveloped land is covered by grass, which is widely used for grazing. The wet weather means that the grass remains green and growing for much of the year. The areas that are wooded, such as De Hoge Veluwe National Park, have mostly been planted with fairly young trees. Even the vegetation on the islands such as Ameland are heavily managed by the government to control erosion.

Fauna

Birds thrive in the watery lands of the Netherlands and the marshes and wetlands are major migration stops for European birds. At various times of the year you can see gulls, terns, herons and many more species. The white stork with its huge nest is protected by numerous laws and the population seems stable. Ravens and many other birds find food aplenty in the pastures and farms.

Larger mammals are mainly found in small numbers in the national parks and reserves. These include deer, fox and badgers. Small mammals such as muskrats are common in the country and less salubrious rodents such as common rats find ample shelter in the cities with their many old and damp places.

A variety of fish species live in the nation's canals and estuaries. One of the most interesting species is the eel, which survives in both fresh and salt water and is common in canals, yet it would have been born from one of 20 million eggs laid by its mother at a depth of 250 metres in the Sargasso Sea off Bermuda! White bream, rudd, pike, perch, stickleback and carp also enjoy the canal environment.

There are 12 crustacean species in the coastal waters, of which the common shrimp and the epidemic import, the Chinese mitten crab, are the most common.

National Parks

There are nine national parks in full operation. Another nine parks are in various stages of creation. Most average a mere 5000 hectares in size and are not meant to preserve some natural wonder but rather are meant to preserve open areas of special interest. There simply aren't that many areas of the Netherlands left untouched. However, the national parks can be fascinating places and they boast good visitor centres with excellent displays explaining contemporary flora and fauna.

De Hoge Veluwe is one of the oldest parks and was once the country retreat of the Kroller-Muller family. Extensive forestation is maintained and it is a good place to see the sandy hills that once were prevalent in this part of the Netherlands.

De Weerribben in Overijssel preserves the land once heavily harvested for peat. Radically altered through the years, the goal now is to allow the land to return to nature. Schiermonnikoog occupies a good portion of its namesake island which was once used by a sect of monks. De Biesbosch, near Rotterdam, has numerous water activities around an area formerly used by reed farmers.

GOVERNMENT & POLITICS

Against the European trend, the Netherlands developed from a republic to a constitutional monarchy, headed today by Queen Beatrix who took over from her mother, Juliana, in 1980. The country's political scene is often compared with the physical landscape – flat and often dull, with coalition governments pursuing policies of compromise.

Officially the country is called The Kingdom of the Netherlands, which includes not just the Netherlands but also the Caribbean islands of Netherlands Antilles and Aruba. A charter drawn up in 1954 sets out the ties between the three nations. This primarily involves policy on foreign relations, defence and immigration issues. In other matters, the three nations operate independently.

The present constitution of the Netherlands dates to 1814. It is continually modified but it continues to give the monarch some official powers that, while primarily ceremonial, can be interpreted as having some influence on government. In recent years this has led to some minor friction between Queen Beatrix and the government.

Parliament, officially known as Staten-General (States-General), consists of two houses: the First Chamber, which has 75 members elected by the province councils, and the Second Chamber, which has 150 members that are directly elected by the populace every four years. The First Chamber may not propose or modify legislation and can only approve or reject it.

The constitution also provides for a High Council of State. This body which dates back to the 16th century serves as an adviser to the elected government and it has the power to propose legislation. However, its advice does not have to be followed and its real power rests in its role as the highest court for appeals on matters between the citizens and government. The 28 members are appointed for life by the monarch who accepts and follows government recommendations in making her selections.

The main parties are the socialist-ecologist Green Left Party, the liberal-centrist parties of the People's Party for Freedom and Democracy (VVD), Democrats 66 (D66) and the Labour Party (PvdA) and the conservative Christian Democratic Appeal. In 1994, the Labour Party, lead by current prime minister, Wim Kok, joined forces with the VVD and D66 in forming a successful cabinet which gained even more seats at the most recent general election in 1998. Because of the colours of the coalition parties (red and blue), it's commonly referred to as the *paars* (purple) government. The next national elections are scheduled for 2002.

Kok is easily the country's most popular politician. He has presided over a period of economic success and he is appreciated for having a common touch. His favourite dish is a casserole of potatoes and beans, he's been known to turn up at government receptions on his bicycle and he's a big football fan.

The country consists of 12 provinces, one of which, Flevoland, only came into existence in 1967 after it had been claimed from the sea. The province of Holland was split into Noord Holland (North Holland; capital: Haarlem) and Zuid Holland (South Holland; capital: Den Haag) during the Napoleonic era. The Catholic half of the population lives mainly in the south-eastern provinces of North Brabant and Limburg. The province of Zeeland gave New Zealand its name (Australia used to be known as New Holland).

As with Belgians and Luxembourgers, the Dutch view the European Union as a fact of life, and further integration is taken for granted.

ECONOMY

Despite its small size, the Netherlands has a strong economy. It is a leader in service industries such as banking, electronics (Philips) and multimedia (Polygram), and also has a highly developed horticultural industry dealing in bulbs and cut flowers. Agriculture plays an important role, particularly dairy farming and glasshouse fruits and vegetables. Rotterdam Harbour, which handles the largest shipping tonnage in the world, is vital to the economy as are the country's large supplies of natural gas in the north-east.

The Dutch economy is the envy of Europe. In the late 1990s it was averaging a healthy growth of 3.4% a year, while figures for unemployment and annual inflation were remarkably low at 2.7% and 2.2% respectively. Many Dutch say their economic success is due to their status as a small country with a long tradition of trading. Globalisation, the economic trend sending shudders elsewhere, is an economic force the Dutch have been used to for centuries. Workers often work for short-term contracts, which means that the workforce is flexible and can move from a dying industry to a growing one fairly easily. Social stability is assured by a generous welfare system for those caught between jobs.

POPULATION & PEOPLE

Western Europe's most densely populated country has 15.6 million people, and a lot of Friesian cows in its 34,000 sq km. The concentration is 459 humans per sq km (the cow concentration varies widely). Human habitation is especially high in the Randstad – the western hoop of cities including Amsterdam, Den Haag and Rotterdam which is one of the most densely populated conurbations on earth.

More than 90% of the population are ethnically Dutch. Several ethnic groups with ties to former colonies are part of the balance of the population: Indonesia (1.2%), Surinam (1.2%) and the Netherlands Antilles and Aruba (0.6%). Other groups include those born in EU countries (1.9%) and Turkey (1%). Large cities tend to have slightly higher concentrations of non-Dutch residents.

EDUCATION

More than 75% of primary and secondary schools in the Netherlands are private. The Dutch constitution allows any group of people to set up a school based on religious or philosophical beliefs or educational principles. However, the government is responsible for setting education standards and seeing that the schools achieve them. It also sets the curriculum and each year determines teacher salaries in schools whether public or private. The literacy rate is over 99%.

The government gives large block grants each year to all schools that make the grade scholastically and these payments in fact account for all of the school's budgets. Schools may only charge parents for extracurricular activities, otherwise tuition is free. In typical Dutch tradition of tolerance, schools rarely require students to wear uniforms.

Children are required to attend school from ages five to 18, however the last two years may include a combination of practical skills and classroom instruction. Over 22% of those aged 18 to 27 attend college or university part- or full-time. Tuition at all institutions is set nationally and students are given block grants as well as low-interest loans to cover their costs. There are few dormitories.

SCIENCE & PHILOSOPHY
Science

It should come as no surprise that the Dutch lead the world in hydraulic engineering. However, they are also known for their electrical engineering expertise. Philips, the Dutch electrical giant, has research laboratories in Eindhoven that have invented a number of consumer electronic products including the cassette tape and compact disks.

There have been numerous notable Dutch scientists. Jan Swammerdam (1637–80) was a naturalist and was probably the first to detect red blood cells. Christiaan Huygens (1629–95) was a mathematician and physicist who studied astronomy and was the first person to correctly identify the ring structure surrounding Saturn. He was the first to use a pendulum in clocks. Hendrik Antoon Lorentz (1853–1928) and Pieter Zeeman (1865–1943) shared the 1902 Nobel Prize in physics for their work postulating the existence of electrons.

There have been many notable Dutch botanists. The French-born Carolus Clusius (1526–1609) spent the last 20 years of his life on the faculty of Leiden University where he did pioneering work in the classification of plants. He introduced new species into Holland including the potato, and much more prophetically, the tulip.

Hugo de Vries (1848–1935) was a botanist who specialised in studying evolution through plant research. He maintained that new species develop via mutations.

Philosophy

Desiderius Erasmus (1469–1536) stands not only as a great Renaissance philosopher but as a classic Dutchman as well. See the boxed text 'The Prototypical Dutchman?' for details. Hugo Grotius (1583–1645) was a humanist who also wrote the first definitive text on international law. He said that natural law should govern nations as well as humans and he maintained that there were only certain just causes for war.

Baruch Spinoza (later Benedict; 1632–77) was an Amsterdam Jew who was excommunicated for heretical thought. He rejected the concept of free will, contending that human action is motivated by one's concept of self-preservation. His belief that mind and body (or ideas and the physical universe) are simply different aspects of a single substance,

---

The Prototypical Dutchman?

MW

Desiderius Erasmus

Desiderius Erasmus (1469-1536) was born in Rotterdam and went on to become one of the great figures of the Renaissance. A philosopher and humanist, he was an ordained Roman Catholic priest. Yet he didn't doggedly follow church dogma and walked a middle ground between radicals like Martin Luther and those who considered any criticism of the church as heresy.

As a scholar he studied the Greeks extensively and translated the New Testament into Latin based on the original Greek text. He was a high-profile figure during his time and his works which include *In Praise of Folly* and *The Education of a Christian Prince* were widely read. He resolutely followed a middle path throughout life and his reputation suffered during the centuries of religious war which followed his death. In recent decades Erasmus' tolerance, moderation and humour have received wide-spread appreciation. His work is a foundation for humanism and liberal thought.

Erasmus left a large body of work which is endlessly quotable. A few of his thoughts on various subjects include the following:

Books
When I get a little money, I buy books; if any is left I buy food and clothes.

Gullibility
Man's mind is so formed that it is far more susceptible to falsehood than to truth.

Parties
Whether a party can have much success without a woman present I must ask others to decide, but one thing is certain, no party is any fun unless seasoned with folly.

Hunters
They take unbelievable pleasure in the hideous blast of the hunting horn and baying of the hounds. Dogs' dung smells sweet as cinnamon to them.

which he called alternately God and Nature, got him in no end of hot water.

The great French philosopher René Descartes (1596–1650) who is often thought of as the pioneer of modern philosophy spent many of his most productive years in the Netherlands after he registered at the University of Leiden in 1630. Philosopher John Locke (1632–1704) also found a home in the Netherlands from 1683 to 1689 while he was in exile from an England torn by religious strife.

ARTS

The Netherlands has a strong legacy of art and architecture. Brilliant and world-class examples of both can be found throughout the country.

The Dutch also have a rich tradition of music, although Amsterdam's pre-eminence and easy accessibility from all points of the country mean that much of the action in this medium is concentrated there.

Painting

Dutch painting can be found at numerous galleries nationwide. The most important are the Rijksmuseum and the Van Gogh Museum in Amsterdam, the Frans Hals Museum in Haarlem, the Mauritshuis and Gemeente Museum in Den Haag and the Kroller-Muller Museum near Arnhem.

The Prototypical Dutchman?

Sanity

I doubt if a single individual could be found from the whole of mankind free from some form of insanity. The only difference is one of degree. A man who sees a gourd and takes it for his wife is called insane because this happens to very few people.

Human Nature

Now I believe I can hear the philosophers protesting that it can only be misery to live in folly, illusion, deception and ignorance, but it isn't – it's human.

Intellectuals

Ask a wise man to dinner and he'll upset everyone by his gloomy silence or tiresome questions. Invite him to a dance and you'll have a camel prancing about. Haul him off to a public entertainment and his face will be enough to spoil the people's entertainment.

Socrates

As an example of just how useless these philosophers are for any practice in life there is Socrates himself, the one and only wise man, according to the Delphic Oracle. Whenever he tried to do anything in public he had to break off amid general laughter. While he was philosophising about clouds and ideas, measuring a flea's foot and marvelling at a midge's humming, he learned nothing about the affairs of ordinary life.

Lawyers

Amongst the learned the lawyers claim first place, the most self-satisfied class of people, as they roll their rock of Sisyphus and string together 600 laws in the same breath, no matter whether relevant or not, piling up opinion on opinion and gloss on gloss to make their profession seem the most difficult of all. Anything which causes trouble has special merit in their eyes.

Old Age

The nearer people approach old age the closer they return to a semblance of childhood, until the time comes for them to depart this life, again like children, neither tired of living nor aware of death.

The distinction between Dutch and Flemish painting dates from the late 16th century, when the Protestant northern provinces of the Low Countries kicked out the Spaniards but couldn't dislodge them from the provinces in the south. Until then, most paintings in the Low Countries originated in the southern, 'Flemish' centres of Ghent, Bruges and Antwerp, and dealt with the biblical and allegorical subject matter popular with patrons of the day – the Church, the court and, to a lesser extent, the nobility.

Famous names include Jan van Eyck (died 1441), the founder of the Flemish School who perfected the technique of oil painting; Rogier van der Weyden (1400–64), whose religious portraits showed the personalities of his subjects; Hieronymus (Jeroen) Bosch (1450–1516), with macabre allegorical paintings full of religious topics; and, Pieter Bruegel the Elder (1525–69), who used Flemish landscapes and peasant life in his allegorical scenes.

In the northern Low Countries, meanwhile, artists began to develop a style of their own. In Haarlem, painters were using freer, more dynamic arrangements in which people came to life. Jan Mostaert (1475–1555), Lucas van Leyden (1494–1533) and Jan van Scorel (1494–1562) brought realism into their works, modifying the mannerist ideal of exaggerated beauty. Around 1600 the art teacher Karel van Mander proclaimed that Haarlem was creating a distinctively Dutch style of painting.

In Utrecht, however, followers of the Italian master Caravaggio, such as Hendrick ter Bruggen (1588–1629) and Gerrit van Honthorst (1590–1656), made a much more fundamental break with mannerism. They opted for realism altogether and played with light and shadow, with night scenes where a single source of light created dramatic contrasts – the *chiaroscuro* (clear-obscure) approach used to such dramatic effect by Caravaggio in Rome.

Golden Age (17th Century) Both these schools influenced the golden age of Dutch painting in the 17th century with stars like Rembrandt, Vermeer and Frans Hals. Unlike earlier painters or some contemporaries, none of this trio made the almost obligatory pilgrimage to Italy to study the masters. Their work showed that they no longer followed, but led – much like the young Republic that seemed to burst out of nowhere.

Artists suddenly had to survive in a free market. Gone was the patronage of Church and court. In its place was a new, bourgeois society of merchants, artisans and shopkeepers who didn't mind spending 'reasonable' money to brighten up their houses and workplaces with pictures they could understand. Painters rose to the occasion by becoming entrepreneurs themselves, churning out banal works, copies and masterpieces in studios run like factories. Paintings became mass products that were sold at markets among the furniture and chickens. Soon the wealthiest households were covered in paintings from top to bottom like wallpaper – carefully composed snapshots of a world that had ceased to be a mysterious place. Foreign visitors commented that everyone, even bakeries and butcher shops, seemed to have a painting or two on the wall.

Artists specialised in different categories. There was still a market for religious art but it had to be 'historically correct' rather than mannerist, in line with the Calvinist emphasis on 'true' events as described in the Bible. Greek or Roman historical scenes were an extension of this category. Portraiture, in which Flemish and Dutch painters had already begun to excel, was a smash hit in this society of middle-class upstarts brimming with confidence, though group portraits cost less per head and suited a republic run by committees and clubs. Maritime scenes and cityscapes sold well to the government, and landscapes, winter scenes and still lifes (especially of priceless, exotic flowers and delicious meals) were found in many living rooms. Another favourite in households was genre painting, which depicted domestic life or daily life outside.

These different categories may help visitors to Dutch art galleries understand what they're looking at, but some painters defy such easy classification.

Rembrandt The son of a miller, Rembrandt van Rijn (1606–69), the greatest and most versatile of 17th-century artists, excelled in all these categories and pioneered new directions in each. Sometimes he was centuries ahead of his time, as with the emotive brush strokes of his later works.

He grew up in Leiden and was already an accomplished chiaroscuro painter when he came to Amsterdam in 1631 to run Hendrick van Uylenburgh's painting studio. Portraits were the most profitable line and Rembrandt and his staff (or 'pupils') churned out scores of them, including group portraits such as *The Anatomy Lesson of Dr Tulp* (1632). In 1634 he married Van Uylenburgh's Friesian niece, Saskia, who often modelled for him.

Rembrandt fell out with his boss, but his wife's capital helped him buy the sumptuous house next door (the current Rembrandthuis) where he set up his own studio, with staff who worked in a warehouse in the Jordaan. These were happy years: his paintings were a success and his studio became the largest in Holland, though his gruff manners and open agnosticism didn't win him dinner-party invitations from the elite.

Rembrandt became one of the city's main art collectors and often sketched and painted for himself, urging staff to do likewise. Residents of the surrounding Jewish quarter provided perfect material for his dramatic biblical scenes.

In 1642, a year after the birth of their son Titus, Saskia died and business went downhill. Rembrandt's majestic group portrait, *The Nightwatch* (1642), was considered innovative by the art critics of the day (it's now the Rijksmuseum's prize exhibit), but the people in the painting had each paid f100 and some were unhappy that they were pushed to the background. Rembrandt told them where to put the painting and suddenly he received far fewer orders. He began an affair with his son's governess but kicked her out a few years later when he fell for the new maid, Hendrickje Stoffels, who bore him a daughter, Cornelia. The public didn't take kindly to the man's lifestyle and his spiralling debts, and in 1656 he went bankrupt. His house and rich art collection were sold and he moved to the Rozengracht in the Jordaan.

No longer the darling of the wealthy, he continued to paint, draw and etch – his etchings on display in the Rembrandthuis are some of the finest ever produced in this medium – and received the occasional commission. His pupil Govert Flinck was asked to decorate the new city hall, and when Flinck died Rembrandt scored part of the job and painted the monumental *Conspiracy of Claudius Civilis* (1661). The authorities disliked it and soon had it removed. In 1662 he completed the *Staalmeesters* (the 'Syndics') for the drapers' guild and ensured that everybody remained clearly visible, but it was the last group portrait he did.

The works of his later period show that Rembrandt lost none of his touch. No longer constrained by the wishes of wealthy clients, he enjoyed a new-found freedom and his works became more unconventional while showing an even stronger empathy with their subject matter, for instance in *A Couple: the Jewish Bride* (1665). The many portraits of Titus and Hendrickje, and his ever gloomier self-portraits, are among the most stirring in the history of art.

A pest epidemic in 1663–64 killed one in seven Amsterdammers, among them his faithful companion Hendrickje. Titus died in 1668, aged 27 and just married, and Rembrandt died a year later, a broken man.

Hals & Vermeer Another great painter of this period, Frans Hals (1581/85–1666), was born in Antwerp but lived in Haarlem. He devoted most of his career to portraits, dabbling in occasional genre scenes with dramatic chiaroscuro. His ability to render the expressions of his subjects was equal to that of Rembrandt though he didn't explore their characters as much. Both masters used the same expressive, unpolished brush strokes, and seemed to develop from a bright exuberance in their early careers to a darker, more solemn approach later on.

A good example of Hals' 'unpolished' technique is *The Merry Drinker* (1630) in the Rijksmuseum, which could almost have been painted by one of the 19th-century impressionists who so admired his work. His famous children's portraits are similar. Hals was also an expert of beautiful group portraits in which the groups almost looked natural, unlike the rigid line-ups produced by lesser contemporaries – though he wasn't as tactless as Rembrandt in subordinating faces to the composition. A particularly good example is the pair of paintings known collectively as *The Regents & the Regentesses of the Old Men's Alms House* (1664) in the Frans Hals Museum in Haarlem, which he painted near the end of his long life.

The grand trio of 17th-century masters is completed by Jan Vermeer (1632–75) of Delft. He produced only 35 meticulously crafted paintings in his career and died a poor man with 10 children – his baker accepted two paintings from his wife as payment for a debt of more than f600. His work is devoted mainly to genre painting, which he mastered like no other. Other paintings include a few historical/biblical scenes in his earlier career, his famous *View of Delft* (1661) in the Mauritshuis, and some tender portraits of unknown women, such as the stunningly beautiful *Girl with a Pearl Earring* (1666), also in the Mauritshuis. His Catholicism and lingering mannerism help explain the emphasis on beauty rather than the personalities of the people he portrayed.

The Little Street (1658) in the Rijksmuseum is Vermeer's only street scene; the others are set indoors, bathed in serene light pouring through tall windows. The calm, spiritual effect is enhanced by dark blues, deep reds and warm yellows, and by supremely balanced compositions that adhere to the rules of perspective. Good examples include the Rijksmuseum's *The Kitchen Maid* (also known as *The Milkmaid*, 1658) and *Woman in Blue Reading a Letter* (1664), or, for his use of perspective, *The Love Letter* (1670). In *Woman in Blue*, note the map on the wall, a backdrop he used in several other works, as did many other artists of the period. Maps were appreciated as valuable works of art in 17th-century Dutch society just like paintings, which might say something about Dutch

appreciation for spatial relationships (something to do with the flat country and ongoing land reclamation perhaps?).

Baroque Around the middle of the 17th century the atmospheric unity in Dutch paintings, with their stern focus on mood and the subtle play of light, began to make way for the splendour of the baroque. Jacob van Ruysdael went for dramatic skies and Albert Cuyp for Italianate landscapes, while Ruysdael's pupil Meindert Hobbema preferred less heroic and more playful bucolic scenes full of pretty detail.

This almost frivolous aspect of baroque also announces itself in the genre paintings of Jan Steen (1626–79), the tavern-keeper whose depictions of domestic chaos led to the Dutch expression 'a Jan Steen household' for a disorderly household. A good example is the animated revelry of *The Merry Family* (1668) in the Rijksmuseum. It shows adults having a good time around the dinner table, oblivious to the children in the foreground pouring themselves a drink. There's a lot going on in this painting and it all comes together well, but it's also very busy as baroque art often is.

18th & 19th Centuries The golden age of Dutch painting ended almost as suddenly as it began, when the French invaded the Low Countries in the 'Disaster Year' of 1672. The economy collapsed and with it the market for paintings. A mood of caution replaced the carefree optimism of the years when world lay at the Republic's feet. Painters who stayed in business did so with 'safe' works that repeated earlier successes, and in the 18th century they copied French styles, pandering to the awe for anything French.

They produced many competent works but nothing ground-breaking. Cornelis Troost (1697–1750) was one of the best genre painters, sometimes compared to Hogarth for introducing quite un-Calvinistic humour into his pastels of domestic revelry, which were reminiscent of Jan Steen.

Gerard de Lairesse (1640–1711) and Jacob de Wit (1695–1754) specialised in decorating the walls and ceilings of buildings

– De Wit's trompe l'oeuil decorations in the current Theatermuseum and Bijbels Museum are worth seeing.

The late 18th century and most of the 19th century produced little of note, though the landscapes and seascapes of Johan Barthold Jongkind (1819–91) and the gritty, almost photographic Amsterdam scenes of George Hendrik Breitner (1857–1923) are a bit of an exception. They appear to have inspired French impressionists, many of whom visited Amsterdam at the time.

The work of these two painters also reinvented 17th-century realism and influenced the Hague School in the last decades of the 19th century, with painters such as Hendrik Mesdag (1831–1915), Jozef Israels (1824–1911) and the three Maris brothers (Jacob, Matthijs and Willem). The landscapes, seascapes and genre works of this school are on display in the Mesdag Museum in Den Haag, where the star attraction is Mesdag's *Panorama Mesdag* (1881), a gigantic, 360° painting of the seaside town of Scheveningen viewed from a dune. It's quite impressive.

Van Gogh Without a doubt the greatest 19th-century Dutch painter was Vincent van Gogh (1853–1890), whose convulsive patterns and furious colours were in a world of their own and still defy comfortable categorisation. Van Gogh (pronounced 'khokh', rhymes with Scottish 'loch') had a short and tortured but very productive life. He didn't begin painting until 1881 and produced most of his works in the four years he spent in France, before shooting himself to escape mental illness in 1890 (he had already cut off his own ear after an argument with Gauguin). Famous works on display at the Van Gogh Museum in Amsterdam include *The Potato Eaters* (1885), a prime example of his sombre Dutch period, and *The Yellow House in Arles* (1888), *The Bedroom at Arles* (1888) and several self–portraits, sunflowers and other blossoms that show his vivid use of colour in the intense Mediterranean light. One of his last paintings, *Wheatfield with Crows* (1890), is an ominous work foreshadowing his suicide.

20th Century In his early career, Piet Mondriaan (1872–1944; he dropped the second 'a' in his name when he moved to Paris in 1910) painted in the Hague School tradition, but after discovering theosophy he began reducing form to its horizontal (female) and vertical (male) essentials. After flirting with cubism he began painting in bold rectangular patterns, using only the three primary colours of yellow, blue and red set against the three neutrals (white, grey and black), a style known as 'neoplasticism' – an undistorted expression of reality in pure form and pure colour. His *Composition in Red, Black, Blue, Yellow & Grey* (1920) in the Stedelijk Museum is an elaborate example of this. His later works were starker (or 'more pure') and became dynamic again when he moved to New York in 1940. The world's largest collection of his paintings resides in the Gemeente Museum of his native Den Haag.

Mondriaan was one of the leading exponents of De Stijl (The Style), a Dutch design movement that aimed to harmonise all the arts by bringing artistic expressions back to their essence. Its advocate was the magazine of the same name, first published in 1917 by Theo van Doesburg (1883–1931). Van Doesburg produced works similar to Mondriaan's, though he dispensed with the thick, black lines and later tilted his rectangles at 45°, departures serious enough for Mondriaan to call off the friendship.

Throughout the 1920s and 1930s, De Stijl attracted not just painters but also sculptors, poets, architects and designers. One of these was Gerrit Rietveld (1888–1964), who designed the Van Gogh Museum and several other buildings, but is best known internationally for his furniture, such as the Mondriaanesque *Red Blue Chair* (1918) on display in Amsterdam's Stedelijk Museum, and his range of uncomfortable zigzag chairs that, viewed side-on, are simply a 'Z' with a backrest.

Other schools of the prewar period included the Bergen School, with the expressive realism of Annie 'Charley' Toorop (1891–1955), daughter of the symbolist painter Jan Toorop; and De Ploeg (The

Plough), headed by Jan Wiegers (1893–1959) in Groningen, who were influenced by the works of Van Gogh and German expressionists. In her later works Charley Toorop also became one of the exponents of Dutch surrealism, more correctly known as 'magic realism', which expressed the magical interaction between humans and their environment. Leading magic realists included Carel Willink (1900–83) and the almost naive autodidact Pyke Koch (1901–91).

One of the most remarkable graphic artists of this century was Maurits Cornelis Escher (1902–72). His drawings, lithos and woodcuts of blatantly impossible images continue to fascinate mathematicians. Strange loops defy the laws of Euclidean geometry: a waterfall feeds itself, people go up and down a staircase that ends where it starts, a pair of hands draw each other. He also possessed an uncanny knack for tessellation, or 'tiling' – the art of making complex, preferably 'organic' shapes fit into one another in recurring but subtly changing patterns. Though sometimes dismissed as novelties that belong in poster shops, Escher's meticulously crafted works betray a highly talented artist who deserves credit for challenging our view of reality.

After WWII, artists rebelled against artistic conventions and vented their rage in abstract expressionism, the more furious the better. In Amsterdam, Karel Appel (1921–) and Constant (Nieuwenhuis; 1920–) drew on styles pioneered by Paul Klee and Joan Miró, and exploited bright colours and 'uncorrupted' children's art to produce incredibly lively works that leapt off the canvas. In Paris in 1945, they met up with the Dane Asger Jorn (1914–73) and the Belgian Corneille (Cornelis van Beverloo, 1922–), and together with several other artists and writers formed a group known as CoBrA (Copenhagen, Brussels, Amsterdam).

Their first major exhibition, in the Stedelijk Museum in 1949, aroused a storm of protest with predictable comments along the lines of 'My child paints like that too'. Still, the CoBrA artists exerted a strong influence in their respective countries even after they disbanded in 1951. The Stedelijk

Museum has a good collection of their works but the CoBrA Museum in Amstelveen displays the more complete range, including the most colourful ceramics you're ever likely to see.

It is probably too early to say much about the significance of Dutch art from the 1960s onwards. Works include the op art of Jan Schoonhoven, influenced by the Zero movement in Germany; the abstracts of Ad Dekkers and Edgar Fernhout; the media collages of Rob Scholte and Marlene Dumas; and the photographic collages of Jan Dibbets.

Architecture
The Netherlands has been a leader in architecture for centuries. From 17th-century Amsterdam to 20th- and 21st-century Rotterdam, the nation has splendid examples of design from a myriad of eras and styles. While there are scores of individual buildings that are especially well designed, you will soon realise that the nation as a whole doesn't have any truly flamboyant stand-outs like a St Peter's Cathedral or a Louvre. This is entirely in keeping with the Dutch character.

Romanesque The windy plains of the north are the best places to find surviving examples of the sturdy brick churches erected in the 12th and 13th centuries. The lonely church perched on a man-made hill in Hogebeintum in Friesland shows the simple patterned brick decoration used to enliven the exteriors of churches during this time.

Gothic The Netherlands didn't see the kind of huge Gothic cathedrals that were raised in France in the 14th and 15th centuries. However, the Catholics of Noord Brabant did their best to erect a few churches of stone with soaring vaults and buttresses. Sint Janskathedraal in Den Bosch and Breda's Grote Kerk are both good examples of what came to be called the Brabant Gothic style. Note the timber vaulting (the marshy ground precluded the use of heavy stone) and the widespread use of brick rather than stone. Stone was not only heavy but also scarce; there was plenty of clay and sand to produce bricks.

Flamboyant Gothic made its mark on the town halls of Gouda and Middleburg. The former has a delicate yet stately feel while the latter benefited from the talents of its Belgian architects who had worked on some of the finest structures in their country.

Mannerism Perhaps the Netherlands was just too far away to feel much influence from the Italian Renaissance in the 16th century but it did go for mannerism, a sort of toned-down baroque, in a big way. It was a unique style with rich ornamentation that merged classical and traditional elements. In the facades they used mock columns, so-called pilasters, and they replaced the traditional spout gables with step gables richly decorated with sculptures, columns and obelisks. The playful interaction of red brick and horizontal bands of white or yellow sandstone was based on strict mathematical formulas that pleased the eye.

Certainly the biggest examples of this are the three churches in Amsterdam designed by Hendrik de Keyser and built in the early 1600s: the Zuiderkerk, the Noorderkerk and the Westerkerk. All three show a major break from the sober and stolid brick churches found out in the provinces. Their steeples are ornate and built with a variety of contrasting materials. The windows are framed in white stone which is set off by the brown brick, while a profusion of details enliven the walls and roof lines.

17th Century This was the Golden Age when the Netherlands was the richest nation in Europe, with money pouring in from its successful trading worldwide.

Befitting its role as a world power, Dutch architecture of this period was solid and impressive with imposing lines and looming decoration that was meant to pronounce the building's – and by default the owner's – importance. Greek and Roman classical design was an inspiration. The pilasters looked more like columns, with pedestals and pediments. In order to accentuate the vertical lines, the step gable changed to a neck gable with decorative scrolls, topped by a triangular or rounded frontispiece to imitate a temple roof. Soft red brick was made more durable with brown paint. Built as Amsterdam's town hall in 1648 by Jacob van Campen, the building which is now the Royal Palace exudes gravity with its solid lines and shape.

Along city canals, the prosperous traders did their best to let the world know that they were successful. Despite the limitations imposed by the narrow plots, each building makes a statement at its gable through a myriad of shapes, forms and sculpture. Follow the details right up to the gable where you will see the ubiquitous projecting beam with pulley that became standard in this era as most houses were also used by their owners to store their goods.

Elsewhere in the land, Den Haag is graced by its own Royal Palace and the Mauritshuis (which is now a museum). There are scores of other examples and you'd be hard pressed to walk the canals of Leiden, Delft, Maastricht or other classic Dutch towns without finding your own favourites.

18th-Century French Influence The wealthy class now began to enjoy the fortunes amassed by their predecessors. Many turned to banking and finance and conducted their business from the comfort of opulent homes. Those who still engaged actively in trade no longer stored goods in the attic but in warehouses elsewhere. The Louis XV and rococo styles were pervasive in their influence.

The preoccupation with all things French provided fertile ground for Huguenot refugees, such as Daniel Marot and his assistants Jean and Anthony Coulon, who introduced French interior design with matching exteriors. Interiors were bathed in light thanks to stuccoed ceilings and tall sash windows (a French innovation), and everything from staircases to furniture was designed in harmony. A number of examples of their work can be found along the Lange Voorhout in Den Haag.

Neoclassicism The Napoleanic Wars and associated economic chaos suppressed architectural development in the late 18th century. However when in doubt there are always the buildings of ancient Greece and Rome and these indeed were the inspiration for construction during this time. The Groningen Town Hall built over an extended period due to the bad economy (1774–1811) is an example of the return to pillars, although the heavy use of brick for the walls is a purely Dutch accent.

Late 19th Century As the 19th century progressed, architects continued turning to past styles for inspiration. The main Dutch styles in the latter half of the 1800s were neo-Gothic, harking back to the grand Gothic cathedrals in which no design element was superfluous, and also neo-Renaissance, which brought De Keyser's Dutch Renaissance architecture back into the limelight. The former suited the boom in Catholic church-building now that Catholics were free to build new churches in Protestant parts of the country; the latter appealed to local architects because houses in this style were being demolished at a rapid rate.

One of the leading architects of this period was Pierre Cuypers, who built several neo-Gothic churches but often merged the two styles, as can be seen in Amsterdam's Centraal Station and Rijksmuseum which have Gothic structures and Dutch Renaissance brickwork. His Saint Catherine's Church in Eindoven was a soaring example of neo-Gothic until it was destroyed by German bombs in WWII.

Neo-Renaissance buildings that at first look like well-polished veterans of the 16th century were built throughout the country. Their stepped gables and gable ends along with alternating stone and brickwork for many symbolise classic Dutch architecture.

Berlage & the Amsterdam School As the 20th century approached, the neo-styles and their reliance on the past were strongly criticised by Hendrik Petrus Berlage, the father of modern Dutch architecture. Instead of expensive construction and excessive decoration, he favoured simplicity and a rational use of materials. His 1902 Beurs (Bourse, or Stock Exchange) in Amsterdam

displayed his ideals to the full. He cooperated with sculptors, painters and tilers to ensure that ornamentation was integrated into the overall design in a supportive role, rather than being tacked on as an embellishment to hide the structure.

Berlage's residential architecture approached a block of buildings as a whole, not as a collection of individual houses. In this he influenced the young architects of what became known as the Amsterdam School, though they rejected his stark rationalism and preferred more creative designs. Leading exponents were Michel de Klerk, Piet Kramer and Johan van der Mey. The latter heralded the Amsterdam School in his Scheepvaarthuis at Prins Hendrikkade.

These architects built in brick and treated housing blocks as sculptures, with curved corners, oddly placed windows and ornamental, rocket-shaped towers. Their Amsterdam housing estates, such as De Klerk's 'Ship' in the Oostzaanstraat and Kramer's Cooperatiehof in the Pijp neighbourhood, have been described as fairy-tale fortresses rendered in a Dutch version of Art Deco. Their preference for form over function meant that their designs were interesting to look at but not always fantastic to live in, with small windows and inefficient use of space.

Many architects of this school worked for the Amsterdam city council and designed the buildings of the ambitious 'Plan South'. This was a large-scale expansion of good-quality housing, wide boulevards and cosy squares between the Amstel and what was to become the Olympic Stadium. It was mapped out by Berlage and instigated by the Labour Party alderman FM Wibaut, though Berlage didn't get much of a chance to design the buildings, with council architects pushing their own designs. Subsidised housing corporations provided the funding here and elsewhere in the 1920s, a period of frantic residential building activity beyond the canal belt and in other parts of the country, especially around Rotterdam.

Functionalism While Amsterdam School-type buildings were being erected all over their namesake city, a new generation of architects began to rebel against the school's impractical (not to mention expensive) structures. Influenced by the Bauhaus School in Germany, Frank Lloyd Wright in the USA and Le Corbusier in France, they formed a group called *de 8* (the 8) in 1927.

Architects such as B Merkelbach and Gerrit Rietveld believed that form should follow function and sang the praises of steel, glass and concrete. Buildings should be spacious, practical structures with plenty of sunlight, not masses of brick treated as works of art to glorify architects.

The all-important Amsterdam Committee of Aesthetics Control didn't agree with this, however, and kept the functionalists out of the canal belt, relegating them to the new housing estates on the outskirts of the city. In other cities, the functionalists made more of an impact on the centre, the 1930 De Bijenkorf department store in Rotterdam was a tour de force for the style. It, however, was another casualty of WWII.

Functionalism continued after the war and put its stamp on new suburbs west and south of Amsterdam as well as during the rebuilding of Rotterdam and other war-damaged cities. High-rise suburbs were built on a larger scale than originally planned, yet they still weren't sufficient to keep up with the population boom and increasing urbanisation of Dutch life. However, resistance to functionalism grew as the subtle aspects of good design were lost from these huge projects and the emphasis instead put on cheap and quick construction.

Modernism and Beyond With construction booming throughout much of the Netherlands, especially in the Randstad, there has been ample opportunity to flirt with numerous architectural styles such as structuralism, neorationalism, postmodernism, supermodernism and more. Many examples of these styles can be found in Rotterdam (see the boxed text 'Rotterdam Architecture' in the Zuid Holland & Zeeland chapter), where city planners have encouraged bold designs that range from Pet Blom's visually startling cube-shaped apartments to Ben van Berkel's graceful Erasmusbrug (Erasmus Bridge).

Dance

Ballet and dance companies can be found in several Dutch cities. The most prestigious troupe is the Netherlands Dance Theater, which is directed by Jiri Kylian in Den Haag. Other well-respected companies include the Scapino Ballet in Rotterdam and the National Ballet in Amsterdam.

Music

The dour church elders of the Calvinist era dismissed music as frivolous, even though they did begin to allow organ music in churches in the 17th century because it kept people out of pubs. Therefore, the Netherlands contributed relatively little to the world's music heritage, which makes its vivid music scene today all the more remarkable.

Especially in Amsterdam, the world's top acts are billed matter-of-factly, and Dutch musicians excel in (modern) classical music, jazz and techno/dance. In towns filled with college students, such as Leiden and Groningen, the local music scene will be far larger than the town's size would otherwise suggest.

Classical The country's best symphony orchestras and classical musicians perform in the Concertgebouw in Amsterdam. You can't go wrong with tickets for the world-renowned, Riccardo Chailly-conducted Concertgebouw Orkest, which plays music by 'big' composers but also highlights modern and unknown works.

If the pianist Ronald Brautigam is on the bill you'll be guaranteed a top-flight performance. He often collaborates with violinist Isabelle van Keulen. Cellists of note (so to speak) are Quirine Viersen and Pieter Wispelwey. The pianist Wibi Soerjadi is one of the most successful classical musicians in the country. He specialises in romantic works, and elderly ladies swoon over this handsome youngster who looks like a Javanese prince. Soprano Charlotte Margiono and mezzo-soprano Jard van Nes are worth catching too.

The Nederlandse Opera is based in the Stopera (officially called the Muziektheater), which is also in Amsterdam, where it stages world-class performances.

Major regional cities such as Den Haag, Rotterdam and Maastricht also benefit from generous state funding and have full schedules of performances by local orchestras and groups.

Modern Classical & Experimental

Dutch modern composers include Louis Andriessen, Theo Loevendie, Klaas de Vries and the late Ton de Leeuw. Worthwhile performers include The Trio, Asko Ensemble, Nieuw Ensemble and, last but not least, the Reinbert de Leeuw-conducted Schönberg Ensemble. A frequent venue for these performers is the IJsbreker in Amsterdam.

Jazz The distinction between modern classical and improvised music can be vague. Jazz band leaders such as Willem Breuker and Willem van Manen of the Contraband have a decades-long reputation for straddling the two genres.

More recently, the Dutch jazz scene has become more mainstream with gifted young chanteuses such as Fleurine and especially Surinam-born Denise Jannah, widely recognised as the country's best jazz singer. The latter is the first singer from Surinam to be signed to the legendary Blue Note label where she recently released her third CD. Her repertoire consists mainly of American standards but she adds elements of Surinamese music on stage.

Astrid Seriese and Carmen Gomez operate in the crossover field, where jazz verges on, or blends with, pop. Father and daughter team Hans and Candy Dulfer, tenor and alto saxophonists respectively, are a bit more daring. Dad, in particular, constantly extends his musical boundaries by experimenting with sampling techniques drawn from the hip-hop genre. Daughter is better known internationally, thanks to her performances with Prince, Van Morrison, Dave Stewart, Pink Floyd and Maceo Parker, among others.

Trumpeter Saskia Laroo mixes jazz with dance but is also respected in more traditional circles. In instrumental jazz, you can't go past pianist and Thelonious Monk Award-winning Michiel Borstlap and his

soul and label-mate, bass player Hein van de Geyn. The North Sea Jazz Festival, Europe's largest, is held in Den Haag each summer.

Pop & Dance Amsterdam is really the centre of modern music in the Netherlands. Bands and DJs that develop elsewhere in the country quickly seek out the scene in Amsterdam, and – as the Dutch will often mention sadly – if they're really good, soon leave for London or LA. The country's small size also means that groups can perform in Amsterdam and still be sought out relatively easily by fans from the farthest provinces.

Amsterdam may have been a 'Magic Centre' in the 1960s but its pop scene was slow to develop (the country's pop centre in those days was Den Haag, with bands like Shocking Blue and Golden Earring, who both hit No 1 in the USA). Famous Amsterdam bands in the 60s were the Outsiders – a wild band whose lead singer, Wally Tax, was reputed to be the man with the longest hair in the country – and the Hunters, an instrumental guitar group that included Jan Akkerman, who later achieved international fame in the progressive rock band Focus and was proclaimed the best guitarist in the world in a readers' poll by English magazine *Melody Maker* in 1973.

In the late 1970s the squatter's movement provided fertile ground for a lively punk music scene, followed by synthesiser-dominated New Wave. In the mid-1980s Amsterdam was a centre for guitar-driven rock bands, such as the still-active garage rockers Claw Boys Claw.

Since then Amsterdam has evolved into a capital of the dance genre, from house to techno to R&B, centred around the dance club Roxy which spectacularly burned down in 1999. Perhaps the best known Dutch dance variant internationally is the so-called 'gabber', a style in which the number of beats per minute and the noise of buzzing synthesisers goes beyond belief. Amsterdam also boasts a vital hip-hop scene, spearheaded by the Osdorp Posse who rap in their mother tongue.

Rave parties are organised in Amsterdam dance clubs and also at typically impromptu settings. Worthwhile DJs who do the club rounds include the Belgian grandmaster and Amsterdam resident, Eddy de Clerq, as well as Dimitri, Marcello and 100% Isis. Quazar is an excellent dance project set up by Gert van Veen, music critic with the newspaper De Volkskrant.

Alternative rockers Claw Boys Claw, 1960s pop legend Wally Tax and the Dutch-language rockers The Scene, De Dijk and Trockener Kecks have survived everything new, but rock bands are making a comeback and promising new bands are surfacing. The Excelsior Records label is home to Daryll Ann and upstarts such as Caesar, Johan, Benjamin B and Scram C Baby.

World Music Cosmopolitan Amsterdam offers a wealth of world music. Surinam-born Ronald Snijders, a top jazz flautist, often participates in world music projects. Another jazz flautist heading towards 'world' is the eternal Chris Hinze, for instance with his album *Tibet Impressions*, though most of his repertoire falls in the new age category.

Fra-Fra-Sound plays 'paramaribop', a unique mixture of traditional Surinamese kaseko and jazz (the moniker is a contraction of Paramaribo, the capital of Surinam, and bebop), but the bulk of world repertoire from Amsterdam is Latin, ranging from Cuban salsa to Dominican merengue and Argentinean tango. Try the following bands to get a taste of the Dutch world scene: Nueva Manteca (salsa), Sexteto Canyengue (tango) and Eric Vaarzon Morel (flamenco).

Literature

Dutch literature has been neglected by the English-speaking world, which is a shame. The lack of English translations is partly to blame. Interestingly, Flemish authorities are happy to subsidise translations of their authors but Dutch authorities are less inclined to do so.

The Dutch Shakespeare, Joost van den Vondel, is heavy going in his tragedy *Gijsbrecht van Aemstel* (1637), which is available in translation. It recounts the agony of the local count who had to go into exile after losing out to the count of Holland and his toll privileges. Vondel's best tragedy, *Lucifer* (1654), which describes the rebellion of the archangel against God, has also been translated. Other big authors of this period, Bredero (comedies) and Hooft (poems, plays, history, philosophy), have yet to appear in English.

The most interesting 19th-century author was Eduard Douwes Dekker, a colonial administrator and Amsterdam native who wrote under the pseudonym Multatuli (Latin for 'I have suffered greatly'). His *Max Havelaar: or the Coffee Auctions of the Dutch Trading Company* (1860) exposed colonial narrow-mindedness in the dealings of a self-righteous coffee merchant. It shocked Dutch society and led to a review of the 'culture system' in the East Indies (the forced production of tropical crops for export). Den Haag author Louis Couperus (*The Hidden Force*, 1900) explored the mystery of the East Indies from the colonialist's perspective.

The WWII occupation was a traumatic period that spawned many insightful works. *The Diary of Anne Frank* is the famous moving account of a Jewish girl's thoughts and yearnings while hiding in an annexe to avoid deportation by the Germans. In recent years Frank's words have inspired an entire literary subculture that re-examines and debates her work and life.

Etty Hillesum's *Etty: An Interrupted Life* is in a similar vein but more mature. Marga Minco *(The Fall, An Empty House, Bitter Herbs)* explores the war years from the perspective of a Jewish woman who survived.

Amsterdam author Harry Mulisch focuses on Dutch apathy during WWII (*The Last Call and The Assault*, which was made into an Oscar-winning film), but he has written many other books that don't involve the war. His works have their ups and downs but he is one of the great authors of Dutch literature. The war made its mark on the works of other major Dutch writers such as Gerrit Kouwenaar *(I Was Not a Soldier)* and Willem Frederik Herman *(The Dark Room of Damocles)*.

Jan Wolkers shocked Dutch readers in the 1960s with his provocatively misogynist but powerful *Turkish Delight*, which was made into a (Dutch) film by Paul Verhoeven starring Rutger Hauer. Xaviera Hollander (Vera de Vries) titillated the USA with an account of her call girl experiences in *The Happy Hooker*.

Simon Carmiggelt *(A Dutchman's Slight Adventures, I'm Just Kidding)* wrote amusing vignettes of Pijp neighbourhood life in his column in the newspaper *Het Parool*. Nicolas Freeling *(A Long Silence, Love in Amsterdam, Because of the Cats)* created the BBC's Van der Valk detective series. Jan-Willem van der Wetering *(Hard Rain)* is another author of offbeat detective stories. Hugo Claus *(The Sorrow of Belgium)* and Harry Mulisch *(The Discovery of Heaven)* both produced bestselling works.

Cees Nooteboom *(A Song of Truth and Semblance, In the Dutch Mountains)* is accessible and amusing. Lieve Joris, a Flemish author who lives in Amsterdam, writes about cultures in transition in Africa, the Middle East and Eastern Europe. Her *Gates of Damascus*, about daily life in Syria, has been published in the Lonely Planet Journeys series, as has *Mali Blues*, an account of her quest to get to know a Mali musician. Another book in this series is *The Rainbird: a Central African Journey* by Jan Brokken, a highly regarded novelist, travel narrator and literary journalist. It's a fascinating account of white explorers, missionaries, slavers and adventurers who traipsed through the jungles of Gabon.

Any Dutch town of any reasonable size will have at least one well-stocked and serious bookstore that will include a fair number of English-language titles. Used bookstores are also common. The third week in March is the national Boekenweek, when buyers who spend more than a certain amount in a bookshop receive a free (Dutch) book.

Cinema

Dutch films haven't exactly set the world of cinema on fire, though this has more to do with the language barrier and funding problems in a modest distribution area than with lack of talent.

One of the most 'important' Dutch directors of all time was Joris Ivens (1898–1989), who was influenced by Russian filmmakers but added his own impressionistic lyricism. He made award-winning documentaries about social and political issues – the Spanish Civil War, impoverished Belgian miners, Vietnam – but was also an accomplished visual artist in his own right; for instance in *Rain* (1929), a 15-minute impression of a rain shower in Amsterdam that took four months to shoot.

Directors, actors and camera operators who made the jump to English have done quite well for themselves. Paul Verhoeven *(Robocop, Total Recall, Basic Instinct, Starship Troopers)* is perhaps the best known director abroad, though his reputation has suffered from his disastrous *Showgirls*. George Sluizer *(Spoorloor)*, Dick Maas *(Flodder in Amerika, Amsterdamned)*, Fons Rademakers *(The Assault)* and Marleen Gorris *(Antonia's Line*, which won the Oscar for best foreign film in 1996) have also made a name internationally, if not always among the general public. Gorris' follow-up is an English-language film adaptation of Virginia Woolf's *Mrs Dalloway* starring Vanessa Redgrave. Jan de Bont, who won accolades for his camera work in *Jewel of the Nile* and *Black Rain*, directed the box-office hits *Speed* and *Twister*.

Rutger Hauer began his acting career at home as the lead in Paul Verhoeven's *Turks Fruit* (Turkish Delight, an Oscar nominee for best foreign film in 1974), but has since gained glory in Hollywood with convincing bad-guy performances in disturbing films such as *The Hitcher* and *Blade Runner*. Jeroen Krabbé also became a well-paid Hollywood actor *(The Fugitive, The Living Daylights, Prince of Tides)* after starting out in Dutch films and has now turned to directing, with his first film being *Left Luggage* starring Isabella Rosselini.

Purely Dutch productions are limited to under 20 films a year, usually with the sponsorship of major television networks. The Filmmuseum in the Amsterdam's Vondelpark is the national museum on this subject – it's not a museum with regular displays but screens interesting films from its huge archive. In addition, the Dutch have a keen appreciation of films beyond Hollywood blockbusters and in most medium-sized and larger cities there is at least one cinema that specialises in screening obscure, unusual and offbeat films from around the world. Rarely ever are films dubbed, but instead merely subtitled into Dutch – as any film purist will tell you it should be.

Theatre

Amsterdam has a rich theatrical tradition dating back to medieval times. In the Golden Age, when Dutch was the language of trade, local companies toured the theatres of Europe with Vondel's tragedies, Bredero's comedies and Hooft's verses. They're still performed locally in more modern renditions.

Theatre was immensely popular with all levels of society, perhaps because the city lacked a decent theatre building and plays were often performed outdoors. Gradually, however, the patrician class and their preoccupation with French culture turned theatre into a more elitist affair, and towards the end of the 19th century it had become snobbish, with little room for development.

This attitude persisted until the late 1960s, when disgruntled actors began to throw tomatoes at their older colleagues and engaged the audience in discussion about the essence of theatre. Avant-garde theatre companies such as Mickery and Shaffy made Amsterdam a centre for experimental theatre, and many smaller companies sprang up in the 1970s and 1980s.

Most of these have now merged or disappeared as a result of cutbacks in government subsidies, while musicals and cabaret are enjoying a revival. But survivors and newcomers are still forging ahead with excellent productions – visual feasts with striking sets, lighting and creative costumes. The language barrier is, of course, an issue with Dutch productions, though with some of them it's hardly relevant.

English-language companies often visit Amsterdam, especially in summer. In addition, the college town of Groningen hosts a summer festival for small theatre troupes from around Europe.

SOCIETY & CONDUCT
Stereotypes

The Netherlands in general and Amsterdam in particular can be 15 years ahead of the rest of the world on some moral and social issues (drugs, abortion, euthanasia, homosexuality). On others they're 15 years behind, for instance with media policy, where every religious and ideological affiliation can broadcast but commercial motivation is still more or less frowned upon. Sometimes they step 15 years sideways, for instance in preaching to the rest of the world about right and wrong – perhaps the only other preachers with similar drive are the Americans.

Critics attribute this to the 'minister's mentality' of moral rectitude epitomised by the Calvinist minister scowling from the pulpit. Indeed, an acute sense of moral right and wrong comes through in the earnest insistence that it hardly matters *how* you say something, it's *what* you say that counts, which gives the Dutch a bit of a reputation for bluntness. And they do get carried away, hence the English term 'Dutch uncle' for someone who criticises frankly and severely.

It also gives them a reputation for a lack of humour, yet they have an unusual ability to laugh at themselves and will cut down people who take themselves too seriously. 'Act normal, that's crazy enough,' goes the saying.

The Dutch have little nationalist pride except on the soccer field. They love to talk about their 'irrelevant' country and how they have had to find a way to fit into a world where they are so insignificant. You frequently hear some variation on the theme 'not many people in the world speak Dutch so it is better if we speak English.'
The country has few monumental buildings or projects. Most attempts at grandeur have traditionally been criticised, ridiculed and sabotaged, though Calvinist frugality has played a role too. Every separate house or building shines in its own individual way; grandeur is considered gross. It's almost as if people are proud of not being proud, except in their opinions.

It is said that the Calvinist Dutch, like the Presbyterian Scots, are careful with money, and they certainly have proven to be astute traders. It's worth remembering that the Netherlands and especially Amsterdam have always had a money culture: there was little or no traditional aristocracy with large landholdings. The people who dominated society built their own wealth and did so entirely on money – if they squandered it, they had nothing to fall back on. It determined prosperity and thus virtue.

Pillarisation & Tolerance

During much of the first half of the 20th century, Dutch society was characterised by *verzuiling* (pillarisation), a social order sanctioned by the 1917 'Pacification' compromise in which each religion and/or political persuasion achieved the right to do its own thing, with its own schools, political parties, trade unions, cultural institutions, sports clubs etc. Each persuasion represented a pillar that supported the status quo in a general 'agreement to disagree'. This elegant solution for a divided society, however, had to make way for a society where the old divisions were increasingly irrelevant. In the 1960s people began to question the status quo and the pillars came tumbling down.

Verzuiling's social and cultural segmentation is considered outdated now, but it has left a strong legacy in a culture of tolerance and willing acceptance of an endless string of petty rules and regulations to make things work fairly. The Dutch will deliberate endlessly before they issue a planning permit or form a government. Everyone is expected to have an opinion and to voice it, but meddling in others' affairs is 'not done' – at least not without following the proper procedures.

For instance, many foreigners have commented that thick cigarette smoke not just in pubs seems at odds with the high level of ecological concern. But it flows out of the Dutch commandment to be 'reasonable', to let everyone have their place and live their own life even if this puts some burdens on society. Public smoking is slowly being pushed back but these things take time. Can't get more Dutch than that.

Do's & Don'ts

The accepted greeting is a handshake – make it firm but not bone-crushing. Cheek kissing (two or three pecks) is common between men and women (and between women) who know one another socially.

The typically pragmatic convention for queuing is to take a numbered ticket from a dispenser and await your turn. Always check whether there's a dispenser if you're in a post office, government office, bakery, at a delicatessen counter in a supermarket etc.

If you're invited home for dinner, bring something for the host: a bunch of flowers or a plant, a bottle of wine, or some good cake or pastries. It's polite to arrive five to 15 minutes late (never early) but business meetings start on time.

Dress standards are casual (most concerts, most restaurants) or smart casual (theatre, opera, up-market restaurants and some business dealings); and slightly formal (most business dealings) or quite formal (bankers).

A special note for drug tourists: it is 'not done' to smoke dope in public. At coffeeshops it's OK and in some other situations

Good to the Last Scrape – or Drop

Arguably no household item represents Dutch thrift better than the *flessenlikker* (bottle-scraper). With a little practice, this miracle tool (which culminates in a disk on the business end) can tempt the last elusive smears from a mayonnaise jar or salad-dressing bottle. The flessenlikker is a hit in the Netherlands but oddly, not in its country of origin – Norway. Another item you'll find in Dutch supermarkets is the traditional Grolsch beer bottle with the resealable ceramic cap. This design was first introduced in the Calvinist north where the steely-eyed imbibers considered the contents of a bottle far too much to drink in one sitting and wanted to be able to store their brew from sober sip to sober sip.

too, but even the hippest locals detest foreigners who think they can just toke up anywhere. The same applies to drinking out on the street: the fact that you can do it doesn't mean it's accepted.

RELIGION

The number of former churches that these days house art galleries is the most obvious sign of today's attitude to religion and art. Fully 40% of the Dutch say they have no religious affiliation.

After the Alteration of 1578, when Amsterdam went over to the Protestant camp and Calvinism became the leading faith in the northern Netherlands, authorities still promoted religious tolerance (though not freedom), even towards those who didn't belong to any church. Civil marriages (sanctioned by public officials rather than clergy) were legally recognised as early as the 17th century in Amsterdam, a first in Europe.

Two nationwide trends reflect the limited role traditional religious dogma plays in daily life. The Netherlands is the only country in the world where doctors openly practise euthanasia. Official figures show that this accounts for 4000 deaths a year, however it is thought that as many as 30,000 people are euthanased a year. Although technically illegal, doctors who assist in suicide or practise euthanasia are not prosecuted as long as the patient has unbearable physical and/or mental suffering and personally takes the decision to die.

In schools, sex is taught as something that is enjoyable and healthy. By not saddling the topic with guilt or shame, it is hoped that this will lead to an open atmosphere where safe sex and family planning are both easier to discuss and practice.

Catholics account for the largest portion of people expressing religious affiliation at 32%. The term 'Catholic' should be used in preference to 'Roman Catholic' because many Dutch Catholics disagree with the pope on church hierarchy, contraception and abortion. Among Protestants there are two major groups. In the late 19th century a growing minority of low-income strugglers disagreed with the tolerance of the Hervormde Kerk (Dutch Reformed Church) and broke off to form the Gereformeerde Kerk ('Re-reformed' Church) in pursuit of orthodox-Calvinist doctrine. The schism persists to this day though it affects an ever smaller number of people. The Dutch Reformed Church claims 14% of the population while the break-away Calvinists account for 7%. Another 7% of the population claims affiliation with other churches with Muslim at 4.3% and Hindu at 0.5% being the two largest segments of this category.

The Dutch Reformed Church is known for its liberal views and it is one of few churches to support same sex marriages.

LANGUAGE

Most English speakers use the term 'Dutch' to describe the language spoken in the Netherlands, and 'Flemish' for that spoken in the northern half of Belgium and a tiny north-western corner of France. Both are in fact the same language, the correct term for which is Netherlandic, or *Nederlands*, a West Germanic language spoken by about 25 million people worldwide. The differences between Dutch and Flemish (*Vlaams*) are similar to those between British and North American English.

The people of the northern Friesland province speak their own language. Although Friesian is actually the nearest relative of the English language, you won't be able to make much sense of it, although you'll have to go to a small-town shop or a farm to really hear it. It's not the dominant language in the province, but most of the locals know some as a sign of cultural pride.

Almost every Dutch person from age five onwards seems to speak English, often very well and better than you'll ever learn Dutch, so why bother? That's a good question because you'll rarely get the opportunity to practise: your Dutch acquaintances will launch into English, maybe to show off, but also because knowledge of the language is so widespread that they're happy to accommodate you. But a few words in Dutch show goodwill which is always appreciated and you might begin to understand a bit more of what's going on around you. The phrase *Spreekt u Engels?* (Do you speak English?) before launching into English is best used with older people. The young, thanks to years of English in school, as well as exposure to vast amounts of English language media (movies are usually subtitled rather than dubbed), will likely look at you like you've gone around the bend if you ask about their English skills.

For more extensive coverage of Dutch see the Language chapter. You can also pick up Lonely Planet's *Western Europe phrasebook*.

Facts for the Visitor

SUGGESTED ITINERARIES

Depending on the length of your stay, you might want to see and do the following things:

Two days Visit Amsterdam

One week Spend two days in Amsterdam, one day each in Haarlem (visit the Keukenhof gardens in season), Delft, Den Haag and the remaining two days visiting Rotterdam and the Kinderdijk windmills

Two weeks Spend three days in Amsterdam, one day each in Haarlem (Keukenhof in season), Den Haag, Leiden and Delft, two days in Rotterdam (Kinderdijk), one day around the Delta Region (Middelburg) Hoge Veluwe National Park, Deventer and two days in Maastricht

One month This should give you enough time to have a look around the whole country

PLANNING

The Netherlands is one of the easiest places in which to travel. Up-to-date information is plentiful, transport connections are easy and there are a wealth of things to do. All this means that you can allow a fair amount of spontaneity in your trip.

Conversely, however, if there are certain sights you absolutely must see – such as the tulip fields or many of the outdoor attractions – then you will want to plan your trip to coincide with the months they are open or blooming. Also, the best of the less expensive places to stay can book up early, even in Amsterdam with its wealth of good choices. And some towns just don't have that many places to stay, so it makes sense to get your reservations in advance.

If this is your first trip to Europe, the Netherlands is a good destination for the above reasons plus the minimal language problems and overall 'ease of use'. You may find it very helpful to check out Lonely Planet's *Read This First: Europe*, which is a great predeparture tool for planning your trip.

WHEN TO GO

Any time can be the best time to visit. The summer months are delightful as the Dutch

seem to live outdoors and things happen everywhere. It's also the peak tourist season; accommodation is harder to find and prices are high. Many Dutch go on holidays in summer – especially in August – and some businesses close down or adapt their activities, eg, museums and orchestras.

From mid-October to mid-March the climate is miserable but there are fewer tourists. Accommodation is relatively cheap (except around New Year) though some hotels might be closed. You'll mingle with 'real' Dutch in cosy pubs and be able to enjoy the country's cultural life at its most authentic. The shoulder seasons, roughly from mid-March to late May and late August to mid-October, can offer the best of both worlds, though you might want to avoid Easter in Amsterdam with its hordes of tourists and expensive hotels.

A festival or special event can enhance your visit – see Public Holidays & Special Events later in this chapter – but it won't be a secret and you might have trouble finding accommodation. If weather is your main concern, see Climate in the Facts About the Netherlands chapter.

Maps

The best road maps of the Netherlands are those produced by Michelin (scale: 1:200,000) and the ANWB (scale: 1:300,000). The ANWB also puts out provincial maps detailing cycling paths and picturesque road routes (scale: 1:100,000). You will find a wide variety of maps for sale at any VVV office, as well as at bookstores and newsstands. Lonely Planet also produces a handy and – more importantly – water-repellent Amsterdam map that's good for carrying during your city exploration.

What to Bring

It's very easy to find almost anything you need in the Netherlands and, since you'll probably buy things as you go along, it's better to start with too little rather than too much.

Travelpacks, a combination backpack/ shoulder bag, are very popular. The backpack straps zip away inside the pack when they are not needed, so you almost have the best of both worlds. Some packs have sophisticated shoulder-strap adjustment systems and can be used comfortably even on long hikes. Backpacks or travelpacks are always much easier to carry than a bag, and can be made reasonably theft-proof with small padlocks.

A pure backpack is a popular method of carrying gear as it is convenient, especially for walking. On the downside, a backpack doesn't offer too much protection for your

valuables, the straps tend to get caught on things and some airlines may refuse to accept responsibility if the pack is damaged or tampered with.

Another alternative is a large, soft zip bag with a wide shoulder strap so it can be carried with relative ease but this is only good for relatively short distances as your shoulder will soon ache. Travel suitcases with the built-in wheels and handles that deploy are very popular, but are really only good if you'll be going between your transport and hotels as they're not great for dragging long distances.

Forget a pure suitcase without wheels or other oversized luggage as you'll soon understand where the 'lug' in luggage comes from. A burdensome bag such as these will soon turn your trip into one of misery and you'll want to toss it into the nearest canal.

As for clothing, the climate will have a bearing on what you take along, but be prepared for rain at any time of year. Remember that insulation works on the principle of trapped air, so several layers of thin clothing are warmer than a single thick one (and will be easier to dry). You'll also be much more flexible if the weather suddenly turns warm. Bearing in mind that you can buy virtually anything on the spot, a minimum packing list could include:

underwear, socks and swimming gear (if planning on hitting the beaches)
a pair of dark jeans or even better a dark pair of comfortable pants that don't run afoul of any 'no jeans' rules
maybe a pair of shorts or skirt
a few shirts
a warm sweater
a solid pair of walking shoes
sandals or thongs for showers
a raincoat, waterproof jacket or umbrella
a medical kit of essentials from home, otherwise pharmacies are common
a Swiss Army knife
soap and towel
toiletries, just sufficient for the trip's duration

A padlock is useful to lock your bag to a luggage rack in a bus or train; it may also be needed to secure your hostel locker. A Swiss Army knife comes in handy for all sorts of things. *Any* pocketknife is fine, but make sure it includes such essentials as a bottle opener and strong corkscrew! Toiletries and toilet paper are readily obtainable, but you'll need your own supply of paper in many public toilets and at those in camping grounds. Tampons are available at pharmacies and supermarkets. Condoms are widely available in the Netherlands.

A tent and sleeping bag are vital if you want to save money by camping. A sleeping sheet with pillow cover (case) is necessary if you plan to stay in hostels. You may have to hire or purchase one if you don't bring your own. Make one yourself out of old sheets (include a built-in pillow cover) or buy one from your hostel association.

Other optional items include a compass, a torch (flashlight), a pocket calculator for currency conversions, an alarm clock, an adapter plug for electrical appliances (such as a cup or immersion water heater to save on expensive tea and coffee), a universal bath/sink plug (a film canister sometimes works), sunglasses, a few clothes pegs and premoistened towelettes. During city sightseeing, a small daypack is better than a shoulder bag for deterring thieves. Many travelpacks have one that zips off.

Consider using plastic carry bags or bin liners inside your backpack to keep things separate, for isolating dirty laundry, but also dry if the pack gets soaked.

If you are going to be cycling, consider bringing your favourite bike helmet, although you can buy a reasonable one in the Netherlands.

RESPONSIBLE TOURISM

The Netherlands is firmly in the first world. Its population is affluent and the population is well used to the comings and goings of people from around the world. So you need not worry about trying to minimise your impact on Dutch society. Indeed, a fair part of the economy is based on tourism.

However, given the tolerant nature of the Dutch, many practices that are considered vices in other countries are openly practised in the Netherlands. Amsterdam is well known for its huge red-light district where prostitution is on open display. So too the city's 'coffeeshops', where people openly smoke pot. Even in fairly small towns, you may be surprised to round a corner and find women lit by red lights sitting in windows. And every town has at least one coffeeshop. That said, most Dutch seem to actively ignore such places. If they disapprove, they keep it to themselves.

Legally, the government is in line with the populace. Prostitution, which is legal, is subject to numerous regulations designed to protect the health and the rights of all parties involved. In fact, brothels were scheduled to be made legal in October 2000 in order to allow tighter government regulation. One other important point to remember with prostitution is that most of the prostitutes are not Dutch. Hailing from Third World nations and Eastern Europe, the prostitutes are, despite government regulations, prone to abuse and exploitation from those they work for and by customers.

Drugs are subject to a welter of regulations. Small amounts of cannabis may be openly smoked in coffeeshops but local regulations may make the actual purchase difficult. Further, open pot smoking is deplored by many and there is little tolerance – and less laxity in laws – for hard drug use and sales.

Finally, it is perhaps best to remember that while activities frowned upon in a traveller's home country may be allowed here, the Netherlands really should be visited first and foremost for its culture, sights and people. Those who visit the country purely for an orgy of pot-smoking and sexual excess are missing the point entirely and doing the Dutch themselves a disservice.

TOURIST OFFICES
Local Tourist Offices

Within the Netherlands, tourist information is supplied by the VVV (Vereniging voor Vreemdelingenverkeer; Society for Foreigner Traffic), which has offices throughout the country. Although each office is locally run, they all have a huge amount of information that covers not just their area but the rest of the country as well. However, most VVV publications cost money and there are commissions for services (f6 per person to find a room, f2.50 to f5 on theatre tickets etc). The offices are often very crowded but it can be worth the wait at busy times to buy locally available items. An example is the Amsterdam Culture & Leisure Pass available from the Amsterdam VVV. With their universal English skills, VVV offices are also good for buying such things as local transport tickets.

See the individual city listings for details on local services – such as lists of private accommodation – as well as opening hours.

Tourist Offices Abroad

The Nederlands Bureau voor Toerisme (NBT) handles tourism inquiries outside the country. It is an excellent contact during your predeparture planning. There is the added advantage that many publications sent for free from the NBT cost money once you arrive in the Netherlands.

The VVV offices include:

Belgium (plus Luxembourg) (☎ 02-543 08 00, fax 534 21 94) NBT, Louizalaan 89, PO Box 136, 1050 Brussels

Canada (☎ 416-363 1577, fax 363 1470) Netherlands Board of Tourism, 25 Adelaide St East, Suite 710, Toronto, Ont, M5C 1Y2

France (☎ 1 43 12 34 20, fax 12 34 21) Office Néerlandais du Tourisme, 9 rue Scribe, 75009 Paris

Germany (☎ 0221-9257 1727, fax 9257 1737) Niederländisches Büro für Tourismus, Friesenplatz 1, Postfach 270580, 50511 Cologne

Japan (☎ 03-32 22 11 15, fax 32 22 11 14) Netherlands Board of Tourism, NK Shinwa Building 5f 5–1, Koijmachi, Chiyoda-ku, Tokyo 102

Sweden (plus Denmark, Norway & Finland) (☎ 08-5560 0750, fax 714 8434) Holländska Turistbyrån, Högbergsgatan 50–1tr, 1118 26 Stockholm

UK (plus Ireland) (☎ 020-7828 7900, fax 7828 7941) Netherlands Board of Tourism, 18 Buckingham Gate, PO Box 523, London SW1E 6NT

USA (☎ 212-370 7360, fax 370 9507) Netherlands Board of Tourism, 355 Lexington Ave, New York, NY, 10017

The NBT office in Sydney, Australia has closed down. The embassy in Canberra, consulates in the major cities or the KLM office in Sydney will be able to help.

The NBT Web site, www.visitholland .com, has email links to all of the above offices, plus other NBT offices worldwide and other useful links.

Other Information Sources

The VVV is useful for mainstream tourist information but other places might serve you better. Both Amsterdam and Rotterdam have information sources that offer specialised help for cultural and other matters. See the city listings for details.

The Dutch automobile association ANWB has free or discounted maps and brochures and provides a wide range of useful information and assistance if you're travelling with any type of vehicle (car, bicycle, motorcycle, yacht etc). In many cities the VVV and ANWB share offices. You'll probably have to show proof of membership of your automobile club (see Useful Cards in the following section).

VISAS & DOCUMENTS
Passport

Your most important travel document is your passport, which should remain valid until well after you return home. If it's just about to expire, renew it before you go. This may not be easy to do overseas, and some countries insist that your passport remains valid for a specified period (usually three months) beyond the date of your departure from that country.

Applying for or renewing a passport can take anything from an hour to several months, so don't leave it till the last minute. Bureaucratic wheels usually turn faster if you do everything in person rather than relying on the post or agents, but check first what you need to take with you: photos of a certain size, birth certificate, population register extract, signed statements, exact payment in cash etc.

Visas

Tourists from Australia, Canada, Israel, Japan, South Korea, New Zealand, Singapore, the USA and most of Europe need only a valid passport – no visa – for a stay of up to three months. EU nationals can enter for three months with just their national identity card or a passport expired less than five years.

Nationals of most other countries need a so-called Schengen visa, named after the Schengen Agreement that abolished passport controls between the EU member states (except the UK and Ireland) plus Norway and Iceland. A visa for any of these countries should in theory be valid throughout the area for 90 days, but it pays to double-check with the embassy or consulate of each country you intend to visit because the agreement is not yet fully implemented – some countries may impose additional restrictions on some nationalities. Residency status in any of the Schengen countries negates the need for a visa, regardless of your nationality.

Schengen visas are issued by Dutch embassies or consulates and can take a while to process (up to three months if you're unlucky), so don't leave it until the last moment. You'll need a valid passport (valid until at least three months after your visit) and 'sufficient' funds to finance your stay. Fees vary depending on your nationality – the embassy or consulate can tell you more.

Visas for study purposes are complicated – check with the Dutch embassy or consulate. For work visas, see the Work section later in this chapter.

Visa Extensions The Netherlands is the most densely populated country in Europe and voters seem to support the government crackdown on people who don't have the proper immigration documents. Tourist visas can be extended for another three months maximum, but you'll need a good reason and the extension will only be valid for the Netherlands, not the Schengen area.

Visa extensions and residence permits are handled in Amsterdam by the Vreemdelingenpolitie (Aliens' Police; ☎ 020-559 63 00), Johan Huizingalaan 757 out in the southwestern suburbs, 8 am to 5 pm Monday to Friday. Bring something to read: you'll probably have to wait a couple of hours. You can call them for information on visa extensions from other parts of the country.

Travel Insurance

Medical or dental costs might already be covered through reciprocal health-care arrangements (see Health later in the chapter). But you'll still need cover for theft or loss, and for unexpected changes to travel arrangements (ticket cancellation etc). Check what's already covered by your local insurance policies or credit card issue; you might not need separate travel insurance. In most cases, though, this secondary type of cover is very limited with lots of tricky small print. For peace of mind, nothing beats straight travel insurance at the highest level you can afford.

Driving Licence & Permits

Of course you'll need to show a valid driving licence when hiring a car. Visitors from outside the EU should also consider an international driving permit (IDP). Car-rental firms will rarely ask for one but the police might do so if they pull you up. An IDP can be obtained for a small fee from your local automobile association – bring along a valid licence and a passport photo – and is only valid (for a year) together with your original licence.

Useful Cards

A Hostelling International (HI) card is useful at the official youth hostels – non-members are welcome but pay f5 more per night. Other hostels may give small discounts. If you don't pick up a HI card before leaving home you can buy one at youth hostels in the Netherlands.

An International Student Identity Card (ISIC) will get some admission discounts and might pay for itself through discounted air and ferry tickets, and the GWK exchange offices will charge 25% less commission when exchanging cash. The same applies to hostel cards, as well as the GO 25 card for people aged under 26 who aren't students, issued by the Federation of International Youth Travel Organisations (FIYTO) through student unions or student travel agencies.

The Cultureel Jongeren Paspoort (CJP, Cultural Youth Passport) is regarded as a national institution that gives people aged under 27 whopping discounts to museums and cultural events around the country – any young person with a particular interest in the arts is well advised to get one. It costs f22.50 a year and is available at VVV offices. You don't have to be Dutch but you do need decent ID.

Teachers, professional artists, museum conservators and certain categories of students may get discounts at a few museums or even be admitted free – it sometimes depends on the person behind the counter. Bring proof of affiliation, eg, an International Teacher Identity Card (ITIC).

Many VVV offices sell local culture cards that give a break on admission to local attractions. See the relevant city listings for availability. A good example is the Amsterdam Culture & Leisure Pass sold by the city's VVV offices and some large hotels. This contains 31 vouchers that give free entry or substantial discounts to the most important museums, a free canal cruise, and discounts on land and water transport and some restaurants. The pass represents a total value of f170 and sells for f39.50, which could be a good investment depending on your interests.

If you're travelling with any type of vehicle, the Dutch automobile association ANWB (see Other Information Sources in the previous section) will provide a wide range of services free of charge if you can show proof of membership of the equivalent association at home, preferably in the form of a letter of introduction such as the yellow Entraide Touring Internationale document. Your automobile club should be able to provide this; if the staff have never heard of it, ask for someone who knows their stuff.

Copies

All important documents (passport data page and visa page, credit cards, travel insurance policy, air/bus/train ticket, driving licence etc) should be photocopied before you leave home. Leave one copy with someone at home and keep another one with you, separate from the originals.

It's also a good idea to store details of your vital travel documents in Lonely Planet's free online Travel Vault in case you lose the photocopies. Your password-protected Travel Vault is accessible online anywhere in the world – create it at www.ekno.lonelyplanet.com.

EMBASSIES & CONSULATES
Dutch Embassies and Consulates

Diplomatic representation abroad includes:

Australia (☎ 06-273 3111) 120 Empire Circuit, Yarralumla, Canberra, ACT 2600

Belgium (☎ 02-679 17 11) ave Herrmann-Debroux 48, 1160 Brussels

Canada (☎ 613-237 50 30) Suite 2020, 350 Albert St, Ottawa, Ont K1R 1A4

Denmark (☎ 33-70 72 00) Toldbodgade 33, 1253 Kopenhagen K

France (☎ 01-40 62 33 00) 7–9 Rue Ebie, 75007 Paris

Finland (☎ 09-66 17 37) Skillnadsgatan 19 B, 00130 Helsinki

Germany (☎ 030-20 95 60) Friedrichstrasse 95, 10117 Berlin

Ireland (☎ 01-269 34 44) 160 Merrion Road, Dublin 4

Luxembourg (☎ 22 75 70) 5 Rue CM Spoo, L-2546

New Zealand (☎ 04-473 8652) 10th fl, Investment House, Ballance & Featherston St, Wellington

Norway (☎ 22 60 21 96) Oscarsgate 29, 0352 Oslo

South Africa (☎ 012-344 39 10) 825 Arcadia Street, Arcadia

Sweden (☎ 08-24 71 80) Götgatan 16A, Stockholm

United Kingdom (☎ 0171-584 5040) 38 Hyde Park Gate, London SW7 5DP

USA (☎ 202-244 5300) 4200 Linnean Ave, NW Washington, DC 20008

Embassies & Consulates in the Netherlands

Amsterdam is the country's capital but the government and ministries are based in Den Haag, so that's where all the embassies are. They include:

Australia (☎ 070-310 82 00) Carnegielaan 4
Belgium (☎ 070-312 34 56) Lange Vijverberg 12
Canada (☎ 070-311 16 00) Sophialaan 7

Denmark (☎ 070-365 58 30) Koninginnegracht 30
France (☎ 070-312 58 00) Smisplein 1
Finland (☎ 070-363 85 75) Groot Hertoginnelaan 16
Germany (☎ 070-342 06 00) Groot Hertoginnelaan 18–20
Ireland (☎ 070-363 09 93) Dr Kuijperstraat 9
New Zealand (☎ 070-346 93 24) Carnegielaan 10-IV
Norway (☎ 070-311 76 11) Prinsessgracht 6a
South Africa (☎ 070-392 45 01) Wassenaarseweg 40
Sweden (☎ 070-412 02 00) Van Karnebeeklaan 6A
United Kingdom (☎ 070-427 04 27) Lange Voorhout 10
USA (☎ 070-310 92 09) Lange Voorhout 102

Consulates in Amsterdam include:

Denmark (☎ 020-682 99 91) Radarweg 503
France (☎ 020-530 69 69) Vijzelgracht 2
Germany (☎ 020-673 62 45) De Lairessestraat 172
Luxembourg (☎ 020-301 56 22) Reimersbeek 2
Norway (☎ 020-624 23 31) Keizersgracht 534-I
United Kingdom (☎ 020-676 43 43) Koningslaan 44 near the Vondelpark
USA (☎ 020-575 53 09) Museumplein 19 near the Concertgebouw

Your Own Embassy

It's important to realise what your own embassy – the embassy of the country of which you are a citizen – can and can't do to help you if you get into trouble.

Generally speaking, it won't be much help in emergencies if the trouble you're in is remotely your own fault. Remember that you are bound by the laws of the country you are in. Your embassy will not be sympathetic if you end up in jail after committing a crime locally, even if such actions are legal in your own country.

In genuine emergencies you might get some assistance, but only if other channels have been exhausted. For example, if you need to get home urgently, a free ticket home is exceedingly unlikely – the embassy would expect you to have insurance. If you have all your money and documents stolen, it might assist with getting a new passport, but a loan for onward travel is out of the question.

Some embassies used to keep letters for travellers or have a small reading room with home newspapers, but these days the mail holding service has usually been stopped and even newspapers tend to be out of date.

CUSTOMS

Visitors from EU countries can bring virtually anything they like, provided it's for personal use and they bought it in an EU country where the appropriate local tax was levied. Duty-free allowances on cigarettes and alcohol have been abolished within the EU, but allowances on other products (perfume etc) remain in place. The staff at duty-free shops will ask to see your ticket and will tell you in no uncertain terms how much (or rather, little) they're willing to sell you – though you're welcome to buy your whisky at the local, taxed price.

Visitors from a European country outside the EU and not resident in the EU can import goods and gifts valued up to f125 (bought tax-free) as well as 200 cigarettes (or 50 cigars or 250g of tobacco), 1L of liquor more than 22% by volume or 2L less than 22% by volume, plus 2L of wine and 8L of nonsparkling Luxembourg wine, 60g of perfume and 0.25L of eau de toilette.

Visitors from outside Europe and residents outside Europe can bring in 400 cigarettes (or 100 cigars or 500g of tobacco) plus other goods, spirits, wines and perfumes as for non-EU Europeans.

Tobacco and alcohol may only be brought in by people aged 17 and over.

MONEY
Currency

The unit of currency is the guilder (gulden; abbreviated as f, fl, Hfl or Dfl), divided into 100 cents. There are f1000, f250, f100, f50, f25 and f10 banknotes, and f5, f2.50, f1, f0.25, f0.10 and f0.05 coins. One-cent coins no longer exist; prices in supermarkets are still indicated in cents (eg, f5.99) but the bill is rounded off to the nearest five cents when paid in cash.

The Dutch flair for graphic design shows in the eye-catching banknotes, in particular the f100 note with its Escher-type 'building blocks', or the stunning f10 bill. If you're on the sort of budget where you would receive a f1000 note from the bank, ask to have it broken down into f100 and f50 notes because many places refuse the larger denominations.

Note that the Dutch have f2.50(!) as well as f25 and f250 coins. This flouts the more typical standard of at least having bills in divisions of 20s.

The Euro On 1 January 1999 a new currency, the euro, was introduced in Europe and on that date the exchange rates of the participating countries were irrevocably fixed to the euro – in the case of the Netherlands, at f2.20371 to the euro. Denmark, Greece, Sweden and the UK refused to participate (for the time being), but the other EU members including the Netherlands are gradually phasing out their local currencies in favour of the euro. One of the main benefits will be that you can easily compare prices in the participating countries without all those tedious calculations.

At the time of writing, the euro is used for 'paper' accounting and prices are often displayed in guilders as well as euros, though cash payments are still entirely in guilders. On 1 January 2002 euro banknotes and coins will come in a period of dual use as guilders are withdrawn from circulation. By July 2002 only euro notes and coins will remain.

The €5 note in the Netherlands is the same €5 note you will use in other EU countries that have adopted the euro. Notes will come in denominations of 500, 200, 100, 50, 20, 10 and five euros. Coins will come in denominations of two and one euros, then 50, 20, 10, five, two and one cents. On the reverse side of the coins each participating state will be able to use their own designs, but all euro coins can be used anywhere that accepts euros.

It is uncertain exactly what practices will be adopted until the euro takes over completely. The Dutch, in general, are happy to adopt the euro but some shops might be more ready to do so than others. For the time being, it's wise to check euro bills and coins carefully to make sure that any conversion from guilders has been calculated

correctly. The most confusing period will probably be between January and July 2002 when there will be two sets of notes and coins in circulation.

After that date, you won't need to change money at all when travelling to other single-currency members. Banks may still charge a handling fee (yet to be decided) for travellers cheques but they won't be able to profit by buying the currency from you at one rate and selling it back to you at another.

The Lonely Planet Web site which can be found at www.lonelyplanet.com has a link to a currency converter and up-to-date news on the euro integration process.

Exchange Rates

At the time of going to press, exchange rates for the guilder and the euro were:

country	unit		guilder (f)
Australia	A$1	=	1.42
Canada	C$1	=	1.63
Denmark	10Dkr	=	2.95
euro	€1	=	2.20
France	10FF	=	3.36
Germany	DM1	=	1.12
Ireland	IR£1	=	2.79
Japan	Y100	=	2.24
New Zealand	NZ$1	=	1.11
Norway	10Nkr	=	2.70
South Africa	R10	=	3.47
Sweden	10Skr	=	2.62
United Kingdom	UK£1	=	3.63
United States	US$1	=	2.43

country	unit		euro (€)
Australia	A$1	=	0.65
Canada	C$1	=	0.74
Denmark	10Dkr	=	1.34
France	10FF	=	1.52
Germany	DM1	=	0.51
Ireland	IR£1	=	1.26
Japan	Y100	=	1.02
New Zealand	NZ$1	=	0.50
Netherlands	f1	=	0.45
Norway	10Nkr	=	1.22
South Africa	R10	=	1.51
Sweden	10Skr	=	1.18
United Kingdom	UK£1	=	1.65
United States	US$1	=	1.10

Exchanging Money

Cash Cash is still common and nothing beats cash for convenience – or risk of theft/loss. Plan to pay cash for most daily expenses, though staff at upmarket hotels might cast a furtive glance if you pay a huge bill with small-denomination notes rather than a credit card, and car-rental agencies will probably refuse to do business if you only have cash. Keep the equivalent of about US$50 separate from the rest of your money as an emergency stash.

Travellers Cheques & Eurocheques

Banks charge a commission to cash travellers cheques (with ID such as a passport). American Express and Thomas Cook don't charge commission on their own cheques but their rates might be less favourable. Shops, restaurants and hotels always prefer cash; a few might accept travellers cheques but their rates will be anybody's guess. Eurocheques (with guarantee card) – not to be confused with the new currency (though you can, of course, write them in euros) – are much more widely accepted, and because you write the amount in guilders there's no confusion about exchange rates; they get charged to your account at the more favourable interbank rate.

ATMs Automatic teller machines can be found outside most banks, though in some cases you might have to swipe your card through a slot to gain entry to a secure area. There are ATMs around the airports and most of the train stations. Credit cards like Visa and MasterCard/Eurocard are widely accepted, as well as cash cards that access the Cirrus network. Logos on ATMs show what they accept, although these days most seem unconcerned about where your card comes from. If in doubt, shove the card in and see what happens. Beware that if you're limited to a maximum withdrawal per day, the 'day' will coincide with that in your home country. Also note that using an ATM can be the cheapest way to exchange your money from home – but check with your home bank for extortionate service charges before leaving.

Credit Cards All the major international cards are recognised and you will find that most hotels, restaurants and major stores accept them. But always check first to avoid, as they say, 'disappointment'. Shops often levy a cheeky 5% surcharge (sometimes more) on credit cards to offset the commissions charged by card providers.

To withdraw money at a bank counter instead of through an ATM, go to a GWK branch (see the following Moneychangers section). You'll need to show your passport.

Report lost or stolen cards to the following 24-hour numbers:

American Express – ☎ 020-504 80 00 (9 am to 6 pm Monday to Friday), ☎ 020-504 86 66 (other times)
Diners Club – ☎ 020-557 34 07
Eurocard and **MasterCard** have a number in Utrecht (☎ 030-283 55 55) but foreigners are advised to ring the emergency number in their home country to speed up things
Thomas Cook – ☎ 0800-022 8630
Visa – ☎ 020-660 06 11

International Transfers Transferring money from your home bank will be easier if you've authorised somebody back home to access your account. In the Netherlands, find a large bank (preferably in a major city) and ask for the international division. A commission is charged on telegraphic transfers, which can take up to a week but usually less if you're well prepared; by mail, allow two weeks.

The GWK (see the following Moneychangers section) is an agent for Western Union and money is transferred within 15 minutes of lodgment at the other end. The person lodging the transfer pays a commission that varies from country to country. Money can also be transferred via American Express and Thomas Cook at their Amsterdam offices.

Moneychangers Avoid the private exchange booths dotted around tourist areas; they're convenient and open late hours but rates and/or commissions are lousy, though competition is fierce and you may do reasonably well if you hunt around. Banks and post offices (every post office is an agent for Postbank) stick to official exchange rates and charge a commission of around f6, as does GWK (Grenswisselkantoren; ☎ 0800-566 free information service). Keep in mind that exchange rates between euro currencies are fixed and it all comes down to commissions these days.

Generally your best bet for exchanging money as you travel around the Netherlands is to use GWK. Offices are in almost every medium-sized and larger train station as well as at the borders on major highways. Many locations, such as those at Amsterdam's Centraal Station and at Schiphol airport are open 24 hours. See the individual city listings for details on GWK offices and opening hours.

Costs

Prices in the Netherlands are similar to those in other Western European countries and the USA and Australia. The sky is the limit in Amsterdam: you can easily throw hundreds of guilders down the drain each day with little to show for it. At rock-bottom, if you stay at a camp site or hostel and eat cheaply, you might get away with f60 a day. A (very) cheap hotel, pub meals and the occasional beer and sundries will set you back f100. Things become a bit more comfortable on f150 a day.

Tipping & Bargaining

Tipping is not compulsory, but if you're pleased with the service by all means round up the bill by 5% to 10%. Such a tip is expected in a taxi. A tip of 10% is considered generous, but is becoming increasingly common. In pubs with pavement or table service it's common practice to leave the small change. Service is usually efficient but hardly ever formal and sometimes quite indifferent; shouting or 'talking down' to staff will ensure they ignore you. Toilet attendants should be tipped 25 to 50 cents, though in some clubs they demand f1.

Ironically for a country with such a rich trading history, there's very little bargaining – it's definitely not done in shops. People do bargain at flea markets, though you'll have to

be pretty good at this if your Dutch isn't fluent. Prices at food markets are generally set but become more negotiable later in the day. The so-called Dutch auction, where the auctioneer keeps lowering the price until somebody takes the item, is still practised at flower and plant auctions such as the huge flower market in Aalsmeer and the Monday plant market on Amstelveld.

Discounts

Students or those aged under 26 won't get a lot of discounts with their ISIC or GO 25 cards, but a CJP card (see the earlier Useful Cards section) can pay for itself many times over. Seniors get discounts on a wide range of services (see Senior Travellers later in this chapter).

Taxes & Refunds

Value-added tax (Belasting Toegevoegde Waarde, or BTW) is calculated at 19% for most goods except consumer items like food and books, which attract 6%. The usual high excise (accijns) is levied on petrol, cigarettes and alcohol – petrol prices here are among the most expensive in Europe. The price for a packet of cigarettes is indicated on an excise sticker, and it will cost the same wherever you buy it, separately or by the carton.

Hotel accommodation is often subject to 'city hotel tax' used to fund the local tourism authority. The amount – when charged – averages 5% and is usually included in the quoted price except at the more expensive hotels.

Travellers from non-EU countries can have the BTW refunded on goods over f300 if they're bought from one shop on one day and are exported out of the EU within three months. To claim the tax back, ask the shop owner to provide an export certificate when you make the purchase. When you leave for a non-EU country, get the form endorsed by a Dutch customs official, who will send the certificate to the supplier, who in turn refunds you the tax by cheque or money order. If you want the tax as you leave the country, it's best to buy from shops displaying a 'Tax Free for Tourists' sign, though you'll lose about 5% of the refund in commissions. In this case the shopkeeper gives you a stamped cheque that can be cashed when you leave.

Buying with a credit card is the best system as you won't pay tax so long as you get customs to stamp the receipt the shop owner gave you and you send the receipt back to the shop.

POST & COMMUNICATIONS
Post
Post offices are open 9 am to 6 pm weekdays and 10 am to 1 pm Saturday, more or less. Poste restante is best handled in Amsterdam, see the city listing for details.

Mail is delivered locally six days a week. Unless you're sending mail within the post office's local region, the slot to use in the rectangular, red letter boxes is Overige Postcodes (Other Postal Codes).

Postal Rates Letters within Europe (only air mail, known as 'priority') cost f1 up to 20g; beyond Europe they are f1.60 (priority) or f1.25 (standard). Postcards (only priority) cost f1 to anywhere outside the country. An aerogramme (*priorityblad*) is f1.30. Within the country, letters (up to 20g) or postcards cost f0.80.

Standard mail (also available within Europe for parcels and printed matter) is not much cheaper than priority and takes about twice as long to reach the destination. For instance, a priority parcel to the UK takes two to three days, whereas standard takes four to five; to the USA, it's four to six days as opposed to eight to 12.

Addresses The postal code (four numbers followed by two letters) comes in front of the city or town name, eg, 1017 LS Amsterdam. The codes are complicated and there's little apparent logic to them, but they pinpoint an address to within 100m. The telephone book provides the appropriate postal code for each address. Most post offices stock a complete set of the country's phone books.

There are a few peculiarities with street numbers. Sometimes they're followed by a letter or number (often in Roman numerals). Letters (eg, No 34A or 34a) usually indicate the appropriate front door when two or more share the same number, whereas numbers (34–2, 34r² or 34-II) indicate the appropriate floor. In modern dwellings, letters often indicate the appropriate apartment irrespective of the floor. The suffix 'hs' (34hs) stands for *huis* (house) and means the dwelling is on the ground floor, which may be half a floor above street level (in which case it's sometimes called *beletage*, the floor behind the door bell). The suffix 'bg' (34bg) stands for *begane grond* (ground floor). The suffix 'sous' (34sous) stands for *souterrain* and means the dwelling is in the basement (or rather, a basement that's half under street level; it can't be much deeper because of ground water).

Telephone
The country code for calling the Netherlands is ☎ 31.

This used to be one of the more expensive European countries for phone calls but prices keep coming down with the new phenomenon of competition for the former monopoly of KPT-Telecom. Most public phones accept credit cards as well as various phonecards sold by the public phone owner. As always, using a hotel phone is much more expensive than any other type of phone.

For local directory information, call ☎ 0900-80 08 (f0.95 for up to three numbers, free from a phone box). International directory inquiries can be reached on ☎ 0900-84 18 (f1.05 for up to two numbers). To place a collect call (*collect gesprek*), ring ☎ 0800-01 01 (free call). For other operator-assisted calls, ring ☎ 0800-04 10 (free call, though you'll be charged a f7.70 service fee if you could have rung the country direct).

Mobile Phones The Netherlands uses GSM 900/1800, which is compatible with the rest of Europe and Australia but not with the North American GSM 1900 or the totally different system in Japan (though some North Americans have GSM 1900/900 phones that do work here). If you have a GSM phone, check with your service provider about using it in the Netherlands, and beware of calls being routed internationally (very expensive for a 'local' call). You can also rent one at the KPN-Telecom Rent Centre (☎ 020-653 09 99) at Schiphol airport (to the left of the central exit at Schiphol Plaza) for around f150 a week depending on the phone. In this case, however, you can't use your existing number.

For a cheaper alternative, you might consider a prepaid deal from one of the private mobile phone operators, eg, Libertel or Dutchtone. You'll have to buy a handset, but it's subscription-free and you can recharge the prepaid cards via a toll-free number. Check with local independent telecom shops for the best offers. At the time of research the cheapest deal we found was f149 for the handset including a card with a half-hour's local calling time, but that's likely to decrease.

Dial Tones Tones are similar to those used throughout most of Continental Europe: an even dial tone at fairly lengthy intervals means the number is ringing; a similar tone at shorter intervals means the number is engaged; a three-step tone means the number isn't in use or has been disconnected.

Costs Calls within the metropolitan area are time-based, and the official, KPN-Telecom public phone boxes cost a flat f0.20 a minute regardless of when you ring (public phones in cafes, supermarkets and hotel lobbies can charge anything up to f0.50 a minute). The minimum charge from a public phone is f0.25. Private phones cost f0.06 a minute from 8 am to 8 pm weekdays, f0.03 a minute in the evenings, and f0.02 a minute from 8 pm Friday to 8 am Monday. For calls outside the metropolitan area, KPN's public phones charge f0.30 a minute regardless of when you ring, whereas private phones cost f0.125 a minute between 8 am and 8 pm weekdays and half that at other times.

The cost of international calls varies with the destination and changes frequently due to competition. At the time of writing, Britain cost f0.21 a minute, the USA f0.19, and Australia f0.80 to f0.90 – but don't forget to add f0.20 a minute to these rates when ringing from a KPN phone box.

Phonecards Most public telephones are cardphones and there may be queues at the few remaining coin phones. KPN-Telecom cards are available at post offices, train station counters, VVV and GWK offices and tobacco shops for f5, f10 and f25, and calls cost the same regardless of the value of the card, ie, you get no discount. Note that railway stations have Telfort phone booths that require a Telfort card, though there should be KPN booths outside.

Lonely Planet's eKno Communication Card (see the insert at the back of this book) works from private as well as public phones and is aimed specifically at independent travellers. It provides budget international calls (for local calls you're better off with a KPN card), a range of messaging services, free email and travel information. You can join online at www.ekno.lonelyplanet.com, or by phone from the Netherlands by dialling ☎ 0800-022 35 16 (free call). Once you have joined, to use eKno from the Netherlands, dial ☎ 0800-022 36 05.

0800, 0900 & 06 Numbers Many information services, either recorded or live, use phone numbers beginning with ☎ 0800 (free) or ☎ 0900 (which cost between f0.22 and f1.05 a minute depending on the number). To avoid running up big phone bills, care should be taken whenever dialling ☎ 0900. Businesses that quote an 0900 number are required by law to state the cost, but this can vary depending on where you ring from and so isn't always clear.

Numbers beginning with ☎ 06-5 or ☎ 06-6 are mobile and pager numbers. Numbers beginning with ☎ 0909 are for paid amusement (radio and TV games, for instance); ☎ 0906 numbers are for sex and chat lines.

Using Phone Books Similar surnames are listed alphabetically by address and not by initials, because local research has shown that people recall an address more readily than someone's initials. Confusingly, Dutch dictionaries and most other listings put the contracted vowel 'ij' after the 'i' but phone books treat it as a 'y'. Note that surnames beginning with 'van', 'de' etc are listed under the root name, eg, 'V van Gogh' would be listed as 'Gogh, V van'. For married women and widows who use their husbands' names, the maiden name traditionally comes after the name of the husband.

The phone book lists postal codes for each entry and fax numbers where relevant. The pink pages at the front are business or 'yellow' pages but business names are repeated in the white pages as well.

Phone Codes To ring abroad, dial ☎ 00 followed by the country code for your target country, the area code (you usually drop the leading 0 if there is one) and the subscriber number. Area codes for Dutch cities covered in this book are given at the start of the city's listing.

Home Country Direct Instead of placing a collect call through the local operator you could dial directly to your home country operator and then reverse charges, charge the call to a phone company credit card or perform other credit feats. This is possible to many (not all) countries and costs a fair bit – check with your home phone company before you leave, though you might not get the full story on costs. The following is a selection (with the relevant country codes for reference); ring international directory inquiries if your country isn't listed or the number appears to have changed:

country	country code	phone number
Australia		
(Telstra)	61	☎ 0800-022 00 61
(Optus)		☎ 0800-022 55 61
Belgium	32	☎ 0800-022 11 32
Canada	1	☎ 0800-022 91 16
Finland	358	☎ 0800-022 03 58
France	33	☎ 0800-022 20 33
Germany	49	☎ 0800-022 00 49
Ireland	353	☎ 0800-022 03 53
Japan	81	☎ 0800-022 00 81
Luxembourg	352	☎ 0800-022 03 52
New Zealand	64	☎ 0800-022 44 64
Norway	47	☎ 0800-022 00 47
South Africa	27	☎ 0800-022 02 27
Sweden	46	☎ 0800-022 00 46
UK	44	☎ 0800-022 99 44
USA		
(AT&T)	1	☎ 022 91 11
(MCI)		☎ 0800-022 91 22
(Sprint)		☎ 0800-022 91 19

Fax

It's difficult to send or receive faxes as a visitor. Some of the more upmarket hotels are happy to help if you announce your requirements in advance, and most hotels with fax (some of the cheaper hotels don't have one) will at least let you receive the occasional message. (Business travellers take note: this might convince the boss that you need to stay at something a bit more upmarket.)

Many local post offices now have coin-operated fax machines. But these are good for sending, not receiving. One solution if you have Internet access and a laptop is to register with eFax (www.eFax.com), which provides you with a free telephone fax number in one of several countries. Faxes received at this number are then emailed to you as documents that you can view with eFax software installed on your laptop. The service is free as you get to view a couple of ads before you open your faxes.

Email & Internet Access

Email Travelling with a portable computer is a great way to stay in touch with life back home, but unless you know what you're doing it's fraught with potential problems. Most of the Netherlands still uses an old-style four-prong socket for plugging in phones. However most phones use the standard RJ-11 plug, so you can always unplug the phone from the cord and then use that cord to plug into your modem. Alternatively, four-prong to RJ-11 cords are sold in any electronics store.

Your laptop itself will require power. Often the AC adapters are universal and able to handle a range of power supplies.

But don't assume this. See the Electricity section later in the chapter for details. For more information on travelling with a portable computer, see www.teleadapt.com or www.warrior.com.

Once you have your laptop hooked up to a phone line and power, you need to get on-line. Major Internet service providers such as AOL, AT&T, Earthlink etc, have access numbers at least in Amsterdam if not other Dutch cities. The key here is to check with your ISP's Web site (or actual human support person) before you leave. You'll need to know what technical details are required to access your account as well as telephone access numbers you can call in the Netherlands. This information is usually easy to come by. If you access your Internet email account at home through a smaller ISP or your office or school network, your best option is either to open an account with a global ISP, like those mentioned above, or to rely on cybercafes and other public access points to collect your mail.

To access your email, whether through your laptop or public access point in a cybercafe or library, you'll need to carry three pieces of information with you to enable you to access your account: your incoming (POP or IMAP) mail server name, your account name and your password. Your ISP or network supervisor will be able to give you these. Armed with this information, you should be able to access your Internet mail account from any net-connected machine in the world, provided it runs some kind of email software (remember that Netscape and Internet Explorer both have mail modules). It pays to become familiar with the process for doing this before you leave home.

If you use one of the free Web-based email services which can be found at Yahoo.com, Lycos.com, Excite.com, Hotmail.com or eKno with its Web site at www.ekno.lonely planet.com) then you can check your email from any computer with Internet access.

Internet Access Many Dutch cities have cybercafes, however the market seems quite volatile. Twice while researching this book we were directed to 'new' cybercafes that

had already closed. Fortunately there is an excellent alternative: most Dutch libraries offer free or cheap Internet access. The listings for important cities and towns in this book give library details and opening hours.

Many hostels and other budget-orientated accommodation also offer Internet access.

INTERNET RESOURCES

The World Wide Web is a rich resource for travellers. You can research your trip, hunt down bargain air fares, book hotels, check on weather conditions or chat with locals and other travellers about the best places to visit (or avoid!).

There's no better place to start your Web explorations than the Lonely Planet site (www.lonelyplanet.com). Here you'll find succinct summaries on travelling to most places on earth, postcards from other travellers and the Thorn Tree bulletin board, where you can ask questions before you go or dispense advice when you get back. You can also find travel news and updates to many of our most popular guidebooks, and the sub-WWWay section links you to the most useful travel resources elsewhere on the Web.

Lonely Planet's 'Destination the Netherlands', is an unparalleled Web site at www. lonelyplanet.com/dest/eur/net.htm. There you'll find news and information from travellers like yourself about the Netherlands.

There are scores of additional Web sites devoted to the Netherlands. Many are listed in the relevant sections of this book. However, good general-purpose sites include one operated by the Dutch Ministry of Foreign Affairs that has a wealth of background facts and information (www.minbuza.nl). For any virtual visitor to Amsterdam, the Digital City (www.dds.nl) remains a good first stop, with hundreds of information resources (many in English), interaction opportunities, home pages and links.

The Dutch Tourism Board has a useful Web site at www.visitholland.com which includes a schedule of upcoming events.

BOOKS

There are many, many books about the Netherlands. But note that most books are published in different editions by different publishers in different countries. As a result, a book might be a hardcover rarity in one country while it's readily available in paperback in another. Fortunately, bookshops and libraries search by title or author, so your local bookshop or library is best placed to advise you on the availability of the following recommendations.

Lonely Planet

Lonely Planet has several products that are worth considering. *Amsterdam* is a detailed guide to the city that includes information useful for long-term residents.

Amsterdam Condensed has all the essentials on the capital and fits easily in your pocket. The *Amsterdam City Map* is a handy size and has the added benefit of being laminated to protect it from the frequent rains.

Visitors to neighbouring countries should consider LP's *Brussels, Brugges & Antwerp, France, Germany* and *Britain.* Longer travels would benefit from *Western Europe* or *Europe on a shoestring.* For help with the Dutch language beyond the language section in this book (as well as other key European languages), there is the *Western Europe phrasebook.*

Guidebooks

There are more guidebooks to the Netherlands than you can shake a bicycle spoke at. Women might wish to consult Catherine Stebbings' *Amsterdam – the Woman's Travel Guide* published by Virago. The *Best Guide to Amsterdam & the Benelux* is the definitive gay guide.

If you plan to settle in the Netherlands for a while, get hold of *Live & Work in Belgium, The Netherlands and Luxembourg* from Vacation Work Publications, with detailed explanations of the necessary paperwork and more. *Living & Working in the Netherlands* by Pat Rush (How To Books) isn't bad either.

The Good Beer Guide to Belgium and Holland by Tim Webb takes a detailed look at the hundreds of little-known beers available in the Netherlands.

History

CR Boxer's *The Dutch Seaborne Empire 1600–1800,* first published in 1965, remains one of the most readable academic textbooks on how this small corner of Europe dominated world trade. Simon Schama's *The Embarrassment of Riches: an Interpretation of Dutch Culture in the Golden Age* (1987) deals with the tensions between vast wealth and Calvinist sobriety, and much more. Peter Burke's *Venice and Amsterdam* (1994) discusses the obvious similarities and less obvious differences between these trading empires. *Tulipomania: The Story of the World's Most Coveted Flower and the Extraordinary Passions It Aroused* by Mike Dash takes an engaging look at the bizarre run on tulip prices and futures in the 17th century. It should give any dot.com millionaire pause. And, in fact, there seems to be a bit of a publishing mania sparked by tulips. Also on offer are *The Tulip* by Anna Pavord, which also looks at the bulb speculation, and *Tulip Fever,* a comic historical novel set during the mania.

Amsterdam, A Short History (1994) by Dr Richter Roegholt provides a good, concise summary but few insights. Serious students should track down Pieter Geyl's *The Revolt of the Netherlands, 1555–1609* (1958) and *The Netherlands in the 17th Century, 1609–1648* (1961/64). Johan Huizinga's *The Waning of the Middle Ages: A Study of the Forms of Life, Thought, and Art in France and the Netherlands in the 14th and 15th Centuries* (1924) is world famous (among historians at least) and is as much a literary work as a study. For an entertaining romp through the Golden Age of Dutch painting, read Michael Frayn's *Headlong,* a novel filled with artistic details.

If you read Dutch, Geert Mak's *Een Kleine Geschiedenis van Amsterdam* (1994) offers revelations and potted dramas, and a perceptive analysis of the cultural revolution that swept the city from the mid-1960s to mid-1980s – Mak calls it the '20-year city war'. *Spinoza: A Life* by Steven M Nadler covers the amazing life of the 17th-century philosopher.

The famous *Diary of Anne Frank,* an autobiography written by a Jewish teenager, movingly describes life in hiding in Nazi-occupied Amsterdam. There are numerous more books available that explore Frank's life as well as look at the issues surrounding the diaries themselves.

General

For practical architecture and engineering, see *Building Amsterdam* by Herman Janse (De Brink, 1994), with clear drawings showing how it was done, from houses and churches to bridges and locks. Hans Ibelings covers the fascinating subject of *20th Century Architecture in the Netherlands* well in a beautifully illustrated book.

Dutch Painting (1978) by RH Fuchs is a good introduction. *Dear Theo: The Autobiography of Vincent Van Gogh* is a fascinating study of the artist's troubled life through his own letters to his brother. There are many, many more good books on Dutch art available in most art museum bookshops.

The UnDutchables (1989) by Colin White & Laurie Boucke takes a humorous look at Dutch life; sometimes it's spot-on and sometimes so wide of the mark it becomes slapstick. A more realistic appraisal of Dutch customs, attitudes and idiosyncrasies is Hunt Janin's very readable *Culture Shock! Netherlands* (1998), or the rather serious but knowledgable *Dealing with the Dutch* by Jacob Vossestein who runs the Royal Tropical Institute's 'Understanding the Dutch' training programs for businesspeople and expatriates.

John Irving's bestselling *A Widow for One Year* has numerous important scenes set in Amsterdam, especially in the red-light district.

For literature by Dutch authors, see the Arts section in the Facts About the Netherlands chapter.

FILMS

Films shot in the Netherlands have been few and far between. The main Hollywood movie entirely set in the country was *A Bridge Too Far* (1977), the story of Operation Market Garden and the failed assault on Arnhem. It was shot on location in Arnhem and at Deventer and Nijmegen. There is a memorable Amsterdam canal scene in the James Bond film *Diamonds Are Forever* (1971).

NEWSPAPERS & MAGAZINES

The European editions of *The Economist, Newsweek* and *Time* are easily found, as are most of the major international magazines and newspapers (and many of the more obscure ones). The main British newspapers are available the same day, while the *International Herald Tribune* – which has a publishing plant in Den Haag – has fairly late news. Look to large bookstores or train station newsstands for these titles.

By far the largest national newspaper is the Amsterdam-based *De Telegraaf,* a right-wing daily with sensationalist news but good coverage of finance. The populist *De Volkskrant* is a one-time Catholic daily with leftist leanings. *Algemeen Dagsblad* is thin and dull. The highly regarded *NRC Handelsblad*, a merger of two elitist papers from Rotterdam and Amsterdam, sets the country's journalistic standards.

The *Financieele Dagblad*, the country's leading financial daily, includes a useful one-page summary in English.

RADIO & TV

The BBC World Service broadcasts on 648 kHz medium wave, loud and clear on any AM radio. The broadcast differs from the short-wave world service in that it is almost entirely in English. Given the proximity of the Netherlands to the UK, it is possible to pick up BBC Radio Five Live, a talk radio and live sports station at 693 kHz medium wave and BBC Radio Four, the cherished news and information station, at 198 kHz long wave.

Dutch TV sends insomniacs to sleep, though the large proportion of ad-free, English-language sitcoms and films with Dutch subtitles is a plus. Fortunately the Netherlands has the highest density cable-TV network in the world, with the percentage of households hooked up to cable is approaching 100%. Cable means access not just to Dutch and Belgian channels but many channels from Britain, France, Germany, Italy and Spain, and all sorts of other so-called Euro-channels with sport and music clips, as well as Turkish and Moroccan stuff. In most hotel rooms, you will have cable TV with access usually to CNN International, BBC1, BBC2, BBC World and possibly more. Given that so many of the programs are subtitled, you may find your English-language choices in the dozens at certain times.

PHOTOGRAPHY & VIDEO

Film is widely available but fairly expensive by European standards – a Kodak 64 (36-exposure) slide film costs about f22 – so it's best to stock up tax-free on your way over. High-speed film (200 ASA or higher) is sensible because the sky is often overcast and, even if it's not, buildings and trees tend to cast unwanted shadows. If there's a blanket of snow with sunshine (a rare combination but a fantastic photo opportunity) you might want slower film. Film developing is easy and quick, and costs f5.50 plus f1 per print. Cassettes for video cameras are about f7.50/24 for 30/90 minutes. *Travel Photography: A Guide to Taking Better Pictures* is written by internationally renowned travel photographer, Richard I'Anson. It's full colour throughout and designed to take on the road.

Living-room video cassette recorders use the PAL image-registration system, the same as most of Europe and Australia, which is incompatible with the NTSC system used in North America and Japan or the SECAM system used in France. This means that if you buy a prerecorded video tape here you might not be able to play it at home – check your unit's requirements before leaving home. Shops might stock NTSC versions but very few have tapes in SECAM.

TIME

The Netherlands is on Central European time, GMT/UTC plus one hour. Noon is 11 am in London, 6 am in New York, 3 am in San Francisco, 6 am in Toronto, 9 pm in Sydney and 11 pm in Auckland, and then there's daylight-saving time. Clocks are put forward one hour at 2 am on the last Sunday in March and back again at 3 am on the last Sunday in October.

When telling the time, beware that Dutch uses *half* to indicate 'half before' the hour. If you say 'half eight' (8.30 in many forms of English), a Dutch person will take this to mean 7.30. Dutch also uses constructions like *tien voor half acht* (7.20) and *tien over half acht* (7.40), and less surprisingly, *kwart voor acht* (7.45) and *kwart over acht* (8.15).

ELECTRICITY

Electricity is 220V, 50 Hz and plugs are of the Continental two-round-pin variety. If you need an adapter, get it before you leave home because most of the ones available in the Netherlands are for locals going abroad.

WEIGHTS & MEASURES

The Netherlands, like all of the EU (with the exception of those feet-dragging Brits and Irish), fully uses the metric system. See the inside back cover for a conversion table between metric and imperial measures.

LAUNDRY

A self-service laundry is called a *wasserette* or a *wassalon* and the Netherlands could do with more of them. It normally costs about f8 to wash 5kg; add a few f1 coins for the dryer. You can also get the staff to wash, dry and fold a load (a full garbage bag) for around f15 – drop it off in the morning, pick it up in the afternoon. Upmarket hotels will, of course, do your laundry too, but at a price.

The major problem is that most of the staffed laundries are closed on weekends. Given that these are often the same places that do laundry for hotels, you may be unable to get clean clothes from Friday until Monday no matter what the cost. Outside of college towns, self-service laundries can be hard, if not impossible, to find.

TOILETS

Public toilets are scarce but there are plenty of bars or other establishments you can pop into. Their toilets aren't always the cleanest – public facilities in department stores are more hygienic. Toilet attendants (of which there are a lot) should be tipped 25 to 50 cents, though some attendants in clubs will demand fl.

Dutch toilets outside of hotels usually include a feature called – and we use this term with our noses held – the 'inspection shelf'. The name says it all.

HEALTH

The Netherlands is a very healthy place and no special precautions are necessary when visiting. The biggest risks are likely to be viral infections in winter, sunburn (you hope the weather will allow this precaution!) and insect bites in summer and foot blisters from too many happy days hiking.

For a medical emergency dial ☎ 112; visit a local pharmacy or medical centre if you have a minor medical problem and can explain what it is. Hospital casualty wards will help if the problem is more serious. Nearly all health professionals in the Netherlands speak English; tourist offices and hotels can make recommendations.

Predeparture planning

Immunisations are not necessary for travel to the Netherlands. But it is always a good idea to ensure that your normal childhood vaccinations (against measles, mumps, rubella, diphtheria, tetanus and polio) are up to date. You may want to consider vaccinations for hepatitis A and B, as these illnesses can occur anywhere.

Health Insurance Make sure that you have adequate health insurance. The Netherlands has reciprocal health arrangements with other EU countries and Australia – check with your public health insurer which form to include in your luggage (E111 for British and Irish residents, available at post offices). You still might have to pay on the spot but you'll be able to claim back home. Citizens of other countries are well advised to take out travel insurance – medical or dental treatment is less expensive than in North America but still costs plenty.

Travel Health Guides There are also a number of excellent travel health sites on the

Internet. From the Lonely Planet home page there are links at www.lonelyplanet.com/weblinks/wlheal.htm to the World Health Organization and the US Centers for Disease Control & Prevention.

Other Preparations Make sure you're healthy before you start travelling. If you are going on a long trip make sure your teeth are OK. If you wear glasses take a spare pair as well as your prescription.

If you require any medication, make certain that you bring along the generic name for the drug, so that if you lose your supply it will be easier to obtain a replacement. Also, if there are some commonly used drugs such as penicillin that you are allergic to, wear a bracelet stating this.

Environmental Hazards

Jet Lag Jet lag is experienced when a person travels by air across more than three time zones (each time zone usually represents a one-hour time difference). It occurs because many of the functions of the human body (such as temperature, pulse rate and emptying of the bladder and bowels) are regulated by internal 24-hour cycles. When we travel long distances rapidly our bodies take time to adjust to the 'new time' of our destination, and we may experience fatigue, disorientation, insomnia, anxiety, impaired concentration and loss of appetite. These effects will usually be gone within three days of arrival, but to minimise the impact of jet lag:

• Rest for a couple of days prior to departure
• Try to select flight schedules that minimise sleep deprivation; arriving late in the day means you can go to sleep soon after you arrive. For very long flights, try to organise a stopover
• Avoid excessive eating (which bloats the stomach) and alcohol (which causes dehydration) during the flight. Instead, drink plenty of noncarbonated, nonalcoholic drinks such as fruit juice or water
• Avoid smoking
• Make yourself comfortable by wearing loose-fitting clothes and perhaps bringing an eye mask and ear plugs to help you sleep
• Try to sleep at the appropriate time for the time zone you are travelling to

Motion Sickness Eating lightly before and during a trip will reduce the chances of motion sickness. If you are prone to motion sickness try to find a place that minimises movement – near the wing on aircraft, close to midships on boats, near the centre on buses. Fresh air usually helps; reading and cigarette smoke don't. Commercial motion-sickness preparations, which can cause drowsiness, have to be taken before the trip commences. Ginger (available in capsule form) and peppermint (including mint-flavoured sweets) are natural preventatives.

Infectious Diseases

Diarrhoea Simple things like a change of water, food or climate can all cause a mild bout of diarrhoea, but a few rushed toilet trips with no other symptoms is not indicative of a major problem.

Dehydration is the main danger with any diarrhoea, particularly in children or the elderly as dehydration can occur quite quickly. Under all circumstances *fluid replacement* (at least equal to the volume being lost) is the most important thing to remember. Weak black tea with a little sugar, soda water, or soft drinks allowed to go flat and diluted 50% with clean water are all good. With severe diarrhoea a rehydrating solution is preferable to replace minerals and salts lost. Commercially available oral rehydration salts (ORS) are very useful; add them to boiled or bottled water. In an emergency you can make up a solution of six teaspoons of sugar and a half teaspoon of salt to a litre of boiled or bottled water. You need to drink at least the same volume of fluid that you are losing in bowel movements and vomiting. Urine is the best guide to the adequacy of replacement – if you have small amounts of concentrated urine, you need to drink more. Keep drinking small amounts often. Stick to a bland diet as you recover.

Gut-paralysing drugs such as loperamide or diphenoxylate can be used to bring relief from the symptoms, although they do not actually cure the problem. Only use these drugs if you do not have access to toilets, eg, if you *must* travel. Note that these drugs are not recommended for children under 12 years.

In certain situations antibiotics may be required: watch out for diarrhoea with blood or mucus (dysentery), any diarrhoea with fever, profuse watery diarrhoea, persistent diarrhoea not improving after 48 hours and severe diarrhoea. These suggest a more serious cause of diarrhoea and in these situations gut-paralysing drugs should be avoided.

In these situations, a stool test may be necessary to diagnose what bug is causing your diarrhoea, so you should seek medical help urgently. Where this is not possible the recommended drugs for bacterial diarrhoea (the most likely cause of severe diarrhoea in travellers) are norfloxacin 400mg twice daily for three days or ciprofloxacin 500mg twice daily for five days. These are not recommended for children or pregnant women. The drug of choice for children would be co-trimoxazole with dosage dependent on weight. A five-day course is given. Ampicillin or amoxycillin may be given in pregnancy, but medical care is necessary.

Hepatitis Hepatitis is a general term for inflammation of the liver. It is a common disease worldwide. There are several different viruses that cause hepatitis, and they differ in the way that they are transmitted. The symptoms are similar in all forms of the illness, and include fever, chills, headache, fatigue, feelings of weakness and aches and pains, followed by loss of appetite, nausea, vomiting, abdominal pain, dark urine, light-coloured faeces, jaundiced (yellow) skin and yellowing of the whites of the eyes. People who have had hepatitis should avoid alcohol for some time after the illness, as the liver needs time to recover.

Hepatitis A is transmitted by contaminated food and drinking water. You should seek medical advice, but there is not much you can do apart from resting, drinking lots of fluids, eating lightly and avoiding fatty foods. Hepatitis E is transmitted in the same way as hepatitis A; it can be particularly serious in pregnant women.

There are almost 300 million chronic carriers of **hepatitis B** in the world. It is spread through contact with infected blood, blood products or body fluids, for example through sexual contact, unsterilised needles and blood transfusions, or contact with blood via small breaks in the skin. Other risk situations include having a shave, tattoo or body piercing with contaminated equipment. The symptoms of hepatitis B may be more severe than type A and the disease can lead to long-term problems such as chronic liver damage, liver cancer or a long-term carrier state. Hepatitis C and D are spread in the same way as hepatitis B and can also lead to long-term complications.

There are vaccines against hepatitis A and B, but there are currently no vaccines against the other types of hepatitis. Following the basic rules about food and water (hepatitis A and E) and avoiding risk situations (hepatitis B, C and D) are important preventative measures.

HIV, AIDS & STDs

HIV & AIDS Infection with the human immunodeficiency virus (HIV) may lead to acquired immune deficiency syndrome (AIDS), which is a fatal disease. Any exposure to blood, blood products or body fluids may put the individual at risk. The disease is often transmitted through sexual contact or dirty needles – vaccinations, acupuncture, tattooing and body piercing can potentially be as dangerous as intravenous drug use.

If you do need an injection, ask to see the syringe unwrapped in front of you.

Fear of HIV infection should never preclude treatment for serious medical conditions which can be alleviated with surgery.

Sexually Transmitted Diseases HIV/AIDS and hepatitis B can be transmitted through sexual contact – see the relevant sections earlier for more details. Other STDs include gonorrhoea, herpes and syphilis; sores, blisters or rashes around the genitals and discharges or pain when urinating are common symptoms. In some STDs, such as wart virus or chlamydia, symptoms may be less marked or not observed at all, especially in women. Chlamydia infection can cause infertility in men and women before any symptoms have been noticed. Syphilis symptoms eventually disappear completely but the disease continues and can cause severe problems in later years. While abstinence from sexual contact is the only 100% effective prevention, using condoms is also effective. The treatment of gonorrhoea and syphilis is with antibiotics. The different sexually transmitted diseases each require specific antibiotics.

Treatment & Information There are numerous STD clinics in the Netherlands. Don't be afraid to check them out if you think you may have contracted something.

Free testing for sexually transmitted diseases is available in Amsterdam at the Municipal Medical & Health Service, GG&GD (☎ 020-555 58 22), Groenburgwal 44 in the old town. It's open 8 to 10.30 am and 1.30 to 3.30 pm weekdays, but you must arrive in the morning to be tested that day. Bring along a book or magazine as you'll probably have to wait a couple of hours. If a problem is diagnosed the service will provide free treatment immediately, but the results of blood tests are only available after a week (you can get the results over the phone if you aren't returning to Amsterdam). This excellent service is available to everyone and it's not necessary to give an address or show identification (English is spoken). There's also a gay STD and HIV clinic (tests etc), which is open 7 to 9 pm on Friday, but you have to make an appointment between 9 am and 12.30 pm or 1.30 and 5.30 pm weekdays.

The spread of HIV/AIDS has been contained to some extent by practical education campaigns and free needle-exchange programs. Telephone help lines include:

AIDS Information Line (☎ 0800-022 22 20, free call) – questions about HIV and AIDS answered 2 to 10 pm weekdays; discretion guaranteed
AIDS-HIVpluslijn (☎ 020-685 00 55) – telephone support line for people with HIV, or for their friends and relatives; 1 to 4 pm Monday, Wednesday and Friday, 8 to 10.30 pm Tuesday and Thursday

Cuts, Bites & Stings

Cuts & Scratches Wash well and treat any cut with an antiseptic such as povidone-iodine. Where possible avoid bandages and Band-Aids, which can keep wounds wet.

Bedbugs & Lice Bedbugs live in various places, but particularly in dirty mattresses and bedding, evidenced by spots of blood on bedclothes or on the wall. Bedbugs leave itchy bites in neat rows. Calamine lotion or a sting relief spray may help.

All lice cause itching and discomfort. They make themselves at home in your hair (head lice), your clothing (body lice) or in your pubic hair (crabs). You catch lice through direct contact with infected people or by sharing combs, clothing and the like. Powder or shampoo treatment will kill the lice and infected clothing should then be washed in very hot, soapy water and left in the sun to dry.

Bites & Stings Bee and wasp stings are usually painful rather than dangerous. However, in people who are allergic to them severe breathing difficulties may occur and require urgent medical care. Calamine lotion or a sting relief spray will give relief and ice packs will reduce the pain and swelling.

Ticks You should always check all over your body if you have been walking through a potentially tick-infested area as ticks can cause skin infections and other more serious diseases. If a tick is found attached, press down around the tick's head with tweezers, grab the head and gently pull upwards. Avoid pulling the rear of the body as this may squeeze the tick's gut contents through the attached mouth parts into the skin, increasing the risk of infection and disease. Smearing chemicals on the tick will not make it let go and is not recommended.

Everyday Health

Normal body temperature is up to 37°C (98.6°F); more than 2°C (4°F) higher indicates a high fever. The normal adult pulse rate is 60 to 100 per minute (children 80 to 100, babies 100 to 140). As a general rule the pulse increases about 20 beats per minute for each 1°C (2°F) rise in fever.

Respiration (breathing) rate is also an indicator of illness. Count the number of breaths per minute: Between 12 and 20 is normal for adults and older children (up to 30 for younger children, 40 for babies). People with a high fever or serious respiratory illness breathe more quickly than normal. More than 40 shallow breaths a minute may indicate pneumonia.

Women's Health

Antibiotic use, synthetic underwear, sweating and contraceptive pills can lead to fungal vaginal infections, especially when travelling in hot climates. Fungal infections are characterised by a rash, itch and discharge and can be treated with a vinegar or lemon-juice douche, or with yoghurt. Nystatin, miconazole or clotrimazole pessaries or vaginal cream are the usual treatments.

Sexually transmitted diseases are a major cause of vaginal problems. Symptoms include a smelly discharge, painful intercourse and sometimes a burning sensation when urinating. Medical attention should be sought and male sexual partners must also be treated. For more details see the section on Sexually Transmitted Diseases earlier. Besides abstinence, the best thing is to practise safer sex using condoms.

WOMEN TRAVELLERS

Dutch women attained the right to vote in 1919, and in the late 1960s and 1970s the Dolle Minas women's movement ('Mad Minas'; after the radical late 19th-century feminist Wilhelmina Drucker) made sure that abortion on demand was more or less accepted and paid for by the national health service. There is some way to go before it can be said that women are fully emancipated (their participation rate in the labour force, for instance, is one of the lowest in Europe, with the highest proportion of part-time work), but Dutch women on the whole are a rather confident lot. On a social level, equality of the sexes is taken for granted and women are almost as likely as men to initiate contact with the opposite sex.

There's little street harassment and the Netherlands is generally safe. Amsterdam, for that matter, is probably as safe as it gets in the major cities of Europe. Just take care in the red-light district, where it's best to walk with a friend to minimise unwelcome attention.

The feminist movement is less politicised than elsewhere, more laid-back and focused on practical solutions such as cultural centres and archives, bicycle repair shops run by and for women, or support systems to help women set up businesses. For more about feminism, or a full rundown of the many women's groups, contact the following organisations in Amsterdam (where most national groups are based):

Het Vrouwenhuis (The Women's House; ☎ 020-625 20 66) Nieuwe Herengracht 95 near the Botanical Garden – a centre for several women's organisations and magazines, with workshops, exhibitions and parties; there's also a bar and a library

IIAV (International Information Centre & Archives of the Women's Movement; ☎ 020-665 08 20) Obiplein 4 east of Muiderpoort-station – centre for feminist studies; extensive collection of clippings, magazines and books

Outside of Amsterdam, it can be useful to look under *Vrouwenhuis* in the phone directory.

Organisations

The following organisations may prove useful in times of crisis. Although based in Amsterdam, they can provide valuable leads to organisations in other parts of the country:

De Eerste Lijn (The First Line; ☎ 020-613 02 45) – for victims of sexual violence

Vrouwengezondheidscentrum Isis (Women's Health Centre; ☎ 020-693 43 58) Obiplein 4 – advice, support and self-help groups

Rechtshulp voor Vrouwen (Legal Aid for Women; ☎ 020-638 73 02) Willemsstraat 24B

GAY & LESBIAN TRAVELLERS

Partisan estimates put the proportion of gay and lesbian people in Amsterdam at 20% to 30%. This is probably an exaggeration, but there's no doubt that Amsterdam is the gay and lesbian capital of Europe – although the lesbian scene, as always, is less developed than the gay one. Mainstream attitudes have always been reasonably tolerant but it wasn't until the early 1970s that the age of consent for gay sex was lowered to 16, in line with hetero sex, and in 1993 it became an illegal act to discriminate against job-seekers

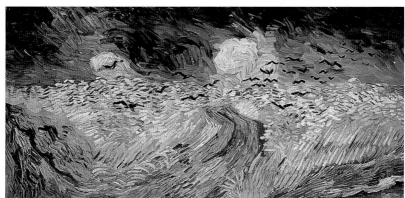

Vincent van Gogh's *Crows in the Wheatfield* is one of many displayed at the Van Gogh Museum.

Irises

Leaving the Church at Nuenen

Self-Portrait at the Easel

The Potato Eaters

DAVID STANLEY

Celebrating Koninginnedag in style

MARTIN MOOS

Half-pipe in front of Rijksmuseum

DOEKES LOLOFS

Watch out for the thin ice

EDWARD A M SNIJDERS

Rowing on the Bosbaan, south of Amsterdam

RICK GERHARTER

Music while you munch in Vondelpark

JULIET COOMBE

MARTIN MOOS

Cycling through Dam Square

Dam pigeons in front of the Royal Palace

(including teachers) on the basis of sexual orientation.

The fact that Christian parties are in opposition for the first time since 1917 has finally made it possible to tackle issues relating to family law. Same-sex marriage has finally been recognised, though the attendant right to adopt children could take a bit longer to be sorted out. The government has long subsidised the national organisation COC – one of the world's largest organisations for gay and lesbian rights – but now trade unions are busy researching the lot of homosexual employees, the police advertise in the gay media for new applicants, and the acceptance of homosexuality in the army is greater than ever.

With the gay and lesbian scene so well developed in Amsterdam it may come as a surprise to find it so undeveloped elsewhere. The further one gets from the capital, the more likely it is that gay and lesbian bars and clubs will operate behind dark windows. In some towns you may not be able to find a gay or lesbian establishment. The exception is Rotterdam and the many university towns with their large – albeit largely transient – gay and lesbian populations.

Organisations

The obvious contact point for gay and lesbian information is COC (☎ 020-6234596, fax 6267795, ✉ info@coc.nl, postal address: Postbus 3836, 1001 AP Amsterdam). It is the most important and the largest organisation for gay and lesbians in the Netherlands and the oldest in Europe. It can give advice on a myriad of subjects and has contacts throughout the country. COC also has an informative Web site at www.coc.nl which has numerous links.

Special Events

The biggest party in Amsterdam each year is *Koninginnedag* (Queen's Day) which celebrates the Queen Mother's birthday on 30 April. Ex-queen Juliana and her daughter Queen Beatrix are very popular among the gay community and this day is celebrated with great enthusiasm, causing some confusion among foreign gays about the 'queen' everyone is so happy about. On this day a big gay and lesbian party called the *Roze Wester* (Pink Wester) is held at the Homomonument, with bands and street dancing; the Reguliersdwarsstraat and Amstel also get very lively. It helps if you like beer because you can hardly get anything else.

June is the usual month for Gay Pride Week, there are special events, parties and parades in many Dutch cities (see Public Holidays & Special Events later in this chapter).

DISABLED TRAVELLERS

Travellers with a mobility problem will find the Netherlands fairly well equipped to meet their needs, certainly considering the natural limitations of some of the older buildings. A large number of government offices and museums have lifts and/or ramps. Many hotels, however, are in old buildings with steep stairs and no lifts; restaurants tend to be on ground floors, though 'ground' sometimes includes a few steps. Train and public transport stations have lifts, many trains have wheelchair access, and most train stations and public buildings have toilets for the disabled. People with a disability get discounts on public transport. Train timetables are published in Braille and banknotes have raised shapes on the corners for identification. Netherlands Railways has an excellent information line (☎ 030-235 55 55) with details of all their services for travellers with disabilities.

Organisations

Many Dutch organisations work with and for people with disabilities but unfortunately there's no central information service. However, the helpful Nederlands Instituut voor Zorg & Welzijn (NIZW, ☎ 030-230 66 03, fax 231 96 41), Postbus 19152, 3501 DD Utrecht, can provide extensive information on accessible places to stay throughout the country and can refer you to other organisations if your request is more specific.

Another good source of accessibility information is Mobility International Nederland (☎ 0343-521 795, fax 516 776), Heidstein 7, 3971 ND Driebergen.

Bartiméus Zeist (☎ 030-698 22 11, fax 698 23 75), Postbus 1003, 3700 BA, Zeist, is an organisation for the blind and partially sighted which has useful information for Dutch travel.

In Britain, the Royal Association for Disability & Rehabilitation (RADAR; ☎ 020-7250 3222), 12 City Forum, 250 City Rd, London EC1V 8AF, may be able to help plan your trip. Its guide, *European Holidays & Travel Abroad – A Guide for Disabled People,* gives a good overview of facilities in Europe (published in even-numbered years). Web site: www.radar.org.uk.

In the USA, the Society for the Advancement of Travelers with Handicaps (SATH; ☎ 212-447 7284, postal address: 347 Fifth Ave, Suite 610, New York, NY 10016) has information sheets on a wide range of destinations or will research your specific requirements. Membership is $45 a year ($30 for seniors and students); the information charge for nonmembers is $5, which covers costs. Web site: www.sath.org.

Mobility International (☎ 541-343 1284, mailing address: PO Box 10767, Eugene, OR 97440) offers international educational exchanges but will also answer questions and help travellers with special needs. Web site: www.mobility-international.org.

Finally, it's well worth checking some of the many links at www.access-able.com, a Web page for travellers with disabilities.

SENIOR TRAVELLERS

The minimum age for senior discounts is 65 (60 for the partner) and they apply to public transport, museum entry fees, concerts and more. You could try flashing your home-country senior card but you might have to show your passport to be eligible.

Senior travellers who are concerned about personal safety can perhaps take heart from the fact that people up to 24 years of age are six times more likely to become a victim of crime here than those aged over 65.

THE NETHERLANDS FOR CHILDREN

Lonely Planet's *Travel with Children* by Maureen Wheeler is worth reading if you're unsure about travelling with kids. Much of her advice is valid in the Netherlands, where there is much to keep them occupied. Unfortunately the country also has a lot of open water (all Dutch children learn to swim at school).

Attitudes to children are very positive, apart from some hotels with a no-children policy – check when you book. Most restaurants have high chairs and children's menus. Facilities for changing nappies (diapers), however, are limited to the big department stores, major museums and train stations and you'll pay 50 cents to use them.

You might want to be on the lookout for *The Cow Who Fell in the Canal* by Phyllis Krasilovsky. It's a wonderful children's book about the adventures of Hendrika, a cow who experiences the joys of canal and market life.

DANGERS & ANNOYANCES

Much of the Netherlands is utterly safe. Caution is most important in the larger towns with their accompanying urban tensions and concerns.

Amsterdam is a small city by world standards but requires big-city street sense, though it's positively tame if you're used to New York or Johannesburg. Violent crime is unusual but theft, especially pickpocketing, is a real problem. Don't carry more money around than you intend to spend – use a secondary wallet or purse and keep your main one safe. Don't walk around conspicuously with valuables, or give away that you're a tourist with map, camera or video. Walking purposefully helps.

A car with foreign registration is a popular target, and if it's parked along a canal it will probably get broken into. Don't leave things in the car: definitely remove registration and ID papers and, if possible the radio.

If something is stolen, by all means get a police report for insurance purposes but don't expect the police to retrieve your property or to apprehend the thief – put the matter down to experience. This might seem weak but it's not a police state and usually there's very little they can do.

Mosquitoes can be a nuisance in summer. They breed in stagnant parts of the canals and in water under houses. In some parts of the country they're no problem, but in other parts people sleep under mosquito nets six months of the year (no kidding!).

All those bicycles are great for the environment, individual health etc, but they can also be quite a menace to pedestrians. When crossing the street, don't just look for cars but also for speeding bikes. They're quiet so you won't hear them coming. Don't stray into a bike lane without looking in both directions. At rush hours in cities, you may actually find yourself waiting for an opening in the flow of bikes for what seems like forever.

All that Dutch development means that in the cities there is often not a discreet patch of grass for Fido to foul. In some areas you'll spend more time watching where you step than watching the sights around you. Also, North Americans and Australians should accept that nonsmokers have few rights here; tobacco smoke in pubs can be thick enough to deter all but the most committed smokers, and unfortunately the Dutch seem allergic to open windows.

EMERGENCIES
The national emergency number (police, ambulance, fire brigade) is ☎ 112.

LEGAL MATTERS
The Dutch police *(politie)* are a pretty relaxed and helpful lot. If you do something wrong, they can hold you up to six hours for questioning (another six hours if they can't establish your identity, or 24 hours if they consider the matter serious) and do not have to grant you a phone call, though they'll ring your embassy or consulate.

Since 1994 there's a 'limited' requirement for anyone over 12 years of age to carry ID (eg, in public transport without a valid ticket, at soccer stadiums, in the work place and when opening a bank account). Typically, theory doesn't always match practice and everyone is confused, but it seems that foreigners should carry their passport. Then again, a photocopy of the relevant data pages should be OK unless there's reason to suspect you're an illegal immigrant. Sounds logical, doesn't it? A driving licence is not OK because it doesn't show your nationality.

Drugs
Contrary to what you may have heard, cannabis products are illegal. The confusion arises because the authorities have had the sense to distinguish between 'soft' drugs (cannabis) and addictive 'hard' drugs (heroin, crack, pills) when deciding where to focus their resources. Soft drugs for personal use (defined as up to 5g, down from 30g after table-thumping from France) are unofficially tolerated, but larger amounts put you in the prosecutable 'dealer' category.

The key phrase is *gedogen* (sometimes translated as 'tolerating'), a wonderful Dutch term that means official condemnation but looking the other way when common sense dictates it. Hard drugs (including LSD) are treated just as seriously as anywhere else and can land you in big trouble, although the authorities tend to treat genuine, registered addicts as medical cases rather than as serial killers. Amsterdam was an early adopter of methadone and needle-exchange programs and of safe-injecting houses.

Neighbouring countries take a dim view of such tolerance now that border controls have been abolished in theory, and the government is under EU pressure to clamp down – never mind that most hashish reaches the Netherlands through France and Belgium and most heroin through Germany. In typical Dutch fashion this has led to some tightening of rules and regulations without losing sight of the commonsense approach.

One of the positive results of this approach has been to move cannabis out of the criminal circuit and into registered 'coffeeshops', driving a wedge between cannabis users and predatory street dealers who would rather sell the more profitable hard stuff. Since the late 1980s the number of heroin addicts in the Netherlands has stabilised at around 1.6 per 1000 inhabitants, slightly more than in Germany, Norway, Austria or Ireland; but in hard-line France the proportion is 2.6 per 1000, and in Greece, Spain and Italy it's higher still. Dutch addicts have the best average survival rate in Europe and the lowest incidence of HIV infection.

These tolerant policies attract many drug tourists; drugs are cheaper and more readily available, and generally of better quality, in the Netherlands than elsewhere. The country has become a major exporter of high-grade marijuana (grown locally) and is the European centre for the production of ecstasy. Much of Europe's cocaine passes through Rotterdam harbour.

For more about (soft) drugs, see the boxed text 'Coffeeshops'.

Warning Never, *ever* buy drugs on the street: you'll get ripped off or mugged. And *don't* light up in view of the police, or in an establishment without checking that it's OK

Cafe Society

When locals say *cafe* they mean a pub, also known as a *kroeg*, and there are over 1000 of them in the city. Proprietors prefer the term *cafe* (yes, they serve coffee as well, but very much as a sideline). Of course, when they say *coffeeshop* they mean another thing all together.

Many cafes have outside seating on a *terras* (terrace) that may be covered and heated in winter. These are great places to relax and watch passers-by, soak up the sun, read a paper or write postcards for a few hours. Once you've ordered a drink you'll be left alone but you might be expected to order the occasional top-up. If all tables are occupied, don't be shy about asking if a seat is taken and sharing a table.

A good tradition in many cafes, especially the so-called grand cafes, is the indoor reading table with the day's papers and news magazines, including one or two in English.

The price for a standard beer varies from around f2.75 to f4.50. If you occupy a table or sit at the bar, it's common to put drinks on a tab and to pay when you leave. If things are busy or you sit outside you'll probably have to pay per service.

TYPES OF CAFES

Once upon a time cafes only served a few perfunctory snacks but many these days have proper menus. Those that take their food seriously (or would like their customers to think they do) call themselves *eetcafe* and their food can be very good indeed. Many cafes in the following categories serve food.

"This coffee is *strong*"

Brown Cafe

The most famous type is the brown cafe *(bruin cafe)*. The true specimen has been in business for a while, is stained by smoke (recent aspirants simply slap on the brown paint), has sand on the wooden floor, and provides an atmosphere conducive to deep and meaningful conversation. There might be Persian rugs on the tables to soak up spilled beer.

Grand Cafes

Grand cafes are spacious with comfortable furniture. They're all the rage, and any pub that installs a few solid tables and comfortable chairs will call itself a grand cafe. Some are grand indeed, and when they open at 10 am they're perfect for a lazy brunch with relaxing chamber music tinkling away in the background.

to do so. The Dutch detest drug tourists who think they can just smoke dope anywhere.

Prostitution

Prostituting oneself is legal in the Netherlands and in October 2000 the government was due to make brothels legal as well. This tolerance stems from a widespread view that prostitutes are victims rather than criminals. Numerous laws regulate the industry

and prostitutes are liable for tax. Health checks are performed and there are plans afoot for pensions and other social schemes. Much of this open policy stems from a desire to undermine the role of pimps and the underworld in the sex industry.

This said, most prostitutes are immigrants from Third World countries and Eastern Europe. Exploitation is inevitable in such a business. On the main streets of

Cafe Society

Other Cafes

Theatre cafes attract performing artists and other types who do a lot of drinking. There are also a few **tasting houses** *(proeflokalen)* that used to be attached to distilleries (a holdover from the 17th century when many small distilleries were in operation in Amsterdam and around the Netherlands), where you can try dozens of *genevers* and liqueurs.

Some cafes straddle these categories and others don't really fit in, such as the relatively new phenomenon of Irish pubs.

Opening hours depend on whether the cafe has opted to be a 'day business' (7 am to 1 am, weekends to 3 am), an 'evening business' (8 pm to 3 am, weekends to 4 am) or a 'night business' (10 pm to 4 am, weekends to 5 am). Cafes are free to adjust their hours within these limits but very few open before 9 am.

COFFEESHOPS

Many establishments that call themselves *koffieshop* (as opposed to *koffiehuis*, espresso bar or sandwich shop) are in the cannabis business, though they do serve coffee. There are also a few *hash-cafes* serving alcohol that are barely distinguishable from pubs.

You'll have no trouble finding a coffeeshop; they're all over town, seemingly on every corner. The ubiquitous hemp leaves have been taken down to appease concerned politicians, but it's a safe bet that an establishment showing palm leaves and perhaps Rastafarian colours (red, yellow and green) will have something to do with cannabis – take a look at the clientele and ask at the bar for the list of goods on offer, usually packaged in small bags for f25. In some places, like Rotterdam, regulations require you to do your buying in a separate place. Fear not, in any town the staff will clue you in on local regulations.

Another concession to politics is that 'space' cakes and cookies are sold in a rather low-key fashion, mainly because tourists had problems. If you're unused to their effects, or the time they can take to kick in and run their course, you could indeed be in for a rather involved experience. Ask the staff how much you should take and heed their advice, even if nothing happens after an hour. Many coffeeshops sell magic mushrooms, which is quite legal because it's an untreated, natural product (though this may change, with the argument that drying the mushrooms is a treatment, which makes them illegal).

Cannabis products used to be imported but these days the country has top-notch home produce, so-called *nederwiet* (NAY-der-weet) developed by diligent horticulturists and grown in greenhouses with up to five harvests a year. Even the police admit it's a superior product, especially the potent 'superskunk' with up to 13% of the active substance THC (Nigerian grass has 5% and Colombian 7%). According to a government-sponsored poll of coffeeshop owners, nederwiet has captured over half the market and hash is in decline even among tourists.

Most shops are open from 10 am to 1 am Sunday to Thursday, to 3 am Friday and Saturday.

Amsterdam's red-light district, you have little to fear as they are as much of a well-policed tourist attraction as elsewhere. However the back alleys are more dubious as are the characters you'll see lurking about. This advice goes for other Dutch cities, such as Rotterdam and Den Haag, which have their own red-light areas. Even towns such as Leiden and Groningen have their red-light areas seemingly plopped down amid otherwise quiet streets.

Road Laws

Drink driving is considered a major crime in the Netherlands, as all those roadside warning placards will remind. See the Car & Motorcycle section of the Getting Around chapter for details on the rules of the road in the Netherlands.

BUSINESS HOURS

As a general rule, bank opening hours are 9 am to 4 pm Monday to Friday, offices 8.30 am to 5 pm Monday to Friday, and shops 9 am to 5.30 pm Monday to Saturday. Now for the exceptions:

On Monday many shops don't open till noon but they stay open until 8 or 9 pm on Thursday night. Department stores and supermarkets generally close around 6 pm weekdays and at 5 pm on Saturday, but most supermarkets near city centres stay open till 8 pm.

Most regular nontourist shops outside the city centres close at 5 or 6 pm weekdays and at midday Saturday, depending on their line of trade, and almost all are closed on Sunday.

In the centres, however, most shops are open 9 am (noon on Monday) to 5 pm (9 pm on Thursday) throughout the week including Saturday, and many are open noon to 5 pm Sunday (especially the first Sunday of the month). Rotterdam in particular is pushing Sunday shopping.

Government offices, private institutions, monuments and even museums follow erratic and sometimes very limited opening hours to suit themselves; they're mentioned in this book where possible. Many museums are closed Monday.

PUBLIC HOLIDAYS & SPECIAL EVENTS

Public Holidays

People take public holidays seriously and you won't get much done. Most museums adopt Sunday hours on the days below (except Christmas and New Year) even if they fall on a day when the place would otherwise be closed.

The holidays are:

New Year's Day *(Nieuwjaarsdag)*

Easter Good Friday *(Goede Vrijdag)*; Easter Sunday and Easter Monday *(Eerste and Tweede Paasdag)*

Queen's Day *(Koninginnedag)* 30 April

Liberation Day *(Bevrijdingsdag)* 5 May Note that this day is not a universal holiday: government workers have the day off but almost everyone else has to work.

Ascension Day *(Hemelvaartsdag)*

Whit Sunday (Pentecost) and **Monday** *(Eerste and Tweede Pinksterdag)* Ascension Day and Whit Sunday and Monday fall at different times depending on Easter. Usually they occur between mid-May and mid-June.

Christmas Day and Boxing Day *(Eerste and Tweede Kerstdag)*

Remembrance Day 4 May official commemoration day that many treat as a day off.

Note too that *Carnaval* – again a day tied to Easter – is celebrated rigorously in the Catholic south. Huge parties occur in the five days leading up to Shrove Tuesday. Little work is done, much lager is guzzled and hotels are filled.

Special Events

Local special events are noted in the individual listings for cities and towns. The following are some of the very largest and most important events in the country, which may well be an excuse for a trip in themselves.

January

New Years Day Big in most city centres but especially in Amsterdam where there are many impromptu fireworks.

February/March

Carnaval Celebrated often on the weekend before Shrove Tuesday in a manner that would do Brazil, Venice or New Orleans proud in the mostly Catholic provinces of Noord Brabant,

A Moment in Time

We were hanging out over beers one May 4th a couple of years ago in an Amsterdam bar filled with fairly raucous people in their 20s who were laughing, carousing and listening to some fairly cutting-edge rock. At about 7:30 pm we noticed that the bartender, a guy with a shaven head and numerous tattoos, was setting up a TV on the bar. 'A football match?' we wondered. But the young and trendy black-clad types around us didn't seem like sports fanatics.

Close to 8 pm the TV came on with pictures of the Queen standing solemnly on Dam Square. Noise in the bar diminished, conversations ceased, and attention turned to the screen. We were intrigued. We hadn't really thought of the Dutch as people who got worked up because the Queen stood at attention. At 8 pm exactly the bar went quiet. Many stood, and each seemed to be lost in thought. After a few moments, the TV went off, talk resumed and the music returned.

Chatting with our neighbours, we learned about Remembrance Day. Every May 4th at 8 pm the entire nation comes to a halt for two minutes silence in honour of those who died during WWII. Those remembered include military personnel who died defending the country, civilians killed by fighting and bombing, the many who starved to death during the winter of hunger 1944-45 and Jews murdered by the Nazis.

Given that memories of the war have all but faded from public conscience in most countries more than five decades on, we were struck by what one young man said: 'To forget would be a crime and give an excuse for it to happen again.'

Gelderland and Limburg. Towns have huge parties. The one in Maastricht is famous and features days of drinking and dancing while bands prowl the streets.

March
Maastricht Art Show Europe's largest art show is held each year in Maastricht. Here's your chance to pick up a Monet, or at least do some serious browsing.

April
Queen's Birthday Celebrations on 30 April are held throughout the nation and feature much wearing of orange and much drinking as well. There's processions, dances, live music etc.

May
National Mill Day Just about every working windmill in the nation is open for visits on National Mill Day, usually on the second Saturday of the month. Look for windmills flying blue flags.

July
North Sea Jazz Festival Held in Den Haag this festival attracts the best talent from around the world.

August
Holland Festival and the **Uitmarkt** in Amsterdam are huge events, see the Amsterdam chapter for details.

ACTIVITIES

If it involves water, frozen or not, you'll find scores of enthusiasts doing it in the Netherlands. Other activities aided by flat land – biking and walking – are naturals and part of the national image.

Cycling

The Netherlands is nirvana for cyclists. Dedicated bike lanes and paths, huge guarded parking areas in most towns and cities and road rules that increasingly favour cyclists over cars are just some of the reasons why.

See the special section on Biking for all the details.

Walking

A close second to cycling, walking is popular throughout the country. If you want to put some hills on your itinerary, try the Maastricht area and Limburg Province in the south. De Hoge Veluwe National Park is good if you want to get out into nature. The islands off the north and west coasts are all good for long walks on the beach and dunes. Every VVV office has information on local routes, or you can just head out

Sinterklaas, the Original Santa Claus

Every year on 6 December the Dutch celebrate Sinterklaas in honour of St Nicholas, the inspiration for Santa Claus (Klaas is a nickname for Nicholas).

A few weeks beforehand, the white-bearded saint, dressed as a bishop with mitre and staff, arrives in Amsterdam by ship 'from Spain' (a legacy of Spanish colonial rule over the Netherlands) and enters the city on a grey or white horse to receive the city keys from the mayor. He is accompanied by a host of mischievous black servants called Black Peters (Zwarte Pieten) who throw sweets around. Well-behaved children get presents in a shoe that they've placed by the fireplace with a carrot for the saint's horse (he stays on the roof while a Black Peter climbs down the chimney). Recent efforts to diffuse the politically incorrect aspects of Black Peter (who's usually played by a Dutch person wearing black face make-up) by renaming him Blue Peter or Green Peter have been largely shunned. Instead, the legend that Black Peter puts naughty children in his bag and takes them back to Spain has been repositioned to emphasise his role as a bestower of gifts.

On the evening of 5 December people give one another anonymous and creatively wrapped gifts accompanied by funny/perceptive poems about the recipient written by Sinterklaas. The gift itself matters far less than the wrapping and poetry.

The commercialisation of Christmas has weakened the impact of this charming festival. Ironically, the American Santa Claus who dominates the Christmas spirit these days evolved from the Sinterklaas celebrations at the Dutch settlement of New Amsterdam (New York).

Sinterklaus coming to town.

along a dike, confident that it's very hard in this mostly flat land to ever get very lost.

For really unusual walking, see the boxed text 'Pounding Mud' in the Groningen & Drenthe chapter.

Skating

When the canals freeze over in winter (which doesn't happen often enough) everyone goes for a skate. Lakes and waterways in the countryside also fill up with colourfully clad skaters making trips tens of kilometres long. It's a wonderful experience, though painful on the ankles and butt if you're learning.

People drown under ice every year. Don't take to a patch of ice unless you see large groups of people, and be very careful at the edges and under bridges (such areas often don't freeze properly).

You can only rent skates at a skating rink. A pair of simple hockey skates costs upwards of about f100 at a department store (sports shops might have a wider selection but tend to be more expensive). Hockey skates are probably the best choice for learners; figure skates (with short, curved blades) are difficult to master, and speed skates (with long, flat blades) put a lot of strain on the ankles. Check for second-hand skates on notice boards at supermarkets or libraries. Old wood-framed skates that you tie under your shoes can be picked up cheaply at antique and bric-a-brac shops. Don't dismiss them; they're among the fastest skates around if they're freshly sharpened, and make great souvenirs.

For details on the legendary *Elfstedentocht* or '11 Cities' skating race, see the boxed text 'A Day at the Races' in the Friesland chapter.

Boating

The Dutch are avid sailors. On weekends a fleet of restored flat-bottomed boats, called the 'brown fleet' because of their (reddish) brown sails, crisscross the watery expanse of the IJsselmeer and the many lakes of

Friesland. Some are privately owned but many are rented, and sailing one is an unforgettable experience. The cheapest option is *botters,* former fishing boats with long, narrow leeboards and sleeping space (usually for around eight people) below deck. Larger groups could rent a converted freight barge known as a *tjalk,* originally with jib and spritsail rig though modern designs are made of steel and have diesel motors. Other vessels include anything from ancient pilot boats to massive clippers. You can also find motorboats for gliding along the countryside canals.

Costs are quite reasonable if you can muster a group of fellow enthusiasts. Some places only rent boats for day trips but it's much more fun to go for the full weekend experience. The usual arrangement is that you arrive at the boat at 8 pm Friday, sleep on board, sail out early the next morning, and visit several places around the IJsselmeer before returning between 4 and 6 pm on Sunday. Food is not included in the package, nor is cancellation insurance (trips are cancelled if wind is stronger than 7 Beaufort or wind force 7), but you do get a skipper.

During the summer, weekly rentals are also very popular. You check in on Saturday afternoon and return the next Saturday morning.

The following companies have typical rates. To find the deal that suits you best, bear in mind that everything is negotiable:

Hollands Glorie (☎ 0294-27 15 61, fax 26 29 43) Ossenmarkt 6, Muiden – weekend trips from 8 pm Friday to 5 pm Sunday; in the high season (May to September), a tjalk costs f1400 (maximum 14 people), and a clipper for a large group of people is f4700; there are also weekly arrangements, eg, a tjalk from Monday to Sunday from f3000, and many other options; in March, April and October prices are discounted by 10%

Zeilcharter Volendam (☎ 0299-36 97 40, fax 36 34 42) Enkhuizerzand 21, Volendam – a botter costs f800 per day (10 am to 6 pm, maximum 12 people); there are also more expensive boats, eg, a modern yacht for up to 8 people at f995 per day (f2400 for a weekend, f4890 for a week)

Holland Zeilcharters (☎ 0299-65 23 51, fax 65 36 18) Het Prooyen 4a, Monnickendam – botters

from f650 per day (12 to 14 people) and many other options

Muiden Jacht Charter (☎ 0294-26 14 13, fax 26 10 04) Naarderstraat 10, Muiden – has four botters costing from f600 per day (10 am to 6 pm, maximum 20 people); a weekend costs from f1250

Marco van den Berg (☎ 06-53 65 72 30) Oede Doelenkade 55, Hoorn – has yachts for up to 80 passengers from f500 per day, and larger ones for up to 150 people from f800 in Medemblik

Enkhuizen Yachtcharter (☎ 0228-32 32 00) Oosterhavenstraat 13, Enkhuizen –charges from f1900 per week to rent its luxury ocean-going yachts

Flevo Sailing (☎ 0320-26 03 24) Oostvaardersdijk 59C, Lelystad – rents out yachts for four to six passengers from f500 per day

Friesland Boating (☎ 0514-522 607, fax 522 620) de Tille 5, Koudam – has canal boats for weekly hire ranging in size from those suitable for four people (from f1200 per week) to those suitable for 12 people (from f2700)

Top of Holland Yacht Charter (☎ 058-216 08 54, fax 234 06 80) Postbus 1742, Leeuwarden – represents a score of companies in Friesland renting out everything from small sailboats to large cabin cruisers
Web site: www.topofholland.com

Boat Charter Holland (☎ 0515-424 617, fax 423 290) Eeltjebaasweg 3, Sneek – represents rental firms all over the Netherlands with a concentration of Friesland

Finally, the Netherlands Board of Tourism Web site at www.visitholland.com/geninfo/ has an excellent interactive boat rental feature that will match you up with rental firms depending on your budget, what type of boat you want and where you want to rent it. Follow the 'boat rental' link.

Windsurfing

There's lots of water and the wind blows all the time, hmmm, seems like a good place for windsurfing...

It is. Windsurfing is popular throughout the Netherlands. At most developed beaches along the coast and the islands you will find a number of places which will rent windsurfing equipment.

See the appropriate sections in the individual chapters. You can also inquire at any VVV office, who count this as one of their most frequent questions.

COURSES

The Foreign Student Service (☎ 020-671 59 15), Oranje Nassaulaan 5, 1017 AH Amsterdam, is a support agency for foreign students. It provides information about study programs and intensive language courses, and helps with accommodation, insurance and personal problems. It's open 9 am to 5.30 pm weekdays.

Language

Dutch is a close relative of English but that doesn't make it easy to learn. 'Normal' courses take months and intensive courses last several weeks. Plan ahead and make inquiries well in advance.

The Volksuniversiteit Amsterdam (☎ 020-626 16 26), Rapenburgerstraat 73, 1011 VK Amsterdam, offers a range of day and evening courses that are well regarded and don't cost a fortune. The Tropeninstituut (Royal Institute for the Tropics) has intensive language courses with a large component of 'cultural training', aimed specifically at foreigners moving to the Netherlands; it's fairly expensive but very effective. Contact the Language Training department (☎ 020-568 85 59) at Postbus 95001, 1090 HA Amsterdam. Web site: www.kit.nl.

The British Language Training Centre (☎ 020-622 36 34), Nieuwezijds Voorburgwal 328E, 1012 RW Amsterdam, is also expensive and has a good reputation.

There is a good Web site, found at www.learndutch.org, where you can learn Dutch online through structured courses.

Other Courses

The Volksuniversiteit (see previous section) offers a range of courses, some in English. The Amsterdam Summer University (☎ 020-620 02 25), Keizersgracht 324, 1016 EZ Amsterdam, conducts all of its courses and workshops in English. Subjects focus on arts and sciences, as befits the traditions of the Felix Meritis building that houses it.

WORK

Nationals from EU countries (as well as Iceland, Norway and Liechtenstein) may work in the Netherlands but they need a renewable residence permit, a tedious formality. There are few legal openings for non-EU nationals and the government tries to keep immigrants out of this already overpopulated country. You may be eligible if you are filling a job that no Dutch or EU national has the (trainable) skill to do, are aged between 18 and 45, and have suitable accommodation, but there will be a mound of red tape. (Forget about teaching English: there's very little demand.) All this has to be set in motion before you arrive (with the exception of US nationals, who may look for work within three months after they arrive as a tourist).

As a rule, you need to apply for temporary residence before an employer can apply for a work permit in your name. If all goes well, you will be issued a residence permit for work purposes. The whole rigmarole should take about five weeks. For more information, contact the Dutch embassy or consulate in your home country. Alternatively, for residence permits you can contact the Immigratie en Naturalisatiedienst (☎ 070-370 31 24, fax 370 31 34), Postbus 30125, 2500 GC Den Haag. For work permits and details of the Aliens Employment Act, contact the Landelijk Bureau Arbeidsvoorziening, Postbus 415, 2280 AK Rijswijk.

Au pair work is easier to organise, provided you are aged between 18 and 25, hold medical insurance and your host family earns at least f3000 a month after tax. The maximum period is one year. Nationals of the EU, Australia, Canada, Japan, Monaco, New Zealand, Switzerland and the USA can organise the necessary residence permit with the Vreemdelingenpolitie (Aliens' Police – see Visa Extensions in the earlier Documents section) after arrival in the Netherlands; others must organise this with the Dutch embassy or consulate in their home country.

Nationals of Australia, Canada and New Zealand can apply for a one-year working holiday visa if they're aged between 18 and 30. These visas are intended for people whose purpose of the visit is primarily for pleasure but who also hope to bolster their income with work. The details are complex and applying for the visa will include a meeting with a visa officer at a Dutch embassy who will try to determine if you have the means to return home if you can't find work. Contact the Dutch embassy or consulate in your home country's capital city for further details.

Illegal jobs (working 'black') are pretty rare these days, with increased crackdowns on illegal immigrants working in restaurants, pubs and bulb fields (traditional employers of 'black' labour). Some travellers' hotels in Amsterdam still employ touts to pounce on newly arrived backpackers; the pay isn't much but you may get free lodging.

If you're fortunate enough to find legal work, the minimum adult wage is about f1700 a month after tax.

ACCOMMODATION

There is a range of accommodation available in the Netherlands. However, much of the country suffers from the 'Amsterdam effect': because transport links are so good and Amsterdam is such a draw, many people stay in Amsterdam even when they plan on visiting, say, Leiden or Utrecht. However, Rotterdam and Maastricht have numerous places to stay.

Visitors to the Randstad may want to stay in one of the beach towns such as Scheveningen or Zandvoort, since they have huge numbers of B&Bs and other budget accommodation in season. However the beach towns are not as salubrious as they might seem and suffer from massive crowds and development.

Outside of resort areas, you won't find a lot of B&Bs or homestays. Some VVV offices maintain a list of people offering rooms, but this is by no means as universal as you'll find in Germany or Austria.

Camping

The Dutch like to camp, even in their own country. There are scores of camping grounds throughout the Netherlands. Facilities vary, but tend to be complete, with playgrounds, shops, cafes and the like.

Camping grounds are classified under a one to five-star system for sanitary facilities and amenities by the Stichting Classificatie Kampeer- en Bungalowbedrrijven (☎ 070-324 54 83), Postbus 93008, 2509 AA Den Haag. The ANWB publishes an annual list of Dutch camping grounds with facility listings and prices. Any VVV office can also provide you with detailed lists for the entire country.

Expect to pay f15 to f40 and more for two people and a tent overnight, depending on facilities. Many camping grounds also have simple bungalows that sleep two or more and cost from f80. Note too that few towns have camping areas in easy walking distance to the centre and that public transportation lines may not come close.

Many farms also make some land available for camping, although the law limits this to five sites or less. Besides the restful sounds of cattle, you'll probably enjoy a simpler and less crowded existence than at major camping grounds, especially in season. Local VVV offices usually can steer you to an accommodating farm, although who's participating tends to vary from year to year.

Camping grounds of all kinds are usually only open from April to October. The listings in this book note exceptions.

It's also worth noting *trekkershutten* (camping huts), which can be rented at camp sites and other recreational areas throughout the Netherlands. The typical hut is a simple wooden affair (100 sq metres) with four bunks, a cooking range, bicycle shelter, light and electricity. You'll need sleeping bags and your own cooking utensils, dishes and cutlery if you want to cook. All sites have sanitary facilities, and some a camp store and canteen. Costs are f55 per night for up to four people (maximum three nights in the same hut). Reserve through the VVV tourist offices or, for a f25 administration fee, at the Netherlands Reservation Centre (☎ 070-419 55 25), PO Box 404, 2260 AK Leidschendam. You can also order a brochure listing the trekkershutten from Stichting Trekkershutten Nederland (fax 0224-563 318), Ruigeweg 49, 1752 HC Sing Maartensbrug.

Hostels

Official Youth Hostels The head office of the Netherlands Youth Hostel Association (NJHC, ☎ 020-551 31 55, fax 639 01 99) is at Professor Tulpplein 4, 1018 GX Amsterdam (ironically, in front of the Amstel Inter-Continental Hotel, one of the most luxurious hotels in the country). The association uses the Hostelling International logo for the benefit of foreigners but has kept the 'youth hostel' name. Web site: www.njhc.org.

A youth hostel card (or rather, an International Guest Card) costs f30 at this office or at the hostels; alternatively, nonmembers pay f5 a night more for a bed and after six nights, which can be accumulated at various hostels, they become a member. HI or NJHC members can get discounts on international travel, eg, 10% discount on Eurolines bus tickets, and pay less commission on money exchange at the GWK (official exchange) offices. Members and nonmembers have the same rights at the hostels and there are no age limits.

Bookings are strongly advised in summer – a phone call or fax to the hostel is enough (most don't accept email reservations). Facilities at the 34 NJHC hostels vary widely and, apart from the usual dormitories, may include rooms for two, four, six and eight people that are often used by families. These should be booked well ahead in busy periods (spring, summer and autumn holidays) and rates vary considerably – inquire at the hostel. Locations range from Amsterdam to Ameland Island but there are not as many in cities as one would hope.

Nightly rates vary with the hostel, but range from f23 to f39 per person depending on location and season.

Other Hostels Amsterdam is home to a large number of non-NJHC hostels. The qualities of these places is wildly variable. There are not many elsewhere in the country, again due to the 'Amsterdam effect'.

'Unofficial' hostels are reluctant to take bookings over the phone and seem to prefer walk-in trade. Try getting there by 10 am and you should stand a reasonable chance.

Hotels

Ratings & Facilities The star-rating system for hotels goes up to five stars; accommodation rating less than one star can call itself a pension or guesthouse but not a hotel. The ratings are not very helpful because they have more to do with the amenities – lifts (elevators), phones in the rooms, minibar etc – and the number of rooms than with the quality of the rooms themselves.

Many hotels (like many of the houses) have steep and narrow stairs but no lifts, which make them inaccessible for people with mobility problems. Check when you make inquiries. Of course the top-end hotels do have lifts, and some mid-range ones too.

Rooms usually come with TV, though in the cheaper places you might have to feed coins into a timer to help pay for the cable subscription. Then again, there might be no room TV even in some expensive hotels, so if this means a lot to you, check when making inquiries.

Hotels tend to be small – any hotel with more than 20 rooms is 'large' – so if you book a room with shower or toilet in the corridor you probably won't have to share it with too many other guests. If you book a room with private shower, this will usually include a toilet but not always. Hotels in the top price bracket have bathrooms with real baths attached to the rooms; cheaper hotels tend to have showers but might have a few rooms with baths for the same price – ask.

Bookings VVV offices can book hotel rooms anywhere in the Netherlands. They usually charge a fee – excluding any deposit – that varies from f3 to f10 (mostly f10). GWK offices, such as the ones in Amsterdam, will often take reservations. They charge f5 commission and you pay 10% of the room charge in advance.

The Netherlands Reservation Centre (☎ 70-419 55 19; fax 419 55 44), Postbus 404, 2260 AK Leidschendam, accepts hotel bookings from abroad. Web site: www.hotelres.nl.

Hotels tend to charge a bit more if you come to them through these services – you can save money by booking directly with the hotel. Many of them won't accept credit card details over the phone (if they accept cards at all) and may insist on a down payment by cheque or money order before they'll confirm the booking.

When booking for two people, make it clear whether you want a twin (two single beds) or double (a bed for two). It should make no difference to the price, but the wrong bed configuration could be impossible to fix on the spot when rooms are fully booked in summer.

Many hotels have their own web sites these days: try keying in www.(hotelname).nl.

Prices Generally you get what you pay for. Hotels in the lowest price bracket (below f125 for a double) can be run down and invariably seem to suffer from mouldy smells due to the damp climate, coupled with the Dutch aversion to decent ventilation. Still, they can be good value, especially if they've just been renovated. Hotels above this price bracket are more pleasant, and may even have doubles for less than f125 depending on the season and whether or not you want breakfast or a shower in the room. Breakfast in the hotel is a good idea because few food establishments open early.

Single rooms cost about two-thirds of the rates quoted here for doubles; add a third to a half for triples. Hotels that accept children (many of them don't) often have special rates for families. Prices at many hotels drop a bit in the low season (roughly October to April excluding Christmas/New Year and Easter) but it's always worth asking for 'special' rates, especially if you're staying a few nights. Top-end hotels, on the other hand, often rely on business travellers and tend to be cheaper in the summer months and on weekends.

FOOD

Dutch food in the traditional sense is not exactly world famous, but international influences have made modern Dutch cuisine quite palatable. In fact, in recent years the Netherlands has undergone a bit of a culinary revolution and you can eat very well

indeed. If you prefer traditional Chinese, Italian, Thai, Mexican or whatever, you'll find it in even fairly small towns. Prices are very reasonable by European standards and servings are generous.

Smoking is still an entrenched habit in Dutch restaurants. A few places have non-smoking sections but even serious vegetarian establishments have trouble banning smokers altogether.

Where & When

Don't overlook the many *eetcafes*, which are pubs that also serve meals; most of them could just as well be listed here as places to eat and many are good to excellent, though they don't always take reservations. They're affordable and lively, and if you enjoy the ambience you can hang around for drinks afterwards. The grand cafes, in particular, are good places for lunch. Many pubs also have food and thus the differences between restaurant and pub can get fuzzy. For most towns in this book we have combined them under the category Places to Eat & Drink.

The main meal of the day is dinner, from around 6 to 9.30 pm. More popular places fill up by 7 pm (the Dutch eat early). Book ahead or arrive early, or be prepared to wait at the bar. You could also arrive late; films, concerts and other performances usually start at 8.30 or 9.30 pm and tables may become available then for a 'second sitting', but keep in mind that many kitchens close by 10 pm (though the restaurants may stay open longer). Vegetarian restaurants tend to close earlier.

Lunch is more modest, with sandwich and salad menus, though you'll find places that serve full meals if you really want one.

Cuisines

Cuisines such as Italian, Spanish, Mexican, Thai, Chinese, Indian and Turkish will be similar to what you're used to, though they might be adapted a bit to suit the Dutch palate and ingredients available locally. Vegetarians are well catered for and most restaurants have one or more vegetarian dishes on the menu, though we also list several dedicated vegetarian places.

Dutch The standard Dutch meal consists of potatoes, meat and vegetables in large portions (though meat is expensive, so don't expect plate-filling steaks). Few restaurants serve exclusively Dutch cuisine but many places have several Dutch staples on the menu, especially in winter, that are filling and good value for money.

stamppot (mashed pot) – potatoes mashed with vegetables (usually kale or endive) and served with smoked sausage or strips of pork
hutspot (hotchpotch) – similar to stamppot, but with carrots, onions and braised meat
erwtensoep (thick pea soup) – a spoon stuck upright in the pot should fall over slowly; with smoked sausage and bacon
asperges (asparagus) – always white; very popular in spring; served with ham and butter
kroketten (croquettes) – dough-ragout with meat (sometimes fish or shrimp) that's crumbed and deep-fried; often in the form of small balls called *bitterballen* served with mustard, a popular pub snack
mosselen (mussels) – popular, and best eaten, in the months that contain an 'R', ie, September to April; cooked with white wine, chopped leeks and onions, and served in a bowl or cooking pot with a side dish of French fries *(frites* or *patat)*; use an empty shell as a pincer to pluck out the bodies; don't eat mussels that haven't opened properly as they can be poisonous

Seafood doesn't feature as prominently as one might expect in a seafaring nation, though there's plenty of it. Popular fish include *schol* (plaice), *tong* (sole), *kabeljauw* (cod), and freshwater *forel* (trout). *Garnalen* (shrimps, prawns) are also found on many menus, often large species known by their Italian name of *scampi. Haring* (herring) is a national institution, eaten lightly salted or occasionally pickled but never fried or cooked; *paling* (eel) is usually smoked. Don't dismiss herring or eel until you've tried them – see the Fast Food section later in this chapter.

Typical Dutch desserts are fruit pie (apple, cherry or other fruit), *vla* (custard) or pancakes. Many snack bars and pubs serve *appeltaart* (apple pie) and coffee throughout the day.

Cheese is hugely popular and varies far more than those who only associate the

Netherlands with mild gouda. At the very least, try some old *(oud)* gouda with mustard. It is hard and rich in flavour and is a popular bar snack.

Finally, most towns have at least one place serving *pannekoeken* (pancakes). These come in a huge array of flavours and cost around f10. Kids love 'em.

Fusion It's the sort of food that Australians, Californians and more recently, Londoners have been enjoying for years. The idea is to combine Asian/Pacific Rim ingredients and cooking techniques with local produce on the one plate.

Indonesian This is a tasty legacy of Dutch colonial history. Some dishes, such as the famous *rijsttafel* (rice table – white rice with heaps of side dishes, take your time), are colonial concoctions rather than traditional Indonesian, but that doesn't make them less appealing.

One slight problem, however, is that most places serving Indonesian food are Chinese-Indonesian, run by Chinese (some with Indonesian backgrounds) who have perfected bland dishes to suit Dutch palates. The food is OK and can be great value, but if you want the real thing, avoid places that call themselves *Chinees-Indonesisch* (or order Chinese dishes there instead).

Even at 'genuine' Indonesian restaurants, rijsttafel can be a bit of a rip-off and the ingredients don't always taste authentic – once you've had a really good one you'll know the difference. Instead of a rijsttafel, you might prefer ordering *nasi rames* (literally: boiled rice), a plate of rice covered in several accompaniments that would be served in separate bowls in a rijsttafel. The same dish with thick noodles (more a Chinese-Indonesian variant and quite filling) is called *bami rames.*

Gado-gado (lightly steamed vegetables and hard-boiled egg, served with peanut sauce and rice) feels good in all respects. *Saté* or *sateh* (satay) is marinated, barbecued beef, chicken or pork on small skewers; unfortunately it's often cooked electrically and smothered in peanut sauce.

Other stand-bys are *nasi goreng* (fried rice with onions, pork, shrimp and spices, often topped with a fried egg or shredded omelette) and *bami goreng* (the same thing but with noodles).

Indonesian food is usually served mild for sensitive western palates. If you want it hot (*pedis,* pronounced 'p-DIS'), say so but be prepared for the ride of a lifetime. It's better to play it safe by asking for *sambal* (chilli paste), if it isn't already on the table, and helping yourself. Usually it's *sambal oelek,* which is red and hot; the dark-brown *sambal badjak* is based on onions and is mild and sweet.

Indonesian food should be eaten with a spoon and fork (chopsticks are Chinese) and the drink of choice is beer or water.

International Many restaurants fall into this category, which mixes cuisines from different parts of the world depending on the skill or preference of the cook.

Surinamese Food from this former South American colony is similar to Caribbean food – a unique African/Indian hybrid – with Indonesian influences contributed by indentured labourers from Java. Chicken features strongly, along with curries (chicken, lamb or beef), potatoes and rice, and delicious *roti* (unleavened bread pancakes).

Fast Food
There are any number of sandwich shops *(broodjeszaken)* or snack bars to still your immediate hunger. The latter have an amazing range of multicoloured treats in a display case. Usually based on some sort of meat and spices, these items – like anything else you order – are dumped into a deep-fryer when you order. Some snack bars take the concept of fast food even further and have a long rows of coin-operated windows. Insert f2 or f3 and you have immediate access to a fried treat, cooked usually the same day.

Vlaamse frites (Flemish fries) are French fries made from whole potatoes rather than the potato pulp you'll get if the sign only says 'frites'. They're supposed to be smothered in mayonnaise (though you can ask for ketchup, curry sauce, garlic sauce or a myriad of other gloopy toppings) and will fill your stomach for around f3. They are a national institution and you can find stands everywhere.

Also try seafood at one of the seafood stalls found in every town. Raw, slightly salted herring (about f4, cut into bite-sized bits and served with optional onion and pickles) might not sound appealing, but you could very well think differently once you've tried it. The same applies to smoked eel, which, like herring, is quite filling, especially if taken in a bun. If you still can't bear the thought, go for shrimps or *gerookte makreel* (smoked mackerel).

Israeli or Lebanese snack bars specialise in *shoarma,* a pitta bread filled with sliced lamb from a vertical spit, salad and a choice of sauces, which makes a filling snack. In some parts of the world it's known as a *gyros* or *doner kebab.* Such places also do a mean *felafel* (spiced chickpea patties, deep-fried).

Poffertjes are miniature pancakes topped with butter and sprinkled with caster sugar – absolutely delicious.

Self-Catering
Albert Heijn, the country's dominant supermarket chain, seems pretty much to have sewn up the centre of most towns. Although prices are higher than some other chains, it tends to have a greater range of baked goods and ready-to-eat and deli foods.

Most cities and towns have markets in one or more locations on one or more days. Here you can buy everything from fresh produce to fresh fish.

Costs
The prices quoted in this book are probably the minimum you'll end up spending; add something to drink and one or two other dishes and you could spend twice as much. Drinks other than *pils* (draught beer) will pad out the bill, and wine can be a blatant rip-off in restaurants, with bottles that cost f10 in the shops going for anything up to f45. 'House wines' are no different: a half-litre carafe of acidic house red will cost at

least f15, though some restaurants do serve drinkable stuff.

Many places list a *dagschotel* (dish of the day) or *dagmenu* that will be good value, but don't expect a culinary adventure. On the other hand, the trend in many places is to limit the menu to two or three options that change daily, in which case the food can be quite exciting.

Service is included in the bill and tipping is at your discretion, though most people leave some change (5% to 10%). The protocol is to say how much you're paying in total as you settle the bill.

Beware that many restaurants do *not* accept credit cards; ask in advance to avoid embarrassment.

DRINKS
Nonalcoholic
Dutch tap water is fine, but people always seem to prefer mineral waters. Note that, except for the smallest sizes, water either comes in returnable – and heavy – glass or thick plastic containers. Dairy drinks include chocolate milk, Fristi (a yoghurt drink), *karnemelk* (buttermilk) and of course milk itself, which is good and relatively cheap. A wide selection of fruit juices and all the international soft drinks are available too.

Tea & Coffee
Tea is usually served as a cup of hot water with a tea bag, though many places do offer a wide choice of bags from a special box. If you want milk, ask *met melk, graag* ('with milk, please'); many locals prefer to add a slice of lemon instead.

The hot drink of choice is coffee, which should be strong. If you simply order *koffie* you'll get a sizeable cup of the black stuff with a separate jug (or small airline container) of *koffiemelk*, a slightly sour-tasting cream similar to unsweetened condensed milk that enhances the flavour. *Koffie verkeerd* (coffee 'wrong') comes in a bigger cup or mug with plenty of real milk. If you order *espresso* or *cappuccino* you'll be lucky to get a decent Italian version; most cappuccinos are just covered in watery froth, though the blandness may be disguised by a sprinkle of cinnamon. Don't count on finding decaffeinated coffee, and if you do it's likely to be some vile instant stuff. The Dutch have an interesting history with coffee. See the boxed text 'Coffee: from Yemen to You' for details.

Alcoholic
Lager beer is the staple drink, served cool and topped by a two-finger-thick head of froth – supposedly to trap the flavour. Brits

Coffee: from Yemen to You

The coffee plant is said to have come from Ethiopia, but it was the Yemenis who first commercialised the product. In 1616 a Dutch visitor to Al-Makha, a Red Sea port in Yemen, noted a caravan of 1000 camels carrying goods including fruit, spices, pottery and coffee – the latest craze in Europe – grown in the Yemeni mountains. Two years later the Dutch built Al-Makha's first coffee factories.

By the 1630s coffee houses were operating in the Netherlands, and the demand for coffee rose to such heights that Yemen was unable to meet demand. Prices soared, bringing prosperity to the coffee merchants of Al-Makha, who built gorgeous villas in the city. During those years Yemen had a virtual world monopoly on the beans, and the term 'mocha' (*mokka* in Dutch) has survived to the present day to indicate the strongly flavoured, dark-brown coffee from Arabia, or an equally dark and tasty mixture of coffee and chocolate.

Eventually, however, the plant was smuggled out by scheming Dutch traders and, after being studied and propagated in Amsterdam's Hortus Botanicus, it was cultivated in Ceylon (Sri Lanka) and Java by the early 1700s. With its monopoly broken, Al-Makha began a slow decline.

Today, there is a popular scheme in the Netherlands run by the Max Havelaar Foundation to ensure that the Third World producers of this popular drink get a price that affords them a decent living, see the boxed text 'Seal of Fairness' later in the chapter.

requesting 'no head please' will meet with a steely response. *Een bier* or *een pils* will get you a normal glass; *een kleintje pils* is a small glass and *een fluitje* is a small, thin, Cologne-style glass. Many places also serve half-litre mugs *(een grote pils)* to please tourists.

For more on the wide range of beers served in the Netherlands, see the boxed text 'A Tasty Brew'.

Dutch gin *(genever)* is made from juniper berries and is drunk chilled from a tiny glass filled to the brim. Most people prefer *jonge* (young) genever, which is smooth and relatively easy to drink; *oude* (old) genever has a strong juniper flavour and can be an acquired taste. A common combination, known as a *kopstoot* (head butt), is a glass of genever with a beer chaser – few people

can handle more than two or three of those. Brandy is known as *vieux* or *brandewijn*. There are plenty of indigenous liqueurs, including *advocaat* (a kind of eggnog) and the herb-based *Beerenburg*, a Friesian schnapps.

Wines in all varieties are very popular thanks to European unity. Great French and Italian wines are widely available at fairly cheap prices in liquor stores.

ENTERTAINMENT

Dutch cultural funding is generous and even in medium-sized towns you will find classical music, opera and dance companies. Live music is always popular and the Dutch are big fans of jazz. Many towns have bars with regular live jazz performances. There are also the usual rock bands of widely differing talents. However, many cafes and pubs don't regularly have live music, so

A Tasty Brew

The Dutch have been brewing beer for centuries and, indeed, towns like Groningen built their fortunes on brewing.

Today, popular brands of pilsner include Heineken, Amstel, Grolsch, Oranjeboom, and the cheap Brouwersbier put out by the Albert Heijn supermarket chain. These brands generally contain 5% alcohol by volume in the bottle and close to 5% on tap, so a few of those seemingly small glasses can pack quite a wallop.

Of these huge brands, Heineken may have the biggest name outside of the Netherlands, including in the USA where it is ironically considered a 'high-end' beer. At home, Heineken has a bit of an image problem, being considered 'the beer your cheap father drinks' to quote one wag. Grolsch is very popular – particularly in the Catholic parts of the country – and has an excellent reputation for taste. Grolsch and Heineken both market seasonal beers several times a year – suds tastier than their mainstream brands (although Grolsch's standard brew is pretty decent). Try Grolsch's *Lentebok* (Spring bock).

The Netherlands also has scores of smaller beer producers. Brand is known for its fine pilsner and speciality beers. That the company was recently snapped up by Heineken hasn't seemed to have dulled its output – a credit to its huge new owner. Most of the smaller breweries make a range of products; your best bet is to gleefully try anything you haven't seen before. The small size of Dutch beer portions means that you won't be stuck with much if the brew isn't to your liking. Some noted small brewers include Gulpen, Bavaria, Drie Ringen, Leeuw and Utrecht.

The beers by Amsterdam's windmill-based *Brouwerij 't IJ* (on tap there but also sold bottled in many local pubs) are simply, to quote an LP author, 'awesome' – you can taste the fresh grain and alcohol content up to 8% (its 'Colombus' brew).

Several widely available beers come from Belgium. De Koninck, Palm, Duvel and Westmalle Triple all have strong and crisp flavours that cause the mass-market Dutch pilsners to pale. You can easily find at least one on tap in most bars.

Throughout this guide, we've listed cafes and bars where you can select from a good range of beers.

performances tend to be centred on venues specialising in live music.

The Dutch are also big moviegoers and their tastes are eclectic and wide-ranging. Cities have several cinemas and the films are almost always shown with subtitles rather than being dubbed. There are also numerous cinemas showing offbeat and unusual films and you may find products from your own country that you'd never find at home.

In Amsterdam you can find just about any entertainment imaginable.

SPECTATOR SPORTS

Football (soccer) is far and away the main spectator sport in the Netherlands.

Teams are divided into professional and amateur categories. The former are organised nationally, while the latter are separated into Saturday and Sunday leagues. This finds its roots in the religious backgrounds of the Dutch. Protestants used to insist on leaving Sunday sacred so they played on Saturday while the Catholics were happy to play on Sunday. The amateur football season runs from September through May. Being crowned amateur champion in the Netherlands is a very big deal.

The professional football league has recently been sponsored by PTT-Telecom and thus you'll see their name in every reference to the league. The season is the same as the amateur season. Most of the teams have huge stadiums that are sold out far in advance to ticket subscribers. Don't count on being able to buy a ticket.

The best teams are: AJAX (based in Amsterdam), Feyenoord (Rotterdam) and PSV (Eindhoven). The latter was the national champion of the 1999–2000 season.

Other teams with large followings include: FC Twente (Enschede), Vitesse (Arnhem), Willem II (Tilburg), Roda JC (Kerkrade), Heerenveen (Heerenveen), NEC (Nijmegen) and De Graafschap (Doetinchem).

The teams that finish in the top two spots also play in the Champions League, the Europe-wide competition. Dutch fans at matches pitting their squad against another European team are known for painting their faces – among other parts – orange.

For more information on Dutch football, contact the Royal Dutch football Association (KNVB, ☎ 0343-499 211, fax 491 615), Woudenbergseweg 56, 3707 ZX Heist.

The Elfstedentocht skating race brings out tens of thousands of spectators, but is run very sporadically due to the weather. See the boxed text 'A Day at the Races' in the Friesland chapter.

SHOPPING

With a few exceptions – dope, pornography, flower bulbs, rounds of cheese, obscure types of *genever* (Dutch gin) – there's nothing to be found in the Netherlands that you won't find elsewhere, and fantastic bargains are rare.

Amsterdam however is known for its speciality shops and markets. You might be able to find a glow-in-the-dark toothbrush or banana-flavoured condom back home, but Amsterdam has whole shops devoted to toothbrushes or condoms – or hammocks, mosquito nets and of course clogs, to name just a few of the eccentric goods on offer.

Amsterdam is also known for its diamonds. The city has been a major diamond centre since Sephardic Jews introduced the cutting industry in the 1580s (one of the few occupations open to them at the time). The *Cullinan*, the largest diamond ever found (3106 carats), was split into more than 100 stones here in 1908, after which the master cutter spent three months recovering from stress. The *Kohinoor* or Mountain of Light was cut here too – a very large, oval diamond (108.8 carats) acquired by Queen Victoria that now forms part of the British crown jewels.

WWII dealt a serious blow to the industry but there are about a dozen diamond factories in the city today – some of which offer tours, see the Amsterdam chapter for details. Diamonds aren't necessarily cheaper here than elsewhere but prices are fairly competitive.

Generally Dutch stores are open 9.30 am to 6 pm weekdays and until 4.30 weekends. There are a few exceptions; in many towns, such as Den Haag, stores don't open until 11 am or later on Monday; stores stay open

Seal of Fairness

In 1859, Douwes Dekker, a Dutch diplomat, wrote a book about the abuses by his own countrymen in the Dutch East Indies (today's Indonesia). His book, which was really an autobiography, centred on a character named Max Havelaar who railed against policies which forced the local people to work for Dutch coffee plantations, to the detriment of their own food production.

Generations of Dutch have read *Max Havelaar, or the Coffee Auctions of the Dutch East India Company*, and its tale of colonial abuse has touched many. In 1986, a group of Mexican coffee-growers told the Dutch government that they would forego development aid if they could just get a fair price for their coffee. This resonated with many and led to the formation of the modern-day Max Havelaar Foundation.

Its goal is simple: to ensure Third World producers are able to receive payment for their products allowing them a living wage. Products that meet this important criteria are able to be sold with the Max Havelaar logo. The foundation uses auditors to ensure that products with the label were purchased at a fair price from the producers and that no middle agents imposed themselves extracting unfair profit. In addition, producers must have access to capital so they can finance their crops in advance and they must be able to work in decent working conditions that don't impose undue stress on the environment.

In 1988, the first packet of coffee bearing the Max Havelaar logo was sold in a Dutch shop. In 1993, cocoa was added to the range and the first chocolate bar with the logo appeared. Since then, tea, honey and bananas have been added. Over 90% of Dutch supermarkets carry goods with the Max Havelaar logo – the foundation allows qualifying firms to use the logo, it doesn't produce the products itself – and the market share is growing. Already 6% of the bananas sold in the Netherlands bear the logo.

The foundation is spreading its mission to other parts of Europe as well. You can find the Max Havelaar logo in Danish, German and Belgian supermarkets, among others. Producers that are part of the scheme include over 200 coffee co-operatives in 18 countries. In the case of all the products, the members of the co-operatives have to be small producers, in that one family works on the farm rather than large numbers of hired labourers.

For more information, contact the Max Havelaar Foundation (☎ 030-233 46 02, fax 233 29 92, ✆ maxhavelaar@maxhavelaar.nl), Lucasbolwerk 7, 3512 EG Utrecht.

Sign of fairness in trade

late one night a week – usually Thursday – until 9 pm and Sunday shopping, from about 11 am to 5 pm is catching on in many cities such as Rotterdam.

For information about a popular program to sell food items in shops at prices that actually benefit their Third World farmers, see the boxed text 'Seal of Fairness'.

Getting There & Away

The Netherlands is an easy place to reach. Amsterdam's Schiphol airport has copious air links worldwide, including many on low-cost European airlines. Train links on high-speed trains are good, especially from France, Belgium and Germany. Other land options are easy and the many border crossings are invisible, thanks to the Schengen agreement which obviates document checks between many EU counties including the Netherlands and its neighbours. There are also several ferry links with Britain.

AIR
Airports & Airlines
Schiphol airport, near Amsterdam, is not only the Netherlands' main international airport, but also the third busiest airport in Europe. It is the hub for KLM, the Dutch carrier with close ties to America's Northwest. Most of the world's major airlines serve Schiphol. There are direct flights and connections to all continents. See the Getting There & Away section for Amsterdam for a list of airlines and their local contact numbers. Schiphol is easily reached by rail from all points of the country in under 2½ hours.

Rotterdam Airport trails Schiphol by a huge margin, not least because of its proximity. It has handy links to London operated by KLM uk, one of KLM's myriad of regional operators as well as Belgian-based VLM and British Airways. The latter also serves Birmingham and Manchester. KLM exel serves Paris.

Eindhoven and Maastricht airports are mainly for business travellers. From the former, KLM exel serves Hamburg, London, Manchester and Paris. British Airways flies to/from London, Manchester and Birmingham.

Buying Tickets
An air ticket alone can gouge a great slice out of anyone's budget, but you can reduce the cost by finding discounted fares. Recent stiff competition has resulted in widespread

discounting – good news for travellers! The only people likely to be paying full fare these days are travellers flying in 1st or business class. Passengers flying in economy can usually manage some sort of discount. But unless you buy carefully and flexibly, it is still possible to end up paying exorbitant amounts for a journey.

For long-term travel there are plenty of discount tickets which are valid for 12 months, allowing multiple stopovers with open dates. For short-term travel cheaper fares are available by travelling midweek, staying away at least one Saturday night or taking advantage of short-lived promotional offers.

When you're looking for bargain air fares, go to a travel agent rather than directly to the airline. From time to time, airlines do have promotional fares and special offers, but generally they only sell fares at the official listed price. One exception to this rule is the expanding number of 'no-frills' carriers operating in Europe, which mostly sell direct to travellers. Unlike the 'full-service' airlines, no-frills carriers often make one-way tickets available at around half the return fare, meaning that it is easy to put together a return ticket when you fly to one place but leave from another. Easy-Jet, from Britain, is the main no-frills airline serving the Netherlands.

The other exception is booking on the Internet. Many airlines, full-service and no-frills, offer some excellent fares to Web surfers. They may sell seats by auction or simply cut prices to reflect the reduced cost of electronic selling. Many travel agents around the world have Web sites, which can make the Internet a quick and easy way to compare prices, a good start for when you're ready to start negotiating with your favourite travel agency. Online ticket sales work well if you are doing a simple one-way or return trip on specified dates. However, online super-fast fare generators are no substitute for a travel agent who knows all about special deals, has strategies for avoiding layovers and can offer advice on everything from which airline has the best vegetarian food to the best travel insurance to bundle with your ticket.

The days when some travel agents would routinely fleece travellers by running off with their money are, happily, almost over. Paying by credit card generally offers protection, as most card issuers provide refunds if you can prove you didn't get what you paid for. Similar protection can be obtained by buying a ticket from a bonded agent, such as one covered by the Air Transport Operators Licence (ATOL) scheme in the UK. Agents who only accept cash should hand over the tickets straight away and not tell you to 'come back tomorrow'. After you've made a booking or paid your deposit, call the airline and confirm that the booking was made. It's generally not advisable to send money (even cheques) through the post unless the agent is very well established – some travellers have reported being ripped off by fly-by-night mail-order ticket agents.

You may decide to pay more than the rock-bottom fare by opting for the safety of a better-known travel agent. Firms such as STA Travel, which has offices worldwide, Council Travel in the USA and usit Campus (formerly Campus Travel) in the UK are not going to disappear overnight and they do offer good prices to most destinations.

If you purchase a ticket and later want to make changes to your route or get a refund, you need to contact the original travel agent. Airlines only issue refunds to the purchaser of a ticket – usually the travel agent who bought the ticket on your behalf. Many travellers change their routes halfway through their trips, so think carefully before you buy a ticket which is not easily refunded.

Student & Youth Fares Full-time students and people under 26 have access to better deals than other travellers. The better deals may not always be cheaper fares but can include more flexibility to change flights and/or routes. You have to show a document proving your date of birth or a valid International Student Identity Card (ISIC) when buying your ticket and boarding the plane. There are plenty of places around the world where nonstudents can get fake student cards, but if you get caught using a fake card you could have your ticket confiscated.

Frequent Flyers Most airlines offer frequent flyer deals that can earn you a free air ticket or other goodies. To qualify, you have to accumulate sufficient mileage with the same airline or airline alliance. Many airlines have 'blackout periods', or times when you cannot fly for free on your frequent-flyer points (Christmas and Chinese New Year, for example). The worst thing about frequent-flyer programs is that they tend to lock you into one airline, and that airline may not always have the cheapest fares or most convenient flight schedule.

Courier Flights Courier flights are a great bargain if you're lucky enough to find one. Air-freight companies expedite delivery of urgent items by sending them with you as your baggage allowance. You are permitted to bring along a carry-on bag, but that's all. In return, you get a steeply discounted ticket.

There are other restrictions: Courier tickets are sold for a fixed date and schedule changes can be difficult to make. If you buy a return ticket, your schedule will be even more rigid. You need to clarify before you fly what restrictions apply to your ticket, and don't expect a refund once you've paid. Booking a courier ticket takes some effort. They are not readily available and arrangements have to be made a month or more in advance. You won't find courier flights on all routes either – just on the major air routes.

Courier flights are occasionally advertised in the newspapers, or you could contact air-freight companies listed in the phone book. You may even have to go to the air-freight company to get an answer – the companies aren't always keen to give out information over the phone. *Travel Unlimited* (PO Box 1058, Allston, MA 02134, USA) is a monthly travel newsletter based in the USA that publishes many courier

Air Travel Glossary

Cancellation Penalties If you have to cancel or change a discounted ticket, there are often heavy penalties involved; insurance can sometimes be taken out against these penalties. Some airlines impose penalties on regular tickets as well, particularly against 'no-show' passengers.

Courier Fares Businesses often need to send urgent documents or freight securely and quickly. Courier companies hire people to accompany the package through customs and, in return, offer a discount ticket which is sometimes a phenomenal bargain. However, you may have to surrender all your baggage allowance and take only carry-on luggage.

Full Fares Airlines traditionally offer 1st class (coded F), business class (coded J) and economy class (coded Y) tickets. These days there are so many promotional and discounted fares available that few passengers pay full economy fare.

Lost Tickets If you lose your airline ticket an airline will usually treat it like a travellers cheque and, after inquiries, issue you with another one. Legally, however, an airline is entitled to treat it like cash and if you lose it then it's gone forever. Take good care of your tickets.

Onward Tickets An entry requirement for many countries is that you have a ticket out of the country. If you're unsure of your next move, the easiest solution is to buy the cheapest onward ticket to a neighbouring country or a ticket from a reliable airline which can later be refunded if you do not use it.

Open-Jaw Tickets These are return tickets where you fly out to one place but return from another. If available, this can save you backtracking to your arrival point.

Overbooking Since every flight has some passengers who fail to show up, airlines often book more passengers than they have seats. Usually excess passengers make up for the no-shows, but occasionally somebody gets 'bumped' onto the next available flight. Guess who it is most likely to be? The passengers who check in late.

Promotional Fares These are officially discounted fares, available from travel agencies or direct from the airline.

Reconfirmation If you don't reconfirm your flight at least 72 hours prior to departure, the airline may delete your name from the passenger list. Ring to find out if your airline requires reconfirmation.

Restrictions Discounted tickets often have various restrictions on them – such as needing to be paid for in advance and incurring a penalty to be altered. Others are restrictions on the minimum and maximum period you must be away.

Round-the-World Tickets RTW tickets give you a limited period (usually a year) in which to circumnavigate the globe. You can go anywhere the carrying airlines go, as long as you don't backtrack. The number of stopovers or total number of separate flights is decided before you set off and they usually cost a bit more than a basic return flight.

Transferred Tickets Airline tickets cannot be transferred from one person to another. Travellers sometimes try to sell the return half of their ticket, but officials can ask you to prove that you are the person named on the ticket. On an international flight tickets are compared with passports.

Travel Periods Ticket prices vary with the time of year. There is a low (off-peak) season and a high (peak) season, and often a low-shoulder season and a high-shoulder season as well. Usually the fare depends on your outward flight – if you depart in the high season and return in the low season, you pay the high-season fare.

flight deals from destinations worldwide. A 12-month subscription to the newsletter costs US$25, or US$35 for readers outside the USA. Another possibility (at least for US residents) is to join the International Association of Air Travel Couriers (IAATC). The membership fee of $45 gets members a bimonthly update of air-courier offerings, access to a fax-on-demand service with daily updates of last minute specials and the bimonthly newsletter, *Shoestring Traveler*. For more information, contact IAATC (☎ 561-582 8320) or visit its Web site, www.courier.org. However, be aware that joining this organisation does not guarantee that you'll get a courier flight.

Second-hand Tickets You'll occasionally see advertisements on youth hostel bulletin boards and sometimes in newspapers for 'second-hand tickets'. That is, somebody purchased a return ticket or a ticket with multiple stopovers and now wants to sell the unused portion of the ticket.

The prices offered look very attractive indeed. Unfortunately, these tickets, if used for international travel, are usually worthless, as the name on the ticket must match the name on the passport of the person checking in. Some people reason that the seller of the ticket can check you in with their passport, and then give you the boarding pass – wrong again! Usually the immigration people want to see your boarding pass, and if it doesn't match the name in your passport, then you won't be able to board your flight.

What happens if you purchase a ticket and then change your name? It can happen – some people change their name when they get married or divorced and some people change their name because they feel like it. If the name on the ticket doesn't match the name in your passport, you could have problems. In this case, be sure you have documents such as your old passport to prove that the old you and the new you are the same person.

Ticketless Travel Ticketless travel, whereby your reservation details are kept within an airline computer, is becoming more common. On simple return trips the absence of a ticket can be a benefit – it's one less thing to worry about; however, if you are planning a complicated itinerary which you may wish to amend en route, there is no substitute for the good old paper version.

Travellers with Special Needs

Most international airlines can cater to people with special needs – travellers with disabilities, people with young children and even children travelling alone.

Travellers with special dietary preferences (vegetarian, kosher etc) can request appropriate meals with advance notice. If you are travelling in a wheelchair, most international airports can provide an escort from check-in desk to plane where needed, and ramps, lifts, toilets and phones are generally available.

Airlines usually allow babies up to two years of age to fly for 10% of the adult fare, although a few may allow them free of charge. Reputable international airlines usually provide nappies (diapers), tissues, talcum and all the other paraphernalia needed to keep babies clean, dry and half-happy. For children between the ages of two and 12, the fare on international flights is usually 50% of the regular fare or 67% of a discounted fare.

Departure Tax

There is a small percentage departure tax included in the cost of tickets from Dutch airports.

The UK

KLM (and its many subsidiaries), British Airways, British Midland and EasyJet fly to Netherlands from the UK. Watch for special fares and sales that can be as low as UK£50 return.

Airline ticket discounters are known as bucket shops in the UK. Despite the somewhat disreputable name, there is nothing under-the-counter about them. Discount air travel is big business in London. Advertisements for many travel agents appear in the travel pages of the weekend broadsheets, such as the *Independent* on Saturday and the *Sunday Times*. Look out for the free magazines, such as TNT, which are widely available in London – start by looking outside the main railway and underground stations.

For students or travellers under 26, popular travel agencies in the UK include STA Travel (☎ 020-7361 6161), which has an office at 86 Old Brompton Rd, London SW7 3LQ, and other offices in London and Manchester. Visit its Web site at www.statravel.co.uk. Usit Campus (☎ 0870-240 1010), 52 Grosvenor Gardens, London SW1WOAG, has branches throughout the UK. The Web address is www.usitcampus .com. Both of these agencies sell tickets to all travellers but cater especially to young people and students. Charter flights can work out as a cheaper alternative to scheduled flights, especially if you do not qualify for the under-26 and student discounts.

Other recommended travel agencies in London include:

Trailfinders (☎ 020-7938 3939) 194 Kensington High St, London W8 7RG
Bridge the World (☎ 020-7734 7447) 4 Regent Place, London W1R 5FB
Flightbookers (☎ 020-7757 2000) 177–178 Tottenham Court Rd, London W1P 9LF

Continental Europe

Amsterdam is well connected to almost all other European cities with airports. KLM and the major airlines of each country all serve each other.

You should be able to find return fares from the major hub airports such as Copenhagen, Frankfurt, Paris and Madrid for US$150 to US$200.

Though London is the travel discount capital of Europe, there are several other cities in which you will find a range of good deals. Generally, there is not much variation in air fare prices for departures from the main European cities. All the major airlines are usually offering some sort of deal, and travel agents generally have a number of deals on offer, so shop around.

Across Europe many travel agencies have ties with STA Travel, where cheap tickets can be purchased and STA-issued tickets can be altered (usually for a US$25 fee). Outlets in major cities include:

ISYTS (☎ 01-322 1267, fax 323 3767) 11 Nikis St, Upper Floor, Syntagma Square, Athens
Passaggi (☎ 06-474 0923, fax 482 7436) Stazione Termini FS, Galleria Di Tesla, Rome
STA Travel (☎ 030-311 0950, fax 313 0948) Goethestrasse 73, 10625 Berlin
Voyages Wasteels (☎ 08 03 88 70 04 only from within France, fax 01 43 25 46 25) 11 rue Dupuytren, 756006 Paris

France has a network of student travel agencies which can supply discount tickets to travellers of all ages. OTU Voyages (☎ 01 44 41 38 50) has a central Paris office at 39 Ave Georges Bernanos (5e) and another 42 offices around the country. The Web address is www.otu.fr (only in French). Acceuil des Jeunes en France (☎ 01 42 77 87 80), 119 rue Saint Martin (4e), is another popular discount travel agency.

General travel agencies in Paris which offer some of the best services and deals available include:

Nouvelles Frontières (☎ 08 03 33 33 33) 5 Ave de l'Opéra (1er)
Web site: www.nouvelles-frontieres.com
Voyageurs du Monde (☎ 01 42 86 16 00) 55 rue Sainte Anne (2e)

Belgium, Switzerland and Greece are also good places for buying discount air tickets. In Belgium, Acotra Student Travel Agency (☎ 02-512 86 07) at rue de la Madeline, Brussels, and WATS Reizen (☎ 03-226 16 26) at de Keyserlei 44, Antwerp, are both well-known agencies.

In Switzerland, SSR Voyages (☎ 01-297 11 11) specialises in student, youth and budget fares. In Zurich, there is a branch at Leonhardstrasse 10 and there are others in most major Swiss cities. The Web address is www.ssr.ch.

In Athens, check the many travel agencies in the backstreets between Syntagma and Omonia Squares. For student and non-concessionary fares, try Magic Bus (☎ 01-323 7471, fax 322 0219).

The USA

Continental Airlines, Delta Air Lines, Northwest Airlines and United Airlines all have nonstop services to Amsterdam from the cities in the USA. Fares vary by season, from a low of US$300/500 from the east coast/west coast in winter to a high of US$700/900 in summer.

Discount travel agents in the USA are known as consolidators (although you probably won't see a sign on the door saying 'Consolidator'). San Francisco is the ticket consolidator capital of America, although some good deals can be found in Los Angeles, New York and other big cities. Consolidators can be found through the *Yellow Pages* or the major daily newspapers. The *New York Times*, the *Los Angeles Times*, the *Chicago Tribune* and the *San Francisco Chronicle* all produce Sunday travel sections in which you will find a number of travel agency ads. Ticket Planet is a leading ticket consolidator in the USA and is recommended. Web site: www.ticketplanet.com.

Council Travel, America's largest student travel organisation, has around 60 offices in the USA; its head office (☎ 800-226 8624) is at 205 E 42 St, New York, NY 10017. Call it for the office nearest you or visit its Web site at www.counciltravel.com. STA Travel (☎ 800-777 0112) has offices in Boston, Chicago, Miami, New York, Philadelphia, San Francisco and other major cities. Call the toll-free 800 number for office locations. Web site: www.statravel.com.

Canada

Canadian Airlines serves Amsterdam from Toronto. Fares vary with the seasons; from C$400 in winter to C$700 in summer.

Canadian discount air ticket sellers are also known as consolidators and their air fares tend to be about 10% higher than those sold in the USA. The *Globe & Mail*, the *Toronto Star*, the *Montreal Gazette* and the *Vancouver Sun* carry travel agents' ads and are good places to look for cheap fares.

Travel CUTS (☎ 800-667 2887) is Canada's national student travel agency and has offices in all major cities. Web site: www.travelcuts.com.

Australia

Qantas has connecting flights to Amsterdam from Sydney. Otherwise you can go through one of the many Asian connection hubs on a variety of airlines. Apex fares average A$1400, but you should be able to beat that by shopping around.

For flights to Europe from Australia, Round-the-World (RTW) tickets are often real bargains and since Australia is pretty much on the other side of the world from Europe, it can sometimes work out cheaper to keep going right round the world on a RTW ticket than do a U-turn on a return ticket.

Cheap flights from Australia to Europe generally go via South-East Asian capitals, involving stopovers at Kuala Lumpur, Bangkok or Singapore. If a long stopover between connections is necessary, transit accommodation is sometimes included in the price of the ticket. If it's at your own expense, it may be worth considering a more expensive ticket.

Quite a few travel offices specialise in discount air tickets. Some travel agents, particularly smaller ones, advertise cheap air fares in the travel sections of weekend newspapers, such as the *Age* in Melbourne and the *Sydney Morning Herald*.

Two well-known agents for cheap fares are STA Travel and Flight Centre. STA Travel (☎ 03-9349 2411) has its main office at 224 Faraday St, Carlton, Vic 3053, and offices in all major cities and on many university campuses. Call ☎ 131 776 Australia-wide for the location of your nearest branch or visit its Web site at www.statravel.com.au. Flight Centre (☎ 131 600 Australia-wide) has a central office at 82 Elizabeth St, Sydney, and there are dozens of offices throughout Australia. Web site: www.flightcentre.com.au.

New Zealand

Reaching Amsterdam from Auckland means you have a choice of transiting though Los Angeles or via one of the Asian hubs. Apex fares average NZ$1800.

Round-the-World (RTW) and Circle Pacific fares for travel to or from New Zealand are usually the best value, often cheaper than a return ticket. Depending on which airline you choose, you may fly across Asia, with possible stopovers in India, Bangkok or Singapore, or across the USA, with possible stopovers in Honolulu, Australia, one of the Pacific Islands or California.

The *New Zealand Herald* has a travel section in which travel agents advertise fares. Flight Centre (☎ 09-309 6171) has a large central office in Auckland at National Bank Towers (corner Queen and Darby Sts) and many branches throughout the country. STA Travel (☎ 09-309 0458) has its main office at 10 High St, Auckland, and has other offices in Auckland as well as in Hamilton, Palmerston North, Wellington, Christchurch and Dunedin. Web site: www.statravel.com.au.

Asia

The major Asian carriers, such as Singapore Airlines, Cathay Pacific, Japan Airlines, Malaysia Airlines and Garuda Indonesia serve Amsterdam. It's worth your time shopping around as fares vary widely; consider US$600 to US$700 to be average for an Apex ticket.

Although most Asian countries are now offering fairly competitive air fare deals, Bangkok, Singapore and Hong Kong are still the best places to shop around for discount tickets. Hong Kong's travel market can be unpredictable, but some excellent bargains are available if you are lucky.

Khao San Rd in Bangkok is the budget travellers headquarters. Bangkok has a number of excellent travel agents, but there are also some suspect ones; ask the advice of other travellers before handing over your cash. STA Travel (☎ 02-236 0262), 33 Surawong Rd, is a good and reliable place to start.

In Singapore, STA Travel (☎ 737 7188) in the Orchard Parade Hotel, 1 Tanglin Rd, offers competitive discount fares for Asian destinations and beyond. Singapore, like Bangkok, has hundreds of travel agents, so you can compare prices on flights. Chinatown Point shopping centre on New Bridge Rd has a good selection of travel agents.

Hong Kong has a number of excellent, reliable travel agencies and some not-so-reliable ones. A good way to check on a

travel agent is to look it up in the phone book: fly-by-night operators don't usually stay around long enough to get listed. Many travellers use the Hong Kong Student Travel Bureau (☎ 2730 3269), 8th floor, Star House, Tsimshatsui. You could also try Phoenix Services (☎ 2722 7378), 7th floor, Milton Mansion, 96 Nathan Rd, Tsimshatsui.

Africa

KLM has numerous services to Africa. Kenya Airways and South African Airways also have frequent links to Amsterdam.

Nairobi and Johannesburg are probably the best places in East and South Africa to buy tickets. Discount tickets from those cities should cost about US$500 and US$600 respectively. Some major airlines have offices in Nairobi, which is a good place to determine the standard fare before you make the rounds of the travel agencies. Getting several quotes is a good idea as prices are always changing. Flight Centres (☎ 02-210024) in Lakhamshi House, Biashara St, has been in business for many years.

In Johannesburg the South African Student's Travel Services (☎ 011-716 3045) has an office at the University of the Witwatersrand. STA Travel (☎ 011- 447 5551) has an office in Johannesburg on Tyrwhitt Ave in Rosebank.

The main international airports in West Africa are Abidjan, Accra, Bamako, Dakar and Lagos. There are also some regular charter flights from some European countries to Banjul (Gambia). It is usually better to buy tickets in West Africa through a travel agency rather than from the airline. Travel agents' fares are generally the same as the fares offered by the airlines, but agents may be more helpful if anything goes wrong.

In Abidjan, there is Saga Voyages (☎ 32 98 70), opposite Air Afrique in Le Plateau. Haury Tours (☎ 22 16 54, fax 22 17 68, ✆ haury@africaonline.co.ci), 2nd floor, Chardy Bldg in Le Plateau, is an affiliate of the French travel group Nouvelles Frontières.

In Accra, try Expert Travel & Tours (☎ 021-775498) on Ring Rd East near the US embassy.

There are several agencies dealing in international and regional flights in Bamako. Two of the best are ATS Voyages (☎ 22 44 35) on Ave Kassa Keita and TAM (☎ 23 92 00, @ tvoyage@sotelma.net) on Square Lumumba, which is open until midnight Monday to Saturday and on Sunday morning. Agencies in Dakar include Senegal Tours (☎ 823 31 81), 5 Place de l'Indépendance, and SDV Voyages (☎ 839 00 81), 51 Ave Albert Sarraut.

In Lagos there are many travel agencies in the Race Course Road complex on the southern side of Tafawa Balewa Square on Lagos Island. Most of the airline offices are also in this area. Try L'Aristocrate Travels & Tours (☎ 01-266 7322), corner Davies and Broad Sts, or Mandilas Travel (☎ 01-266 3339) on Broad St.

LAND
Train
The Netherlands has numerous train links to Germany, as well as Belgium and on to France. Eurail, Inter-Rail, Europass and Flexipass tickets are valid on Dutch trains, which are run by the Nederlandse Spoorwegen (NS). See the Getting Around chapter for more about trains within the country.

Information Major Dutch train stations have international ticket offices. Otherwise you can use the reservations office or, barring that, inquire at the ticket window. In peak periods it's wise to reserve international seats in advance. You can buy tickets on local trains to Belgium and Germany at the normal ticket counters.

For international train information, you can also ring the Teleservice NS Internationaal on ☎ 0900-92 96 (f0.50 a minute). For national trains, simply turn up at the station: you'll rarely have to wait more than an hour for a train to anywhere. NS also has a very good Web site at www.ns.nl, with an English-language option for timetable information only (click on 'Reisinfo' then 'English').

Main Routes There are two main lines south from Amsterdam. One train passes through Den Haag and Rotterdam and on to

Antwerp (f52, 2¼ hours, hourly trains) and Brussels (f62, three hours, hourly trains). The other line south goes via Utrecht and Maastricht to Luxembourg City (f90, six hours, every two hours) and on to France and Switzerland, or branches at Utrecht and heads east via Arnhem to Cologne (f83 plus a f7 EuroCity supplement, 2½ hours, every one to two hours) and farther into Germany. The main line east eventually branches off to the north-east of the country or continues east through Hanover to Berlin (f250, seven hours, three daily).

The fares above are one way in 2nd class; people aged under 26 get a 25% discount. Weekend returns are much cheaper than during the week. For instance, a weekend return Amsterdam-Brussels (departure all day Friday, and returning any time on Monday, or for travel any time in between) costs f75 compared to the normal f124.

The high-speed train, the *Thalys*, runs six times a day between Amsterdam and Antwerp (f61, two hours), Brussels (f72, 2½ hours) and Paris (f161, 4¼ hours). Those aged under 26 get a 45% discount and seniors with a Rail Europe Senior (RES) card are entitled to 30% off stretches outside the Netherlands.

A special weekend deal, a so-called Tourist Ticket, gets you a return on the *Thalys* to Paris for f264.

Late in 2000, another high-speed train, the German *ICE*, is due to begin service between Amsterdam and Cologne and in 2002 on to Frankfurt. Expect travel times to fall and fares to rise.

Once you arrive at rail hubs, such as Cologne, Brussels and Paris, you can find onward connections to much of Europe. There is also a daily night train between Amsterdam and Munich. The fare is f360 plus additional charges if you would like more comfy accommodation than a mere 2nd-class seat.

The UK Rail Europe (☎ 0990-848 848) will get you from London to Amsterdam using the highly civilised Eurostar passenger train service from Waterloo Station through the Channel Tunnel to Brussels, with an onward

Thalys connection from there. This takes about six hours in total and starts from UK£80 return in 2nd class with special deals. Web site: www.raileurope.com.

Train-boat-train combos are cheaper but take a fair bit longer. Stenaline (☎ 0990-707 070) has return fares from London to Amsterdam starting at UK£60 (for those aged under 26) or UK£80 (for those over 26). Special return deals cost £50. The train links go via Harwich in the UK and Hoek van Holland in the Netherlands and take a total of about 7½ hours. Web site: www.stenaline.com.

Bus

Amsterdam and Rotterdam are well connected to the rest of Europe, Scandinavia and North Africa by long-distance bus. For information about regional buses in the Netherlands, for instance to places not serviced by the extensive train network, call the transport information service on ☎ 0900-92 92 (f0.75 a minute).

Eurolines The most extensive European bus network is maintained by Eurolines, a consortium of coach operators. Its Web site, www.eurolines.com, has links to each national Eurolines Web site. See the Amsterdam and Rotterdam sections for details on the Eurolines offices in those cities.

The main lines can be found in the table below.

Eurolines offers a variety of passes which have prices that vary by time of year. A 30-day pass good for unlimited use on the vast network costs f582/465 in low season for adults/under 26ers and f815/652 in high season.

Returns from London to Amsterdam start from UK£45 for adults and UK£41 those under 26. The journeys take 10 to 12 hours and stop at either Rotterdam and Den Haag or Utrecht. Fares may rise or fall considerably depending on cut-throat competition among cross-Channel services. You can reach Eurolines UK on ☎ 08705 143219. Some Eurolines buses cross the Channel via Calais in France; travellers using this service should check whether they require a French visa.

Busabout Busabout (☎ 020-7950 1661, fax 7950 1662), 258 Vauxhall Bridge Road, London SW1V 1BS, is a UK-based budget alternative to Eurolines. Though aimed at younger travellers, it has no upper age limit. It runs coaches along five interlocking European circuits, including one through Amsterdam. Web site: www.busabout.com.

A Busabout pass costs UK£249 (UK£199 for youth and student-card holders) for 15 days on as many of the five circuits as you like. There are also passes available for 21 days at UK£345 (UK£275), one month at UK£425 (UK£325), two months at UK£595

Eurolines

from	to	one way (f) adult	duration under 26	via (hours)	
Rotterdam	Copenhagen	140	125	13	Amsterdam and Groningen
Rotterdam	Hamburg	80	70	9	Amsterdam and Groningen
Rotterdam	Berlin	105	95	12	Amsterdam
Amsterdam	Frankfurt	80	70	7	Utrecht Eindhoven and Venlo
Amsterdam	Prague	135	125	18	Den Haag, Rotterdam and Breda
Amsterdam	Budapest	185	170	20	Utrecht and Arnhem
Amsterdam	Milan	155	140	20	Den Haag, Rotterdam and Breda
Amsterdam	Brussels	30	25	4	Den Haag, Rotterdam and Breda or Utrecht
Amsterdam	Paris	70	65	8	Den Haag, Rotterdam and Breda
Amsterdam	Lyon	135	125	15	Den Haag, Rotterdam and Breda
Amsterdam	Tours	120	110	13	Den Haag, Rotterdam and Breda

(UK£485) and three months at UK£895 (UK£720), as well as Flexipasses entitling you to between 10 and 30 days' travel in a two-month period.

The main drawback is that buses on most loops travel in one direction (ie from Amsterdam to Berlin, but not vice versa), and that you can't just jump on a bus to the next city without buying one of the above passes.

The Busabout service to/from Amsterdam runs from mid-April to the end of October. Coaches stop at the Hotel Hans Brinker in Kerkstraat, smack in the middle of the city.

Gullivers The Berlin-based Gullivers Reisen (☎ 030-311 02 11) connects a few international destinations to Berlin, including Amsterdam (nine hours, DM100, or DM90 for youth and student-card holders) and London-Victoria (16½ hours via Amsterdam, DM185/165). Web site: www.gullivers.de.

Car & Motorcycle

The main entry points from Belgium are the E22 (Antwerp-Breda) and the E25 (Liège-Maastricht). From Germany there are many border crossings, but the main links east are the E40 (Cologne-Maastricht), the E35 (Düsseldorf-Arnhem) and the A1 (Hanover-Amsterdam). For details about car ferries from England see the following Sea section.

Documents Drivers of cars and riders of motorbikes will need the vehicle's registration papers, third-party insurance and an international drivers' permit in addition to their domestic licence. It is a good idea to also have comprehensive coverage. You can get proof of this, a Green Card, from your insurer. If you are travelling in a rental car, check to see what coverage is included and what must be purchased separately. Your auto insurance at home may cover some rentals as will some credit cards, but check on this carefully.

The Dutch automobile association ANWB (See under Tourist Offices in the Facts for the Visitor chapter) provides a wide range of information and services if you can show a letter of introduction from your own association.

Bicycle

For detailed information on cycling see the special section 'Cycling in the Netherlands'. The Netherlands are extremely bike-friendly; once you're in the country you can pedal almost everywhere on dedicated bicycle paths. Everything is wonderfully flat, but that also means powerful wind and it always seems to come from ahead. Beware that mopeds use bike paths too and might be travelling well in excess of their 40km/h speed limit (30km/h in built-up areas). Bikes (or mopeds) are not allowed on freeways at all. Competition cyclists are the main people you'll see wearing bicycle helmets. However, that shouldn't stop you from protecting your own cranium.

If you want to bring your own bike, consider the risk of theft in Amsterdam – rental might be the wiser option. Unless you have an exotic bike parts are not a concern. Repair shops are common especially at the bicycle shops in most train stations.

Transport Bicycles can travel by air. You can take them apart and put them in a bike bag or box, but it's much easier simply to wheel your bike to the check-in desk, where it should be treated as a piece of baggage. You may have to remove the pedals and turn the handlebars sideways so that it takes up less space in the aircraft's hold; check all this with the airline well in advance, preferably before you pay for your ticket.

Your bike can also travel with you on the *Eurostar* and *Thalys* high-speed trains from Belgium, France and the UK provided you can disassemble the bike and fit it into a stowage bag which will fit into the normal luggage storage racks on board.

On regular trains, bike space varies and at busy times you may have to wait for a train with room for your bike. See Bicycles in the Getting Around chapter for more on taking your bike on the train in the Netherlands.

Hitching

Hitching is never entirely safe in any country in the world and we don't recommend it. Travellers who decide to hitch should understand that they are taking a small but potentially serious risk.

Many Dutch students have a government-issued pass allowing free public transport (though this is under review). Consequently the number of hitchhikers has dropped dramatically and car drivers are no longer used to the phenomenon. Hitchers have reported long waits.

On Channel crossings from the UK, the car fares on the Harwich–Hoek van Holland ferry as well as the shuttle through the Channel Tunnel include passengers, so you can hitch to the Continent for nothing at no cost to the driver (though the driver will still be responsible if you do something illegal).

Looking for a ride out of the country? Try the notice boards at public libraries and youth hostels. People also advertise to share fuel costs in the Amsterdam classifieds paper *Via Via* published on Tuesday and Thursday.

SEA

Several companies operate car/passenger ferries between the Netherlands and the UK. Most travel agents have information on the following services but might not always know the finer points – it's easier to catch

---

Warning

The information in this chapter is particularly vulnerable to change: Prices for international travel are volatile, routes are introduced and cancelled, schedules change, special deals come and go, and rules and visa requirements are amended. Airlines and governments seem to take a perverse pleasure in making price structures and regulations as complicated as possible. You should check directly with the airline or a travel agent to make sure you understand how a fare (and ticket you may buy) works. In addition, the travel industry is highly competitive and there are many lurks and perks.

The upshot of this is that you should get opinions, quotes and advice from as many airlines and travel agents as possible before you part with your hard-earned cash. The details given in this chapter should be regarded as pointers and are not a substitute for your own careful, up-to-date research.

---

eels with your bare hands than to pin down who's doing what exactly when it comes to ferries. For information on train-ferry-train services, see the earlier Train section. Once again, expect prices and deals to fluctuate madly depending on cross-Channel competition. Reservations are essential for motorists, especially in the summer high season, though motorcycles can often be squeezed in at the last moment.

Stenaline (☎ 08705-707 070) sails between Harwich and Hoek van Holland, west of Rotterdam. The fast HSS ferries take only 3½ hours and depart in each direction twice a day. Foot passengers pay upwards of UK£25 return. Fares for a car with up to five people range from UK£90 to UK£190 return depending on the season and day of week. Options such as reclining chairs and cabins cost extra and are compulsory on night crossings. Web site: www.stenaline.com.

P&O North Sea Ferries (☎ 01482-377 177) operates an overnight ferry every evening (takes 14 hours) between Hull and Europoort (near Rotterdam). Return fares start at UK£67 for a foot passenger and UK£280 for a car with up to four passengers. The boats boast numerous amenities and a variety of extra-cost cabins which start at UK£26 for two people one-way. Web site: www.ponsf.com.

DFDS Scandinavian Seaways (☎ 0990-333 111) sails between Newcastle and IJmuiden, which is close to Amsterdam. The 14-hour sailings depart daily except in the low season when they depart every other day. Return fares start at UK£54 for a foot passenger plus UK£68 for a car and include reclining seats. Cabins aboard these rather posh ships cost from UK£54 return. Expect these prices to double in high season. Web site: www.dfdsseaways.co.uk.

Most ferries don't charge for a bike and have no shortage of storage space.

ORGANISED TOURS

There are an array of package tours that combine transport and accommodation to the Netherlands. The airlines listed earlier in the chapter, especially those from the UK and USA, all offer packages that can be quite good deals. In addition, they may include valuable extras such as museum passes. The train companies (*Eurostar, Thalys* and the national railways of Belgium, France and Germany) also have packages, as do the ferry companies listed in the preceding section. A visit to a travel agent is bound to yield still more packages.

There are several companies that also offer tours of Holland aboard luxurious river boats. These journeys generally last a week or more and include various bus tours. Aimed at older and well-heeled travellers, these tours are more like cruise ships than actual sightseeing tours. The two biggest operators are Holland River Line River Holidays (☎ 010-414 15 22, fax 433 31 49, Schiedamse Vest 67 71, 3012 BE Rotterdam) and Zee Tours Cruises (☎ 010-282 38 60). Both contract their services with other operators, so you're best off checking with a travel agent.

There are numerous packaged tours for cyclists. Anglo Dutch Tours (☎ 020-8289 2808, fax 8663 3371, 177A High St, Beckenham, Kent, BR3 1AH UK) has a variety of programs throughout the Netherlands. Cyclists ride between each day's destination and their luggage is transported by van. Web site: www.anglodutchsports.co.uk.

Holland Aqua Tours (☎ 0227-545 910, fax 545 999, Dorpsweg K 195, 1676 GM Twisk, Noord Holland) combines tours on bikes during the day with accommodation and transportation on a large canal boat. Web site: www.hat-tours.com.

Elderhostel (☎ 877-426 2167, fax 617-426 0701, 75 Federal St, Boston, MA 02110 USA) is a nonprofit group that runs educational tours aimed at older people. Its programs in the Netherlands include boat trips as well as special interest tours with lectures focusing on Dutch art. Web site: www.elderhostel.org.

Getting Around

The Netherlands is a very easy place to get around. If you are sticking to the major cities and sights, you won't need a car as the train and bus system blankets the country. Or you can do as the Dutch do and provide your power on a bike.

AIR

The only domestic trips possible by air link Amsterdam with Eindhoven and Maastricht. These are intended for business travellers transferring to international flights at Schiphol.

TRAIN

Dutch trains are efficient, fast and comfortable, especially the new double-decker ones. Trains run at regular intervals, usually at least every 30 minutes. Most are operated by the government-owned Nederlandse Spoorwegen (NS; Netherlands Railways). However, some rural lines have now been hived off to combination train and bus operators who coordinate schedules across the region. This scheme is still in the test stages and has produced mixed results, especially in Friesland. A plan to privatise the entire system was permanently shelved after the Dutch looked on in horror at the British experience.

Due to the small size of the country, the longest train journey in the Netherlands only lasts 2½ hours (Rotterdam-Groningen). Only the longest journeys feature on-board services which in any case are limited to a cart selling drinks and snacks. Otherwise the trains are closer to commuter services. Dutch trains have an enviable punctuality record, something unimaginable to the long-suffering commuters just across the Channel in Britain's south-east. Most trains have 1st-class sections, but these are often little different from the 2nd-class areas and, given the short journeys, not worth the extra cost.

Trains can be an all-stops *Stoptrein*, a faster *Sneltrein* (Fast Train, indicated with an 'S'), or an even faster Intercity (IC). EuroCity (EC) trains travel between Amsterdam and Cologne and only stop in Utrecht and Arnhem; they're quite fast (a 10-minute saving to Arnhem) but you pay a f3 supplement at the counter or f6.50 on board the train. From Amsterdam, the high-speed *Thalys* only stops at Schiphol, Den Haag and Rotterdam and requires a special ticket, available at the international ticket counters at the stations where it stops.

Schedules

Services along the major routes stop around midnight (often much earlier on minor routes), but there are night trains once an hour in both directions along the Utrecht-Amsterdam-Schiphol-Leiden-Den Haag-Delft-Rotterdam route.

The national train-timetable book is available for f10.50 from train-station counters and newsagencies, but don't bother unless you're planning numerous trips to small destinations only serviced by local stop-trains. It includes a brief user's guide in English, German, French, Turkish and Arabic. Alternatively, the f2.50 *Intercityboekje* is a handy small booklet listing the schedules of all the IC trains. It also has an excellent map of the entire system.

In stations, schedules are posted by route. Figure out where you're going and look up the schedule which will also show the track numbers. One annoyance, and one of the few failings of NS, is the lack of trip duration and arrival time information. In other words, you can find out when your train will depart but not how long the trip will take or when you will arrive. Station staff will happily provide such information but it's a hassle. On the train, you'll have to watch for your station as you'll have no idea of when you'll arrive. This alone makes the small schedule booklet worthwhile.

For train and ticketing information, ring the national public-transport number, ☎ 0900-92 92 (f0.75 a minute) from 6 am to midnight on weekdays, 7 am on weekends and public holidays. The NS Web site

Westerkerk's crowning glory

Rijksmuseum's windows

The grand orange and white facade of the Magna Plaza

Plenty of time for reflection while strolling Amsterdam's canals

Zuiderkerk's tower

newMetropolis

A blanket of snow provides a different outlook in Amsterdam.

Overlooking Amsterdam's centre – no skyscrapers, plenty of character

Sun sets over Amsterdam with children playing in the 'streets'

Tuschinskitheater

(www.ns.nl) has complete schedules – click on 'Reisinfo' then 'English'.

Stations

Most train stations have luggage lockers which usually cost from f4 depending on size. All but the smallest stations have stores selling newspapers, drinks, snacks, sandwiches and more. Major stations have GWK exchange bureaus that are open long hours. These details are all noted in this book's listings.

The stations are usually a short walk from the city centre. Additionally – just to make it extra easy – the regional and local bus station is inevitably immediately adjacent to the train station.

Bikes

Over 100 stations throughout the country have bicycle facilities for rental, protected parking, repair and sales. Some even sell used bikes at good prices. Details are noted in the city listings in this book.

Bicycles are barred on trains weekdays at rush hours (6.30 to 9 am and 4.30 to 6 pm), except for the Hoek van Holland boat train. There are no restrictions on holidays, weekends or during July and August.

You may bring your bicycle on to any train as long as there is room. Some trains, especially the single-level ICs, have very limited space. However, on popular trains there is often a special bicycle wagon that greatly increases capacity. If the train you want to ride has no room for your bike, you have to wait for the next train.

Just like yourself, your bike needs a ticket to ride the rails. Purchase this from a window or machine before boarding. One-way bike tickets cost f10/15 for trips under/over 80km. Day return tickets cost f15/25. There are no restrictions or fees for collapsible bikes so long as they can reasonably be considered as hand luggage.

For more information on cycling see the special section 'Cycling in the Netherlands'.

Tickets

Tickets cost the same during the day as in the evening, and can be bought at the window (if it's open) or ticketing machines; if you can't buy a ticket beforehand, notify the conductor as soon as you board the train and explain that the ticket windows were closed or the fare machines were all broken. Otherwise, buying a ticket on board (because you didn't have time or you didn't bother) means you'll pay almost double the normal fare.

More and more stations rely on ticketing machines to cut personnel costs and queues at the few remaining counters, which is a bit of a problem for visitors because it is fairly complicated and instructions are in Dutch only. Check where you want to go on the alphabetical list of place names and enter the relevant code into the machine; then choose 1st/2nd class; *zonder/met korting* (without/with discount), eg, if you have a discount card discussed below; and *vandaag geldig/zonder datum* (valid today/without date) – if you choose the latter you can travel some other time but you'll have to stamp the ticket yourself in one of the yellow ticketing machines near the platforms when you do. The machine will then indicate how much it wants to be fed – coins only, though change is given. If you're not sure of the validity of your ticket, stamp it anyway in one of the little machines at the entrances to the platforms.

With a valid ticket you can get out anywhere along the direct route; in other words, with a ticket from Amsterdam to Rotterdam you can visit Haarlem, Leiden, Den Haag and Delft along the way, but backtracking is not permitted. Return tickets are 10% to 15% cheaper than two one-ways but, as with one-way tickets, are only valid on the same day. The only exception is a weekend return *(weekendretour),* which costs the same as a normal return and is valid from 7 pm Friday to 4 am Monday.

Children aged under four travel free if they don't take up a seat; those aged between four and 11 pay a so-called *Railrunner* fare of f2.50 if accompanied by an adult (maximum of three kids, otherwise 40% discount on normal fare) or get a 40% discount on the normal fare if travelling alone.

A *Dagkaart* (Day Card) for unlimited train travel throughout the country costs f81.75 (2nd class) or f122.75 (1st class), which is the same as you'll pay for a return ticket to any destination more than 233km away. Add f12 for a *Stad/Streek-Dagkaart* (City/Region Day Card) and you'll have use of trams, buses and metros as well.

A *Meerman's Kaart* (Multiple-Person Card) provides unlimited train travel for up to six people during the same periods as the *Voordeel-Urenkaart* discussed in the next paragraph; for two people this costs f112 (2nd class) or f174 (1st class).

If you plan to do a lot of travelling, consider investing f99 in a *Voordeel-Urenkaart* (Advantage Hours Card) valid for one year, which gives 40% discount on train travel weekdays after 9 am, as well as all weekend, on public holidays and throughout July and August. The discount also applies to up to three people travelling with you on the same trip. As well, the card gives access to evening returns valid from 6 pm (but not on Fridays) that are up to 65% cheaper than normal returns. A similar version for those aged 60 and over gives an additional seven days' free travel a year. The card is available at train station counters (passport photo required, plus driving licence or passport for the 60-plus version).

In July and August you can buy a *Zomertoer* (Summer Tour) ticket that allows three days' unlimited train travel within the country during any 10-day period for f99 (only 2nd class); two people travelling together pay f129. Stamp your ticket in the yellow machines at the stairways to the platforms. If you pay an extra f19 (f27 for two) the ticket becomes a *Zomertoer Plus* which is also valid for all trams, buses and metros during those three days. If you start the ticket on 31 August it can be used until 9 September.

A *Waddenbiljet* (Wadden Ticket) combines the train, ferry and bus tickets required for a visit to one of the Wadden Islands in the north of the country (Texel, Vlieland, Terschelling, Ameland or Schiermonnikoog), and so long as you don't take more than a day each way you can stay there for up to a year if you like. The ticket costs the same as two one-way train fares

and a 40% discount applies if you hold a *Voordeel-Urenkaart,* though pensioners may be better off buying all tickets separately because of ferry discounts.

Train Passes There are several train pass options for people living outside the Netherlands. These can be purchased in Europe or in the Netherlands, by showing your passport.

The Holland Rail Pass lets you travel on any three days of your choice in a one-month period. It costs UK£38/US$65 for adults and UK£31/US$52 for seniors over 60 and youths under 26, in 2nd class. In 1st class the pass costs UK£57/US$98 for adults and UK£46/US$78 for seniors and youths.

A five-day version is also available. The pass costs UK£57/US$98 for adults and UK£46/US$79 for seniors aged over 60 and youths under 26, in 2nd class. In 1st class the pass costs UK£84/US$147 for adults and UK£68/US$119 for seniors and youths. In addition, when two people travel together, they can purchase a second identical pass for 50% of the price of the first one. Children under 12 pay 50% of the adult pass cost. The pass represents good value if you are going to cover a fair amount of the country.

If your trip will encompass all three Low Countries, the Benelux Tourrail Card is useful as it covers Belgium and Luxembourg in addition to the Netherlands. The pass is good for any five days in one month and includes a substantial *Eurostar* discount if you are travelling from the UK. In 2nd class it costs UK£82/US$155 for adults and UK£58/US$104 for youths under 26. A 1st-class version costs UK£122/US$217 and there is no age discount.

Eurodomino passes are good for travel on the railways of one country, and are available for most of the countries of Europe. The version for the Netherlands is generally not as good value as the Holland Rail Pass discussed above.

Inter-Rail passes are good for people who can show they have lived in Europe for at least six months. They're divided by zones; a pass good for Zone E, which covers the Netherlands, Belgium, Luxembourg and

France, costs UK£229/159 for adults/youths and is good for unlimited travel for 22 days.

All of the above passes can be bought from Holland Rail (☎ 01962-773 646, fax 773 625, Chase House, Gilbert St, Ropley, Hampshire SO24 OBY UK). Web site: www.hollandrail.com.

Outside Europe, the Eurailpass is heavily marketed. Good for 17 countries, it's more than overkill if you're just visiting the Netherlands or even Benelux. A 15-day pass costs US$610/427 for adults/youths and is only available for 1st-class travel. You can buy these at travel agents. Europe Rail, an international sales arm of the French railways, markets these as well as the Holland Rail Pass and the Benelux Tourrail Card. Web site: www.europerail.com.

Rail Idee The NS offers numerous Rail Idee day trips throughout the country (and even to Antwerp, Brussels, Ghent or Brugge in Belgium, with the possibility to return the next day). These packages include a return 2nd-class ticket plus selected admissions, brochures, bicycle hire and even meals. The price is sometimes less than a return ticket by itself. These trips are not advertised to foreign tourists and the illustrated *Er-op-Uit!* booklet (f6.75) describing the trips is only in Dutch, but of course anyone can sign up. The booklet is available at train-station counters, where you can also book the actual trips.

NS Reisburs (Travel Bureau; ☎ 0900-92 92 for domestic, ☎ 0900-92 96 for international) in major stations might be able to help you choose the trip, but its main focus is organised tours and other packages offered by more than 30 companies.

Treintaxi More than 100 train stations offer an excellent *treintaxi* (train taxi) service that takes you to/from the station within a limited area. This costs f7.50 per ride if you buy your special taxi ticket at a train-station counter or ticketing machine; buy another one for the return ride or else it's f9.50 from the driver. The service operates daily from 7 am (from 8 am Sunday and public holidays) till the last train, which varies per

station. At stations where it operates, there's now usually a special call box outside near the normal tax rank. Use this to summon a treintaxi if none is waiting.

These are special taxis (normal taxis don't take part in this scheme) and it's a shared service – the driver determines the route and the ride might take a bit longer than with a normal taxi, but it's usually much cheaper. Ask the counter operator or taxi driver for a pamphlet listing all participating stations and the relevant phone numbers for bookings. There is also a central information number (☎ 0900-TREINTAXI or 0900-873 468 294, f0.75 a minute).

The treintaxi service is handy for reaching places far from stations that don't have frequent bus services. It can be useful on day trips, which is noted in the individual chapters. As its radius of operation varies, it's always worth checking where it operates in advance if you're going far.

Unfortunately some major stations (Amsterdam CS, Den Haag CS or HS, Rotterdam CS) are excluded but other useful ones including Delft, Leiden Centraal and Utrecht CS are in the scheme – and what's more, the treintaxis there operate all night because of night trains.

BUS

Buses are used for regional transport rather than for long distances, which are better travelled by train. They provide a vital service, especially in parts of the north and east, where trains are less frequent or nonexistent. The national *strippenkaart* (see the following Local Transport section) is used on most regional buses. The fares are zone-based, but figure on roughly one strip for every five minutes of riding. Details of useful buses for reaching places where trains don't is included in the listings.

Bus stations are almost always adjacent to the main train station in every town. In towns without a train service, there is usually a major stop near the centre.

CAR & MOTORCYCLE

Dutch freeways are extensive but are prone to congestion. Those around Amsterdam and the A4 south to Belgium and the A2 south-east to Maastricht are especially likely to be jammed at rush hours and during busy travel periods. Smaller roads are usually well maintained. However, the campaign to discourage car use means that you will find all manner of obstacles placed in your path. At entrances to towns, you may find the road narrows to a single lane which means cars in opposite directions must take turns entering and leaving. On other two-lane roads, the middle line has been eliminated and wide bike lanes marked along the sides. In many places you'll find an assortment of speed-bumps and other 'traffic-calming schemes'.

Like much of Western Europe, petrol is very expensive. At the time of research it was about f2.60 per litre (about US$4 per gallon). Unleaded gas is *loodvrij*. For other motoring information, contact the Royal Dutch Touring Association (ANWB; ☎ 070-314 71 47) at Wassenaarseweg 220, 2596 EC, Den Haag.

Road Rules

Like the rest of continental Europe, traffic travels on the right. The minimum driving age is 18 for vehicles and 16 for motorcycles. Seat belt use is required for everyone in a vehicle and children under 12 must ride in the back as long as there is room.

The standard European road rules and traffic signs apply. Trams always have the right of way. If you are trying to turn right, bikes have priority.

Speed limits are 50km/h in built-up areas, 80km/h in the country, 100km/h on major through-roads and 120km/h on freeways (sometimes 100km/h, clearly indicated). The blood-alcohol limit when driving is 0.05%.

Rental

Car There are many places to rent cars in the Netherlands. However, outside Amsterdam, the locations can be in suburban and other inconvenient locations if you are

Road Distances (km)

	Amsterdam	Apeldoorn	Arnhem	Breda	Den Bosch	Den Haag	Dordrecht	Eindhoven	Enschede	Groningen	Haarlem	Leeuwarden	Leiden	Maastricht	Nijmegen	Rotterdam	Tilburg	Utrecht
Amsterdam	---																	
Apeldoorn	86	---																
Arnhem	99	27	---															
Breda	101	141	111	---														
Den Bosch	88	91	64	48	---													
Den Haag	55	133	118	72	102	---												
Dordrecht	98	133	102	30	65	45	---											
Eindhoven	121	109	82	57	32	134	92	---										
Enschede	161	75	98	212	162	224	200	180	---									
Groningen	203	147	172	260	236	252	248	254	148	---								
Haarlem	19	117	114	121	103	51	94	136	184	204	---							
Leeuwarden	139	133	158	248	222	188	234	240	163	62	148	---						
Leiden	45	125	110	87	99	17	60	132	192	242	42	178	---					
Maastricht	213	201	167	146	124	223	181	86	274	348	228	334	239	---				
Nijmegen	122	63	18	101	44	135	98	62	134	208	135	194	131	148	---			
Rotterdam	73	128	118	51	81	21	24	113	195	251	70	206	36	202	114	---		
Tilburg	114	115	88	25	25	102	60	34	186	260	129	246	117	123	68	81	---	
Utrecht	37	72	64	73	55	62	61	88	139	195	54	181	54	180	85	57	81	---

arriving by train. You can look for local car rental firms in telephone directories under the heading *Autoverhuur*. Major international rental firms that have central reservations offices include:

AutoEurope (☎ 0800-022 35 70) – often has excellent rates
Budget (☎ 0800-023 82 38)
Europcar (☎ 0800-022 22 30)
Hertz (☎ 0800-23 54 37 89)

Motorcycle Renting a car is cheaper than renting a motorcycle but sometimes a car just won't do, will it? The following rental outlets are in the Amsterdam area:

KAV Autoverhuur (☎ 020-614 14 35) Johan Huizingalaan 91 in the south-west of the city – 47 different types of motorcycles ranging in price from f70 a day plus f0.25 per km (first 100km free) to f218 a day and f0.40 per km (after the first 100km), tax included; insurance waiver f29.50 a day; credit card and international driving permit required
Kuperus BV (☎ 020-668 33 11) Van der Madeweg 1–5 – Yamaha Virago at f99 a day including insurance, tax and 100km (extra kilometres f0.25 each); three-day, unlimited-kilometre hire is f425 all inclusive; a Honda VT750, CB750 or Suzuki Marauder, which will cost f164 a day including 100km; credit card and international driving permit required
Motorsport Selling (☎ 020-465 66 67) Spaklerweg 91 – a range of big touring bikes at f105 a day plus f0.25 per km (the first 125km are free), tax and insurance included; on a weekly basis it's f840 with 875km free; f1000 deposit required; cash is fine

Purchase

Car Buying and selling a vehicle privately is possible if you have sufficient time and expertise. You can transfer registration at the post office but don't forget about motor vehicle tax for Dutch-registered vehicles, which is due quarterly. For information about registration documents, call the Department of Road Transport on ☎ 0598-62 42 40 from 8 am to 5 pm weekdays. The Central Office for Motor Vehicle Tax is on ☎ 0800-07 49 (free call), also from 8 am to 5 pm weekdays.

Camper Van In Amsterdam, Braitman & Woudenberg (☎ 020-622 11 68), Droogbak 4A at Singel diagonally opposite Hotel Ibis, sells camper vans to travellers with a guaranteed repurchase agreement. A good VW Westfalia costs f10,000, and if you return it in good condition within three months you'll get 75% back, within six months 65%, and within a year 60%; longer periods are negotiable. Occasionally there are cheaper vans at around f5000.

BICYCLE

With 10,000km of cycling paths, a *fiets* (bicycle) is *the* way to go. The ANWB publishes cycling maps for each province and VVV offices always have numerous routes and suggestions. Major roads have separate bike lanes, and, except for motorways, there's virtually nowhere bicycles can't go. That said, in places such as the Delta region and along the coast you'll often need muscles to combat the North Sea headwinds. While about 85% of the population own bikes and there are more bikes than people, they're also abundantly available for hire. In most cases you'll need to show your passport, and leave an imprint of your credit card or a deposit (from f50 to f200). Private operators charge f10 to f12.50 per day, and f50 per week. Train-station hire shops (called *Rijwiel* shops), uniformly charge f9.50/38 a day/week. You must return the bike to the same station.

Alternatively, it can work out much cheaper to buy a 'second-hand' bike from a street market for upwards of f25, bearing in mind it's probably part of the stolen bike racket.

For complete details on biking in the Netherlands, including cycling laws, tours and more, see the special section 'Cycling in the Netherlands'.

HITCHING

Hitching is never entirely safe in any country in the world, and we don't recommend it. Travellers who decide to hitch should understand that they are taking a small but potentially serious risk. People who do choose to hitch will be safer if they travel in pairs and let someone know where they are planning to go.

BOAT

Ferries connect the mainland with the five Frisian Islands. See the relevant sections in the Friesland chapter for details. Other ferries span the Westerschelde in the south of Zeeland, providing road links to the bit of the Netherlands south of here and Belgium. These are popular with people using the Zeebrugge ferry terminal and run frequently year-round. There is also a frequent ferry service on the IJsselmeer linking Enkhuizen with Stavoren and Urk. You'll also find a few small river ferries providing crossings for remote stretches of the IJssel and other rivers.

Rental

Renting a boat is a popular way to tour the myriad of canals, rivers, lakes and inland seas. Boats come in all shapes and sizes from canoes to motor boats to small sailing boats to large and historic former cargo sloops. Prices span the gamut and there are hundreds of rental firms throughout the country. See the Boating section of the Facts for the Visitor chapter.

LOCAL TRANSPORT

Buses and/or trams operate in most cities, and Amsterdam and Rotterdam also have metro systems.

There is a national fare system. You buy a *strippenkaart* (strip card) which is valid throughout the country, and stamp off a number of strips depending on how many zones you plan to cross. The ticket is then valid on all buses, trams, metro systems and city trains for an hour, or longer depending on the number of strips you've stamped. Around central Amsterdam, for example, you'll use two strips (one for the journey plus one for the zone), with an additional strip for each additional zone.

In the central areas of cities and towns, you usually will only need to stamp two strips – the minimum fee. When riding on trams and metros it is up to you to stamp your card (fare dodgers will face an on-the-spot fine). On trams the machines are usually on-board while for the metros they are at the entrance to the platforms. Maps will usually help give an idea of how many zones you'll be travelling through. Simply start with two strips and then add one for each additional zone; thus a three-zone journey would require that you stamp four strips (and you don't need to stamp each one, just the last one will suffice).

The buses are more conventional, with drivers stamping the strips as you get on. Bus and tram drivers sell two/three-strip cards for f3/4.50. More economical are 15-strip cards for f11.75 or 45-strip ones for f34.50, which you must purchase in advance at train or bus stations, post offices, many VVV offices or tobacconists. More than one person can use a single strip – simply stamp enough strips to cover all the riders. Children and pensioners pay f7 for a 15-strip ticket that has to be bought in advance. And note that if you get caught without a properly stamped strip, playing the ignorant foreigner (the 'dufus' strategy) will guarantee that you get fined.

Taxi

Usually booked by phone (officially you're not supposed to wave them down on the street), taxis also hover outside train stations and hotels and cost roughly f25 for 5km. Even short trips in town can get expensive quickly. There are also treintaxis: see the section earlier in the chapter under Train for details.

ORGANISED TOURS

Almost every town of any size has organised tours, especially during the summer months. These are often canal and harbour tours that last from one hour to all day. In addition, you will often find guided walks and other tours organised by local VVVs. See the city listings in this book for local options. In Amsterdam, especially, there are several firms offering organised day trips around the country. Other choices include boats operated from Ameland Island that venture off the coast to view wildlife, and the hugely popular Rotterdam harbour tours.

Cycling in the Netherlands

There are more bicycles – 16 million – than people in the Netherlands and more than 500,000 in Amsterdam alone. For most Dutch, having a bike is just as important as owning a car, and even Prime Minister Wim Kok rides one to work. They're also an excellent way to see the country, and the largely flat Dutch landscape means you don't have to be as fit as an Olympian to do so, either.

Information Your first stop is the ANWB, which has its head office in Den Haag (☎ 070-314 76 81), at Wassenaarseweg 220, as well as offices in Amsterdam (☎ 020-673 08 44), at Museumplein 5, and other cities. The Dutch motoring organisation sells a welter of route maps as well as camping, recreation and sightseeing guides aimed especially at cyclists. The ANWB's 1:100,000 series of 20 regional maps (f13.95 each) include circular routes of 30km to 50km, and numbers correspond to their signs on the way (six-sided, green print on white background).

Staff will help once you prove membership of your own national motoring association, or you can join the ANWB for f34.50 per year. Many VVV tourist offices also sell ANWB materials and book cycling holidays. Web site: www.anwb.nl (only in Dutch).

Clothing & Equipment Wind and rain are an all-too-familiar feature of Dutch weather. A lightweight nylon jacket will provide protection, but be sure to buy a 'breathing' variety (Gore-Tex or the like) or the sweat will gather, even in a strong wind. The same thing applies to cycling trousers or shorts.

As for the bike itself, a standard touring model is probably the best choice. Gears are useful for riding against the wind, or for tackling a hilly route in Overijssel or Limburg (rest assured, though, the Alps it ain't).

Most Dutch prefer a 'Holland' touring bike – a sturdy, stable beast which is ideal for carting around a tent and provisions. Other popular items include a frame bag for a windcheater, camera or packed lunch, as well as a handlebar map-holder so you'll always know where you're going. Few locals wear a bicycle helmet, although they're sensible protection (especially for children, who tend to fall more often than adults).

Above all, make sure there's a bell. Bike paths can get terribly crowded and it becomes a bore if you have to ask to pass every time.

Another necessity is a repair kit. Most Rijwiel shops will equip their bikes with a kit or will provide one on request.

Renting Rental shops are available in abundance. Many day trippers avail themselves of the train-station hire points, called Rijwiel shops, where you can park, rent and buy bicycle parts from early until late. For rentals they uniformly charge f9.50/38 a day/week. You'll have to show a passport or national ID card, as well as leaving a credit card imprint or paying a deposit (usually f50 to f200). The main drawback is you must return the bike to the same station – a problem if you're not returning to the same place. Private shops charge similar rates, but may be more flexible on the form of deposit. In summer, it's advisable to reserve ahead as many shops regularly rent out their entire stock. The useful NS excursions book *Er-op-Uit* (f6.75) lists telephone numbers of the 60-odd Rijwiel shops nationally, in addition to the ones listed in this book, so you can reserve your bike ahead wherever you go. Also see the Getting Around section of individual towns for details of local rental options.

On the Train You can take your bike on the train, but it's usually cheaper to rent one wherever you're going. A ticket costs f10/17.50 for one-way/return tickets to destinations up to 80km away, and f15 for singles for one-way journeys farther afield (no returns available). A day pass is f25. Collapsible bikes are considered hand luggage and go for free, provided they're folded up.

Dutch trains have special sections for loading two-wheelers – look for the bicycle logos on the side of the carriage. Remember that you can't take your bike along during rush hour (6.30 to 9 am and 4.30 to 6 pm from Monday to Friday). The railways publish a free brochure, *Fiets en Trein* (in Dutch) which will tell you which stations have bicycle hire and storage facilities – pick one up at the NS ticket counter.

Road Rules & Security Most major roads have separate bike lanes, with their own signs and traffic lights. Generally, the same road rules apply to cyclists as to other vehicles, even if few cyclists seem to observe them (notably in Amsterdam). In theory, you could be fined for running a traffic light or reckless riding, but it rarely happens. Watch out at roundabouts: unlike elsewhere in Europe, vehicles *approaching* the traffic circle have the right of way.

Be sure you have one or two good locks – eg, the hardened chain-link or T-hoop variety – and that you attach the frame *and* front wheel to something solid, like a canal railing. However, even the toughest lock won't stop a determined thief, so if you have an expensive model it's probably safer to buy or rent a bike locally. Many train-station rental shops also run *fietsenstallingen*, secure storage points where you can leave your bike for about f2 per day. In some places you'll also encounter rotating bicycle 'lockers' which can be accessed electronically.

Don't ever leave your bike unlocked, even for an instant. Second-hand bikes are a lucrative trade, and hundreds of thousands are stolen in the Netherlands each year. Even if you report the theft to the police, chances of recovery are virtually nil.

Camping Apart from the camping grounds listed in this book, there are plenty of *natuurkampeerterreinen* (nature campsites) along bike paths, often adjoined to a local farm. They tend to be smaller, simpler and cheaper than the regular campgrounds, and many don't allow cars or caravans. The Stichting Natuurkampeerterreinen publishes a map guide to these sites, on sale at the ANWB.

You might also try the *trekkershutten*, basic camping huts with a bicycle shelter available at many campsites. They sleep up to four people for a mere f55 per night. See Accommodation section in the Facts for the Visitor chapter for a full description and how to reserve.

Routes You're spoilt for choice in the Netherlands. Easy day trips can be found in the Er-op-Uit book (mentioned under Renting), and we've listed four day trips later in this section.

The Rijwiel shops sell pamphlets of the routes described in Er-op-Uit (f4, or f2.50 if you show your train ticket).

If you're seeking more of an odyssey, there are droves of cross-country and international routes to harden your calves. Most have some sort of theme – medieval settlements, for instance, or some natural feature such as rivers or dunes.

The ANWB sells guides to signposted paths such as the Noordzeeroute, a 470km trek that starts in Den Helder and meanders along dunes and delta to Boulogne-sur-Mer in France (f17.50), and the Saksenroute from the Waddenzee to Twenthe (230km).

CYCLING ROUTES

Baronie Route
(52km; 2½-3¾ hrs)

The province of Noord Brabant in the southern part of the country has a definite Flemish-Belgian feel to it, in the cuisine and the ornate architecture. The **Baronie** is the area around the town of Breda, which belonged to the princedom of Brabant until the 17th century; the counts of Nassau resided here between 1403 and 1567.

Starting point is **Breda** train station, which has a bicycle hire shop (☎ 076-521 0501). The gravel-and-sand Baronierroute (well-signposted) leads along the municipal park to Breda's 16th-century **kasteel** (fort), which houses a military academy. It takes a while to get out of town as you pass through the suburb of Ginneken, but eventually you'll reach a lush forest which girds the town. Between Ulvenhout and Alphen you can pedal about 15km on continuous forest paths. In the **Prinsebos** (Prince's Forest), planted in the early 20th century, you may see sturdy Brabant horses at work hauling timber.

At route marker 23570 you can either turn right to reach Chaam, a Protestant village amid predominantly Catholic Brabant, or follow the Maastrichtse Baan (Maastricht Route) towards Alphen, the birthplace of artist Vincent van Gogh. Shortly before Alphen you'll pass a Gothic chapel from the 16th century – but the tower was built after WWII. From here a number of routes cross over into Belgium, including the **Smokke-laarsroute** (Smugglers' Route).

The path here is pretty and follows the old **Bels Lijntje** (Belgium Line), the train line opened in 1867 to link Tilburg with Turnhout. The last passenger train ran in 1934; the route was converted to a cycle path in 1989.

If you have time, stop off for a look around the border town of **Baarle-Nassau**, which has been the object of border disputes since the 12th century. The Belgian and Dutch governments finally settled a 150-year difference in 1995 – and as a result, Belgian territory grew by 2600 sq m.

Before Baarle-Nassau, veer right and you'll eventually pass a pretty heath, the **Strijbeekse Heide**. Just beyond at the village of Galder, you can cross the bridge

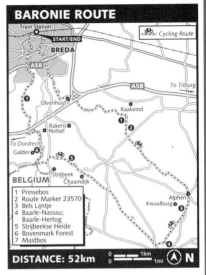

BARONIE ROUTE

Train Station · · · · · Cycling Route

START/END
BREDA
A58
A58   To Tilburg

7 Ulvenhout
Raakeind
Rakens Notsel
To Dordrecht
Galder
5
Strijbeek
BELGIUM   Chaamdijk
1 Prinsebos
2 Route Marker 23570
3 Bels Lijntje   Alphen
4 Baarle-Nassau;   Kwaalburg 3
   Baarle-Hertog
5 Strijbeekse Heide
6 Bovenmark Forest
7 Mastbos   4

DISTANCE: 52km   0 ▬▬ 1km
0 ▬▬ 1mi   N

and turn right into the **Bovenmark Forest** before doubling back to the main path, the **Frieslandroute** (LF9). Cross the highway A58 to reach the forestry station at **Mastbos**, but take care of the loose sand and rocks on the final stretch back into Breda.

Mantelingen Route
(35km; 1¾-2½ hrs)

Depart from **Domburg**, a popular beach resort in the south-west coastal province of Zeeland. In the 19th century, Domburg lured the well-to-do to its spa facilities and chic hotels. Its most famous son was painter Piet Mondriaan, a leading light of the modernist De Stijl movement. The Domburg VVV tourist office (☎ 0118-581 342), Schuitvlotstraat 32, has a list of bicycle hire shops.

Start your tour at 't Groentje, an eastern suburb of Domburg. The opening stretch is sheltered from the brisk winds by a hedge on both sides; the adjacent fields are dotted with **schuren**, farmhouses with black-tar roofs and green doors. The doorframes are painted white to make them easier to see against the oft-dark sky. Just outside the village of Serooskerke stands a cheerily decorated windmill, **De Hoop**.

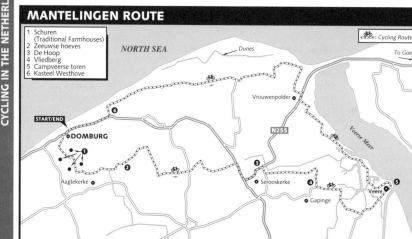

MANTELINGEN ROUTE

1 Schuren (Traditional Farmhouses)
2 Zeeuwse hoeves
3 De Hoop
4 Vliedberg
5 Campveerse toren
6 Kasteel Westhove

NORTH SEA

Dunes

To Goes

Cycling Route

Vrouwenpolder

Veere Meer

START/END

DOMBURG

N255

Aagtekerke

Serooskerke

Veere

Gapinge

DISTANCE: 35km

0 — 3km
0 — 2mi

N

Farther on, as you approach the town of Veere, you'll see a **vliedberg**, an artificial rise laid in the 12th century as a defence post and refuge in times of floods. The town sits on the south shore of the Veerse Meer, a large lake which was created by closing off an arm of the North Sea. Veere was a wool trading centre in the 16th century, especially for imported Scottish wool. The most striking building in town is the enormous **Vrouwekerk**, a Gothic-style church designed by Andrews Keldermans; the well alongside was once used by Scottish traders to wash their wool for market.

The route leads beyond the church to the Markt; turn right to glimpse the **Campveerse Toren**, towers which formed part of the old city fortifications. Local youths have been known to dare a dive from the turrets into the cold waters of the bay, sometimes over boats moored on the shore.

Continuing west along the quay in Veere, you'll pass a row of handsome 19th-century houses; at the bridge, turn around for an idyllic scene worthy of a snapshot. West of town, cycle along the Veerse Meer and cross over the N255 road; here begins the chain of **dunes** that protect the Walcheren

Forest from the North Sea. This leafy expanse between the coast and *polders* (drained lands) gives the route its name, Manteling, which roughly translates as mantle or overcoat. There are lots of bicycle storage areas between the dunes if you want to climb up for a sea view.

Near the end of the route, as you turn left (east) away from the dunes, you'll come to the **Kasteel Westhove**, a 16th-century fort (restored in 1977) that was long owned by the local deacons. Today it houses a youth hostel; in the adjacent orangery there's a biological museum and a garden of local flora.

Amstel Route
(30km; 1½-2¼ hrs)

This is an attractive, convenient route for visitors to Amsterdam, beginning in the southern suburb of Amstelveen and taking in a section of the Amstel River and some unexpectedly bucolic surrounds. You can rent two-wheelers at the bike shops at Amsterdam-Zuid WTC station (☎ 020-673 1513) or at Amsterdam-Amstelstation (☎ 020-692 3584).

Departure point is the **Amstelpark**, a pretty municipal park about 300m south of the A10 motorway. Cycling isn't allowed in the park, which has a rose garden, open-air theatre, cafes and other facilities.

A couple of kilometres south of the route's start you'll come to **Oudekerk aan de Amstel**, a pretty, affluent village with plenty of riverside cafes and handsome houses. Once you pass under the busy A9 highway, turn left on the signposted path. From here you'll get a good view of the **De Ronde Hoep**, a wild, sparsely populated area drained by local settlers about 1000 years ago. The Amstel narrows here and changes names to Waver, or farther south, Oude Waver. When you come to the two hand-operated bridges, you'll clearly see that the land is below water level.

At the south-westernmost part of our route lies a squat, riverside **bunker**, which is one of 38 defensive forts built around Amsterdam at the turn of the 20th century (they were already outmoded by the 1920s). Just to the north, the village of Nes aan de Amstel, on the west side of the river, has some delightful wooden, cafe-filled terraces – admire them from a distance, as there's no bridge close by.

Crossing north under the A9 again, the final leg of the journey gives you a view to the east of Amsterdam-Zuidoost. It's home to the depressing modern suburb of Bijlmermeer, which made headlines in 1993 when a cargo jet crashed into an apartment block, killing at least 50 people. Farther north, the path curls around the fringes of the green Amstelland area, with oodles of all-too-cute garden allotments. The Amstelpark, your starting (and finishing) point, lies just to the north.

Paterwoldsemeer Route (40km; 2-2¾ hrs)

This circuit begins in the lively northern city of Groningen, taking in some attractive green areas to the south. You can rent wheels from the bike shop (☎ 050-312 4174) at Groningen train station.

With the station entrance at your back, turn right and ride to the Museum voor Moderne Kunst (Modern Art Museum), a yellow-and-green building behind the blue-arched pedestrian bridge. Then turn right again to reach the busy Herenweg. You'll pass rows of shops and then some handsome manor houses as you approach Haren, an unexciting dormitory town.

Its most redeeming feature is **Hortus Haren**, a delightful garden with tropical greenhouses and a number of themed outside gardens including a Chinese walled garden, complete with waterfall and arched wooden bridges. From Haren, continue south to Noordlaren; on your right lie the **Appelbergen** forests, while on your left in the distance you'll see the industrial skyline of Hoogezand, on the fringes of a large natural gas field.

Just east of the church in Noordlaren lies the **Noordlarenvaartje**, a 560-hectare lake created in the last ice age that's just 1m deep. To get to the lake follow signs to the De Bloemert watersports centre.

Returning to the church, ride north-west through the Appelbergen nature reserve, one of the prettiest spots on this route. After the tiny village of Glimmen, you come to **Oosterbroek**, a grouping of large farms in leafy surrounds. To the north you'll see the garish colours of the Gasunie complex, one of Europe's largest natural gas producers.

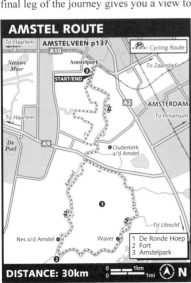

AMSTEL ROUTE

To Haarlem | AMSTELVEEN p137
Nieuwe Meer
Amstelpark
START/END
To Haarlem
De Poel
Ouderkerk a/d Amstel
Nes a/d Amstel
Waver
To Zaanstad
AMSTERDAM
To Hilversum
To Utrecht

🚲 = Cycling Route

1 De Ronde Hoep
2 Fort
3 Amstelpark

DISTANCE: 30km
0 — 1km
0 — 1mi
N

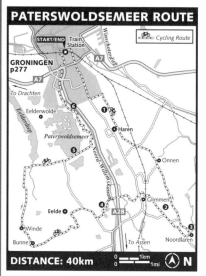

PATERSWOLDSEMEER ROUTE

START/END Train Station

GRONINGEN p277

To Drachten

Winschoterdiep

A7

A7

Cycling Route

Eelderwolde

Paterswoldsemeer

Noord-Willemskanaal

Eelderdiep

Haren

Onnen

Glimmen

Eelde

Winde

Bunne

To Assen

Noordlaren

DISTANCE: 40km

0 — 1km
0 — 1mi

N

Once you emerge from the forest you'll see the landing field of Eelde, where KLM's aviation school is located. The landscape really opens up here, and after a stretch of well-developed bike path you'll come to the **Paterswoldsemeer**, a lake created by harvesting peat in the 18th and 19th centuries. You can stop off at the De Paalkoepel cafe, which has a nice spot overlooking the lake on the east side.

Moving north along the busy A28 highway near the canal, you won't miss seeing a large **power mast** sporting the time 10:40. This is Groningen's official marker, and the number – which actually refers to the year of the city's founding – lights up every morning for one minute at the appointed time.

Once you pass the lake called Hoornse Meer, you're back at the outskirts of Groningen, and only a couple of kilometres from the train station.

Amsterdam

☎ 020 • pop 731,000

Personal freedom, liberal drug laws, the gay centre of Europe – these images have been synonymous with the Dutch capital since the heady 1960s and 1970s, when it was one of Europe's most radical cities.

While the exuberance has dimmed somewhat since, it has not been extinguished. Tolerance is still a guiding principle that even serious social problems (such as a chronic housing shortage) have failed to dent.

Just as enduring is the lively mix of the historical and contemporary that you'll experience when exploring the myriad art galleries and museums, relaxing in the canalside cafes or enjoying the open-air entertainment that pulsates throughout the city in summer. Amsterdam buzzes 24 hours a day, and is the kind of place where you get the feeling that something is always 'happening'.

Amsterdam is often called the Venice of the north, and for good reason. Both cities struggle against water to survive; both had maritime trading empires, and both have a giant reputation in the art world. Both had a ruling class whose wealth was based not on inheritance, but on money created through commerce and finance. But, unlike Venice, Amsterdam is no museum piece and thrives on constant change.

Since the Middle Ages the city has lured migrants and nonconformists, making it one of the world's earliest melting pots. Despite (or because of) this transient mix, people accept each other as they are and strive to be *gezellig*, a typically Dutch term which means 'convivial'. This mood is best experienced over a drink in one of its famous brown cafes.

Because Amsterdam is compact, a single day can hold a cross-section of the contrasts – the old and the new, the Calvinist ethic and the sleaze, the traditional and alternative cultures – that visitors find at once baffling and delightful.

HIGHLIGHTS

- Rijksmuseum – view Rembrandt's *Nightwatch* and other Golden Age masterpieces
- Van Gogh Museum – gape at the phenomenal paintings of a tortured soul
- Canal tour – admire the gabled 16th- and 17th-century facades
- Artis Zoo – enjoy the wild and wonderful creatures, especially in the aquarium
- Vondelpark – take in a free summer concert
- Brown cafes – sample Dutch conviviality over a drink or three
- Leidseplein – watch the performance artists between club visits
- Albert Cuypmarkt – browse wares from the far reaches of the globe
- Reguliersgracht and Keizersgracht – admire the view from this intersection

Map 1 - Greater Amsterdam pp238-9
Map 2 - Amsterdam p241
Map 3 - Amsterdam pp242
Map 4 - Amsterdam pp244
Map 5 - Amsterdam p246
Map 6 - Amsterdam p247
Map 7 - Amsterdam pp248-9
Amsterdam Transport System pp250-1

AMSTERDAM

HISTORY

From around AD 1200 there was a fishing community here known as 'Aemstelredamme' – meaning the dam over the Amstel River. In 1275 the count of Holland granted the community freedom from paying tolls on Holland's locks and bridges. Amsterdam grew rapidly on sea trade and managed to stay independent of the Hanseatic League of trading cities. By the late 1400s, nearly two-thirds of ships bound to and from the Baltic Sea were from Holland, and most of them had Amsterdam owners.

During the Reformation, the stern Calvinist movement took hold in the Low Countries. This guided the region's struggle against the Spanish, who had taken these 17 provinces as their colonial possession. In 1578 Calvinist brigands captured Amsterdam and the seven northern provinces (led by Holland and Zeeland) declared themselves a republic.

Merchants and artisans flocked to Amsterdam in the late 16th century, creating a new class of monied intellectuals and ushering in the Golden Age. The world's first regular newspaper was printed in Amsterdam in 1618. Dutch ships dominated sea trade between England, France, Spain and the Baltic countries, and had a virtual monopoly on North Sea fishing and Arctic whaling. The mighty Dutch East India Company controlled European trade with Asia.

By the late 17th century, Holland didn't have the resources to match the growing might of France and England, and Dutch merchants directed their fortunes into banks rather than daring sea voyages. Amsterdam was revitalised when the country's first railway opened in 1839. Colonial profits from the Dutch East Indies funded the building of the North Sea Canal, helping Amsterdam to benefit from the Industrial Revolution.

Luckily, the city's stunning architecture was spared bombing during WWII. Postwar growth was rapid, and by the late 20th century, Amsterdam had shed much of its old shipping industries in favour of the services sector. But its reputation as a cultural and arts centre remains unchallenged.

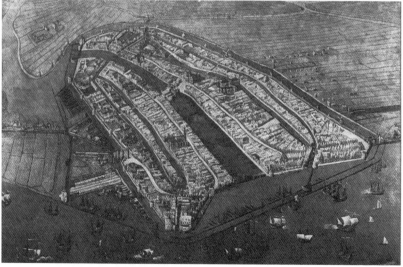

AMSTERDAM HISTORISCH MUSEUM

Bird's eye view of Amsterdam, painted in 1538 by Cornelis Anthonisz, looking southwards. This is the oldest surviving 'map' of the city.

Genuine emerald center stone.
Solid sterling silver. Gleaming 24 karat gold accents.

A genuine emerald glows at the center of a shining Celtic cross, shown here at approximate actual size.

IRELAND FOREVER. It is a land unchanged by time. Where ancient stone crosses stand firm and strong. Eternal markers of a powerful Irish heritage that will endure forever.

Here is a shining symbol of the spirit of a proud people. A bold man's ring masterfully crafted of solid sterling silver. Its intricate sculpture inspired by the distinctive artistry of an ancient Celtic cross. Gleaming 24 karat gold accents reflect the wealth of centuries. And at its center, a genuine, finely polished emerald glows in the vibrant green hue of the Irish countryside.

This dramatic ring is offered *exclusively* through The Franklin Mint, Franklin Center, PA 19091-0001. It will arrive in a deluxe presentation case, complete with a Certificate of Authenticity, attesting to its bold Irish heritage.

THE FRANKLIN MINT. SHARING YOUR PASSION FOR COLLECTING.

NO POSTAGE
NECESSARY
IF MAILED
IN THE
UNITED STATES

BUSINESS REPLY MAIL
FIRST-CLASS MAIL   PERMIT NO. 1   FRANKLIN CENTER PA

POSTAGE WILL BE PAID BY ADDRESSEE

THE FRANKLIN MINT
PO BOX 2760
FRANKLIN CENTER PA 19092-2760

Out of the mist of an ancient Irish past...
comes a bold symbol of pride and heritage.

The Power of the Emerald Isle
Celtic Cross Ring

A distinctive
man's ring
inspired by a land
and people
of mythic spirit,
determination
and pride.

Shown larger to enhance intricate detail.

ORIENTATION

Most of Amsterdam lies south of the IJ, an arm of a vast lake, the IJsselmeer. Crowned to the north by the Centraal Station (CS), the old city is encased by two layers of *grachten* (canals): an old, medieval core and a 'newer' 17th-century district which surrounds it.

The city's central point is Dam Square, a five-minute walk south down Damrak from Centraal Station. Other centres of activity include Leidseplein, with its cornucopia of entertainment; Rembrandtplein, with its many clubs and cafes; and Nieuwmarkt Square, with open-air markets and pubs.

Maps

Lonely Planet's *Amsterdam City Map* is a handy, concertina-folded overview with a street index covering the popular parts of town in detail – and it's laminated to make it rain-proof. The VVV tourist offices also sell an adequate map (f4).

For something that includes the outer suburbs, buy the Dutch-produced *Cito Plan* or the German *Falkplan*. The Cito is clearer, in either the ring-bound booklet or large sheet version. The Swiss Hallwag sheet map is also good and very clear but the smallest streets aren't labelled. Michelin also produces a city map of Amsterdam.

INFORMATION
Tourist Offices

Amsterdam's busy main tourist office, VVV (Map 4), in front of Centraal Station, is open 9 am to 5 pm daily. The VVV's central information number (☎ 0900-400 40 40) operates 9 am to 5 pm Monday to Friday and costs f1 a minute. The VVV fax number is 625 28 69 and the mailing address is Postbus 3901, 1001 AS Amsterdam. It charges f6 per person to find a room and a f2.50 to f5 surcharge on theatre and concert tickets.

Other VVV branches include:

Centraal Station (Map 4) inside along track 2 (spoor 2), open 8 am to 7.45 pm Monday to Saturday and 9 am to 5 pm Sunday
Leidseplein 1 (Map 6), open 9 am to 7 pm Monday to Friday and weekends to 5 pm

Van Tuyll van Serooskerkenweg 125 by Stadionplein, open 9 am to 5 pm daily
Holland Tourist Information in Schiphol Plaza at the airport, open 7 am to 10 pm daily

The GWK (official exchange office) inside Centraal Station also books rooms for a f5 commission (plus 10% of the hotel fee) and it's usually quieter than the VVV counters. Hours are 7.45 am to 10 pm daily.

For cultural events, the Amsterdam Uitburo (Map 6; ☎ 0900-01 91, f0.75 per minute), Leidseplein 26, offers lots of free magazines and brochures, and sells tickets for a f3 mark-up. The office opens 10 am to 6 pm daily (9 pm Thursday). The telephone line operates 9 am to 9 pm daily for inquiries and ticket reservations. Web site: www.aub.nl.

Discount Passes

The Cultureel Jongeren Paspoort (Cultural Youth Passport, f22.50) gives people aged under 27 big discounts to museums and cultural events around the country. The Museumjaarkaart (Museum Year Card, f55) gives free admission to most of the city's museums. (See the Facts for the Visitor chapter for details of other useful national cards).

The VVV offices and some large hotels sell the Amsterdam Culture & Leisure Pass. This 31-voucher booklet allows free entry or major discounts to important museums, to land and water transport and to some restaurants. There's also a free canal cruise. The pass represents a total value of f170 and sells for f39.50 – generally worthwhile, although it's unlikely you'll use all of the available vouchers.

Money

The private exchange booths in tourist areas are convenient but tend to offer lousy rates. Banks and post offices (with branches of the Postbank) stick to official exchange rates and charge a commission of f5 to f6, as do the Grenswisselkantoren (GWK, Border Exchange Offices; ☎ 0800-566). Note that exchange rates between euro currencies are fixed and it all comes down to commissions these days. Reliable exchange centres include:

GWK Centraal Station (Map 4; ☎ 627 27 31) in the station hall – open 24 hours; charges commissions on cash and travellers cheques

GWK Schiphol airport (Map 1; ☎ 653 51 21) – open 24 hours

American Express (Map 4; ☎ 504 87 77) Damrak 66 – open 9 am to 5 pm Monday to Friday, and to noon Saturday; no commission on AmEx cheques

Thomas Cook (Map 4; ☎ 625 09 22) Dam 23–25, with branches on Damrak opposite Centraal Station

Thomas Cook (Map 6; ☎ 626 70 00) Leidseplein 31A – open 9 am to 7 pm weekdays, to 6 pm Saturday, 10 am to 4.30 pm Sunday; no commission on Thomas Cook cheques

VSB Bank (Map 4; ☎ 624 93 40) Singel 548 at the Flower Market – one of several branches, and you can withdraw money over the counter with a credit card; 24-hour exchange machine and ATMs outside

Post

Standard post office hours are 9 am to 5 pm weekdays. The main post office at Singel 250 (Map 3) opens 9 am to 7 pm weekdays and Saturday to noon. The district post office 300m east of Centraal Station, Oosterdokskade 3 (Map 5), is open 9 am to 9 pm weekdays and Saturday until noon. The large branch in the Stopera at Waterlooplein (Map 4) is open 9 am to 6 pm weekdays, and 10 am to 1.30 pm Saturday. For queries about postal services, ring ☎ 0800-04 17 (free).

Unless you're sending mail within the Amsterdam region, use the slot marked *Overige Postcodes* (Other Postal Codes) on the red letterboxes.

Telephone, Fax & Telegram

Most local telephones are card-operated. KPN telephone cards are sold at post offices, train station counters, VVV and GWK offices and tobacco shops. The bigger Amsterdam post offices have send-only fax machines linked to card-operated pay telephones, and you can send telegrams from all post offices. See the Post & Communications section in the Facts for the Visitor chapter for details.

Email & Internet Access

Amsterdam has a slew of bars and coffeeshops offering cheap Internet access. Unless stated otherwise, they charge f2.50 to f3.50 per 20 minutes.

Standard smoking places include Freeworld (Map 2; ☎ 620 09 02), at Korte Nieuwendijkstraat 30, Internet Coffeeshop Tops (Map 6; ☎ 638 41 08), at Prinsengracht 480, and Get Down (Map 6; ☎ 420 15 12), at Korte Leidsedwarsstraat 77.

Just 200m from Centraal Station, the Internet Café (Map 4; ☎ 627 10 52), at Martelaarsgracht 11, opens 9 am to 1 am daily (to 3 am Friday and Saturday) and offers a free email address and 18 PCs. Siberie (Map 2; ☎ 623 59 09), Brouwersgracht 11, opens 11 am to 11 pm daily (to midnight Friday and Saturday); though it has just one PC, it's free with a drink (20 minutes max).

Another tip for the cash-poor is the Waag (Map 4; ☎ 557 98 98), the old weigh house on Nieuwmarkt Square. It offers free Netsurfing in an atmospheric public reading room-cum-bar as long as you consume something. It opens 10 am to 1 am daily (Monday from 11 am).

EasyEverything (Map 4; ☎ 320 62 94), Reguliersbreestraat 22, run by EasyJet airline magnate Stelios Haji-Ioannou, operates Europe's biggest Net cafe with its 600-odd terminals over 7500 sq m accessible 24 hours a day. It charges f2.50 per hour of Web surfing.

The Cyber C@fe (Map 4; ☎ 623 51 46), Nieuwendijk 19, is a classy oasis in a grubby street offering three Windows machines and four Macs. It opens 10 am to 1 am weekdays, till 3 am weekends.

Mad Processor (Map 3; ☎ 421 14 82), Bloemgracht 82, aims to be a sort of 'Kinko's for the masses'. It offers 14 buffed-for-graphics Pentium III PCs connected to the Net by fibre-optic cable (f2.50 for 10 minutes or f12.50 per hour).

The University library (Map 4; ☎ 525 22 66), at Singel 425, has a score of Internet terminals available for just f5 per day (pay at the desk); a month-long Web pass costs f10.

Internet Resources

For useful English-language Web sites on the Netherlands in general see the Internet Resources section in the Facts for the Visitor chapter.

The definitive Web site for Amsterdam is www.amsterdam.nl, with a mind-boggling amount of information and links, plus a useful map-finder function. Also try www.visit amsterdam.nl, a site run by the Netherlands Board of Tourism (which supplies the tourist information for www.amsterdam.nl). Both have an online hotel booking function.

The Digital City site (www.dds.nl) has hundreds of information resources (many in English), interaction functions, home pages and links.

Travel Agencies

The best advice is to shop around, beginning with the following agents:

Amber Reisbureau (Map 3; ☎ 685 11 55) Da Costastraat 77 – open 10 am to 5 pm weekdays, Saturday to 3 pm; has a great travel bookstore and good prices on tickets to Asia

Ashraf (Map 2; ☎ 623 24 50, fax 622 90 28) Haarlemmerstraat 140 – runs overland adventure tours to Africa, Asia and Latin America for young people

Budget Air (Map 4; ☎ 627 12 51) Rokin 34 – free brochure published every two months with 700 fares for cheap flights; pick up a copy and don't rely on staff for the best deals

D-Reizen (Map 1; ☎ 200 10 12) Linnaeusstraat 112 – open weekdays 9.30 am to 6 pm (to 8 pm Thursday), Saturday 10 am to 3 pm; really friendly service and some good last-minute deals from Lufthansa, Sabena, KLM and others

Kilroy Travels (Map 3; ☎ 524 51 00) Singel 413 – special deals for those aged under 33

NBBS (Maps 3 & 4; ☎ 423 44 33) with an office at the main post office, Singel 250 and also on Rokin – the official student travel agency; prices are not the best, so compare other discount travel agencies

Bookshops

Amsterdam has a number of Anglo-oriented bookshops:

The American Book Center (Map 4; ☎ 625 55 37) Kalverstraat 185 – 10% discount with a valid student card; interesting sales; good travel guide section, cheaper than competitors; many US newspapers and magazines

The English Bookshop (Map 3; ☎ 626 42 30) Lauriergracht 71 – interesting selection of English books; open 1 to 6 pm Tuesday to Friday, 11 am to 5 pm Saturday

Waterstone's (Map 4; ☎ 638 38 21) Kalverstraat 152 – specialist in English-language books; strong on travel guidebooks, maps and novels; translated Dutch literature on the 1st floor

Travel Bookshops which specialise in travel guides include:

à la Carte (Map 7; ☎ 625 06 79) Utrechtsestraat 110 – travel books, maps and globes

Amber (Map 3; ☎ 685 11 55) Da Costastraat 77 – behind the travel agency is a crammed bookshop with many hard-to-find travel guidebooks in Dutch, English, German and French

Evenaar Literaire Reisboekhandel (Map 3; ☎ 624 62 89) Singel 348 – travel literature

Joho (Map 4; ☎ 471 50 94) Taksteeg 8 – a treasure-trove of maps, camping and trekking supplies; stunning choice of Lonely Planet guides

Pied à Terre (Map 3; ☎ 627 44 55) Singel 393 – specialist in hiking and cycling books, maps and travel guides

Gay & Lesbian For a collection of gay and lesbian literature:

Intermale (Map 4; ☎ 625 00 09) Spuistraat 251 – gay photo books, magazines and videos

Vrolijk (Map 4; ☎ 623 51 42) Paleisstraat 135 – most of the major gay and lesbian magazines worldwide

Xantippe Unlimited (Map 3; ☎ 623 58 54) Prinsengracht 290 – large selection of women's books, from classical fiction to modern research; gay books too

Other Bookshops Other bookshops in Amsterdam include:

Athenaeum Bookshop & Newsagency (Map 3; ☎ 622 62 48) Spui 14–16 – vast assortment of unusual books for browsers; the separate newsagency has the city's largest choice of international newspapers and magazines

Scheltema Holkema Vermeulen (Map 3; ☎ 523 14 11) Koningsplein 20 – the largest bookshop in town has recently expanded; a true department store with many foreign titles, a restaurant and good New-Age and multimedia sections

De Slegte (Map 4; ☎ 622 59 33) Kalverstraat 48 – specialist in second-hand or remaindered titles; a lot of dirt-cheap books on the ground floor but some gems upstairs

Libraries

The main public library, the Centrale Bibliotheek (Map 3; ☎ 523 09 00), is at Prinsengracht 587 and opens 1 to 9 pm Monday, 10 am to 9 pm Tuesday to Thursday, 10 am to 5 pm Friday and Saturday, and (October to March) 1 to 5 pm Sunday. It has a wide range of English-language newspapers and magazines, a coffee bar and a useful notice board. You're free to browse and read.

The main Amsterdam university library (Map 4; ☎ 525 22 66) at Singel 425 opens 9.30 am weekdays and closes at 5 pm (Monday, Wednesday and Friday) or 8 pm (Tuesday and Thursday). Saturday hours are 9.30 am to 1 pm.

Universities

Amsterdam has two universities and over 40,000 students. About 27,000 attend the Universiteit van Amsterdam (UvA), whose buildings are spread throughout the city. Some 13,500 students attend the Vrije Universiteit (VU, Free University) established by orthodox Calvinists in 1880.

For information about international education programs in English offered by the University of Amsterdam, contact Universiteit van Amsterdam, Service & Informatiecentrum (☎ 525 33 33, fax 525 29 21, 🖳 uva-info@bdu.uva.nl), Binnengasthuisstraat 9, 1012 ZA Amsterdam. Tuition fees are about f10,000 per academic year; fees for regular study programs in Dutch are approximately f2300 per academic year.

The Foreign Student Service (☎ 671 59 15), Oranje Nassaulaan 5, 1017 AH Amsterdam, provides information about study programs and intensive language courses, and helps with accommodation, insurance and personal problems. Hours are 9 am to 5.30 pm weekdays.

Cultural Centres

The many cultural centres and institutes in town include:

British Council (☎ 550 60 60) Keizersgracht 269 – educational and cultural exchanges, open 9.30 am to 5.30 pm Monday to Friday; information centre open 1 to 5 pm Tuesday and Wednesday, to 6 pm Thursday

De Balie (☎ 553 51 51, recording in Dutch and English) Kleine Gartmanplantsoen 10 at Leidseplein – cafe, restaurant, theatre, seminars, political debates, lectures etc; new-media hang-out of intellectuals; open 9 am to 5 pm weekdays

Goethe Institut (Map 7; ☎ 623 04 21) Herengracht 470 – German cultural centre with lectures, films (some with English subtitles), plays and discussions, plus German language courses at all levels and Dutch courses for Germans; office hours 9 am to 6 pm weekdays (to 4.30 pm Friday); library open 1 to 6 pm Tuesday to Thursday, to 4 pm Friday

Jewish Cultural Centre (☎ 646 00 46) Van der Boechorststraat 26 – by appointment only

John Adams Institute (☎ 624 72 80, with recording of upcoming events in English) Herenmarkt 97 in the former West Indisch Huis – Dutch-US friendship society that organises lectures, readings and discussions on US culture and history led by heavyweight authors such as Saul Bellow, Gore Vidal and Annie Proulx

Maison Descartes (Map 7; ☎ 622 49 36) Vijzelgracht 2A – office opens 9.30 am to 4 pm weekdays, library 1 to 6 pm (Tuesday and Thursday to 8 pm); many events are organised by the Alliance Francaise (☎ 625 65 06) at Keizersgracht 708

Business Services

The luxury hotels (and Schiphol airport) all offer business services. Some have full-service business centres with steep prices. A cheaper option is Mini Office (Map 3; ☎ 625 84 55, fax 638 78 94, 🖳 moffice@xs4all.nl), Singel 417, with services for the short-term business visitor including hardware and software that can be rented by the hour, bindings and mailings, email and fax service and lots more.

Kinko's offers roughly the same services as Mini Office and opens 24 hours (but has pretty lousy service). It's at Overtoom 62 near Leidseplein (Map 6; ☎ 589 09 10, fax 589 09 20).

If you're looking for a fully set-up facility, the Euro Business Center (Map 2; ☎ 520 75 00, fax 520 75 10), Keizersgracht 62–64, will supply an office with furniture, phone, computer and more for f1250 to f5000 a month. Secretarial and other services are also available. Regus Business Centre (Map 1; ☎ 301 22 00), Strawinskylaan 3051, 1077 ZX Amsterdam (and two other locations) is similar and also does video-conferencing.

For translations, contact Berlitz Translation Services (Map 4; ☎ 639 14 06, fax 620 39 59), Rokin 87, though it's not cheap.

Laundry

Local *wasserettes* or *wassalons* normally cost about f8 to wash 5kg; add a few f1 coins for the dryer. You can also get the staff to wash, dry and fold a load (a full garbage bag) for around f15 – drop it off in the morning, pick it up in the afternoon.

The Clean Brothers (Map 3; ☎ 622 02 73) Kerkstraat 56 off Leidsestraat – f8 to wash up to 5kg plus f1.25 to dry, or leave it with them for f13.50; open 7 am to 9 pm daily

Happy Inn (Map 4; ☎ 624 84 64) Warmoesstraat 30 near Centraal Station – f14.50 to wash, dry and fold up to 6kg; open 9 am to 6 pm Monday to Saturday

Wasserette Van den Broek (Map 4; ☎ 624 17 00) Oude Doelenstraat 12, the eastern extension of Damstraat – full-service (f15 to wash, dry and fold up to 5kg) or self-service, open 8.30 am to 7 pm Monday to Friday, 10 am to 4 pm Saturday

Wasserette (Map 2) Haarlemmerstraat 45 – open 9 am to 7 pm Monday to Saturday, 10 am to 5 pm Sunday

Toilets

Public toilets are scarce; your best bet is to pop into a department store. Toilet attendants are usually tipped 25 to 50 cents. Men can also resort to public urinals installed around town.

Amsterdam for Children

Places or activities designed to keep the little ones occupied include:

Vondelpark (Map 6) – a green oasis with a children's playground, ducks and a petting zoo with sheep and llamas

Amsterdamse Bos (Map 1) – a huge recreational area with an animal enclosure, children's farm and forestry museum

Tram Museum Amsterdam (Map 1) – a historic tram which runs past the Amsterdamse Bos

Tropenmuseum (Map 1) – has a children's section with activities focusing on exotic locations

Artis Zoo (Maps 5 & 7) – the planetarium and aquarium are favourites

Canals – hire a paddle boat or take a harbour cruise

Mirandabad swimming pool (Map 1) – wave machines and covered slides

Theater Carré (Map 7) – holds a circus mid-December to early January

newMetropolis (Map 5) – a hands-on science and technology museum

Jaap Edenbaan (Map 1) – ice skating year-round

Baby-sitters charge between f5 and f12.50 an hour depending on the time of day, sometimes with weekend and/or hotel supplements. The agencies, which use male and female students, get busy on weekends so book ahead. Try Oppas-Centrale Kriterion (☎ 624 58 48, 5.30 to 7 pm daily), Roetersstraat 170hs, which has been in business for a long time.

Emergency & Medical Services

In an emergency, the national telephone number for police, ambulance and fire brigade is ☎ 112.

For minor health concerns, pop into a local *drogist* (chemist) or *apotheek* (pharmacy; to fill prescriptions).

For more serious problems, go to the casualty ward of a *ziekenhuis* (hospital) or ring the Centrale Doktersdienst (☎ 0900-503 20 42), the 24-hour central medical service that will refer you to a doctor, dentist or pharmacy.

Forget about buying flu tablets at supermarkets; for anything more medicinal than toothpaste you'll have to go to a drogist or apotheek.

Hospitals with 24-hour emergency facilities include:

Onze Lieve Vrouwe Gasthuis (Map 7; ☎ 599 91 11) Eerste Oosterparkstraat 1 at Oosterpark near the Tropenmuseum – the closest public hospital to the city centre

Academisch Ziekenhuis der VU (Map 1; ☎ 444 44 44) De Boelelaan 1117, Amsterdam Buitenveldert – this hospital has made a name for itself in sex-change operations

Academisch Medisch Centrum (☎ 566 91 11) Meibergdreef 9, Bijlmer – hospital of the Universiteit van Amsterdam; famous for its AIDS research

Dangers & Annoyances

Amsterdam is a pretty safe place. Violent crime is unusual in the city but theft, particularly pick-pocketing, is a real problem. Don't carry more money than you need, and keep your passport in a concealed pouch or a hotel safe. Walking around with valuables or obvious tourist gear will only invite trouble.

A car with foreign numberplates is a popular target for smash-and-grab theft, especially on the canals. Remove valuables, ID papers and, if possible, the radio when you park.

If something is stolen, report it to the police for insurance purposes, but don't expect to see your property again – the officers are inundated with such cases.

Drugs Contrary to what you may have heard, cannabis products are illegal. Soft drugs for personal use (defined as up to 5g) are tolerated, but larger amounts make you liable to prosecution. Hard drugs (including LSD) can land you in big trouble, although the authorities tend to treat genuine, registered addicts as medical cases.

For more about (soft) drugs, see the boxed text 'Coffeeshops' in the Facts for the Visitor chapter.

Lost & Found Items found on buses, trams or the metro often turn up at the GVB head office (Map 4; ☎ 551 49 11), at Prins Hendrikkade 108–114. Hours are 9 am to 4.30 pm Monday to Friday. If something goes missing on a train contact the Gevonden Voorwerpen (Lost & Found office; ☎ 557 85 44) at Centraal Station near the luggage lockers. It is open 24 hours.

THINGS TO SEE & DO

Amsterdam is full of hidden gems and unexpected delights. The attractions described in this chapter are the more 'important' ones; no doubt you'll find some of your own, and begin to understand what keeps drawing people back to the city.

It's easy to spend a fortune in Amsterdam but some of the most enjoyable in the city things cost nothing:

- Wander the red-light district and try to admire the architecture
- Enjoy peace and quiet in the Begijnhof
- Stroll through the Civic Guard Gallery
- Take a tour of a diamond factory
- Visit the Zuiderkerk
- Wander through the Rijksmuseum garden
- Catch a free lunch-time concert in the Concertgebouw or the Stopera
- Join over 2000 in-line skaters on a skate through the city each Friday night (weather permitting); meet outside the Nederlands Filmmuseum in the Vondelpark at 8 pm
- Watch horse training indoors at the Hollandse Manege
- Hear a carillon recital while walking along a canal (the VVV has up-to-date schedules)

One of the charms of the centre of town – Amsterdam Centrum – is that its history is still so evident in its layout. The Damrak, Dam Square and Rokin, which run down the middle of the old medieval core, used to form the final stretch of the Amstel River. The east bank was called Old Side (Oude Zijde), the west bank was the New Side (Nieuwe Zijde). New neighbourhoods were needed to house an influx of workers after the Industrial Revolution. De Pijp, between the Amstel and Hobbemakade, was the first area to be added in the 1860s, full of shoddily-built tenement blocks. Upper-class housing rose around the Vondelpark in the 1860s and 1870s. Towards the end of the 19th century, new residential areas sprang up beyond the canal belt, often with little planning or foresight.

Damrak, Dam & Rokin (Map 4)

Most visitors arrive at **Centraal Station** (1889), a Dutch-Renaissance edifice with Gothic additions built to a design by Pierre Cuypers, who was also responsible for 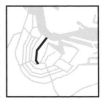 the Rijksmuseum, and AL van Gendt, who designed the Concertgebouw. Its structure – a central section flanked by square towers with wings on either side – is similar to Cuypers' Rijksmuseum.

Leaving the station towards the city, the cupola and twin towers of the neobaroque **St Nicolaaskerk** (1887) are to your left. Designed by AC Bleijs, it is the city's main Catholic church but is under threat of closure. The interior contains many paintings and a high altar with the crown of Holy Roman Emperor Maximilian I.

Damrak The Damrak (Dam Reach), the former harbour area, stretches south of the train station. Today it's an agonising stretch of gaudy souvenir shops, exchange bureaus and claustrophobic hotels. At No 18 is **Seksmuseum Amsterdam** (also known as 'De Venustempel'), open 10 am to 11.30 pm daily and well worth the f4.50 admission for its bizarre collection of pornographic material, including sketches by John Lennon.

At the southern end of the Damrak stands the 1903 **Beurs van Berlage** (☎ 530 41 41), the exchange building named after the architect HP Berlage. The functional lines and stark, square clock tower are considered a landmark of Dutch urban architecture. The central hall, with its steel and glass roof, was the commodities exchange. Traders later moved to the neoclassical **Effectenbeurs** (Stock Exchange), built in 1913 by Pierre Cuypers on the east side of Beursplein.

The bourse is now a cultural centre, with concert performances and changing exhibitions. The public entrance to Beurs van Berlage is on the Damrak side, next to the bicycle shop. It opens 10 am to 4 pm Tuesday to Sunday; entry costs f6 (students/ seniors f4). Climb the clock tower for a good view of the old town.

Dam Square The Damrak ends at Dam Square (Dam for short), the original market square where the dam was built across the Amstel, giving the city its name. It seems a bit empty now, inhabited by thousands of pigeons and the occasional fun fair.

At the eastern end looms the **Nationaal Monument**, a phallic obelisk erected in 1956 in memory of those who died during

AMSTERDAM HISTORISCH MUSEUM

Procession of the Lepers, painted by Adriaen van Nieulandt in 1633. Left to right: the old city hall, the Nieuwe Kerk, the Weigh House and the Damrak with small freighters drying their sails. The procession, to gather donations, was last held in 1603.

WWII. The fallen are honoured in a Remembrance Day ceremony on 4 May. The statues symbolise war, peace and resistance; the urns at the rear contain earth from the 11 provinces and the Dutch East Indies.

The imposing hulk on the opposite side is the **Royal Palace**, or Koninklijk Paleis, built as a grand city hall in 1665. Architect Jacob van Campen spared no cost for this display of wealth. A century and a half later it became the palace of Napoleon's brother-king Louis, who stocked it with a rich collection of Empire furniture. Nowadays it's the official residence of Queen Beatrix, although her real home is in Den Haag.

The interior, particularly the Civic Hall, is more lavish than the sober facade suggests. Opening times vary; you might be lucky between 12.30 and 5 pm, but ring ☎ 624 86 98 to check. Admission costs f7/5 (for adults/students and seniors).

Next to the Royal Palace is the 15th-century **Nieuwekerk** (New Church), the coronation church of Dutch royalty. This late-Gothic basilica is only 'new' in relation to the Oudekerk (Old Church). Of particular interest are the magnificent carved oak chancel, the bronze choir screen, massive organ and stained-glass windows. Exhibitions and organ concerts are held here, but no church services. Opening hours and admission fees vary – ring ☎ 638 69 09 for details.

Rokin South of the Dam, the Damrak becomes the Rokin – a corruption of *rak-in*, or 'inner reach' – most of which was filled in the 19th century. It's more upmarket than the Damrak, with office buildings, snazzy shops and art dealers.

At Grimburgwal, where the water begins again, the bank opposite the Rokin is called Oude Turfmarkt. Near the corner, at Oude Turfmarkt 127, is the **Allard Pierson Museum** (☎ 525 25 56), with a rich collection of archaeological material. The museum's exhibits (Egyptian, Mesopotamian, Roman and Greek, among others) provide a good insight into the daily life of Amsterdam in ancient times. The museum opens 10 am to 5 pm from Tuesday to Friday, and from 1 pm at weekends. Admission will cost f9.50 (students/seniors f7). Its Web site is at www.uba.uva.nl/apm.

The Rokin ends at Muntplein, a busy intersection dominated by the **Munttoren** (Mint Tower). This was part of the 15th-century Regulierspoort, a city gate that burned down in 1619. When the French occupied much of the republic in the 19th century, the national mint was transferred here from Dordrecht for safe-keeping.

Old Side (Oude Zijde; Map 4)

East of the Damrak-Rokin axis is the Old Side of the medieval city. The name is misleading because the New Side to the west is actually older. In the 1380s the Old Side began  to expand eastwards towards the Oudezijds Voorburgwal (front fortified embankment) and soon farther towards to the Oudezijds Achterburgwal (rear fortified embankment).

Originally the city didn't extend farther south than Grimburgwal, where the filled-in part of the Rokin ends today. In the 1420s, however, the newly dug Geldersekade and Kloveniersburgwal added more space for the growing population.

Warmoesstraat One of the original Amstel dikes ran along Warmoesstraat, where the city's wealthiest merchants used to live. Today it's a run-down strip of restaurants, cheap hotels and sex shops, with the busiest police station in town (No 44–50). **Geels & Co** (☎ 624 06 83) at No 67 is a tea and coffeeshop with an interesting little museum upstairs (free admission). The museum opens 2 to 4 pm on Tuesday, Friday and Saturday.

Oudekerk A few paces east is the mighty Oudekerk, the Gothic Old Church built in the 14th century to honour the city's patron saint, St Nicholas. The city's oldest surviving building, the church is sadly demeaned by the red-light district around it. The original basilica was replaced in 1340 by a vaulted triple-hall church of massive proportions.

Note the stunning Müller organ (1724), the gilded oak vaults and the stained-glass windows (1555). Some of the 15th-century carvings on the choir stalls are downright rude. As in the Nieuwekerk, many famous Amsterdammers are buried under worn tombstones, including Rembrandt's first wife, Saskia van Uylenburgh. The church opens 11 am to 5 pm daily, from 1 pm Sunday; admission costs f5 (students/seniors f3.50).

The church's **tower** (1565) is arguably the most beautiful in Amsterdam and affords a magnificent view. The tower can only be visited by a special tour for f65 per hour (maximum 25 people). Ring ☎ 612 68 56 to book.

Red-Light District Amsterdam's (in)famous red-light district is known colloquially as the *wallen* or *walletjes* for the canals that run down the middle. From the 14th century onward, its houses of ill repute and distilleries were the undoing of countless sailors. The distilling vats have gone but the seaminess remains, with porn theatres, sex shops and prostitutes displaying themselves behind neon-lit windows.

That said, the ambience is laid-back and far less threatening than in red-light districts elsewhere. Crowds of sightseers mingle with pimps, drunks, weirdos and Salvation Army soldiers; police chat with prostitutes. Streetwalking is illegal, so female sightseers tend to be left alone. *Don't* take photos of prostitutes or talk to drug dealers.

At Oudezijds Voorburgwal 40 is the **Museum Amstelkring** (☎ 624 66 04), home to **Ons' Lieve Heer op Solder** (Our Dear Lord in the Attic). This is one of several 'clandestine' Catholic churches set up after the Calvinists seized power in 1578. The small attic church remained in use until 1887, when it was converted to a rich display of Catholic church art. The 17th-century living quarters are remarkable, too. Hours are 10 am to 5 pm daily and from 1 pm Sunday; admission costs f10 (students/seniors f7.50).

Other places in the red-light district include the **Hash & Marihuana Museum** (☎ 623 59 61), at Oudezijds Achterburgwal 148, and the renowned **Tattoo Museum** (☎ 625 15 65), at Oudezijds Achterburgwal

---

Sinning in Safety

For tourists who flock to Amsterdam for sex and drugs, the Dutch police has published a guide to the red-light district. The English-language leaflet, called 'Police Red Light Guide', was written by officer Wim Schild, a local resident and 12-year veteran of the red-light district beat.

The guide tells visitors not to buy cannabis from street dealers, but only from the coffeeshops which are authorised to sell it. It also gives tips on how to deal with Amsterdam's prostitutes, who display themselves behind large windows. Prostitution was legalised in the Netherlands in autumn 2000.

'If you visit one of the women, we would like to remind you, they are not always women', says Schild. Visitors to the red-light district should not hesitate to approach a police officer with a problem, because the police 'knows why you're here and you can hardly surprise us anymore'.

Schild also notes that anyone planning to eat 'space cakes' – cookies laced with marihuana, hashish or other drugs – should be sure to drink lots of sweet liquids.

---

130. The **Erotic Museum** (☎ 624 73 03), at Oudezijds Achterburgwal 54, is less entertaining than Seksmuseum Amsterdam on Damrak (see the earlier Damrak, Dam & Rokin section).

Zeedijk North of the red-light district is the Zeedijk, once sailors' first port of call with its abundance of wine, women and song. The house at **Zeedijk 1** dates from the mid-1500s and is one of only two timber-fronted houses left in the city (another, older one is in the Begijnhof).

East of the Zeedijk is the Geldersekade. The small brick tower (1480) at the pointy tip of this canal is called the **Schreierstoren** from the old Dutch word for 'sharp'. Tourist leaflets inaccurately call it the 'wailing tower' (from *schreien*, to weep or wail) and claim that sailors' wives cried their lungs out here when ships set off for distant lands.

English captain Henry Hudson also set sail from here in 1609 to find a northern passage to the East Indies, but ended up buying Manhattan instead.

Nieuwmarkt Square In the 17th century, ships used to load and unload produce at Nieuwmarkt (New Market). The imposing **Waag** (weigh house) dates from 1488, when it formed part of the city fortifications. Public executions took place at the Waag from the early 19th century. Later it housed a fire station, a vault for the city archives, and two museum collections. Today it's a cafe-restaurant with Web terminals in the bar (see Email & Internet Access in the Information section of this chapter).

South of Nieuwmarkt Square On the east side of Kloveniersburgwal at No 29 is the **Trippenhuis**, built in 1660–64 for the wealthy Trip brothers, who made their fortune in metals, artillery and ammunition (note the mortar-shaped chimneys). A ridiculously narrow house stands across the canal at No 26 (see the boxed text 'In a Tight Spot').

To the south-east, on the opposite side of the canal at the corner of Oude Hoogstraat is the **Oostindisch Huis**, the former head office of the mighty VOC, the United East India Company. Designed by Hendrick de Keyser, the structure was rented to the VOC in 1603 and now belongs to the University of Amsterdam. Enter the courtyard through the small gate at Oude Hoogstraat 24 to spot the door-top emblem across the courtyard – the only trace of the VOC's history here.

Old Side, Southern Section The Old Side south of Damstraat, Oude Doelenstraat and Oude Hoogstraat is distinctly residential

Facade detail of the Oostindisch Huis

In a Tight Spot

Tourist guides like to point out the narrowest house in Amsterdam, and explain that property was taxed on frontage – the narrower the house the lower the tax. It seems, however, as if each guide has a different 'narrowest' house.

The house at Oude Hoogstraat 22 (Map 4), east of Dam Square, is 2.02m wide and 6m deep. Occupying a mere 12 sq m, it could well be the least space-consuming self-contained house in Europe (though it is a few storeys high). Singel 144 measures only 1.8m across the front, but widens to 5m at the rear.

The Kleine Trippenhuis (Small Trippenhouse; Map 4) at Kloveniersburgwal 26 is 2.44m wide. It is located opposite the 22m-wide house of the Trip brothers at No 29, one of the widest private residences in the city. The story goes that their coachman exclaimed, 'If only I could have a house as wide as my masters' door!' and that his wish was granted.

---

and the red-light district seems miles away. The University of Amsterdam has a stronghold at the southern end of Oudezijds Voorburgwal, as the jumble of parked bicycles you'll find here implies.

At Oudezijds Voorburgwal 231 is the **Universiteitsmuseum De Agnietenkapel** (☎ 525 33 39), with changing exhibitions on the history of the university. It opens 9 am to 5 pm weekdays (ring the door bell; admission f3.50). The complex originally housed the convent of St Agnes in 1397 and the beautiful Gothic chapel was added in 1470.

Just south of the Agnietenkapel is the **Huis aan de Drie Grachten** (House on the Three Canals, 1609), a beautiful building that was owned by a succession of prominent Amsterdam families. It's now a linguistics and literature bookshop.

Across Oudezijds Achterburgwal, just before the corner with Grimburgwal, is a small, arched gateway called the **Oudemanhuispoort** (Old Man's House Gate). Note the spectacles above the gateway: an almshouse for elderly men and women was built here in 1601 from the proceeds of a public lottery. A market for second-hand books operates in the passage.

A few steps south of the Oudemanhuispoort, another gateway leads to the former inner-city hospital, the **Binnengasthuis**, dating from 1582. It's now a mini-campus of the University of Amsterdam.

New Side (Nieuwe Zijde; Map 4)

West of the Damrak-Rokin axis is the New Side of the medieval city, which was actually settled earlier than the Old Side – the name dates from the construction of the Nieuwekerk.

Nieuwendijk This dike, the oldest in the city, used to link up with the road to Haarlem, and its businesses fleeced many travellers on their way to the market on Dam Square. This pedestrian-only shopping street still has a downmarket image, though some of the narrow side streets are picturesque.

Singel, Northern Section On the east side of the Singel stands the imposing baroque **Ronde Luthersekerk** (Round Lutheran Church; Map 2), built in 1668–71. The only round Protestant church in the country, it now serves as a conference centre for the nearby Renaissance Hotel, and holds free chamber-music performances on Sunday morning.

Across the canal, tied up at No 40, is the **Poezenboot** (Cat Boat), which is owned by an eccentric woman who looks after several hundred stray moggies. Visitors are welcome from 1 pm to 3 pm daily – in return for a donation towards cat food.

Farther along the Singel is **Torensluis**, one of the widest bridges in the city. The ghastly statue is of Multatuli (Latin for 'I have suffered greatly'), the pen name of the brilliant 19th-century author Eduard Douwes Dekker, who exposed colonial narrow-mindedness in a novel about a coffee merchant. The nearby **Multatuli Museum** (☎ 638 19 38), at Korsjespoortsteeg 20,

end

Magna Pl...
Nieuwezijds ...
Royal Palace, is th...
facade of Magna Plaza...
government architect CH...
main post office, the complex...
verted into a shopping centre. Che...
columned galleries and the many clo...
shops (there's also a huge Virgin Megasto...
in the basement).

Kalverstraat South of Dam Square is Kalverstraat, the car-free extension of Nieuwendijk. The name (Calves Street) presumably refers to the cattle that were led to market on Dam Square. Shops here are less grungy than those on Nieuwendijk and it gets awfully crowded, especially at weekends. Near Muntplein there's a shopper's temple called the **Kalvertoren** (Kalver Tower); the snack bar in the complex tower affords a 360° view.

South along Kalverstraat, there's a gateway at No 92 that leads to the **Amsterdams Historisch Museum** (☎ 523 18 22). Housed in the former civic orphanage, the museum provides an engaging overview of the city's history. The restaurant (free entry) serves delicious pancakes. The museum opens 10 am to 5 pm weekdays, and from 11 am at weekends. Admission costs f11 (various discounts). Pick up a free English-language booklet. Web site: www.ahm.nl.

For the orphanage's courtyard (note the cupboards where the orphans used to store their possessions), walk through to the **Civic Guard Gallery** (same hours as the museum, free entry). The group portraits of civic guards recall Rembrandt's groundbreaking work in *The Nightwatch*, which hangs in the Rijksmuseum.

Begijnhof Hidden just north of Spui Square is the Begijnhof, a former convent dating from the early 14th century. This surreal oasis consists of tiny houses grouped around a well-kept courtyard (open daily). The house at **No 34** dates from around

...house here belonged to a chalk
...hence the name.

...uld turn left here towards Kalver-
...ong the **Heiligeweg**, the Holy Way
...d by pilgrims on their annual pro-
...n to the chapel of the Miracle of Am-
...am. A procession still takes place every
...on the Sunday closest to 15 March.

...3ack along the Singel, the southern side of
...e canal between Koningplein and Vijzel-
...raat is occupied by the **Bloemenmarkt**
(Flower Market), open 9 am to 5 pm Monday to Saturday. Amsterdam has specialised
in flower markets since the first Tulipmania
in the 17th century (see the boxed text 'Mad
About Tulips' in the Facts about the Netherlands chapter). The place is packed with
tourists and pickpockets, and prices are steep
by local standards, but it's a pretty sight.

Western Canal Belt (Maps 2 & 3)

In the late 16th cen-
tury, the city burst its
medieval walls with
a flood of Jewish
refugees from Portu-
gal and Spain and
Protestant refugees
from Antwerp. In the
1580s new land was
reclaimed from the IJ and Amstel in the
east, while in the west the Singel became a
residential canal. A new moat was added
that became Herengracht.

In 1613 the authorities embarked on the
ambitious canal-belt project that more than
tripled the city's area. These canals, with
their many bridges and connecting roads,
were all built in one huge effort. The whole
city was enclosed by a new outer moat, the
zigzag outer moat now known as the
Singelgracht. The moat's outer quays became the current Nassaukade, Stadhouderskade and Mauritskade.

By 1625 the western canal belt was completed down to the radial Leidsegracht before money ran out. The project was picked
up again later, but at a much slower pace,
and by the end of the 17th century it petered
out just short of its original goal (see the
Southern Canal Belt section).

...use...
marked the...
with Grimburgw...
sion across Rokin. The...e'
(or rather, the area inside a slu...

A book market is held Fridays in front of
the Begijnhof entrance. The statuette on the
west side is of an Amsterdam street-brat
called the *Lieverdje* (Little Darling). The
focal point for Provo 'happenings' in the
mid-1960s, it's now a meeting spot for the
intelligentsia who congregate in the pubs
and bookshops nearby. The classicist building between Voetboogstraat and Handboogstraat is the **Maagdenhuis**, the Virgins'
House built in 1787 as a Catholic girls' orphanage (now the administrative seat of the
university). The handsome **Lutheran Church**
next door (1633) still holds services.

Singel, Southern Section The **University Library** is at Singel 421–425. The citizen's 'hand-bow' militia used to meet in No
421 and the 'foot-bow' militia in No 425 –
the nearby Handboogstraat and Voetboogstraat are named after them. The building at No 423 was constructed by Hendrick
de Keyser in 1606 as the city arsenal.

On the opposite canalside are the soaring
turrets of the neo-Gothic **Krijtberg** (Chalk
Mountain; Map 3) church, completed in
1883 to a design by Alfred Tepe. The lavish
paintings and statuary make this one of the
city's most beautiful churches. You can visit
during Mass from noon to 1 pm and 5 to
6 pm daily, or Latin Mass at 9.30 and 11 am

AMSTERDAM

AMSTERDAM HISTORISCH MUSEUM

Herengracht on the corner with Leidsegracht, painted in 1783 by Isaak Ouwater

The new canals split society into haves and have-nots. Until then, merchants lived more or less in their warehouses, mingling with their labourers and suppliers. After the new canals were built, the wealthiest escaped to residential mansions along the Herengracht (named after the '17 Gentlemen' of the United East India Company). The Keizersgracht (the 'emperor's canal' in honour of Maximilian) was similarly upmarket, and businesses that could be deemed annoying or offensive were banned. The Prinsengracht (so named to keep the House of Orange happy) was a 'cheaper' canal with smaller residences, warehouses and workshops. The canal acted as a barrier against the working-class Jordaan beyond.

Western Islands (Map 2) The wharves and warehouses of the Western Islands were a focus of the harbour in the early 17th century. The **Prinseneiland** and **Realeneiland** are the prettiest of the islands – the narrow bridge linking the two, the Drieharingenbrug (Three Herrings Bridge), replaced a pontoon bridge that used to be pulled aside to let ships through.

Don't miss the photogenic **Zandhoek**, the 17th-century sand market on the eastern waterfront of Realeneiland. The Zandhoek escaped demolition this century thanks to Jan Mens's 1940 novel *De Gouden Reael*, named after the bar-restaurant at Galgenstraat 14 (Gallows Street). It used to provide a view over the IJ to the gallows at Volewyck, the uninhabited tip of what was to become Amsterdam North.

Haarlem Quarter (Map 2) The Haarlem Quarter (Haarlemmerbuurt) attracts few tourists and thus retains a relatively 'authentic' feel. **Haarlemmerstraat** and its western extension **Haarlemmerdijk** were part of the original sea dike along the IJ. The area has a charming range of shops, pubs and restaurants.

The former meat hall at the north end of **Herenmarkt Square** became the **Westindisch Huis** in 1623, head office of the West India Company. When Admiral Piet Heyn captured the Spanish silver fleet off Cuba in 1628, the booty was stored here. His deeds are immortalised in a Dutch nursery rhyme which is sung by soccer fans at international matches:

Piet Heyn, zijn naam is klein
Zijn daden benne groot, zijn daden benne groot,
Die heeft gewonnen de Zilveren Vloot.

(Piet Heyn, his name is small,
his deeds are great, his deeds are great,
they won [triumphed over] the Silver Fleet).

Walk through the east entrance into the courtyard with its statue of Pieter Stuyvesant, the unpopular governor of New Netherlands, which included the Hudson Valley, Delaware and several Caribbean islands. Today the building houses the John Adams Institute, a Dutch-US friendship society (see Cultural Centres in the Information section earlier in this chapter).

The busy road to Haarlem led through the **Haarlemmerpoort** (Haarlem Gate) on Haarlemmerplein, where travellers heading into town had to leave their horses and carts. The current building structure (1840) was built as a tax office and a gateway for King William II to pass through on the way to his coronation.

Brouwersgracht (Map 2) The Brewers' Canal, named after the breweries that used to operate here, was an industrious canal full of warehouses, workshops and smelly factories banned from the residential canal belt. Note the almost uninterrupted row of former warehouses, now apartment houses, from No 172 to 212. Houseboats add to the lazy, residential character of this picturesque canal.

Herengracht (Map 3) The first section of Herengracht, south from Brouwersgracht, shows a mixture of expensive 17th- and 18th-century residences and warehouses. The **White House** (1620) at No 168 houses the **Theatermuseum** (☎ 623 51 04), open 11 am to 5 pm Tuesday to Friday, weekends from 1 pm (admission f7.50, or f4 with discounts). It has a stunning interior which was completely restyled in the 1730s, with intricate plasterwork and extensive paintings by Jacob de Wit and Isaac de Moucheron; a magnificent spiral staircase was also added at this time.

The museum spills over into the **Bartolotti House** at No 170–172, which has one of the most stunning facades in the city – a red-brick, Dutch-Renaissance job that follows the bend of the canal. It was built in 1615 by Hendrick de Keyser and his son Pieter by order of the wealthy brewer Willem van den Heuvel.

Just beyond, Herengracht is crossed by **Raadhuisstraat**, which links the Jordaan with the Dam. Note the shopping arcade on the far side, which was designed by AL van Gendt (the Concertgebouw architect) for an insurance company, with sculptures of vicious animals to stress the dangers of life without insurance.

Continuing along Herengracht, the quartet of sandstone neck gables at No 364–370 is known as the Cromhouthuizen, designed in 1662. They now house the **Bijbels Museum** (☎ 624 24 36), open 10 am to 5 pm Monday to Saturday, Sunday from 1 pm (admission f5, discounts f3.50), which includes beautiful 18th-century ceiling paintings by Jacob de Wit and the *Delft Bible* printed in 1477.

Keizersgracht (Map 3) The three **Greenland warehouses** (Map 2) with their step gables at Keizersgracht 40–44 belonged to the Greenland (or Nordic) Company, which dominated Arctic whaling from the early 17th century. Many houses along here used to belong to whaling executives and still bear decorations of their trade.

Farther south on the opposite side is the **House with the Heads** at No 123. The beautiful step gable has six heads at door level representing the classical muses. Folklore has it that the heads represent six burglars decapitated by an axe-wielding maid as they tried to break into the cellar.

The tall **Greenpeace Building** at No 174–176, which houses the organisation's international headquarters, is a rare example of Art-Nouveau architecture in Amsterdam. It was built in 1905 for a life insurance company – note the guardian angel who seems to be peddling an insurance policy.

On the same side of the canal, you'll see the pink granite triangles of the unique

Homomonument at Westermarkt just before you get to Raadhuisstraat. It commemorates those who were persecuted for their homosexuality by the Nazis.

Farther along Keizersgracht stands the **Felix Meritis building** at No 324. It was built in 1787 for a society which promoted the ideals of the Enlightenment through the study of science, arts and commerce. The colonnaded facade served as a model for that of the Concertgebouw, and Brahms, Grieg and Saint Saëns performed in its oval concert hall. Today, the Felix Meritis Foundation stages European performing arts events.

Prinsengracht (Map 3) Prinsengracht, named for Prince William of Orange, is the least posh of the main canals. Instead of stately offices and banks, it's peppered with cafes and shops. The houses are smaller and narrower than along the other canals, and houseboats line the quays.

The **Noorderkerk** (Map 2) at Noordermarkt, near the northern end of the canal, was completed in 1623 as a Calvinist church for the 'common' people in the Jordaan. It's shaped like a Greek cross (four arms of equal length) around a central pulpit. A sculpture near the entrance commemorates the bloody Jordaan riots of July 1934, when five people died in protests over government austerity measures. The **Noordermarkt** hosts a flea market on Monday morning and a farmers market on Saturday morning.

On the opposite side of Prinsengracht is the **Anne Frankhuis** at No 263, probably Amsterdam's most famous canal house that draws half a million visitors a year. Interest focuses on the *achterhuis*, the 'rear house' or annexe where the Jewish Frank family hid to escape deportation.

Anne's father, Otto Frank, was a businessman who emigrated with his family from Frankfurt to Amsterdam in 1933. As the German occupiers tightened the noose around the city's Jewish inhabitants, Otto – together with his wife, two daughters and several friends – moved into the rear of the building in July 1942. The entrance was concealed behind a revolving bookcase.

They were betrayed to the Gestapo in August 1944 and deported; Anne died in Bergen-Belsen concentration camp in March 1945, only weeks before it was liberated. After the war Otto published Anne's diary which was found among the litter in the annexe. Translated into 55 languages, the diary gives a moving account of wartime horrors through a young girl's eyes.

In 1957 the Anne Frank Foundation opened a museum here illustrating the Jews' plight in WWII and the dangers of present-day racism and anti-Semitism. The museum (☎ 556 71 00) opens 9 am to 7 pm daily (to 9 pm from April to August). Admission costs f10 (children 10 to 17 years, f5; children under 10, free). Early evening is the best time to go, after the queues have disappeared. Web site: www.annefrank.nl.

Just to the north-east stands the **Westerkerk** (☎ 624 77 66), with the tallest steeple in the city (85m). It's topped by a gaudy version of the imperial crown that Habsburg emperor Maximilian I bestowed to the city's coat of arms. The tower, the tourist logo of Amsterdam today, affords a tremendous view over the city.

The church is the main gathering place for Amsterdam's Dutch Reformed community. This showcase Protestant church was built to a 1620 design by Hendrick de Keyser, who copied his design of the Zuiderkerk. The nave, 29m wide and 28m high, is the largest of any Dutch Protestant church.

The huge main organ dates from 1686, with panels decorated with biblical scenes and instruments. Rembrandt, who died bankrupt in 1669 at nearby Rozengracht, is buried somewhere in the church – perhaps near the grave of his son Titus, where there's a commemorative plaque. The church opens 11 am to 3 pm Monday to Friday, Easter to mid-September (also Saturday in July and August). The tower opens 10 am to 5 pm Monday to Saturday from April to September. Entry costs f3.

Jordaan (Maps 2 & 3) The Jordaan neighbourhood was built to house canal workers in the early 17th century. Here too came the tanneries, breweries, sugar refineries and other smelly or noisy industries banned from the inner canal belt.

The origin of the name Jordaan is unclear: it may be a corruption of the French *jardin* (garden), as many French Huguenots settled here in what used to be the market gardens beyond the city walls. But some historians contend that there's a biblical connection to the Jordan River.

For centuries, the Jordaan remained thoroughly working-class. By the early 20th century one in seven Amsterdammers lived here in squalid conditions. New housing estates in Amsterdam's suburbs brought some relief, and in the 1960s and 1970s many Jordanese moved away. Students, artists and white-collar professionals have transformed the Jordaan into a trendy area, though it still retains some of its original flavour.

The Jordaan is well endowed with lively **markets**, such as:

Noordermarkt (Map 2) – see the earlier Prinsengracht section
Lindengracht (Map 2) – general market on Saturday, very much a local affair
Westermarkt on Westerstraat (Map 3) – clothes and textiles on Monday
De Looier at Elandsgracht 109 (Map 3) – bargain antiques and bric-a-brac at indoor stalls most days 11 am to 5 pm, Thursday to 9 pm, closed Friday

In the late 19th and early 20th centuries many of the Jordaan's ditches and narrow canals were filled in, though their names remain: Palmgracht, Lindengracht, Rozengracht (now a busy thoroughfare), Elandsgracht. **Bloemgracht** was the most upmarket of the canals and, for that reason, was never filled in: here wealthy artisans built smaller versions of patrician canal houses. Note the row of three step gables at No 87–91, now owned by the Hendrick de Keyser Foundation and known as the Three Hendricks.

The Jordaan also has many private **hofjes**, courtyards surrounded by almshouses built by wealthy benefactors. Some hofjes are real gems, with beautiful restored houses and stunning gardens. If the entrance is unlocked, residents probably won't mind if you take a quick peek.

Southern Canal Belt (Maps 3, 4, 6 & 7)

This second section of the city's grand canal project took some 40 years to complete. The corner of Herengracht and Leidsegracht is a tranquil spot, surrounded by 17th- and 18th-century houses. The buildings along Leidsegracht and the southern canal belt are almost entirely residential, with few of the warehouses seen in the western section. The facades are also more restrained.

Herengracht (Maps 4 & 7) Along the southern section of Herengracht the buildings are larger than in the western section. By the mid-17th century many Amsterdam merchants had amassed stupendous fortunes, and they saw to it that restrictions were relaxed on the size of canalside plots.

The Herengracht between Leidsestraat and Vijzelstraat, known as the **Golden Bend** (Map 4), had some of the largest private mansions in the city. Most of them now belong to financial and other institutions. Dutch architectural themes are still evident but the dominant styles are Louis XIV, XV and XVI – French culture was all the rage among the city's wealthy class.

A prime example is the interior of the **Goethe Institut** at No 470 (Map 7; see Cultural Centres under Information in this chapter).

Another Golden Bend house open to the public is the **Kattenkabinet** (Cats' Cabinet; Map 4; ☎ 626 53 78) across the canal at No 497. This museum, devoted to the feline presence in art, was founded by a wealthy financier in memory of his tomcat. It opens 11 am to 7 pm Tuesday to Saturday and from noon Sunday (entry f10).

Back on the even side of Herengracht, the corner with Vijzelstraat is dominated by the colossal **ABN-AMRO bank building** (Map 7) that continues all the way to Keizersgracht. It was completed in 1923 as head office for the Netherlands Trading Society, a Dutch overseas bank that later became the ABN Bank and merged with the AMRO Bank in 1991. The ABN-AMRO is the largest bank in the country and the largest foreign bank in the USA.

Beyond Vijzelstraat, past the mayor's residence at No 502, is the **Geelvinck Hinlopen Huis** (Map 7; ☎ 639 07 47) at No 518, a 17th-century house with stylish rooms, a formal garden and art in the coach house. It's worth a look if you can be bothered organising a private tour for f150 (maximum 15 people).

A few steps past this house is the start of the radial **Reguliersgracht** (Map 7), the beautiful 'canal of the seven bridges' cut in 1664. Canal tour boats halt here for photos, especially at night when the bridges are lit up and their graceful curves are reflected in the water. This canal was almost filled at the turn of the century to accommodate a tram line.

Walk down Reguliersgracht to take in its serenity and lively mix of architectural styles. Sights include:

- the house at No 34 with its massive eagle gable commemorating the original owner, Arent van den Bergh, and its unusual twin entrance for the upstairs and downstairs dwellings
- the superb scene back towards Herengracht from the east-west bridge at Keizersgracht, and the photogenic lean of the two houses on the corner
- the Dutch/German woodwork fantasy at No 57–59 reminiscent of the city's medieval wooden houses, built in 1879 for a carpentry firm (the same architect, Isaac Gosschalk, designed No 63)
- the Amstelveld with the white, wooden Amstelkerk at Prinsengracht
- the statuette of a stork set into the corner house at No 92 (storks were a protected species; canal-boat operators fantasise that a midwife lived here)

North of here across Herengracht towards the centre of town is **Thorbeckeplein** (Map 4), with a statue of Jan Rudolf Thorbecke, the Liberal politician who created the Dutch parliamentary system in 1848. An art market (mostly modern pictures) is held here 10.30 am to 6 pm Sunday from mid-March to mid-October.

Beyond Thorbeckeplein is the raucous **Rembrandtplein** (Map 4), focused on the proud statue of the painter unveiled in 1852. The grassy square is lined with pubs, grand cafes and restaurants, and attracts suburbanites looking for a noisy good time under the neon lights.

The street running west from Rembrandtplein to the Munt is Reguliersbreestraat. On its left side is the **Tuschinskitheater** (Map 4; ☎ 626 26 33) at No 26–28, established in 1921 and still the most glorious cinema in the country. The blend of Art Deco and Amsterdam School architecture with almost camp interior decorations is a visual feast. Guided tours in July and August (Sunday and Monday at 10.30 am) cost f7.50.

At the eastern end of Rembrandtplein is **Utrechtsestraat**, a lively street with interesting shops, restaurants and cafes that's worth a wander.

Farther east at Herengracht 605 is the **Museum Willet-Holthuysen** (Map 4; ☎ 523 18 22), a beautiful house with a sumptuous interior bequeathed to the city a century ago. Dating from 1687, it has been remodelled several times and underwent extensive renovations recently. It opens 10 am to 5 pm weekdays and from 11 am at weekends, and costs f7.50 (f5.50 with discounts).

Keizersgracht (Maps 3, 6 & 7) The **Metz department store** (Map 3) at Keizersgracht 455 was built in 1891 to house the New York Life Insurance Company, but soon passed to the purveyor of luxury furnishings. The functionalist designer and architect Gerrit Rietveld added the top-floor gallery, where you can have lunch with a view.

Across the canal at No 508 is the former **PC Hooft store** (Map 3), built for a cigar manufacturer in 1881. The name refers to poet, playwright and national icon Pieter Cornelisz Hooft, whose 300th birthday was commemorated in this Dutch-Renaissance throwback with a Germanic tower.

Farther along on this side of the canal, beyond Leidsestraat, is the solid yet elegant **Keizersgrachtkerk** (Map 6) at No 566. It dates from 1888 and was built to house the orthodox-Calvinist Gerevormeerd community who left the Dutch Reformed Church two years before.

AMSTERDAM

Gables & Hoists

A gable not only hid the roof from public view but also helped to identify the house until the French-led government introduced house numbers in 1795 (the current system of odd and even numbers dates from 1875). The more ornate the gable, the easier it was to recognise. Other distinguishing features included facade decorations, signs or wall tablets (cartouches).

There are four main types of gables. The simple **spout gable** with semicircular windows or shutters, a copy of the earliest wooden gables, was used mainly for warehouses from the 1580s to the early 1700s. The **step gable** was a late-Gothic design favoured by Dutch-Renaissance architects from 1580 to 1660. The **neck gable**, also known as bottle gable, was introduced in the 1640s and proved most durable, featuring occasionally in designs of the early 19th century. Some neck gables incorporated a step. The **bell gable** first appeared in the 1660s and became popular in the 18th century.

Many houses built from the 18th century onwards no longer had gables but straight, horizontal cornices that were richly decorated, often with pseudo-balustrades.

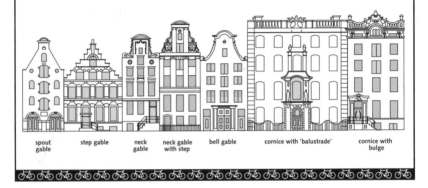

| spout gable | step gable | neck gable | neck gable with step | bell gable | cornice with 'balustrade' | cornice with bulge |

The next side street is **Nieuwe Spiegelstraat** (Map 6), lined with shops selling luxury antiques and other collectables. Even if you're skint, at least have a look at the goods on offer. The extension of this street, the pretty Spiegelgracht with more antique shops and especially art galleries, leads to the Rijksmuseum.

Farther along Keizersgracht from Spielgracht, across windswept Vijzelstraat, is the **Museum Van Loon** (Map 7; ☎ 624 52 55) at No 672, built in 1672 for a wealthy arms dealer. The house, acquired by the wealthy Van Loon family in the late 1800s, recalls canalside living in Amsterdam when money was no object for the wealthy, with a rococo rose garden. The museum inside the house opens from 11 am to 5 pm Friday to Monday, and costs f7.50 for adults (f5 with discounts).

Prinsengracht (Maps 3, 6 & 7) Near the corner with Leidsegracht is the **Paleis van Justitie** (Court of Appeal; Map 3) at No 436, a huge, neoclassical edifice. It served as an orphanage, and by the early 19th century more than half the city's 4300 orphans were crammed in here. A royal decree in 1822 relocated orphans over the age of six to other towns, despite local protestations over this 'theft of children'.

A hundred metres or so down Leidsestraat is **Leidseplein** (Map 6), one of the liveliest squares in the city and the undisputed centre of nightlife. It has always been busy: in the 17th century it was the gateway to Leiden and other points south-west, and travellers had to leave their carts and horses here when heading into town.

The **Stadsschouwburg** (City Theatre; Map 6) with its balcony arcade located at

Overlooking Jordaan from Westerkerk's tower

Singel – one of the city's first residential canals

Biking – the only way to get around

Afternoon stroll in Vondelpark

Keeping the canals clean

Muiderslot – visitors welcomed for 700 years

Nightlife abounds on Lijnbaansgracht.

Bridges everywhere on Reguliersgracht

Welcoming sign: Grasshopper and Oudekerk

Walter Suskin Bridge: coming together at night

Nieuwe Spiegelstraat: home of the antiques

Red lights lead the way

Leidseplein 25 dates from 1894. Public criticism of the building's design stopped funding for the facade, and the architect, Jan Springer, promptly retired. Large-scale plays and operettas are held here. South across Marnixstraat, the **American Hotel** (Map 6) is an Art-Nouveau landmark from 1902. No visit to Amsterdam would be complete without a coffee in its stylish Café Americain.

The sidewalk cafes at the north end of the square are perfect for watching street artists and eccentric passers-by. There's something for everyone here: pubs and clubs that continue till daylight, and a smorgasbord of restaurants, cinemas and even a casino shaped like a roulette table.

Farther east, beyond the intersection of Prinsengracht and Reguliersgracht, stands the wooden **Amstelkerk** (Map 6). The city planners had envisaged four new Protestant churches in the southern canal belt, but the only one that materialised was the Oosterkerk (Map 5). The Amstelkerk (1670) was meant to be temporary, but funds were lacking for a more permanent church, slated for the adjacent **Amstelveld Square**. The 'temporary' church still conducts services today.

Continue to the Amstel and you'll see the **Amstelsluizen** (Map 7). These impressive sluices (1674) allowed the canals to be flushed with fresh water from the Amstel rather than salt water from the IJ (see the boxed text 'Canal Cleaning', in the Facts about the Netherlands chapter). They were still operated by hand until recently. Across the river is the **Theater Carré**, built as a circus in 1868 and now the city's largest theatre (1700 seats).

To your left is the **Magere Brug** (Map 7), the most photographed drawbridge in the city. It links Kerkstraat with Nieuwekerkstraat and dates from the 1670s, when it was a very narrow pedestrian drawbridge. Often incorrectly translated as the 'Skinny Bridge', it was actually named after the Mager sisters who lived on opposite sides of the canal, and who had a footbridge built so they could see each other more easily.

Nieuwmarkt Neighbourhood (Maps 4 & 5)

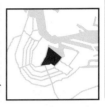

For information about Nieuwmarkt Square, see the earlier Old Side section. East of this square is the Nieuwmarkt neighbourhood, the birthplace in 1975 of the organised squatter movement. People occupied houses that stood to be demolished for the new metro line, and much of the area was eventually razed in favour of modern housing estates.

Until WWII the area was the focal point of Amsterdam's Jews, a thriving community who made the city a centre for diamonds, tobacco, printing and clothing. They also gave Amsterdam an exceptional variety of lively markets, some of which still exist as sad reminders (eg, the flea market on Waterlooplein).

Lastage (Map 5) East of Nieuwmarkt Square was an area known as the Lastage, a jumble of wharves, docks, rope yards and warehouses. In the early 16th century the Lastage was fortified by means of the wide **Oude Schans** canal and guarded by a gun turret, the **Montelbaanstoren** – its octagonal tower was added in 1606. Today the spot offers panoramic views over expanses of water.

North-west of here, on the corner of Binnenkant and Prins Hendrikkade, is the **Scheepvaarthuis**, the Shipping House completed in 1916 to a design by Johan van der Mey. This remarkable building which resembles a ship's bow was the first in the Amsterdam School style, and remains one of the finest examples of the movement. It's now home to the municipal transport company that runs the trams and buses.

Nieuwmarkt Islands (Map 5) In the 1580s, the sudden influx of Sephardic Jews from Spain and Portugal prompted the newly Calvinist authorities to reclaim land from the IJ in the form of several rectangular islands east of Oude Schans, one of which, **Uilenburg**, is still recognisable as an island today.

On Uilenburg, the vast Gassan diamond factory (☎ 622 53 33), abutting a synagogue at Nieuwe Uilenburgerstraat 173–175, was the first to use steam power in the 1880s. The factory was recommissioned in 1989 after thorough renovations. See Diamonds in the Shopping section of this chapter for details of free guided tours of diamond grinderies.

Southern Nieuwmarkt Neighbourhood (Map 4) South of here, inside the sea dike, the 16th-century authorities reclaimed land from the Amstel, creating the island of Vlooienburg (the current Waterlooplein), that would become the heart of the Jewish quarter.

The street that runs from Nieuwmarkt Square in the direction of Waterlooplein is St Anthoniesbreestraat. Note the **Pintohuis** at No 69 which used to belong to a wealthy Sephardi, Isaac de Pinto, who had it remodelled with Italianate pilasters in the 1680s. It's now a library annexe – pop inside to admire the beautiful ceilings.

A passageway in the modern housing estate across St Anthoniesbreestraat leads to the **Zuiderkerk**, the Southern Church built by Hendrick de Keyser in 1603–11. This was the first custom-built Protestant church in Amsterdam – still a Catholic design but without the choir – and served as a blueprint for De Keyser's Westerkerk. The final church service was held here in 1929 and at the end of WWII it served as a morgue.

It now houses the Municipal Centre for Physical Planning and Public Housing (☎ 622 29 62) with an interesting exhibit on all aspects of urban planning, open noon to 5 pm Monday to Friday and Thursday to 8 pm (free admission). A large, computerised laser map answers questions about the city in English. From June to September, you can climb the tower for a great view over the city (2, 3, and 4 pm Wednesday to Saturday; f3).

South of here, across the beautiful **Raamgracht**, is the narrow **Ververstraat** with a mix of old and new architecture typical of this area. The name, Painters' Street, refers to the polluting paint factories that

were limited to this street (originally a canal) beyond the city walls. At the end of Ververstraat, turn right to the steel drawbridge over the pretty **Groenburgwal**, which affords a good view of the Zuiderkerk. Note the slight tilt in its tower.

Jodenbreestraat (Map 4) St Anthoniesbreestraat opens on to the wide Jodenbreestraat, a remnant of a never-built freeway. Note the picturesque, leaning lockkeeper's house at the lock to the left, where you can have a quiet beer out in the sun.

Across the road, at Jodenbreestraat 4–6, is **Museum Het Rembrandthuis** (☎ 520 04 00), a beautiful house dating from 1606 where Rembrandt lived and worked. The master painter bought the house for a fortune in 1639, but chronic debt forced him to move to the Jordaan in 1658. The years in this house were the pinnacle of his career, when he ran the largest painting studio in Holland, but he ruined it all by making enemies and squandering his earnings.

The museum is notable for its near-complete collection of Rembrandt's etchings (250 of 280 he is known to have made). It has recently been refurbished and expanded with a modern section, and opens 10 am to 5 pm daily. Admission costs f12.50 (various discounts). Web site: www.rembrandthuis.nl.

Next to the Rembrandthuis is **Holland Experience** (☎ 422 22 33), at Waterlooplein 17. This hype-fest starts with a plotless half-hour film that lurches from tulips to windmills to threatened dikes, with hoky effects (eg, cheap perfume puffed in while the tulips are on screen). When an on-screen dike crumbles, room temperature falls and the audience is sprinkled with water. If you can't resist, Holland Experience opens 10 am to 6 pm daily and costs f17.50 with minimal discounts, or f25 in combination with the Rembrandthuis.

Waterlooplein (Map 4) South of this is Waterlooplein, once the heart of the Jewish quarter. Here looms the **Stopera**, the city hall and music theatre complex that opened in 1986 after nearly two decades of controversy (the name derives from 'Stop the

Opera' protests). One critic remarked that the building, which is officially called the Muziektheater, 'has all the charm of an Ikea chair'. There are free lunch-time concerts on Tuesday. Note the little display in the arcade between the city hall and the theatre that shows the country's water levels.

A flea market is held just north of the Stopera from Monday to Saturday, with a wide range of goods, including some genuine junk. Beware of pickpockets.

The neoclassical **Mozes en Aäronkerk**, a Catholic church built in 1841 on the northeastern corner of Waterlooplein, shows that this wasn't an exclusively Jewish area. It is still used as a church and also as a centre for social and cultural organisations.

Jewish Centres (Maps 4 & 5) On the east side of the big Mr Visserplein roundabout is the majestic **Portuguese-Israelite Synagogue** (Map 5; ☎ 624 53 51), built between 1671 and 1675 by the Sephardic community. It was the largest synagogue in Europe at the time and is still impressive. The architect, Elias Bouman, was inspired by the Temple of Solomon but the building's classicist lines are typical of Amsterdam. The large library of the Ets Haim seminary is one of the most important Jewish libraries in Europe. The synagogue, at Mr Visserplein 3, opens 10 am to 4 pm Sunday to Friday. Admission costs f7.50 (f5 with discounts).

South of the synagogue, at JD Meijerplein 2–4, is the **Joods Historisch Museum** (Map 4; ☎ 626 99 45), the Jewish Historical Museum, a beautifully restored complex of four Ashkenazic synagogues linked by glass-covered walkways. These are the Grote Sjoel (Great Synagogue, 1671), the first public synagogue in Western Europe; the Obbene Sjoel (Upstairs Synagogue, 1686); the Dritt Sjoel (Third Synagogue, 1700 with a 19th-century facade); and the Neie Sjoel (New Synagogue, 1752), the largest in the complex.

The Great Synagogue contains religious objects as well as displays showing the rise of Jewish enterprise and its role in the Dutch economy. The New Synagogue focuses on aspects of Jewish identity and the history of Jews in the Netherlands. There's also a kosher coffeeshop serving Jewish specialities. The complex opens 11 am to 5 pm daily (except Yom Kippur) and costs f8 (f4 with discounts). Web site: www.jhm.nl.

Plantage (Maps 1, 5 & 7)

In the 19th century, the Jewish elite began to move into the Plantage (Plantation), where they built imposing town villas. Until then the Plantage had been a district of parks and gardens.

The University of Amsterdam's **Hortus Botanicus** (Botanical Garden; Map 5; ☎ 625 84 11), Plantage Middenlaan 2A, was founded in 1638 as a herb garden for the city's doctors. It became a repository for tropical seeds and plants brought by Dutch ships from the East and West Indies. Coffee, pineapple, cinnamon and oil palm were distributed from here throughout the world.

The wonderful mixture of colonial and modern structures includes a restored, octagonal seed house; a modern, three-climate glasshouse with subtropical, tropical and desert plants; and a monumental palm house (don't miss the 400-year-old cycad, the world's oldest potted plant). The Hortus Medicus, the medicinal herb garden, attracts students from around the globe.

The garden opens 9 am to 5 pm on weekdays, and from 11 am at weekends. In winter it closes at 4 pm. Admission costs f7.50 (children f4.50); guided tours on Sunday at 2 pm cost f1.

Several buildings in the area serve as reminders of its Jewish past. The **Nationaal Vakbondsmuseum** (National Trade Union Museum; Map 5; ☎ 624 11 66) at Henri Polaklaan 9 used to house the powerful General Netherlands Diamond Workers' Union. The displays aren't of great interest to foreigners, but the building (designed by HP Berlage) is magnificent. The museum opens 11 am to 5 pm Tuesday to Friday and

1 to 5 pm Sunday. Admission costs f5 (f3 with discounts).

Around the corner, at Plantage Kerklaan 61A, is the **Verzetsmuseum** (Resistance Museum; Map 5; ☎ 620 25 35), which provides an excellent insight into the difficulties faced by those who fought the German occupation from within. The exhibits (labelled in Dutch and English) explain issues such as active and passive resistance, how the illegal press operated, and how 300,000 people were kept in hiding. It opens 10 am to 5 pm Tuesday to Friday, noon to 5 pm at weekends, and costs f8 (f4 with discounts). There's also a library.

At Plantage Kerklaan 38–40 is the **Artis Zoo** (Map 5; ☎ 523 34 00), the oldest zoo on the European continent, founded in 1838. Famous biologists have studied and worked here among the rich collection of creatures – from the tiniest insects up to elephants and giraffes. Some of the enclosures are cramped, but the zoo's layout is very pleasant, with ponds, statues and leafy winding pathways.

The fascinating aquarium (Map 7) has some 2000 fish and exhibits including a cross-section of an Amsterdam canal. There's also a planetarium (Dutch commentary with a summary in English). The zoo opens 9 am to 5 pm daily; entry costs f26.50 (children 4 to 11 years, f18.50, free for toddlers). Check the board for feeding times. The fee includes the museums and the hourly shows at the planetarium. Admission is cheaper in September. Web site: www.artis.nl .

The **Hollandsche Schouwburg** (Holland Theatre; Map 5; ☎ 626 99 45) at Plantage Middenlaan 24 played a tragic role during WWII. The Germans turned it into a theatre by and for Jews, and after 1942 the theatre became a detention centre for Jews while awaiting deportation.

In 1961 the theatre was demolished except for the facade and the area immediately behind it. There's a memorial room and an exhibition room with videos and documents on the building's history. It opens 11 am to 4 pm daily; admission is free.

South-east of Artis Zoo stands an 18th-century grain mill known as **De Gooyer** (Map 1), the sole survivor of five windmills from this corner of the city. In 1985 the former public baths alongside, at Funenkade 7, were converted into **Bierbrouwerij 't IJ** (Map 1; ☎ 622 83 25), a small brewery producing 10 different beers. They can be quaffed 3 to 7.45 pm Wednesday to Sunday. There's a tour of the brewery on Friday at 4 pm.

About 200m north-east of Artis Zoo, just south of the converted warehouses called Entrepotdok, is the **Museumwerf 't Kromhout** (Map 1; ☎ 627 67 77), an 18th-century shipyard at Hoogte Kadijk 147. It still repairs boats, but also houses a museum devoted to shipbuilding and early marine engines. The museum opens 10 am to 4 pm weekdays, and costs f3.50.

Eastern Islands (Map 5)

Several new islands were constructed in the 1650s: the islands of Kattenburg, Wittenburg and Oostenburg, largely devoted to the sea trade. Admiralty offices and buildings 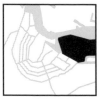 arose on the western island of **Kattenburg**, and warships were fitted out in the adjoining naval dockyards that are still in use today.

The Republic's naval arsenal was housed in an imposing building at Kattenburgerplein 1, completed in 1656. It houses the **Nederlands Scheepvaartmuseum** (Netherlands Shipping Museum; ☎ 523 22 22), with one of the most extensive collections of maritime memorabilia in the world. If you only visit a couple of Amsterdam museums, make this one of them.

Displays trace the fascinating history of Dutch seafaring from ancient times to the present, covering maritime trade, naval combat, fishing and whaling. Don't miss the film re-enactment of a trip to the East Indies. There are some 500 ship and boat models, a stunning collection of charts and navigational matter and a periscope on the top floor – offering an unexpected panorama of the city.

A replica of the 700-tonne *Amsterdam* is moored alongside the museum. The ship set sail on its maiden voyage in the winter of 1748–49 with 336 people on board but was wrecked off Hastings, on the English coast. You can board the ship and watch actors in 18th-century costume recreate life at sea.

The museum opens 10 am to 5 pm Tuesday to Sunday, and costs f14.50 (various discounts). Admission to the *Amsterdam* is included in the entry fee. Web site: www.generali.nl/scheepvaartmuseum.

West of this museum, the green structure resembling a ship's bow is the **newMetropolis Science & Technology Center** (☎ 0900-919 11 00, f0.75 per minute), designed by the Italian architect Renzo Piano. It offers many interactive displays that are a delight, especially for children. Hours are 10 am to 6 pm Tuesday to Sunday; admission costs f24 (children f16). The (free) rooftop 'plaza' affords a great view over the city. Web site: www.newmet.nl.

Old South (Oud Zuid; Map 6)

This wedge-shaped district, roughly bordered by the Vondelpark in the west and Hobbemakade in the east, is variously called the Museum Quarter, Concertgebouw area or Vondelpark area. Wealthy investors saw to it that tenement blocks or businesses were prohibited here.

In the 1920s, plots in the south were filled with Amsterdam School-designed apartments commissioned by subsidised housing corporations. Good examples can be seen along **JM Coenenstraat** by architect JF Staal and in the adjoining **Harmoniehof**, featuring the robust designs of JC van Epen.

Rijksmuseum The Museum Quarter's gateway – literally, with its pedestrian and bicycle underpass – is the 1885 Pierre Cuypers-designed Rijksmuseum (☎ 674 70 47). It bears a striking resemblance to Centraal Station, conceived by the same architect

and completed four years later. The style is a mixture of neo-Gothic and Dutch Renaissance. Aspects of the former (towers, stained-glass windows) elicited criticism from the Protestant king, who dubbed the building 'the archbishop's palace' (Cuypers was Catholic, which shows in his architecture).

The Rijksmuseum became a repository for several national collections, including the royal art collection that was first housed in the palace on Dam Square. It's the country's premier art museum and one that no self-respecting visitor to Amsterdam can afford to miss – in fact, 1.2 million visitors flock here each year.

Some 5000 paintings and many other works of art are displayed in 200-odd rooms, so it pays to be selective if you don't want to spend days here. Grab a free floor plan and home in on the areas that interest you most – there are five major collections. The museum shop on the 1st floor sells useful guidebooks.

The most important collection, Paintings, consists of Dutch and/or Flemish masters from the 15th to 19th centuries, with emphasis on the Golden Age. Pride of place is taken by Rembrandt's huge *Nightwatch* (1650), showing the militia led by Frans Banningh Cocq, a future mayor of the city – the painting only acquired this name in later years because it had become dark with grime (it's nice and clean now). Other 17th-century Dutch masters on this floor include Jan Vermeer *(The Kitchen Maid,* also known as *The Milkmaid,* and *Woman in Blue Reading a Letter)*, Frans Hals *(The Merry Drinker)* and Jan Steen *(The Merry Family)*.

The other exhibits are Sculpture & Applied Art (delftware, beautiful doll's houses, porcelain, furniture), Asiatic Art (including the famous 12th-century *Dancing Shiva),* Dutch History and finally the Print Room, with changing exhibitions from the museum's store of 800,000 prints and drawings.

From 2003 to 2005 most sections of the museum will be closed for a sweeping renovation that will cost several hundred million guilders. Only the top attractions will be on display, and it's not yet clear what will happen with the rest.

The museum opens 10 am to 5 pm daily and costs f15 (f7.50 with discounts, no student discount). The main entrance faces the city centre at Stadhouderskade 42. The **garden** at the back (free entry), with flowerbeds, fountains and an eclectic collection of stone memorabilia, opens 10 am to 5 pm Tuesday to Saturday, and 1 to 5 pm Sunday.

Behind the museum lies the sprawling **Museumplein**, which hosted the World Exhibition in 1883. It has only recently been transformed into a huge park, with an underground Albert Heijn supermarket under the conspicuous 'dog-ear' bulge opposite the Concertgebouw.

Van Gogh Museum The next museum down, with its main entrance at Paulus Potterstraat 7, is the recently refurbished and expanded Van Gogh Museum (☎ 570 52 00) designed by Gerrit Rietveld (its separate annexe on Museumplein, designed by Kishio Kurosawa, is commonly known as 'the Mussel'). The museum opened in 1973 to house the collection of Vincent's younger brother Theo, which consists of about 200 paintings and 500 drawings by Vincent and his friends or contemporaries, such as Gauguin, Toulouse-Lautrec, Monet and Bernard.

Born in 1853, Vincent van Gogh (pronounced 'khokh') had a short but very productive life. He didn't begin painting until 1881 and produced most of his works in the four years he spent in France, where the painter shot himself to escape mental illness in 1890. Famous works on display include *The Potato Eaters* (1885), a prime example of his sombre Dutch period, and *The Yellow House in Arles* (1888), *The Bedroom at Arles* (1888) and several self-portraits, sunflowers and other blossoms that show his vivid use of Mediterranean light and colour. One of his last paintings, *Wheatfield with Crows* (1890), is an ominous work foreshadowing his suicide.

His paintings are on the 1st floor; other floors display his drawings and Japanese prints, as well as works by friends and contemporaries. The museum opens 10 am to 6 pm daily and costs f12.50 (children f5, free under 12 years). The library opens 10 am to

12.30 pm and 1.15 to 5 pm Monday to Friday. Web site: www.vangoghmuseum.nl.

Stedelijk Museum Next to the Van Gogh Museum is the Stedelijk Museum, the City Museum (☎ 573 29 11). It's one of the world's leading collections of modern art from 1850 to the present. On display are modern classics by Monet, Van Gogh, Cezanne, Matisse, Picasso, Chagall and many others. There are also abstract works by Mondriaan, Van Doesburg and Kandinsky, and a large, post-WWII selection of creations by Appel (great mural in the cafe-restaurant). The list of famous artists goes on and on – De Kooning, Newman, Ryman, Judd, Warhol, Lichtenstein, to name a few. Sculptures include works by Rodin, Renoir and Moore; some can be viewed in the sculpture garden (which is overlooked by a cafe-restaurant).

The museum, at Paulus Potterstraat 13, displays most of its permanent collection in the summer months; at other times there are changing exhibitions. An extension onto Museumplein is scheduled to open by 2002. The museum opens 11 am to 5 pm daily and costs f9 (f4.50 with discounts); special exhibitions might cost extra. Web site: www.stedelijk.nl.

Concertgebouw The Concert Building at the end of Museumplein, at Concertgebouwplein 2–6, was completed in 1888 to a neo-Renaissance design by AL van Gendt. The venue attracts 800,000 visitors a year, making it the busiest concert hall in the world. Its Grote Zaal (Great Hall) has near-perfect acoustics.

Conductors and soloists consider it an honour to perform here. Under the 50-year guidance of composer and conductor Willem Mengelberg (1871–1951), the Concertgebouw Orchestra (with the epithet 'Royal' since 1988) developed into one of the world's finest orchestras.

In the 1980s the Concertgebouw was thoroughly restored to mark its 100th anniversary. Architect Pi de Bruin added an ugly glass foyer which, despite ongoing criticism, has proved quite functional.

The Grote Zaal seats 2000 people and is used for concerts. Recitals take place in the Kleine Zaal (Small Hall), a replica of the hall in the Felix Meritis building. Tickets are available on ☎ 671 83 45 between 10 am and 5 pm daily, or at the door till 7 pm (after 7 pm you can only get tickets for that evening's performance). The VVV and Amsterdam Uitburo (see Tourist Offices in the Facts for the Visitor chapter) also sell tickets. Free lunch-time concerts take place Wednesday at 12.30 pm. Web site: www.concertgebouw.nl.

Vondelpark & Surroundings This English-style park with ponds, lawns, thickets and winding footpaths was laid out in the 1860s and 1870s for the bourgeoisie. It was named after the poet and playwright Joost van den Vondel (1587–1679), the Shakespeare of the Netherlands.

About 1.5km long and 300m wide, the park is a mecca for joggers, in-line skaters, street musicians, couples in love, families with kids – in short, anybody who enjoys lush green surroundings. From June to August, free concerts are held in its **open-air theatre** (☎ 523 77 90 for information), and there are always musicians performing throughout the park. The functionalist **Round Blue Teahouse** (1936) serves coffee with wonderful cake. A stand near the Amstelveenseweg entrance at the southwestern end of the park rents in-line skates and gloves for about f7 an hour.

At Vondelpark 3 is the **Nederlands Filmmuseum** (☎ 589 14 00), which houses memorabilia and a priceless archive of the films screened in its two theatres. One theatre contains the Art-Deco interior of Cinema Parisien, an early Amsterdam cinema. You can visit 10 am to 5 pm daily (closed Monday). Entry is free unless a film is being shown. The museum's charming Café Vertigo (☎ 612 30 21) is a popular meeting place, and an ideal spot to people-watch; on summer evenings films are shown on the outdoor terrace. Web site: www.nfm.nl.

The impressive library and study centre (☎ 589 14 35) opens 10 am to 5 pm Tuesday to Friday and from 11 am Saturday.

A few steps down the road at Vondelstraat 140 is the neoclassical **Hollandse Manege** (1882) designed by AL van Gendt, an indoor riding school inspired by the famous Spanish Riding School in Vienna. Walk through the passage and up the stairs to the cafe, where you can sip a beer or coffee while watching the instructor put the horses through their paces. The school should be open daily but times vary – ring ☎ 618 09 42 to avoid disappointment.

South of the park, at Amstelveenseweg 264 just north of the Olympic Stadium, is a former train station which houses the **Tram Museum Amsterdam** (☎ 673 75 38). Historic trams run between here and Amstelveen – a great outing for kids and adults. An 1¼-hour return trip costs f5 (f2.50 with discounts) and stops at the Amsterdamse Bos recreational area. Services operate 11 am to 5 pm Sunday from April to October, and Wednesday afternoon from May to September.

De Pijp (Map 7)

This district, which lies south of the broad Stadhouderskade, probably got its name from its straight, narrow streets that are said to resemble the stems of old clay pipes. This was the city's first 19th-century slum.

Its shoddy tenement blocks provided cheap housing for workers drawn by the city's industrial revolution. In the past few years the Pijp has attracted a slightly wealthier breed of locals who are doing up apartments and lending the neighbourhood a gentrified air. The Pijp area is still often called the 'Quartier Latin' thanks to its lively mix of people – labourers, intellectuals, new immigrants, prostitutes and, more recently, yuppies.

The locals are best viewed at the **Albert Cuypmarket**, Amsterdam's largest and busiest market, Monday to Saturday along Albert Cuypstraat. Here you'll find food, clothes and other general goods of every description and origin, often cheaper than anywhere else. If you want to experience the 'real' Amsterdam at its multicultural best, this market is not to be missed.

The area's other main draw is the **Heineken Museum** (☎ 523 94 36) at Stadhouderskade 78, still commonly known as the Heineken Brewery. The brewery closed in 1988 due to inner-city congestion; since then, the building has been used only for administration. Guided visits take place at 9.30 and 11 am weekdays (also at 1 and 2.30 pm from June to mid-September). Entry costs f2 (a donation to charity). The visit ends with a generous beer-tasting, and if it's your birthday you get a free Delft-blue beer mug.

South of Albert Cuypstraat is the **Sarphatipark**, an English-style park named after 19th-century Jewish doctor and chemist Samuel Sarphati (1813–66). With its ponds, fountains and bird life, it's a lovely place for a picnic lunch.

At Amsteldijk 67 is the neo-Renaissance **Gemeentearchief** (Map 7; ☎ 572 02 02), the Municipal Archives. You can peruse the archives for research free of charge, and it holds occasional exhibitions. Hours are 10 am to 5 pm Monday to Saturday (closed Saturday in July and August).

Oosterpark District (Map 7)

This south-eastern district, named after the lush, English-style park at its centre, was built in the 1880s for diamond-industry workers. The area is home to the **Tropenmuseum**

(☎ 568 82 00) at Linnaeusstraat 2, an impressive complex completed in 1926 to house the Royal Institute of the Tropics, one of the world's leading research institutes for tropical hygiene and agriculture.

Its three tiers of galleries offer reconstructions of daily life in several tropical countries – among them a north African street, Javanese house, Indian village, and an African market. Other exhibits cover music, theatre, religion, crafts, world trade and ecology, and there are special displays throughout the year. The children's section (☎ 568 82 33) offers guides for six to 12-year-olds – book ahead. There's an extensive library, a shop selling books and gifts and unique CDs, a pleasant cafe, a restaurant serving Third World cuisine, and the Tropeninstituut Theater, a theatre that screens films but also hosts music, dance, plays and other performances by visiting international artists.

The museum opens 10 am to 5 pm Monday to Friday (weekends from noon). Entry costs f12.50 (students/seniors f7.50). It's a good place to spend a lazy Monday when most of the other museums are closed. Web site: www.kit.nl.

New South (Nieuw Zuid; Map 1)

The New South, the area between the Amstel and the Olympic Stadium, was the result of a 1901 housing act that set minimum building standards and required proper

blueprints for city expansion. Urban planners, architects and municipal authorities had not worked together so closely since the canal-belt project, creating a successful blend of solid housing, wide boulevards and cosy squares.

Among the first residents were Jewish refugees from Germany and Austria, many of them writers and artists, who settled around Beethovenstraat. The Frank family lived at Merwedeplein farther to the east, where Churchillaan and Rooseveltlaan merge around the **'Skyscraper'** (1930), a 12-storey building with spacious luxury apartments designed by JF Staal.

South-west of here is the **RAI** exhibition and conference centre (☎ 549 12 12, fax 646 44 69) at Europaplein 8, the largest such complex in the country. There's always some sort of exhibition or trade fair going on: cars, two-wheelers, boats, camping gear – ring to find out.

Amstelveen (Map 1)

This calm suburb south of Amsterdam is home to a huge recreation area: the **Amsterdamse Bos** (Amsterdam Woods). It's the result of a 1930s job-creation scheme, and urbanites flock to its 940 hectares of lakes, wooded areas and meadows at weekends. Its only drawback is that it's close to Schiphol airport and a lot of low-flying aircraft.

The visitors centre (Map 1; ☎ 643 14 14) at Nieuwe Kalfjeslaan 4 opens 10 am to 5 pm daily. Besides loads of walking and cycling paths you'll find an animal enclosure with bison, a goat farm, and a rowing course (the Bosbaan) with several water craft for hire. The forestry museum (☎ 645 45 75) has displays about the development and flora and fauna of the area; it opens 10 am to 5 pm daily, and Sunday from 1 pm (free). Take the historic tram from the Haarlemmermeer Station (see the earlier Vondelpark section) or bus No 170, 171 or 172 from Centraal Station. There's a bike rental at the main entrance at Van Nijenrodeweg.

Nearby is the **CoBrA Museum** (☎ 547 50 50), at Sandbergplein 1–3, just opposite the Amstelveen bus terminal (bus No 170, 171 or 172 from Centraal Station). After WWII the CoBrA movement was formed by postwar artists from Denmark, Belgium and the Netherlands – the name consists of the first letters of their respective capital cities. This treasure trove of painting, ceramics, statuary and more is open 11 am to 5 pm from Tuesday to Sunday and will cost you f7.50 (students/children f5/3.50). Web site: www.cobra-museum.nl.

Amsterdam North (Noord; Map 1)

Amsterdam North was once considered to be beyond the pale – a place where, several hundred years

ago, the bodies of executed criminals were dumped. Since the 19th century the area across the IJ river has been distinctly working-class, and offers glimpses of daily life well away from the tourists. It's worth half a day to explore the older sections on foot or by bicycle.

Take the free pedestrian ferry marked 'Buiksloterwegveer' (between Pier 8 and Pier 9) from behind Centraal Station across the IJ to the Shell Oil installations at Buiksloterweg, where you'll disembark next to the **Noordhollands Kanaal**. The VVV tourist office has maps of bicycle routes of the area; the prettier stretches include the **Florapark**, due north along the canal, and the comely old wooden houses along Nieuwendammerdijk to the east (follow signs towards Schellingwoude).

WALKING TOURS

Amsterdam is tailor-made for walking. You could simply follow your nose or, if a particular area takes your fancy, you could explore it with the previous text.

Alternatively, you could follow one or more of the official VVV walks designed by the ANWB (the Dutch automobile association), which take you through the most interesting parts of the city.

ACTIVITIES

Fitness Centres To pump iron to loud disco music head for Barry's Fitness Centre (Map 7; ☎ 626 10 36), Lijnbaansgracht 350. A day card is f20 and a monthly pass is f110. For aerobics and feel-good activities, including sauna, massage, physiotherapy and dietary advice, try the Garden Gym (Map 4; ☎ 626 87 72), Jodenbreestraat 158. A one-day pass ranges from f16.50 to f23.50, a monthly pass from f77.50 to f122.50.

Saunas Saunas are mixed and most guests go nude, so check your modesty at the front desk – or rent a towel. Deco (Map 4; ☎ 623 82 15), Herengracht 115, is a respectable, elegant sauna with good facilities including a snack bar. Its wonderful Art Deco furnishings used to grace a Parisian department store. Hours are 11 am to 11 pm

Monday to Saturday, and 1 to 6 pm Sunday. Admission costs f19.50 11 am to 2 pm on weekdays; at other times it's f27.50.

The Eastern Bath House/Hammam (Map 2; ☎ 681 48 18), Zaanstraat 88 in the northwest beyond the Haarlemmerpoort, is a Turkish bath house for women only (Sunday and Monday men only).

Mandate (Map 6; ☎ 625 41 00), Prinsengracht 715, is a beautiful 18th-century canal house with a very modern, gay-only sport school and sauna. It opens 11 am to 10 pm weekdays, noon to 6 pm Saturday and 2 to 6 pm Sunday.

Swimming Pools Ring ahead to ensure the pool is open to the general public, because special-interest sessions are often scheduled throughout the week.

Flevoparkbad (Map 1; ☎ 692 50 30) Zeeburgerdijk 630 east of the city centre – outdoor pool only; open 10 am to 5.30 pm May to September
Marnixbad (Map 2; ☎ 625 48 43) Marnixplein 5–9 at the western end of Westerstraat – indoor pool only, closed in July and August, admission f4.75/4 for adults/children
De Mirandabad (Map 1; ☎ 642 80 80) De Mirandalaan 9 south of the city centre – tropical 'aquatic centre' complete with beach and wave machine; indoor and outdoor pools; entry costs f6.25
Sloterparkbad (Map 1; ☎ 613 37 00) Slotermeerlaan 2 in the western suburbs next to the terminus of tram No 14 – in an attractive recreational area with yacht harbour; both indoor and outdoor pools; admission costs f5

Ice Skating The canals rarely freeze over in winter, but Amsterdam's many ponds make for good ice skating. Don't take to a patch of ice unless you see large groups of people, and be very careful at the edges and under bridges (such areas often don't freeze properly).

You can now rent skates at a skating rink. A pair of simple hockey skates costs upwards of about f100 at a department store (sports shops tend to be more expensive). Hockey skates are probably the best choice for learners; figure and speed skates are tough to master.

Jaap Eden IJshockeyhal (☎ 694 98 94), Radioweg 64 in the eastern suburb of Watergraafsmeer (tram No 9), has an indoor and outdoor rink. Skate rentals cost f7 to f9.

Tennis & Squash The huge Borchland Sportcentrum (☎ 563 33 33), Borchlandweg 8–12, next to the Amsterdam ArenA stadium in the Bijlmer (metro: Duivendrecht or Strandvliet) has tennis, squash and badminton courts, bowling alleys and other facilities including a restaurant.

Tenniscentrum Amstelpark (Map 1; ☎ 301 07 00), Karel Lotsylaan 8, has 42 open and covered courts and runs the country's biggest tennis school. It's conveniently close to the World Trade Center and RAI exhibition buildings.

Squash City (Map 2; ☎ 626 78 83), Ketelmakerstraat 6 at the railway line at Bickerseiland (west of Centraal Station), charges f28 (f37 in the evenings) for two people to use a squash court; a combined ticket for court, gym and sauna costs f23.50 per person (evenings f28.50)

Bungy Jumping Bungy Jump Holland (Map 2; ☎ 419 60 05), Westerdoksdijk 44, about 600m north-east of Centraal Station., offers 75m jumps from a waterside crane, from noon to 9 pm daily in July and August (Thursday to Monday in May and June, Thursday to Sunday in October). It costs f100 for the first jump, f75 for the second, and f400 for 10.

LANGUAGE COURSES

Dutch is a close relative of English but that doesn't make it easy to learn. Mainstream courses take months and intensive courses last several weeks.

At the Volksuniversiteit Amsterdam (Map 1; ☎ 626 16 26), Rapenburgerstraat 73, 1011 VK Amsterdam, there is a range of well-regarded day and evening courses that don't cost a fortune.

The Tropeninstituut (Royal Institute for the Tropics) has intensive courses with a large cultural component aimed at foreigners moving to the Netherlands; they're expensive but effective. Contact the Language

Training department (☎ 568 85 59) at Postbus 95001, 1090 HA Amsterdam. Web site: www.kit.nl.

The British Language Training Centre (☎ 622 36 34), Nieuwezijds Voorburgwal 328E, 1012 RW Amsterdam, is also expensive and has a good reputation.

ORGANISED TOURS

Quite a few organisations offer tours that provide a quick overview of the sights. Prices may vary depending on special exhibitions at the Rijksmuseum:

Holland International (Map 4; ☎ 625 30 35) Damrak 90 – 3½-hour bus tour includes the Rijksmuseum and a diamond factory; 2.30 pm daily (f48)

Keytours (Map 4; ☎ 623 50 51) Dam 19 next to Thomas Cook and the Krasnapolsky Hotel – 3½-hour city sightseeing tours in summer: the tour at 9.30 am is by bus and boat (f40) while the 2.30 pm tour is by bus to the Rijksmuseum and a diamond factory (f48); only afternoon tours in winter

Lindbergh Tours (Map 4; ☎ 622 27 66) Damrak 26 – 2½-hour city sightseeing tours by bus 10 am and 2.30 pm daily in summer (f27.50), or f35 bus plus one-hour canal boat tour; only afternoon tours in winter

Canal Tours

A horde of tour boats leave from in front of Centraal Station, along Damrak and Rokin and also in the area near the Rijksmuseum, and charge around f15 for a one-hour cruise. The tour boats are all pretty similar, and you can just hop on board. The Lovers boat opposite Centraal Station charges f10 for students.

Boom Chicago (Map 3; ☎ 423 01 01), Korte Leidsedwarsstraat 12, conducts 'smoking' boat tours round the canals in the warmer months. The 1¼-hour circuit goes through the tiny canals of the red-light district, and you can bring your own smokes and snacks. Tours (15 people maximum, f20 each) are usually at 1, 3 and 5 pm, and often 9 pm in summer. The Boom Chicago tour is very popular, so book a couple of days ahead. Check out their Web site at www.boomchicago.nl.

Bicycle Tours

Several operators offer bike tours from April to October. Yellow Bike Tours (Map 4; ☎ 620 69 40), Nieuwezijds Kolk 29 off Nieuwezijds Voorburgwal, is the largest of its kind and offers three-hour bicycle tours around town for f32.50, or longer, 6½-hour tours to Broek in Waterland north of Amsterdam for f42.50.

Let's Go (Map 3; ☎ 600 18 09), Keizersgracht 181, offers 6½-hour bike tours to Edam and Volendam, or a Castle & Windmills tour east of the city, for f45 (train tickets not included). Tours start at the VVV office in front of Centraal Station and you take the train to the bikes. Web site: http://come.to/letsgo.

For information on a 30km bicycle tour, the Amstel Route, which begins and ends south of the city at Amstelveen, see the chapter 'Cycling in the Netherlands'.

PLACES TO STAY

Amsterdam is a mecca for tourists year-round, so book well ahead. It's worth paying a bit extra for something central so you can enjoy the nightlife, without resorting to night buses or taxis. This doesn't imply you'll have to stay in the canal belt: the Museum Quarter or the Vondelpark area, for instance, are only a short walk from the action at Leidseplein.

Ask about parking if travelling by car. In most cases parking is a major problem and the best you'll do is a (payable) parking permit on the street or a security-guarded garage (from about f60 per day). The top-end hotels have their own parking, but like to be warned in advance.

Bookings

The VVV offices or the GWK (money exchange office) at Centraal Station have hotel-booking services that are useful during busy periods – see Tourist Offices in the Information section of this chapter for details.

The price categories for doubles are as follows: Budget (under f125), Mid-Range (f125 to f275) and Top End (from f275). Singles cost about two-thirds of the prices quoted here.

For something novel, Lindbergh Travel (Map 4; ☎ 639 01 90, fax 622 27 69), at Damrak 26/27, books accommodation on small passenger barges less than 500m from Dam Square. Doubles start around f130 with shared facilities and from f150 with private shower and toilet.

Gay & Lesbian Hotels

Amsterdam's hotels are generally gay- and lesbian-friendly, but we've listed some establishments which cater especially to homosexuals.

The *Aerohotel (Map 3; ☎ 622 77 28, fax 638 85 31, Kerkstraat 49)*, in the middle of the gay action, is a popular gay hotel that charges f110 to 175 for a double.

Hotel Orfeo (Map 6; ☎ 623 13 47, reception ☎ 622 81 80, Leidsekruisstraat 14) is a very laid-back place with a decent sauna which charges f100 for a double. The *Stablemaster Hotel (Map 4; ☎ 625 01 48, fax 624 87 47, Warmoesstraat 23)* caters for the leather crowd and has doubles for f160.

The sole women-only establishment is *Liliane's Home (Map 7; ☎ 627 40 06, Sarphatistraat 119, 1018 GB Amsterdam)*, which has three rooms from f185 for a double. It's not really a hotel but a private home and isn't geared up for walk-in trade – best to write in advance.

Hotel Quentin (Map 6; ☎ 626 21 87, fax 622 01 21, Leidsekade 89) is popular with lesbians, though heteros and gays also stay here; a double costs f125 to f130 with private shower, f97.50 without.

The *Black Tulip Hotel (Map 4; ☎ 427 09 33, fax 624 42 81, Geldersekade 16)* caters to gay men, and S&M fetishists in particular. Rooms have a mind-boggling array of equipment, including cages, bondage chairs, slings hooks and more. Doubles start at f195, including breakfast. Web site: www.blacktulip.nl.

PLACES TO STAY – BUDGET
Camping Grounds

Camping Vliegenbos (Map 1; ☎ 636 88 55, fax 632 27 23, Meeuwenlaan 138), Amsterdam North, opens April to September and is the most convenient site for people without

a car. Tent campers pay f14.75 per person (a car is f5.50 extra). There are also camping huts for up to four people for f85 (reserve by fax or letter). From Centraal Station, take bus No 32 or night bus No 72, or the free ferry from Pier 8 behind Centraal Station. Once on the other side, it's a 20-minute walk or five-minute ride by bicycle.

Camping Het Amsterdamse Bos (off Map 1; ☎ 641 68 68, fax 640 23 78, Kleine Noorddijk 1) opens April to October. It's a long way south-west of town in the pretty Amsterdamse Bos (woods), but there's a swift bus (No 171) from Centraal Station. The noise from nearby Schiphol airport can be annoying. It costs f8.75 per person, f5.50 per tent and f4.75 per car.

Gaaspercamping (off Map 1; ☎ 696 73 26, fax 696 93 69, Loosdrechtdreef 7), Gaasperdam, is in a large park-cum-recreational area in the south-eastern suburbs (metro to Gaasperplas, then a 500m walk). It costs f6.75 per person, f7.25 per tent and f6.25 per car, and opens mid-March to December.

Hostels

Bookings are strongly advised in summer at the HI hostels; the others usually don't take telephone reservations, so you'll just have to turn up.

The HI *Stadsdoelen Youth Hostel (Map 4; ☎ 624 68 32, Kloveniersburgwal 97)*, near the red-light district in the old town, is very central and charges f28 for members. There's a 2 am curfew, though the door is opened at a quarter past the hour to let people in and out.

The *City Hostel Vondelpark (Map 6; ☎ 589 89 96, Zandpad 5)* on the Vondelpark is the cheerier of the two HI hostels and clearly the busiest, with 300,000 guests a year. There have been reports of theft, so mind your valuables. Members pay f35/38 for a dorm bed in the low/high season including breakfast, and double rooms go for f90/125. There's no curfew.

Christian backpackers will feel right at home in *Christian Youth Hostel Eben Haëzer (Map 3; ☎ 624 47 17, fax 627 61 37, Bloemstraat 179)* in the Jordaan. A bed costs f23 including breakfast, there's a 2 am curfew, and the age limit is 35.

Bob's Youth Hostel *(Map 4;* ☎ *623 00 63, fax 675 64 46, Nieuwezijds Voorburgwal 92)*, four blocks from Centraal Station, is devoid of Christian leanings and has a very relaxed policy on dope. A bed is f26 including breakfast, and there's no age limit. It's a basic and convenient place to crash if you roll into Amsterdam exhausted.

The ***Flying Pig Downtown Hostel*** *(Map 4;* ☎ *420 68 22, fax 421 08 02,* **℮** *headoffice@flyingpig.nl, Nieuwendijk 100)* is a popular choice run by backpackers, with comfortable rooms and rock music downstairs. Dorm beds cost f26.50 to f41.50, and doubles go for f120 with shower and toilet, breakfast included. The ***Flying Pig Palace Hostel*** *(Map 6;* ☎ *400 41 87, fax 421 08 02, Vossiusstraat 46)* at the Vondelpark has similar rates.

Also check out ***Haarlem Youth Hostel*** in the Haarlem section of the Noord Holland chapter.

Hotels

These budget places are popular with backpackers, and some have lounges filled with happy smokers who'd be in jail if this weren't Amsterdam. Budget hotels often won't take telephone bookings, so start door-knocking from 10 am.

Frisco Inn *(Map 4;* ☎ *620 16 10, Beursstraat 5)*, off Damrak, is a youth hotel with doubles for f90 with or without shower (luck of the draw), breakfast not included; triples/quads with bunk beds cost f40 to f45 a head. There's a bar downstairs.

Centrumhotel *(Map 4;* ☎ *624 35 35, fax 624 86 66,* **℮** *centrumhotel@xs4all.nl, Warmoesstraat 15)*, near Centraal Station, is a cheerful, renovated place charging f100 for a double with shared shower, f115 with private shower, f135 with shower and toilet. All rooms have TV and there's a bar downstairs.

Hotel Kabul *(Map 4;* ☎ *623 71 58, fax 620 08 69, Warmoesstraat 42)*, next to the red-light district police station, really packs the customers in. A dorm bed starts at f35 and a double room at f125, both including breakfast.

Hotel Winston *(Map 4;* ☎ *623 13 80, fax 639 23 08,* **℮** *winston@winston.nl, War-*

moesstraat 123), a block from the Dam, is also a multimedia centre with a trendy bar. Brightly coloured doubles with shared facilities cost f95 and up; breakfast is f10.

Hotel Crown *(Map 4;* ☎ *626 96 64, fax 420 64 73, Oudezijds Voorburgwal 21)*, in the red-light area, has tidy doubles with shared shower for f100 to f120 depending on the season, or f110 to f130 with private shower – good value for the location. Dorm beds cost f30 to f50.

Hotel Brian *(Map 4;* ☎ *624 46 61, fax 625 39 58,* **℮** *hotelbrian@hotmail.com, Singel 69)*, near Centraal Station, is a shabby but friendly canalside place charging f40 per person in doubles, triples or quads, breakfast included. The ***Liberty Hotel*** *(Map 4;* ☎ *620 73 07, Singel 5)* has the same prices and setup (and is run by the same owners). Avoid both hotels if you can't handle funny or even normal smoke.

Also near the station, ***Hotel BA (Budget Amsterdam)*** *(Map 4;* ☎ *638 71 19, fax 638 88 03, Martelaarsgracht 18)* has doubles with shared shower for f75 to f120 depending on the season, including breakfast. Dorm beds start at f25 to f35.

The ***Euphemia Budget Hotel*** *(Map 7;* ☎*/fax 622 90 45,* **℮** *euphemiahotel@budgethotel.A2000.nl, Fokke Simonszstraat 1)* occupies a former monastery on a quiet street off busy Vijzelgracht. Doubles without shower cost f70 to f150 depending on the season, with shower f90 to f150; buffet breakfast is f8.50 per person extra.

The ***International Budget Hotel*** *(Map 3;* ☎ *624 27 84, fax 626 18 39,* **℮** *euphemia hotel@budgethotel.a2000.nl, Leidsegracht 76)* is in an attractive old canal house (run by Euphemia's owners). A double without shower costs f120, and a bed in a four-bed dorm starts at f35 depending on the season; breakfast costs extra.

Hotel Pension Hortus *(Map 5;* ☎ *625 99 96, fax 416 47 85, Plantage Parklaan 8)* faces the Botanical Garden. Small doubles with or without shower (luck of the draw) are f90 including breakfast. A bed in a quad dorm costs f45 including breakfast. Its relaxed clientele includes young and happy smokers.

On a quiet street near the Concertgebouw is *Hotel Peters (Map 6; ☎ 673 34 54, fax 623 68 62, Nicolaas Maesstraat 72)*. It's a private home where they've done little to create a hotel atmosphere. A double with or without shower is f100 (rooms with shower are smaller), or f130 with shower and toilet, breakfast included; all rooms have a TV and fridge.

PLACES TO STAY – MID-RANGE
Inside the Canal Belt

The *Amstel Botel (Map 5; ☎ 626 42 47, fax 639 19 52, Oosterdokskade 2–4)* is a floating hotel a few minutes walk east of Centraal Station. Doubles cost f147, or f157 on the water side. All rooms have shower, toilet, TV and phone; breakfast is f12 extra. It's a bit like sleeping on the ferry.

Hotel van Onna (Map 3; ☎ 626 58 01, Bloemgracht 102–108) consists of 41 rooms in three houses along a beautiful, quiet canal in the Jordaan. Well-kept, modern doubles cost f140 with shower and toilet, breakfast included. There are no phones or TVs in the rooms. Front rooms are for heavy sleepers: the nearby Westerkerk's bells peal every half-hour until 1.30 am and start again at 6.30 am.

Hotel Agora (Map 3; ☎ 627 22 00, fax 627 22 02, Singel 462), near the Flower Market, has doubles without shower for f120 to f150, or f175 to f215 with breakfast included. It's a comfortable hotel in an old building with a large, stylish lobby and breakfast area.

Hotel Hans Brinker (Map 6; ☎ 622 06 87, fax 638 20 60, Kerkstraat 136) is a large, slick place that prides itself on its spartan rooms and lack of facilities, and it's often full. Small, clean doubles with shower and toilet cost f145 including breakfast; dorm beds cost f41.50. There's a f2.50 surcharge per person for one-night stays. Web site: www.hans-brinker.com.

Among the string of slightly musty hotels near Leidseplein, *Hotel Impala (Map 6; ☎ 623 47 06, fax 638 92 74, Leidsekade 77)* has doubles without shower for f120 to f130, with shower for f150, and with toilet and shower for f160.

Hotel Prinsenhof (Map 7; ☎ 623 17 72, fax 638 33 68, Prinsengracht 810) near Utrechtsestraat is in a beautiful old canal house with an electric luggage hoist in the staircase. The two attic rooms with their diagonal beams are popular. Doubles cost f125/175, breakfast included.

Near the Artis Zoo, try *Hotel Rembrandt (Map 5; ☎ 627 27 14, fax 638 02 93, Plantage Middenlaan 17)*. Smallish doubles without shower cost f110, larger doubles with bath or shower are f160. This includes breakfast in the stunning, wood-panelled breakfast room with 17th-century paintings. It faces a noisy tram line; ask for a room at the back.

The *Canal House Hotel (Map 3; ☎ 622 51 82, fax 624 13 17, ✉ info@canalhouse.nl, Keizersgracht 148)* is an olde-worlde place spread over three grand canal houses. All rooms have antique furniture but no TVs (though there are modem sockets). A double with bath costs f265 to f345, which includes breakfast.

Near Rembrandtplein, the *Seven Bridges (Map 7; ☎ 623 13 29, Reguliersgracht 31)* has nine doubles with shower and toilet for f200 to f350, room-delivered breakfast on fine china included. The well-kept, beautiful rooms are tastefully decorated with expensive furniture. It's a lovely hotel on one of the loveliest canals – and popular, so book well ahead.

Outside the Canal Belt

Hotel Smit (Map 6; ☎ 676 63 43, fax 662 91 61, PC Hooftstraat 24) has doubles with bath and toilet for f190 to f220 depending on the season, including breakfast. This clean, reasonably new and lift-equipped place is close to Leidseplein and the museums.

Hotel De Filosoof (Map 1; ☎ 683 30 13, fax 685 37 50, ✉ filosoof@xs4all.nl, Anna van den Vondelstraat 6) is a stately hotel devoted to deep themes next to the Vondelpark. There's a Nietzsche room, a Wittgenstein room, a Humanism room and so on. A double with bath or shower and TV costs f195, including breakfast.

Hotel Arena (Map 7; ☎ 694 74 44, fax 663 26 49, ✉ info@hotelarena.nl, 's Gravesandestraat 51) is a huge complex on the lush Oosterpark. Its double rooms all have own shower and toilet, for f150 to f210 in summer and f110 to f160 in winter. Parking costs just f5 whenever you leave the parking area. There's a cafe and restaurant, live music in the bar, and dance nights on Thursday, Friday and Saturday.

PLACES TO STAY – TOP END

Hotels in this category change rates often to match the competition, so call around. All rooms have bathrooms with proper bath, shower and toilet.

Inside the Canal Belt

The family-owned *Hotel Estheréa (Map 3; ☎ 624 51 46, fax 623 90 01, ✆ estherea@xs4all.nl, Singel 305–307)* occupies three canal houses. It has doubles for f260 to f365 depending on the season, breakfast not included (f27.50). The newly redone rooms come with all the mod cons, and there's a pleasant bar.

The *Ambassade Hotel (Map 3; ☎ 626 23 33, fax 624 53 21, ✆ info@ambassade hotel.nl, Herengracht 341)* is a stylish, almost grand hotel spread over 10 canal houses. All rooms are different and tastefully appointed. Check out the antique clock (1750) in the lounge, with its rocking ships and mermaids. Doubles cost f350 and breakfast another f27.50.

The *Grand Hotel Krasnapolsky (Map 4; ☎ 554 91 11, fax 622 86 07, ✆ info@ krasnapolsky.nl, Dam 9)*, behind the national monument, is an elegant, historic hotel on Amsterdam's main square. Doubles cost f545 to f660. The highlight is its renowned 'winter garden' with its steel and glass roof (1879).

The *Pulitzer Hotel (Map 3; ☎ 523 52 35, fax 627 67 53, ✆ sales_amsterdam@ sheraton.com, Prinsengracht 315–331)* occupies a row of 17th-century canal houses with beautifully restored facades and some original (restored) interiors. Doubles cost f695 to f870.

Grand Westin Demeure (Map 4; ☎ 555 31 11, fax 555 32 22, ✆ reservations@ thegrand.nl, Oudezijds Voorburgwal 197) is housed in the former admiralty building where Queen Beatrix's civil wedding took place in 1966. It charges f730 for doubles; weekend deals go for f590, or f650 including dinner in one of eight banquet chambers. The five-star frills include an indoor swimming pool.

Hotel De l'Europe (Map 4; ☎ 531 17 77, fax 531 17 78, ✆ hotel@leurope.nl, Nieuwe Doelenstraat 2–8) has doubles for f655 to f755. It's an impressive red-brick building near Muntplein that oozes Victorian elegance. The attached Excelsior Restaurant is very good.

The Art-Deco *American Hotel (Map 6; ☎ 556 30 00, fax 556 30 01, ✆ american@ interconti.com, Leidsekade 97)*, just off Leidseplein, is a listed monument built in 1902. Doubles cost f565 to f650 but aren't as luxurious as you might expect. Breakfast in the stylish Café Americain is another f35. Cheaper deals are available when booked in conjunction with a KLM flight to Amsterdam.

Another Art-Deco monument, the *Golden Tulip Schiller (Map 4; ☎ 554 07 00, fax 624 00 98, ✆ sales@gtschiller .goldentulip.nl, Rembrandtplein 26–36)* has recently been restored to its original 1912 splendour. Works by the artist-hotelier Frits Schiller adorn the walls. Tastefully furnished doubles go for f420 to f495.

The *Amstel Inter-Continental Hotel (Map 7; ☎ 622 60 60, fax 622 58 08, ✆ amstel@ interconti.com, Professor Tulpplein 1)* has an imposing location on the Amstel. It's probably the country's finest hotel and attracts the glitterati (the Rolling Stones stay here while on tour). A double with bath on the river side costs f650 at weekends (f600 on the land side) but on weekdays you're looking at f995/895. Breakfast costs f48.50. Facilities include a limousine service, health club and swimming pool. It also boasts La Rive, Amsterdam's only restaurant with two Michelin stars.

Outside the Canal Belt

The *Bilderberg Garden Hotel (Map 1; ☎ 664 21 21, fax 679 93 56, ✆ garden@ bilderberg.nl, Dijsselhofplantsoen 7)*, south-west of the centre, has doubles with jacuzzi for f250 to f590, breakfast not included (f37.50). It's a small five-star hotel in a low-rise building and prides itself on its home-away-from-home ambience.

The **Hilton Amsterdam** (Map 1; ☎ 710 60 00, fax 710 60 80, Apollolaan 138–140), south-west of the city centre, has doubles for f445 to f650. Your standard Hilton, but it's in a stately area and boasts a marina with handsome old boats for hire. In 1970, John Lennon and Yoko Ono stayed in bed here for world peace, and you can do the same in their suite. Web site: www.hilton.com.

PLACES TO EAT

Amsterdam has hundreds of restaurants and *eetcafes* catering to all tastes and budgets. The Dutch eat dinner early and the more popular places fill up by 7 pm, so book ahead or arrive early (or be prepared to wait at the bar). Or arrive late: films, concerts and other performances usually start at 8.30 or 9.30 pm, when tables may suddenly become available. But keep in mind that many kitchens close at 10 pm, although the restaurants stay open longer. Vegetarian restaurants and some eetcafes tend to close earlier.

Lunch is a more modest affair, with sandwich and salad menus, though you'll find places that serve full meals if you really want one.

The streets around Leidseplein (Lange Leidsedwarsstraat and Korte Leidsedwarsstraat) are packed with restaurants – a veritable culinary melting-pot. But quality at these touristy places can be mediocre; take a short stroll to another area, and the chances of a memorable meal will improve.

Breakfast & Lunch

You may have trouble finding places (other than hotels) that serve before 9 or even 10 am. But if you know where to look, you'll discover plenty of small, inexpensive cafes serving hearty breakfasts and good quality sandwiches, soups and cakes for lunch. The more interesting ones are in the side streets of the canal belt, in the Jordaan and around Nieuwmarkt.

Nielsen (Map 3; ☎ 330 60 06, Berenstraat 19) is spread over two levels often filled with vases of fresh flowers. The set breakfast – eggs, toast, fruit, juice and coffee for f13.75 – is hard to beat. For lunch, the extra-big turkey club sandwich (f12.50) is fantastic. It opens 8 am to 5 pm Tuesday to Saturday and from 9 am Sunday.

Hein (Map 3; ☎ 623 1048, Berenstraat 20) across the street also does wonderful breakfasts. The owner, Hein, is happy to cook just about anything that takes your fancy in the open, industrial-style kitchen. It opens 9 am to 6 pm Wednesday to Monday.

In the Jordaan, **Foodism** (Map 3; ☎ 427 51 03, Oude Leliestraat 8) is a hip joint run by a fun crew. Open 11 am to 10 pm daily, it serves filled sandwiches and all-day breakfasts, and pasta at night. Try the 'Miss Piggy' – egg and bacon fettuccine for f15.50.

Dimitri's (Map 3; ☎ 627 93 93, Prinsenstraat 3) looks like a Parisian brasserie and serves lots of salads, pastas and burgers. Mornings see media types nibbling on croissants or, if they're feeling perky, ordering the champagne breakfast for f22.50.

Goodies (Map 3; ☎ 625 61 22, Huidenstraat 9) looks a little like a 1970s country kitchen and serves big sandwiches during the day and pasta at night. It opens 9.30 am to 10.30 pm Monday to Saturday and Sunday from 11 am.

Café Reibach (Map 2; ☎ 626 77 08, Brouwersgracht 139) is a charming gay-and-straight establishment that serves a massive breakfast for f22.50. The pear tart (f5) sells out within minutes of coming out of the oven.

Metz & Co Café (Map 3; ☎ 520 70 36, Keizersgracht 455), on the top floor of the swanky department store, does breakfasts, brunches and afternoon teas for f19.50 to f22.50.

Restaurants – Medieval Centre

Argentinian There are quite a few Argentinian steak houses dotted along the tourist eat streets. **Gauchos** (Map 4; ☎ 626 59 77, Geelvincksteeg 6) plates up rib-eye steaks (f26.50 to f47) and as many spareribs as you like for f26.50. It's part of a chain of six Gauchos around town.

Chinese For 'real' Chinese at affordable prices, visit the strip of Chinese restaurants along the Zeedijk near Nieuwmarkt Square. *Hoi Tin (Map 4; ☎ 625 64 51, Zeedijk 122)* is far from glamorous, but the menu features over 200 dishes with most mains priced around f17. It opens noon to midnight

Oriental City (Map 4; ☎ 626 83 52, Oudezijds Voorburgwal 177–179) is a large, efficient restaurant serving tasty main dishes from f17.50 to f45. Many Chinese eat here.

Dutch *De Roode Leeuw (Map 4; ☎ 555 06 66, Damrak 93)* used to be a stronghold of Dutch tourists but attracts a wider clientele these days. The food is still well prepared, with main dishes under f35.

d'Vijff Vlieghen Restaurant (Map 3; ☎ 624 83 69, Spuistraat 294–302) caters to splurging foreigners keen to sample good Dutch food in authentic surroundings (and that's what they get). Mains start at f48 and there are four-course menus for f82.50. Book ahead.

Dorrius (Map 4; ☎ 420 22 24, Nieuwezijds Voorburgwal 5) serves a wide range of Dutch dishes in olde-worlde surroundings. It's one of the city's premier Dutch restaurants, and the prices (many main dishes under f40) are worth it.

Haesje Claes (Map 4; ☎ 624 99 98, Nieuwezijds Voorburgwal 320) is slightly cheaper but no worse, with dark wooden panelling to enhance the experience. It opens noon to 10 pm daily; reservations are recommended.

If you're low on cash, try *Keuken van 1870 (Map 4; ☎ 624 89 65, Spuistraat 4)*, a former soup kitchen still serving dirt-cheap meals from an old-fashioned open kitchen. Nothing is over f21, and the set menu weekdays is f12. It opens 12.30 to 8 pm weekdays, weekends from 4 to 9 pm.

Fusion *Tom Yam (Map 4; ☎ 622 95 33 Staalstraat 22)* is a real treat. Former Michelin-star chef Jos Boomgaardt has turned his sights east and now dishes up fragrant, Thai-inspired soups, curries and noodle dishes. The set menu for f55 is a good option. It opens 6 to 10 pm daily.

Greek *Grekas (Map 3; ☎ 620 35 90, Singel 311)* is actually a catering shop, but you can also sit down for generous portions of the best Greek home cooking. Low overheads (snack-bar ambience) ensure very reasonable prices.

International *Pier 10 (Map 1; ☎ 624 82 76, De Ruijterkade Steiger 10)*, behind Centraal Station, offers a great harbour view as you dine by candlelight. Its French/Dutch/Italian dishes are on the pricey side (mains from f35) but worth the money. Book a table in the waterside rotunda and watch the sun set over the North Sea Canal.

The *Supper Club (Map 4; ☎ 638 05 13, Jonge Roelensteeg 21)* has theme nights: you may find yourself in downtown Naples with the laundry hanging from the ceiling, or in a sophisticated Paris salon. Menu prices vary according to day of the week (f85 to f95).

Eetcafé de Staalmeesters (Map 4; ☎ 623 42 18, Kloveniersburgwal 127) is a cosy place with inventive, reasonably priced mains under f30 and a three-course menu for f39.50.

Italian *Caprese (Map 4; ☎ 620 00 59, Spuistraat 261)* does good and affordable Italian food, and not just pizzas and pasta either. Many Italians eat here.

North American For a modern take on burgers and bagels, head to *Caffe Esprit (Map 4; ☎ 622 19 67, Spui 10)*. Gorgeous waiters (they're all models) scurry around the terrace area serving mega-sandwiches to too-thin glamour girls. The salads (from f11.75 to f19.75) are meals in themselves.

Seafood *De Visscher (Map 4; ☎ 623 73 37, Kalverstraat 122)* is a fast-food chain serving inexpensive, good seafood, open from 10 am to 7.30 pm, Thursday till 9.30 pm.

Restaurants – Western Canal Belt
Dutch One of the best places to try delicious, filling pancakes (savoury or sweet) is *The Pancake Bakery (Map 3; ☎ 625 13 33, Prinsengracht 191)*, in the basement of

AMSTERDAM

a restored old warehouse. It has dozens of varieties for f8 to f19, as well as omelettes, soups and desserts. The kitchen opens noon to 9.30 pm daily.

French *Jean Jean (Map 2; ☎ 627 71 53, Eerste Anjeliersdwarsstraat 12)* has meat and fish dishes for under f33, as well as crepes, soups and salads. It's nothing special but honest and affordable.

Bordewijk (Map 2; ☎ 624 38 99, Noordermarkt 7) has a minimalist interior that focuses your palate on the spectacular French/Italian cuisine. Prices are lower than at most French restaurants this good, with three-course set menus for f60 to f80. It opens 6.45 to 11 pm (closed Monday).

One very famous place is *Christophe (Map 3; ☎ 625 08 07, Leliegracht 46)*. Jean Christophe's subtly swanky, Michelin-starred restaurant is constantly filled with diners enjoying dishes like warm oysters with saffron and caviar (f45) and roasted lobster with sweet garlic and potatoes (f60).

Fusion *!Zest (Map 3; ☎ 428 24 55, Prinsenstraat 10)* is popular with local media types and business diners. Dishes like prawns atop a coriander and coconut coulis (f36.50) are served in a beautifully understated deluxe room. It opens 6 to 11.30 pm daily (reserve ahead).

Summum (Map 2; ☎ 770 0407, Binnen Dommersstraat 13) is a small place with crisp white tablecloths and napkins. The quiet formality of the room contrasts with the punchy Italian and Thai dishes. Mains are priced from f22 to f 37.

Indian *Koh-I-Noor (Map 3; ☎ 623 31 33, Westermarkt 29)* has a pretty gaudy interior but serves good curries, tandoori and biryani dishes. Mains are around f25 and it opens 5 to 11 pm daily.

International *De Belhamel (Map 2; ☎ 622 10 95, Brouwersgracht 60)* charms with its Art Nouveau interior and good French-inspired food. Most mains cost under f37. (Entrance is around the corner in Binnen Wieringerstraat.)

Stoop (Map 2; ☎ 639 24 80, Eerste Anjeliersdwarsstraat 4) serves some of the best bistro-style food in Amsterdam. Tasty mains like lambshanks on mashed potatoes (f32.50) and moreish desserts (f11.50) make bookings essential. It opens 6.30 to 11 pm daily.

Italian *Toscanini Caffè (Map 2; ☎ 623 28 13, Lindengracht 75)* is a convivial place in a former courtyard, with mains under f33 and three-course menus for f57.50. It's always busy, so book ahead.

Burger's Patio (Map 3; ☎ 623 68 54, Tweede Tuindwarsstraat 12) serves Italian food (not burgers, despite the name) in the evenings only. The three-course set menu (Tuscan tomato soup, grilled lamb cutlets and tiramisu) for f40 is good value.

Mexican *Rozen & Tortillas (Map 3; ☎ 620 65 25, Prinsengracht 126)* packs in students and locals with dishes like chicken quesadillas (f18.50) and beef fajitas (f28.50 for two). Order a caipirinha (f7.50) or two, and you'll salsa out into the night.

Seafood *Albatros (Map 3; ☎ 627 99 32, Westerstraat 264)* is a good fish restaurant with a somewhat camp decor and a smoke-free section. Main courses cost f32.50, three-course menus start at f53. The kitchen opens 6 to 11 pm (closed Wednesday).

Spanish It's not much to look at, but *Casa Juan (Map 2; ☎ 623 78 38, Lindengracht 59)* does fantastic Spanish food – some say the best in Amsterdam and they could well be right – at more than reasonable prices.

Paso Doble (Map 2; ☎ 421 26 70, Westerstraat 86) has a wonderful tiled interior and almost matches Casa Juan in the quality of its food.

Thai *Pathum Thai (Map 2; ☎ 624 49 36, Willemsstraat 16)* is busy and cheap, with mains around f24. *Rakang Thai (Map 3; ☎ 627 50 12, Elandsgracht 29)* is a hip restaurant with over-the-top decorations and delicious cooking. The menu includes mains for around f30.

Turkish *Avare (Map 2; ☎ 639 31 67, Lindengracht 248)* is a Turkish eetcafe with wonderfully kitsch interior trimmings found in old-fashioned Jordaan cafes. The food isn't bad either.

Turqoise (Map 3; ☎ 624 20 26, Wolvenstraat 22) is another Turkish eetcafe, less over-the-top than Avare but the food is good, the service is great and it's cheap.

Vegetarian *De Vliegende Schotel (Map 3; ☎ 625 20 41, Nieuwe Leliestraat 162)* in the Jordaan is a popular, homy little place with a blackboard menu. Meals are inexpensive (under f15) and are served daily from 5.30 to 10.15 pm.

De Bolhoed (Map 3; ☎ 626 18 03, Prinsengracht 60–62) is one of the most popular vegetarian restaurants in town. It serves organic food and amazing cakes in arty surroundings. It has a three-course *dagmenu* for f35. It opens noon to 10 pm.

Restaurants – Southern Canal Belt

Dutch *De Blauwe Hollander (Map 6; ☎ 623 30 14, Leidsekruisstraat 28)* is a cosy little place that serves the types of dishes you might get in a Dutch home, daily from 5 to 10 pm. All meals are under f30.

At *Hollands Glorie (Map 7; ☎ 624 47 64, Kerkstraat 220–222)*, off Vijzelstraat, the 'authentic' 17th-century interior puts you in the right mood for the well-prepared dishes (most main dishes under f36).

French For a satisfying splurge, try the *Zuidlande (Map 7; ☎ 620 73 93, Utrechtsedwarsstraat 141)*. The restaurant's cook, who trained under star chef Paul Bocuse, prepares a number of creative French and Mediterranean dishes with an excellent balance of flavours. Main dishes (generous servings) are under f40.

Indian One of the city's best is *Memories of India (Map 4; ☎ 623 57 10, Reguliersdwarsstraat 88)*. This restaurants clone from London has great vegetarian menus for f35, nonvegetarian for f39.50, and main dishes around f29.

Indonesian *Indonesia (Map 6; ☎ 623 20 35, Korte Leidsedwarsstraat 18)* is one of the few places that does a really good *rijsttafel*. Prices start at f39.50 for a 'small' version that'll fill most stomachs. Book ahead.

Nearby, *Bojo (Map 6; ☎ 622 74 34, Lange Leidsedwarsstraat 51)* is open 5 to 2 am weekdays (4 am on weekends) and is an institution with late eaters. The quality varies, but it's cheap for the Leidseplein area.

Tempo Doeloe (Map 7; ☎ 625 67 18, Utrechtsestraat 75) is regarded as a top-notch Indonesian restaurant (although the food can be quite variable). Unless you ask for mild the food will be served quite spicy, but in such a way as to enhance the subtle flavours, not kill them. Expect f50 to f70 per head, and reserve to avoid disappointment.

Tujuh Maret (Map 7; ☎ 427 98 65, Utrechtsestraat 73) next door is less up-market but just as good and more consistently so. Mains cost around f25 and the food can be quite spicy.

International *Dwars (Map 7; ☎ 620 66 90, Derde Weteringdwarsstraat 17)* proves that the Dutch can cook very well indeed. Eight tables are served from a one-chef open kitchen. A three-course menu costs f47.50, or f50 for the chef's surprise 'Carte Blanche'. It's closed Sunday.

Szmulewicz (pronounced smoolerwitch; Map 4; ☎ 620 28 22, Bakkersstraat 12) has a filling dish of the day for f19.50; other dishes are around f25. The food – a smattering of Mexican, American and European dishes – is really well priced. Live bands play on the terrace in summer.

Pygma-lion (Map 7; ☎ 420 70 22, Nieuwe Spiegelstraat 5A) is a South African bistro plating up all those animals you normally see in a game park. Expect antelope curry (f38.50), crocodile in sage sauce (f39.50) and sandwiches filled with oven-roasted zebra (f10.75).

Italian *Piccolino (Map 6; ☎ 623 14 95, Lange Leidsedwarsstraat 63)* is a busy Italian place in the touristy Leidseplein area. Try the pizza calzone (f16), and book ahead.

Panini (Map 7; ☎ 626 49 39, Vijzel-gracht 3–5) serves delicious focaccias for lunch and homemade pastas, eg, fettuccine with ricotta cheese and tomato sauce, in the evenings. Most mains are under f25.

Pastini (Map 3; ☎ 622 17 01, Leidsegracht 29) is a small romantic restaurant overlooking two canals. The antipasto starters (f19.50 for five dishes) are as substantial as the perfectly cooked pasta dishes (f17.50 to f22.50).

Pasta e Basta (Map 7; ☎ 422 22 26, Nieuwe Spiegelstraat 8) is a scream, with a camp rococo interior. Opera singers serenade you while you are served a variety of antipasto and pasta. Prices are reasonable (f60 for a three-course set menu). It opens 6 pm to midnight daily, but you'll have to book weeks ahead.

Japanese Sushi bars are popping up all over Amsterdam. *Bento (Map 6; ☎ 622 42 48, Kerkstraat 148)*, at Nieuwe Spiegelstraat, serves organic Japanese cuisine in a room decorated with rice-paper skylights and bamboo trees. For a treat, order the royal bento box (f65) filled with sushi, sashimi, grilled fish and more. It opens 6 to 10.30 pm (closed Monday).

Mexican *Rose's Cantina (Map 4; ☎ 625 97 97, Reguliersdwarsstraat 38)* was one of the first Mexican restaurants in town and is still going strong. Big main portions a la Dutch go for around f28, and litre pitchers of margarita for f56.50. You can't reserve but it's worth waiting for a table. Food is served 5.30 to 11 pm daily.

North American *Gary's Muffins (Map 4; ☎ 420 24 06, Reguliersdwarsstraat 53)* serves great fresh bagels, warm chocolate brownies and sweet and savoury muffins to all those clubbers. There are other branches at Marnixstraat 121, Prinsengracht 454, Jodenbreestraat 15 and in the basement of the American Book Center at Kalverstraat 185. It opens noon to 3 am daily and on weekends to 4 am.

Seafood *Sluizer (Map 7; ☎ 622 63 76, Utrechtsestraat 43–45)* consists of two restaurants: a renowned fish restaurant at No 45 and a 'meat' restaurant at No 43. It's an Amsterdam institution and always busy, so book ahead.

Le Pêcheur (Map 4; ☎ 624 31 21, Reguliersdwarsstraat 32) is renowned for its beautiful courtyard and fantastic fish. Try the mixed seafood platter at f39.50 and, if you're not too full, the tarte tatin with caramel ice cream. It opens noon to midnight Monday to Friday, Saturday from 5 pm. Bookings are advisable.

Spanish The stunning tiled facade at *Pata Negra (Map 7; ☎ 422 62 50, Utrechtsestraat 142)* is matched by equally beautiful ones inside. It attracts a young (and loud) crowd enjoying the array of fine tapas (from f5). Give the sangria a miss, though, unless you like wine mixed with Fanta. It opens 6 pm to midnight.

Restaurants – Nieuwmarkt Neighbourhood

Fusion *Zosa (Map 4; ☎ 330 62 41, Kloveniersburgwal 20)* is a sunny, ultra-mod restaurant serving a mix of French/Italian dishes with a definite Asian influence. Starters such as Vietnamese rice-paper rolls (f12.50) and desserts like stuffed flambeed figs (f12.50) are particularly good.

International If cheese fondue is your thing, try *Café Bern (Map 4; ☎ 622 00 34, Nieuwmarkt 9)*; book ahead. Also in this area is *Hemelse Modder (Map 4; ☎ 624 32 03, Oude Waal 9)*, a popular, beautifully decorated, modern restaurant whose speciality is chocolate mousse ('heavenly mud', hence the name of the place). Most mains are under f30 and the three-course set menu costs f47.50.

Restaurants – De Pijp

This somewhat bohemian part of town sees relatively few tourists in its often busy eateries. You'll mingle with the locals.

Assyrian *Eufraat (Map 7; ☎ 672 05 79, Eerste van der Helststraat 72)* serves Middle Eastern food, but the speciality, as the name implies, is Assyrian. The service is friendly and the food excellent and good value, with mains around f23, three courses for under f35.

Surinamese Surinamese restaurants are small and specialise in takeaway food. They close early and some only open for lunch. Stroll around the backstreets near the Albert Cuypmarkt (Map 7), or try *Albert Cuyp 67 (Map 7; ☎ 671 13 96, Albert Cuypstraat 67)* or *Albina (Map 7; ☎ 675 51 35)* next door at No 69.

Vegetarian *Harvest (Map 7; ☎ 676 99 95, Govert Flinckstraat 251)* is fully vegetarian and purchases the ingredients at the nearby Albert Cuypmarkt. *Dagschotels* are under f22, and there's a terrace out the back and even a nonsmoking section. It opens Monday to Saturday 5.30 to 11.30 pm (kitchen closes at 9.30 pm).

Self-Service Cafeterias
The *Hema department store (Map 4; ☎ 623 41 76, Nieuwendijk 174)* has a good, inexpensive cafeteria upstairs, open 11 am to 5.15 pm Monday to Friday (8.15 pm Thursday), to 4.45 pm Saturday, and noon to 4.15 pm Sunday. It's also good for coffee and ice cream. Other department stores *(Vroom & Dreesmann, Bijenkorf)* also have decent cafeterias.

The *Atrium (Map 4; ☎ 525 39 99)* is a student cafeteria in the Binnengasthuis university complex. The quality is middling, but where else can you eat for well under f10? It opens noon to 2 pm and 5 to 7 pm weekdays.

Fast Food
Amsterdam has scores of places where you can grab a quick sandwich, burger or pizza slice. The areas around Leidseplein and Rembrandtplein are a sight for sore eyes when you're starving.

One of the best *frites* places is the *Vlaamse Friteshuis (Map 4; Voetboogstraat 31)* off Spui Square. It opens 11 am to 6 pm Monday to Saturday, from noon to 5.30 pm Sunday.

MAOZ Falafel (Map 4; Muntplein 1) does its flagship sandwich for f6, crispy

and hot, with endless toppings from the self-service salad bar. The half-dozen branches around town include one at Leidsestraat 85.

If you'd prefer something sweeter (and typically Dutch), the *poffertjes* (minipancakes) at the *Carrousel* (Map 7) on Weteringcircuit are a real treat.

Self-Catering
Albert Heijn, the country's dominant supermarket chain, has branches throughout the city, including:

Nieuwezijds Voorburgwal 226 (Map 4), with great stand-up or takeaway meals
Koningsplein 6 (Map 3)
Museumplein (Map 6).

Other locations are marked on the maps. They're expensive, but well stocked and open long hours, including weekends.

Other food shops include:

Hema (Map 4; ☎ 623 41 76, Nieuwendijk 174) – good food section at the back of this department store
Dirk van den Broek (Map 7; ☎ 673 93 93, Eerste van der Helststraat 25), behind the Heineken Museum – one of the country's least expensive supermarket chains
Aldi Supermarket (Map 7; Nieuwe Weteringstraat 28), near Vijzelgracht – cheaper still, but quite depressing

ENTERTAINMENT
Amsterdam is many things to many people, but no-one in their right mind would call it boring. It's one of the entertainment capitals of Europe, with wonderful pubs; music, theatre and film programs to suit all tastes; and frantic nightlife that arouses even the most jaded party animals.

Listings
The free *Uitkrant* is the definitive publication for art and entertainment. It's in Dutch, but you can usually decipher enough information to go on. Pick up a copy at the Amsterdam Uitburo or anywhere with free publications, such as Centraal Station, bookshops or newsagents.

The VVV's English-language *What's On in Amsterdam* is published monthly and costs f4.50. It has entertainment schedules and an address listing but is less comprehensive than the *Uitkrant*. It's sold by the VVV, large book and magazine shops and many hotels.

Cafes

There are many varied types of cafes in Amsterdam – and throughout the Netherlands – and much can be learned about local culture in an hour at a brown cafe or a tasting house. For a detailed explanation of the different types of Dutch cafes see the boxed text 'Cafe Society' in the Facts for the Visitor chapter.

Brown Cafes

The medieval centre teems with brown cafes, including:

Hoppe (Map 3; ☎ 420 44 20, Spui 18) – visit one of the best known cafes in the city, on Spui Square. It has been enticing drinkers behind its thick curtain for more than 300 years, and its beer sales are among the highest in the city.

Lokaal 't Loosje (Map 4; ☎ 627 26 35, Nieuwmarkt 32–34) – one of the oldest and prettiest in the Nieuwmarkt area, this cafe has beautiful etched-glass windows and tile tableaus on the walls.

Pilsener Club (Map 4; ☎ 623 17 77, Begijnesteeg 4) – also known as Engelse Reet, this is a narrow, ramshackle place from 1893 and one of a number of brown cafes worth seeking out around Spui Square. Beer comes straight from the vat behind the draughting alcove and connoisseurs say they can taste the difference.

De Schutter (Map 4; ☎ 622 46 08, Voetboogstraat 13–15) – a student eetcafe open daily from 11 am (with food from 5.45 to 10 pm). Dagschotels start at f15 and mains go up to f17.50.

The Jordaan area is also packed with wonderful cafes, including:

Café Nol (Map 3; ☎ 624 53 80, Westerstraat 109) – the epitome of the Jordaan cafe, a place where the original Jordanese still sing oompah ballads with drunken abandon. The kitsch interior is a must-see.

Café 't Smalle (Map 3; ☎ 623 96 17, Egelantiersgracht 12) – this charming cafe was opened in 1786 as a genever distillery and tasting house. The interior has been restored with antique porcelain beer pumps and leadlight windows.

Eylders (Map 6; ☎ 624 27 04, Korte Leidsedwarsstraat 47) – an artists' cafe with exhibits and attractive leadlights. During WWII it was a meeting place for artists who refused to toe the cultural line imposed by the Nazis.

Het Papeneiland (Map 2; ☎ 624 19 89, Prinsengracht 2) – a 17th-century gem with Delft-blue tiles. The name, Papists' Island, goes back to the Reformation, when a clandestine Catholic church across the canal was supposedly linked by a tunnel from here.

De Pieper (Map 3; ☎ 626 47 75, Prinsengracht 424) – unassuming but unmistakably old (from 1664), and is considered by some to be the king of the brown cafes.

Van Puffelen (Map 3; ☎ 624 62 70, Prinsengracht 377) – farther north on Prinsengracht, this cafe-restaurant is popular among students and intellectuals. It opens from 3 pm weekdays, noon at weekends; the kitchen opens at 6 pm.

De 2 Zwaantjes (Map 3; ☎ 625 27 29, Prinsengracht 114) – an authentic Jordaan cafe and refuge of card-playing locals. Weekends are raucous, with sing-along Dutch ballads. Note the imposing leadlight awning over the bar.

Grand Cafes

Café Americain (Map 6; ☎ 556 32 32, Leidsekade 97) – the most stylish grand cafe is in the American Hotel just off Leidseplein. This Art-Deco monument attracts rafts of celebrities, and prices are stiff.

Café Dante (Map 3; ☎ 638 88 39, Spuistraat 320) – this is a large, Art-Deco-style space with an art gallery upstairs. Peaceful during the day, in the evening it turns into a boisterous bar for suits.

Café de Jaren (Map 4; ☎ 625 57 71, Nieuwe Doelenstraat 20) – a huge, bright place overlooking the Amstel from its sun deck. People here are in their 20s and 30s, slightly yuppyish. The great reading table has foreign publications.

Café de Vergulde Gapper (Map 3; ☎ 624 89 75, Prinsenstraat 30) – a former pharmacy decorated with old chemists' bottles and vintage posters. The terrace fills with media types in the late afternoons.

Luxembourg (Map 3; ☎ 620 62 64, Spui 22–24) – on Spui Square, this cafe is indeed a grand place, with tasty breakfasts, great sandwiches and lunch-time surprises. Pick up a paper and read it in the morning sun.

Mediacafé De Kroon (Map 4; ☎ 625 20 11, Rembrandtplein 17–1) – the pearl of the grand cafes, this neocolonial gem overlooks Rembrandtplein from a covered terrace. The restaurant food (mains around f38) is good.

Tasting Houses

De Drie Fleschjes (Map 4; ☎ 624 84 43, Gravenstraat 18) – behind the Nieuwekerk, this place dates from 1650, with old vats rented out to groups for members to help themselves. It opens noon to 8.30 pm Monday to Saturday, and 3 to 7 pm Sunday.

Proeflokaal Wijnand Fockinck (Map 4; ☎ 639 26 95, Pijlsteeg 31) – by Dam Square, this is a small tasting house serving scores of genevers and liqueurs. Its pretty courtyard serves lunch and snacks 10 am to 6 pm.

Other Cafes

Bar Bep (Map 4; ☎ 626 56 49, Nieuwezijds Voorburgwal 260) – one of Nieuwezijds Voorburgwal's 'see and be seen' bars, this looks like a 1950s Eastern European cabaret lounge.

Café De IJsbreker (Map 7; ☎ 665 30 14, Weesperzijde 23) – south-east of the canal belt, this pleasant cafe on the Amstel belongs to the IJsbreker centre for contemporary music and has a great riverside terrace. In 2002 the centre moves to the Eastern Docklands. Service can be slow.

Café Schiller (Map 4; ☎ 624 98 46, Rembrandtplein 26) – not to be confused with the hotel – has a stylish, Art-Deco interior with portraits of Dutch actors and cabaret artists. It does good dagschotels from f20. Hours are 4 pm to 1 am Sunday to Thursday, and Friday and Saturday till 2 am.

Diep (Map 4; ☎ 420 20 20, Nieuwezijds Voorburgwal 256) – next door to Bar Bep, with changing decorations – everything from bubble-wrap chandeliers to a fibreglass hammerhead shark.

Gollem (Map 3; ☎ 626 66 45, Raamsteeg 4), north of Spui Square, this is the pioneer of Amsterdam 'beer cafes'. Choose from 200 beers on tap or bottled. Its small interior swims in beer paraphernalia (coasters, bottles and posters).

Maximiliaan (Map 4; ☎ 626 62 80, Kloveniersburgwal 6–8) – off Nieuwmarkt Square, this is a rambling brew-pub with copper kettles. It has a restaurant, tasting area, tours and beer seminars, and home-brewed beers on tap.

De Waag (Map 4; ☎ 422 77 72, Nieuwmarkt 4) – housed in the former 15th-century weigh house. Hundreds of candles hang from wrought-iron candelabras. You can surf the Web here free with a drink, but give the restaurant food a miss. It opens 10 am to 1 am daily.

Coffeeshops

Listed here are some popular coffeeshops and a few quirky ones, too. Price and quality are reasonable – you won't get ripped off like you would on the street. Most shops open 10 am to 1 am Sunday to Thursday, and to 3 am Friday and Saturday.

Barney's (Map 2; ☎ 625 97 61, Haarlemmerstraat 102) – a mixture of trippy New-Age art and Lord of the Rings-inspired furniture

The Bulldog (Map 6; ☎ 627 19 08, Leidseplein 13–17) – this famous coffeeshop chain has five branches around town; this is the largest, with Internet facilities, two bars, pool tables and a cafe serving food.

Greenhouse (Map 4; ☎ 627 17 39, Oudezijds Voorburgwal 191) – the recipient of many awards at the annual High Times festival, this Indonesian-inspired coffeeshop has undersea-themed bathrooms and high-quality weed and hash.

Grey Area (Map 3; ☎ 420 43 01, Oude Leliestraat 2) – owned by a couple of laid-back American guys, this tiny shop introduced the extra-sticky, flavourful 'Double Bubble Gum' weed to the city.

Homegrown Fantasy (Map 4; ☎ 627 56 83, Nieuwezijds Voorburgwal 87A) – quality Dutch-grown product, pleasant staff and good tunes; see the toilets for a visual treat.

Cinemas

Amsterdam's 14 cinemas always have a good choice, including 'art' movies for the discerning viewer. Film listings are pinned up at cinemas and in many pubs, or you can check the paper on Thursdays. *AL* means *alle leeftijden* (all ages); 12 or 16 are the restrictions. The mainstream Hollywood cinemas around Leidseplein have half-price matinee tickets for their first screening weekdays.

The following cinemas have the most atmosphere:

Kriterion (Map 7; ☎ 623 17 09, Roetersstraat 170) – an Amsterdam School/Art-Deco building showing cult movies, with occasional sneak previews

The Movies (Map 2; ☎ 638 60 16, Haarlemmerdijk 161) – another Art-Deco gem, a real classic with a restaurant

Nederlands Filmmuseum (Map 6; ☎ 589 14 00, Vondelpark 3) – shows films daily and has live jazz in the cafe Sunday afternoon

Tuschinskitheater (Map 4; ☎ 626 26 33, Reguliersbreestraat 26) – probably the country's most beautiful cinema, with a sumptuous Art-Deco interior

De Uitkijk (Map 6; ☎ 623 74 60, Prinsengracht 452) – the city's oldest surviving cinema, a cosy affair in an old canal house

Music

Classical & Contemporary

A number of venues offer free lunch-time concerts from 12.30 to 1.30 am (except June to August). The Muziektheater (Stopera) holds free concerts of 20th-century music Tuesday; on Wednesday the Concertgebouw has chamber music or classical concerts, sometimes also jazz; and on Friday the Bethaniënklooster puts on anything from medieval to contemporary.

Bethaniënklooster (Map 4; ☎ 625 00 78, Barndesteeg 6B) – small former monastery near Nieuwmarkt Square; ticket office open 30 minutes before performances

Beurs van Berlage (Map 4; ☎ 627 04 66, Damrak 243) – two small concert halls housed in the former commodities exchange; ticket office open 2 to 5 pm Tuesday to Friday and 1¼ hours before performances

Churches – check the Amsterdam Uitburo for performances (not just organ recitals) in the Oudekerk, Nieuwekerk, Engelsekerk and others

Concertgebouw (Map 6; ☎ 671 83 45, recording in Dutch, Concertgebouwplein 4–6) – world-famous concert hall with near-perfect acoustics; ticket office open 10 am to 7 pm (telephone only to 5 pm); after 7 pm tickets only for that evening's performance

Koninklijk Theater Carré (Map 7; ☎ 622 52 25, Amstel 115–125) – opera, operetta, ballet, musicals, cabaret; ticket office open 10 am to 7 pm (Sunday from 1 pm)

Muziekcentrum De IJsbreker (Map 7; ☎ 693 90 93, Weesperzijde 23) – centre for contemporary music; ticket office open 9.30 am to 5.30 pm, and from 7.45 pm on event nights; will move to the Eastern Docklands in 2002

Muziektheater (Map 4; ☎ 625 54 55, Waterlooplein 22) – large-scale ballet and opera in the Stopera; ticket office open Monday to Saturday 10 am to 6 pm, Sunday and public holidays from 11.30 am

Stadsschouwburg (Map 6; ☎ 624 23 11, Leidseplein 26) – opera and operetta; ticket office

open Monday to Saturday from 10 am to start of performances

Jazz, Blues & Latin American Jazz is popular and there's a lot happening in cafes around town; blues thrives less. The world's largest jazz festival is the North Sea Jazz Festival in Den Haag in July (see Special Events in the Facts for the Visitor chapter).

Jazz Café Alto (Map 6; ☎ 626 32 49, Korte Leidsedwarsstraat 115) – live jazz and blues at this small brown cafe; music 10 pm to 3 am Sunday to Thursday and to 4am Friday and Saturday; catch tenor saxophonist Hans Dulfer on Wednesday night

Bimhuis (Map 4; ☎ 623 33 73, Oude Schans 73–77) – Amsterdam's main jazz venue for over 25 years; excellent auditorium and pretty spiffy bar; open 8 pm Thursday to Saturday, concerts start at 9 pm, closed July and August; planning to move to the Eastern Docklands in 2002

Bourbon Street Jazz & Blues Club (Map 6; ☎ 623 34 40, Leidsekruisstraat 6–8) – blues, funk and rock & roll; open 10 pm to 4 am weekdays, to 5 am weekends

Canecão (Map 6; ☎ 626 15 00, Lange Leidsedwarsstraat 70) – samba and salsa to live Brazilian music; open 10 pm to 4 am Sunday to Thursday, to 5 am Friday and Saturday

Heeren van Aemstel (Map 4; ☎ 620 21 73, Thorbeckeplein 5 off Rembrandtplein) – open 3 pm daily; office workers and students; live pop and jazz begins around 10 pm; grand cafe interior and eetcafe

Maloe Melo (Map 3; ☎ 420 45 92, Lijnbaansgracht 163) – this small, smoky venue is home to the city's blues scene; pub opens at 9 pm, the hall at 10.30 pm, and live music begins at 11 pm

Modern Information and tickets for pop, dance and rock events are available at the Amsterdam Uitburo or at the venues direct. For large concerts you can also ring the Ticketlijn on ☎ 0900-300 12 50. Top venues include:

ArenA Stadium (☎ 311 13 33 for information) – in the Bijlmer, the ultimate stadium venue (seats 52,000) for the top crowd-pullers

De Koe (Map 3; ☎ 625 44 82, Marnixstraat 381) – *the* place in the Amsterdam pop scene, with regular performances 4 pm Sunday (free admission)

Korsakoff (Map 3; ☎ 625 78 54, Lijnbaansgracht 161) – open 10 pm to 4 am daily; hard rock and alternative music venue for a young crowd; bouncers could be picky

Melkweg *(Milky Way; Map 6; ☎ 624 17 77, Lijnbaansgracht 234)* – membership f5 a month, extra admission depending on what's on; cinema, art gallery, cafe, multimedia entertainment; live music almost every night

Paradiso *(Map 6; ☎ 626 45 21, Weteringschans 6)*, off Leidseplein – membership f5 a month, extra admission for live music, housed in a former church; open between 8 and 10 pm when there's a concert, 11.30 pm when it's a club; big-name groups have been appearing here since the 1960s

Theatre

There are about 50 theatres – the ones listed below are merely a selection. Performances are often in Dutch, sometimes in English (especially in summer) and sometimes it doesn't matter.

Boom Chicago *(Map 3; ☎ 423 01 01, Korte Leidsedwarsstraat 12)* – English-language standup and improv comedy throughout the year; foyer cafe

De Balie *(Map 6; ☎ 623 29 04, Kleine Gartmanplantsoen 10)* – productions focusing on multicultural and political issues for intellectuals; new media facilities and a stylish bar

Felix Meritis *(Map 3; ☎ 623 13 11, Keizersgracht 324)* – the former cultural centre of the city, now with experimental theatre, music and dance; lots of co-productions between Eastern and Western European artists

Koninklijk Theater Carré *(Map 7; ☎ 622 52 25, Amstel 115–125)* – the largest theatre in town (1700 seats), with mainstream international shows, musicals, cabaret, circuses etc; backstage tours 3 pm Saturday and Wednesday

Melkweg *(Map 6; ☎ 624 17 77, Lijnbaansgracht 234A)* – world-renowned cultural centre, with anything from music and film to plays, dance and multimedia productions

Stadsschouwburg *(Map 6; ☎ 624 23 11, Leidseplein 26)* – the city's most beautiful theatre (1894); large-scale productions, operettas, English-language productions in summer

Vondelpark Theatre *(☎ 673 14 99, Vondelpark)* – large (1800-seat) open-air amphitheatre in the middle of the Vondelpark, with a wide range of performing arts in June, July and August

Clubs

Not much happens before 10 pm and some places don't open till well after midnight.

Many clubs are *alleen voor leden* (only for members), but you can 'join' at the door if the bouncer likes the look of you. Dress standards are generally casual, and admission varies from f5 to f45. The venues listed below close at 4 or 5 am.

Some popular clubs include:

Arena *(Map 7; ☎ 694 74 44, 's-Gravesandestraat 51)* – club parties at Hotel Arena; two floors of tunes (everything from rock, house and techno); Thursday to Saturday 10 pm to 5 am

Dansen bij Jansen *(Map 4; ☎ 620 17 79, Handboogstraat 11)* – popular student club that's been going for 25 years; it's often too busy to dance

Escape *(Map 4; ☎ 622 11 11, Rembrandtplein 11)* – this commercial club is the largest in Amsterdam with a capacity of 2000; Saturday's house/techno night is wildly popular; expect a dressed-up crowd, laser shows and heavy security; open 10 pm to 4am Thursday to Saturday

iT *(Map 4; ☎ 625 01 11, Amstelstraat 24)* – Thursday to Sunday from 11 pm (Saturday gays

---

Roxy Burns

The lyrics *Burn baby burn, disco inferno* must have come to mind as over 4000 people watched in shock as Amsterdam's most famous nightclub, the Roxy – originally a cinema near the Muntplein at the end of Kalverstraat – burnt down one sunny July afternoon in 1999.

Fireworks were let off in the club during a party held after the funeral of the Roxy's designer and co-founder, Peter Giele, whose body had been sailed down the Amstel to its resting place accompanied by flame-cannons. The flamboyant Giele had been quite entranced by the theme of fire, being one of the first promoters to introduce fireworks shows *inside* a club (quite legal, apparently). Sparks entered the ventilation system and within minutes the club was ablaze. All that remained were the walls and the facade.

Nightclubbers and industry insiders always knew that Peter Giele and the Roxy were inextricably linked, but no-one could have predicted that the demise of one would be so connected with the destruction of the other.

---

only); originally a gay club, this huge venue draws a flamboyant crowd of glam club kids, professional dancers and drag queens

Melkweg (Milky Way; Map 6; ☎ 624 17 77, Lijnbaansgracht 234) – regular club nights (Thursday and Saturday) and one-off parties at this multimedia centre

Odeon (Map 3; ☎ 624 97 11, recording in Dutch, Singel 460) – open nightly at 11 pm; 'three floors of dancing' with house, hip-hop and a jazz cellar

Paradiso (Map 6; ☎ 626 45 21, Weteringschans 6) – operates as a club from Friday to Sunday; expect future funk, big-beat, hip-hop and classic house; open 11.30 pm to late

Sinners in Heaven (Map 4; ☎ 620 13 75, Wagenstraat 3–7) – frequented by well-dressed thirtysomethings; decorated to resemble a castle/dungeon; open 11 pm to 4 am Thursday, to 5 am Friday and Saturday

Soul Kitchen (Map 4; ☎ 620 23 33, Amstelstraat 32) – retro soul and funk music for 'elderly youngsters' (minimum entry age 25) who love the club's African-inspired interior; Thursday to Sunday from 11 pm

Trance Buddha (Map 4; ☎ 422 82 33, Oudezijds Voorburgwal 216) – Amsterdam's trance temple, open 11 pm to 4 am (5 am Friday and Saturday)

Gay & Lesbian Venues

Amsterdam's gay scene is the biggest in Europe, with close to 100 gay and lesbian bars, cafes, clubs, shops and hotels. Apart from the commercial venues listed below there's an active alternative circuit. Ask around or contact the Gay & Lesbian Switchboard to find out about the latest 'in' places.

Many popular gay places are along Reguliersdwarsstraat, while Rembrandtplein is real queen territory. Kinky Amsterdam congregates over on Warmoesstraat in the redlight district. Popular establishments include:

Exit (Map 4; ☎ 625 87 88, Reguliersdwarsstraat 42) – multistorey nightclub playing underground house with a selection of bars and dance floors

Havana (Map 4; ☎ 620 67 88, Reguliersdwarsstraat 17) – camp Art-Deco bar with gorgeous staff (some are drag queens) and thumping club music

iT (Map 4; ☎ 625 01 11, Amstelstraat 24) – one of the most extravagant clubs in town; features weekly gay nights

Monopole (Map 4; ☎ 624 64 51, Amstel 60) – a mixed gay crowd shakes their groove thing to old-school disco classics at this kitschly decorated brown cafe

Montmartre (Map 4; ☎ 620 76 22, Halve Maansteeg 17) – quite an experience: bar staff and patrons belt out Dutch ballads and pop songs (think Abba); it's kind of like a camp Eurovision song contest

Soho (Map 4; ☎ 626 15 73, Reguliersdwarsstraat 36) – currently 'the' in bar; decorated like an old English library; attracts young, friendly guys who enjoy drinking and flirting

Vivelavie (Map 4; ☎ 624 01 14, Amstelstraat 7) – a popular 'lipstick lesbian' cafe, with loud music and large windows so everyone can see out or in

SPECTATOR SPORTS

Few spectator sporting events are worth seeking out apart from soccer, field hockey and the country's own unique sport, korfball. For general information on sporting events, ring the Amsterdam Sport Service on ☎ 552 24 90.

Soccer

Local club Ajax is usually at or near the top of the European league. Ajax plays in the new Amsterdam ArenA stadium (off Map 1; ☎ 311 13 33; metro: Bijlmer), office address: Haaksbergweg 59, which seats 52,000 spectators and has an Ajax museum with cups and other paraphernalia. This massive, expensive, high-tech complex has a retractable roof built over a highway. Matches usually take place Saturday evening and Sunday afternoon during season, which lasts from early September to early June.

Hockey

Unlike soccer, Dutch hockey is still a rather elitist sport played by either sex on expensive club fields. The hockey season is more or less the same as for soccer. For general and match information, contact Hockey Club Hurley (☎ 619 02 33), Nieuwe Kalfjeslaan 21 in the Amsterdamse Bos, which holds mixed training and also games on Monday and Tuesday evening from 9 pm (children also play on Wednesday afternoon and Saturday morning).

Korfball

Korfball, a cross between netball, volleyball and basketball, has a vivid local club scene. For information, contact the Amsterdam Sport Council (☎ 552 24 90) or try SVK Groen-Wit (☎ 646 15 15), Kinderdijkstraat 29.

SHOPPING

With a few exceptions – dope, pornography, flower bulbs, cheese, obscure *genever* (Dutch gin) – there's little in Amsterdam that you won't find elsewhere. Where Amsterdam shines is in its speciality shops and markets.

The most popular shopping streets are lowbrow Nieuwendijk and slightly less lowbrow Kalverstraat, with department stores, clothing boutiques and speciality shops. Pretentious shoppers head for the boutiques along PC Hooftstraat; antique and art buffs check Nieuwe Spiegelstraat and Spiegelgracht. The Jordaan neighbourhood is awash with quirky shops and galleries.

Art & Antiques

Amsterdam teems with art galleries, from the tiniest shops to huge, museum-like complexes. Most of the city's best antique stores are found in or around Nieuwe Spiegelstraat. A sample includes:

Arti et Amicitiae (Map 4; ☎ 626 08 39) Rokin 112 – well-established artists' club displaying contemporary art

Decorativa (Map 7; ☎ 420 50 66) Nieuwe Spiegelstraat 7 – a massive jumble of European antiques, collectibles and weird vintage gifts

Eduard Kramer (Map 6; ☎ 623 08 32) Nieuwe Spiegelstraat 64 – specialising in antique Dutch wall and floor tiles and crammed to bursting with vintage homewares

EH Ariëns Kappers (Map 6; ☎ 623 53 56) Nieuwe Spiegelstraat 32 – prints, etchings, engravings, lithographs and maps from the 17th to 19th centuries

Jaski (Map 6; ☎ 620 39 39) Nieuwe Spiegelstraat 27–29 – paintings, prints, ceramics and sculptures by members of the CoBrA movement

Lieve Hemel (Map 4; ☎ 623 00 60) Nieuwe Spiegelstraat 3 – contemporary Dutch realist painting and sculpture

Prestige Art Gallery (Map 4; ☎ 624 01 04) Reguliersbreestraat 46 near Rembrandtplein – specialist in 17th to 20th-century oil paintings and bronze

Reflex Modern Art Gallery (Map 6; ☎ 627 28 32) Weteringschans 79A opposite the Rijksmuseum – prominent gallery with contemporary art, aimed at tourists

Books

Amsterdam is a major European printing centre. Unfortunately books are expensive whether they're imported or locally produced, especially English-language titles. But bibliophiles will delight in the large number of bookshops, both new and antiquarian. For English-language, gay and lesbian, and travel titles, see Bookshops under Information earlier in this chapter; book markets are covered in the following Markets section.

Antiquariaat Kok (Map 4; ☎ 623 11 91) Oude Hoogstraat 14–18 – wide range of antiquarian stock (literature, coffee-table books, old prints etc)

Athenaeum Bookshop & Newsagency (Map 3; ☎ 622 62 48) Spui 14–16 – vast assortment of unusual books for browsers; the separate newsagency has the city's largest choice of international newspapers and magazines

The Book Exchange (Map 4; ☎ 626 62 66) Kloveniersburgwal 58 – is a rabbit warren of second-hand books

Lambiek (Map 6; ☎ 626 75 43) Kerkstraat 78 – for serious collectors of comic books

Scheltema Holkema Vermeulen (Map 3; ☎ 523 14 11) Koningsplein 20 – the largest bookshop in town, a true department store with many foreign titles, New-Age and multimedia sections

De Slegte (Map 4; ☎ 622 59 33) Kalverstraat 48 – specialist in second-hand or remaindered titles; dirt-cheap books on the ground floor and some gems upstairs

Clothing

Amsterdam is not the place to buy extravagant designer clothes. The Calvinist ethos frowns on conspicuous consumption and demands value for money, so clothing tends to be low-key and reasonably priced.

Analik (Map 3; ☎ 422 05 61) Hartenstraat 36 – feminine, modern pieces for smart young things from Analik, Amsterdam's pre-eminent young designer

Cora Kemperman (Map 3; ☎ 625 12 84) Leidsestraat 72 – floaty, layered separates and dresses in raw silk, cotton and wool

Fun Fashion (Map 4; ☎ 420 50 96) Nieuwendijk 200 – street, surf and skate wear for guys; Carhartt, Stussy, Oakley and Birkenstock

Lady Day (Map 3; ☎ 623 58 20) Hartenstraat 9 – premier location for spotless vintage clothes from Holland and around the world

Mango (Map 4; ☎ 427 27 60) Kalvertoren shopping centre, Singel 457 – the latest street wear, club gear and office separates at reasonable prices

Van Ravenstein (Map 3; ☎ 639 00 67) Keizersgracht 359 – sleek men and women shop here for upmarket Belgian designers (Dries Van Noten, Ann Demeulemeester and Dirk Bikkembergs)

Shoebaloo (Map 4; ☎ 626 79 93) Koningsplein 7 – chic shoes, imports like Patrick Cox, Miu Miu and Prada Sport, and the less expensive house label

Department Stores

With the possible exception of Metz & Co and sections of the Bijenkorf, the department stores stick to safe, mainstream products.

Bijenkorf (Map 4; ☎ 621 80 80) Dam 1 – the city's most fashionable department store; well-chosen clothing, toys, household accessories and books

Hema (Map 4; ☎ 638 99 63) Nieuwendijk 174 among other locations – low prices, reliable quality and a wide range of products including wines and delicatessen goods

Kalvertoren (Map 4) Singel 457 – popular, modern shopping centre containing a small Hema, Vroom & Dreesmann and some mainstream fashion stores

Magna Plaza (Map 4; ☎ 626 91 99) Nieuwezijds Voorburgwal 182 – grand 19th-century building housing over 40 upmarket fashion, gift and jewellery stores

Maison de Bonneterie (Map 4; ☎ 531 34 00) Rokin 140 – exclusive and classic clothes for the whole family; men are catered to with labels like Ralph Lauren, Tommy Hilfiger and Armani

Metz & Co (Map 3; ☎ 520 70 36) Keizersgracht 455 at Leidsestraat – luxury furnishings and homewares, upmarket designer clothes and gifts

Vroom & Dreesmann (Map 4; ☎ 622 01 71) Kalverstraat 201 – large national chain with a wide range of products, slightly more upmarket than Hema; popular for clothing and cosmetics

Diamonds

Amsterdam has been a major diamond centre since the 1580s. There are about a dozen diamond factories in the city today, five of which offer guided tours – the Gassan tour is probably the best. Tours are free and usually conducted seven days a week from 9 am to 5 pm, but ring ahead for details. Diamonds aren't really cheaper in Amsterdam than elsewhere, but prices are fairly competitive.

Amsterdam Diamond Center (Map 4; ☎ 624 57 87) Rokin 1

Coster Diamonds (Map 6; ☎ 676 22 22) Paulus Potterstraat 2–6

Gassan Diamonds (Map 5; ☎ 622 53 33) Nieuwe Uilenburgerstraat 173–175

Stoeltie Diamonds (Map 4; ☎ 623 76 01) Wagenstraat 13–17

Van Moppes & Zoon (Map 6; ☎ 676 12 42) Albert Cuypstraat 2–6

Markets

No visit to Amsterdam is complete if you haven't experienced its lively markets.

Albert Cuypmarkt (Map 7) Albert Cuypstraat – general market with food, clothing, hardware etc, often very cheap; wide ethnic mix; daily except Sunday

Antiques market (Map 2) Noordermarkt in the Jordaan – antiques, fabrics, and second-hand bric-a-brac; Monday morning

Antiques market (Map 4) Nieuwmarkt Square – many genuine articles; Sunday from April to October

Antiques market (Map 3) Elandsgracht 109, in the Jordaan – indoor stalls in De Looier complex; daily except Friday

Art markets on Thorbeckeplein and Spui Square (Map 4) – quality art, mostly modern pictorial, but modest in scope; 10.30 am to 6 pm Sunday from March to October

Bloemenmarkt (Map 4) along Singel near Muntplein – floating Flower Market, colourful in the extreme; daily except Sunday

Boerenmarkt (Farmers Market) on Noordermarkt (Map 2) in the Jordaan and on Nieuwmarkt Square (Map 4) – home-grown produce, organic foods and herbs; Saturday only

Book market (Map 4) Oudemanhuispoort (the old arcade between Oudezijds Achterburgwal and Kloveniersburgwal); obscure in the extreme; weekdays

Book market (Map 4) Spui Square – this venerable market isn't cheap but has a good selection; Friday only

Waterlooplein flea market (Map 4) Waterlooplein – curios, second-hand clothing, music, electronic stuff, erotica, hardware etc; daily except Sunday

Smart Drugs

Smart-drug shops sell legal, organic hallucinogens like magic mushrooms, herbal joints, seeds (opium, marijuana, psychoactive), mood enhancers and aphrodisiacs. Note that these products are probably illegal to bring back home.

Botanic Herbalist (Map 1; ☎ 470 88 89) Cornelius Troostraat 37 – highly recommended for psychoactive plants and huge range of hemp products

Chills & Thrills (Map 2; ☎ 638 00 15) Nieuwendijk 17 – the most commercial smart shop in the city, selling herbal trips, mushrooms, psychoactive cacti, novelty bongs and more; open daily 11 am to 9 pm

Conscious Dreams (Map 6; ☎ 626 69 07) Kerkstraat 117 – Amsterdam's original smart shop still sells magic mushrooms and other natural products that enhance whatever might need enhancing

The Magic Mushroom Gallery (Map 4; ☎ 427 57 65) Spuistraat 249 – magic mushrooms as well as mushroom-growing kits and herbal aphrodisiacs; open 11 am to 10 pm Sunday to Thursday, from 10 am Friday and Saturday

Traditional Souvenirs

Need a traditional reminder of your visit to Amsterdam? Best pick up a pair of clogs, some tulip bulbs or a Delft vase.

Bloemenmarkt along Singel near Muntplein – floating flower market; the traders should be able to tell you if the flower bulbs you wish to purchase can be taken back home

Galleria d'Arte Rinascimento (Map 3; ☎ 622 75 09) Prinsengracht 170 – Royal Delftware, all manner of vases, platters, brooches and Christmas ornaments; 19th-century wall tiles and plaques as well

Heinen (Map 6; ☎ 627 82 99) Prinsengracht 440 – four floors of Delftware; all budgets are catered for (eg, f9 for a spoon to f5000 on an antique vase)

De Klompenboer (Map 4; ☎ 623 06 32) Sint Antoniesbreestraat 51 – clogs painted by the mum of the eccentric owner; open daily 10 am to 6 pm

Speciality Shops

At a loss for souvenirs or gifts? Try some of the following:

Art Unlimited (Map 3; ☎ 624 84 19) Keizersgracht 510 – thousands of well-catalogued postcards on unexpected subjects; beautiful art posters

Beaufort (Map 4; ☎ 625 91 31) Grimburgwal 11 – hand-crafted jewellery; the necklaces and rings are particularly alluring

Condomerie Het Gulden Vlies (Map 4; ☎ 627 41 74) Warmoesstraat 141 – hundreds of kooky condoms; well situated for its trade

Hajenius (Map 4; ☎ 623 74 94) Rokin 92 – renowned for tobacco products and paraphernalia, including leaf cigars (house brand) and clay pipes

Kitsch Kitchen (Map 3; ☎ 428 49 69) Bloemdwarsstraat 21 – everything you need make your home a colourful temple of kitsch; start with the tacky Mexican tablecloths or pink plastic chandeliers

Maranón Hangmatten (Map 4; ☎ 420 71 21) Singel 488 at the floating Flower Market – Europe's largest selection of hammocks

De Ode (Map 1; ☎ 419 08 82) Levantkade 51 on KNSM Island – specialises in coffins and original funerals; buy a bookcase that converts to a coffin when you join the library in the sky

Reina (Map 3; ☎ 428 23 90) Herenstaat 32a – dazzling Moroccan lanterns, Egyptian lamps and giftware from India and Tunisia

Third World & New Age

This is a great city to get in touch with the Third World, nature and the inner you, often all at once.

Abal Wereldwinkel (Map 6; ☎ 664 10 83) Ceintuurbaan 238 – shop run by volunteers selling Third-World crafts, books, toys and food

African Heritage (Map 4; ☎ 627 27 65) Zeedijk 59 – curios and clothing from Africa

Fair Trade Shop (Map 4; ☎ 625 22 45) Heiligeweg 45 – charitable shop featuring Third-World products including gifts and CDs

Himalaya (Map 4; ☎ 626 08 99) Warmoesstraat 56 – a peaceful New-Age oasis in the middle of the red-light district; stock up on crystals, ambient CDs and books on the healing arts

Jacob Hooy & Co (Map 4; ☎ 624 30 41) Kloveniersburgwal 10 – a charming old chemist shop selling medicinal herbs, homeopathic remedies and natural cosmetics

GETTING THERE & AWAY

Amsterdam is well connected to the rest of the world. And if you're looking for cheap deals, advice, or shared rides, this is the best spot in the country.

Air

Most leading airlines fly directly to/from Amsterdam's Schiphol airport, 18km south-west of the city centre. Schiphol, renowned for its tax-free shopping, is one of the world's best international airports. For airport and flight information call ☎ 0900-01 41 (f1 per minute) or check out www.schiphol.nl on the Web.

For information about transport to/from the city, see To/From the Airport in the later Getting Around section.

Airline Offices Airline offices in Amsterdam, listed under 'Luchtvaartmaatschappijen' (Aviation Companies) in the pink pages of the phone book, include:

Aer Lingus (☎ 623 86 20) Heiligeweg 14
Aeroflot (☎ 627 05 61) Weteringschans 26-III
Air France (☎ 446 88 00) Evert van der Beekstraat 7, Schiphol
Air India (☎ 624 81 09) Papenbroeksteeg 2
Air UK (KLM UK) (☎ 474 77 47) Planetenweg 5, Hoofddorp
Alitalia (☎ 577 74 44) Paulus Potterstraat 18
British Airways (☎ 554 75 55) Neptunusstraat 33, Hoofddorp
British Midland (☎ 662 22 11) Strawinskylaan 721
Cathay Pacific (☎ 653 20 10) Evert van der Beekstraat 18, Schiphol
China Airlines (☎ 646 10 01) De Boelelaan 7
Delta Air Lines (☎ 661 00 51) De Boelelaan 7
El Al (☎ 644 01 01) De Boelelaan 7-VI
Garuda Indonesia (☎ 627 26 26) Singel 540
Icelandair (☎ 627 01 36) Muntplein 2-III
Japan Airlines (☎ 305 00 60) Jozef Israelskade 48E
KLM (☎ 474 77 47) Amsterdamseweg 55, Amstelveen
Lufthansa (☎ 560 81 00) Wibautstraat 129
Malaysia Airlines (☎ 626 24 20) Weteringschans 24A
Northwest Airlines (☎ 648 71 11) Weteringschans 85C
Qantas (☎ 683 80 81) Stadhouderskade 6
Singapore Airlines (☎ 548 88 88) De Boelelaan 1067
South African Airways (☎ 554 22 88) Polarisavenue 49, Hoofddorp
Thai Airways (☎ 622 18 77) Singel 466–468
Transavia (☎ 601 56 66) Westelijke Randweg 3
United Airlines (☎ 504 05 55) Strawinskylaan 831-B8

Train

Amsterdam's main train station is Centraal Station (CS) which has regular links nationally and to neighbouring countries. See the Getting Around chapter for general information about trains within the country.

For international train information and reservations, use the NS international office inside the station (open daily 6.30 am to 10.30 pm). Be prepared for number-taking and long waits. There's another international office at Amstelstation, open daily 10 am to 5 pm, which is far less crowded but a bit out of the way.

Bus

Amsterdam has good long-distance bus links with the rest of Europe, Scandinavia and North Africa. For information about regional buses in the Netherlands, call the transport information service on ☎ 0900-92 92 (f0.75 a minute). Specific fares and travel durations are covered under individual towns in the regional chapters.

Eurolines & Busabout Eurolines tickets can be bought at most travel agencies and Netherlands Railways (NS) Reisburo (Travel Bureau) in Centraal Station. The most convenient Eurolines Amsterdam office (Map 4; ☎ 560 87 87) is at Rokin 10 near Dam Square. It supplies free time tables and fare information, and fares are consistently lower than the train. Buses leave from the bus station (☎ 694 56 31) next to Amstelstation, easily accessible by metro.

Busabout tickets can bought through its London office (UK ☎ 020-7950 1661) or on the coaches themselves. Services to/from Amsterdam run from mid-April to the end of October. Coaches stop at Hotel Hans Brinker (Map 6) on Kerkstraat, smack in the middle of the city.

For details of Eurolines, Busabout, and other bus services, see the Getting There & Away chapter.

Car & Motorcycle

Freeways link Amsterdam to Den Haag (A4/E19 and A44), Rotterdam (A4/E19) and Utrecht (A2/E35) in the south, and

Amersfoort (A1/E231) and points farther east and north-east. The A10/E22 ring freeway encircles the city, with tunnel sections under the IJ. Amsterdam is about 480km (six hours' drive) from Paris, 840km from Munich, 680km from Berlin and 730km from Copenhagen.

The ferry port at Hoek van Holland is about 80km away; the one at IJmuiden is just up the road along the North Sea Canal (see the Sea section in the Getting There & Away chapter for ferry details). For more about driving (or rather, not driving) in Amsterdam and about rental cars, see Car & Motorcycle in the Getting Around chapter.

The Dutch automobile association, ANWB (Map 6; ☎ 673 08 44), Museumplein 5, provides a wide range of information and services if you can prove membership of your own association.

Bicycle

Once you're in the country you can easily pedal to/from Amsterdam on dedicated bike paths. For details of bicycle rental in Amsterdam, see the following Getting Around section.

Hitching

Looking for a ride out of Amsterdam? Try the notice boards at the Science and Economics complex at Roetersstraat 11, the main public library at Prinsengracht 587, the museum or the youth hostels. People also advertise to share fuel costs in the classifieds paper *Via Via* published on Tuesday and Thursday.

Boat

Fast Flying Ferries (☎ 639 22 47 or 0900-92 92) runs a hydrofoil ferry from Pier 7 behind Amsterdam Centraal Station to Velsen (hourly on the hour, half-hourly during peak times), which costs f14/8.25 return for adults/children. The 25-minute trip drops you in Velsen, 3km short of IJmuiden, where you catch Connexxion bus No 70 into town. From IJmuiden, Scandinavian Seaways sails to Newcastle in the UK (see Sea in the Getting There & Away chapter for details).

GETTING AROUND
To/From the Airport

A taxi into the city from Schiphol airport takes 20 to 45 minutes (maybe longer in rush-hour traffic) and costs about f65. Trains to Centraal Station leave every 15 minutes, take 15 to 20 minutes and cost f6.50 (f10.75 return). Train-ticket counters are in the central court of Schiphol Plaza – buy your ticket before taking the escalator down to the platforms (you might want to buy a *strippenkaart* while you're at it – see the following Public Transport section).

Some city hotels have their own free shuttle service. A KLM shuttle bus runs between the airport and 15-odd major hotels every 30 minutes until mid-evening (f17.50 one way, f30 return). Connexxion bus No 172 runs a regular service between the airport and Centraal Station.

By car, take the A4 freeway to/from the A10 ring road around Amsterdam. A short stretch of A9 connects to the A4 close to Schiphol. Car-rental offices at the airport are in the right corner near the central exits of Schiphol Plaza.

Parking The airport's P1 and P2 short-term parking garages (under cover) charge f3.50 per half-hour for the first three hours, then f4 per hour. The maximum charge is f47.50 a day for the first two days, f25 a day thereafter. The P3 long-term parking area (open air) is a fair distance from the terminal but is linked by 24-hour shuttle bus. The charge is f85 for up to three days (minimum charge) and f7.50 for each day thereafter – a good alternative to parking in the city.

Public Transport

Amsterdam is a compact city, but public transport (tram, *sneltram*, bus and metro) is comprehensive. Most tram and bus lines as well as the metro converge at Centraal Station. The GVB (Municipal Transport Company) information office (Map 4) in front of the station opens 7 am to 9 pm weekdays (7 pm from late October to March), weekends from 8 am, and sells all types of tickets and passes. Pick up its free *Tourist Guide to Public Transport Amsterdam* booklet. For transport information, call ☎ 0900-92 92 weekdays 6 am to midnight, weekends from 7 am (f0.75 a minute).

Tickets & Passes Ticketing is based on zones. Most of Amsterdam proper (the canal belt and surrounding districts) is one zone; travel to the outer suburbs is two to three.

The strip ticket *(strippenkaart)* is valid on all buses, trams and metros and costs f12 for 15 strips or f35.25 for 45. They're available at tobacco shops, post offices, train-station counters and ticketing machines, many bookshops and newsagencies, and the GVB office (Map 4) in front of Centraal Station. The GVB also sells day passes valid for all zones at f12; a one-week pass for the centre (one zone) costs just f42.

Night buses take over shortly after midnight, when the trams and regular buses stop running. Drivers sell single tickets for f4, or you can stamp two strips off your strip card and pay a f2 supplement (which works out more expensively). The privately run Connexxion night buses cost more.

Circle Tram Tram No 20 is the useful Circle Tram that loops through the city along the major tourist sights. It goes either direction from Centraal Station about every 10 minutes from 9 am to 6 pm. Normal strip tickets (one zone, ie, two strips) and passes are valid.

Train You're most likely to use the train in Amsterdam when travelling to/from Schiphol airport. The options are Centraal Station; Lelylaan, De Vlugtlaan and Sloterdijk in the western suburbs; Zuid WTC and RAI (near the exhibition centre) in the southern suburbs; or Duivendrecht and Diemen-Zuid in the south-eastern suburbs. You can use strip tickets for trains in the Amsterdam region, but *not* to/from Schiphol, which requires a regular train ticket.

Car & Motorcycle

There's *no* free parking within the centre, and pay-and-display ticket machines are set up in or near every street. Paid parking applies 9 am to 11 pm Monday to Saturday,

noon to 11 pm on Sunday, and costs f3 to f5 per hour. Nonpayers will find a yellow *wielklem* (wheel clamp) attached to their car and it will cost f130 to have it removed. The notice on your windscreen will give the location of the closest City Surveillance (Stadstoezicht) office, where you must go personally to pay in cash. Foreigners with credit cards can ring the number on the notice and pay at their car.

Alternatively, you can park in the outer suburbs and just take the tram or metro. The Transferium parking garage (☎ 400 17 21) under the Amsterdam ArenA stadium in the Bijlmer charges f2.50 per hour or f12.50 per day, including transfers to the metro and two return tickets to Centraal Station – an excellent deal. There's a similar parking garage (same deal) in front of the VVV office at Stadionplein in the south-western outskirts.

It's also possible to buy a city parking permit from the Stadstoezicht (there's one at Bakkerstraat 13 off Rembrandtplein) for f33/185.50 a day/week. It's one-third cheaper for outside the canal belt or Museum Quarter. Monthly permits are also available. Day permits can also be bought from the street-side ticket machines.

Parking garages in the city centre (eg, on Damrak, near Leidseplein and under the Stopera) are often full and cost more than a parking permit.

Motorcyclists can park on the pavement (sidewalk) free of charge provided they don't obstruct anybody.

Car Rental Local companies are usually cheaper than the multinationals (Avis, Budget, Hertz, Europcar) but don't offer as much backup or flexibility (eg, one-way rentals within or outside the Netherlands). Rates change almost weekly, so it pays to call around. Rentals at Schiphol airport incur an extra f70.50 'airport company tax'.

AutoEurope
(☎ 0800-022 35 70) a US firm that works with the big rental car agencies; also offers competitive deals
Avis
(☎ 430 96 09) international reservations weekdays only

ELLIOT DANIEL

TWE KANEFAS BALE 1632

LEANNE LOGAN

INT·LAT·VAN BEL OFTEN
IN DE·NIEVE STADT

LEANNE LOGAN

·CHRISTIAAN·
·HUYGENS·

ELLIOT DANIEL

REIKT HAAR DE HAND

ELLIOT DANIEL

Wall murals and plaques give away the secret of what went on behind closed doors.

A dike in Marken – keeps the sea at bay, but not the tourists.

Hoorn harbour – home to many explorers

Enkhuizen harbour – chock-a-block with boats

(☎ 683 60 61) Nassaukade 380, not far from Leidseplein

(☎ 644 36 84) President Kennedylaan 783

(☎ 430 95 11) Klokkenbergweg 15

Budget

(☎ 0800-023 82 38) central number (free call, 8 am to 8 pm Monday to Friday, 8 am to 5 pm Saturday)

(☎ 070-384 43 85) international reservations

(☎ 612 60 66) Overtoom 121

(☎ 604 13 49) Schiphol Plaza

Europcar

(☎ 070-381 18 91) international reservations (weekdays only)

(☎ 683 21 23) Overtoom 197

(☎ 316 41 90) Schiphol Plaza

Hertz

(☎ 0800-23 54 37 89) central number

(☎ 504 05 54) international reservations (daily 8 am to 8 pm)

(☎ 612 24 41) Overtoom 333

(☎ 623 61 23) Engelsesteeg 4

Kuperus BV

(☎ 693 87 90, fax 665 98 78) Middenweg 175 on the south-eastern side of town (tram No 9)

Safety Rent-a-Car

(☎ 636 63 63) Papaverweg 3B, near the Galaxy Hotel, Amsterdam North

One great option is available through the Dutch post office, where you buy a voucher for the smallest Budget car for f55 a day or f85 a weekend, including insurance, tax and 200km (f0.20 per extra kilometre). The vouchers are valid for six months, and you must book the car directly at a Budget office at least 24 hours in advance. For information, call ☎ 0900-15 76 from 8 am to 8 pm weekdays, to 5 pm Saturday.

Taxi

Amsterdam taxis are among the most expensive in Europe. To call a taxi, dial ☎ 0900-677 77 77. You're not supposed to hail taxis on the street but nobody seems to care much. Taxis cost the same day or night; flag fall is f3.50 to f4, and a tip of 5% to 10% is expected.

The excellent *treintaxi* service (see the Getting Around chapter) only operates to/from Amsterdam Zuid WTC station and is limited to Amstelveen, Buitenveldert and a few other outlying areas – call ☎ 645 18 52.

Bicycle & Moped

Bicycles are an ideal way to get around – nothing within the canal belt is more than 10 minutes away by bike. Most bikes carry locks worth more than the thing itself, indicative of the fact that up to 200,000 bicycles are stolen each year.

You could also buy a bike, an option worth considering if you're spending a month or so in town. Bicycle shops sell second-hand bikes for f140 to f200; add f60 to f100 for one or two good locks to attach the frame and front wheel to something solid. Drug addicts might offer bikes for as little as f25, but it's highly illegal.

The Dutch automobile association, ANWB (Map 6; see Tourist Offices under Information earlier in this chapter), provides cycling maps and information if you show a letter of introduction from your automobile association (or your cycling association, but that may depend on the person behind the counter).

For details on bicycling laws, tours and more, see the special section 'Cycling in the Netherlands'.

Bicycle Rental Many visitors rent a bike, but the chaotic traffic can be challenging. Take care, and watch those tram tracks.

The companies listed below require ID plus a credit-card imprint or a cash deposit.

How-To Guide to Bike Theft

Watch out for your bicycle on your next visit to Amsterdam. Chiel van Zelst, a former drug addict, has written a memoir, *100,000 Bike Valves*, which includes tips on how to steal a bike. In his book, 35-year-old Van Zelst admits he stole 'at least' 50,000 bicycles in the 1980s, when he roamed the streets desperate for money to support his habit. Amsterdam police say addicts and petty criminals steal as many as 180,000 bicycles each year. The bikes usually are resold within hours – sometimes to their original owners – for as little as f25. The police have appointed a special coordinator to crack down on bicycle theft, the city's most common crime.

Prices are for standard, 'coaster-brake' bikes; gears and hand brakes cost more.

Amstel Stalling (Map 1; ☎ 692 35 84) Amstelstation – f9.50/38 a day/week, f100 deposit

Bike City (Map 3; ☎/fax 626 37 21) Bloemgracht 68–70, in the Jordaan opposite the Anne Frankhuis – f12.50/50 a day/week, f50 deposit and no advertising on the bikes, so you can pretend you're a local

Damstraat Rent-a-Bike (Map 4; ☎ 625 50 29) Pieter Jacobsdwarsstraat 7–11, near Dam Square – f15/67.50 a day/week, f50 deposit

Holland Rent-a-Bike (Map 4; ☎ 622 32 07) Damrak 247, in the Beurs van Berlage – f12.50/50 a day/week, f50 deposit with a passport or f200 without

MacBike (Map 4; ☎ 620 09 85) Meester Visserplein 2, near Gassan Diamond factory – f12.50/60 a day/week, f50 deposit or a credit-card imprint, passport required. Other MacBike outlets are at Marnixstraat 220 (Map 3; ☎ 626 69 64) next to the Europarking complex

Rijwielshop (Map 4; ☎ 624 83 91) Stationsplein 12 – access at the far east end of the building near the city bus stops; f9.50 a day, f38 a week, f200 deposit

Moped Rental Moped Rental Service (Map 3; ☎ 422 02 66), Marnixstraat 208, rents neat little mopeds from f12.50 an hour or f35/60 a half/full day including insurance and a full tank of petrol. You'll need a licence (a car licence will do). The place opens 9 am to 7 pm daily in summer, to 6 pm in winter.

Boat

Ferries The free ferry to Amsterdam North marked *Buiksloterwegveer* leaves between Pier 8 and Pier 9 behind Centraal Station (Map 1). It runs every five minutes from 6.30 am to 9 pm, then every 10 minutes from 9 pm to 6.30 am daily, and only takes a few minutes to get across. The *Adelaarswegveer* from Pier 8 goes diagonally across the IJ. It operates every seven or 15 minutes from 6.27 am to 8.57 pm weekdays, every 15 minutes on Saturday, but not Sunday. Cars and motorbikes are not allowed on either ferry.

Canal Boat, Bus & Bike For information about organised canal tours, see Canal Tours in the earlier Organised Tours section.

The Lovers Museum Boat (Map 1; ☎ 622 21 81) leaves every 30 or 45 minutes from in front of Centraal Station and stops at all the major museums. A day ticket costs f25 (f15 after 1 pm). A single stop costs f7.50, two stops cost f10, and three or four stops f12.50. The day ticket gives 10% to 50% admission discounts to most museums en route.

The Canal Bus (☎ 623 98 86) does a circuit between Centraal Station and the Rijksmuseum between 10.15 am and 6.45 pm. A day pass costs f22 (f32.50 including entry to the Rijksmuseum).

Canal 'bikes' (paddle-boats) can be hired from kiosks at Leidseplein, Keizersgracht/Leidsestraat, the Anne Frankhuis and the Rijksmuseum; two/four-seaters cost f25/40 an hour.

Noord Holland

After the non-stop buzz of Amsterdam, the surrounding region of Noord Holland (North Holland) is bucolic sedation. It's the most populous province after Zuid Holland, and knows how to package its charms for tourists – the windmills, cheese markets and sweet little towns that attract the multitudes in summer. This is also easy hiking and cycling country, with well-marked trails meshing the villages with lush pastures and marshlands.

West of Amsterdam, you should under no circumstances miss Haarlem, a stylish town with an aura of 17th-century grandeur – not to mention some great museums and very cosy pubs.

It's also a good place to stay if you're going to the Keukenhof bulb fields (see the Zuid Holland & Zeeland chapter). Unless you enjoy ridiculous crowds and exhaust fumes, we'd recommend you give most beach resorts on the west coast a wide berth (Zaandvoort, Bergen and Egmond among others). Nonetheless, there are some brilliant trails in the dunes, particularly in coastal nature reserves such as Kennemerduinen.

A half-hour's drive north of Amsterdam, the Gouwzee Bay towns of Edam, Volendam and Marken can seem utterly fake and fill to bursting in summer, although they have their charms in the evenings after the tour buses depart.

Monnickendam is a less obvious choice and perfect if you're into 17th-century architecture. Moving north, the former Golden Age ports of Hoorn and Enkhuizen have a more genuine air about them, both with attractive old harbours (the latter also has an excellent open-air museum).

The cheese auction at Alkmaar is a durable, if kitschy attraction. The North Sea island of Texel offers some of the country's finest beaches and outdoor recreation, but can get very crowded in summer. To the east of the capital, the leafy forests of Het Gooi are a refuge for urbanites,

HIGHLIGHTS

- Watching the old yachts come in at Enkhuizen
- Hiking or cycling on Texel Island
- Haarlem's Frans Hals Museum and old town
- The period rooms of Muiden Castle
- Clambering in the windmills at Zaanse Schans
- Eating smoked fish with a brew portside

while the towns of Muiden and Naarden nearby have remarkable old fortresses worth a visit.

Visitors to Amsterdam might consider staying in Noord Holland, as you'll generally get better value for your money. Moreover, public transport to the capital is excellent. The regional tourist board has a comprehensive Web site at www.noord-holland-tourist.nl.

Getting There & Around

The region is well served by the national rail and, where the train ends, the bus networks begin. Motorways run north-south

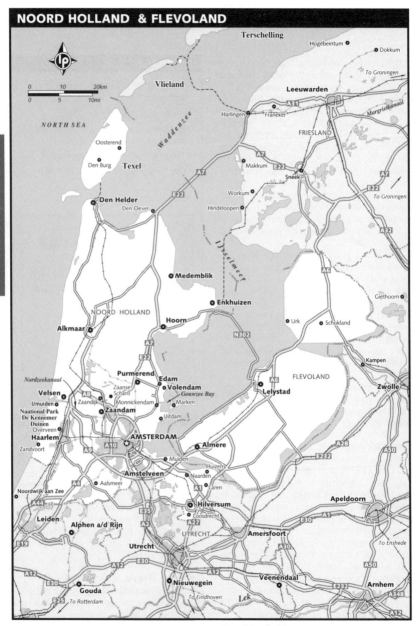

from Haarlem to Alkmaar (the A9), and from Amsterdam to Den Oever (the A7), which continues on to Friesland Province via the 30km-long Afsluitdijk. From Enkhuizen there's another fast dike road, the N302, running across the IJsselmeer to Lelystad in Flevoland. See the Getting There & Away sections under individual towns for full details of train and bus schedules.

North of Amsterdam, a fun way to see some IJsselmeer towns is on the *Historische Driehoek* (Historic Triangle) train/boat/train tour that operates from April to October. This involves a train from Amsterdam to Enkhuizen, a connecting boat to Medemblik, a narrow-gauge steam train from Medemblik to Hoorn, and the train from Hoorn back to Amsterdam. You'll need to get an early start to take in the Zuiderzee Museum in Enkhuizen before catching the boat. This whole *Rail Idee* package (tickets from train stations) costs f53.50 per person.

Many of the IJsselmeer port towns, including Enkhuizen, Hoorn, Monnickendam, Muiden and Naarden, have yachts and *botters* (old fishing boats) for rent, but they don't come cheap at around f600 per day for a botter. See the Facts for the Visitor chapter for a listing of boat rental firms and prices.

North of Amsterdam

The large peninsula north of Amsterdam, known in the extreme north as West Friesland, is exceedingly popular with day-trippers from the capital. On sunny days the area teems with visitors, particularly the coastal towns along the IJsselmeer, where clog-wearing inhabitants pose wearily in front of their quaint wooden houses. Places tend to feel more authentic the further north you go, and it's a good idea to rent a bicycle to get off the beaten track – but you'll rarely find yourself alone, even in the remotest corners.

ZAANSTAD & ZAANSE SCHANS
☎ 075 • pop 130,000

The urban sprawl north-west of Amsterdam is known as Zaanstad, a collection of seven separate communities merged in the 1970s. The biggest is Zaandam, a modern town with a chocolate factory that spreads its enticingly sweet fumes over a wide radius. It has had two famous residents: Russia's Peter the Great and, nearly two centuries later, Claude Monet (who painted a series of watery landscapes).

Several authentic working **windmills** – probably the closest together you'll ever see – stand along the Zaan River just north of Zaandam. They're part of the open-air museum-piece village, **Zaanse Schans**. Sure, it's kitschy but does have its merits with some authentic workshops, historic exhibits and traditional old wooden houses. All its structures, mills included, were carted in from around the country to recreate a 17th-century community, and on a sunny day it's a lovely spot despite the inevitable crowds.

Some attractions are free, such as the Albert Heijn colonial goods shop, a cheesemaker's shops (free samples) and a clog factory that copies the footwear with a device similar to that of a keymaker. One mill sells fat jars of its tasty mustard from f1.75. The bakery, clock and period museums (all costing admission) aren't worth the trouble. Half the fun is clambering about inside the old windmills that shake like the devil in the North Sea breeze. A tourist boat does 45-minute cruises on the Zaan several times a day for f9/4.50 for adults/children from April to September.

Visitors to the area should not miss the old quarter called **Zaandijk** directly east across the river from Zaanse Schans. It's ignored by tourists and shows more authentically what 'old Holland' was like.

The museum visitors centre (☎ 616 22 21) at Kalverringdijk 5 opens 10 am to 5 pm, Tuesday to Sunday, from March to October. The rest of the year it's open weekends only. The local tourist office (☎ 616 22 21, fax 670 53 81) is at Gedempte Gracht 76 in Zaandam.

In **Zaandam** itself, drop by Krimp 23, where Peter the Great of Russia lived for

NOORD HOLLAND

five months in 1697. He arrived incognito as a sailor, Peter Mikhailov, to garner support for western forces against the Turks, and stayed at the two-room wooden cabin belonging to Gerrit Kist, a former employee of his highness. Peter worked as an apprentice on the nearby wharves, learning much about shipbuilding, drinking and swearing in Dutch. Check out the old graffiti, left mainly by Russians who visited on a kind of pilgrimage during the 19th century. Hours are 10 am to 1 pm and 2 pm to 5 pm from Tuesday to Friday, and 1 to 5 pm at weekends. Entry is f2.50/1.50.

Getting There & Away

Trains from Amsterdam take about half an hour (twice hourly). From Centraal Station, take the *Stoptrein* towards Alkmaar and get off at Koog Zaandijk – it's an eight-minute, well-signposted walk to the Zaanse Schans open-air museum.

To continue to Zaandam, cross the large bridge to the left of Zaanse Schans, take the first street on your right into Zaandijk and board the southbound bus No 89. Ask the driver to let you out at the large canal in the centre of town; Zaandam's pedestrian shopping mall (Gedempte Gracht) faces the bus stop.

MONNICKENDAM

☎ 299 • pop 17,800

Monnickendam's restored 17th-century houses and old fishing cottages are picture-postcard material. The name comes from Benedictine monks who built a dike near here in the 13th century. The town was an important Zuiderzee fishing centre until the construction of the Afsluitdijk – as elsewhere in the region – killed the fishing industry. So Monnickendam reinvented itself as a resort for water sports, as its yacht-filled old harbour testifies.

Information & Orientation

The old town lies in the sea-faced crook of two highways, the N247 and the N518 (Bernhardlaan). The tourist office (☎ 65 19 98, fax 65 52 68), which also represents nearby Marken, is on the south side of the

intersection at Nieuwpoortslaan 15. Hours are 1 to 5 pm on Monday and 9.30 am to 5 pm, Thursday to Saturday from September to May. The rest of the year it opens an hour longer on the same days. From April to September it also opens 1 to 5 pm on Sunday.

The office sells a leaflet with a self-guided tour of the town (in English, f2.50). Staff will reserve local accommodation, but for a whopping f30 fee – so you're probably better off doing it yourself.

There's an ING Bank at the corner of Gooische Kaai and Zuideinde, and a Rabobank at Nieuwezijds Burgwal 34 in the centre; the latter has an ATM outside. The post office is at H Reyntjeslaan, 100m southeast of the old centre across Bernhardlaan.

Things to See & Do

The 15th-century tower of the **Speeltoren**, the former town hall, has a beautiful carillon with mechanical knights that plays, sadly, only Saturday morning at 11 am and noon. It also houses the **Historisch Museum**, an unremarkable display of local history that includes archaeological finds, ceramics and some model ships. It opens 10 am to 4 pm from Tuesday to Saturday, and 1 to 4 pm from Sunday and Monday, June to mid-September; the rest of the year it closes on Sunday. Entry costs f2.50/1.

It's worthwhile having a look at the Gothic **Grotekerk**, notable for its triple nave, tower galleries and a dazzling oak choir screen from the 16th century. Just north-east of the tourist office on De Zarken, it opens 10 am to 4 pm from Tuesday to Saturday, and 2 to 4 pm on Sunday and Monday from June to August.

The old harbour along Haringburgwal is interesting for its eel-smoking shops. Check out the statue, on the corner of Grote Noord and 't Prooyen, of the fisherman curing the slippery critters on a stick.

Windsurfing & Boating Bootvloot (☎ 65 34 84), Burg. Versteegstraat 25, rents windsurf boards for f40/70 per half-day/day. Holland Zeilcharters (☎ 65 23 51), Het Prooyen 4a, has botters from f650 per day.

Cheese Farms At Katwoude, about 3km north-east of Monnickendam, there are three cheese farms that can be visited daily: Irene Hoeve, Jacobs Hoeve (both on Hoogedijk, bus No 114 to Lagedijk) and Simone Hoeve on Wagenweg. The presenters don pretty traditional duds but the demonstrations, while informative, bear all the hallmarks of tourist routine. Irene Hoeve also has a clog-making shop in back.

Places to Stay & Eat
Camping Uitdam (☎ 020-403 14 33, fax 403 14 33, Zeedijk 2), in Uitdam, 5km south-east of Monnickendam, has a beach, laundry, snack bar and bicycle rental. It charges f39 for two people plus a tent and car, and opens March to October. Take the dike road (Waterlandse Zeedijk) from Monnickendam, or walk/cycle along the dike.

The *Hotel Lake Land (☎ 65 37 51, fax 65 45 87, Jachthaven 1)* is the sole hotel – a large, rather charmless complex on the north harbour. It has comfortable rooms with private amenities from f80 per person.

De Roef (☎ 65 18 60, Noordeinde 40) is a splendid fish-and-barbecue restaurant, serving mains from f25. It shows the Dutch *can* cook a good steak. Hours are 5 to 11 pm daily.

't Markerveerhuis (☎ 65 16 75, Brugstraat 6) offers lunch and dinner in its pretty, glassed-in harbour terrace. Soups start at f7.25, salads at f12.75 and the day's specials cost f19.50.

't Wapen (☎ 65 74 84, Havenstraat 7) in the beautiful old **Waag** (weigh house) on the central canal, has good fish dishes and a three-course *menu* for f48.50.

Getting There & Around
Connexxion bus No 111 goes to/from the centre of Monnickendam to Amsterdam Centraal Station, harbour side (25 minutes, twice to four times an hour); bus No 115 makes the trip hourly. Bus No 111 continues on to Marken (12 minutes, hourly). Bus Nos 114 and 117 go north to Edam (18 minutes) and Hoorn (45 minutes) twice an hour.

Ber Koning (☎ 65 12 67) at Noordeinde 12 and Van Driel (☎ 65 32 64) at Dirksznlaan 109 both rent touring bikes for f9 per day. The local camp site also has two-wheelers (see Places to Stay & Eat section earlier).

VOLENDAM & MARKEN
☎ 0299
Some 22km north-east of Amsterdam lies Volendam, a former fishing port turned tourist trap with a population of 26,750. It's quaint all right, with its rows of wooden houses and locals who don traditional dress for church and during festivals. But the hordes of camera-toting visitors spoil the fun – you'll encounter fewer of them when you explore some of the pretty streets behind the harbour.

Across Gouwzee Bay, 2km to the east, lies picturesque Marken with a population of 2000. This was an isolated fishing community in the Zuiderzee until 1957, when a causeway was built to the mainland. Since then it's become a museum-piece village, earning its keep from the same day-trippers who besiege Volendam. Expect to spend half a day poking around both places.

Information & Orientation
The tourist office (☎ 36 37 47, fax 36 84 84, ✉ info@volendam.nl) is at Zeestraat 39; Connexxion buses stop at Zeestraat. The old harbour district is about 400m to the south-east. The office opens 10 am to 5 pm daily from April to September, and 10 am to 3 pm from Monday to Saturday the rest of the year. You can pick up a brochure with a self-guided tour of Volendam (f1.50). Staff will reserve accommodation for a f3.50 fee per person. Web site: www.vvv-volendam.nl

There's no tourist office in Marken, but the VVV in Monnickendam can supply information (see that section).

Money In Volendam, there's an ABN-Amro bank with an ATM at the corner of Juianaweg and Prins Bernhardlaan, 150m south-west of the tourist office.

Post & Communications The post office is at Europaplein 1, about 200m south-east of the tourist office. The public library at Foksiastraat 10, about 250m north-east of the

NOORD HOLLAND

tourist office off busy Julianaweg, has a few Internet terminals (f2.50 per 15 minutes). Library hours are 2.30 to 8.30 pm on Monday, Wednesday and Friday, 2 to 5.30 pm on Monday and 11 am to 2 pm on Saturday.

Things to See & Do

The **Volendams Museum** (☎ 36 92 58), at Zeestraat 37, is great if you're a cigar aficionado, but there's not much else on offer. Besides some traditional costumes, prints and paintings of harbour scenes, the museum has 11 million cigar bands plastered on its walls. Hours are 10 am to 5 pm daily; admission costs f3.50/2.

In Marken, the colourful **Kerkbuurt** is the most authentic area, with tarred or painted houses raised on pilings to escape the Zuiderzee floods. A row of eel-smoking houses here has been converted to the **Marker Museum** (☎ 60 19 04), a display at Kerkbuurt 44 devoted to local culture and traditions (more colourful costumes). It opens 10 am to 5 pm from Monday to Saturday, and noon to 4 pm on Sunday, from Easter to October. Entry is free.

Windsurfing Slobbeland (☎ 36 36 99), in a little hut 300m south-west of the harbour at Slobbeland 1a, rents windsurf boards for f40 per half-day from April to October.

Places to Stay

If you must stay here, the tourist office has lists of B&B places charging from f35 per person. On the harbour, the huge, *Hotel Spaander* (☎ 36 35 95, fax 36 96 15, Haven 15–19), run by Best Western, is a charming affair with an old-world facade including traditional carved balconies. Picasso was among the artists who stayed here, and the downstairs is crammed with historic paintings. It charges from f75/150 for singles/doubles with private shower and toilet.

The *Hotel Lutine* (☎ 36 32 34, fax 36 22 54, Haven 80), with just eight rooms, is much more intimate and has just as nice a view. Rooms with en-suite shower and toilet start at f65/130. The *Hotel van den Hogen* (☎ 36 37 75, fax 36 94 98, Haven 106) nearby has similar rooms for f70/140.

Places to Eat

The fishing industry may have dried up, but seafood remains king in Volendam. The *Grand Café Van Diepen* (☎ 36 37 05, Haven 35) is a cut above the other tourist eateries, with its lunch specials a bargain, including baked cod fillet with salad and chips for f19.75. The atmospheric *Hotel Spaander* (see Places to Stay) does big sandwiches from f7.50, and a soup and main course for f22.50.

The tiny *KL Leek* supermarket is at Zeestraat 7, about 25m north of the harbour. The street running along the seashore is lined with fish vendors selling smoked cod, eel and herring sandwiches from about f4. *P&P* at Nordeinde 1 sells tasty filled fish rolls from f2.50.

Getting There & Around

There's no train station in Volendam. Connexxion bus No 110 runs between Volendam and Amsterdam (45 minutes) and Edam (12 minutes) every hour until about midnight. Bus No 111 goes from Amsterdam via Monnickendam to Marken (30 minutes, half-hourly).

From mid-March to September, the *Marken Express* ferry makes the 20-minute crossing from Volendam to Marken every half hour from 10.30 am to 6 pm. Return tickets cost f12.50/7.50; one-way fares are f6.50/6. In Volendam, the ferry leaves from the docks at Havendijkje.

In Volendam, Ber Koning (☎ 65 12 67), at Noordeinde 12, rents bicycles for f12.50 per day. In Marken, Hollander (☎ 65 14 52) at the Parkeerterrein (main car park) charges similar rates. The VVV in Volendam sells cycling maps of the area (f6.95).

EDAM

☎ 0299 • pop 7000

Once renowned as a whaling port, this scenic little town is a surprisingly calm place after the tourist rabble of Volendam. In its 17th-century heyday it had 33 shipyards that built the fleet of legendary admiral Michiel de Ruijter. Its storybook canals, drawbridges and old shipping warehouses make Edam a lovely place to wander, and it

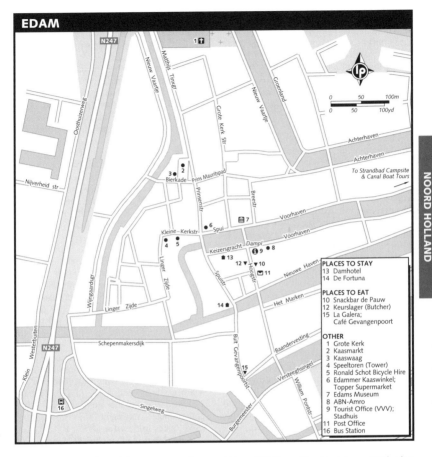

EDAM

PLACES TO STAY
13 Damhotel
14 De Fortuna

PLACES TO EAT
10 Snackbar de Pauw
12 Keurslager (Butcher)
15 La Galera;
    Café Gevangenpoort

OTHER
1 Grote Kerk
2 Kaasmarkt
3 Kaaswaag
4 Speeltoren (Tower)
5 Ronald Schot Bicycle Hire
6 Edammer Kaaswinkel;
   Topper Supermarket
7 Edams Museum
8 ABN-Amro
9 Tourist Office (VVV);
   Stadhuis
11 Post Office
16 Bus Station

NOORD HOLLAND

attracts relatively few visitors – except during its famous cheese market in summer.

Information

The tourist office (☎ 37 42 36, fax 37 42 36, ℮ Info@vvv-edam.nl) is in the splendid 18th-century Stadhuis (Town Hall) on Damplein, the main square. Hours are 10 am to 5 pm from Monday to Saturday from April through October; and 10 am to 3 pm the same days from November to March. It also opens 1 to 4 pm on Sunday in July and August. The office sells an English-language booklet, *A stroll through Edam* (f5) for self-guided tours. Web site: www.vvv-edam.nl.

The ABN-Amro branch at Haven 141 (next to the tourist office) exchanges money and has an ATM that takes international credit cards. The post office, with a Postbank that also changes currency, is at Hoogstraat 8.

Things to See & Do

In the 16th century, William of Orange bestowed on Edam the right to hold a **Kaasmarkt** (Cheese Market), the town's economic anchor right through the 1920s.

At its peak 250,000 rounds of cheese were sold here every year. On the western side of Kaasmarkt stands the old **Kaaswaag** (cheese weigh house) that holds exhibitions on the town's chief product (open 10 am to 5 pm from April to October; free admission). The cheese market, smaller than the one in Alkmaar but just as touristy, is held 10 am to noon on Wednesday mornings in July and August.

The 15th-century **Grotekerk** is the town's chief monument. The stunning stained-glass windows depicting coats of arms and historical scenes were added after 1602, when the church (and most of the town) burned to a crisp after a lightning strike on the steeple. The present tower, which has vaulted ceiling to take weight off the base, was built much shorter than its predecessor. It opens 2 to 4.30 pm daily from April to October. The taller and older **Speeltoren**, leaning slightly over Kleine Kerkstraat about 100m further south, is all that remains of the 15th-century Kleine Kerk.

Edams Museum (☎ 37 24 31), at Damplein 8, has a so-so collection of old furnishings, porcelain and silverware; it's more famous for its **floating cellar**, a metre-high tub designed by a retired ship's captain who yearned for the sea. The ornate brick structure is Edam's oldest, dating from 1530. The museum opens 10 am to 4.30 pm from Monday to Saturday, and 1.30 to 4.30 pm on Sunday from April to mid-October. Admission is f10/5.

Boat Tours The tourist office organises 1½-hour excursions on botters in the IJsselmeer in summer, weather permitting. Departure is from the Strandbad Edam camp site (see Places to Stay). Boats go every two hours from 11 am to 7 pm on Wednesday and Saturday; tickets cost f21/13.50 at the VVV. You can also rent one yourself (from f425 for an afternoon) from the VVV.

Places to Stay
Strandbad Edam (☎ 37 19 94, fax 37 15 10, Zeevangszeedijk 7a) lies on the shores of the IJsselmeer. Open April to October, the camp site has a swimming beach, a laundry

and a restaurant and charges f5/8/5.75 per adult/tent/car. From Damplein, walk 2km east along the northern side of the Voorhaven canal.

At the tourist office you can get a list (f1) of private accommodation from about f30 per person. Edam has just two hotels. The **Damhotel** (☎ 37 17 66, fax 37 40 31, Keizersgracht 1) is a pleasant, middle-of-the-road place on the central canal. Its well-equipped singles/doubles with private shower and toilet cost f115/190, including breakfast.

The swanky **De Fortuna** (☎ 37 16 71, fax 37 14 69, @ fortuna2@wxs.nl, Spuistraat 7) consists of six 17th-century houses, some of which overlook a pretty terraced garden on the canal's edge. Rooms with private amenities start at f122/172, breakfast included.

Places to Eat
La Galera (☎ 37 19 71, Gevangenpoortsteeg 3) is a restaurant-pizzeria serving pastas and pizzas for f10 to f20 and meat dishes from f27.50. It opens 5 to 9 pm daily (till 10 pm at weekends). The **Café de Gevangenpoort** next door is a pleasant pub selling burgers, sandwiches and light meals till after midnight.

The **restaurant** at the Damhotel has a fine three-course menu (eg, smoked quail with bacon in port wine sauce) for f52.50. Main dishes average f25 to f30. The **De Fortuna** does elaborate three and four-course meals starting at f55; reserve ahead. (See Places to Stay for details.)

Keurslager butcher shop at Hoogstraat 5 sells wonderful filled rolls from f3.50; the **Snackbar de Pauw** across the street has shoarma pockets for f6.50 and full meals (fish, pork or chicken with chips) from f12.50.

If you can't resist, pick up some cheese in the oh-so-quaint **De Edammer Kaaswinkel** at the corner of Spui and Prinsenstraat, but don't expect any bargains. There's a small supermarket, **Topper**, next door.

Getting There & Around
Edam isn't on the railway line. Connexxion bus No 110 stops twice an hour at the bus station on the south-western side of town and

continues south to Monnickendam (20 minutes) and Amsterdam (45 minutes). Bus No 114 travels north to Hoorn (25 minutes, twice an hour), and No 113 makes jaunts to Volendam (12 minutes, one to two times an hour).

Ronald Schot (☎ 37 21 55) at Kleine Kerkstraat 8 rents touring bikes for f7.50/10 per half-day/day.

HOORN
☎ 0229 • pop 62,000
This lively little port was once capital of West Friesland and, boosted by the presence of the Dutch East India Company, a mighty trading city. Its 17th-century glory is still palpable around the central square and the harbour – nowadays a yachting marina that's chock-a-block with old wooden fishing boats and barges.

Its most famous son was explorer Willem Schoutens, who named the tip of South America – Cape Horn – after his home town in 1616. Another Hoorn seaman, Abel Tasman, left his mark a few years later by putting New Zealand and Tasmania on the map.

Orientation & Information
Hoorn's old town begins about 1km southwest of the train station. From the station, walk south along broad Veemarkt to Gedempte Turfhaven, turn right and take the first left into Grote Noord, the pedestrianised shopping street. At the end is the scenic main square, Rode Steen, and the harbour area is a stone's throw further south, down Grote Havensteeg.

The local Hoorn ANWB/VVV office (☎ 0900-403 110 55, fax 0229-21 50 23, ✉ vvvhoorn@planet.nl) is at Veemarkt 4, about 100m south of the train station. From June to August it opens 1 to 6 pm on Monday, 9.30 am to 6 pm Tuesday to Friday, 9.30 am to 5 pm on Saturday and 1 to 5 pm on Sunday. The rest of the year it closes an hour earlier on weekdays; from September to March it's closed on Sunday. Staff will book local accommodation for a f3.50 fee per person (plus f1 for the phone call).

Money Rabobank at Veemarkt 21 will change money, and has an ATM that takes international credit cards. The post office also has a Postbank exchange desk.

Post & Communications The post office is at Grote Oost 28, which leads east from Rode Steen. The public library at Wisselstraat 8 charges f2.50 per ¼-hour of Internet use (four terminals). It opens 1 to 8.30 pm on weekdays, with a one-hour break at 5.30 (closed Tuesday evening), and 10 am to 1 pm on Sunday.

Things to See & Do
Hoorn's heyday as a shipping hub is long gone, but the imposing **statue of Jan Peterszoon Coen**, founder of the Dutch East India Company, still looks over the Rode Steen ('red stone'), so named for the blood that used to flow from the town gallows there. On the north-eastern side of the square is the 17th-century **Waag** (weigh house) which now houses a pleasant grand cafe.

On the opposite side is the impressive **Westfries Museum** (☎ 21 48 62), the former state college, a wedding-cake gable fronted by the coat of arms of Oranje-Nassau. Its collection includes archaeological finds, weapons, maritime instruments, grandfather clocks and ornate furnishings recalling Hoorn's past riches. Impressive, too, are its 17th- to 19th-century paintings, including some 2.5m-high group portraits of bigwigs from the Dutch East India Company. The museum opens 11 am to 5 pm from Monday to Friday, and 2 to 5 pm at weekends. Admission costs f5/2.50.

Less compelling is the **Museum of the 20th Century** (☎ 21 40 01), a historical overview of major events after 1900. The best things here are a 30-sq-metre scale model of Hoorn in 1650 and an audiovisual presentation about the town's role during the Golden Age. The museum, at Bierkade 4 in two old cheese warehouses, opens 10 am to 5 pm from Tuesday to Sunday. Entry costs f5/4.

The scenic harbour, which is lined by stately gabled houses, is overlooked by the massive **Hoofdtoren**, a defensive gate from 1532 that now houses a bar and restaurant. The tiny belfry was added a century later.

NOORD HOLLAND

Steam Train A shiny old locomotive, the Museum Stoomtram, puffs the hour-long journey between Hoorn and Medemblik daily in the summer months. Trains depart from Hoorn station at 11.05 am from Tuesday to Saturday, April to October (also Monday in July and August). One-way tickets cost f14.50/11; returns 23.50/17.50. You can combine train and boat, eg, from Hoorn to Medemblik by train, and back by boat and train via the Zuiderzee Museum at Enkhuizen for f23.50/17.50. Other combinations are available.

Places to Stay

The hostel *Jeugdherberg de Toorts* (☎ 21 42 56, Schellinkhouterdijk 1a), in a pretty seaside spot 2km east of town, charges f25 for a dorm B&B (open July and August only). Take bus No 47 from the train station to the De Dregt stop in Schellinkhout.

There are few hotels in the old town, but the VVV has a list of B&B places from f30 per person.

The friendly *Isola Bella* (☎ 21 71 71, Grote Oost 65), is the closest to the harbour, with nice rooms above its Italian restaurant from f65 per person.

Hotel de Keizerskroon (☎ 21 27 17, fax 21 10 22, Breed 31), a large hotel-restaurant 100m south-west of the tourist office, has basic singles with hall shower for f70, and singles/doubles with private facilities for f100/140.

The *Hotel de Magneet* (☎ 21 50 21, fax 23 70 44, Kleine Oost 5D), just across the canal on the eastern side of the old centre, is spacious and comfortable with shared facilities and breakfast for f70/100. Rooms with private bath and toilet cost f105/130. Parking is free.

Places to Eat

The *Gasterij de Korenmarkt* (☎ 27 98 26, Korenmarkt 1) is a quaint cafe-restaurant with a nice terrace and view of the marina. Soups start at f8.50, and most mains cost under f15. Try the beef *stoofpotje* (hearty beef-and-vegetable stew; f10.50) and baked goat's cheese in strawberry sauce (f9.50). It's open for lunch and dinner.

The cosy, pub-like *Brasserie Bonteke* (Nieuwendam 1, ☎ 21 73 24) does soups and sandwiches, lamb, pork and chicken dishes from f22, and a good vegie curry for f20 (closed Monday and Tuesday).

Isola Bella (see Places to Stay) has pizzas and pasta for f11 to f21 (open 5 to 11 pm, closed Monday).

La Bascule Grand Café (☎ 21 51 95, Rode Steen 8) is a nice place for lunch in the old weigh house, with hot filled ciabatta sandwiches and salads from f8 each. There are plenty of other cafes around Rode Steen and along the harbourfront.

Markets are held Wednesday and Saturday along Breed. The *Aldi* supermarket at Dubbele Buurt 40, five minutes' walk west of the VVV, opens daily till 6 pm (8 pm on Thursday, 5 pm on Saturday). *Delikaas* (Breed 38) in an ornate colonial-style building, stocks cheese, freshly roasted nuts, dried meats and wine.

Next to the Hoofdtoren at the harbour, the tiny *Vishandel Leen Parlevliet* takeaway sells wonderful seafood rolls from f5.

Getting There & Around

There are frequent trains to Hoorn from Amsterdam (f13.25, 40 minutes, every half hour), Enkhuizen (f6.50, 1¼ hours, twice hourly), and Alkmaar (f6.50, 25 minutes, half-hourly).

The bus station is right outside Hoorn train station. Interliner bus No 305 goes hourly to Den Helder (one hour) Leeuwarden (2½ hours) and Alkmaar (one hour). Connexxion bus No 114 serves Edam (30 minutes, every half-hour) and the harbour side of Amsterdam Centraal Station (one hour, twice hourly).

The bicycle shop (☎ 21 70 96) at Hoorn train station charges f9.50/38 per day/week for touring bicycles. It opens 5.45 am to 11.30 pm daily (from 6.30 am on Saturday, 7.30 am on Sunday).

ENKHUIZEN

☎ 0228 • pop 16,500

Like other IJsselmeer ports, Enkhuizen shot to fame as a strategic harbour for the Dutch merchant fleet during the Golden Age. Its fortunes declined as the Zuiderzee began to silt up in the late 17th century. It still possesses a large fleet – of carefully tended old pleasure boats, especially wooden windjammers. But its main draw today is the superb Zuiderzeemuseum, which re-creates life in the region before the bay was sealed off in 1932. With its meandering canals and rows of gabled houses, Enkhuizen is one of the prettiest towns on the West Frisian peninsula.

Information & Orientation

The train station, a terminus on the line to Amsterdam, is on the southern edge of town. The yacht-filled Buitenhaven and the narrower Oude Haven bisect the town roughly east to west; canals encircle the old centre. Dijk is the main cafe-and-restaurant drag, on the northern bank of Oude Haven. About 200m further north, the long, pedestrianised Westerstraat runs parallel and is lined with lovely homes and impressive historic buildings.

The tourist office (☎ 31 31 64, fax 31 55 31, @ vvvenkhuizeneo@hetnet.nl) is at Tussen Twee Havens 1, about 50m east of the train station. It opens 9 am to 5 pm from Monday to Friday, and 9 am to 2 pm on Saturday, November to Easter and 9 am to 5 pm from Monday to Saturday, from Easter to June. In July and August, it closes at 5.30 pm from Monday to Saturday, and opens 9 am to 5 pm on Sunday. The office sells ferry tickets and a self-guided tour booklet (in English) to the town's sights (f3.50).

The laundrette in the train station (entrance on the north side) opens 7 am to 11 pm daily.

Money There's an ABN-Amro at Venedie 8, about 50m north of the Dijk canal street. ING Bank has a branch across the road at Melkmarkt 1.

Post & Communications The post office is about 1km west of the old centre at Molenweg 7. The public library, about 500m further west on the canal at Kwakespad 3, charges f2.50 per 15 minutes of Internet use (one terminal). It opens 1.30 to 9 pm on Monday and Friday, 1.30 to 5.30 pm on Tuesday and Wednesday and 10 am to 12.30 pm on Saturday (closed Thursday and Sunday).

Things to See & Do

In the eastern section of Westerstraat you'll find the remarkable **Westerkerk**, a 15th-century Gothic church with a removable wooden belfry. The ornate choir screen (1542) and imposing pulpit (1568) are worth a look. Opposite the church is the **Weeshuis**, a 17th-century orphanage with a sugary, curlicued portal.

At the other end of Westerstraat stands the 16th-century **Waag** (weigh house) on the old cheese market, and nearby the classical **Stadhuis**, modelled after the Amsterdam town hall that once stood on Dam Square. You can peek through the windows at the lavish Gobelins and tapestries (closed to the public).

Between the Buitenhaven and the Oude Haven, the **Drommedaris** was built as a defence tower as part of the 16th-century town walls. Once a formidable prison, it now serves as a youth hostel (see Places to Stay), but its clock-tower carillon still tinkles a playful tune on the hour.

Zuiderzeemuseum This impressive historical museum (☎ 31 82 60) actually consists of two parts: the open-air museum (Buitenmuseum) with 130-odd rebuilt dwellings and workshops, and the indoor (Binnenmuseum) which is devoted to farming, fishing and shipping. They are linked by a 15-minute ferry ride (you can walk there in about the same time).

The Buitenmuseum is by far the more captivating. It consists of a mock village whose inhabitants (all in traditional dress) live and work in a Zuiderzee village as it looked around the start of the 20th century. Buildings were trucked in from all over the region; the **lime kilns** from Akersloot, a **row of Monnickendam houses**, and the **post office** from Den Oever are but a few highlights. Don't miss the **Urk quarter**, which is raised to simulate the island the town once occupied. There are plenty of shops open to the public, including a chemist, a bakery and a rather steamy laundry (from the era before detergents).

NOORD HOLLAND

Each section (both ☎ 31 82 60) charges admission. The Buitenmuseum at Wierdijk 12 opens 10 am to 5 pm from Monday to Saturday (till 6 pm on Sunday), September to June. In July and August it opens till 6 pm daily. Entry costs f18.50 (children and seniors f13). The Binnenmuseum opens 10 am to 5 pm daily, year-round, and charges f8/7 for adults/children and seniors.

Places to Stay

Camping Enkhuizer Zand (☎ 31 72 89, fax 31 22 11, Kooizandweg 4), next to the Zuiderzeemuseum's open-air museum on the sea, costs f10.20/5.75/2.35 per adult/tent/car. Open April to September, this sprawling site has an indoor pool, grocery and tennis courts. The much smaller *de Vest* (☎ 31 12 21, Noorderweg 31), about 1km to the west, operates April to September and charges similar prices.

Jeugdhotel de Drommedaris (☎ 31 20 76, Paktuinen 1) is a quirky student hostel in the Drommedaris on the old harbour. Beds in the circular dorm cost a mere f12.50 and breakfast f7.50. Bring your own sheets or sleeping bag, as none are lent out. It's open year-round.

The VVV has a list of private accommodation from f25, including breakfast. *Hotel du Passage* (☎ 31 24 62, fax 31 81 33, Paktuinen 8) about 300m north-east of the train station has well-kept rooms despite the dingy corridors. Singles/doubles with breakfast cost f65/115. Reception is in the Chinese restaurant on the ground floor.

The *Appartement Hotel Driebanen* (☎ 31 61 81, fax 32 14 54, Driebanen 59), in a quiet canalside location 500m north of the old harbour, has singles/doubles with hall shower and toilet for f85, with private amenities for f125. Its weekly rates start at f350/588 for low/high season.

Villa Oud Enkhuizen (☎ 31 42 66, fax 31 81 71, ✉ villa_oud@wxs.nl, Westerstraat 217) is in a stately old villa about 1.5km west of the old town. Breakfast is served in the conservatory with a view of the manicured garden. Singles/doubles with private amenities cost f110/165 and triples f210.

Hotel Centrum (☎ 31 28 27, fax 31 64 73, ✉ info@hetcentrum.com, Westerstraat 153) has clean, modern rooms up the steep stairs above an atmospheric brown cafe. Doubles are f125.

Places to Eat

De Kapel Vlaaierij Proeverij (☎ 32 32 72, Westerstraat 128a), in the nave of a renovated 17th-century chapel opposite the Oude Weeshuis, has a great midday menu with soups for f7.50, ciabatta and club sandwiches for f10 to f11, salads, quiches and wonderful cakes and pies. It also opens for dinner (mains from f32.50).

The *Dikke Mik* (☎ 31 64 04, H.J. Schimmelstraat 10), is a tiny *eetcafe* near the Dijk with daily specials from f15. The clientele can get a bit crunchy after dark. The *Schipperscafe 't Ankertje* (Dijk 6) is a pub with a wonderful terrace on the canal across from the Drommedaris tower, serving pancakes, sandwiches and apple pie.

Restaurant De Boei (☎ 31 42 80, Havenweg 5), is known for its splendid fish dishes, particularly skate, from about f30. Its great spot on the outer harbour pulls in the tourists. It opens all day (closed November to February).

The posh *Restaurant de Drie Haringhe* (☎ 31 86 10, Dijk 28) offers Dutch and seafood mains f25 to f43, and three-course meals from f60 (try the seawolf fillet in green mustard sauce). It serves lunch and dinner (closed Tuesday).

A *market* is held Wednesday mornings on Westerstraat. The *Aldi* supermarket at Torenstraat 10 (near the Zuiderkerk) opens till 6 pm on weekdays (8 pm on Thursday), and to 4 pm on Saturday. *Vishandel Jacco Dekkers* (☎ 13 58 41, Bocht 1) is a terrific fish takeaway with a charming terrace on the water out back. Deep fried portions of shrimp, cod, eel and herring start at f5 (closed Monday).

Getting There & Away

There are regular trains to Amsterdam (f17.25, one hour, half-hourly), Den Helder (f19.25, 1¼ hours, change at Hoorn and Heerhugowaard), Hoorn (f6.50, 25 minutes, half-hourly), and Alkmaar (f13.25, one hour, change at Hoorn).

The bus station is behind Enkhuizen train station. Most connections involve a change at Hoorn (bus No 43, one hour, hourly). From the harbour side of Amsterdam Centraal Station, take bus No 114 to Hoorn (one hour, half-hourly) and switch to No 43.

There are ferries, all offering single and day return tickets, three times daily from Enkhuizen-Spoorhaven to Urk (1¾ hours), Stavoren (1¼ hours) and Medemblik (1¼ hours). All single/return tickets cost f12.50/18.

Getting Around

Dekker Tweewielers (☎ 31 29 61) at Nieuwstraat 2–6 has regular and three-speed bikes for f9.50/day. Leave a passport or national ID card as deposit. It opens daily to 9 pm (6 pm on Sunday). Hotel Driebanen (see Places to Stay) rents bikes for f9/day.

De Waterspiegel (☎ 31 74 56), at Olifantsteiger 3, rents six-person rowboats for f25/75 per hour/day, with f100 deposit. Kayaks and larger rowboats are also available. Enkhuizen Yachtcharter (☎ 32 32 00), Oosterhavenstraat 13, charges from f1900 per week to rent its ocean-going yachts.

MEDEMBLIK

☎ 0227 • pop 7300

About 12km north-west of Enkhuizen lies Medemblik, the oldest port on the IJsselmeer with a history going back to the 12th century. Known predominantly as a yachting centre, the town also has a medieval castle and a historic train museum well worth a visit.

Information & Orientation

The bus station is on the northern side of the old town, which sits largely on a peninsular. The harbours are about 500m to the south. The castle is on another, tiny peninsula on the eastern fringe, and is signposted from the harbour. Richly decorated facades on Kaasmarkt, Torenstraat, Nieuwstraat and along the Achterom canal are a lovely sight.

There's a tiny tourist office (☎/fax 54 28 52, ✉ vvv.medemblik@wxs.nl) in the train station at Dam 2. Hours are 10 am to noon and 2 to 4 pm from Monday to Saturday, November to March; and 10 am to 5 pm from Monday to Saturday, April to October. It also opens 10 am to 5 pm on Sunday in July and August. There's a Rabobank at Nieuwstraat 74, and a post office at Bagijnhof 10.

Things to See & Do

Kasteel Radboud (☎ 54 19 60), one of the few castles ever built in Noord Holland, was a precaution by Count Floris V in 1282 against further rebellion from the recently conquered West Frisians. It later served as a prison and fell into disrepair before a sweeping 19th-century restoration led by Pierre Cuypers, the designer of Amsterdam's Rijksmuseum. The imposing **Ridderzaal** (Knights' Hall) looks much as it did in the Middle Ages. Exhibitions give insights into the castle's history and inhabitants. Hours are 10 am to 5 pm from Tuesday to Friday, and 2 to 5 pm on Saturday, mid-May to mid-September. Entry costs f5/2.50.

The town's other main draw is the **Stoommachine Museum** (Steam Engine Museum, ☎ 54 47 32). Some of its 30 or so locomotives, in the old pump station, at Oosterdijk 4, are fired up for demonstrations in the summer months. It opens 10 am to 5 pm from Tuesday to Saturday, and from noon to 5 pm on Sunday from April to October. Admission is f5/2.50.

Places to Stay & Eat

Camping Zuiderzee (☎ 54 23 45, fax 54 42 47, Oosterdijk 1), about 1km south-east of the train station, is a big beachside site with a restaurant and laundry. Open April to October, it costs f32.50 for two adults, tent and car.

Herberg Nieuwland (☎ 0227-51 12 72, fax 51 18 99, Gemeenelandweg 116), in Den Oever about 20km north of Medemblik, charges f22 for dorm beds with breakfast. This pretty hostel in a calm spot opens April to October. Take bus No 636 to Wieringerwerf and change to No 130, which will take you to Den Oever.

The simple but friendly *Hotel B&B de Waeg (☎/fax 54 12 03, Oostersingel 5)*

NOORD HOLLAND

about 1km south-east of the train station, charges f50 per person, breakfast included.

Eetcafé Royal (☎ 54 12 04, Nieuwstraat 38) does good daily specials from f12 (closed Monday). *De Tijd (☎ 54 13 86, Westerhaven 1)* has pancakes from f8 and other Dutch specialities (closed Tuesday). There are other restaurants on Oosterhaven and Achter Eiland.

Getting There & Around

The nearest train station is in Hoorn, where you'll have to change to Connexxion buses for most destinations. From Amsterdam, take bus No 114 to Hoorn (one hour, twice hourly) and change to bus No 40 (another hour, every hour). From Enkhuizen, take bus No 43 and change to No 234 at Wervershoof.

A ferry runs three times daily from Medemblik to Enkhuizen-Spoorhaven. Single/return tickets cost f12.50/18 (1¼ hours each way).

Smit (☎ 54 12 00) at Vooreiland 1 rents touring bikes for f8.50 per day. The Zuiderzee camp site also rents two-wheelers (see Places to Stay).

ALKMAAR
☎ 072 • 93,000

One hour's train journey north of Amsterdam lies the picturesque small town of Alkmaar. It holds a special place in Dutch hearts as the first town, in 1573, to repel occupying Spanish troops; locals opened the locks and flooded the area with sea water, forcing the perplexed invaders to retreat. The victory also won the town weighing rights, which laid the foundation for its fame today – the cheese market. This rather overrated ceremony really packs in the tourists, but little cheese actually changes hands; nowadays that's left to the modern dairy combines.

The Afsluitdijk

For nearly three centuries plans were made, and shelved, to close off the Zuiderzee (South Sea) and increase the amount of arable land in the area north-east of Amsterdam.

The Zuiderzee, which opened into the North Sea beyond, was lined with villages dependent on the sea waters for fishing and, further north, ports such as Enkhuizen and Hoorn that kept the goods flowing to and from the Dutch colonies during the Golden Age.

Unfortunately the area was prone to flooding, but only in the late 19th century did new construction methods allow Cornelis Lely to come up with a blueprint for a retaining dike. Four years after the 1916 flood catastrophe, work began in earnest amid protests from fishermen who worried (quite rightly as it turned out) about the effect on their livelihoods.

Engineers, on the other hand, warned that the Wadden Islands might flood as the sea level rose. In 1932, the Zuiderzee was finally sealed off by what became known as the Afsluitdijk (Barrier Dike) and the IJsselmeer (IJssel Lake) was created. The much-dreaded rise in water level never occurred, but the fishing industry to the south was effectively killed.

This impressive 30km dam – it's not really a dike because there's water on either side – connects the provinces of North Holland to the west and Friesland (Fryslân) to the east. Driving east from Den Oever, you'll pass a **Memorial to Cornelius Lely**, who died in 1929 and never saw his project completed. Further east are the **Stevinsluizen**, two sets of sluices named after the 17th-century engineer Henri Stevin, who first mooted the idea of reclaiming the Zuiderzee.

You can cross the Afsluitdijk on the hourly Interliner bus No 350 from Alkmaar to Leeuwarden, but not by train. Singles/returns cost f30/51 and you can buy your ticket on the bus (strip cards aren't valid).

A second dike from Enkhuizen slices this inland sea in half; the southern portion is officially known as the Markermeer. Another plan foresaw the drainage of these seas to reclaim the land, as happened in the province of Flevoland, but these schemes were shelved for environmental reasons. On a nice day you'll see hundreds of yachts and traditional Zuiderzee fishing and cargo boats (see Sailing under Activities in the Facts for the Visitor chapter for rental details).

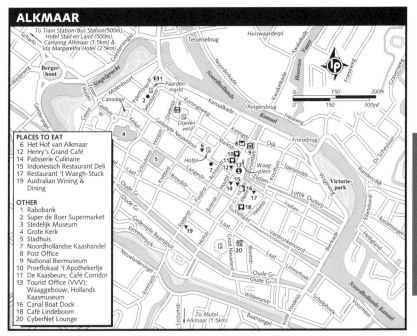

ALKMAAR

PLACES TO EAT
6 Het Hof van Alkmaar
12 Henry's Grand Café
14 Patisserie Culinaire
15 Indonesisch Restaurant Deli
17 Restaurant 't Waegh-Stuck
19 Australian Wining & Dining

OTHER
1 Rabobank
2 Super de Boer Supermarket
3 Stedelijk Museum
4 Grote Kerk
5 Stadhuis
7 Noordhollandse Kaashandel
8 Post Office
9 National Biermuseum
10 Proeflokaal 't Apothekertje
11 De Kaasbeurs; Café Corridor
13 Tourist Office (VVV);
   Waaggebouw; Hollands
   Kaasmuseum
16 Canal Boat Dock
18 Café Lindeboom
20 CyberNet Lounge

Information & Orientation

The pretty, canal-bound centre is 500m
south-east of the train station. The main arteries are Gedempte Nieuwsloot, which leads
you to the main square (Waagplein), and
Langestraat, a long and dull pedestrianised
shopping street. The eastern part is the most
charming, with lots of restaurants and bars
around the Waag and the area near Bierkade.

The tourist office (☎ 511 42 84, fax 511
75 13, ✉ vvvalkeo@wxs.nl) is at Waagplein
2, unmissable in the Waaggebouw, the towering old weigh house. It opens 10 am to
5.30 pm on Monday, 9 am to 5.30 pm on
Tuesday and Wednesday, 9 am to 9 pm on
Thursday, 9 am to 6 pm on Friday and
9.30 am to 5 pm on Saturday. Staff will book
local accommodation for a f10 fee. Web site:
www.noord-holland-tourist.nl/nl/alkmaareo
(Dutch only).

Money There are few banks in the old centre. The Rabobank at Paternosterstraat 1

changes money and has an ATM that takes
international credit cards.

Post & Communications The main post
office is at Houttil 4. The CyberNet Lounge
(☎ 520 54 20), Laat 75, charges f0.20 per
minute of Internet use as you sink into its
massive couches. It opens 10 am to 10 pm
daily.

Things to See & Do

Cheese Market Alkmaar is one of the few
Dutch towns where cheesemakers' guilds
still operate. At 10 am every Friday morning the famous round slabs – mostly Gouda,
Edam, and Leidse – are stacked on Waagplein, and the buyers insert a hollow rod
into the rounds to extract a sample. After a
taste-test (which also involves a lot of sniffing and crumbling to check fat and moisture
content), the auction opens and bidders sig-
nal their interest with hand claps. As deals
are struck the porters, clad in white save for

their brightly coloured straw hats, whisk the cheeses on sledges to the old scale, accompanied by a zillion camera clicks from the tourists lining the square. Arrive early if you want a good view from the throng (mid-April to mid-September).

Other Attractions The **Waaggebouw** served as a chapel in the 14th century before it was converted to a weigh house two centuries later. The tower carillon (with mechanical jousting knights) plays at 6.30 and 7.30 pm on Thursday and noon and 1 pm on Saturday; during cheese market season it also chimes at 11 am and noon on Friday. Apart from the tourist office it houses the **Hollands Kaasmuseum** (Dutch Cheese Museum; ☎ 511 42 84), a display of historical cheese-making utensils, photos and a curious collection of paintings by 16th-century female artists. The museum opens 10 am to 4 pm from Monday to Saturday (Friday from 9 am). Admission costs f5/3.

Housed in the old De Boom brewery at Houttil 1, the **Nationaal Biermuseum** (☎ 511 38 01) has a fun collection of beer-making equipment, explanations and the usual wax dummies showing how the suds were once made. You can buy beer in the top-floor shop or down a few at the well-stocked bar downstairs. It opens 10 am to 4 pm from Tuesday to Saturday, and 1 to 4 pm on Sunday. Entry is f4.50/2.50.

Highlight of the **Stedelijk Museum** (Municipal Museum; ☎ 511 07 37), at Doelenstraat 3, is its collection of Golden Age paintings by Dutch masters. Kids will also enjoy the displays of 19th-century toys. The museum opens 10 am to 5 pm from Tuesday to Friday, and 1 to 5 pm at weekends. Admission costs f3/2.

Among the main historic buildings, the **Stadhuis** (Town Hall) on Langestraat is a mish-mash of ostentatious 16th- and 17th-century styles. You can take a peek at the antique Renaissance interiors from 9 am to noon and 2 to 4 pm from Monday to Friday (free).

The Gothic **Grotekerk**, restored to its present glory in 1996, is just as famous for its two fantastic **organs**. The smaller one (the

'Swallow Organ') in the north ambulatory is one of the country's oldest (1511), while the huge and ornate nave organ (1643) was designed by Jacob van Campen, the leading organ-maker of the day. Organ concerts take place some Fridays during summer – check with the tourist office for times.

Canal Boat Tours Open-topped canal boats make 45-minute tours with commentary (also in English) departing from Mient, near the Waag. Tours run at 11 am from Monday to Thursday and Saturday from April to October; and also on Sunday from May to August. On Friday, during cheese market season, boats go every 20 minutes starting at 9.30 am. Tickets cost f7.50/4.50.

Places to Stay
Camping Alkmaar (☎ 511 69 24, Bergerweg 201) has a pleasant woodside location about 1km west of the train station. It charges f8/7/4 per adult/tent/car, and opens April to mid-September. Take bus Nos 160 or 162 to Sportpark (10 minutes).

Alkmaar has only three hotels and no hostel. The tourist office has a list of private accommodation from about f30 per person.

One of the best choices is opposite the train station. *Hotel Stad en Land* (☎ 561 39 11, fax 511 84 40, Stationsweg 92) has modern, quiet singles/doubles for f90/130, all with private shower and toilet, TV and phone. Breakfast is included. Rear rooms overlook a little pond.

Ida Margaretha (☎ 561 39 89, fax 564 51 02) is a well-kept, family run place in a residential area 2km north of the train station. It's comfy but unexciting and starts at f55 per person, including private amenities. Take bus No 156 to Kanaldijk.

The three-star *Motel Alkmaar* (☎ 540 14 14, fax 540 12 32, Arcadialaan 2) is your standard suburban option, clean and with all mod cons, about 1.5km south of the old centre. Rates are from f80/160. Take bus No 25 from the train station to Arcadialaan.

Places to Eat
Alkmaar has a huge variety of restaurants and cafes. The *Indonesisch Restaurant*

Deli (☎ 515 40 82, Mient 8) offers good-value dishes such as maduras beef (f13.50) and more elaborate *rijsttafels* for f40. It opens 5 to 10 pm (closed Wednesday).

The *Patisserie Culinaire (☎ 511 29 27, Houttil 11)* is an artsy lunch place, with lots of freshly-made filled baguettes and croissants from f6, quiche for f4 and big salads from f14. Hours are 9 am to 6 pm (closed Sunday).

Henry's Grand Café (☎ 511 32 83, Houttil 34) is a convivial place serving soups, salads, sandwiches and set meals including pork or chicken satay at f16.50. There's a good beer selection. Evening dishes cost f20 to f35. It opens till 12.30 am.

Het Hof van Alkmaar (☎ 512 12 12, Hof van Sonoy 1), a former 15th-century cloister overlooking a lovely courtyard, offers up-market Dutch cuisine. Starters are from f9.75 and mains from f30 (we enjoyed the marinated Victoria bass with vegies in chilli-coconut sauce). Three-course menus cost f40. It opens for lunch and dinner (closed Monday). *Restaurant 't Waegh-Stuck (☎ 512 11 14, Fridsen 101)* is a swish Dutch-French place serving vegie lasagne for f24.50 and three-course dinners for f41.25.

Homesick Aussies might try *Australian Wining & Dining (☎ 512 28 79, Ridderstraat 17)*. Outback specialities include crocodile soup (f12.50) and kangaroo fillet in port wine (f35). It's open evenings till 11 pm (closed Monday and Tuesday).

There's a *Super de Boer* supermarket at Paardenmarkt 2. For a quick bite, try *Deniz Bakkerij*, a Turkish bakery at Stationsweg 72 opposite the train station, with *böreks* (meat pastries) for f3 and sandwiches from f3.50. *Noordhollandse Kaashandel (☎ 511 34 22, Magdalenenstraat 11)* has an excellent selection of Dutch and French cheeses.

Entertainment Bars and brown cafes line the north side of Waagplein. *De Kaasbeurs (Houttil 30)* has regular jazz concerts on its rear stages; *Café Corridor* two doors down plays rock and pop till the wee hours. The *Proeflokaal 't Apothekertje (☎ 512 41 07, Waagplein 16)* is an old-style drinking hole done up like a chemist shop. Over by the old fish market, *Café Lindeboom (☎ 512 17 43, Verdronkenoord 114)* is a cosy bar with a lively crowd.

Getting There & Away

There are trains twice an hour from Amsterdam Centraal Station (f11.50, 30 minutes). Other frequent services include Hoorn (f6.50, 25 minutes, half-hourly), Den Helder (f13.25, 35 minutes, hourly), Haarlem (f10.50, 30 to 45 minutes, half-hourly) and Enkhuizen (f13.25, one hour, with a change at Hoorn).

Alkmaar is served by many regional bus lines, but key destinations involve changes. From Amsterdam Centraal Station, take bus 94 via Zaandam (10 minutes, half-hourly) to Beverwijk and change to bus Nos 167 or 168 to Alkmaar.

Getting Around

The cheese market is a 15-minute walk south-east of the train station. You can also take Connexxion bus Nos 10, 22 or 127 to Kanaalkade (5 minutes).

The bicycle shop (☎ 511 79 07) at the train station charges f9.50/38 per day/week to rent touring bicycles. Bring your passport or national ID card as deposit. It opens Monday to Friday, 8 am to 11.30 pm (Saturday from 6.30 am, Sunday from 7.30 am).

TEXEL ISLAND
☎ 0222 • pop 13,000

The biggest and oldest of the Wadden Islands, Texel (pronounced 'tessel'), just 20 minutes north of Den Helder by ferry, is a remarkably diverse place with broad white beaches, lush nature reserves, forests and a few picture-book villages. Texel – 25km long and 9km wide – consisted of two islands until 1835, when a sliver of land to Eyerland Island to the north was reclaimed from the sea and gradually widened.

Before the North Sea Canal was opened in the 19th century, Texel was a main stop for ships en route to and from Asia, Africa and North America; the first trade mission to the East Indies (1595–97) began and ended here. It was also the site of a spectacular maritime disaster. On Christmas

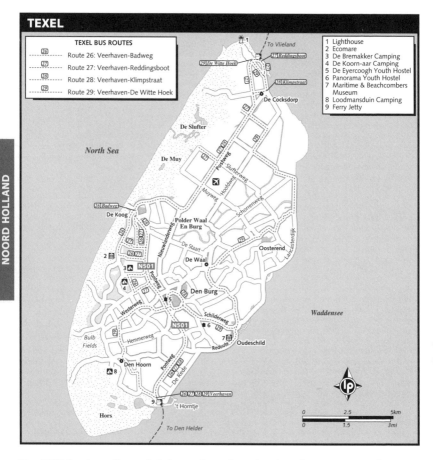

TEXEL

TEXEL BUS ROUTES
- 26 ----- Route 26: Veerhaven-Badweg
- 27 ----- Route 27: Veerhaven-Reddingsboot
- 28 ----- Route 28: Veerhaven-Klimpstraat
- 29 ----- Route 29: Veerhaven-De Witte Hoek

1 Lighthouse
2 Ecomare
3 De Bremakker Camping
4 De Koorn-aar Camping
5 De Eyercoogh Youth Hostel
6 Panorama Youth Hostel
7 Maritime & Beachcombers Museum
8 Loodmansduin Camping
9 Ferry Jetty

Day 1593, hurricane-force winds battered a merchant fleet moored off the coast and 44 vessels sank, drowning some 1000 seamen.

Texel lives chiefly from tourism, with the majority of visitors being either Dutch or German. Its beaches, particularly near touristy De Koog, fill to bursting in June when the world's largest catamaran race for the Cisco Trophy takes place.

Information & Orientation

The main town is Den Burg, located 6km north of the ferry jetty and home to the tourist office. To the south-east, Oudeschild

has a beachcombers museum and a pretty little harbour for fishing-boat excursions; Den Hoorn is a peaceful village close to tulip fields to the south-west. Oosterend has some of the Texel's most picturesque architecture (including its oldest church), while tiny De Cocksdorp, due north near the lighthouse, is a good place to really get away from it all.

There's a friendly VVV office in Den Burg at Emmalaan 66 (☎ 31 47 41, fax 31 00 54, @ info@texel.net), on the southern fringe of town and well signposted from the centre. It opens 9 am to 6 pm from Monday

euro currency converter €1 = f2.20

to Friday, and 9 am to 5 pm on Saturday from November to March. From April to November it stays open to 9 pm on Friday, and in July and August, from 10 am to 1.30 pm on Sunday, too. Staff book accommodation on the spot for a f10 fee. Web site: www.texel.net.

Money In Den Burg, the ABN-Amro at the corner of Binnenburg and Kantoorstraat, about 50m east of the imposing **Hervormde Kerk** (Reform Church), has an ATM and a currency-exchange machine. Other banks are located in De Koog and De Cocksdorp. The larger post offices also exchange money.

Post & Communications The main post office in Den Burg is at Parkstraat 3, open 9 am to 5.30 pm from Monday to Saturday with a one-hour break at 12.30. Surf the Internet at the Den Burg public library, Drijverstraat 7, for f2.50 per quarter-hour. It opens 9 am to 6 pm Monday to Friday (Thursday to 8 pm), and 10 am to 5 pm on Saturday.

Things to See & Do
Texel's wonderful **beaches** (on the eastern North Sea shore only) are marked by numbered pilings; lifeguards are on duty from No 9 south-east of Den Hoorn to No 21 near De Koog in summer. There are two nudist beaches, at No 9 near Den Hoorn and at No 27, close to the tidal gully at De Slufter. Swimming is prohibited between Nos 31 and 33 by the lighthouse, due to the treacherous currents between Texel and Vlieland.

The **Ecomare** (☎ 31 77 41) has exhibits covering Texel's huge array of bird life and some fascinating aquariums – try going eye-to-eye with a shark or seaskate. It's also a refuge for sick seals and birds retrieved from the oft-polluted Wattenmeer. The museum, which is south of De Koog at Ruyslaan 92 (bus No 26), opens 9 am to 5 pm daily; seal feedings are at 11 am and 3 pm. Admission costs f12.50/10/5 for adults/students/children under 13.

The **Maritime and Beachcombers Museum** (☎ 31 49 56) has some extraordinary

junk recovered from sunken ships – it's a bit like perusing the inventory of *The Titanic*, including old-time spectacles, passengers' diaries, barbershop gear etc. The museum, in the old windmill at Barentszstraat 21 in Oudeschild, opens 10 am to 5 pm from Tuesday to Saturday; entry is f8/4. To gather your own beach treasure, board a horse-drawn wagon run by **Jutters Plezier** (☎ 31 62 25) in De Cocksdorp. Tours (f15/9 for adults/children up to 12 years) depart from the lighthouse in De Cocksdorp – check with the VVV for times.

Maritime Museum
On the way to Texel, the only real attraction in the unspectacular naval town of **Den Helder** (population 60,000) is the Maritime Museum (☎ 0223-65 75 34), housed in the former arsenal of the Dutch Royal Navy. Visitable vessels include a minesweeper and a submarine – definitely not for the claustrophobic – moored on the docks outside. The museum is a 10-minute walk south-west of the ferry terminal at Hoofdgracht 3. Hours are 10 am to 5 pm from Monday to Friday and noon to 5 pm at weekends. Entry costs f7.50/5.

Cycling & Hiking The tourist office sells a useful booklet of bike routes (f2; in Dutch) and can advise on the hiking trails that crisscross the island. The well-marked 80km-long 'Texel Path' takes you through the dunes and over the mud flats before veering inland through the island's villages; the circular local routes along the way make for nice one-to-three-hour hikes or bike trips. The marshy De Slufter and De Muy nature reserves are a mecca for bird-watchers (don't forget your wellies).

Boat Trips Several shrimp trawlers in Oudeschild take tourists along on their daily fishing runs. The *Emmie TX 10* departs at 10.30 am and 2 pm daily (except Sunday) for a two-hour trip including a run by the local seal colony that suns itself on the sandbanks. Tickets cost f12 (children up to 10 years cost f10). Book ahead at the VVV or on ☎ 31 36 39.

NOORD HOLLAND

NOORD HOLLAND

Pleasure Flights Tessel Air (☎ 31 14 36) offers short spins over Texel and the nearby islands of Vlieland and Terschelling. It charges f45/75/95/120 for flights of 15/30/45/60 minutes (you can choose a *reachable* destination for the latter two). For more adventurous types, **parachute jumping** together with an instructor costs f320 per jump. It's a good idea to book ahead.

Places to Stay

Camping Texel's dozen camp sites get crowded in summer; the VVV in Den Burg can tell you which sites have vacancies. The cheapest is *De Bremakker* (☎ 31 28 63, fax 31 37 78, ✉ bremakker@wxs.nl, Templierweg 40) between Den Burg and De Koog by the woods 1km from the beach. It's open April to October and is f23.50 for two people and a tent. There's a laundry, snack bar, shower and sports facilities. Take bus No 26 to Templierweg.

Close by, *De Koorn-aar* (☎ 31 29 31, fax 32 22 08, ✉ koorn_aar@etrade.nl, Grensweg 388) is a sprawling family oriented site with a swimming pool and supermarket nearby. Open April to October, it charges f37.75 for up to four people and a tent. Take bus No 26 to Grensweg.

For camping in isolation, head to *Loodsmansduin* (☎ 31 92 03, fax 31 92 03, Rommelpot 19) amid the dunes by Den Hoorn. It costs f38.50 for two people and tent. Take bus No 29 to Den Hoorn, and follow the signs for the 15-minute trip to Loodsmansduin.

Hostels There are two youth hostels on Texel. About 2km east of Den Burg, *Panorama* (☎ 31 54 41, fax 31 38 89, Schansweg 7), is in a pretty thatched house next to the *Hoge Berg* (the 15m-high 'Tall Mountain'). It opens year-round and charges f28 for dorm beds including breakfast. The *De Eyercoogh* (☎/fax 31 29 07, Pontweg 106) is a 10-minute walk southwest of the centre of Den Burg. It's a simpler place with six large dorms, costs f25 for B&B and operates April to October. For both hostels, take bus No 28 from the ferry jetty (also No 29 for Panorama).

Hotels Hotels tend to be expensive on Texel and prices can rise in July and August. The VVV also has a B&B list from f35 per person per night. Add f1.30 tourist tax per night to your bill.

In Den Burg, *Hotel De Merel* (☎ 31 31 32, fax 31 03 33, Warmoesstraat 22) has rooms for f65 per person. *'t Koogerend* (☎ 31 33 01, fax 31 59 03, Kogerstraat 94) charges f81/112 for singles/doubles, all with TV, phone and private amenities.

The three-star *Hotel de Lindeboom* (☎ 31 20 41, fax 31 05 17, Groeneplaats 14) is a nice option on the main square. Spacious, modern rooms with private facilities start at f95/128.

Het Wapen van Texel (☎/fax 31 96 23, Herenstraat 34) in Den Hoorn is a stylish, old-fashioned place with a good restaurant. Doubles with private bath and toilet start at f130. It's handily close to a nudist beach to the south-east.

The intimate, family run *'t Anker* (☎/fax 31 62 74, Kikkertstraat 24) in a quiet spot in De Cocksdorp, has homey doubles with private shower and toilet from f134.

If you must stay in charmless De Koog, *Hotel Brinkzicht* (☎ 31 72 58, fax 32 71 29, Dorpsstraat 210) offers basic but clean doubles from f99 (f119 with private shower and toilet).

Places to Eat

Restaurants With thousands of sheep roaming the island, lamb dishes get top billing. In Den Burg, try the *Eetcafé Ploff Inn (Kantoorstraat 3)*, a popular little eatery tucked away behind the ABN-Amro bank. It does tasty lamb satay for f17.50, sandwiches from f3 and also daily specials for f15.

The pleasant *Grand Café* at Hotel de Lindeboom (see Places to Stay) has pancakes from f8, club sandwiches for f11, and fish or lamb dishes from f18.50. Both places are open for lunch and dinner.

In Den Hoorn, *Loodman's Welvaren* (☎ 31 95 17, Herenstraat 12) is an inviting *cafe-eethuis* with three-course menus for f35 and a big choice of pancakes. It's open all day till 10 pm.

The best bet in De Koog is the *Vogelhuis Orangerie* (☎ *31 72 79, Dorpsstraat 204*), which serves local dishes, such as baked butterfish in mustard sauce for f24.50, in its glass-roofed veranda all day (closed Monday and Tuesday). There are many restaurants in Dorpsstraat.

If you're feeling flush, the *Rôtisserie Kerckeplein* (☎ *31 89 50, Oesterstraat 6*) in Oosterend has splendid Texel-French cuisine. Lamb or fish dishes start at f39 and a set four-course dinner costs f72.50 (closed Monday and Tuesday). Wash it all down with a dark *Texels Speciaalbier*.

Self-Catering There's a *Super de Boer* supermarket in Den Burg on the corner of Gasthuisstraat and Gravensstraat. In De Koog, try the big *Spar* at Dorpsstraat 29. Both open weekdays till 6 pm and on Saturday to 5 pm.

There are plenty of fish takeaway joints, but the top pick is arguably *Vispaleis-Rokerij* (*Heemskerckstraat 13*), which cures its own catch in a shop behind the harbour dam in Oudeschild. It does a great fish soup for f6.50 and eel/herring sandwiches for f7.50. In Den Burg, the *Viscenter Waddenzee* on Stenenplaats has wonderful *kibbeling* (deep-fried cod cheeks) from f5.

Getting There & Away
Train & Ferry Trains from Amsterdam to Den Helder (1½ hours, f22.50) are met by a bus that whisks you to the awaiting, hourly car ferry. The ferry trip to 't Horntje on Texel takes 20 minutes, and costs f5/10/48.50/71 per child/adult/car/caravan.

Ferries from Den Helder leave at 35 minutes past the hour (6.35 am to 9.35 pm), while those from 't Horntje go at five minutes past (6.05 am to 9.05 pm). If you're driving, show up at the docks at least half an hour before departure in summer – there'll be a queue.

From May to mid-September, the ferry firm De Vriendschap (☎ 31 64 51) makes the half-hour crossing from near De Cocksdorp to car-free Vlieland, the next of the Wadden Islands to the north. In July and August it departs at 10.30 am and returns from Vlieland at 5 pm; service is irregular

the rest of the summer, so check times with the VVV. The return fare is f24.50 (f15 for children 4 to 11 years). For more details, see the Friesland chapter.

Getting Around
Connexxion/AOT (☎ 0900-92 92) operates four routes, three of which run frequently; consider buying a day pass for the whole island, which costs just f6. Bus No 26 links incoming ferries in 't Horntje with Den Burg (seven minutes, hourly from 7 am to almost 10 pm) and De Koog (another 16 minutes) and the northern hamlet of De Cocksdorp (20 minutes from De Koog). Bus No 28 goes to De Koog and circles back by a clutch of camp sites (and the Ecomare museum). Bus No 29 links 't Horntje to Den Hoorn and Den Burg and snakes along the eastern shore to Oudeschild, Oosterend and Cocksdorp. The one infrequent service is Bus No 27 which links 't Horntje and De Cocksdorp.

Bicycle The welter of rental shops include Zegel (☎ 31 25 30), 14 Parkstraat, in the centre of Den Burg, which charges f7.50/32.50 for touring bikes per day/week and f10/40 for three-speeds. Near the ferry terminal, the shop 't Horntje (☎ 31 95 88), Pontweg 2, charges similar rates.

Taxi The Telekom Taxi (☎ 32 22 11) takes you between any two destinations on the island for f7 per person. Book at least an hour in advance, or buy a ticket at the Teso counter in the Den Helder ferry terminal; taxis wait by the ferry jetty in 't Horntje.

West of Amsterdam

HAARLEM
☎ 023 • pop 150,000
The capital of Noord Holland province, Haarlem has retained more of its 17th-century character than any other Randstad city. The wealth of historic buildings, private courtyards and posh antique shops exude an air of refined elegance, and its Frans Hals Museum is one of the country's most impressive. With

NOORD HOLLAND

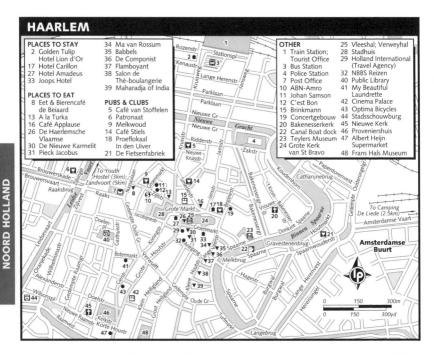

HAARLEM

PLACES TO STAY
2 Golden Tulip Hotel Lion d'Or
17 Hotel Carillon
27 Hotel Amadeus
33 Joops Hotel

PLACES TO EAT
8 Eet & Bierencafé de Beiaard
13 A la Turka
16 Café Applause
26 De Haerlemsche Vlaamse
30 De Nieuwe Karmelit
31 Pieck Jacobus

34 Ma van Rossum
35 Babbels
36 De Componist
37 Flamboyant
38 Salon de Thé-boulangerie
39 Maharadja of India

PUBS & CLUBS
5 Café van Stoffelen
6 Patronaat
9 Melkwoud
14 Café Stiels
18 Proeflokaal in den Uiver
21 De Fietsenfabriek

OTHER
1 Train Station; Tourist Office
3 Bus Station
4 Police Station
7 Post Office
10 ABN-Amro
11 Johan Samson
12 C'est Bon
15 Brinkmann
19 Concertgebouw
20 Bakenesserkerk
22 Canal Boat dock
23 Teylers Museum
24 Grote Kerk van St Bravo

25 Vleeshal; Verweyhal
28 Stadhuis
29 Holland International (Travel Agency)
32 NBBS Reizen
40 Public Library
41 My Beautiful Laundrette
42 Cinema Palace
43 Optima Bicycles
44 Stadsschouwburg
45 Nieuwe Kerk
46 Proveniershuis
47 Albert Heijn Supermarket
48 Frans Hals Museum

several reasonably priced hotels as well as a vibrant pub and restaurant scene, Haarlem also makes a good base for visiting Amsterdam, just 19km to the east, or the Keukenhof bulb fields to the south.

History

The name Haarlem derives from *Haarloheim*, meaning a place on high, wooded sandy soil. Its origins date back to the 10th century, when the counts of Holland set up a toll post on the Spaarne River and built lavish residences nearby. Granted a charter by Count William II in 1245, Haarlem came into its own as an inland port, second only to Amsterdam. The Spanish laid siege to Haarlem in 1572, finally cutting off the town's supplies by blocking the Haarlemmermeer with their fleet. The city surrendered after seven months, but worse was yet to come: Spanish commander Frederick of Toledo ordered the massacre of virtually the city's entire population, including the

Protestant clerics (inscriptions on buildings around town recall the horror). Five years later the invaders were repelled by William of Orange (aka William The Silent) and Haarlem embarked on its period of Golden Age prosperity, attracting renowned painters and artists from throughout Europe.

Orientation

The main train station – an Art Deco masterpiece in its own right – is on the north side of the old town. Grote Markt is the main square, a 10-minute walk to the south. The centre has a large pedestrianised section, with lots of pubs and restaurants along Zijlstraat, Grote Houtstraat and especially Lange Veerstraat.

Information

Tourist Offices The tourist office (☎ 0900-616 16 00, fax 534 05 37, ✉ info@vvvzk.nl) is outside the front door of the train station at Stationsplein 1. Hours are 9.30 am to 5.30 pm from Monday to Friday and 10 am to 2 pm on Saturday. Staff will reserve local accommodation for a f10 fee. Website: www.haarlem.nl.

Money In the train station, there's a GWK exchange office and a Postbank ATM that takes international credit cards. ABN-Amro has a branch, also with an ATM, in the old town at Zijlstraat 86, the neo-Gothic former post office. The Postbank in the main post office also changes money.

Post & Communications The main post office is at Gedempte Oude Gracht 2. The public library (☎ 515 7600), at Doelenplein 1, has five Internet terminals that can be used for free; hours are 10 am to 6 pm from Monday to Friday, and noon to 5 pm on Saturday.

Laundry My Beautiful Laundrette at Botermarkt 20 opens 8.30 am to 8.30 pm daily (last load at 7 pm).

Travel Agencies NBBS Reizen (☎ 531 69 29) at Anegang 17 specialises in cut-rate air tickets for students and last-minute offers. Holland International (☎ 532 11 40) is a good all-purpose travel agency at Grote Houtstraat 3.

Things to See & Do
The Old Town The main square is the **Grote Markt**, flanked with restaurants and cafes and a clutch of historical buildings. At the western end stands the florid, 14th-century **Stadhuis** (Town Hall), which grew many extensions in the centuries that followed, including a balcony where judgments from the high court were pronounced. The counts' hall contains 15th-century panel paintings and is normally open during office hours.

At the opposite end looms the **Grotekerk van St Bavo**, the Gothic cathedral with a 50m-high steeple that can be seen from almost anywhere in the city. It contains some fine Renaissance artworks, but the star attraction is its stunning Müller organ – one of the most magnificent in the world, standing 30m high with about 5000 pipes. It was played by Handel and Mozart (the latter was 10 years old at the time). The church opens 10 am to 4 pm from Monday to Saturday; entry is f2.75/1.75 for adults/children and seniors. There are tours in English on request (f4.50). Free organ recitals take place at 3 pm every Saturday and also at 8.15 pm every Tuesday from April to September.

In the centre of Grote Markt stand the 17th-century **Vleeshal**, a former meat market, and the **Verweyhal**, an old fish market; both serve as modern art annexes of the Frans Hal Museum. On the square north of the Grotekerk is a statue of Laurens Coster, whom Haarlemmers believe has a claim, along with Gutenberg, to be called the inventor of moveable type.

Off Grote Houtstraat to the south-west stands the **Proveniershuis**, the former headquarters of St Joris Doelen (the Civic Guards of St George), which started life as an almshouse. Its wonderful old *hofje* is one of Haarlem's prettiest (see also boxed text 'Haarlemmer Hofjes'). Around the corner to the west, down charming Korte Houtstraat, is the 17th-century **Nieuwekerk**; the capricious tower by Lieven de Key is supported by a rather boxy design by Jacob van Campen.

North-east of the Teylers Museum, at the corner of Vrouwestraat and Bakenesserstraat, stands the lovely **Bakenesserkerk**, a late 15th-century church with a lamp-lit tower of sandstone. The stone was employed here when the Grote Kerk proved too weak to support a heavy steeple – hence the wooden tower of the cathedral today.

Museums The **Frans Hals Museum** (☎ 023-511 57 75), at Groot Heiligland 62, features the master's portraits and works by other great artists – a must-see for fans of Dutch painting. Kept in an almshouse where the artist spent his final, impoverished years, the collection focuses on the 17th-century **Haarlem School**, which is regarded as the pinnacle of Dutch mannerist art. Eight group portraits by Hals, detailing the companies of the Civic Guard, are the museum's pride and joy, revealing the painter's exceptional attention to mood and

NOORD HOLLAND

psychological tone. Don't miss his two paintings known collectively as *The Regents & the Regentesses of the Old Men's Alms House* (1664). Among other treasures are the curious works by Hals' teacher, Flemish artist Carel van Mander: ceiling-high illustrations of the human anatomy with Biblical and mythological allusions. The museum opens 11 am to 5 pm from Monday to Saturday, and 1 to 5 pm on Sunday. Admission costs f7.50/3.50.

On Grote Markt, the **Vleeshal** holds contemporary art exhibitions; the **Verweyhal** next door, in a fancy Renaissance building designed by Lieven de Key, houses the Frans Hals Museum's collection of modern art, including works by Dutch impressionists and the CoBrA movement. (Don't miss Piet van Leeuwen's surreal work, including one of tuna tails protruding from a tulip field.) Known collectively as **De Hallen**, the museums open 11 am to 5 pm from Monday to Saturday, and 1 to 5 pm on Sunday. Entry costs f3.50/1.75.

The **Teylers Museum** (☎ 023-531 90 10) is the oldest museum in the country (1778), named for philanthropist-merchant Pieter Teyler van der Hulst. This eclectic collection at Spaarne 16 comprises drawings by the Italian Renaissance artists, notably Michelangelo and Raphael, and paintings from the Dutch and French schools. Its stunning *Ovale Zaal* (Oval Room) contains a display of natural history specimens in elegant glass cases spread over two galleries; elsewhere you'll find fossils, mineral crystals, and old whizz-bang scientific devices, such as an 18th-century electrostatic machine. Hours are 10 am to 5 pm from Tuesday to Saturday, and noon to 5 pm on Sunday. Admission costs f10/2.50.

Canal Boat Tours Woltheus Cruises (☎ 535 77 23) runs 75-minute canal boat tours with commentary in English five times a day (10.30 am, and then every 1½ hours till 4.30 pm) from April to October. Tickets cost f12.50/10/7.50 for adults/ seniors/children under 12. Departure is from opposite the Teylers Museum (south side of the river).

Haarlemmer Hofjes

The first of Haarlem's many residential *hofjes* or courtyards were laid out for monks in the 12th century. Later, they were used as lodging for travellers and as hospitals. Most are private but you can usually take a peek.

Ask the VVV tourist office for its free brochure, *Hofjeswandeling*, which includes the following:

Teylershofje, Koudenhorn 64 – built by the founder of the Teyler Museum (1787)
Hofje van Staats, Jansweg 39 – originally for poor women of the Reformed Church (1733)
St Jorisdoelen, Grote Houtstraat 144 – a proveniershuis (1591)
Hofje van Loo, Barrevoetstraat 7 – a guesthouse built by mayor Sijmon van Loo (1489)
Brouwershofje, Tuchthuisstraat 8 – for members of the brewers' guild (1472)
Frans Loenen Hofje, Witte Herenstraat 24 – almshouses built from a merchant's estate (1607)

The VVV also runs a guided tour of hofjes at 10 am every Saturday, and also 10 am Wednesday in July and August. Tickets cost f10/7.50. Commentary is in Dutch but most guides will take questions in English.

Places to Stay

Camping *De Liede* (☎ 533 23 60, fax 535 86 66, Lieoever 68), 2.5km east of the old centre, charges f5.50 for each adult/tent/car, and opens all year. It also rents canoes and paddle boats. Take bus No 2 (direction 'Zuidpolder') to Zoete Inval and walk north for 10 minutes. Summer-only sites dot the dunes near Zandvoort.

Hostels The newly renovated *Haarlem Youth Hostel* (☎ 537 37 93, fax 537 11 76, Gijzenpad 3) 3km north-east of the train station charges f28/33 for juniors/seniors, including breakfast. There are surcharges for doubles and quads. Rules include 10 pm silence but there's no curfew (room key is also the front door key). It operates late March to

December. Laundry and cooking facilities are available. Take bus No 2 (direction Haarlem Noord) from the train station to the Haarlem Youth Hostel stop (10 minutes).

Hotels The tourist office has a list of B&Bs from f35 per person. Add f3.50 tourist tax per person per night to the prices given below.

The friendly *Joops Hotel (☎ 532 20 08, fax 512 53 00, @ Joops@multiweb.nl, Oude Groenmarkt 20)* is the best deal in town. Its 100-odd comfortable, spacious rooms are spread over an entire block along Warmoestraat by the Grote Kerk. Singles/doubles with hall shower and toilet start at f55/105, while small studios with a kitchenette cost from f115. The breakfast buffet is f17.50. Reception is on the ground floor in the Belly & Bolly antique shop.

Hotel Amadeus (☎ 532 45 30, fax 532 23 28, @ info@amadeus-hotel.com, Grote Markt 10) has comfortable rooms, all with TV, phone, private shower and toilet. It charges f95/140/180 for singles/doubles/triples, breakfast included. Guests can surf the Web at the bar for f7.50 per half-hour.

The *Hotel Carillon (☎ 531 05 91, fax 531 49 09, Grote Markt 27)* in the shadow of the Grote Kerk has ageing but pleasant singles with hall shower and toilet for f60, and singles/doubles with private facilities for f110/142. Breakfast is included and served in the cafe downstairs.

Right outside the train station, the *Golden Tulip Hotel Lion d'Or (☎ 532 17 50, fax 532 95 43, @ reservations@hotelliondor.nl, Kruisweg 34)*, has very modern but cramped rooms, and you pay for the location. Rates start at f210/280 with private amenities.

In Zaandvoort, the Hogeweg is littered with places. Try *Pension Schier (☎/fax 571 95 41, Hogeweg 45)*, with rooms from f65/90. Take bus No 81 from Haarlem train station to Zaandvoort bus station (20 minutes).

Places to Eat & Drink

Restaurants Lange Veerstraat is a treasure-trove of enticing restaurants. It's a good idea to reserve ahead, although the huge selection means you'll find a table somewhere.

Ma van Rossum (☎ 551 06 808, Lange Veerstraat 14) has some wonderfully lacy chandeliers and mains from f20 including crispy battered schnitzel and trimmings (f21.50) on up to chateaubriand (f42.50). It's closed Monday. A few doors down at No 23, *Babbels (☎ 542 35 78)* does very good seafood dishes from f27 including red snapper and shrimp.

De Nieuwe Karmelit (☎ 531 44 26, Spekstraat 6) is a pseudo-Latin American brasserie serving tapas, club sandwiches and satays for lunch; there are well-priced specials (from f17) in the evenings.

The *Pieck Jacobus Restaurant (☎ 532 61 44, Warmoesstraat 18)* is a pleasant little eetcafe with an eclectic menu: sandwiches from f7.50, salads from f10 and good-value specials, including kebab lamb sausages, Turkish bread and yoghurt for f17.50. It opens 10 am to 11 pm (closed Sunday).

For all-out Turkish cuisine, try *A la Turka (☎ 534 11 62, Zijlstraat 95)* for starters under f10 including stuffed grape leaves for f8.50, vegie dishes for f25 and pork and lamb dishes for f26 to f35. It does a four-course *menu* for f28.75. It offers lunch and dinner (closed Monday).

Flamboyant (☎ 542 15 03, Kleine Houtstraat 3) is the town's top Indonesian restaurant. Reckon on paying f50 to f60 per head for a *rijsttafel* including drinks. Hours are 6 to 9.30 pm (closed Tuesday).

The *Maharadja of India (☎ 31 66 49, Kleine Houtstraat 31)* does an unbeatable daily menu: tandoori chicken, bhaji, nan, salad and basmati rice, all for f22. It opens 5 to 10 pm.

De Componist (☎ 532 88 53, Korte Veerstraat 1) is a fancy French-Mediterranean restaurant in a fantastic Art Deco building. Mains start at about f30, and a four-course menu will set you back f62.50.

Pubs & Cafe Haarlem has a slew of atmospheric places to down a few. Among them, the *Eet & Bierencafé de Beiaard (Zijlstraat 56)* has a warm Art Deco interior with billiard tables, darts, and the tasty local *Jopen* beer on its seemingly endless list of brews. It also serves meals (f20 to f27).

NOORD HOLLAND

Café Applause (Grote Markt 3) has an elegant, *fin de siècle* atmosphere. At lunchtime it serves pastas, salads and filled sandwiches (all under f20) but goes seriously upmarket in the evening (set dinners for f42.50).

Het Melkwoud (☎ 531 35 35, Zijlstraat 63) is a great place to nurse a beer with some gritty locals behind those ceiling-high windows. You can't miss the sign – a tree shaped like a woman.

Café Studio (☎ 531 00 33, Grote Markt 25), next to Café Applause, has a see-and-be-seen terrace out front and an intimate, multilayered interior with lots of oak panelling. It opens till 2 am and has occasional live music (see also the Music section below). Other cafes line the north side of Grote Markt.

Self-Catering There's a big *Albert Heijn* supermarket at Grote Houtstraat 174 (also open Sunday mornings). *Johan Samson* at Nieuwe Groenmarkt 39 is an old-fashioned cheese shop that also sells fresh bread, pastas and wine. Around the corner, *C'est Bon*, at Ziljstraat 79, sells nuts, dried fruit and other snack delights.

For your *frites* fix, try *De Haerlemsche Vlaamse* at Spekstraat 3. A medium portion with one of a dozen sauces (including Belgian or Dutch mayo) costs f2.75. There are plenty of fast-food places along Kruisweg by the train station. There's a *Salon de Thé-boulangerie* with baked goodies and Earl Grey served behind the polished wood trim at Kleine Houtstraat 13.

Markets are held at Botermarkt and Grote Markt all day Monday, and at Grote Markt (including a flower market) on Saturday.

Entertainment

To find out what's on, grab a copy of the free local paper *De Haarlemmer* or the listings handout *Luna* at the tourist office or pubs. *Uitloper* is the cinema program guide.

Music The *Concertgebouw (☎ 512 12 12, Klokhuisplein 2)* is the premier concert hall and the *Stadsschouwburg (☎ 512 12 12, Wilsonsplein 23)* the municipal theatre. Together these venues cover a broad spectrum

of stage productions – everything from Tchaikovsky to the Chippendales. The Concertgebouw is also home to the Noordhollands Philharmonisch Orkest, whose season runs from September to June.

For jazz and rhythm & blues, bands play on the back stage of *Café Stiels (☎ 531 69 40, Smedestraat 21)* several times a week. Performances begin at 9 pm. The *Café van Stoffelen (☎ 532 59 40, Kruisstraat 23)* has live pop, soul, Latin and jazz on Sunday evenings from 5 pm. The *Proeflokaal In den Uiver (☎ 532 53 99, Rivierfischmarkt 13)* is a quirky old bar – check out the table china used as lampshades – with jazz on Thursday and Sunday evenings. It opens till 2 am (4 am at weekends).

The *Patronaat (☎ 532 41 03, Zijlsingel 2)* is the top music and dance club, with rock, pop, techno, folk, Latin, Indian, rhythm & blues – you name it. Events usually start around 7 or 9 pm throughout the week, although they do midnight raves from time to time. *De Fietsznfabriek (☎ 542 35 40, Houtmaarkt 7a)* in the new Mondiaal Centrum, has DJ-spun techno, Goa-trance, *rai* and other worldly grooves on Friday and Saturday nights.

Cinemas The *Brinkmann (☎ 532 22 32, Brinkmannpassage 11)* and *Cinema Palace (Grote Houtstraat 111)* both show lots of English-language films with Dutch subtitles. Call ☎ 076-587 75 67 for program details or 0900-93 63 to reserve tickets.

Getting There & Away

Train Haarlem is served by frequent trains on the Amsterdam-Rotterdam line. Services run several times an hour to Amsterdam (f6.50, 15 minutes) and Schiphol airport (f9.50, 35 minutes, change at Amsterdam). There are also main-line links to Den Haag (f13.25, 35 minutes, twice hourly), Rotterdam (f19.25, 50 minutes, twice hourly), Utrecht (f17.25, 45 minutes, change at Amsterdam) and Alkmaar (f13.25, 35 minutes, up to six times hourly).

Bus Connexxion bus No 176 goes to Amsterdam (25 minutes, twice hourly), and

No 80 departs from Amsterdam Marnix-straat to Houtplein south of the centre. Bus No 81 goes to Zaandvoort bus station (25 minutes, twice hourly). IJmuiden Seaport, close to the locks and the beach, can be reached via bus No 70 (40 minutes, twice hourly), while No 236 (No 362 at weekends) serves Schiphol (30 minutes, hourly).

During tulip season, Connexxion also runs a bus from Haarlem to the Keukenhof bulb fields. Return tickets cost f28.50/27/15.50 for adults/seniors/children 4 to 11 years.

Getting Around

Bus Single rides in town cost f2.75; a four-trip Connexxion ticket is f8.25. The bus information kiosk opposite the train station is open daily from 7 am to 6 pm (weekends 9.45 am to 5 pm), and there's a large schedule board at the departure bays. Bus Nos 1, 2, 6 and others stop at Ziljstraat east of Grote Markt.

Bicycle The bicycle shop (☎ 531 70 66) at the front of the train station rents touring bikes for f9.50/38 per day/week. It opens 6 am to 1 am from Monday to Saturday, and 7.30 pm to 12.30 am on Sunday. For a different kind of cycling try Optima Bicycles (☎ 534 15 02), 55 Gierstraat, which rents 'reclining' bicycles for f42.50 per day. Bring your passport or ID card as deposit (closed Monday).

Taxi *Treintaxis* (train taxis) line up in front of Haarlem train station. To order a taxi elsewhere, dial ☎ 515 15 15.

AROUND HAARLEM

The seaside resort of **Zandvoort** lies about 5km west of Haarlem. In summer it seems like half of Amsterdam's residents lie shoulder-to-shoulder on its sandy white beaches, thanks to its proximity to the capital. Don't contemplate driving here on a sunny weekend – there can be traffic jams even in February.

The famous Formula One racetrack in the Zandvoort dunes still hosts motor-sports events. Contests are small fry compared to

the 1970s, when the town hosted the world championship 'Holland Grand Prix'. National pride was dented when the competition was moved abroad – local residents had complained about the noise. The Zand-voort tourist office (☎ 571 79 47, fax 571 7003) at Schoolplein 1 can give you details of upcoming races.

Trains link Zandvoort to Amsterdam Centraal Station twice hourly (f8.25, 35 minutes) via Haarlem (f6.75, 10 minutes). From Haarlem, you can also take the hourly Connexxion bus No 80 or 81.

You might take a stroll into the **Kennemerduinen National Park**, a 1250-hectare coastal tract of dune and forest that stretches from Overveen (immediately north-west of Haarlem) to IJmuiden in the north. You'll be in good company as Prime Minister Wim Kok is known to enjoy hiking here. At a towering 50m, the **Kopje van Bloemendaal** is the highest dune in the country, with a good view of the sea and Amsterdam. The VVV offices in Zaandvoort or Haarlem can provide you with walking maps, but there's also a visitors centre on Zeeweg in tiny Overveen (10 am to 5 pm from Tuesday to Sunday). Take bus No 71 from Haarlem train station.

The **Cruquius Museum** (☎ 528 57 04) is a former steam-driven pump station (with tarantula-like rocker arms outside) that helped to drain the Haarlemmermeer in the 19th century. Displays include a model that cheerfully shows which regions would be flooded if the dikes broke. Hours are 10 am to 5 pm from Monday to Friday, and 11 am to 5 pm at weekends. Entry costs f6/5/3 for adults/seniors/children. From Haarlem, take bus No 140 or 170 to the Cruquius stop (20 minutes).

IJMUIDEN

☎ 0255 ● pop 26,000

Five kilometres north-east of Haarlem is the rather dreary town of IJmuiden, whose huge **North Sea locks** are, however, the main attraction at the mouth of the North Sea Canal. The largest is the Zuidersluis, some 400m long and 45m wide. Few people realise that IJmuiden is also the largest fishing port in

NOORD HOLLAND

Western Europe, home to the factory trawlers that plough the North Atlantic for weeks at a time. The huge beach is a kiteflyer's delight at low tide, but the steel mills north of the locks mar the view.

The tourist office (☎ 51 56 11, fax 52 42 26) is at Plein 1945, No 105. It opens noon to 5 pm Monday, 9.30 am to 5 pm Tuesday to Friday, 9.30 am to 1 pm on Saturday. In winter it closes on Monday.

Getting There & Around

It's a blast taking the hydrofoil (☎ 639 22 47 or 0900-92 92) from Pier 7 behind Amsterdam Centraal Station (hourly on the hour, half-hourly during peak times), which costs f14/8.25 return for adults/children. It skims 25 minutes along the North Sea Canal and deposits you in Velsen, 3km short of IJmuiden, where you catch Connexxion bus No 70 into town.

You could also take a train to Haarlem and catch Connexxion bus No 70, 75 or 86 (25 minutes, six buses an hour Monday to Saturday, four an hour Sunday). Or take Connexxion bus No 82 from Amsterdam Sloterdijk station (25 minutes, two buses an hour weekdays, one an hour weekends).

It's a good idea to take a bicycle (an extra f7 return) because things are spread out. Cycle from Velsen along the dike towards the locks and go across the 'small' and 'middle' locks to the big lock on the far side; along the way you'll find an information centre (open afternoons only).

AALSMEER FLOWER AUCTION

A few kilometres south-west of Amsterdam, the town of **Aalsmeer** hosts the world's biggest **flower auction**, not far from the world's largest tulip garden (see Keukenhof and the boxed text 'Tulips – The Beloved Bulb' in the Zuid Holland & Zeeland chapter). The action takes place in Europe's largest commercial complex (600,000 sq metres, or 100 football fields), and the experience will blow you away. Bidding starts early, so arrive between 7.30 and 9 am to catch the spectacle from the viewing gallery. Selling is conducted (as you might expect) by Dutch auction, with a huge clock showing the

starting price dropping until someone takes up the offer. Admission costs f7.50 (children under 12 free); auctions take place Monday to Friday. Take Connexxion bus No 171 or 172 from Amsterdam Centraal Station.

East of Amsterdam

MUIDEN

☎ 0294 • pop 6800

This historic town at the mouth of the Vecht is renowned for its red-brick castle, the Muiderslot (Muiden Castle). The fortress was built in 1280 by the ambitious Count Florian V, an architecture lover and champion of the poor, who gave it round towers – an innovation unknown at the time in Holland. There's a large yacht harbour and, off the coast, a derelict fort on the island of Pampus.

The tourist office (☎ 26 13 89) is in the old barracks at Kazernestraat 10. It opens 1 to 5 pm Monday, 10 to 5 pm Tuesday to Friday, and 10 am to 2 pm on Saturday, April to mid-October. There's a Rabobank with an ATM at Sluisstraat 11 and a post office next door at No 9.

Castles

The **Muiderslot** (Muiden Castle, ☎ 26 13 25) didn't last long under Florian. The popular count was imprisoned and murdered by jealous colleagues in 1296, and the place razed by the bishops of Utrecht. It was rebuilt in the early 14th century in the form we see today. In the 17th century, the historian-writer Pieter Cornelisz (PC) Hooft, who was bailiff of the castle, entertained some of the century's greatest artists and scientists, including Vondel, Huygens, Grotius and Bredero. This group became known as the *Muiderkring* (Muiden Circle).

It's the most visited castle in the country, and for good reason as the precious furnishings, weapons, and Gobelin hangings are spectacular. The period rooms can be seen only on guided tours; ring to find out if you can join one in English (and it's worth it). The castle, at Herengracht 1, opens 10 am to 5 pm from Monday to Friday from April to October; and 1 to 4 pm Monday to Friday from November to March. The last tours are an hour before closure. Admission costs f10/7.50.

On an island a few kilometres from Muiden is the **Pampus**, a 19th-century fort built to defend Amsterdam. It fell into disrepair in the 1930s but, as a recent addition to Unesco's World Heritage List, benefits from preservation funds. Ferries to Pampus depart from Muiderslot port at 10.30 am, 12.30 and 2.30 pm from May to September; tickets (covering the ferry and a guided tour) cost f18.50/12.50.

Boating

Boat firms at Muiden harbour rent large, often luxurious motor and sailing boats, but they aren't cheap; prices range from about f600 to f2500 per week. The Watersportcentrum Muiderberg (☎ 26 25 79) rents small sailing boats by the day and windsurf boards and canoes by the hour at Muiderberg harbour (see Getting There & Away for bus links).

Places to Eat

The *Graaf Floris V van Muiden (☎ 26 12 96, Herengracht 72)* is a huge, inviting pub-restaurant (open lunch and dinner) with starters for f8 to f15 and mains for f25 to f33. It has a decent vegetarian menu, too.

For a lighter meal, *Chinso*, at Herengracht 66, has oodles of pizzas, pastas and ice cream.

Getting There & Away

Muiden is a pleasant hour's bicycle trip from Amsterdam in fine weather. The twice-hourly Connexxion bus No 136 leaves from the terminus at Weesperplein metro stop (40 minutes). In Amsterdam, the bus also stops at the Hotel Arena and Amstelstation. The same line goes from Muiden on to Muiderberg (five minutes), Naarden (15 minutes) and Hilversum (25 minutes).

Het Gooi

Along the slow-moving Vecht River east of Amsterdam lies Het Gooi, a shady woodland

speckled with lakes and heath. In the 17th century, this 'Garden of Amsterdam' was a popular retreat for wealthy merchants, and nature-hungry urbanites still flock to its leafy trails to hike and cycle today. The area's main centre is Hilversum, a one-time commuter town given a fresh start by the Dutch broadcasting industry which has its headquarters here (note the hulking transmission tower). The area is roughly bordered by Laren, a town a few kilometres to the northeast with a good modern art museum, Huizen on the Gooimeer to the north, and Loosdrecht, on the artificial lakes known as the Loosdrechtse Plassen to the east. The latter pair are popular water-sport centres, while Naarden, on the Gooimeer to the north, has an intriguing fortress.

NAARDEN
☎ 035 • pop 16,600

The fortifications of Naarden are best seen from the air: a 12-pointed star, with arrowheads at each tip. This defence system, one of the best preserved in the country, was built a century after the Spanish massacred the inhabitants in the 16th century. The bastions were still staffed by the Dutch army through the 1920s, although its strategic importance had already paled before WWI.

Naarden's tourist office (☎ 694 28 36, fax 694 34 24) is at Adriaan Dortsmanplein 1B. It opens 10 am to 5 pm from Monday to Friday, 10 am to 3 pm on Saturday and noon to 3 pm on Sunday, May to October. The rest of the year, hours are 1 to 4 pm from Tuesday to Sunday. You can pick up an English-language leaflet of a self-guided walking tour of the town (f1.50), and the office organises one-hour **boat tours** around the moat (f4).

Things to See & Do

Most of Naarden's quaint little houses date from 1572, the year the Spaniards (under Don Frederick of Toledo) razed the place during their colonisation of North Holland. The bloodbath is commemorated by a **stone tablet** on the building at Turfpoortstraat 7.

The **Vestingmuseum** (Fortress Museum, ☎ 694 54 59), at Westwalstraat 6, gives insights into the finer points of fortresses and

NOORD HOLLAND

fortress-building. Better still, you can wander around the narrow corridors on your own without visiting the museum. Hours are 10.30 am to 5 pm from Tuesday to Friday, and noon to 5 pm at weekends, March to October. Entry is f10/9/7.50 for adults/seniors/children.

Particularly impressive is the **Grotekerk**, a Gothic basilica with stunning, 16th-century vault paintings of biblical scenes. You can climb the tower (265 steps) for a good view of the leafy Gooi and the Vecht River (Wednesday to Saturday afternoons in summer, f3). St Matthew Passion performances are held over Easter.

The 17th-century Czech educational reformer, Jan Amos Komensky (Comenius), is buried here in the Waalse Kapel. His life and work are related next door at the **Comenius Museum** (☎ 694 30 45), Kloosterstraat 33. The museum opens 10 am to 5 pm from Tuesday to Saturday and noon to 5 pm on Sunday from April to October. Entry costs f4.50/2.

Places to Stay & Eat

There's no camp site or hostel close to Naarden, but you can book one of the *trekkershutten* (camping huts) at the *Jachthaven (☎ 694 21 06, Onderwal 4)* for f55 per night for up to four people. Take bus No 136 to Jachthaven (Yacht Harbour; five minutes).

The sole hotel in the old town is *Poorters (☎/fax 694 48 68, Marktstraat 66)*. It's a splendidly renovated place, with four simple but atmospheric rooms (only one has private shower and toilet). There's a cosy bar and a restaurant with regular art exhibitions. Singles/doubles cost f110/130, breakfast included. Reserve ahead.

The *Eetcafé 't Hert (☎ 694 8055, Cattenhagestraat 12)* is a pleasant pub-cafe serving toasted sandwiches (f5), generous salads (from f17) and mains for f18 to f37, including pork satay with salad f18.50. It's open for lunch and dinner.

For a splurge, try *Het Arsenaal (☎ 694 91 48, Kooltjesbuurt1)* in the old weapons store on the eastern side of town. French-style menus start at f70.

Getting There & Away

There are trains twice an hour from Amsterdam Centraal Station to Naarden-Bussum (f6.25, 15 to 20 minutes). There are more trains if you change at Weesp. Bus No 136 also runs to/from Amsterdam (see the Muiden and Hilversum sections).

HILVERSUM
☎ 035 • pop 83,000

With all the plush 19th-century villas on the outskirts, you'd expect Hilversum to have an interesting core. Alas, modern planning has marred many of the highlights designed by Willem Dudok, the city's chief architect in the early 20th century. For visitors' purposes, Hilversum serves as a good launch point for excursions into Het Gooi, although it does have a couple of decent museums of its own.

Information & Orientation

The few attractions are located in or near the pedestrianised centre, which is immediately west of the train station. The tourist office (☎ 624 17 51, fax 623 74 60) is at Noordse Bosje 1, a 10-minute signposted walk up Spoorstraat and Kerkstraat. It opens 9.30 am to 6 pm from Monday to Friday, and 9.30 am to 5 pm on Saturday. A smaller office right at the train station, Schapenkamp 25, keeps similar hours.

There's an ING Bank with ATMs at Oude Torenstraat 15, and the post office is at Kerkbrink 16. The public library at 's Gravelandse Weg 55, a five-minute walk northeast of the Goois Museum, has eight Internet terminals (free; ask at the desk). Hours are 1 to 8 pm from Monday to Friday and 11 am to 2 pm on Saturday.

Things to See & Do

Nearly 100 buildings in Hilversum bear Dudok's stamp, including the beautiful, modernist **Raadhuis** (Town Hall; 1928) at Dudokpark 1, 700m west of the train station. Take a peek at the fabulous interior, with simple, elegant lines that recall Frank Lloyd Wright or the Bauhaus movement. The tower (restored in 1996) is marvellous in its symmetry and inventive arrangement

Enkhuizen is a gateway to the IJsselmeer and home to a flotilla of holiday boats.

Enkhuizen residents get to choose whether to take the car or boat to work.

View from Domtoren, Utrecht

Floating along Oudegracht, Utrecht

Cafes along Oudegracht are definitely the prettiest in town – but you'll pay for the view.

of horizontal and vertical brick. The tourist office sells a walking guide to Dudok's buildings in the town (f6.95).

The Raadhuis also houses the **Goois Museum** (☎ 629 28 26), which isn't a bad idea if you plan to explore the Gooi – 'Amsterdam's Back Garden'. Displays include archaeological finds from early Gooi-dwellers and the history of the region (more interesting than you might think). It opens Tuesday to Sunday, 1 to 5 pm. Entry is f3 (children f1.50).

The **Nederlands Omroepmuseum** (☎ 688 58 88) will tell you more than you ever wanted to know about Dutch radio and television history, with lots of video-and-headset exhibits. It's about 1.5km south-east of the train station; take bus No 134 to Hilversum Sportpark. It opens 10 am to 5 pm, Tuesday to Friday, and noon to 5 pm at weekends. Admission costs f8.50 (kids 4-12 years, f4.75; seniors f7).

In Laren, which is 5km north-east of Hilversum, the **Singer Museum** (☎ 531 56 56), at Oude Drift 1, houses a splendid collection of French and Dutch paintings, mostly modernist and impressionist works from 1880 to 1950. It opens 11 am to 5 pm from Tuesday to Saturday, and noon to 5 pm on Sunday. Entry costs f8.50/7/2.50 for adults/seniors/children. Take bus Nos 136 or 137 from Hilversum train station to Laren Kermisterrein (15 minutes) and follow the signs.

Cycling & Hiking The tourist office sells a huge range of maps to the area, including the *Wandelroutes* and *Fietsroutes in 't Gooi en Omstreeken* ('Hiking Routes' and 'Biking Routes in 't Gooi and Surrounds'), for f1.50 to f1.75 each. If you don't read Dutch, it's no problem as the routes are clearly marked. The cycling series covers 12 paths in the vicinity, all of which are well signposted, with distances of 35 to 70km. Our favourite, *The Last Days of Florian V*, named after the murdered count (see the Muiden section earlier), starts at Muiden and leads via Hilversum to the popular Vriens pancake restaurant in Loenen (67km).

Places to Stay & Eat

Camping Zonnehoek (☎ 577 19 26, Noodweg 50), in the forest about 3km south of Hilversum, charges f5/5 per adult/tent. There's a laundry and snack bar, but cars aren't allowed. It opens April to October.

You probably won't spend the night in Hilversum but, if you do, *Hotel de Waag* (☎ 624 65 17, fax 621 84 60, Groest 17) is a jolly place, with a central location and a nice cafe on the ground floor. Singles/doubles with private shower and toilet cost f75/115.

De Karseboom (☎ 621 21 61, Groest 53) in the pedestrian zone, has a leafy front terrace and three-course menus for f29.50. It also does soups and sandwiches from f6.50.

On the eastern side of the centre are three restaurants all squished together, in a pretty, old white building with forecourt dining. Among them, *De Buren* (☎ 628 14 93, Laanstraat 35) has French-Dutch mains from f34 and three-course menus for f50. Next door at No 37, *De Jonge Graef van Buuren* is a pub-eatery that serves cheaper meals.

Getting There & Around

There are trains, twice to four times hourly, to Amsterdam (f9.50, 55 minutes), Almere (f9.50, 30 minutes, change at Weesp), Utrecht (f6.50, 20 minutes) and Naarden-Bussen (f3, five minutes).

Connexxion bus No 136 links Hilversum train station twice hourly to Naarden (50 minutes), Muiden (one hour) and Amsterdam Amstelstation (1½ hours). No 137 takes a slightly different route to Amsterdam's Bijlmerstation (1¼ hours).

Getting Around

The bicycle shop (☎ 621 30 98) at the train station rents touring bicycles for f9.50/38 per day/week. Bus No 1 goes from the train station to the Goois Museum in the centre (five minutes).

Flevoland

The Netherland's 12th and youngest province, Flevoland, is a masterpiece of Dutch hydro-engineering. In the early

NOORD HOLLAND

1920s, an ambitious scheme to reclaim more than 1400 sq km of land – an idea first mooted in the 17th century – finally went ahead. The completion of the *Afsluitdijk* (Barrier Dike) at the top of the Zuiderzee in 1932 paved the way for ringed dikes to be erected, allowing water to be pumped out at a snail-like pace. The Noordoostpolder, previously part of Overijssel Province, was opened in 1942, followed by the island regions of Eastern Flevoland (1957) and Southern Flevoland (1968). First residential rights were granted to workers who'd helped in reclamation and to farmers, especially from Zeeland, who lost everything in the great flood of 1953.

The cities that sprang up bring to mind anything but the Golden Age. The main hubs – the dormitory towns of Almere and Lelystad in the south, and Emmeloord across the narrow Ketelmeer to the north – are grindingly dull places, laid out in grid patterns with generic housing estates. For the undeterred visitor, the chief points of interest are the museums at Lelystad, opportunities for outdoor recreation and Urk, a delightful former fishing village in the Noordoostpolder.

LELYSTAD
☎ 0320 • pop 60,000
The capital of Flevoland Province, Lelystad is a good example of urban planning gone awry. The town was named for pioneer engineer Cornelius Lely, whose blueprints were adopted in the Zuiderzee Reclamation Act of 1918. The only real reason for visiting this expanse of steel and concrete lies just east of town – a fascinating shipping museum on the IJsselmeer shore.

Information & Orientation
The tourist office (☎ 24 34 44, fax 28 03 18) is at Stationsplein 186, just south-east across the road from the combined train and bus station. It opens 9 am to 5 pm from Monday to Friday and 9 am to 3 pm on Saturday. From April to August it also opens 6.30 to 8.30 pm. The office reserves accommodation free of charge, and sells cycling and hiking maps to the surrounds.

Most shops and restaurants are in the pedestrianised maze of streets opposite the station; the key museums are a short bus ride west on the IJsselmeer shore. There's a big branch of ING Bank at Stationsweg 4, opposite the train station. The post office is at Stadhuisplein 51.

Things to See & Do
The chief point of interest is the **Batavia Werf** (☎ 26 07 99), on the shore of the IJsselmeer 2km east of the train station. Its star attraction is a replica of the Dutch East India Company frigate, the *Batavia*, which took 10 years to reconstruct until its reinauguration in 1985. The original was a 17th-century *Titanic* – big, expensive and supposedly unsinkable. True to comparison, the Batavia, filled to the brim with cannon and goods for the colonies, went down in 1929 on its maiden voyage off the west coast of Australia, taking 341 crewmen to the ocean floor. The wooden skeleton alongside belongs to *The Seven Provinces*, a replica of Admiral Michiel de Ruijter's flagship which is scheduled for completion in 2005. The museum, at Oostvaardersdijk 1, opens 10 am to 5 pm daily (till 9 pm in July to September). Entry costs f17.50/12.50/7.50 for adults/seniors/children six to 17 years.

Virtually next door, in the tubular building looking like a Star Trek reject, the **Nieuw Land Poldermuseum** (☎ 26 07 99) is the country's definitive display on land reclamation. Tried and true techniques of dike and polder-making are illustrated with photos, dioramas and an audio-visual show, much of it in English. There's a restaurant on the ground floor. The museum hours are 10 am to 5 pm from Monday to Friday, and 11.30 am to 5 pm on Saturday. Admission is f8.50/4/7.50 for adults/seniors/children under 17.

To get to the museums, take bus No 150 from the train station to the Nieuw Land stop (eight minutes, at 8.18 am, 12.18, 2.48 and 4.18 pm from Monday to Friday only).

Water Sports The Surfschool Paradiso (☎ 25 68 93), Uilenweg 8 at the Recreatieplas (recreational area) charges f15/55 per hour/day to rent small sailing boats (up to four persons), f15/50 per hour/day for windsurf boards and f7 per hour for canoes (open April to October). Take bus No 1 to the end (Lelystad-Haven). There are other rental services at the harbour, including Flevo Sailing (☎ 26 03 24), which rents yachts for four to six passengers from f450 per day.

Places to Stay

Camping de Houtrib (☎ 23 17 35, *Badweg 1*) offers a simple but very green location. Open April to October, it charges f5/7.50/4.50 per adult/tent/car. Take bus No 3 or 13 to Val van Urk, and walk 100m east on Houtribdreef.

The VVV can book B&B places from f55 per person. *Herberg de Oostvaarder* (☎ 26 00 72, *Oostvaardersdijk 29*), about 2km south-east of the museums, is a youth hostel on the yachting marina. It costs f40 per night including breakfast. Take bus No 1 to Ringdijk.

Of the few cheap hotels, the *Hotel de Lange Jammer* (☎ 26 04 15, *Oostvaardersdijk 31*) near the museum is a modern, clean, family run hotel-pension in a cute working-class house on the water. Rates are f55 to f85 per person for rooms with private amenities, including breakfast. Take bus No 150 to Nieuw Land and walk 100m south along the coastal Oostvardersdijk.

Places to Eat

Cantina Estrellas VIPs (☎ 23 41 68, *Agoraweg 11*), on the windy Agorahof square five minutes' walk east of the station, is an incongruous Mexican-Argentinian place with tortillas from f15.50, salads from f12.50 and empanadas (filled Argentine pastries) from f10. The owner lets down her hair and plays guitar and sings most evenings. It's open 3 pm to midnight.

The *Dubbel-Op* (☎ 28 08 00, *Wold 11–10*) is a popular pancake eatery with an enormous selection from f8. From the train station, walk south on Middenweg past the parking lot at Reaalhof, take the first path on your left, and walk 1km to the east – the odd, double-arched building is unmissable. (Closed Monday and Tuesday at lunchtime.)

There's an *Albert Heijn* supermarket tucked away at the corner of De Wissel and Newingspassage.

Getting There & Around

Trains go three times an hour to/from Amsterdam (f15.25, 40 minutes), Almere (f7.50, 20 minutes) and Utrecht (f19.25, one hour, change at Duivendrecht). Lelystad is a terminus, so there are no direct trains to the Noordoostpolder or Overijssel.

Flevoland is poorly served by regional bus lines. From Amsterdam and other points south, buses go no further than Almere, so the train is your best bet. Bus No 150 goes from Lelystad station to Enkhuizen via the Afsluitdijk (35 minutes, every two to three hours). Bus No 143 goes east to Kampen in Overijssel (40 minutes, half-hourly).

The Stadstaxi (038-339 46 80) is the best way to the museums at weekends, when there's no bus service. It costs f6 per journey. As with the treintaxis, you may have to share your ride. Call half an hour ahead of time. Ring ☎ 22 16 18 for a regular taxi.

Cees Beers (☎ 23 31 22), Stationsplein 10 by the train station, rents bicycles for f8.50 per day. The Herbeg de Oostvaarder (see Places to Stay) has two-wheelers at similar rates.

URK

☎ 0527 • pop 2200

A former island, Urk was swallowed up by anonymous charms of the Noordoostpolder in the 1940s. There are some who say it might wish it had its ferry back.

The town smells of fish because it's the fish-processing centre for much of the Netherlands. This is a holdover from the days when its fleet sailed out into the open Zuiderzee. Today, it's an interesting little place, good for a few minutes if you're in the area.

The main sight is the **memorial overlook** at the far western end of town. Stone tablets around the edges list the seafarers from Urk who have died at sea. There's a lot of names, and the list continues to grow. Otherwise it's an interesting place for about a 15-minute stroll.

NOORD HOLLAND

If you get hungry, the place to sample some fresh fish is **Restaurant De Kaap** *(☎ 68 15 09, Wijk 5)*. The views and the food are good and they have a few rooms for rent as well (from f35 per person). It's closed Monday.

Bus No 141 runs between Urk and Zwolle every hour (one hour, 20 minutes) except on Sunday when there is only one bus all day.

SCHOKLAND
☎ 0527 • pop 450

Recently declared a Unesco World Heritage Site, Schokland was a long and narrow island with a tortured past until it was swallowed up by the Noordoostpolder. It had been populated by an especially plucky group of people until the Dutch government had them removed for their own safety in 1859. Their story and other aspects of Schokland, which has a history that goes back to the last Ice Age, are described at the Schokland Museum (☎ 0527-25 13 96), Middelbuurt 3.

It's open 11 am to 5 pm (closed Monday) and admission is f5/3. There's no easy public transportation to the museum but you can ride a bike from Kampen which is 14km south. Turn west off the N50 on the road at Ens and go another 2.5km.

Utrecht

The small Utrecht province is little more than the its namesake city. In fact it's more of a city-state, than a region. Outside of the capital, Amersfoort provides a diversion in the north-east, there are some interesting old palaces in the south-east and Oudewater is a cute little town in the west.

Otherwise, from a traveller's standpoint, Utrecht is mostly farms with some creeping suburbanisation from Amsterdam in the north-west.

Getting There & Away
Utrecht city and Amersfoort are both major rail junctions. The rest of the sights are accessible by bus or bike.

UTRECHT CITY
☎ 030 • pop 235,000
Utrecht is a historic city; the ecclesiastical centre of the Low Countries from the early Middle Ages. Today it's an antique frame surrounding an increasingly modern interior, lorded over by the tower of the storm-ravaged Dom (Cathedral), the country's tallest church tower. The 14th-century canals, once-bustling wharves and cellars now brim with chic shops, restaurants and cafes. Utrecht is home to the country's largest university, although there's a bit of a rivalry with Leiden University over which can claim the title of the *oldest* university; Utrecht's was founded in 1636. The contemporary student population adds spice to a once largely church-oriented community.

In 1702, centuries of simmering animosity between the bishops of Utrecht and the Roman Catholic Church came to a head when the bishop was booted out of his job for failing to recognise the pope's infallibility. This caused a schism which resulted in the creation of the Old Catholics Church in Utrecht. The religion grew in popularity and peaked in 1889 when scores of disgruntled Catholics had a huge meeting After that the Old Catholics gradually lost its

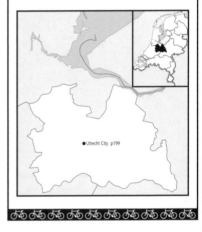

Utrecht City p199

following to the point where there are only about 10,000 members of the church in the Netherlands today.

The most appealing quarter in Utrecht lies between Oudegracht and Nieuwegracht and the streets around the Dom. Note the canals, which are unique to Utrecht with their former warehouse facades below street level. None of this historic character is evident when arriving at the train station, which lies behind Hoog Catharijne, the Netherlands' largest indoor shopping centre and a modern-day monstrosity.

Orientation
Utrecht is a travel hub. Train lines and motorways converge on the city from all directions. There is an unattractive sprawl you have to penetrate to reach the centre

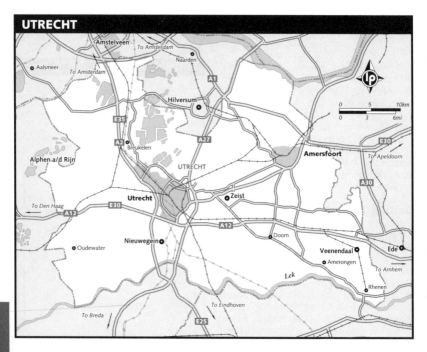

UTRECHT

from whichever direction you approach. West of Utrecht Centraal Station (CS) is an unappealing modern area. The historic quarters are to the east, but reaching the streets means traversing Hoog Catharijne, which will leave you gasping for air when you finally get outside.

But your travails aren't over! Press on past the rapidly ageing Muziekcentrum, built in 1979, where the VVV office is located, and close your eyes through the commercial excesses of Lange Viestraat. At Oudegracht, hang a right along the canal and slow your pace. As you round the bend with the Domtoren (Dom Tower) firmly in sight, you can start to soak up some of Utrecht's emerging charms. Most of the interesting bits lie within 10 minutes walk of the Dom, although the Museum Quarter is a pleasant 15-minute stroll south. Note that the streets along Oudegracht change their names several times in quick succession in the area near the Stadhuis and Domtoren.

Information

Tourist Offices The VVV (☎ 0900-414 14 14, f0.50 per minute, fax 296 66 35, ✆ info@vvvutrcht.nl), Vredenburg 90, is five minutes from the station; it's open from 9 am to 6 pm weekdays, until 5 pm Saturday and until 4 pm holidays. The good free map has a full street index.

Money The GWK Exchange is in the Centraal Station concourse near track No 12. It's open 7.30 am to 9 pm. There are ATMs nearby and along the main pedestrian streets.

Post The main post office (☎ 0800 00 12), Neude 11, is open 10 am to 6 pm weekdays and until 4 pm Saturday.

A handy branch (☎ 233 24 81) in Hoog Catharijne is open 8 am to 6 pm weekdays and 10 am to 1 pm Saturday. It's in the south-eastern corner of the rabbit warren; good luck.

Libraries The city library (☎ 286 18 00), Oudegracht 167, couldn't be more central or have better views.

Internet access costs f2.50 per 30 minutes. It's open 1 to 9 pm on Monday, 11 am to 6 pm on Tuesday to Friday and 10 am to 2 pm on Saturday.

Travel Agencies NBBS (☎ 231 45 20) is at Oudkerkhof 27.

Bookshops Broese Wristers (☎ 223 52 00), Stadhuisbrug 5, has a good selection of travel and English-language books.

Laundry Kolman Wasserette (☎ 231 82 62), Oudegracht 177, is open 7 am to 9 pm daily. A load of laundry costs f10.

Emergency Call the police at ☎ 239 71 11.

Around the Domtoren

Some 465 steps lead up to excellent views from the 112m **Domtoren** (Dom Tower; ☎ 233 30 36). Besides the views, you can ponder the size of the former church. Built in the 14th century, the church and its tower were medieval landmarks. In 1674 the North Sea winds got a mite stronger than

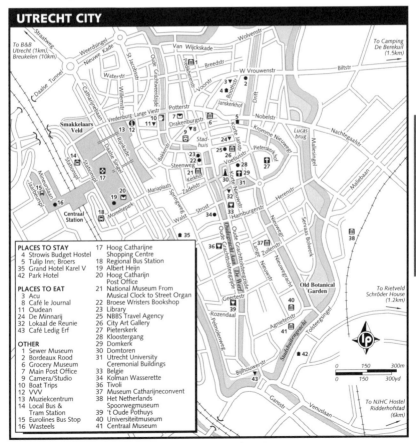

UTRECHT CITY

PLACES TO STAY
4 Strowis Budget Hostel
5 Tulip Inn; Broers
35 Grand Hotel Karel V
42 Park Hotel

PLACES TO EAT
3 Acu
8 Café le Journal
11 Oudean
24 De Minnarij
32 Lokaal de Reunie
43 Café Ledig Erf

OTHER
1 Sewer Museum
2 Bordeaux Rood
6 Grocery Museum
7 Main Post Office
9 Camera/Studio
12 Boat Trips
12 VVV
13 Muziekcentrum
14 Local Bus & Tram Station
15 Eurolines Bus Stop
16 Wasteels

17 Hoog Catharijne Shopping Centre
18 Regional Bus Station
19 Albert Heijn
20 Hoog Catharijn Post Office
21 National Museum From Musical Clock to Street Organ
22 Broese Wristers Bookshop
23 Library
25 NBBS Travel Agency
26 City Art Gallery
27 Pieterskerk
28 Kloostergang
29 Domkerk
30 Domtoren
31 Utrecht University Ceremonial Buildings
33 Belgie
34 Kolman Wasserette
36 Tivoli
37 Museum Catharijneconvent
38 Het Netherlands Spoorwegmuseum
39 't Oude Pothuys
40 Universiteitmuseum
41 Centraal Museum

usual; in fact they reached hurricane force and blew down the church's nave, leaving the tower and transept behind. It is open from 10 am to 5 pm weekdays and noon to 5 pm weekends. Entry costs f7.50/4.50 for adults/children.

Once back on the ground, you can find a row of paving stones marking the extents of the nave. Across this extent is **Domkerk** (☎ 231 04 03), the surviving chancel. It has a few tombs within and is open 10 am to 5 pm weekdays and 10 am to 3.30 pm Saturday from May to September. Through the year it is open 2 to 4 pm on Sunday.

Behind the church is the most charming component of this ecclesiastical troika. The **Kloostergang** is a cloister connecting Domplein with the street called Achter de Dom. It's a peaceful refuge, as the many pigeons and pot smokers will attest.

The 19th-century buildings on the western side of Domplein are the **ceremonial buildings** of Utrecht University. They surround the old church chapter house where the Treaty of Utrecht was signed in 1579 forming a military alliance of the northern provinces.

Walking down Voetiusstraat from behind the Domkerk leads one to **Pieterskerk**. Built in 1048, it is the oldest Romanesque church in the Netherlands. Much damage was caused during the storm of 1674 and more during a dubious 1965 restoration. Should you get inside – opening hours are sporadic but try on Friday or Saturday.

Canals

Scene of a million tourism brochure covers, the bend in the **Oudegracht** where the Bakkerbrug crosses is undeniably photogenic. It is cheerily illuminated by lots of little lights at night, and hundreds sit outside at the many cafes by day. However, it's south of this point where the canal is at its most evocative. The streets are quieter and stretch 1km to where the waters meet the Stadsbuitengracht. It is a memorable stroll that will make you forget about your entrance to the city.

The **Stadsbuitengracht** has its own turn as a lovely canal on the eastern side of the old quarter where it follows many parks built on the site of the old fortifications.

Museum Quarter

There are 14 museums, many of them bizarre hideaways for odd pursuits – a sewer museum is one example. However, those around the Museum Quarter, about 1km south of the Domtoren, are reasonably serious.

The pick of the litter by far is the **Museum Catharijneconvent** (☎ 231 72 96), Nieuwegracht 63, which has the finest collection of medieval religious art in the Netherlands. It's housed in a Gothic former convent and an 18th-century canalside house. The history of Christianity in the country is presented here amid the trappings of the old convent. It's an excellent museum and all but the most jaded will marvel at the many beautiful illuminated manuscripts. The museum is open 10 am to 5 pm from Tuesday to Friday and from 11 am on weekends. Admission costs f10/5. Bus No 2 from CS passes the front entrance.

The **Centraal Museum** (☎ 236 23 62), Agnietenstraat 1, has a wide-ranging collection that always seems to be getting rearranged. There's applied arts dating back to the 17th century as well as paintings by some of the Utrecht School artists. There's even a 12th-century boat that was dug out of the local mud. It's open 10 am to 5 pm Tuesday to Saturday and from noon Sunday. Cost is f6/3. Take bus No 6 from CS.

The **Universiteitmuseum** (☎ 253 80 08), Lange Nieuwstraat 106, is another mixed bag. There's a re-created late-19th-century classroom, historic dentistry tools (ouch!) and just way too many models of medical maladies. You can find refuge out back in the **Old Botanical Garden** with lots of old trees and plants, none of which will make you wince. The museum is open 10 am to 5 pm Tuesday to Friday and from 1 pm weekends. Admission costs a rather high f7.50/3.75. Bus No 2 from CS passes the front entrance.

Across the Stadsbuitengracht, it's the Netherlands Railways' chance to show off what's in its attic; the company's headquarters are in Utrecht. The **Het Netherlands Spoorwegmuseum** (☎ 230 62 06), Maliebaanstation, is housed in an old train station and has the expected collection of old Dutch railway equipment. It also has a miniature railway outside that's loved by children, who can go for rides behind a mini-*Thalys* high-speed train. It's open 10 am to 5 pm from Tuesday to Friday and from 11.30 am weekends. Admission costs a 1st class f15/9.50. Take bus No 2 from CS to Catharijneconvent and walk east for five minutes.

Small Museums
The following are all within a 10-minute walk from the Domtoren. Whether you want to make the walk is another matter.

The **Grocery Museum** (☎ 231 66 28) at Hoogt 6 is worth 10 minutes; the one-room collection sits above a sweet shop filled with the popular Dutch *drop* (sweet or salted liquorice). It's open 12.30 to 4.30 pm from Tuesday to Saturday and entry is free until you make the inevitable purchase of candy.

The **National Museum From Musical Clock to Street Organ** (Nationaal Museum Van Speelklok tot Pierement; ☎ 231 27 89), Buurkerkhof 10, has a colourful collection of musical machines from the 18th century onwards, demonstrated with gusto on hourly tours. It's open 10 am to 5 pm Tuesday to Saturday and from noon Sunday. Cost is f12/7.50.

The previously mentioned **Sewer Museum** (Nederlands Waterleidingmuseum; ☎ 248 72 11), Lauwerhof 29, takes a hard look at what happens to water before and after humans use it. Just so that no-one will think it doesn't have something for everyone, the museum also has displays of historic irons and ironing boards. Admission costs f2.50/1.25.

Boat Trips
There are boat trips (☎ 272 01 11) along Utrecht's canals from 11 am to 6 pm daily. Each lasts one hour and costs f12.50/10. The landing is on Oudegracht near the Viebrug.

Architecture
After some of Utrecht's museums you may be ready to get out of town. The **Rietveld Schröder House** (☎ 236 23 62) is an excellent excuse. It was built in 1924 by Utrecht architect Gerrit Thomas Rietveld to the principles of the De Stijl movement and in fact is the only house that can make this claim. Everything inside and out is drawn from a palette of red, blue, yellow, white, grey and black. The house is one of the most important accomplishments of European architecture in the 20th century and is a place of pilgrimage for many architecture buffs. It's open 11 am to 5 pm from Wednesday to Saturday and from noon on Sunday. Tours are given on the hour and cost f9/6. The house is 4km east from the centre at Prins Hendriklaan 50. Take bus No 4 from CS to the De Hoogstraat stop.

Special Events
Holland Festival of Ancient Music (☎ 236 22 36) – just what the name implies, the event held in late August brings in musicians specialising in music from long ago.

Netherlands Film Festival – the Dutch may only produce about 20 films annually, but each year in late September all are shown at this festival which culminates in the awarding of the coveted Golden Calf to the lucky winner. Web site: www.filmfestival.nl.

Places to Stay
Camping *Camping De Berekuil* (☎ 271 38 70, Ariënslaan 50), is easily reached by bus No 57 from the station; get off at the Biltse Rading stop (about 10 minutes, every 15 minutes). It's open all year and sites go from f20.

Hostels The university means that Utrecht is blessed with plenty of budget accommodation.

In town, it's hard to beat *Strowis Budget Hostel* (☎ 238 02 80, fax 241 54 51, @ strowis@xs4all.nl, Boothstraat 8). Run by a clever group of ex-squatters, it is in a 17th-century building near the centre that has been lovingly restored and converted into a hostel. It's open 24 hours a day and the list of services includes free email access. Prices start at f20 per person in a 12-bed room, rising to f40 per person for two sharing a double. It's a 15-minute walk from CS, or take bus No 3, 4, 8 or 11 to the Janskerkhof stop.

UTRECHT

B&B Utrecht (☎ 504 34 884, fax 244 87 64, ✉ amitie@xs4all.nl, Egelantierstraat 25) has several buildings in a quiet neighbourhood north of the centre. It's a friendly place and rooms come in all flavours costing f55/75 single/double. A dorm bed costs f22.50. It's popular with students, some of whom work for their rent. There's free Internet access and someone may pick you up from CS, try calling. Otherwise it's a 15-minute ride on frequent bus No 3 from CS to Watertoren, then walk two blocks west.

The NJHC hostel *Ridderhofstad (☎ 656 12 77, fax 657 10 65, Rhijnauwenselaan 14)* is 8km east of the city centre in Bunnik. It's in a charming old mansion and rooms come in all sizes. The fee is f26.50 to f30 per person depending on the season. It's an easy bike ride or 20 minutes away on frequent bus No 40, 41 or 43 (ask the driver for Bunnik).

Hotels The *Park Hotel (☎ 251 67 12, fax 254 04 01, Tolsteegsingel 34)* has comfy rooms with private facilities for f78/125, which includes parking. It has a nice garden out back. The hotel is a 25-minute walk from the station, or take bus No 2 to Tolsteegbrug.

The *Tulip Inn (☎ 231 31 69, fax 231 01 48, ✉ tiutrecht@wxs.nl, Janskerkhof 10)* is part of the chain, but this one is in a nice old building on a pleasant square. The rooms have the usual conveniences a business traveller would expect and cost from f210/275.

The best place to stay in Utrecht is the recently opened *Grand Hotel Karel V (☎ 233 75 55, fax 233 75 00, ✉ info@karelv.nl, Geertebolwerk 1)*. It's in a building that dates back to the 14th century, which the hotel lavishly converted. The service and decor are understated but flawless. Rooms start at f395, but weekend specials can bring the price down to f300.

Places to Eat

Do as the discerning locals do: avoid the bend in the **Oudegracht** where the Bakkerbrug crosses. It's a pretty spot but you'll pay for and be rewarded by the views alone. Some of Utrecht's best restaurants lie elsewhere.

Restaurants & Cafes *Acu (☎ 231 45 90, Voorstraat 71)* is run by the same collective who runs the Strowis hostel, which is around the corner. It has a small and cool bar staffed by volunteers. The menu changes daily, but there's always vegetarian specials for f7.50. On Wednesday everything served is vegan and organic. It's popular, so arrive early for dinner. There's live music after 10 pm.

Lokaal de Reunie (☎ 231 01 00, 't Wed 3A) is one of many good cafes on this street near the Domtoren. There's sawdust on the floors and it has an attractive airy atmosphere, even the candles are a cut above the norm. The menu has salads (f14), sandwiches and more. Food is served until 11 pm, drinks until at least 1 am.

Café Ledig Erf (☎ 231 75 77, Tolsteegbrug 3) is a classic brown cafe overlooking a confluence of canals. It's well away from the centre and has a vast terrace. The menu is short and simple – sandwiches for f7 – and it's open until at least 1 am.

Oudean (☎ 231 18 64, Oudegracht 99) is the best choice on this popular stretch of the canal. Set in a restored 14th-century banquet hall, it has a varied menu of salads from f18 and mains from f28. Best of all, it brews its own beer, guaranteeing high times under the high ceilings. Opening hours are until 2 am daily.

Café le Journal (☎ 236 48 39, Neude 32–34) is a classy, nearly grand cafe on this busy square. The salads are inventive (from f10) and the brown bread has many local fans. Food is served from 9 am to 9.30 pm and the bar is open until midnight.

Broers (☎ 234 34 06, Janskerkhof 9) is a stylish and modern version of a brown cafe. It sprawls over several rooms and there are good views out onto the streets and square. On some nights there's live music and dancing. Next door, it has an elegant dinner restaurant with three-course meals of pasta, steak and the like for f49.

De Minnarij (☎ 231 29 58, Korte Jansstraat 4) has a basement tapas bar where the little plates average f6. On the ground floor, the dining room is lovely and relaxed. The changing menu reflects a broad range of influences and depends on what's fresh. Mains average f32. It's open 4 pm to midnight, from noon weekends.

Self-Catering *Albert Heijn (☎ 231 89 20)* has a large store in the Hoog Catharijne shopping centre by the post office. It's open 8 am to 8 pm (closed Sunday).

Vredenburg is the site of large markets on Wednesday and Saturday.

Entertainment

Belgie (☎ 231 26 66, Oudegracht 196) is a lively and fun bar that's watched over by a large inflatable shark. The beer selection is good and it's open until at least 2 am.

A basement pub, *'t Oude Pothuys (☎ 231 89 70, Oudegracht 279)* is small and dark. There's jam sessions every night with locals trying their hand at rock and jazz.

Tivoli (☎ 231 14 91, Oudegracht 245) is popular with students who ponder the offerings of the video jockey while dancing to techno or hanging in the long hallway. Cover charge averages around f5.

Bordeaux Rood (Voorstraat 81) is a coffeeshop on a mellow street with a few unpretentious cafes.

Utrecht has many theatres, one of the more professional is *Camera/Studio (☎ 231 77 08, Oudegracht 156)* which is known for its productions by contemporary Dutch playwrights.

The *Muziekcentrum (☎ 231 45 44)* sprawls around Vredenburg and is the main performing arts complex. The ticket office is at Vredenburgpassage 77.

Shopping

There are interesting boutiques and special interest stores on the less frenetic stretch of Oudegracht south of the Domtoren.

City Art Gallery (☎ 318 97 51) at No 33 is one of several good art galleries on Oudkerkhof, just north of the Domtoren.

Getting There & Away

Train You'll be overwhelmed by Utrecht's Centraal Station (CS) even before you're swallowed up by the adjoining Hoog Catharijne complex. Lockers are by track

No 4 on the main concourse, which, despite having all kinds of services, has a crummy newsstand. Utrecht is a hub for Dutch rail services, and even if you're not visiting the city, you'll probably change trains here at some point.

Some of the main services include:

destination	price (f)	duration (mins)	frequency (per hr)
Amsterdam	11.50	33	4
Den Helder	30.50	120	2
Enschede	33	100	1
Groningen	45	120	1
Maastricht	42	120	2
Rotterdam	15.25	35	2

Bus Eurolines buses stop at Jaarbeursplein out the back of the train station; tickets can be bought from Wasteels (☎ 293 08 70), a travel agent at Jaarbeurstraverse 6 (on the covered walkway which joins CS to Jaarbeursplein). For information on the services, see the Getting There & Away chapter.

Getting Around

Local Transport Local buses and trams leave from a trash-strewn area underneath and north of the passage from CS to Hoog Catharijne. Services are provided by GVU and Connexxion.

There is a useful information office (call ☎ 0900-9292 for all local transport info, f0.75 per minute) there that is open 6.30 am to 7 pm weekdays and 9 am to 5 pm weekends. Regional buses leave from the adjoining area to the south.

Taxi For a taxi, dial ☎ 230 04 00. Utrecht CS is part of the treintaxi scheme (☎ 230 20 20).

Bicycle The CS bicycle shop (☎ 231 11 59) is down by the local buses. It's open 5 am to 1 am weekdays, from 6 am Saturday and from 7 am Sunday.

AROUND UTRECHT

About 10km north-west from Utrecht is the town of Breukelen (no points awarded for guessing the US city that adopted this name). While unremarkable in itself, the

UTRECHT

town is the gateway to the **Loosdrechtse Plassen**, a large series of lakes formed from the flooded digs of peat harvesters.

There are all manner of bike paths around the waters and quite a bit of interesting scenery. Parts of the lakes are desolate, while others are surrounded by lovely homes on small islands which are joined to the road by cute little bridges.

The best way to visit is by bike from Utrecht. Follow the signs to Breukelen. Otherwise, the short run from Utrecht CS to Breukelen is made by several trains per hour.

AMERSFOORT
☎ 033 • pop 118,000

Another Dutch town that made its fortune from the 16th-century beer and wool trades, Amersfoort is a quiet place for stroll if you want to escape the masses of the more popular towns to the east.

The train station is a 10-minute walk from the centre via Vlasakkerweg and Utrechtseweg. Langestraat is the commercial spine of the town and just about everything is within a couple of minutes' walk.

Information
The VVV (☎ 0900-112 23 64, fax 465 01 08, ✆ info@vvv-amersfoort.com), Stationsplein 9–11, is just to the left as you exit the train station. It's open 9.30 am to 5.30 pm on weekdays and 10 am to 2 pm on Saturday. However, you might not bother as staff are loathe to part with information you can't pay for.

The GWK in the train station is open 8 am to 8 pm (until 5 pm Sunday). The post office (☎ 465 55 59), at Utrechtseweg 8, is open 9 am to 6 pm on weekdays and 10 am to 2 pm on Saturday.

Things to See & Do
Much of Amersfoort's appeal comes from wandering the old centre, which has a couple of attractive little canals and over 300 buildings from before the 18th century. **Zuidsingel** is a fine place to start.

Onze Lieve Vrouwe Toren is the surviving 15th-century Gothic tower of the church that used to stand on this spot. Like so many

Dutch churches it was destroyed in a tragedy, this time a gunpowder explosion in 1787. You can explore the interior from 10 am to 5 pm Tuesday to Saturday only in July and August. Admission is f5. The square out front, **Lieve Vrouwekerkhof**, is the most charming place in town. It's the site of a **flower market** on Friday mornings.

Amersfoort's surviving old church, **Sint Joriskerk**, was rebuilt in a sort of Gothic-cum-airplane-hangar style in the 16th century after the original Romanesque one had burnt down (obviously insuring Dutch churches has never been a lucrative proposition). The interior is open 2 to 4.30 pm (closed Sunday) from June to September. Admission is f1.

The **Museum Flehite** (☎ 461 99 87), Westsingel 50, looks better from the outside than within. The buildings are attractively set at the junction of canals and you enter the museum courtyard over a bridge. The collections cover local geology, history and decorative arts. It is open 11 am to 5 pm (from 1 pm weekends, closed Monday) and costs f6/3 for adults/children.

The town has three surviving gateways on the canals. The **Koppelpoort** guards the north and was built in the 15th century, the **Kamperbinnenpoort** is at the eastern end and dates from the 13th century, while **Monnikendam** that sits to the south-east was built in 1430.

Possibly the most fun you'll have in Amersfoort is touring the **Drie Ringen Brewery** (☎ 462 03 00), at Kleine Spui 18, near Koppelpoort. Open 1 to 7 pm from Thursday to Saturday, you can wander around this much-heralded micro-brewery and then try one of the five beers on tap.

Places to Stay & Eat
Camping Recreatiepark Bokkeduinen (☎ 461 99 02, fax 465 43 93, Borchman Wuytierslaan 81) is 2km west of the train station. Sites cost from f20. Take bus No 70 in the direction of Soest and tell the driver where you want to get off.

Amersfoort makes a fine day trip, but if you wish to linger, then you can't go wrong at *Logies de Tabaksplant (☎ 472 97 97, fax 470 07 56, @ tabaksplant@wxs.nl, Coninckstraat 15)* Just beyond the Kamperbinnenpoort, the small hotel is run by a lovely owner and the rooms are smart and cheery. Singles/doubles cost f50/100. From the station, the best transport is by a treintaxi.

***Verse Friet Van Gogh** (Langestraat 143)* is a small place that really is the artist of frites. All the potatoes are freshly hand-cut and cost f3.50 per portion. It's open noon to 7 pm daily.

***Het Filmhuis** (☎ 465 55 50, Groenmarkt 8)* is one of several cafes in the shadow of the hulking Sint Joriskerk. This one is bright and airy and has a typical menu with sandwiches for f10. It's open 11 am to midnight.

The top pick in town is ***Mariëhof** (☎ 463 29 79, Kleine Haag 2)*, which is set in elegant gardens. The French menu is ambitious and a complete meal will run to f120 for dinner, but a mere f65 for lunch – before drinks.

Getting There & Around
The train station is nearly new. Lockers are near track No 4. Some fares and schedules include:

destination	price (f)	duration (mins)	frequency (per hr)
Amsterdam	13.25	31	2
Groningen	42	90	2
Utrecht	7.50	14	4

Buses stop on the right, as you leave the station.

Amersfoort is part of the treintaxi scheme (☎ 462 24 44).

The bicycle shop (☎ 461 49 85) in the train station is open 6 am to 1 am (from 8 am weekends).

SOUTH-EAST UTRECHT
Doorn
☎ 0343 • pop 10,100
Built as a true castle in the 14th-century, **Huis Doorn** was turned into the sort of indefensible mansion still called a castle in the 1700s. It's had numerous owners during its time, but none more infamous than Kaiser Wilhelm II of Germany who lived

there in exile from 1920 until his death in 1941 – after Germany had gone to battle in another world war.

There is a fine collection of German art that the Kaiser seems to have brought along with him from various German palaces. You can stroll the grounds and ponder the fate of the Kaiser, who had been allowed into exile by the Dutch as long as he remained under 'house arrest' (some house!). The mansion (☎ 42 10 20) and grounds are open 10 am to 5 pm Tuesday to Saturday, mid-March to October. The rest of the year and every Sunday it's open from 1 to 5 pm. Admission is f9/4.50.

Bus 50 from Utrecht CS makes the 20km journey to the small town of Doorn (50 minutes) every 30 minutes. The castle is right near the bus stop.

Amerongen
☎ 0343 • pop 7300
The countryside around this small town on the Nederrijn River is dotted with old wooden tobacco drying sheds. A further 8km east from Doorn on the N225, Amerongen was the first stop on the Kaiser's flight from Germany. **Kasteel Amerongen** (☎ 45 42 12, Drostestraat 20, has had a string of owners among Europe's old aristocracy. It was actually a fortified castle in the 13th century, taking on its present twee appearance in the late 1600s. The house and grounds are open 10 am to 5 pm from Tuesday to Friday and from noon weekends from mid-March to October. Admission is f7/5.

You might not want to see both places, but visits can be a good excuse to explore the countryside.

OUDEWATER
☎ 0348 • pop 9900
A pretty little small town, there is one reason to visit Oudewater: witchcraft.

In the 16th and 17th centuries, the **Heksenwaag** (Witches Weigh House) in the centre of town was thought to have the most accurate scales in the land. Women came from far and wide to be weighed. The reason was simple; popular belief held that a

UTRECHT

woman who weighed too little for her size was obviously a witch. Whereas any woman who seemed to weigh the proper amount for her size was obviously too heavy to ride a broom and thus not a witch. We're not making any of this up!

Women who passed the weight test were given a certificate good for life proclaiming them non-witch. Those who didn't pass the test, which was entirely subjective, were best advised to start eating a lot, although many were put to painful death. Fans of the movie *Monty Python and the Holy Grail* will be familiar with the procedure.

The Heksenwaag (☎ 56 34 00), Leeuweringerstraat 2, is open 10 am to 5 pm (from noon Sunday, closed Monday), April to October. Admission, which includes many witchcraft and historical displays, is f3/1.50.

Oudewater is on the route of bus No 180 which runs in either direction between Gouda (22 minutes) and Utrecht CS (40 minutes) every 30 minutes.

Zuid Holland & Zeeland

Once visitors leave Amsterdam to explore the Netherlands, Zuid (South) Holland and Zeeland are likely to be the first areas they will visit. The major cities are all worthy of visits for a day or more: Leiden for its university culture, history and extensive canals and old town; Den Haag (The Hague) for its art museums; Delft for its simple charms and beauty; and, Rotterdam for its energy and vibrant modern architecture.

In addition, the area has several smaller places worth your time. Gouda is a perfect little old canal town and Dordrecht surprises all those who don't overlook it. South of Rotterdam, Zeeland is the dike-protected province that people so often associate with the Netherlands when they think of its huge areas below sea level. Middelburg is a delightful regional centre.

Besides dikes and the profusion of windmills, that other Dutch icon, the tulip, is much in evidence. The Keukenhof gardens are a place of pilgrimage for lovers of the plant and a place of conversion for sceptics. The land around the gardens and along the border with Noord Holland is the centre of the Dutch tulip industry and every April it comes alive with colour.

The area is, of course, perfect for biking and hiking, and trails and paths are everywhere, especially along the dikes. The built-up beaches of Noordwijk aan Zee and south to Scheveningen are disappointing and popular mostly with locals. But in between the developments there are rural stretches easily reached by bike. Things improve along the coast in Zeeland which, while popular, is not as built-up.

Zuid Holland

Along with the provinces of Noord Holland and Utrecht, Zuid Holland is part of the Randstad, the population and economic centre of the Netherlands. Two of the nation's most important cities, Den Haag, the royal

family's and government's seat, and Rotterdam, Europe's busiest port, are here. In addition, Leiden is one of the world's great old university towns and Gouda and Delft are just plain enjoyable. Just east of lovely Dordrecht is Biesbosch, a natural area along the border with Noord Brabant that includes a fascinating national park. East of Rotterdam, Kinderdijk is a must-see for windmill lovers.

It's hard to envisage a trip to the Netherlands that doesn't include time spent in Zuid Holland.

The Web site at www.zuid-hollandinfo.nl has plenty of information on the region.

ZUID HOLLAND & ZEELAND

Getting There & Away

The Netherlands Railways cover the province of Zuid Holland like a spilled bowl of spaghetti. Trains are frequent and link all the major centres.

LEIDEN

☎ 071 • pop 118,300

Home to the country's oldest university, Leiden is an effervescent town with an intellectual aura generated by the 20,000 students who make up a sixth of the population. The university was a present to the town from William the Silent for withstanding two

Spanish sieges in 1574. It was a terrible time that was only ended when the Sea Beggars arrived and chased out the Spaniards. According to lore, the retreating Spanish left in such a hurry that they abandoned a kettle of hotpot (stew). This along with herring and bread brought by the rescuers was the cause for a celebration that is recalled annually on 3 October, now the date of Leiden's biggest festival (see the Special Events section later).

A few decades after the siege, Protestants fleeing persecution elsewhere in the Low Countries, France and England arrived in Leiden to a somewhat warmer welcome.

Most notable was the group led by John Robinson, who were eventually to sail to America and into history as the pilgrims aboard the *Mayflower*. See the boxed text 'Pilgrims' Progress' for details.

Wealth from the linen industry contributed to Leiden's prosperity, and during the 17th century the town also produced several artists. Most notable was Rembrandt, who was born in Leiden in 1606 and lived there for 26 years before going on to greater fame in Amsterdam.

The town's other truly notable event happened in 1807 when a canal barge laden with gunpowder blew up, wiping out a large area around Steenschur.

Today the town is a typical old Dutch town with a refreshing overlay of vibrancy from the students. Look for the literary quotes painted on many walls in their original language. Leiden is well worth a visit, but be sure to get away from the crowded centre to some of the outlying areas along the canals, where you might just get a taste for hotpot.

Orientation

Old Leiden is a classically compact canal town. Arriving at the station (Centraal) you may be tempted to stay on the train or bus as the area in front of the station has been rather grimly redeveloped in a rather Eastern-bloc style. But five minutes' walk brings you to Beetenmarkt where the views improve.

Haarlemmerstraat and Breestraat are the town's two pedestrian arteries and most sights are within five minutes of either. You may not realise it while walking, but the ring canal follows the saw-tooth angles of the old fortifications.

The town is bisected by many waterways, the most notable being the Oude Rijn and also the Nieuwe Rijn which meet at Hoogstraat to form a canal called simply the Rijn.

Of course, anyone who has seen the Rhine in all its wide glory in Germany will realise that these are but just a couple of the welter of Rhine tributaries throughout Zuid Holland province.

Information

Tourist Offices The VVV (☎ 0900-222 23 33, f0.99 per minute, fax 516 12 27, ✉ mailbox@leidenpromotie.nl) is five minutes' walk from the station on the way into town at Stationsweg 2D. It is open 10 am to 6.30 pm weekdays and 10 am to 2 pm Saturday. It has a good number of printed guides for walks around town. Worth special mention are 'In the Young Rembrandt's Footsteps' (f4) and the lavish 'A Walk Around Locations Related to the 17th-Century Painters' (f6.95). It also rents 'Talking Walls' audio walking tours of the city for f15. These excellent CDs present events and history keyed to specific sites. The town's Web site is www.leiden.nl.

Money The GWK in the train station is open 7 am to 9 pm daily. There are ATMs outside the station and many more along Stationsweg.

Post & Communications The most convenient post office is at Breestraat 46 (☎ 514 17 88). It's open 9 am to 6 pm weekdays and 10 am to 1.30 pm Saturday.

For Internet access, see the following Bookshops and Libraries sections.

Travel Agencies NBBS (☎ 513 23 90), Breestraat 46, is a big agency offering a full range of services and supplying the town's university students with cheap tickets.

Bookshops Leiden is well served by bookshops catering to the needs of travellers. The Joho Company (☎ 514 50 07), Stille Rijn 8–9, is an oasis for the traveller, and not just because it stocks every LP title published. It has other books and maps, travel gear and supplies and unlimited Internet access for f5. It's open the usual shopping hours.

Nearby, Reisboekhandel Zandvliet (☎ 512 70 09), Stille Rijn 13, stocks nothing but travel books and maps.

Kooyker Ginsburg (☎ 516 05 00), Breestraat 93, is a large mainstream bookshop with lots of English-language choices and a good magazine selection.

ZUID HOLLAND & ZEELAND

Pilgrims' Progress

In 1608 a group of Calvinist Protestants who had split with the Anglican Church left persecution in Nottinghamshire, England, for a journey that would span decades and thousands of miles. Travelling first to Amsterdam under the leadership of John Robinson, they found their welcome there less than, well, welcoming. They encountered theological clashes with local Dutch Protestants who, in an attempt at a 'smear campaign', accused the English arrivals of child molestation and other perversions.

In Leiden they found a more liberal atmosphere thanks to the university and some like-minded Calvinists who already lived there. They also found company with other refugees from persecution elsewhere, which included French Huguenots. In fact, by 1610 as much as one-third of Leiden's population consisted of refugees.

The English Calvinists lived somewhat communally. A few had money while others worked in the booming local textile industry. However, their past was eventually to catch up with them. In 1618 King James I of England announced he would assume control over the Calvinists living in Leiden. In addition, the local Dutch were becoming less tolerant of splinter religious groups.

The first group of English left Leiden in 1620 for Delfshaven in what is today Rotterdam, where they bought the *Speedwell* with the intention of sailing to the New World in hopes of putting their problems behind them once and for all. Unfortunately the *Speedwell* didn't live up to its name and after several attempts at sailing the Atlantic, they gave up and, against their better judgement, put into Southampton in England. Here they swapped the leaky *Speedwell* for the much more seaworthy *Mayflower* and sailed, as it were, into history as the Pilgrims.

Of course nothing is ever quite so neat and that legendary voyage was actually just one of many involving the Leiden group. It wasn't until 1630 that most had made their way to the American colonies founded in what is today New England. And they had a few passengers as well; some 1000 people made the voyages, including a number of Dutch who were considered oddballs for their unusual beliefs. Many French Huguenots also made the trip, including the Delano family, who in conjunction with some of the Dutch started the family that produced a number of notables including two US presidents named Roosevelt.

Traces of the Pilgrims today in Leiden are elusive. The best place to start is the **Leiden American Pilgrim Museum** (☎ 512 24 13), Mandenmakerssteeg 11, an absolutely fascinating restoration of a house occupied around 1610 by the soon-to-be Pilgrims. For the price of admission (f3) you get a personal tour given by curator and noted historian Jeremy Bangs. The house itself dates from 1375, but the furnishings are contemporary to the Pilgrims' period. Note the tiles on the floor, which are the originals from the 14th century. The house is open 1 to 5 pm Wednesday to Saturday. Pick up a walking-tour brochure (f1) which helps you explore the surviving parts of 17th-century Leiden.

One of the few other sites with direct links to the Pilgrims is the surviving wall of the **Vrouwenkerk**, the church where the Pilgrims worshipped. Although it's not much to look at, its significance is unquestioned and it's been the cause of controversy of late. Developers who want to build a disco on the site are at loggerheads with preservationists led by Bangs. The site's future is not helped by Leiden's surprisingly mixed record on historic preservation. This is the town, after all, that tore down Rembrandt's birthplace during the 20th century to expand a printing plant.

Around the **Pieterskerk** are the other significant sites with a Pilgrim connection. It's here that John Robinson is buried, having never made it to America. See the section A Walk through Old Leiden for details.

The Leiden municipal archives are housed in a new building at Vliet 45, south of Rapenburg. Inside, the **Pilgrim Fathers Center** (☎ 512 01 91) has displays and is the place to check out whether your ancestors came from Nottinghamshire by way of Leiden. It's open 9.30 am to 5 pm weekdays and until noon Saturday.

Libraries The Centrale Bibliotheek (☎ 514 99 43) is in a restored old building at Nieuwstraat, near Hooglandse Kerk. It has Internet access (f5 per 30 minutes) and is open 11 am to 5 pm daily (closed Sunday from June to August).

Laundry There's a Zelf Was (self-wash, but you could figure this one out, right?) at Morsstraat 50 (☎ 512 03 38). It's open daily 8 am to 8 pm.

Emergency For all emergencies call ☎ 112. For non-immediate matters call the Leiden police on ☎ 525 88 88. If you need a doctor after hours and on public holidays, call ☎ 0900-776 33 37. Otherwise, the VVV has lists of local physicians.

Rijksmuseum van Oudheden
Learn to walk like an Egyptian – you'll get lots of clues from the hieroglyphs on display at the Rijksmuseum van Oudheden (National Museum of Antiquities; ☎ 516 31 63), Rapenburg 28, which has a world-class collection. Its striking entrance hall contains the Temple of Taffeh, a gift from Egypt in 1969 for the Netherlands' help in saving ancient monuments from inundation when the Aswan High Dam was built. A huge reconstruction was due to be completed in late 2000 that will provide a new home for the museum's other collections that span the Middle East, Greece and Rome. There are also artefacts from the early mud-dwellers who were the first Dutch.

The museum is open Tuesday to Saturday from 10 am to 5 pm, Sunday from noon, and costs f7/6 for adults/children.

A Walk Through Old Leiden
From the Rijksmuseum van Oudheden, cross the Rapenburg and turn south to No 73. This is the administrative building of **Leiden University**, which was founded here in 1575. The building is a former convent and many of the offices are in what was once a chapel. Follow the signs on the 1st floor to the 'sweating room' where terrified students did just that while waiting for their examinations, proof that some things don't

change. You can wander around the complex during business hours. An **academic museum** (☎ 527 72 43) has old teaching instruments and the like and is open 1 to 5 pm Wednesday to Friday (free).

Behind this, the **Hortus Botanicus** (☎ 527 72 49), Europe's oldest botanical garden, was begun in 1587. This is where Carolus Clusius from Vienna set up shop in 1592 when he was hired by the university to research medicinal plants. Besides the helpful herbs, he also planted some bulbs from Turkey called tulips. The bulb fields a short distance from Leiden are the direct result (see the boxed text 'Tulips – The Beloved Bulb'). The garden has much more than herbs and bulbs, though. It has many rare and old species of plants dating back to its founding. It's open daily from 9 am to 5 pm (Sunday from 10 am) but is closed Saturday from October to March. Admission costs f5/2.50.

Cross the Rapenburg and at No 76 turn into the alley where you'll find the remains of the **Begijnhof**. The white building at the end is the former chapel where the Pilgrims once prayed.

Turn up Kloksteeg to **Pieterskerk**, the 15th-century Gothic church that's the burial place for numerous Leiden notables, including painter Jan Steen and Pilgrim leader John Robinson. It's far from graceful, the heavy lines indicating the need for structures that can withstand the often violent North Sea breezes. Like many Dutch churches, opening hours are short: 1.30 to 4 pm. But it's free.

Facing the front of the Pieterskerk, look to the left and you'll see the **Gravensteen**, a former prison that now makes an appropriate home for the university's law faculty. There have been a few renovations...

Look to the right from the same spot and you'll see **Jean Peijnhof** on a little alley off Kloksteeg. It was one of many almshouses in Leiden like the Begijnhof over the rear wall where old people received accommodation and food. Built on the site of John Robinson's house in 1683, it has a plaque in his honour.

Walk to the rear of Pieterskerk and walk up narrow Pieterskerk Choorsteeg to

ZUID HOLLAND & ZEELAND

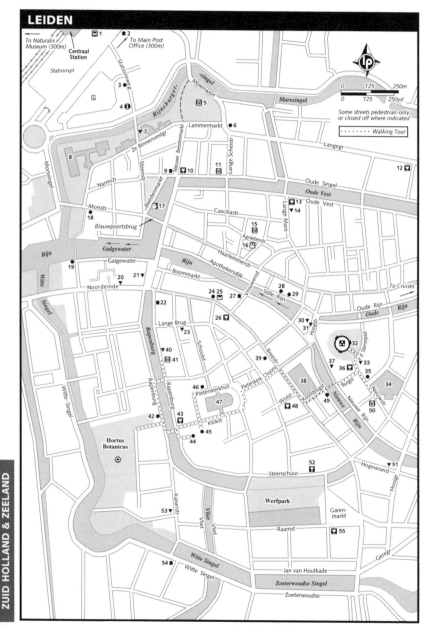

LEIDEN

To Naturalis Museum (300m)

Centraal Station

To Main Post Office (300m)

Stationspl

Stationsweg

Rijnsburgersingel

singel

Molenwerf

Maresingel

0   125   250m
0   125   250yd

Some streets pedestrian-only or closed off where indicated

········· Walking Tour

Lammermarkt

2e Binnenvestgr

Nieuwe Beestenmarkt

Lange Scheistr

Langegr

Oude Singel

Oude Vest

Narmstr

Steenstr

Beestenmarkt

Caeciliastr

Lange Mare

Morsstr

Blauwpoortsbrug

Galgewater

Agnietenstr

Haarlemmerstr

Rijn

Rijn

Galgewater

Apothekersdijk

Boommarkt

Vrouwenstr

Stille Rijn

Noordeinde

To Cruises

Oude Rijn

Oude   Rijn

Witte   Singel

Lange Brug

Rapenburg

Scholstr

Breestr

Choorsteeg

Hoogstr

D Sterrepad

Burgst

Nieuwe   Rijn

Nieuwstr

Koornbrugst

Pieterskerkhof

Pieterskerk Choorst

Rapenburg

Wolst

Klokst

Hortus Botanicus

Kaiserstr

Vliet

Vliet

Vliet

Steenschuur

Werfpark

Garen-markt

Raamst

Hogewoerd

Hooigr

Jan van Houtkade

Witte Singel

Zoeterwoudse Singel

Zoeterwoudse

LEIDEN

PLACES TO STAY
2 Golden Tulip Leiden
9 Pension Rose
22 Hotel de Doelen
27 Hotel Nieuw
   Minerva
54 Pension Witte
   Singel

PLACES TO EAT
7 Stadscafé
14 Brasserie
20 Splinter Eethuis
21 De Gouvernante
23 Big Easy
30 Annie's B-Day
31 Fu's Loempia Kiosk
33 Koetshuis De Burcht
37 Café Einstein
40 Augustinus
51 Eethuis Odessa
53 Verboden Toegang

OTHER
1 Bus Station
3 Super de Boer
   Supermarket
4 VVV
5 De Valk Windmill
6 In Casa
8 Rijksmuseum voor
   Volkenkunde
10 Duke
11 Lakenhal
12 COC
13 In de Oude Maren Poort
15 Museum Boerhaave
16 Kijkhuis
17 Boat Tours
18 Zelf Was
19 Canoe Rentals
24 NBBS Travel Agency
25 Post Office
26 Bacchus
28 The Joho Company

29 Reisboekhandel Zandvliet
32 Burcht
34 Hooglandse Kerk
35 Centrale Bibliotheek
36 De Burcht Bar
38 Stadhuis
39 Kooyker Ginsburg
41 Rijksmuseum van
   Oudheden
42 Leiden University
   Administration Building
43 Barrera
44 Begijnhof
45 Jean Peijnhof
46 Gravensteen
47 Pieterskerk
48 Café de WW
49 Vismarkt
50 Leiden American Pilgrim
   Museum
52 St Lodewijk Church
55 Bonte Koe

Breestraat and turn right. There on the left is the **Stadhuis**, built in the early 17th century. There's a reason it looks so good: it burnt down in 1929 and was rebuilt.

Turn left on Koornbrugsteeg. You can see the stones of the old **Vismarkt** and there are usually a few fish vendors about even today. Cross the covered bridge, where the corn market used to be held. The roof dates from 1825.

Continue a short way up Burgsteeg to Nieuwstraat. Turn to the left and you'll see a **gateway** featuring a lion bearing the town's coat of arms. Pass through to the courtyard in front of the **Burcht**, a hill that was built as a fortress in the 11th century. There's a good view of Leiden from the hill and you can view the route you just walked.

Afterwards you can visit the **Leiden American Pilgrim Museum** (see the earlier boxed text 'Pilgrims' Progress') and the **Hooglandse Kerk**, both down Nieuwstraat. This huge hulk of a church dates from the 15th century. It's open odd hours; try the door.

Other Attractions
The 17th-century **Lakenhal** (Cloth Hall; ☎ 516 53 60), Oude Singel 28–32, houses the Municipal Museum, with an assortment of works by old masters, as well as period rooms and temporary exhibits. The 1st floor has been restored to the way it would have looked when Leiden was at the peak of its prosperity from the cloth trade. Other displays cover the rest of the city's history. It's open weekdays 10 am to 5 pm, weekends from noon, and costs f5/2.50. Its Web site is www.lakenhal.demon.nl.

Leiden's landmark windmill, **De Valk** (The Falcon; ☎ 516 53 53), at Tweede Binnenvestgracht 1, is a museum that will blow away notions that windmills were a Dutch invention. It's been carefully restored and once inside you'll see how, in both construction and operation, Dutch windmills have much in common with the sailing ships of their day. It's open Tuesday to Saturday 10 am to 5 pm, Sunday from 1 pm, and costs f5/3.

Leiden University was an early centre for Dutch medical research and you can see the often grisly results at the **Museum Boerhaave** (☎ 521 42 24), Lange St Agnietenstraat 10. There's five centuries of pickled organs, surgical tools and an array of skeletons in the self-explanatory Anatomy Theatre. The museum is housed in the hospital where the chronically ill Herman Boerhaave

ZUID HOLLAND & ZEELAND

taught medicine from his sick bed until his death in 1738. It's open 10 am to 5 pm Tuesday to Saturday and from noon Sunday. Admission to the museum is f5/2. Its Web site is www.museumboerhaave.nl.

A big stuffed elephant greets you at **Naturalis – Nationaal Natuurhistorisch Museum** (National Museum of Natural History; ☎ 568 76 00), Darwinweg 2, a large and well-funded collection of all the usual dead critters, including the one-million-year-old Java man, discovered by Dutch anthropologist Eugene Dubois in 1891. Interactive exhibits let you create your own ecosystem, a treat for rain-drenched kids dreaming of the sun. The museum and its striking building is 300m west from behind the train station. Naturalis is open noon to 6 pm (closed Monday) and costs f12.50/5. Its Web site is www.naturalis.nl.

Big **Werfpark** is built on the site of the worst damage from the 1807 explosion of a gunpowder barge. Damage extended for several hundred metres in all directions. Just across the Steenschuur, **St Lodewijk Church** somehow survived the worst of the destruction. King Louis Napolean took the entire catastrophe as a sign from God and made St Lodewijk the first openly Catholic church in Holland.

The **Rijksmuseum voor Volkenkunde** (National Museum of Ethnology; ☎ 516 88 00), near the station at Steenstraat 1, focuses almost entirely on the former Dutch colonies and has a larger collection of Indonesian stuff than the Tropenmuseum in Amsterdam. However, at the time of writing, it was getting a complete revamp and the regular collection may be entirely closed when you read this, so check in advance. A series of temporary exhibitions is planned to tide things over until construction is finished (due by summer 2001). Currently, it's open 10 am to 5 pm daily except Monday (from noon Saturday), and costs f10/5. Its Web site is www.rmv.nl.

Activities

You can paddle your way around the canals on a rented **canoe** or **kayak** year-round. Botenverhuur 't Galgewater (☎ 514 97 90) is

open 11 am to 6 pm daily (until 10 pm June to September). Rentals cost from f8 per hour.

Organised Tours

Except during the worst weather, Rederij Rembrandt (☎ 513 49 38) gives one-hour **boat tours** of Leiden at various times through the year. Check the schedules from the dock at Beestenmarkt. Tickets cost f9/5.

There are longer **cruises** of the waterways and lakes around Leiden from late June until September. Operated by Rederij Slingerland (☎ 521 98 75), cruises depart from a dock at Haven, 700m east of the Burcht. The three-hour tours depart at 1 pm Sunday to Wednesday and cost f20/12.50.

Special Events

Leiden's wheels of commerce all grind to a halt on 3 October to commemorate the day the starvation caused by the Spanish ended in 1574. The revelry is undiminished even four centuries later and there is much eating of the ceremonial hotpot, herring and bread. But more than anything, consumption focuses on liquid bread (beer) and a drunken time is had by all, especially the night before.

Places to Stay

Leiden has less accommodation than you'd expect since many visitors choose to stay in Amsterdam.

Camping The closest seaside grounds are in Katwijk aan Zee, 8km to the west. *De Zuidduinen (☎ 401 47 50, fax 407 70 97, ✉ info-zuidduinen@tours.nl, Zuidduinseweg 1)* and *De Noordduinen (☎ 402 52 95, 403 39 77, ✉ info-noordduinen@tours.nl, Campingweg 1)* are open from April to October and rates start at f30 per site in the off-season. Both can be reached from Leiden on bus No 31 or 41.

De Wasbeek (☎ 301 13 80, Wasbeeklaan 7), at Warmond, a few kilometres north of Leiden, charges a mere f20 for sites and is a short ride on bus No 50 or 51. It's open all year.

Hostels The nearest NJHC hostel, *De Duinark (☎ 0252-37 29 20, fax 37 70 61, Langevelderlaan 45)* is 45 minutes away near Noordwijk aan Zee. Take bus No 57 or 90 (last bus is at 11 pm) to Sancta Maria hospital and walk 10 minutes. Prices per person are f26.50 to f30, depending on the season.

Hotels & Pensions The canal-front *Pension Witte Singel (☎ 512 45 92, 514 28 90, Witte Singel 80)* is on a peaceful canal south of the town centre. Bathless rooms are f60/95 for a single/double, or f85/110 with bath. It's a 15-minute walk from the station and one of the best values in town.

About the cheapest place is *Pension Rose (☎ 514 66 30, fax 521 70 96, Beestenmarkt 14)*, which is above a cafe of the same name. It's a casual place, so casual that you may end up wandering the darkened halls late at night looking for toilet paper. Basic rooms cost from f75/100.

Hotel de Doelen (☎ 512 05 27, 512 84 53, ✆ dedoelen@tref.nl, Rapenburg 2) is a stately and classic place. Some of the canalside rooms are palatial. More basic rooms – still with bath and TV, though – cost from f100/150.

Hotel Nieuw Minerva (☎ 512 63 58, fax 514 26 74, ✆ hotel@nieuwminerva.nl, Boommarkt 23) has a traditional look and a quiet canalside location. The rooms are quite comfy and well equipped and cost f150/200.

The *Golden Tulip Leiden (☎ 522 11 21, fax 522 66 75, ✆ reservations@golden tulip-leiden.nl, Schipholweg 3)* is large and modern. The rooms, aimed at business travellers who will trade architectural charm for amenities, cost from f233.

Places to Eat

Restaurants *Koetshuis De Burcht (☎ 512 16 88, Burgsteeg 13)* is in the shadow of the Burcht. It has a well-prepared Dutch menu with meals from f35. The bar is long and there are comfortable wicker chairs for relaxing with a cold one. It's open for lunch, dinner and drinks daily.

Brasserie (☎ 512 54 40, Lange Mare 38) is a classic brasserie that's very popular with locals. There are lunch specials from f10, while at night, things are fancier and you can easily spend f50 before you add on drinks. It's open daily.

Big Easy (☎ 566 34 20, Papengracht 6A) honours the flavours of Louisiana with an array of spicy dishes that include jambalaya (f28.50). It's a big place and is open for dinner daily.

De Gouvernante (☎ 514 88 18, Kort Rapenweg 17) has traditional Dutch food with French touches. It's a lovely place and besides the regular menu, there's a special 'surprise' menu for f79 per person that depends on what's fresh as well as the chef's whim. It's open daily for dinner.

Verboden Toegang (☎ 514 33 88, Kaiserstraat 7) is more welcoming than the name implies: Entrance Forbidden. Signs to this effect – 'borrowed' from around Europe – decorate the dining room. The fine Dutch food is carefully prepared and dinner with drinks will run to f75 per person.

Cafes The best value in town is *Augustinus (☎ 516 23 33, Rapenburg 24)*, a cafe aimed at students but which welcomes everybody. Service is sit-down and the specials are dirt cheap. The daily steak is f10 and the main special is f12.50. It's open from 5 to 9.30 pm and reservations are recommended.

The austere *Splinter Eethuis (☎ 514 95 19, Noordeinde 30)* has good-value, two-course meals for f16.50 and a selection of vegetarian dishes (closed Monday to Wednesday).

Annie's B-Day (☎ 512 57 37, Hoogstraat 1A) is a below-street-level cafe right on the confluence of the two Rijns. You can watch the fluids flow from the open-air deck. The simple menu averages under f25.

Students love *Eethuis Odessa (☎ 514 63 98, Hogewoerd 18)*, which has pasta dishes under f17 and pitchers of red wine for f23.50. It's dark inside but bright outside in the summer, when there are tables on a floating terrace.

Stadscafé (☎ 512 61 20, Stationsweg 7–9) is in a leafy stretch on the site of the old fortifications. It's bright, with the usual cafe menu, and is open until midnight daily.

Café Einstein (☎ 512 53 70, Nieuwe Rijn 19) bustles with locals popping in for a drink, a snack and a chat from early to late. There is a skylit room in the rear and chairs next to the canal.

ZUID HOLLAND & ZEELAND

Fast Food & Self-Catering *Fu's Loempia Kiosk* on Hoogstraat is an especially good example of this Dutch fast-food staple (similar to a large spring roll). A huge *loempia* costs f3.25 and there are numerous noodle and rice dishes.

There's a **Super de Boer** supermarket *(☎ 516 16 60, Stationsweg 44)* for all your picnic needs.

Entertainment
Bars & Clubs Evenings revolve around the town's lively cafes. Unless otherwise noted, the following are usually open until at least midnight daily.

De Burcht (☎ 514 23 89, Burgsteeg 14) is a literary bar next to the Burcht, that's popular with professorial types.

Bacchus (☎ 514 34 44, Breestraat 49) is popular with the students of the folks who frequent De Burcht. It's big, noisy and most people are in the 16 to 21 age range.

Barrera (☎ 514 66 31, Rapenburg 56) is a classic brown cafe with a good corner location for people-watching.

In de Oude Maren Poort (☎ 514 32 15, Lange Mare 36) overlooks Oude Vest Canal and has very pleasant outside seating. It's open until 3 am weekends.

Bonte Koe (☎ 514 10 94, Hooglandsekerk-Choorsteeg 13) was built for a butcher, which explains the cow decor. An interesting selection of neighbourhood characters matches the interesting beer list.

COC (☎ 522 06 40, Langegracht 65) is a bar run by the national gay and lesbian organisation, and is open Thursday to Saturday.

Live Music *In Casa (☎ 512 49 38, Lammermarkt 100)* is huge and has live music, a dance floor, comedy and a variety of events. It's usually open well into the morning and cover charge depends on what's on.

Tulips – The Beloved Bulb

Tulips have captured the fancy of the Dutch, and humans in general, for centuries. In fact, at times this love has become an absolute mania (see the boxed text 'Mad about Tulips' in the Facts about the Netherlands chapter).

While it's easy for some to pooh-pooh such adoration of a simple flower, there's no denying the magnificence of their displays each year during tulip season. Thousands of people arrive from all over the world to see the bulbs in bloom. Postcards just don't do justice to the vast fields of colour.

The first stop on any tulip tour is the **Keukenhof**, the world's largest flower garden. Located between the towns of Hillegom and Lisse south of Haarlem. The 32-hectare park attracts a staggering 800,000 people for a mere eight weeks every year. Nature's talents are combined with artificial precision to create a garden where millions of tulips and daffodils bloom every year, perfectly in place and exactly on time.

The gardens stretch on and on and there are greenhouses full of more delicate varieties. Just wandering about can easily take half a day. There are several cafes for when you need a break from the blooms. From the edges of the gardens, you can see the stark beauty of the commercial bulb fields stretching in all directions.

Different plants will be in bloom at different times, but most people home in on the tulip weeks which are *usually* around the middle of April.

The Keukenhof is open from late March to May but dates vary slightly, so check with any VVV office, or the Keukenhof itself (☎ 0252-46 55 55, **@** info@keukenhof.nl). Its Web site is www.keukenhof.com. During its season, the Keukenhof is open 8 am to 7.30 pm daily, and costs f20/10 for adults/children.

There are several options for reaching the park, which is off the N208. By car, you will have to pay a parking fee of f5, but you will have the freedom of exploring the surrounding bulb fields at your leisure. By train, Netherlands Railways sells a special Keukenhof ticket that combines entrance to the

Café de WW (☎ 512 59 00, Wolsteeg 6) plays live rock to a young crowd most Fridays. Other nights it has a DJ, and is usually open on weekends past 3 am. The *Duke (☎ 566 15 85, Oude Singel 2)* features jazz in the usual dark and contemplative atmosphere.

Cinemas The *Kijkhuis (☎ 566 15 85, Vrouwenkerksteeg 10)* has an alternative film program.

Getting There & Away

Train Centraal Station (CS) is bright and modern. It has all the usual conveniences and the lockers are near track No 5. Service is frequent in all directions and includes:

destination	price (f)	duration (mins)	frequency (per hr)
Amsterdam	13.25	34	6
Schiphol Airport	9.50	18	4
Den Haag	5.50	10	6

Bus Regional and local buses leave from the bus station directly in front of Centraal Station.

Getting Around

Leiden is compact and you'll have a hard time walking for more than 20 minutes in any one direction, but if you do the smart thing and meander in many directions, you can wander for hours.

If you are in need of a taxi, dial ☎ 521 21 44. Leiden Centraal is in the treintaxi scheme (☎ 521 10 89).

The Bicycle Shop (☎ 512 00 68) in Centraal Station is around the back and is open 6.30 am to 1 am daily.

AROUND LEIDEN

The **Keukenhof** and the heart of the **bulb fields** (see the boxed text 'Tulips – The Beloved Bulb') are about 10km north of Leiden.

Tulips – The Beloved Bulb

gardens and travel on a special express bus between Leiden CS and the Keukenhof, which takes about 20 minutes. It costs f25/16 and can be combined with any rail ticket to Leiden CS. The buses leave Leiden throughout the day until about 4 pm and return to Leiden CS until the park closes.

On regular buses, bus No 54 travels from Leiden through Lisse to Keukenhof. You can also take bus No 50 from Haarlem to Lisse and then change to the No 54 bus for the final leg. Both of these buses run every 30 minutes.

Tulip lovers won't want to limit their time with the plants to just the Keukenhof. The 16,500 hectares of **bulb fields** around the Randstad are also ablaze with colour throughout the tulip-blooming period. The broad stripes of colour stretching as far as one can see are a spectacular feast for the eye. The bulbs are left to bloom fully so that they will gain full strength during the growing season, after which more than one billion guilders' worth of bulbs are exported worldwide.

To appreciate the blooms you have several options. By train, opt for one of the frequent local (meaning slow) trains between Haarlem and Leiden. These pass through the heart of the fields. By car cover the same area on the N206 and N208, branching off down tiny side roads as you wish. But like so much of the Netherlands, perhaps the best way to see the bulb fields is by bicycle. You can set your course along the smallest roads and get lost in a sea of colour.

In **Lisse**, the VVV (☎ 0252-41 42 62), Grachtweg 53A, can give you many, many options for bulb field touring by whatever means of transport you prefer. It's open 9 am to 5 pm weekdays (from noon Monday) and until 4 pm Saturday. Also in Lisse, the small **Museum de Zwarte Tulp** (Museum of the Black Tulip; ☎ 0252-41 79 00), Grachtweg 2A, displays everything you want to know about bulbs, including why there is no such thing as a black tulip. It's open 1 to 5 pm Tuesday to Sunday and admission costs f3.

For details on the Aalsmeer Flower Auction, the world's largest, see the section in the Noord Holland chapter.

The beach towns of **Noordwijk aan Zee** and, 3km to the south, **Katwijk aan Zee** are grim examples that even the Dutch propensity for decent urban planning can go amiss. In fact, there seems to be no planning here, as tower blocks crowd the shore and do their best to block the morning sun. But the sand itself is blameless and on a hot day a trip to these beaches can bring relief from the heat, if you like sharing your solace with about a zillion others.

The best strategy for visiting these places is to bike from Leiden and then head south from Katwijk along the many well-marked trails in the dunes. Just keep riding until the crowds and developments disappear, which even on the hottest days will happen. Alternatively, if for some reason you just want to visit the towns themselves, several buses serve the coast from Leiden CS: Nos 40 and 42 for Noordwijk and Nos 31 and 41 for Katwijk.

DEN HAAG (THE HAGUE)
☎ 070 • pop 445,000

Officially known as 's-Gravenhage ('the Count's Domain') because a count built a castle here in the 13th century, Den Haag (The Hague) is the country's seat of government and residence of the royal family, though the capital city is Amsterdam. It has a refined air, thanks to the many stately mansions and palatial embassies that line its green boulevards. It's known for its prestigious art galleries and a huge jazz festival held annually near the seaside suburb of Scheveningen. There is a poorer side to all the finery, though, and the area south of the centre is far removed from its urbane neighbours to the north.

Prior to 1806, the capital was Den Haag. However, that year, Louis Bonaparte installed his government in Amsterdam. Eight years later, when the French had been sent packing, the government returned to Den Haag, but the title of capital, and the king, remained in Amsterdam.

In the 20th century, Den Haag became the home of several international legal entities including the UN's International Court of Justice and the Academy of International Law. These genteel organisations and the legions of diplomats give the town its rather sedate and urbane air today. If you're looking for ribaldry head to Amsterdam, for old Dutch charm head to Delft.

Den Haag, understated to the point of smugness, is worth a stop mainly for its museums. The beach resort of Scheveningen, about 4km north-west of the centre, is for real beach fanatics only.

Orientation
Den Haag sprawls over a fairly large area, but then all those large 19th-century mansions take room. Centraal Station (CS) is near the heart of town. Hollands Spoor Station (HS), which is on the mainline from Amsterdam to Rotterdam and south, is 1km south of the centre in a less bucolic part of town. Most streets heading west reach the beaches of Scheveningen, 4km distant.

Den Haag has no true central focus; rather, there are several areas of concentration, including the Binnenhof and the nearby Kerkplein. The area immediately south of Herengracht is undergoing a massive facelift as Den Haag creates its New Centre, a bold project to establish a prestigious new commercial and residential area. Construction, including road tunnels, is set to continue for years.

Information
Tourist Offices The main VVV (☎ 0900-340 35 05, f0.75 per minute, fax 346 24 12 for hotel reservations, **@** info@denhaag .com), Koningin Julianaplein 30 next to CS, is open 8.30 am to 5.30 pm Monday to Saturday. It's also open 10 am to 2 pm Sunday in July and August.

The VVV in Scheveningen is at Gevers Deynootweg 1134 in the Palace Promenade shopping centre. It's open 9 am to 5.30 pm Monday to Saturday (until 7 pm, and also 10 am to 2 pm Sunday, in July and August).

Both offices book accommodation (f7), sell transport and entertainment tickets and have a great number of English-language publications. Among the better publications are two with themed walks of art and antique stores and architecture.

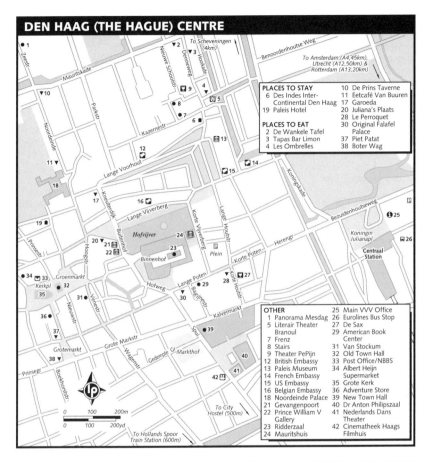

DEN HAAG (THE HAGUE) CENTRE

PLACES TO STAY
6 Des Indes Inter-
Continental Den Haag
19 Paleis Hotel

PLACES TO EAT
2 De Wankele Tafel
3 Tapas Bar Limon
4 Les Ombrelles

10 De Prins Taverne
11 Eetcafé Van Buuren
17 Garoeda
20 Juliana's Plaats
28 Le Perroquet
30 Original Falafel
Palace
37 Piet Patat
38 Boter Wag

OTHER
1 Panorama Mesdag
5 Literair Theater
Branoul
7 Frenz
8 Stairs
9 Theater PePijn
12 British Embassy
13 Paleis Museum
14 French Embassy
15 US Embassy
16 Belgian Embassy
18 Noordeinde Palace
21 Gevangenpoort
22 Prince William V
Gallery
23 Ridderzaal
24 Mauritshuis

25 Main VVV Office
26 Eurolines Bus Stop
27 De Sax
29 American Book
Center
31 Van Stockum
32 Old Town Hall
33 Post Office/NBBS
34 Albert Heijn
Supermarket
35 Grote Kerk
36 Adventure Store
39 New Town Hall
40 Dr Anton Philipszaal
41 Nederlands Dans
Theater
42 Cinematheek Haags
Filmhuis

Money The GWK exchange in CS is open 7 am to 9 pm daily (from 8 am Sunday). ATMs abound, both in the station and around town.

Post & Communications The main post office (☎ 365 38 43) is on Kerkplein 6 next to the Grote Kerk. It's open 7.30 am to 6 pm weekdays and until 4 pm Saturday.

The Internetcafe Den Haag (☎ 363 62 86), Elandstraat 48, is open 5 pm to 1 am (closed Sunday). If you glance away from the screen long enough, you'll notice the funky decor. It also has a full bar and a few snacks.

Travel Agencies NBBS (☎ 360 45 35), Kerkplein 6, has a good location and specialises in discount tickets.

Bookshops The American Book Center (☎ 364 27 42), Lange Poten 23, is a regular US-style bookstore. It has a huge selection of titles and magazines.

Van Stockum (☎ 365 68 08), Venestraat 11, is a large bookshop with a good selection of travel books and magazines.

Libraries The Koninklijke Bibliotheek (☎ 314 09 11), Prins Willem-Alexanderhof 5,

ZUID HOLLAND & ZEELAND

is the national library. Housed in a huge, new, sparkling white building, it has collections of newspapers, magazines, books and more from around the world. It also has all the latest online connections and databases. The Internet day use fee is f5. The library is open 9 am to 5 pm weekdays (until 8 pm Tuesday) and until 1 pm Saturday.

Laundry The coin laundry De Wassalon (☎ 385 84 03), Theresiastraat 250, is a little over 1km east of CS. Take bus No 4 three stops to Laan Van Noi in the direction of Leidschendam 't Lien.

Emergency For all emergencies dial ☎ 112. To contact the police for other reasons call ☎ 310 49 11. The Tourist Assistance Service (TAS, ☎ 310 32 74), Zoutmanstraat 44, helps visitors who've been the victim of a crime or an accident. For general medical information call ☎ 0900-86 00 (after hours ☎ 346 96 69).

Mauritshuis
The Mauritshuis (☎ 302 34 56), Korte Vijverberg 8, is a small but grand museum. It houses the superb royal collection of Dutch and Flemish masterpieces (several famous Vermeers, and a touch of the contemporary with Andy Warhol's *Queen Beatrix*). The building was built as a mansion in 1640 in classical style; all the dimensions are roughly the same (25m) and the detailing shows exquisite care. In 1822 it was made the home of the royal collection.

The small collection is displayed in only 16 rooms on two floors, but what a collection it is! There's no fillers here, as almost every piece is a masterpiece. Rather than slogging along looking for the best stuff, at the Mauritshuis you can see spectacular works in about an hour and then get on your way. Even if you're just passing Den Haag on the train, it's worth hopping off for a visit here.

Highlights include the following (note that some paintings are moved from time to time):

Room 4: *Winter Scene* by Hendrick Avercamp is a delightful evocation of 17th-century life.

Room 8: Pieter Paul Reubens teamed up with Jan Breughel for *Adam and Eve in Paradise*.

Room 9: Three classics by Johannes Vermeer are the stars here: his early *Diana and her Companions* and his famous *Girl with a Pearl Earring* and *View of Delft*.

Room 14: Rembrandt's self-portrait when he was 63 shows a man exhausted by life. Compare this to another self-portrait showing him as a twinkle-eyed young man of 20.

Room 15: More Rembrandts here include the seminal *The Anatomy Lesson of Dr Tulp*, which secured his reputation as a great young painter in his day.

There are excellent guides to each room in English and if you want even more detail, there are audio guides for f5. The gift shop is refreshingly low-key; you won't find any Vermeer toilet seats here. The Mauritshuis is open 10 am to 5 pm Tuesday to Saturday (from 11 am Sunday). Admission is f12.50/6.50 for adults/children.

Binnenhof
The parliamentary buildings around the adjoining Binnenhof (Inner Court) have long been the heart of Dutch politics, though parliament now meets in a modern building (1992) on the south side of the Binnenhof.

The **central courtyard** looks fairly sterile now but it was once used for executions of enemies of the state. A highlight of the Binnenhof complex is the 13th-century **Ridderzaal**, or Knights' Hall. The Gothic dining hall has been carefully restored and you may find yourself wanting to yell, 'More mead!'

The **North Wing** is still home to the Upper Chamber of the Dutch Parliament, who meet in 17th-century splendour. The Lower Chamber used to meet in the **ballroom** which you'll see in the 19th-century wing. It all looks a bit twee and you can see why the politicians were anxious to decamp to the sleek, modern addition nearby.

The best way to see the Binnenhof's buildings is by a tour which leaves from the **visitors centre** (☎ 364 61 44). Here you can see a model showing the hotchpotch of buildings that comprise the Binnenhof and learn about the turbulent past of the Low Countries, where invaders have flooded in more often than the waters. The tours take about an hour and are offered 10 am to 3.45 pm Monday to Saturday. The cost is f6.50/1.50, but note that if the government is busy governing, some parts may be closed.

After your walk you may want to stroll around **Hofvijer**, where the reflections of the Binnenhof and the Mauritshuis have inspired a million snapshots.

Den Haag: Old and New
Across the Hofvijer, the **Gevangenpoort** (Prison Gate; ☎ 346 08 61), Buitenhof 33, is a surviving remnant of the city fortifications from the 13th century. It has hourly tours showing how justice was dispensed in early times – needless to say, it often hurt. It's open 11 am to 4 pm Tuesday to Friday, weekends from noon, and costs f6/4.

Next door, the **Prince William V Gallery** (☎ 362 44 44), Buitenhof 35, was the first public museum in the Netherlands when it opened in 1773. It's been restored to its original appearance and the paintings are hung in the manner popular in the 18th century; not a bit of wall is left bare. Although few of the works are from the original collection, the effect is the same. The gallery is open 11 am to 4 pm Tuesday to Sunday and costs f2.50/1.

Nearby, the **Groenmarkt** is the oddly unatmospheric home to some bits of the old town. The solid **Grotekerk** dates from 1450 and has a fine pulpit constructed 100 years later. The neighbouring 1565 **old town hall** is a splendid example of Dutch Renaissance architecture, but unfortunately you can only admire it from the outside.

The huge **new town hall** at Spui 70, at the corner of Grote Marktstraat, is the much-criticised work by US architect Richard Meier. The 'official' nickname of the building is the 'white swan', but locals prefer the more appropriate 'ice palace'. Even better nicknames are used locally for two enormous government buildings nearby – ride up to the new town hall's 11th floor on an elevator and take a gander at the complex, which has two pointed towers at one end and a dome-topped round tower at the other. See if you agree with the local moniker, 'the tits and penis'.

Local nicknames are more polite for the king and queen's official quarters at **Paleis Noordeinde**, on the Noordeinde. The Renaissance formality of the structure bespeaks regal digs. It's not open to the public and the strong gates ensure security should the populace revolt for having their taxes spent on anatomically suggestive buildings.

You can visit the **Paleis Museum** (☎ 338 11 20) on tree-lined Lange Voorhout. Built in the 18th century, it was the royal home of Queen Emma, mother of Queen Wilhelmina. Now its elegant interior is used for art exhibitions. The opening hours – subject to change – are 11 am to 5 pm Tuesday to Sunday. Admission fees average f10, depending on what's on.

The Hague School of Art
Just past the north end of Noordeinde is another worthwhile art exhibit, the **Panorama Mesdag** (☎ 364 45 44), at Zeestraat 65. The impressive *Panorama Mesdag* (1881) is a gigantic, 360-degree painting of Scheveningen viewed from a dune, painted by Hendrik Willem Mesdag (1831–1915). It's open 10 am to 5 pm daily (Sunday from noon) and costs f7.50/4.

About 500m west, you can see the home of the *Panorama*'s painter at the **Mesdag Museum** (☎ 362 14 34) on Laan van Meerdervoort. Along with others such as Jozef Israëls, Mesdag helped spur a rebirth in Dutch painting through his depictions, in dreamy tones, of the seashore and fishermen, in a style that became known as the Hague School. The museum displays works by these artists, who so influenced Mondriaan in his early years. It's open noon to 5 pm (closed Monday) and admission is f5/2.50.

Peace Palace
The Vredespaleis, or Peace Palace (☎ 302 41 37), at Carnegieplein 2 is home to the UN's **International Court of Justice**. The grand building was donated by American steel maker Andrew Carnegie for use by the International Court of Arbitration, an early international body whose goal was the prevention of war. Sadly, big buildings and grand names can't accomplish what humans

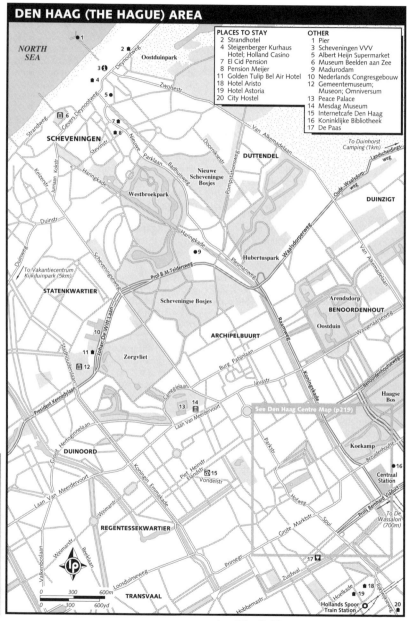

DEN HAAG (THE HAGUE) AREA

PLACES TO STAY
2 Strandhotel
4 Steigenberger Kurhaus Hotel; Holland Casino
7 El Cid Pension
8 Pension Meijer
11 Golden Tulip Bel Air Hotel
18 Hotel Aristo
19 Hotel Astoria
20 City Hostel

OTHER
1 Pier
3 Scheveningen VVV
5 Albert Heijn Supermarket
6 Museum Beelden aan Zee
9 Madurodam
10 Nederlands Congresgebouw
12 Gemeentemuseum; Museon; Omniversum
13 Peace Palace
14 Mesdag Museum
15 Internetcafe Den Haag
16 Koninklijke Bibliotheek
17 De Paas

NORTH SEA

Oostduinpark

SCHEVENINGEN

DUTTENDEL

DUINZIGT

To Duinhorst Camping (1km)

Nieuwe Scheveningse Bosjes

Westbroekpark

Duinweg

To Vakantiecentrum Kijkduinpark (5km)

Hubertuspark

STATENKWARTIER

Scheveningse Bosjes

Arendsdorp

BENOORDENHOUT

Oostduin

ARCHIPELBUURT

Zorgvliet

Haagse Bos

See Den Haag Centre Map (p219)

Koekamp

DUINOORD

Centraal Station

To De Wassalon (700m)

REGENTESSEKWARTIER

Hollands Spoor Train Station

TRANSVAAL

0   300   600m
0   300   600yd

ZUID HOLLAND & ZEELAND

won't and WWI broke out one year after it opened in 1913.

There are hourly guided tours between 10 am and 4 pm weekdays, which cost f5/3, but if the courts are in session these may be cancelled – check with the Peace Palace or the VVV. You need to book seats in advance (security is strict).

To get there, take tram No 7 from CS or tram No 8 from HS.

Gemeentemuseum

Admirers of De Stijl, and in particular of Piet Mondriaan, won't want to miss the HP Berlage-designed Gemeentemuseum (Municipal Museum; ☎ 338 11 11), at Stadhouderslaan 41. It was refurbished in the 1990s at great expense and houses a large collection of works by neoplasticist artists and others from the late 19th century onwards, as well as extensive exhibits of applied arts, costumes and musical instruments.

Mondriaan's unfinished *Victory Boogie Woogie* takes pride of place (as well it should, since the museum paid f84 million for it); stare at it for a couple of minutes and you'll be gripped by the vibrancy of his ode to the USA. There are also a few Picassos and other works by some of the better-known names of the 20th century. The rooms of industrial art shows that commerce can produce good works as well.

The museum is open 11 am to 5 pm Tuesday to Sunday and costs f10/7.50. Take tram No 7 from CS, or No 10 or 11 from HS.

The adjoining **Museon** (☎ 338 13 38, same hours as the Gemeentemuseum) explores the world and its people for school kids, and next door the **Omniversum** (☎ 354 54 54) is an Imax theatre with the usual big-screen thrills (in Dutch). The films usually run until 10 pm.

Madurodam

Towards Scheveningen is Madurodam (☎ 355 39 00), George Maduroplein 1, a miniature town containing everything that's quintessentially Netherlands. There's lots of little buildings, people, airplanes and more. But given that much of the real thing lies within an hour of Den Haag, it seems a little odd to seek out this shrunken and sanitised

version. Not surprisingly, it's big with children, as well as adults with Brobdingnagian leanings. Look away from the glitz for the memorial by the entrance to learn about the history of Madurodam. It was started by JML Maduro as a memorial to his son who fought the Nazi invasion and later died at Dachau.

The site is open from 9 am daily. Closing times vary seasonally from 6 pm in January to 11 pm in August. Admission is f21/14. Take tram No 1 from CS, or tram No 1 or 9 from HS.

Scheveningen

Scheveningen is an overdeveloped seaside resort north of town that makes much of the fact that it has 'the most popular beach' in the Netherlands. Of course, 'most popular' translates to 'obscenely crowded' when the temperature manages to crack about 22°C. The urban planning the Dutch are often rightly praised for is on holiday here and all manner of truly miserable high-rises glower over the sands.

There's lots of the usual seashore schlock – and a long **pier**, which in deference to the dubious North Sea weather was recently glassed over.

Scheveningen makes a stab at the well heeled – or soon to be less so – with the **Holland Casino** (☎ 306 77 77), Kurhausweg 1, next to the landmark Kurhaus Hotel (see Places to Stay). For cultural solace, check out the **Museum Beelden aan Zee** (☎ 358 58 57), Harteveltstraat 1, along the promenade. This indoor/outdoor gallery combines all manner of sculptures of the human form, although you'll see more astonishing sights on the sands below on a hot day. It's open 11 am to 5 pm (closed Monday) and admission is f7.50/4.

You can escape the mobs by heading north along the beach past the end of the tram line. Here the dunes are more pristine and the farther you walk, the greater the rewards. Trails make it an excellent spot for biking.

At the south end of Scheveningen is the harbour, which still sees evidence of the town's original economic activity: fishing.

One oft-repeated story concerns how Dutch resistance fighters during WWII used

ZUID HOLLAND & ZEELAND

'Scheveningen' as a password. It seems that while the Germans could easily learn Dutch, the accent required to properly pronounce 'Scheveningen' was impossible to learn.

See the Getting Around section for all of the transport details between Den Haag and Scheveningen.

Organised Tours

The VVV offers two bus tours that each last two hours. The 'Royal Tour' is a general overview of the area's highlights. It departs at 1 pm from the VVV office at CS and at 1.15 pm from the Scheveningen VVV office Tuesday to Sunday from May to September. The 'Architecture Tour' uses a specialist guide and views buildings old and new. It departs from the CS VVV office at 10.30 am Tuesday from May to September.

Special Events

July

North Sea Jazz Festival (☎ 214 89 00) One of the world's largest events of its kind, the festival draws the some of the best musicians. It's usually held the second weekend of July at the vast Nederlands Congresgebouw, Churchhillplein 10. Rooms are at a premium as thousands of fans descend on the city from all around. You may be best off staying elsewhere and commuting, or booking far in advance.

September

Parliament Opening Held on the third Tuesday of every September. This is one of the best ways to see the Dutch royal family in action as the Queen rides to the Binnenhof in a golden coach.

Places to Stay

Diplomats and royalty call Den Haag home and you can too, for a price; or Scheveningen has oodles of cheap joints catering to holiday-makers.

Camping There are camping sites in the dunes either side of Scheveningen. *Duinhorst* (☎ 324 22 70, fax 324 60 53, Buurtweg 135), to the east, is open from April to September. Prices range from f30 to f55 per site depending on season. Ride bus No 28 from HS or 29 from CS to the end of the line at Oude Waalsdorperweg and then walk about 1km west, or take a treintaxi.

The *Vakantiecentrum Kijkduinpark* (☎ 448 21 00, fax 323 24 57, Machiel Vrijenhoeklaan 450) is open all year. Prices range from f35 to f65 per site depending on season. Ride bus No 23 from CS to one stop before the end of the line at Kijkduin, from where it's a short walk.

Hostels The well-equipped NJHC *City Hostel* (☎ 315 78 88, fax 315 78 77, Scheepmakerstraat 27) is in a grand, restored building south of HS. It has a popular cafe named *Brasserie Backpackers*. Depending on the season, singles range from f67 to f77, doubles from f80 to f100, and dorms from f32.50 to f36.50. It's a five-minute walk from HS or take tram No 1 from HS or CS to the stop 'Rijswijkseplein'; you'll know the hostel at night from its myriad of decorative lights.

Hotels – Den Haag Several budget hotels are clustered in the slightly grotty area near HS. *Hotel Aristo* (☎/fax 389 08 47, Stationsweg 166) is clean and simple with bathless rooms from f70/95 for a single/double.

Hotel Astoria (☎/fax 384 04 01, Stationsweg 139) has rooms with TV and WC from f75/100. It's 20m from HS.

Paleis Hotel (☎ 362 46 21, fax 361 45 33, Molenstraat 26) has an austere style and a great location near Noordeinde. If the sun doesn't shine you can get your own tan in the solarium. The well-equipped rooms cost f165/185.

The *Golden Tulip Bel Air Hotel* (☎ 352 53 54, fax 352 53 53, Johan de Witt Laan 30) overlooks the Gemeentemuseum and is next to the Nederlands Congresgebouw. The standard business-class rooms cost from f250/290, but ask about discounts.

If you're a visiting head of state, fire your assistant if you're not booked into the lovely *Des Indes Inter-Continental Den Haag* (☎ 361 23 45, fax 361 23 50, Lange Voorhout 54–56). The rooms have all the comforts and you might be content to linger in the cafe behind the large orange awnings before heading off to start a diplomatic crisis. Room prices start at f425 and rise faster than an ICBM.

It's 465 steps up, but what a view: Domtoren, Utrecht

Street above and canals at the front door: warehouse living Utrecht style

Passing the time away

A canal with atmosphere, Den Haag

An 'undercover' Police Station, Den Haag

One of the many stately homes in Den Haag

Full of life: Hortus Botanicus, Leiden

Relaxing in Clingendael Park, Den Haag

Hotels – Scheveningen The very basic *Pension Meijer (☎/fax 355 81 38, Stevinstraat 64)* is about 700m from the shore, and has rooms from f45/60.

The friendly *El Cid Pension (☎ 354 66 67, 352 13 81, Badhuisweg 51)* has simple rooms from f45 per person, and is about 500m from the beach.

Strandhotel (☎ 354 01 93, fax 354 35 58, Zeekant 111) is situated on the beach and right above several bars. The rooms have a funky, unreconstructed '50s motif and cost f65/120, rising much higher in summer.

At the top end, the *Steigenberger Kurhaus Hotel (☎ 416 26 36, fax 416 26 46, Gevers Deynootplein 30)* is right on the beach. First built in 1885, it's been added to and restored several times since. The noted thermal baths are there still, as is a casino and many more diversions. Rooms start at f390, but ask about specials, particularly in the off-season.

Places to Eat

Den Haag's gastronomic scene is fairly central. Little action occurs out in the leafy suburbs. There's no shortage of fast-food places in Scheveningen with little to differentiate them.

Restaurants Plan on dining before 9 pm or you'll find closed kitchens and slumbering waiters.

The cobbled streets off Denneweg are one of the livelier areas, with canalside cafes, intimate restaurants, theatres and bars. Nearby you'll find *De Wankele Tafel (☎ 364 32 67, Mauritskade 79)*, a homy little vegetarian haunt with three-course meals from f12.50 to f21.50 that clean out the fruit and veg section of the market. It's open for dinner until 9.30 pm (closed Sunday).

Nearby, the *Tapas Bar Limon (☎ 356 14 65, Denneweg 59A)* has tiled floors, wooden tables and pitchers of sangria. Daily specials are under f20. It's open for dinner daily.

Garoeda (☎ 346 53 19, Kneuterdijk 18A) has a bright, corner location and serves *rijstaffels* from f40 per person. Popular with locals, it's open daily for dinner.

Les Ombrelles (☎ 365 87 89, Hooistraat 4A) is as refined as the fish is fresh. The service is very professional, there's an extensive wine list and the specials are brill and monkfish. Expect to pay more than f60 per person with drinks. It's open for dinner daily.

Cafes *Juliana's Plaats (☎ 365 02 35, Plaats 11)* is a stylish brown cafe with a good wine list. At lunch, baguettes and pancakes go for f9, while at dinner, various Dutch standards average f20. This is a good spot to rest up from viewing priceless paintings.

Le Perroquet (☎ 363 97 86, Lange Poten 1) is one of several places with outdoor seating on the Plein. It serves a wide-ranging, casual menu with satay specials from f15.

Boter Wag (☎ 365 96 86, 10 Grote Markt) is in a restored 17th-century building where butter was once weighed. It has high ceilings and large windows, making for an untypically airy cafe atmosphere. It has a long list of beers on tap and cheap lunch specials for under f9. It's open until at least 1 am nightly.

De Prins Taverne (☎ 364 38 75, Noordeinde 165) straddles the line between cafe and bar, but it does have good lunch salads and sandwiches from f5. It's a classic place with leaded-glass windows and a prime corner location, and is open until at least midnight daily.

Eetcafé Van Buuren (☎ 427 67 26, Noordeinde 90) is another classic place with a good selection of beer. The daily specials are under f20 and later some evenings it has live music.

Fast Food & Self-Catering The *Original Falafel Palace (☎ 427 72 20, Lange Poten 7)* is sparkling and friendly. Buy the namesake sandwich (f6) and peruse the long bar of fillings you ladle on yourself.

Piet Patat (☎ 364 80 19, Grote Markt 3) has some of the best *frites* in town (f3).

The *Markthof* is an area of produce and food stands. You should be able to find just about anything in the many aisles here.

There's a large *Albert Heijn Supermarket (☎ 365 44 69, Torenstraat 27)* that's not far from the Groenmarkt.

ZUID HOLLAND & ZEELAND

In Scheveningen there's an *Albert Heijn Supermarket (☎ 358 81 44, Amsterdamsestraat 9)* near the beach.

Entertainment

Diplomats go to bed early and so does the rest of the town. Amsterdam isn't far and those looking for late-night action catch one of the trains that run all night.

Dance lovers will find plenty of reason to stay put in Den Haag, however, for a performance by the world-renowned Netherlands Dance Theatre.

Bars *De Paas (☎ 392 00 02, Dunne Bierkade 16A)* is a classic brown cafe with small candles on the tables and about 150 beers on offer. It's a friendly yet quiet place with imbibers pondering their brews.

The little bar *De Sax (☎ 346 67 55, Korte Houtstraat 14A)* is just off the Plein. It has a good vibe, not the least of which is due to the cool jazz from the sound system.

Look for the big rainbow flag flying out the front at *Frenz (☎ 363 66 57, Kazernestraat 106)*, a friendly gay bar that's open until late.

Stairs (☎ 364 81 91, Nieuwe Schoolstraat 39) is near a tiny canal and is another gathering place for Den Haag's gays and lesbians. There's dancing until 4 am and later on weekends.

Dance The *Nederlands Dans Theater (☎ 360 49 30, reservations ☎ 360 38 73)* has gained worldwide fame since it was founded in 1959 by a group of dancers frustrated by the ossified creativity of the old Ballet of the Netherlands company.

Today the Netherlands Dance Theatre comprises three companies: NDT1, the main troupe of 32 dancers; NDT2, a small group of 12 young dancers under 21; and NDT3, a group of dancers over age 40 who perform more dramatic works.

Performances are at the Lucent Dance Theatre, Spui 152, which has a 1000-seat main hall under a rippling roof as well as several smaller venues. It's widely thought to be the largest dance-only performance hall in the world.

With three companies, tickets aren't impossible to come by. Check the schedule when you're in town and try the box office which is open 10 am to 6 pm daily. The company's Web site is www.ndt.nl.

Other Entertainment Near the Lucent Dance Theatre, *Dr Anton Philipszaal (☎ 360 98 10, Spui 150)* is home to the Residentie Orchestra, Den Haag's very own local classical symphony.

Theater PePijn (☎ 0900-410 4104, Nieuwe Schoolstraat 21) is a venue for comedy, theatre and cabaret.

The *Literair Theater Branoul (☎ 365 72 85, Maliestraat 12)* has performances of the classics as well as literary lectures.

The *Cinematheek Haags Filmhuis (☎ 345 99 00, Spui 191)* screens foreign and art movies.

Shopping

There are several good streets for galleries, antiques and interesting boutiques; try Denneweg, Noordeinde and Molenstraat. Grosse Marktstraat is lined with major department stores. The Passage, a glass-covered shopping arcade between Spuistraat, Buitenhof and Hofweg, is a stylish affair.

The Adventure Store (☎ 361 69 69), Schoolstraat 19A, has camping and outdoor wear.

Getting There & Away

Train Den Haag has two main train stations, which leads to no end of confusion. Centraal Station (CS) is close to the centre and is a terminus. It has all the usual services and is a hub for local trams and buses. Hollands Spoor (HS) is about 1km south of the centre and is on the main railway line between Amsterdam and Rotterdam and the south. *Thalys* high-speed trains to/from Paris stop here as do many other throughservices. HS also has all the usual services.

Generally, you shouldn't worry too much which station your train will stop at – only pokey locals serve both – as both stations have numerous tram and bus links.

Some sample train services, good for both CS and HS, are:

destination	price (f)	duration (mins)	frequency (per hr)
Amsterdam	17.25	50	4
Leiden	5.50	13	4
Rotterdam	7.50	22	4
Utrecht	17.25	40	4

Bus Eurolines long-distance buses stop on the east side of CS. Regional buses depart from the bus station which is above the tracks at CS.

Getting Around

Public Transport If you're arriving by train at CS and staying near the centre, you probably won't need to use the local services provided by HTM (☎ 384 86 66). However, for anything out of the centre you may want to use the web of tram and bus services. Most routes converge on CS where there is a convenient tram and bus station above the tracks. A number of routes also serve HS, including the jack-of-all-trades tram No 1, which starts in Scheveningen and runs all the way to Delft, passing the centre of Den Haag and CS along the way. A transit map (f1) sold at the VVV offices and at the ticket windows at the train stations covers the region south to Rotterdam.

Tram Nos 1, 8 and 9 link Scheveningen with Den Haag; the fare is three strips. The last tram at night runs in either direction at about 1.30 am. There is also a multiday pass available for the region which is only a good deal if you plan on using public transport a lot. It costs f10/17/21.25 for one/two/three days. A version which includes all the services south to Delft costs f14/21/26. The passes are available from VVVs, hotels and HTM kiosks.

Taxi Call ATC Taxi (☎ 317 88 77) for a cab. You can hail any free taxi, if you can find one.

Bicycle The bicycle shop in CS (☎ 385 32 35) is open 5 am to 2 am daily, and is under the terminal. The HS counterpart (☎ 389 08 30) is open 6 am to midnight (from 7.30 am weekends) and is at the south end of the station. Both rent bikes.

GOUDA
☎ 0182 • pop 73,000

If you think Gouda and you think of mild cheese, then you're not far off the mark. This town's namesake cheese is one of the Netherlands' most well-known exports. However, if you think that Gouda cheese is only the mild – some would say almost tasteless – stuff on your local supermarket's shelf then you are in for a surprise. And like its cheese, Gouda town has a few surprises of its own – not the least of which are the acclaimed 16th-century stained-glass windows in its church. Market day at the overly famous cheese market might actually be the one day not to drop by Gouda during summer. On any day, Gouda is a quick day trip from any city in Zuid Holland. Should you spend the night, the town's charms will be easier to savour after dark and it will be just you and the locals.

Gouda enjoyed economic success and decline in the same manner as the rest of Holland from the 16th century onwards. Its cheese has brought recent wealth as has the country's largest candle factory, which stays busy supplying all those Dutch brown cafes.

The compact centre is entirely ringed by canals and is less than five minutes' walk from the station. The large central square, the Markt, is the focus of the town.

Information

The VVV (☎ 51 36 66, fax 583 210), Markt 27, is open 9 am to 5 pm Monday to Saturday. The GWK exchange in the train station is open 8 am to 7.30 pm daily. The post office (☎ 52 21 00), Westhaven 37, is south of the Markt and open 7 am to 5 pm weekdays and until 1.30 pm Saturday.

The Markt

The central Markt is one of the largest such squares in the Netherlands. Right in the middle is the mid-15th-century **Stadhuis**. Constructed from shimmering sandstone, this regal Gothic structure bespeaks the wealth that Gouda enjoyed from the cloth trade when it was built. The red and white shutters provide a fine counterpoint to the carefully maintained stonework.

ZUID HOLLAND & ZEELAND

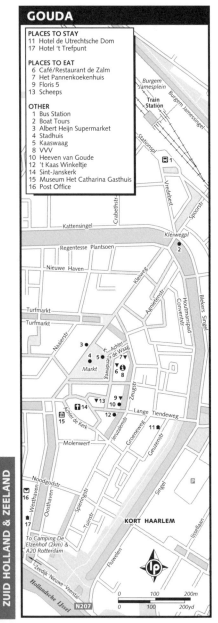

On the north side of the Markt, you can't miss the **Waag**, a former cheese-weighing house built in 1668. If you have any doubt about its use, check out the reliefs carved into the side showing the cheese being weighed. It houses the **Kaaswaag** (☎ 52 99 96), a museum that follows the history of cheese trade in the Netherlands and especially Gouda. It's open 1 to 5 pm Tuesday to Sunday from April to October and costs f5/3.50 for adults/children.

Sint Janskerk and Around

Just to the south of the Markt is Sint Janskerk (☎ 51 26 84), on Achter de Kerk. The church itself had a chequered start: it burned down with ungodly regularity every 100 years or so from 1361 until the mid-16th century when what you see today was finished. As a building, Sint Janskerk is a reasonably attractive late-Gothic church in need of a better steeple. But it's in its huge windows that the church is set apart. The greatest of these were created by Dirck Crabeth, his brother Wouter and Lambert van Noort from around 1550 to 1570. Their works, which are numbered, include the following details:

5   The Queen of Sheba visits King Solomon
6   John the Baptist (the folks on either side paid for the window)
7   The Last Supper
8   Heliodorus, the temple thief, gets scolded by angels
9   The annunciation of the birth of John the Baptist
11 Elisabeth, the mother of John the Baptist
12 The birth of Jesus
13 Young Jesus in the temple
14 John the Baptist preaching
15 John baptises Jesus
16 Jesus preaches for the first time
18 John the Baptist sends messengers to Jesus
22 Jesus purifies the temple (note the look on the face of the money-changer)
23 Jesus washes the disciples' feet
24 Philip preaches
30 Jonah and the whale
31 The speaking ass

You can borrow binoculars from the gift shop for a closer view of the windows. The church is open 9 am to 5 pm Monday to Saturday from March to November (10 am to 4 pm the rest of the year). Admission is f3.50/2.50 for adults/children.

To the immediate south of the church near a small canal, the **Museum Het Catharina Gasthuis** (☎ 58 84 40), Osthaven 10, covers Gouda's history and has a few artworks. It's housed in an old hospital and is open 10 am to 5 pm daily (from noon Sunday); admission is f4.25/2.

Other Attractions

Wandering the streets away from the Markt is rewarding, especially **Lange Tiendeweg** and **Zeugstraat**, with its tiny canal and even tinier bridges. To prove that Gouda cheese really isn't bland, visit **'t Kaas Winkeltje** (☎ 51 42 69), Lange Tiendeweg 30. This cheese shop is filled with fabulous smells and it's here that you can sample some of the aged Goudas that the Dutch wisely keep for themselves. The older the cheese, the sharper the flavour and some of the very old Goudas have an almost Parmesan texture and a rich, smoky taste. With a little mustard smeared on, a hunk of this goes great with beer.

Cheese Market

Once upon a time the Gouda cheese market was the real thing, as the Waag will attest. But the days when more than 1000 dairymen and cheesemakers would assemble in the Markt for a raucous day of buying, selling and trading are long past. Now it's just hundreds of tour buses that assemble every Thursday morning from June to August for an orgy of buying, selling and very little trading. A few men dress up in traditional costume and go through the motions for the mobs of tourists, but the event is really more of an excuse for a huge market to be set up offering not just cheese, but wooden shoes, fake Delft pottery etc. Unless you're into this sort of spectacle, you might want to avoid Gouda at these times.

Boat Tours

In July and August, there are two boat trips a day through the larger canals around Gouda to the nearby Reeuwijk lake district. The tours last three hours and cost f12.50. Contact the VVV office for more details.

Places to Stay

Given that Gouda is such a natural day-trip you might not think of staying here, but you may appreciate its somnolent charms after dark. The VVV has a list of a few private rooms it will book for f3.50. These rooms usually cost f35 to f40 per person.

Camping De Elzenhof (☎ 52 44 56, Broekweg 6) wouldn't be far from town if you were a swallow. But because you have to detour around various canals and waterways and because there is no bus, it becomes a 45-minute haul. Go south from the centre of Gouda, cross the Julianasluis bridge and follow the signs. It has 80 sites which cost from f20 for two people and a tent.

Hotel de Utrechtsche Dom (☎ 52 88 33, fax 549 534, ✉ hotel@rsnet.nl, Geuzenstraat 6) is neat and clean and on a quiet street. Rooms cost from f105 without bath and f125 with bath. In the summer they cost f10 more.

Hotel 't Trefpunt (☎ 51 28 79, Westhaven 46) is a decent and simple place where rooms without bath cost from f85/112 for a single/double.

Places to Eat & Drink

Café/Restaurant de Zalm (☎ 52 53 45, Markt 34) is in an old hotel with big windows looking out on the Markt and has lovely outdoor tables under the porch. Salads and omelettes cost from f11 and it's open 9 am to midnight daily. At dinner they have Dutch and vegetarian main courses for under f30. Run by the same family, *Het Pannenkoekenhuis* is in the old stables of the hotel. It has canalside tables and the usual array of pancakes for under f10.

The best place to dine is *Scheeps* (☎ 51 75 72, Koster Gijzensteeg 5), which specialises in fresh fish. Try the wonderful sea bass stuffed with garlic and pepper (f36). It's open for dinner daily.

Floris 5 (☎ 51 18 60, Zeugstraat 5) is a classic brown cafe with canalside tables when the weather is decent. It's open daily to 1 am. Next door, the same people run *Heeven van*

ZUID HOLLAND & ZEELAND

Goude, a dance club that gets going after 10 pm on Friday and Saturday nights.

There's an *Albert Heijn Supermarket* (☎ 51 28 55, Markt 50) if you're looking at cooking your own meals.

Getting There & Around

Train Gouda's train station is close to the centre and all you'll need are your feet for local transport. The lockers are in the tunnel under the tracks. Sample fares and schedules are:

destination	price (f)	duration (mins)	frequency (per hr)
Den Haag	8.50	19	4
Rotterdam	7.50	19	4
Utrecht	9.50	22	4

For Amsterdam (f17.50) you have to change in either Utrecht or Den Haag.

Bus The bus station is immediately to the left as you exit the train station. The one bus of interest here is to Oudewater. See the listing in the Utrecht chapter for details.

Car & Motorcycle Gouda is near the A12 motorway between Den Haag and Utrecht and the A20 to Rotterdam. There are large parking lots on the periphery of the centre.

Taxi Gouda is part of the treintaxi scheme (☎ 51 22 33).

Bicycle The bicycle shop in the train station (☎ 51 97 51) is open 5.30 am to 8 pm weekdays and from 7 am weekends.

DELFT

☎ 015 • pop 95,000

Had the potters who lived in Delft long ago not been such accomplished copiers, today's townsfolk would probably live in relative peace. But the distinctive blue-and-white pottery which the 17th-century artisans duplicated from Chinese porcelain became famous worldwide as 'delftware'.

If you're here in summer the number of day-tripping tourists will probably make

you wish you weren't; in winter its old-world charm and narrow, canal-lined streets make a pleasant day-trip from Rotterdam or Den Haag. Or you can stay and enjoy the pleasures of Delft – especially at night when the summer mobs leave – and make day-trips to the larger neighbouring cities.

Delft was founded around 1100 and grew rich off weaving and trade in the 13th and 14th centuries. In the 15th century a canal was dug to the Maas River and the small port there, Delfshaven, was eventually absorbed by Rotterdam.

Beyond china, Delft has a strong association with the Dutch royal family and was the home of Vermeer.

Orientation

The train and neighbouring bus station are a 10-minute stroll south of the central Markt.

Information

Tourist Offices The VVV (☎ 212 61 00, fax 215 86 95) is on the Markt at No 83/85. It is open 9 am to 5.30 pm Monday to Saturday; also 11 am to 3 pm Sunday from mid-April to October. It has all the usual services and sells an English-language information book which details a good historic walk (f3.50). It also rents 'Talking Walls' audio walking tours of the city for f15. These excellent CDs talk about events and history keyed to specific sites.

Money The number of ATMs in Delft is in inverse proportion to the number of places selling cheap, fake delftware, ie, infinitesimal. It's best to use the two ATMs just outside the train station to the left as you exit. The GWK office at the same location is open 8 am to 7 pm daily and 8 am to 6 pm weekends.

Post The post office (☎ 212 45 11), Hippolytusbuurt 14, is open 9 am to 5 pm weekdays and 10 am to 1.30 pm Saturday.

Travel Agencies Holland International (☎ 212 19 90), Markt 28, books tours and all manner of tickets and trips.

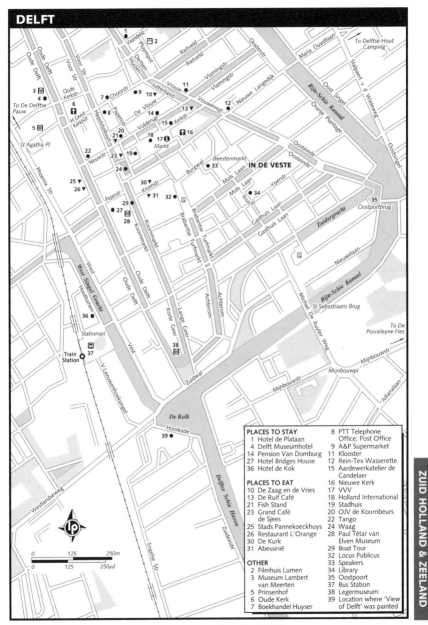

DELFT

PLACES TO STAY
1 Hotel de Plataan
4 Delft Museumhotel
14 Pension Van Domburg
27 Hotel Bridges House
36 Hotel de Kok

PLACES TO EAT
10 De Zaag en de Vries
13 De Ruif Café
21 Fish Stand
23 Grand Café de Sjees
25 Stads Panneckoeckhuys
26 Restaurant L'Orange
30 De Kurk
31 Abessinië

OTHER
2 Filmhuis Lumen
3 Museum Lambert van Meerten
5 Prinsenhof
6 Oude Kerk
7 Boekhandel Huyser
8 PTT Telephone Office; Post Office
9 A&P Supermarket
11 Klooster
12 Rein-Tex Wasserette
15 Aardewerkatelier de Candelaer
16 Nieuwe Kerk
17 VVV
18 Holland International
19 Stadhuis
20 OJV de Koornbeurs
22 Tango
24 Waag
28 Paul Tétar van Elven Museum
29 Boat Tour
32 Locus Publicus
33 Speakers
34 Library
35 Oostpoort
37 Bus Station
38 Legermuseum
39 Location where 'View of Delft' was painted

Bookshops Boekhandel Huyser (☎ 212 38 20), Choorstraat 12–14, has a good travel section and lots of English-language books.

Libraries The library (☎ 212 34 50) is at Kruisstraat 71 at the corner with Molslaan. It has Internet access and is open 10 am to 7 pm weekdays and 10 am to 3 pm Saturday.

Laundry Rein-Tex Wasserette (☎ 214 54 39), Nieuwe Langendijk 4A, is open 10 am to 7 pm weekdays and until 6 pm Saturday.

Delftware

Think Delft and you think delftware, the ubiquitous blue and white china that is almost a cliche. Given that the process was first developed in China, it's ironic that the mass of fake delftware sold in tourist shops also comes from China. The real stuff is produced in fairly small quantities at four factories in and around Delft. See the boxed text 'Making the Blue & White Gold' for details of the manufacturing process.

There are three places where you can see the artists working. The most central and modest outfit is the **Aardewerkatelier de Candelaer** (☎ 213 18 48) at Kerkstraat 14,

Making the Blue & White Gold

The alabaster clay used for delftware comes from England. After it is mixed with water it is poured into moulds and then quickly poured out. The remaining thin coating is then fired at 600°C. The process came from China, where artisans wanted to produce works with corners, which obviously is impossible using pottery wheels, which had been the technique used in Europe until that time.

The resulting piece is then cleaned up and made smooth. The artists then paint their designs. Most people think blue is the only colour used, but there is a rich palette of colours that can be used. Individual artists use time-tested – and saleable designs – as well as developing their own designs each year. Once painted and glazed, the piece makes another trip into the oven and is then ready for sale.

just off the Markt. It has five artists, a few of whom work most days. When it's quiet they'll give you a detailed tour of the manufacturing process. It's open 9 am to 5 pm Monday to Saturday (until 6 pm Sunday until 5 pm from mid-March to mid-October).

The other two locations are really factories and are outside the town centre. **De Delftse Pauw** (☎ 212 49 20), Delftweg 133, is the smaller, employing 35 painters who work mainly from home (take tram No 1 to Pasgeld, walk up Broekmolenweg to the canal and turn left). It has daily tours but you won't see the painters on weekends. It's open 9 am to 4.30 pm daily (11 am to 1 pm on weekends from November to March).

De Porceleyne Fles (☎ 251 20 30), south at Rotterdamseweg 196, is the only original factory operating since the 1650s, and is slick and pricey. Bus No 63 from the train station stops nearby at Jaffalaan, or it's a 25-minute walk from the town centre. Tours aren't free, but cost f5, and are offered between 9.30 am and 5 pm daily (closed Sunday from November to March).

Although complex pieces can be costly, simple bowls that still exhibit the fine qualities of delftware sell for about f20. When in doubt about a piece's authenticity, check the bottom. There should be a number designating which mould was used, the initials of the artist and a two-letter code for the year of manufacture ('AY' designates 2000).

The **Museum Lambert van Meerten** (☎ 260 23 58), Oude Delft 199, has a fine collection of porcelain tiles and delftware dating back to the 16th century. It's open 10 am to 5 pm Tuesday to Saturday (from 1 pm Sunday) and admission is f3.50/1.75 for adults/children.

Vermeer's Delft

One of the greatest Dutch old masters, **Johannes Vermeer** (1632–75) lived his entire life in Delft, fathering 11 children and dying at age 43. His paintings have rich and meticulous colouring and he captures light as few other painters have ever managed. His scenes come from everyday life in Delft, his interiors capturing simple scenes

ZUID HOLLAND & ZEELAND

such as the *Girl with a Pearl Earring*. Vermeer's most famous exterior work, *View of Delft*, brilliantly captures the play of light and shadow of a partly cloudy day. You can visit the location where he painted this work – it's across the canal at Hooikade, southeast of the train station. Unfortunately, none of Vermeer's works remain in Delft. The two works above can be seen at the Mauritshuis in Den Haag.

Churches

The 14th-century **Nieuwekerk** (☎ 212 30 25), next to the Markt, houses the crypt of the Dutch royal family and the mausoleum of William the Silent (due to reopen after restoration at the end of 2000). Note the delicately balanced bronze statue. There are exhibitions about the history of the House of Orange and the church. It's open 9 am to 6 pm Monday to Saturday (until 4 pm from November to March), and costs f4/1.50 for adults/children, which includes entrance to the Oude Kerk.

The Gothic **Oudekerk**, at Heilige Geestkerkhof, looks every one of its 800 years, with its leaning tower 2m from the vertical. Among the tombs inside is Vermeer's. Note also the intricately carved 1548 pulpit. A combination ticket to both churches costs f4/1.50.

Museums

Opposite the Oude Kerk is the **Prinsenhof** (☎ 260 23 58), at St Agathaplein 1. This collection of buildings is a former convent and is where William the Silent held court until he was assassinated in 1584. The bullet hole in the wall has been enlarged by visitors' fingers and is now covered by Perspex. The buildings host displays of historical and contemporary art and are open 10 am to 5 pm Tuesday to Saturday (Sunday from 1 pm); admission is f5/2.50.

The **Legermuseum** (☎ 215 05 00), Korte Geer 1, has a collection of old Dutch military hardware displayed in a restored 17th-century arsenal. There are also displays of the modern role of the Dutch army, including the controversial and disastrous role played as part of the Bosnian peacekeeping

force during the 1990s. It's open 10 am to 5 pm daily (from noon on weekends) and costs f6/3. The **Paul Tétar van Elven Museum** (☎ 212 42 06), Koornmarkt 67, was the home of the 19th-century painter of the same name. It's a good view of the patrician lifestyle during the period. It's open 1 to 5 pm Monday to Saturday from mid-April to November and costs f4/2.

Old Delft

While much of the town dates from the 17th century and is remarkably well preserved, there are some spots where it is possible to get away from the crowds and contemplate the past. Although before you flee the crowded Markt, check out the **Stadhuis** with its unusual combination of Renaissance construction surrounding a 13th-century tower and behind it, the **Waag**, a 1644 weigh house.

East of here, **Beestenmarkt** is a large open space surrounded by fine buildings. Farther east, **Oostpoort** is the sole surviving piece of the town's walls. Its delicate brickwork is beautifully reflected in the canals. **Koornmarkt**, leading south from the Waag, is a quiet and tree-lined canal.

Organised Tours

One of the best ways to see Delft is by a **boat tour** (☎ 212 63 85) on the canals. Boats depart from Koornmarkt 113 from 9.30 am to 6 pm from mid-March to October; a ride costs f8.50/5.50.

The VVV runs a **walking tour** at 2 pm every Wednesday and Friday from April to October. The historic walks last 90 minutes, the narration is in English and Dutch, and they cost f7.50. Register at the VVV office at least 30 minutes in advance.

Places to Stay

Camping The camping ground *Delftse Hout* (☎ 213 00 40, fax 213 12 93, Korftlaan 5) is just to the north-east of town and is open all year. It costs f43 per tent site. Take bus No 64 from the station.

Hotels Delft has a few decent hotels, some in lovely locations, but in summer they are heavily booked.

ZUID HOLLAND & ZEELAND

Pension Van Domburg (☎ 212 30 29, Voldersgracht 24) is no-frills but very centrally located. Look for the entrance next to a cigar shop. The basic rooms without bath cost f75/80 for a single/double.

Hotel de Plataan (☎ 212 60 46, fax 215 73 27, Doelenplein 10) is on a delightful square and has a cool cafe on the ground floor. The breakfast room is downright dignified. The rooms are small but have baths and TVs and cost f130/155.

Hotel de Kok (☎/fax 212 21 25, Houttuinen 14) is a simple place with plenty of parking near the train station. Rooms without bath cost f100/135, and f145/165 with bath.

Delft Museumhotel (☎ 214 09 30, fax 214 09 35, Oude Delft 189) is bright and has spiffy rooms with TVs, baths and more that cost from f190/240.

Hotel Bridges House (☎ 213 36 00, fax 213 36 00, Oude Delft 74) is small and classy and has just 18 rooms overlooking a canal junction. You know it's a good place when you see the rows of books in the lobby. The posh rooms cost from f195/245.

Places to Eat

Restaurants You can sit in comfy straw chairs at *Abessinië (☎ 213 52 60, Kromstraat 21)* where the tasty African fare averages about f21 per plate. It's open daily for dinner.

Stads Pannekoeckhuys (☎ 213 01 93, Oude Delft 113) has dozens of various pancakes from f10. The pea soup is also pretty good. It's open 11 am to 10 pm daily.

De Zaag en de Vries (☎ 213 70 15, Vrouw Juttenland 17) is a cheery orange place with a long vegetarian menu with mains averaging f25. It serves beer and wine, and is open for dinner daily except Monday.

Restaurant L'Orange (☎ 212 36 29, Oude Delft 111B) is a fine French restaurant with an exquisite interior. The sumptuous multicourse meals start at f75. It's open for dinner daily.

Cafes *De Ruif Café (☎ 214 22 06, Kerkstraat 23)* has an attractive terrace and serves generous meals. The *dagschotel* is f15, and there are also vegetarian dishes. It's open daily.

There's great local cuisine at *De Kurk (☎ 214 14 74, Kromstraat 20)*, a classic cafe, open daily, where mains start at f29 or you can opt for the huge menu for f42.

Grand Café de Sjees (☎ 214 46 47, Markt 5) is a classy place with great wicker chairs and two great views: a canal out the back and the Stadhuis in front. Sandwiches and soups average f8 and salads are f15. It's open from 11 am until at least midnight daily.

Fast Food & Self-Catering A *fish stand* on Hippolytusbuurt has a great array of foods from the deep, including smoked herring sandwiches for f3.25.

The *A&P Supermarket (Choorstraat 35)* has the usual assortment of baked goods and pre-prepared meals good for picnics. There's an open-air market on the Markt every Thursday.

Entertainment

The 13,000 students at Delft's technical university ensure that there's no shortage of places to grab a cheap beer and hear some music.

Tango (☎ 213 26 81, Nieuwstraat 2) is a mellow pub with large windows and good magazines. It's open until 1 am daily.

Locus Publicus (☎ 213 46 32, Brabantse Turfmarkt 67) has over 200 beers, including many unusual ones on tap. It's a friendly pub with good music and is open until at least 1 am.

Klooster (☎ 212 10 13, Vlamingstrat 2) has a lot of character and characters in its small space. It has several Trappist beers on tap which flow until at least 1 am.

Speakers (☎ 212 44 46, Burgwal 45–49) is one of several venues on this pleasant and popular street. Big and multilevel, it has live rock, jazz, comedy and DJs on various nights. The cover varies widely and its open usually past 2 am.

OJV de Koornbeurs (☎ 212 47 42, Voldersgracht 1) has an underground dance floor with alternative disco. Cover charge is f7.50 and it usually doesn't get going until after midnight.

The *Filmhuis Lumen (☎ 214 02 26, Doelenplein 5)* screens alternative films.

Getting There & Around

Delft is well served by trains. They include:

destination	price (f)	duration (mins)	frequency (per hr)
Den Haag	4.25	8	4
Rotterdam	5.50	13	4
Amsterdam	19.25	50	2

Lockers are in the main concourse and there are all the usual amenities.

Alternatively, bus No 129 makes the run to/from Rotterdam every hour along a pretty canal. The ride lasts 30 minutes and takes five strips. Buses depart from the front of the station.

Den Haag is linked to Delft not just by trains but by tram No 1. The not-especially-scenic ride takes 30 minutes and takes five strips.

Delft is in the treintaxi scheme (☎ 262 01 85).

The bicycle shop (☎ 214 30 33) in the train station is open 5.45 am to midnight weekdays and from 6.30 am weekends.

ROTTERDAM

☎ 010 • pop 590,000

Nearly destroyed during WWII, the Netherlands' second-largest city spent the second half of the 20th century rebuilding its centre. Although some early efforts were in the typically dire style of the 1950s and '60s, projects of the last two decades have succeeded in giving Rotterdam a look that's not just unique in Europe, but which is also astonishing and impressive. A long walk along the Nieuwe Maas River is an exploration of modern architecture's many variations.

West of the city is Europe's busiest port. Boat tours are justifiably popular and give good views of the huge container ships from around the world.

Rotterdam's history as a major port dates back to the 16th century. In 1572, Spaniards being pursued by the rebel Sea Beggars were given shelter in the harbour. They rewarded this generosity by pillaging the town. Needless to say, Rotterdam soon joined the revolution and became a major port during the revolution.

With its location astride the major southern rivers, Rotterdam is ideally suited to service trading ships. Cargo from abroad can be easily transferred inland and to the rest of Europe. Large canals first constructed in the 1800s and improved ever since link the port with the Rhine River and other major waterways.

On 14 May 1940 the invading Germans issued an ultimatum to the Dutch government: surrender or cities like Rotterdam will be destroyed. The government capitulated, but the bombers were already airborne and the raid was carried out anyway. The historic centre was levelled.

Today Rotterdam has a definite energy that seems in part drawn from the 'anything goes' attitude for reconstruction. The nightlife is good, a large immigrant community adds life and there are some excellent museums.

Rotterdam is a must on any itinerary for the Netherlands and worth at least two days. The city received a polishing-up during 2000 in anticipation of its role as a European City of Culture in 2001.

Orientation

Rotterdam is split by the Nieuwe Maas, a vast channel used for shipping. It is crossed by a series of tunnels and bridges, most photogenic of which is the Erasmusbrug, which opened in 1996 and is nicknamed 'The Swan'.

The mostly reconstructed centre is on the north side of the water. Huge new neighbourhoods are rising to the south. From Centraal Station (CS), a 15-minute walk along the canal-like ponds (they don't flow under the bridges) leads to the waterfront. The commercial centre is to the east, and most of the museums are to the west. The historic neighbourhood of Delfshaven is a further 3km west.

Maps Rudimentary free maps are available in the tourist offices; otherwise there's a f6 Falk map that will be overkill for anyone but an estate agent.

ZUID HOLLAND & ZEELAND

Information

Tourist Offices The VVV office (☎ 0900-403 40 65, fax 412 1763, @ info@vvv .rotterdam.nl), Coolsingel 67, is a five-minute walk from CS and is in a large facility shared with the ANWB. It sells theatre and concert tickets and organises various city tours (see Organised Tours). It's open 9 am to 6 pm weekdays and until 5 pm weekends. The city's Web site is www.rotterdam.nl.

There is another VVV, focusing on the city's architecture, at the Netherlands Architecture Institute (☎ 436 99 09), Museumpark 25. It's open 10 am to 5 pm Tuesday to Saturday, 11 am to 5 pm Sunday and holidays.

Rotterdam has another city-financed tourist service called Use-It (☎ 240 91 58, fax 240 91 59, @ use-it@jip.org) that is right behind CS and next to the long-distance bus terminal at Conradstraat 2. This excellent service is aimed at young travellers but the enthusiastic staff will happily help anyone who is 'young at heart.' They have a range of free English-language publications about attractions and walking tours. There are free day lockers, email access and accommodation discounts. Use-It is open 9 am to 6 pm Tuesday to Saturday (also open Sunday from May to October). Its Web site is www.use-it.nl.

Money GWK in CS is open 7 am to 9 pm daily. There are ATMs everywhere, including right outside the station.

Post The post office (☎ 233 02 55), Coolsingel 42, is in a glorious building that survived the war. It's open 9 am to 6 pm weekdays (until 8.30 pm Thursday) and 9.30 am to 3 pm Saturday.

Travel Agencies Anadolu Actief Reizen (☎ 436 26 00), Nieuwe Binnenweg 1, books cheap tickets worldwide.

Bookshops Donner (☎ 413 20 70), Lijnbaan 150, is a large, multistorey bookseller.

Libraries The Central Library (☎ 281 62 62), Hoogstraat 110, is a destination in itself, with a cafe, an indoor life-sized chess

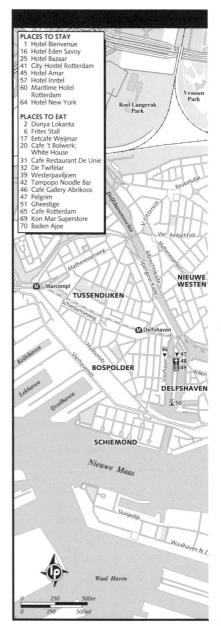

PLACES TO STAY
1 Hotel Bienvenue
16 Hotel Eden Savoy
25 Hotel Bazaar
41 City Hostel Rotterdam
45 Hotel Amar
57 Hotel Inntel
60 Maritime Hotel Rotterdam
64 Hotel New York

PLACES TO EAT
2 Dunya Lokanta
6 Frites Stall
17 Eetcafe Weijmar
20 Cafe 't Bolwerk; White House
31 Cafe Restaurant De Unie
32 De Twifelar
39 Westerpaviljoen
42 Tampopo Noodle Bar
46 Cafe Gallery Abrikoos
47 Pelgrim
51 Gheestige
65 Cafe Rotterdam
69 Kon Mar Superstore
70 Baden Ajoe

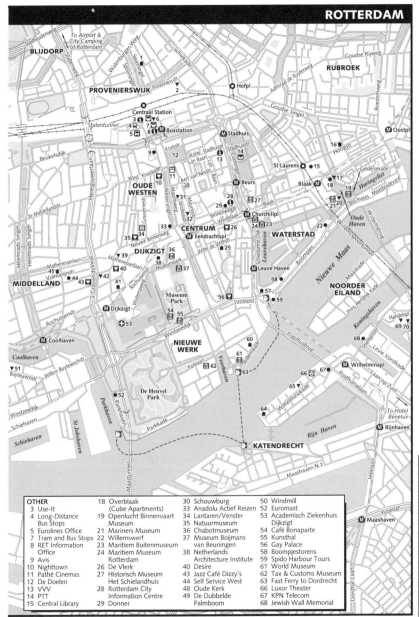

ROTTERDAM

OTHER	18 Overblaak	30 Schouwburg	50 Windmill
3 Use-It	(Cube Apartments)	33 Anadolu Actief Reizen	52 Euromast
4 Long-Distance	19 Openlucht Binnenvaart	34 Lantaren/Venster	53 Academisch Ziekenhuis
Bus Stops	Museum	35 Natuurmuseum	Dijkzigt
5 Eurolines Office	21 Mariners Museum	36 Chabotmuseum	54 Café Bonaparte
7 Tram and Bus Stops	22 Willemswerf	37 Museum Boijmans	55 Kunsthal
8 RET Information	23 Maritiem Buitenmuseum	van Beuningen	56 Gay Palace
Office	24 Maritiem Museum	38 Netherlands	58 Boompjestorens
9 Avis	Rotterdam	Architecture Institute	59 Spido Harbour Tours
10 Nighttown	26 De Vlerk	40 Desire	61 World Museum
11 Pathé Cinemas	27 Historisch Museum	43 Jazz Café Dizzy's	62 Tax & Customs Museum
12 De Doelen	Het Schielandhuis	44 Self Service West	66 Fast Ferry to Dordrecht
13 VVV	28 Rotterdam City	48 Oude Kerk	66 Luxor Theater
14 PTT	Information Centre	49 De Dubbelde	67 KPN Telecom
15 Central Library	29 Donner	Palmboom	68 Jewish Wall Memorial

ZUID HOLLAND & ZEELAND

board and more, including Internet access. It's open 10 am to 9 pm weekdays, 10 am to 5 pm Saturday and 1 to 5 pm Sunday.

Laundry Self Service West (☎ 425 93 74), Nieuwe Binnenweg 251, is open 9 am to 9 pm daily.

Medical Services The Academisch Ziekenhuis Dijkzigt (☎ 463 92 22), Dr Molenwaterplein 40, is a major teaching hospital where the professors will love you if you present with a weird ailment that will challenge the students.

Emergency For all emergencies, dial ☎ 112. To report crimes to the police after the event, call ☎ 247 991.

Dangers & Annoyances Note that the area about 1km west of CS is the scene of many hard drug deals and accompanying dubious behaviour.

Museum Boijmans van Beuningen

Newly expanded in 2000, the Museum Boijmans van Beuningen (☎ 441 94 00), Museumpark 18–20, is Rotterdam's great art museum. The collection spans all eras of Dutch and European art and has a superb Old Masters collection. Among the highlights: *The Marriage at Cana* by Hieronymus Bosch, the *Three Maries at the Open Sepulchre* by Van Eyck, the delightful *Tower of Babel* by Pieter Bruegel the Elder, and *Portrait of Titus* and *Man in a Red Cap* by Rembrandt. Renaissance Italy is well represented; look for *The Wise and Foolish Virgins* by Tintoretto and *Satyr and Nymph* by Titian.

Paintings and sculpture since the mid-19th century are also one of the museum's strengths. There are a number of Monets and other French impressionists, Van Gogh and his pal Gauguin are given space, and there are statues by Degas. Salvador Dali has gained a special room in the expansion and the collection is one of the largest of the odd guy's work.

The applied arts rooms have European works dating from the 13th century. The usability of the museum has improved with the expansion, with works now displayed in logical order by era. There are a number of English-language guides available and a good cafe for resting between masterpieces. On one of Rotterdam's many grey days, the Museum Boijmans van Beuningen can easily fill a day. It's open 10 am to 5 pm Tuesday to Saturday and from 11 am Sunday and holidays. Admission is f10/4 for adults/children. Its Web site is www.boijmans .rotterdam.nl.

Chabotmuseum

Housed in a pre-war Bauhaus-style villa, the Chabotmuseum (☎ 436 37 13), Museumpark 11, not surprisingly is dedicated to the work of Rotterdam expressionist artist Hendrik Chabot. Known for his graphic style, Chabot often focused on the victims of war. Across from the Museum Boijmans van Beuningen, the museum is open 11 am to 5 pm Tuesday to Saturday (from noon Sunday). Admission is f7/4.

Kunsthal

At the south end of Museum Park, the Kunsthal (☎ 440 03 00), Westzeedijk 341, hosts temporary exhibitions. The building is a sight itself, angling up the hill between the park and the dike.

Euromast

Sticking 185m into the Rotterdam sky, the Euromast (☎ 436 48 11), Parkhaven 20, is one of the less successful examples of modern architecture in the city. But if the sky is clear, you can go to the top and once inside you'll see great views of the city that *don't* include the Euromast. To help attract visitors, it has opted for a faux space-flight scenario to get you to the top. The tower is in De Heuvel Park, which is immediately south-west of Museum Park. It's open 10 am to 7 pm daily (until 5 pm from October to March) and admission is a soaring f15/9.50.

Maritime Rotterdam

Near the Erasmus Bridge, the **Maritiem Museum Rotterdam** (☎ 413 26 80), Leuvehaven 1, looks at the Netherlands' rich maritime

Rotterdam Architecture

Architects and architecture buffs will thrill not just to the many stunning buildings lining Rotterdam's streets, but also to the many local educational resources.

A brief tour can begin at the north end of the **Erasmusbrug** (1996), near the Leuve Haven metro station. Ben van Berkel designed the 800m-long Erasmus Bridge with its graceful supports. Walk part of the way across and you'll see the **KPN Telecom** building (2000). It's hard to miss given that it looks like it's about to fall over but for a long pole giving it support. It's the work of Renzo Piano who also did the Pompidou Centre in Paris. Retrace your steps and walk north-east alongside the water on Boompjes. You'll see the three primary-coloured **Boompjestorens** (1988), which are apartment blocks. Continue along the water until you see the striking **Willemswerf** (1988), the headquarters of the huge Nedlloyd shipping company. Note the dramatic lines casting shadows on its sleek, white surface.

Another 100m will bring you to Rotterdam's other signature bridge, the **Willemsbrug** (1981), which makes a bold statement with its red pylons. Turn north at Oude Haven on Geldersekade. The regal 11-storey building on the corner is the **Witte Huis** (White House, 1897), a rare survivor of the pre-war period, giving an idea of the wealth Rotterdam achieved thanks to the shipping industry.

Walk north for about three minutes to Blaak and the metro station of the same name. Here the last stop is the surprising **Overblaak** (1978-84), to your right, marked by the cube-shaped apartments and pencil-shaped tower. Designed by Piet Blom, the project has graced a thousand postcards. One unit, No 70, is open for tours (☎ 414 22 85) 11 am to 5 pm daily (closed Monday to Wednesday in January and February). Admission is f3.50.

The **Netherlands Architecture Institute** (☎ 440 12 00), Museumpark 25, is fittingly in an architecturally stunning building. One side is surrounded by a reflecting moat, while another comprises a sweeping flow of brick along Rochussenstraat. The institute stages a series of ambitious special exhibitions through the year in its cavernous public spaces. There is a good cafe with seats outside, and a large library. It's open 10 am to 5 pm Tuesday to Saturday (until 9 pm Tuesday) and 11 am to 5 pm Sunday and holidays. Admission is f7.50/4.

The VVV in association with the Netherlands Architecture Institute offers **architecture tours** of the city. For information call ☎ 402 32 34 or visit one of the VVV offices, including the one in the institute. The schedules vary by season and the costs depend on the tour.

Rotterdam City Information Centre (☎ 413 40 11), Coolsingel 197, has vast amounts of information – much in English – about the city's architecture and its urban planning. It's open 10 am to 6 pm weekdays and from 11 am Saturday.

Cubicle houses highlight Rotterdam's architectural variety.

traditions. There's the usual array of models that any youngster would love to take into the tub, plus more interesting and explanatory displays. One of the better ones looks at the less-than-salubrious life of a 19th-century seaman. It's open 10 am to 5 pm Tuesday to Saturday and from 11 am Sunday and holidays. Admission is f7.50/4. The **Maritiem Buitenmuseum** (☎ 404 80 72), Leuvehaven 50–72, is the open-air component of the Maritime Museum Rotterdam.

The **Oude Haven** area, near the Blaak train, metro and tram station, preserves bits of the oldest part of the harbour, some of which date back to the 14th century. It's a decent place for a stroll, especially if you take time to look at the large collection of historic boats. The **Openlucht Binnenvaart Museum** (☎ 411 88 67), Konongsdam 1, has a collection of historic inland waterway boats that fills much of the basin. You can see the ongoing restoration and stroll around looking at the boats even outside the official opening hours of 8 am to 8 pm daily. Admission is free. Just around the corner, the small **Mariners Museum** (☎ 412 96 00), Wijnhaven 7–9, has a small collection of material on the lives of those who served in the Dutch navy. Admission is f6/3.

Delfshaven

One of the oldest surviving districts, Delfshaven was once the official seaport for the city of Delft. A reconstructed 18th-century **windmill** overlooks the water at Voorhaven 210. One of the area's claims to fame is that it was where the Pilgrims left Holland for America aboard the *Speedwell*. They could barely keep the leaky boat afloat and eventually transferred to the *Mayflower*, and the rest is history. (See the boxed text 'Pilgrims' Progress' earlier this chapter.) The **Oudekerk** on Voorhaven is where the Pilgrims prayed for the last time before leaving on 22 July 1620.

De Dubbelde Palmboom (☎ 476 15 33), Voorhaven 12, is a history museum housing an excellent collection of items relating to Rotterdam's history as a port. Displays are spread throughout the 1826 warehouse and many have a sociological bent. It's

open 10 am to 5 pm Tuesday to Saturday and from 11 am Sunday and holidays. Admission is f6/3.

Delfshaven is easily reached from the metro stop of the same name by walking 1km west from De Heuvel Park or by taking tram No 4, 6 or 9.

Other Attractions

The city's history is preserved at one of the few surviving 17th-century buildings in the centre at the **Historisch Museum Het Schielandhuis** (☎ 217 67 67), Korte Hoogstraat 31. The eclectic displays include the Atlas Van Stolk collection of prints and drawings of Dutch history. Other exhibits focus on items from everyday life through the ages, such as the purportedly oldest surviving wooden shoe. The museum is open 10 am to 5 pm Tuesday to Saturday and from 11 am Sunday and holidays. Admission is f6/3.

The usual assortment of stuffed critters and fossils populates the halls of the **Natuurmuseum** (☎ 436 42 22), Westzeedijk 345. The highlight is the 15m skeleton of a sperm whale, under a glass roof. The museum is open 10 am to 5 pm Tuesday to Saturday and from 11 am Sunday and holidays. Admission is f5/3.

One of the least favourite professions is honoured at the **Tax & Customs Museum** (☎ 436 56 29) at Parklaan 14–16. Everything to do with government levies from the Egyptians onwards is covered. Many will enjoy learning that it was anger over taxes that led to the Eighty Years' War (1568–1648). The museum is open 11 am to 5 pm (closed Monday) Admission is free.

Nearby, the **World Museum** (☎ 411 22 01), Willemskade 25, is set to reopen its doors late in 2000 after a massive expansion and reconstruction.

The building will be dominated by a huge sculpture of a stylised woman by artist Nikki de Saint Phalle. Once through the entrance between the statue's legs, visitors will encounter oodles of displays relating to the cultures of the world.

On the south side of the Koningshaven, in the middle of an old dock district being reborn as a trendy neighbourhood, there is

ZUID HOLLAND & ZEELAND

a solemn reminder of the recent past. A fragment of a **wall** that once surrounded a warehouse on the spot has been preserved. The site was the departure point for Jews being sent first to Westerbork and then on to concentration camps during WWII.

Organised Tours

There are **harbour tours** offered daily year-round by Spido (☎ 275 99 88). The 75-minute cruises depart every 45 minutes from 9.30 am to 5 pm from June to September, and less frequently the rest of the year. From November to February the last boat leaves at 3.30 pm. Departures are from the pier at Leuvehoofd near the Erasmusbrug and the Leuvehaven metro stop. A ride costs f16/9.50. The company has several longer trips during July and August.

A Tuesday-only tour departs at 10.30 am for a nearly seven-hour trip to the final bit of the Delta Plan which protects the Nieuwe Waterweg. It costs f42.50/31.

Special Events

If you're in Rotterdam during 2001, you'll probably encounter numerous special events tied to the city's designation as a European City of Culture in 2001.

Otherwise, Rotterdam has numerous multicultural festivals. They include:

July
Solero Summer Carnival (☎ 414 17 72) Usually held the last weekend of July. It is a carnival-like bash with music, parades, dancing and parties.

August
FFWD Dance Party (☎ 433 13 00) Turns the centre into one big open-air club with areas for techno, hip hop, big beat etc.

September
World Harbour Festival (☎ 403 40 65) Celebrates the role of the harbour, which directly or indirectly employs over 300,000 people. There are lots of open houses, ship tours and fireworks.

Places to Stay

The VVV will make room reservations for f4.50. Use-It will do the same and they have negotiated several cheap deals with hotels during slow periods, so it's worth checking with them in the off-season.

Camping *City Camping of Rotterdam* (☎ 415 34 40, fax 437 32 15, Kanaalweg 84) is open all year and has a laundry. It costs f9 per person plus f7 per tent. It has little cabins for two for f50. It's a 20-minute walk north-west from CS or take bus No 33 in the direction 'Airport'.

Hostels *City Hostel Rotterdam* (☎ 436 57 63, fax 436 55 69, Rochussenstraat 107–109) is well located near the museums. Most of the beds are in large rooms of six or more. Reception is open until 1 am and beds cost f28 to f31.50, depending on season. It's a 10-minute walk from CS and is close to the Dijkzigt metro stop.

Hotels *Hotel Benelux* (☎ 485 38 07, fax 486 56 25, Beijerlandselaan 47a) has 16 rooms, each with a different decor. Rooms without bath cost f55/99 for a single/double, f75/110 with bath. Take the No 20 tram south of the Nieuwe Maas to the Beijerlandselaan stop.

Hotel Amar (☎ 425 57 95, fax 477 73 21, Mathenesserlaan 316) is a friendly and small place in a leafy neighbourhood. Guests can use bikes for free and all rooms have TV. The hotel is close to where tram Nos 4 and 20 cross.

Maritime Hotel Rotterdam (☎ 411 92 60, fax 411 92 62, ✆ zhuisrot@wxs.nl, Willemskade 13) caters to seamen ashore from their boats, but all are welcome. The modern facility boasts free Internet access, a big breakfast buffet and a cheap bar. Rooms without bath cost f64/118, with bath f79/128. Take the No 20 tram south to the end of the line.

Hotel Bienvenue (☎ 466 93 94, fax 467 74 75, Spoorsingel 24) has 10 rooms and is 200m behind CS near a small park. Rooms have TV and parking is easy. Rooms without bath cost f78/100, with bath f83/130.

Hotel Bazaar (☎ 206 51 51, fax 206 51 59, Witte de Withstraat 16) has a popular restaurant and offers multicultural tours of the city to guests. Each of the 18 rooms has

ZUID HOLLAND & ZEELAND

bath and TV and costs f115/135. Take tram No 5 south from CS two stops, or walk 15 minutes.

Hotel Eden Savoy (☎ 413 92 80, fax 404 57 12, **✉** info.savoy@edenhotelgroup.nl, Hoogstraat 81) is a well-equipped yet fairly nondescript place near Oude Haven. Popular with tour groups, it has rooms with bath and TV for f175/199, but ask about specials. It's about five minutes' walk from the Blaak train, metro and tram station.

Hotel New York (☎ 439 05 00, fax 484 27 01, Koninginnenhoofd 1) is in the grand former headquarters of the Holland America passenger ship line on Wilhelminakade. Often booked far in advance, the hotel is noted for its views, cafe and boat shuttle that takes guests across the Nieuwe Maas to the centre. The posh rooms cost f190/275.

Hotel Inntel (☎ 413 41 39, fax 413 32 33, **✉** inforotterdam@hotelinntel.com, Leuvehaven 80) is in an architecturally interesting building overlooking the harbour. The stylish rooms are equipped with a long list of conveniences, and cost f295/330. The hotel is next to the Leuvehaven metro stop.

Places to Eat
Rotterdam is well served by places to eat. The city's population of immigrants means that choices are varied.

Restaurants **Dunya Lokanta** (☎ 243 06 69, Proveniersstraat 40) is a family-run Turkish place with pictures on the wall of the owner's hometown. It's very friendly, has tables outside in summer and is open daily for dinner. Vegetarian dishes and an array of meaty specials average f15.

Tampopo Noodle Bar (☎ 225 15 22, 's Gravendijkwal 128) is a trendy and stylish Asian restaurant on the corner with Nieuwe Binnenweg. Big bowls of noodle soup loaded with vegies go for f25. It's open 5 to 11 pm daily.

Baden Ajoe (☎ 290 01 56), on Vlif Werelddelen, is part of the huge Vrij Entrepot complex of shops and restaurants in a restored warehouse south of the Nieuwe Maas. The upmarket Indonesian fare is served in lovely surroundings and it has

tables in nice weather outside along the water. Rijsttafels cost f50 per person. It's open daily for dinner.

Café Rotterdam (☎ 290 84 42, Wilhelminakade 699) is actually a smart French brasserie in the old terminal for liners of the Holland America Line. The menu is ambitious and the views are fabulous. Expect to pay at least f50 per person before drinks.

Cafes **De Twifelar** (☎ 413 26 71, Mauritsstraat 173) is a dark cafe whose name means 'the doubter'. Its vegetarian menu is popular with students who like the prices, averaging f15. A DJ provides music until 11 pm weeknights and 2 am weekends.

Westerpaviljoen (☎ 436 26 45, Mathenesserlaan 155) is a classic cafe that gets jammed with joyous locals daily. The inside is steamy but outside there's a great terrace. Most diners only order snacks from the simple menu that averages about f15. It's open daily from lunch-time until 1 am.

Café Gallery Abrikoos (☎ 477 41 40, Aelbrechtskolk 51) is a bright and cheery place filled with art. It has a variety of soups, salads and mains from f20, and is open for lunch and dinner until 10 pm.

Café Restaurant De Unie (☎ 411 73 93, Mauritsweg 34) preserves the 1924 facade of Mondriaanesque red, yellow and blue. The 1986 interior is less successful, although the huge windows open onto the ponds and the toilets are more like shower stalls. The vaguely ambitious Dutch menu has many items for under f30. It also has a small theatre where there are political debates some nights.

Eetcafé Weijmar (☎ 414 88 35, Haringvliet 637) is on Oude Haven and has an ambitious menu for a small cafe. There are lots of fresh ingredients and an open kitchen. Dinner will average f30 per person and you can add to that from the long beer list. The bar is open until 3 am daily.

Café 't Bolwerk (☎ 414 73 03, Gelersekade 1C) is on the ground floor of the historic White House tower on Oude Haven. It has free bowls of peanuts (toss the shells on the floor) and tangerines – to chase away scurvy. The kitchen does steaks and the like for f30. It's popular with the after-work crowd and after midnight on weekends it can get pretty noisy when dancing starts. It's open until at least 4 am daily.

Pelgrim (☎ 477 11 89, Aelbrechtskolk 12) is right near the Pilgrim Fathers church. It brews its own beer – try the Maibock in season – and has good views of the old harbour and a courtyard out the back. The menu has fancy versions of Dutch standards; expect to pay about f33 each. It's open until midnight (closed Monday).

Fast Food & Self-Catering There's a fine *frites stall* right in front of CS. The fries are very crispy, the mayo is real and they cost f3.

Gheestige (☎ 477 20 20, Willem Buytewechstraat 147–149) has takeaway vegie food. It's also an art gallery so you can gaze at the walls while you wait. Delfshaven is nearby, and has some good spots where you can picnic.

The *Kon Mar Superstore (☎ 290 99 88, Vlif Werelddelen 33)* is part of the huge Vrij Entrepot complex of shops and restaurants in a restored warehouse south of the Nieuwe Maas. It has a selection of foods from around the world and lots of deli items good for picnics.

Close to CS, there are loads of markets on West Kruiskade.

Entertainment
Bars & Clubs *Jazz Café Dizzy's (☎ 477 30 14, 's Gravendijkwal 129)* is a big and busy brown cafe that spans two facades and levels. Pictures of the eponymous Mr Gillespie abound and it has open-mike nights often. Needless to say, it plays good tunes from the vast CD collection. It's open until 3 am weekends.

Nighttown (☎ 436 12 10, West Kruiskade 26–28) is a big place with a cool bar from which you can watch the action on the dance floor below. Techno, house and the latest music trends are the rule. During the day there's a slick cafe with outdoor seating out the front. Cover charge varies.

De Vlerk (☎ 411 68 00, Westblaak 80) features small groups playing alternative rock and hoping for fame. It's dark, in a basement and can get wild. The cover

charge varies depending on how recently the band was playing on the pavement for tips. It's open until at least 5 am weekends.

Café Bonaparte (☎ 436 74 33, Nieuwe Binnenweg 117) is a friendly stalwart of Rotterdam's fairly large gay community. It's a classic brown cafe, popular with visitors and locals.

Gay Palace (☎ 414 14 86, Schiedamsesingel 139) has a huge dance floor and is popular with gays, lesbians and straights. Cover charge varies, but averages f10. It's open until at least 5 am weekends.

Coffeeshops *Desire (Nieuwe Binnenweg 148)* is one of several joints, so to speak, on this stretch of street but this one has the best ventilation. The friendly staff will explain the hoops you have to go through to buy something to smoke. It's open 7 am to 4 am daily.

Music & Theatre *Schouwburg (☎ 411 81 10, Schouwburgplein 25)* is the main cultural centre and has a rotating calendar of dance, theatre and drama. Note the cool light fixtures with red necks out the front.

De Doelen (☎ 217 17 17, Schouwburgplein 50), across from the Schouwburg, is the concert centre for the Rotterdam Philharmonic Orchestra.

Lantaren/Venster (☎ 436 13 31, Gouvernestraat 129–133) has several stages for experimental performances. There is also a small cinema that screens off-beat films.

A major new performance venue, the *Luxor Theater (☎ 413 83 26)*, is due to open on the Wilhelminakade in 2001.

Cinemas *Pathé Cinemas (☎ 0900 14 58, Schouwburgplein 101)* is a large and dramatic-looking multiplex with the usual array of Hollywood output and some more interesting lesser-known films.

Shopping
Rotterdam has gone for Sunday shopping in a big way and most stores in the centre are open noon to 5 pm. The Lijnbaan, lined with mainstream shops, was a trendsetter when it began opening over the period 1951

to 1966. The idea of car-free and pedestrianised shopping arcades was copied with more or less success worldwide.

Nieuwe Binnenweg is a vivacious mix of stylish restaurants, old boozers, coffee shops and a range of stores selling used CDs and vintage clothing. West Kruiskade, five minutes south of CS, has a welter of ethnic groceries and stores.

Getting There & Away

Air Rotterdam Airport (☎ 446 34 44) is 4km north-west of the centre, off the E19/A13. It's a sleepy place with basic services, ATMs etc. Various KLM subsidiaries (☎ 020-474 77 47) have flights to/from Paris, London and Manchester. Some are operated by VLM (☎ 415 77 77), a Belgian commuter airline. British Airways (☎ 437 89 11) has flights to/from London, Manchester and Birmingham. On weekends, there are often cheap fares available, so it's worth checking if you don't want to go through Amsterdam's Schiphol.

Train Rotterdam CS is an aging station that is due to get a glitzy replacement in a huge project beginning in 2001. It's on the main line from Amsterdam south and *Thalys* service between Brussels and Paris stop here. See the Train section in the Getting There & Away chapter for details.

Services are frequent to all points on the NS network. They include:

destination	price (f)	duration (mins)	frequency (per hr)
Amsterdam	23.25	60	4
Den Haag	7.50	15	4
Middelburg	33	90	1
Utrecht	15.25	40	2

Bus Rotterdam is a hub for Eurolines bus services to the rest of Europe. See the Bus section of the Getting There & Away chapter for details. The long-distance bus stops are immediately west of CS. The Eurolines office (☎ 412 44 44), Conradstraat 20, is open 9.30 am to 5.30 pm weekdays and until 3 pm Saturday.

Virgin Express Airlines (☎ 0800-022 77 73) operates a frequent bus to/from Brussels Airport that connects with its discount flights around Europe. The price of the bus is included in the ticket. Its Web site is www.virgin-express.com.

Car & Motorcycle Rotterdam is well linked by motorways to the rest of the Netherlands and Belgium.

Car rental firms at the airport include:

Avis (☎ 298 24 24)
Budget (☎ 437 86 22)
Europcar (☎ 437 18 26)
Hertz (☎ 415 82 39)

In addition, Avis (☎ 433 22 33) has a convenient location across from CS at Kruisplein 21. It's open 8 am to 6 pm weekdays and until 1 pm Saturday.

Boat The new Fast Ferry (☎ 0900-266 63 99, f0.22 per minute) links Rotterdam with Dordrecht and is a good option for day trips, or in place of the train. The boat leaves from Willemskade at least once an hour during the day. The fare is f3.75/6.50 one-way/return; bikes cost f2.50/4.

Getting Around

To/From the Airport Bus No 33 makes the 15-minute run from the airport to CS every 12 minutes through the day. A taxi takes 10 minutes to the centre and costs f40.

Public Transport Rotterdam's trams, buses and metro are provided by RET (☎ 0900-92 92, f0.75 per minute). Most converge in front of CS, where there is an information office that also sells tickets. It is open 6 am to 11 pm weekdays and 8 am to 11 pm weekends. There are other information booths in the major metro stations.

Public transport in Rotterdam is easy. For destinations in the centre you won't need to use it, but for Delfshaven and even Oude Haven you might want a lift.

The metro operates in a X pattern of five lines, two of which terminate at CS. Beurs is the interchange station between the lines. Machines to validate tickets are at the station entrances.

Trams cover much of the city and are fast and frequent. Validate your strip ticket on board. On buses, have the driver validate your strips.

RET sells one/two/three-day tickets *(dagkaarts)* for f12/18/24. These are only good value if you plan to use public transport a lot.

Car & Motorcycle Rotterdam has numerous places to park, including along the streets. Look for the blue P signs for large and enclosed garages.

Taxi For a taxi, call ☎ 462 60 60.

Bicycle The bicycle shop at CS (☎ 412 62 20) is underground off the metro station. It is open 5.30 am to 2 am daily (from 7 am Sunday).

NEAR ROTTERDAM

The popular ferries to/from Harwich in the UK dock in **Hoek van Holland**, 28km west of Rotterdam (see the Getting There & Away chapter for details). The town itself is really just a ferry port that has been gussied up with the addition of an artificial beach, just north of the centre on the road to **Monster** (a town in desperate need of a museum named after itself). The beaches here are fairly inaccessible, so if you can get to them, you should be free from crowds. Trains to/from Rotterdam run every 15 minutes (f8.50, 31 minutes) and provide good connections for the ferries.

Across the busy Nieuwe Waterweg from Hoek van Holland is **Europoort**, the huge shipping port right near the entrance to the North Sea. Ferries to/from Hull in the UK dock here. For those not driving, there are buses to/from Rotterdam CS and Amsterdam CS that are timed to connect with the ferries. Reserve these when you buy your ferry ticket.

KINDERDIJK

This is one of the best spots in the Netherlands to see windmills. Named a Unesco World Heritage Site in 1997, it has some 19 windmills strung out on both sides of canals

dug behind the tall dikes at the confluence of the Lek River and several tributaries and channels.

This spot has been a focus of Dutch efforts to reclaim land from the water for centuries. Indeed the name Kinderdijk is said to derive from the horrible St Elizabeth's Day Flood of 1421 when a horrible storm and flood washed a baby in a crib with a cat up onto the dike. Stories aside, it is a starkly beautiful area, with the windmills rising above the empty marshes and waterways like so many sentinels.

Several of the most important types of windmills are here, including hollow post mills and rotating cap mills (see the boxed text 'Blowing in the Wind' for details). The latter are among the highest in the country as they were built to better catch the wind. The mills are kept in operating condition and date from the 18th century.

A visit to Kinderdijk can occupy at least half of a day. From the bus stop and parking area, there are more than 4km of paths along the dikes that run past the windmills. The best day to visit is any Saturday in July and August. From 2 to 5 pm all 19 windmills are in operation, an unforgettable sight that was once common but is now impossible to find anywhere else. At other times, one of the mills functions as a visitors centre and is open 9.30 am to 5.30 pm Monday to Saturday from April to September (f3). Call ☎ 078-613 28 00 for more details.

To reach Kinderdijk, take any of the many local trains from Rotterdam CS to Rotterdam Lombardijen station three stops south-west. From there catch hourly bus No 154 to Kinderdijk. By car, take the N210 12km east from Rotterdam. Watch for the signs for Kinderdijk. There is a car ferry (f3) across the Lek to the parking area.

DORDRECHT
☎ 078 ● pop 118,000

Sitting at the confluence of the Oude Maas River and several tributaries and channels, Dordrecht has also been at the confluence of Dutch history. The first free assembly of Holland and Zeeland was held here in the Het Hof in 1572. It was also the scene of meetings

Blowing in the Wind

Windmills are an icon of the Netherlands. However, long before they starred on a zillion postcards, they played a vital role in the Dutch people's efforts to reclaim land from the sea and in the economic development of the nation.

The earliest known windmills appeared in the 13th century. Simply built around a solid tree trunk, these were called **post mills**. The entire top of the mill could be turned to face the wind. Inside, the shaft of the sails was directly linked to a grinding stone which was used to make flour.

The major innovation came about 100 years later. The **hollow post mill** looked the same from the outside, but inside there was a major innovation. By having the rotating top of the mill mounted on a hollow central core, a drive shaft could be connected to the sails. Through a series of gears, this could then in turn be used for all manner of activities, the most important of which was pumping water. Hundreds of these windmills were soon built on dikes throughout Holland and the mass drainage of land began.

Rotating cap windmill

The next major advancement in Dutch windmill technology came in the 16th century with the invention of the **rotating cap mill**. Rather than having to turn the huge body of the mill top to face the wind, the operators could rotate just the tip which contained the hub of the sails. This made it possible for mills to operated by just one person.

Besides pumping water, mills were used for many other industrial purposes, such as sawing wood, making clay for pottery and, most importantly for art lovers, crushing the pigments used by painters.

By the mid-19th century, there were over 10,000 windmills operating in all parts of the Netherlands. But the invention of the steam engine soon made them obsolete. By the end of the 20th century there were only 950 operable windmills left. But this number seems to have stabilised and there is great interest in preserving the survivors. The Dutch government runs a three-year school for prospective windmill operators, who must be licensed.

Running one of the mills on a windy day is as complex as being the skipper of a large sailing ship, and anyone who's been inside a mill and listened to the massive timbers creaking will be aware of the similarities. The greatest hazard is a runaway, when the sails begin turning so fast that they can't be slowed. This often ends in catastrophe as the mill tears itself apart.

Little can be sadder than the sight of an abandoned mill, stripped of its sails and standing forlorn and denuded. But opportunities to see working windmills abound. **Kinderdijk** in Zuid Holland and **Zaanse Schans** in Noord Holland both have large collections of working mills. See the relative sections for details.

Just about every operable windmill in the nation is open to visitors on **National Mill Day**, usually on the second Saturday of May. Look for windmills flying blue flags.

Hollow post windmill

between Protestant theologians in 1618–19 which resulted in the triumph of the strict Calvinists over the more moderate sects.

With its lovely canals and busy port, Dordrecht enjoyed much affluence, especially from the wine trade during the 17th century. Today, much of this legacy remains and you can spend a delightful day wandering the oval-shaped old town. The large Statenplein is undergoing a massive rebuilding that won't see the dust clear until 2002.

Dordrecht is easily worth a overnight stop and there are numerous cafes and restaurants, some with fine views of the busy waterway along two sides of the city. The town is also the gateway to the lovely Biesbosch National Park.

Orientation

The train station is a good 700m walk from the centre, a journey that passes through some less interesting, newer areas. In the old town, most of the sights are on or near the three old canals, the Nieuwehaven, the Wolwevershaven and the Wijnhaven.

Information

Tourist Offices The VVV (☎ 613 28 00, fax 613 17 83, ✉ vvv.zhz@tref.nl) is near the train station at Stationsweg 1. If you're arriving by car it has a parking lot. It's open 9 am to 5.30 pm weekdays (from noon Monday) and 11 am to 3 pm weekends from June to September. It sells a good walking-tour booklet (f3), and also rents 'Talking Walls' audio walking tours of the city for f15. These excellent CDs talk about events and history keyed to specific sites. The VVV also markets a number of multiday bicycle tours of the region that include accommodation.

Money The GWK exchange in the train station is open 8 am to 8 pm (10 am to 5 pm Sunday). There are ATMs outside the station and in town near the Albert Heijn Supermarket, among many other locations.

Post The post office (☎ 613 21 11) is near the station at Johan de Wittstraat 120. It's open 9 am to 6 pm weekdays and 9 am to 1 pm Saturday.

Libraries The library (☎ 613 00 77), Groenmarkt 53, is in a large, modernised building. It has Internet access and is open noon to 8 pm Tuesday to Friday and 10 am to 1 pm Saturday.

Walking Tour of Dordrecht

Begin the tour on the **Visbrug**, the bridge over Wijjnhaven which gives fine views of the dignified **Stadhuis**. At the north end of Visbrug turn right onto Groenmarkt. As you walk north-east you pass many of the oldest houses in town, many from the early 1600s.

At the next square, Scheffersplein, cross diagonally to Voorstraat. The canal runs under this area, which is home to numerous markets. Voorstraat is the main retail street, and among the typical shops is the **House of Goats** (☎ 674 71 15) at No 281. It has numerous products made courtesy of the omnivorous farm critters, including a whole range of goat cheeses. The goods are all produced in Zuid Holland and neighbouring Noord Brabant.

Just a bit farther on the right is the **Augustinerkerk**, an old church with a facade dating from 1773. Just past it watch carefully for a passage leading to the **Het Hof**. The setting alone – especially at night – is moody and evocative. It's here that the states of Holland and Zeeland met in 1572.

Back out on Voorstraat continue north to the next bridge over the canal (Nieuwbrug). Cross over to **Wijnstraat** and turn right, continuing north. Many of the lopsided houses along here date from the peak of the wine trade, when the nearby canals were filled with boats bearing the fermented stuff.

The street ends at an attractive bridge. Pass along the west or left side of the canal to the river where you will be standing at the **Groothoofdspoort**, once the main gate into town. Walk west along the pavement and view the traffic on the waterways and Oude Maas River.

Circling to the south, you see the **Kuipershaven**, the street along the **Wolwevershaven**, another old canal lined with beautifully restored old wine warehouses and filled with many pleasure boats. As you walk along here, you'll see artists at

ZUID HOLLAND & ZEELAND

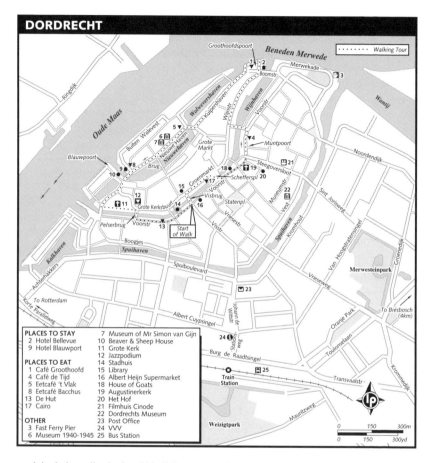

DORDRECHT

PLACES TO STAY
2 Hotel Bellevue
9 Hotel Blauwport

PLACES TO EAT
1 Café Groothoofd
4 Café de Tijd
5 Eetcafé 't Vlak
8 Eetcafé Bacchus
13 De Hut
17 Cairo

OTHER
3 Fast Ferry Pier
6 Museum 1940-1945

7 Museum of Mr Simon van Gijn
10 Beaver & Sheep House
11 Grote Kerk
12 Jazzpodium
14 Stadhuis
15 Library
16 Albert Heijn Supermarket
18 House of Goats
19 Augustinerkerk
20 Het Hof
21 Filmhuis Cinode
22 Dordrechts Museum
23 Post Office
24 VVV
25 Bus Station

work in their studios in the old buildings. At the tiny bridge, cross over to the north side of the **Nieuwehaven**. On the right, watch for the **Museum 1940–1945** (☎ 613 01 72) at No 26. It has a collection of materials from WWII and shows the privations of the region during the war. Look for the propeller prised from a Lancaster bomber in front. It's open 10 am to 5 pm Tuesday to Saturday (from noon Sunday) and costs f2.50/1.50 for adults/children.

Almost next door, the **Museum of Mr Simon van Gijn** (☎ 613 37 93) at No 29. It shows the life of an 18th-century patrician;

however, it was closed at the time of writing, for a major restoration.

While adults will be busy with the museums, kids will be drawn to the **Brug** ('bridge'), the simply named structure arching over the canal that is great fun for running up and down. Continue south-west to the Engelenburgerbrug over the Nieuwehaven's access to the Oude Maas. Then take an immediate right onto the narrow Engelenburgerkade.

At No 18 is the **Beaver & Sheep House**, a structure from 1658 that gets its name from the animals supporting a coat of arms over the door. At the end of the street is **Blauwpoort**, another old trading gate.

Retrace your steps and continue southwest to the base of the **Grotekerk**. Finished 40 years after it was begun in 1460, the church's massive tower was never completed, as it started leaning during construction. You can climb to the top – a mere 279 steps – from where there are excellent views of the town. Inside, the choir stalls are finely carved and there are several lovely stained-glass windows. The church (☎ 614 46 60) is open 10.30 am to 4.30 pm daily from April to October. It is closed much of the rest of the year. Admission is free, but the tower costs f2/1 for all that exercise.

Walk behind the church on curving Kerkstraat to Grote Kerksbuurt. Cross the first bridge, **Pelserbrug**, stopping halfway to admire the view over the tiny canal that runs behind the houses on either side. At the south end of the bridge, turn east (left) onto Voorstraat and follow it back to Visbrug, the starting point.

Dordrechts Museum

Away from the old town, the Dordrechts Museum (☎ 648 21 48), Museumstraat 40, has works by local artists, both new and old. It's the latter that are the most noteworthy, especially several works by Jan van Goyen and Albert Cuyp. The former (1596–1656) was one of the first Dutch painters to capture the interplay of light on landscapes.

Look for his *View of Dordrecht*. The latter lived in Dordrecht his entire life (1620–91) and is known for his many works painted in and around his hometown. The museum is open 11 am to 5 pm (closed Monday) and costs f8/5.

Places to Stay

There is an excellent combined youth hostel, campground and hotel 7km east of the train station on the edge of the Biesbosch National Park. See the following Biesbosch National Park section for details.

Hotel choices in Dordrecht are limited. ***Hotel Blauwpoort*** (☎ 613 60 28, Blauwpoortsplein 9/12) doesn't always accept guests. It has a good location, but call before you go. When open, it offers simple rooms without bath from f45 per person.

By far the best choice – and often the only choice – in the old centre of Dordrecht is the ***Hotel Bellevue*** (☎ 613 79 00, fax 613 79 21, Boomstraat 37). It is a classic old place with brilliant views of the converging waterways and ceaseless shipping. The rooms have been tastefully updated and have baths and TVs plus a few more extras. Rooms start at f75/160 for a single/double.

Places to Eat & Drink

De Hut (☎ 635 20 01, Voorstraat 399) has an innovative fast-food menu that's a fusion of Dutch and Indonesian. It's open until at least 11 pm.

Cairo (☎ 635 23 65, Scheffersplein 5) sits among a bunch of expensive places, but holds its own with excellent falafel treats from f6. It's small, and open until at least 10 pm.

Eetcafé 't Vlak (☎ 613 10 88, Vlak 11) is a local institution housed in a comfy corner building that dates from 1616. Open from noon until at least 10 pm, it has classics like pea soup (f9.50) and pancakes (from f7).

Friendly and idiosyncratic, ***Café de Tijd*** (☎ 613 39 97, Voorstraat 170) has an excellent beer selection including many hard-to-find items. If in doubt ask the friendly owners for advice. Otherwise sit back and take in the scene which can include kids playing, birds chirping, cats lazing, dogs begging and a couple of regulars playing chess. The menu is short and cheap. Try the platter of aged Gouda cheese for f6.

Eetcafé Bacchus (☎ 614 97 22, Blauwpoortsplein 13) is a warmly lit, classic brown cafe with steak and fish dishes under f30. The great tiramisu is f10. It's open noon to 10 pm.

Down by the waterfront, ***Café Groothoofd*** (☎ 613 15 65, Groothoofd 3) has fine food to match the views. It has a stylish dining room and tables outside, and serves excellent fresh dishes from about f20. Later at night it often has live jazz until very late at night.

There is a very centrally located ***Albert Heijn Supermarket*** (☎ 614 22 77, Voorstraat 296) near the Visbrug.

ZUID HOLLAND & ZEELAND

Entertainment

The *Jazzpodium* (☎ 614 08 15, Grotekerks-plein 1) has modern and improvisational jazz and blues. It's open 9 pm to 3 am Wednesday and Friday to Sunday. Cover charge varies depending on the program.

Filmhuis Cinode (☎ 639 79 69, St Jorisweg 76) is a serious cinema devoted to off-beat and artistic films.

Getting There & Away

Train The train station has all the usual services and is right on the main line from Rotterdam south to Belgium. There are also direct trains east to Breda and beyond. Some fares and schedules include:

destination	price (f)	duration (mins)	frequency (per hr)
Amsterdam	29	80	4
Breda	9.50	17	3
Rotterdam	6.50	15	6

Bus Buses leave from the area to your right as you exit the train station. You'll find Bus No 388 serves Utrecht every hour (f18, one hour, 20 minutes).

Car & Motorcycle The busy E19 south to Belgium and north to Rotterdam and beyond passes close to town.

Boat The Fast Ferry (☎ 0900-266 63 99, f0.22 per minute) runs a convenient and the scenic service between Dordrecht and Rotterdam.

The service costs f3.75/6.50 one-way/return and takes a delightful 35 minutes. The boats leave at least once an hour from Merwekade, which is at stop No 12 on the bus No 20 route.

Getting Around

Bus If you don't fancy the 700m walk from the train station to the centre of town, let alone another 500m to the Groothoofds-poort, local bus No 20 makes a circular journey from the train station past most of the major sights in town. These include the Dordrechts Museum (stop No 7) and Kuipershaven (stop No 14).

Car & Motorcycle Plan on parking just outside the old town at one of the many car parks near Statenplein.

Taxi Dordrecht is part of the treintaxi scheme (☎ 613 58 22).

Bicycle The bicycle shop (☎ 614 66 42) in the train station is open 6 am to midnight (from 8 am Sunday).

BIESBOSCH NATIONAL PARK

Covering an area of 7100 hectares, Biesbosch National Park covers a vast area along both banks of the Nieuwe Merwede River east and south of Dordrecht. Before 1421 the area was all reclaimed polder land and had a population of over 100,000 living in over 70 villages.

A huge storm on St Elizabeth's Day that year (18 November) breached the dikes, and floodwaters destroyed all the villages and killed most of the people.

However, out of this calamity grew both new life and a new lifestyle. The floods created several channels in their wake, including what is today called the Nieuwe Merwede River. Linked to the sea, these areas were subject to twice-daily high tides. This led to the growth of tide-loving reed plants, which the descendants of the flood's survivors took to cultivating. By all accounts it was a miserable life, with long days of hard work in a waterlogged land. Residents used the reeds for all manner of goods and the lifestyle continued until the 19th century by which time there was little use for reed in an era of machine-produced goods.

Fast forward to 1970 when one of the first parts of the Delta Project shut off the tides to the area. The reeds, which had been growing wild during the decades since the collapse of the reed markets, began to die. This focused attention on what is one of the largest expanses of natural space left in the Netherlands.

Efforts begun in the 1950s to buy up the land were accelerated and today the Biesbosch National Park is a mixture of nature preserves, ecological study zones and recreational areas.

The park is home to beavers and voles as well as scores of birds. The reeds are dying off, but efforts are being made to preserve some of the fields through cultivation.

The best way to visit the park is to start at the **visitors centre** (☎ 630 53 53), Baanhoekweg 53, some 7km east of the Dordrecht train station. There are all the usual displays about the park's ecology and you can rent kayaks and canoes to explore the park and its many channels and streams. Prices start at f11.50 for 2½ hours.

There are also numerous trails through the marshlands and along the river. The visitors centre is open 9 am to 5 pm (closed Monday except from June to August) and is free.

The centre is also the boarding place for a variety of **boat tours** of Biesbosch which start at f9.25/7.25 for adults/children for a one-hour cruise. The longer cruises are better, though, because they go to more places, including the **Biesboschmuseum** on the southern shore of the Nieuwe Merwede. There are displays here about the lives of the reed farmers.

Places to Stay & Eat
The excellent NJHC-affiliated *Hotel De Hollandse Biesbosch* (☎ 621 21 67, fax 621 21 63, ❷ dordrecht@njhc.org, Baanhoekweg 25) has just about any kind of accommodation you could want. Beds in the four-bed hostel rooms cost from f28. Comfortable rooms with bath and TV cost f88/108 for a single/double. Outside in a natural setting there is a camping area which costs f6 per tent plus f10 for each camper. It's a good idea to reserve any of the accommodation here in advance.

The hotel, which has a bar and restaurant, is in a modern building right next to the park and is 1km west of the visitors centre.

Getting There & Away
The hotel and park are easy bike rides from the train station. Otherwise, bus No 5 (every 30 minutes) travels to within 2km of the hotel and 3km of the park. But if you tell the driver you're going to either, a taxi will be called to take you the rest of the way for only f1.

Zeeland

Look at a map of Zeeland and you can see why there's so much fuss made about water. Its three fingers of land are really just islands set in the middle of a vast delta through which drain many of Europe's rivers, including the Rhine, Schelde and Maas. The name, which means Sea Land, could not be more appropriate as the boundary between the two is thin indeed. For centuries the plucky Zeelanders have been battling the North Sea waters, and not always with success. The St Elizabeth's Day flood of 1421 killed at least 100,000 and forever altered the landscape. The huge flood of 31 January 1953 killed almost 2000, left 500,000 homeless and destroyed 800km of dikes.

The result of this last calamity is the Delta Project, an enormous multidecade construction program that aims to once and for all ensure the security of these lands. It's easily the largest construction project in history and has greatly altered the entire region. See the boxed text 'The Delta Project' for details.

Given the constant battle with the sea, it's no surprise that Zeelanders are a conservative lot of no-nonsense farmers. This is one of the last places in the Netherlands where you find people wearing traditional dress in everyday life. For women this means lots of layers of white lace, and for men, black suits.

Much of Zeeland is farmland. Middelburg is the delightful historic capital, while the coast along the North Sea is lined with beaches beyond the ever-present dikes. Many people venture to this place of tenuous land and omnipresent water just to see the sheer size of the Delta Project dikes and barriers.

Getting There & Away
In Zeeland, Middelburg is easily reached by train, but for most other towns you'll need to rely on the many buses. The most important include bus No 104 which makes a marathon 2½-hour journey between Rotterdam's Centraal Station and Vlissingen that follows the western edge of the province along the Delta Project. It runs every 30 minutes in both directions.

The Delta Project

Begun in 1958, the Delta Project consumed billions upon billions of guilders, millions of labour hours and untold volumes of concrete and rock before it was completed in 1996.

The goal was to avoid a repeat of the catastrophic floods of 1953, when a huge surge of water ahead of a storm rushed far up the Delta estuaries of Zeeland and broke through weak dikes inland. This caused serial failure of dikes throughout the region and much of the province was flooded.

The original goal was to block up all the entrances to the estuaries and create one vast network of freshwater areas. But by the 1960s, environmental conscience had reached a point that this kind of huge-scale ecological transformation was unacceptable to the Dutch public.

The decision was taken to, at great expense, leave the Oosterschelde open to the sea tides while constructing 3km of movable barriers that could be lowered in place ahead of a storm to prevent a surge. This barrier, between Noord Beveland and Schouwen Duiveland, is the most dramatic part of the Delta Project and is the focus of the Delta Expo, which details the enormous effort expended over 10 years to complete the barrier.

Other parts of the Delta Project have included the raising and strengthening of dikes throughout the region and a large movable barrier at the entrance to Rotterdam's harbour, which was the last component completed. However, large areas of water were dammed and made into freshwater lakes by the project before opinion shifted. Veerse Meer between Noord- and Zuid-Beveland is but one example. There the fishing industry has vanished and been replaced by holiday-makers and sailboats.

Elsewhere, the environmental implications of the Delta Project are still being felt. At De Biesbosch National Park near Dordrecht, the reduction of tides is killing the reeds, which have grown there for centuries. But those who recall the terrible floods of the past will probably trade some reeds for their farms any day.

Bus No 2 meets the ferry from Vlissingen at Veer Breskens and then runs south to Brugge in Belgium. The bus journey to the same destination takes 2¼ hours and runs every hour in both directions.

MIDDELBURG
☎ 0118 • pop 45,000

A pleasant and prosperous town, Middelburg is the capital of Zeeland and makes a good place for a pause before exploring the countryside.

Although the Germans destroyed the town's historic centre in 1940, much has been rebuilt and you can still get a solid feel for what life must have been like hundreds of years ago. The fortifications built by the Sea Beggars in 1595 can still be traced in the pattern of the main canals encircling the old town.

As the main town of the Walcheren Peninsula, Middelburg is fairly removed from the rest of the Netherlands and you will find that crowds are seldom a problem. Note that many of the town's sights are closed in winter.

Orientation

The train station for Middelburg is a five-minute walk across two canals from the centre. The Markt is the focus of commercial life but Middelburg's history is concentrated around the Abbey.

Information

Tourist Offices The VVV (☎ 65 99 44, fax 65 99 40, ✆ vvvmid@zeelandnet.nl) shares facilities with the ANWB at Nieuwe Burg 40, near the Abbey. It is open 9.30 am to 5.30 pm Monday to Saturday (Thursday to 9 pm) year-round and noon to 4 pm on Sunday from April to October. It sells a good city walking guide for f6.50 and has a free 'Tourist Pass Middelburg' that gives discounts at most sights in town. There are also over 20 different maps of Zeeland bike-touring routes for sale.

Money There is no GWK exchange in the train station. However, ATMs abound including at ABN/AMRO Bank (☎ 67 25 00),

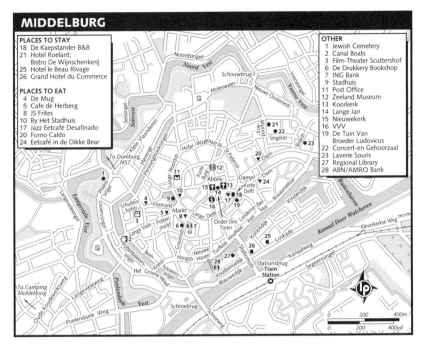

MIDDELBURG

PLACES TO STAY
18 De Kaepstander B&B
21 Hotel Roelant;
   Bistro De Wijnschenkerij
25 Hotel le Beau Rivage
26 Grand Hotel du Commerce

PLACES TO EAT
4 De Mug
5 Cafe de Herberg
8 JS Frites
10 By Het Stadhuis
17 Jazz Eetcafé Desafinado
20 Forno Caldo
24 Eetcafé in de Dikke Bear

OTHER
1 Jewish Cemetery
2 Canal Boats
3 Film-Theater Scuttershof
6 De Drukkery Bookshop
7 ING Bank
9 Stadhuis
11 Post Office
12 Zeeland Museum
13 Koorkerk
14 Lange Jan
15 Nieuwekerk
16 VVV
19 De Tuin Van
   Broeder Ludovicus
22 Concert-en Gehoorzaal
23 Laverie Souris
27 Regional Library
28 ABN/AMRO Bank

Kousteensedijk 3, and ING Bank (☎ 68 44 00), Markt 43.

Post The post office (☎ 64 22 88), Lange Noordstraat 48, is open 8 am to 5.30 pm weekdays and 9 am to 1 pm Saturday.

Bookshops Zeeland's finest bookshop, De Drukkery (☎ 88 68 86), draws customers from as far as Belgium to its large store at Markt 51. There is an excellent magazine selection besides the oodles of books and even an antiquarian section.

Libraries The Zeeland Regional Library (☎ 64 40 00), Kousteensedijk 7, is in a large and modern building on a canal. It has Internet access and is open 5 to 9 pm Monday, 10 am to 9 pm Tuesday to Friday and 10 am to 1 pm Saturday.

Laundry Laverie Souris (☎ 62 34 99), Brakstraat 14, is actually rather nice, for a

coin laundry. You can wash your duds and relax on the wicker furniture 8.30 am to 6 pm weekdays and until noon Saturday.

The Abbey

This huge complex dates from the 12th century. It houses the regional government as well as three churches and two museums. You can start with the **Historama** (☎ 62 66 55) which is in the heart of the complex. Here you can wander some of the oldest corridors trying to sniff out memories of a monk. Displays portray the bleaker aspects of cloistered life and cover the history of the abbey. It's open 11 am to 5 pm (from noon Sunday) from April to October and costs f6/2 for adults/children.

The three churches are all in a cluster. The **Wandelkerk** dates from the 1600s and holds the tombs of Jan and Cornelis Eversten, admirals and brothers killed fighting the English in 1666. It encompasses **Lange Jan**, the rather interesting name given to

ZUID HOLLAND & ZEELAND

Middelburg's symbol, the 91m tower dating from the 14th century. Just east is the **Koorkerk**, parts of which date from the 1300s. Just west is **Nieuwekerk**, which has a famous organ and dates from the 16th century.

The churches (☎ 61 35 96) are open 10 am to 5 pm daily from April to mid-October and are free. During the same hours you can scale the heights of Lange Jan for f3.

In the former monks' dormitories is housed the **Zeeland Museum** (☎ 62 66 55). There's a good range of Zeeland archaeological finds back to the Roman era as well as art from locals artists past and present.

The most interesting stuff relates to the Celtic goddess Nehalennia, who may have been the recipient of offerings from sailors thankful for a safe voyage across the English Channel during Roman times. Then again, she could have been a goddess of flowers. There's no-one left to ask... The stones usually show her with a dog and carrying a basket of fruit. The museum is open 11 am to 5 pm daily (from noon Sunday) and costs f9.50/2.50.

Before leaving the Abbey, you might want to check out the ancient **herb garden** growing in the centre courtyard and, finally, the **Roosevelt Study Centre** (☎ 63 15 90), inside the main building. The centre is dedicated to the study of the Roosevelt family, which produced two US presidents, Theodore and Franklin. Some of their relatives came from nearby Tholen. There are a few free displays that are open for viewing 10 am to 4.30 pm weekdays from April to October.

Stadhuis

Dominating the Markt is the Stadhuis (☎ 67 54 52), a pastiche of styles. The Gothic side facing the Markt is from the 1400s while the portion on Noordstraat is more classical and dates from the 1600s.

Inside there are several sumptuous ceremonial rooms that boast treasures such as the ubiquitous Belgian tapestries. Visits to the building are by guided tours only which last one hour and are offered 11 am to 5 pm daily (from noon Sunday) from April to October. Admission costs f4.

Outside, it's worth exploring the many passages around the Stadhuis.

Other Sights

The area around **Damplein** preserves many 18th-century houses, some of which have recently been turned into interesting shops and cafes.

There is a fairly large old **Jewish Cemetery** on the Walensingel. It has the all-too-common stark memorial to the many Middelburg Jews taken away to their deaths by the Nazis.

Market

Like every other Dutch town, Middelburg has a **weekly market**. However, this one, which takes place Thursdays on the Markt is notable as it attracts many of Zeeland's conservative residents, many of whom still wear traditional dress regardless of whether any tourists are around.

Boat Tours

There are tours of the local canals that depart from the Lange Viele bridge from 11 am to 4 pm daily from April to October. During the warmest months the hours are extended. Rides cost f9/7; call the VVV for more details.

Places to Stay

Camping *Camping Middelburg (☎/fax 62 53 95, Koninginnelaan 55)* is 3km from the train station. Take bus No 56 or 58 (every 30 minutes) and tell the driver where you want to get off. Sites cost from f28 for two people with a tent and there are sometimes little cabins available.

Hostels There is a hostel 10km west near Domburg; see the listing in the Domburg section for details.

Hotels *De Kaepstander (☎ 64 28 48, Koorkerkhof 10)* has four rooms with B&B-style accommodation. Prices are from f50/90 for a simple single/double room with shared bath.

Hotel Roelant (☎ 62 76 59, fax 62 89 73, Koepoortstraat 10) is in a building dating from 1530 and has comfortable rooms with bath from f58/115. There is a nice garden and an excellent restaurant (see Places to Eat).

Hotel le Beau Rivage (☎ *63 80 60, fax 62 96 73, Loskade 19)* is near the train station in a traditional Dutch building with a gabled roof. There are nine rooms, all with TVs and baths, which cost from f85/90.

Also across from the station, ***Grand Hotel du Commerce*** (☎ *63 60 51, fax 62 64 00,* ✆ *info@hotelducommerce.nl, Loskade 1)* is in a building that would look at home on the Cannes beachfront. Well, at least the rooms are warm here and they have all the conveniences. Prices start at f110/140.

Places to Eat
The streets west of the Markt and Damplein are all good hunting grounds for cafes and restaurants, although smart diners avoid Markt.

JS Frites is a stand right on the Markt that has all the usual fried goodies, but these seem to be prepared with an extra bit of elan. It's open after midnight many nights.

Cafe de Herberg (☎ *62 55 39, Pottenmarkt 2)* is one of several similar places in this area. It has a vast terrace and decent daily specials from f10. It's open from 11 am to 10 pm.

Forno Caldo (☎ *64 04 63, Damplein 25)* is a warm and yellow pizza joint that's mostly kitsch-free. A variety of pies cost f18 and the restaurant is open for lunch and dinner daily.

Jazz Eetcafé Desafinado (☎ *64 07 67, Koorkerkstraat 1)* is a delightful place with a huge collection of jazz CDs. The menu leans towards Spanish and Mexican and there's a variety of meals for under f30. The bar is open until midnight, the kitchen until 9.30 pm.

By Het Stadhuis (☎ *62 70 58, Lange Noordstaat 8)* has a casual yet slightly elegant interior. The menu concentrates on fresh seafood such as mussels (f30). It's open for lunch and dinner until 10 pm daily, and is very popular with locals.

Eetcafé in de Dikke Bear (☎ *62 75 75, Damplein 46)* lives up to its name with a motif that has bears all over the interior.

The small but interesting menu doesn't boast bear but it does have local dishes such as seafood which cost f50 for three courses. Kids can opt for the pancake card. It's open daily until 10 pm.

Bistro De Wijnschenkerij (☎ *63 33 09, Koepoortstraat 10)* is run by the same nice people who own Hotel Roelant upstairs. The menu is derived from Provence in France. Four-course menus cost from f42. It's open daily until after 10 pm.

De Mug (☎ *61 48 51, Vlasmarkt 54)* is justifiably famous beyond Middelburg for its menu of dishes prepared with unusual Dutch beers. The choices change often and average f32 for a main. It feels like a great brown cafe and because it's popular, you should book. It shouldn't be a surprise that the beer list is long and boasts many rare brews from the Benelux region.

De Tuin Van Broeder Ludovicus (☎ *62 60 11, Lange Delft 2A)* is a health-food store with an organic bakery, cheese case, produce and more.

Entertainment
Concert-en Gehoorzaal (☎ *61 27 00, Singlestraat 13)* is an old concert hall with a plush interior. There are frequent performances of chamber and other classical music at the hall.

Film-Theater Schuttershof (☎ *61 34 82, Schuttershofstraat 1)* is down a little alley but has a big interior. There's a cinema showing unusual flicks and a large, cool bar area. On some nights it has live music and if you're lucky, local rock sensation 'Busted' will be playing.

The ***carillon*** in Lange Jan rings its many bells every 15 minutes. Longer one-hour concerts are given at noon every Thursday throughout the year and at 7.30 pm Thursday in July and August.

Getting There & Around
Train Middelburg is near the end of the line in Zeeland and the attractive but austere station has that end-of-line feel. Services are limited: there's a very small newsstand and the lockers are hidden away in the bicycle shop. Some fares and schedules are:

ZUID HOLLAND & ZEELAND

destination	price (f)	duration (mins)	frequency (per hr)
Amsterdam	48	150	1
Roosendaal	19.25	45	2
Rotterdam	33	90	1

Bus Regional buses, including No 104, stop along Kanaalweg in front of the train station.

Taxi Middelburg is in the treintaxi scheme (☎ 63 96 45).

Bicycle The bicycle shop (☎ 61 21 78) is to the left as you leave the station. It's open 6.30 am to 10.30 pm (from 8.45 am Sunday).

AROUND MIDDELBURG
The Walcheren Peninsula is a particularly enjoyable place for biking as you can combine journeys to old towns with time at the beach.

Veere
☎ 0118 • pop 5000
Veere is a former fishing village that found a new line of work in tourism when its access to the sea on the Veerse Meer was closed as part of the Delta Project. Happily, tourists and pleasure seekers have been willing to oblige and the town now boasts a busy yacht harbour. Much of the town dates from the early 16th century and it is an atmospheric place to stroll around. Veere is an easy 6km trip north of Middelburg.

Information The VVV (☎ 0900-202 02 80, fax 50 17 92), Oudestraat 28, is in a small building near the Grote Kerk. It is open 10 am to 4.30 pm Monday to Saturday in July and August; from 1.30 pm the rest of the year. Staff can advise on boat rentals and bike routes.

Things to See & Do The best thing to do in Veere is stroll. You'll feel like you've found yourself inside a Veermeer painting. Rich Gothic houses abound, a testament to the wealth brought in by the wool trade with the Scots. At the waterfront, the **Campveerse Toren** was part of the old fortifications. Look

for the indications on the side showing the levels of various floods.

The **Stadhuis** on the Markt dates from 1474 but was mostly completed in 1599. Its tower is still literally stuffed with bells, 48 at last count.

At the south end of town is the 16th-century **Grote Kerk**, another edifice that never matched its designer's intentions. Its stump of a steeple (42m) looms ominously. Relief comes from the nearby **white windmill**.

There are **boat trips** (☎ 41 93 67) on the Veerse Meer from 11 am to 5 pm daily from May to September. Prices vary by trip.

Places to Stay & Eat *Hotel de Capveerse Toren* (☎ *50 12 91, fax 50 16 95,* @ *camp veer@zeelandnet.nl, Kade 2*) is a smart place in a historic building right on the waterfront. Comfortable rooms cost from f63/120 for a single/double in the low season, rising quickly with the thermometer.

Hotel 't Waepen van Veere (☎ *50 12 31, fax 50 60 09, Markt 23–27*) is on the central square. It is a small place, with just 11 rooms from f75/140.

Both of the hotels have *cafes*. In addition there are a few more cafes on Markt as well as a bakery and a grocery.

Getting There & Away Veere is an easy bike ride from Middelburg. Otherwise, bus No 53 makes the 12-minute run every hour (every two hours Sunday).

Domburg
☎ 0118 • pop 900 (winter)
A fairly low-key beach town by Dutch standards, Domburg still gets jam-packed during summer.

Information The VVV (☎ 58 13 42, fax 58 35 46), Schuitvlotstraat 32, is near the entrance to town on Roosjesweg. It's open 9 am to 4.30 pm Monday to Saturday (until 6 pm in July and August). The staff are experts at ferreting out accommodation.

Things to See & Do The **beach** is the main event here. To escape the urban crowds, head south along the tall dunes.

Groot Ammers is one of many windmills on the lakes surrounding Rotterdam

The government's home: Binnenhof, Den Haag

Traditional thatched houses in Den Haag

Ever wonder what to do with those spare coat hangers: Lange Vorhout's sculpture in Den Haag

The French Embassy provides a bold statement in Den Haag

Keep going past the **golf course** until you're right out in the country, a good 4km.

For information on a 38km bicycle route, the Mantelingen Route, which begins and ends at Domburg, see the special section 'Cycling in the Netherlands'.

Places to Stay & Eat *Hof Domburg Camping (☎ 58 82 00, fax 58 36 68,* **@** *info@roompot.nl, Schelpweg 7)* is just west of the centre. It has sites for up to five people for f44 and is open all year.

The hostel *NJHC Kasteel Westhove (☎ 58 12 54, fax 58 33 42, Duinvlietweg 8)* is in a real castle complete with moat, that's 2km east of Domburg and 1km from the beach.

The smallest rooms have four beds and cost f30 per person. The hostel is open from April to October and rents bikes. This is a good one to reserve in advance. Bus No 53 from Middelburg stops along the N287 near the entrance.

The inspirationally named *Hotel Duinlust (☎/fax 58 29 70, Badhuisweg 28)* is central and has simple rooms from f40/62 for a single double. The VVV has a myriad of additional options.

Fast-food stands and restaurants line the beach roads.

Getting There & Away Bus Nos 52 and 53 both link Domburg to Middelburg every hour (every two hours Sunday). Bus No 53 continues south along the beaches.

Vlissingen
☎ 0118 • pop 45,000
Once an important port, Vlissingen is now an unattractive port. Its major feature is the ferry terminal for boats linking the town with Zeeuwsch-Vlaanderen and Belgium to the south across the Westerschelde.

The rather tawdry old town is a 10-minute walk over locks across the channel just west of the ferry port and train station. Buses and cars have to make a long detour around the channel.

Getting There & Away The modern ferry port is the terminus for car ferries that make

the 30-minute run every 30 minutes between Vlissingen and Breskens. The ferries are popular with people using the channel ferry ports of Zeebrugge and Oostende in Belgium. The fare is f13 per car and the boats have few amenities for the short and unscenic trip.

Next to the ferry port is the train station. This is the terminus of the line through Middelburg, 6km north. Trains run every hour. Bus No 104 terminates at the train station.

BEVELAND
The lands east of Walcheren are known collectively as Beveland. This is the heart of Zeeland's farms and in the summer you'll see orchards of fruit trees in bloom. Otherwise, Beveland, both Noord and Zuid, is primarily a place you'll pass through on the way to Middelburg.

Goes
☎ 0113 • pop 34,200
This is the main town of Beveland. It's of interest for the **Grote Markt**, the main square which has an 18th-century rococo **Stadhuis**. The weekly market is held here on Tuesdays, which is definitely the best day to stop by. There are a few of the usual cafes on the square.

The VVV (☎ 0900-168 16 66, fax 25 13 50) is near the train station at Stationsplein 3, a five-minute walk from the Grote Markt. It's open 10 am to 4.30 pm weekdays and until 1 pm Saturday.

Goes is on the train line between Middelburg and Roosendaal. There are two trains per hour in each direction. Bus No 132 links Goes with Zierikzee to the north.

DELTA EXPO
Travelling the N57, the main road north from Middelburg through western Zeeland, you can't help but notice the many massive projects of the Delta Project. You will see a succession of huge dikes and dams, all designed to avoid a repeat of the many floods.

Possibly the most impressive stretch is the portion between Noord Beveland and Schouwen Duiveland, further to the north. The long causeway built atop the massive movable inlets is designed to allow the sea tides in and out of the Osterschelde. This **storm surge barrier** is over 3km long, spans three inlets and two artificial islands. It took 10 years to build, beginning in 1976.

At about the midway point, the **Delta Expo** (☎ 0111-65 27 02) is an excellent museum and visitors centre for the Delta Project (for more information, see the boxed text 'The Delta Project'). There is a huge model showing how the tides and floods affect the entire Delta region. Many more exhibits on several floors deal with the effects of the floods as well as showing how the entire massive project was built. At the very top is an observation deck with fine views. You can also visit one of the nearby complex pylons of the storm surge barrier and see how the huge movable gate works.

On the other side of the N57 is **Water-Land**, a seasonal park that operates in conjunction with the Expo. There's a dolphin rescue station here for treating beached dolphins, all sorts of water slides and pools, exhibits on the flora and fauna of the Delta and more. Between the two sites, you can easily spend a day out here on what is an artificial island built for the project.

The Expo and WaterLand are open daily 10 am to 5 pm (until 9 pm in July and August) from 1 April to 31 October. The rest of the year only the Expo is open 10 am to 5 pm Wednesday to Sunday. Admission for both attractions is f21.50/16.50 for adults/children; for the Expo only in the off season it's f14.50/9.50.

Bus No 104 stops right at the Expo on its run between Rotterdam's Centraal Station and Vlissingen. The buses take two hours from Rotterdam and 30 minutes from Middelburg and run every 30 minutes.

SCHOUWEN-DUIVELAND

The middle 'finger' of the Delta, Scouwen-Duiveland is a compact island of dunes.

Zierikzee

☎ 0111 • pop 13,300

The town grew wealthy in the 14th century from trade with the Hanseatic League. Things took a turn for the worse in 1576 when a bunch of Spaniards waded over from the mainland at low tide and captured Zierikzee, precipitating a long economic decline.

Information The VVV (☎ 41 24 50, fax 41 72 73), Meelstraat 4, is in the Stadhuis. It is open 9 am to 5 pm weekdays and 10 am to 1 pm Saturday (until 3 pm from May to September). Its town booklet (f2) is filled with facts and a decent little map.

There are banks and ATMs on Havenpark. The post office (☎ 41 55 55), Poststraat 39, is open 9 am to 5.30 pm weekdays and 10 am to 1 pm Saturday. The library (☎ 41 45 48), Haringvlietplein 2, has Internet access and is open 2 to 5 pm weekdays (closed Tuesday) as well as 9.30 am to noon Wednesday and Saturday.

Things to See Long, open **Havenpark** makes a good entrance to the old town after the boat-lined Oude Haven. It is lined with cafes and shops. The unusual **Gasthuiskerk** with the deep arcades is the site of a flower market.

The **Maritiem Museum** (☎ 45 44 64), Mol 25, is just off Havenpark. It is in the 's-Gravensteen, a sturdy 16th-century prison that still has its bars. Besides the displays on local seafaring, there's a fine garden out the back. It's open 10 am to 5 pm (from noon Sunday) and costs f4/2 for adults/children.

The **Stadhuis**, Meelstraat 6–8, has a unique 16th-century wooden tower topped with a statue of Neptune. Its museum (☎ 45 44 64) has a few displays of local history. It's open the same hours as the Maritiem Museum and a combined admission ticket to both costs f6/3.

At Oude Haven at the east end of town, the **Noordhavenpoort** and the **Zuidhaven-poort** are old city gates from the 16th and 14th centuries respectively.

Places to Stay & Eat The VVV has a list of local rooms for overnight stays. Otherwise, *Pension Beddegoed (☎ 41 59 35, Meelstraat 53)* is very centrally located. Simple rooms cost from f50 per person.

Stadsbakkerij (☎ 45 04 65, Applemarkt 8) has cheap snacks and sandwiches. It's closed Sunday.

Next door, *Pannekoekenhuis 't Zeeuwse* *(☎ 41 61 79, Appelmarkt 6)* has crayons on the tables for kids, and pancakes from f10. It's open 10 am to 6 pm and is closed Sunday.

Concordia (☎ 41 51 22) dominates the end of Havenpark with its terrace. The broad cafe menu has numerous dinners from f20. It's open until 11 pm daily.

Getting There & Away The bus stop is north of the centre, a five-minute walk across the canal along Grachtweg. Bus No 132 makes the 30-minute run to Goes at least every 30 minutes. Bus No 133 runs to Rotterdam's Zuidplein metro station. The 75-minute ride leaves at least every hour.

Westerschouwen
☎ 0111 • pop 17,900
This small town at the west end of Scouwen-Duiveland is sheltered by tall dunes. It adjoins **Beschermd Natuur-Monument**, a vast park set among the sands and woods.

There are all sorts of hiking and biking trails availabe to the outdoor enthusiast. Although predictably busy in summer, you can easily find solitude in some of the more remote parts of the park.

The VVV (☎ 65 15 13, fax 65 28 33), Noordstraat 45A in the neighbouring inland town of Burgh-Haamstede, can help with all manner of camping, private room and hotel accommodations. It's open 9 am to 5 pm weekdays and until 2 pm Saturday.

Camping Irenehoeve (☎ 65 15 86, fax 65 42 88, Lageweg 18) is one of several family-run campgrounds. Fees vary widely depending on the season.

Hotel De Zilvermeeuw (☎ 65 22 72, fax 65 82 55, Lageweg 21) has nine decent rooms with baths from f65/85 for a single/double.

Lageweg is lined with casual food places, including one at the very end of the road at the bus stop.

Bus No 133 from Rotterdam via Zierikzee and Bus No 134 from Zierikzee both stop right at the sand dunes. Both run every 30 minutes. Bus No 104, the Vlissingen-Rotterdam bus, stops about 2km from Westerschouwen in Burgh-Haamstede.

ZEEUWS-VLAANDEREN
This often neglected part of the Netherlands runs along the Belgian border south of the Westerschelde. It is an unremarkable place with numerous farms and a few chemical plants.

The many small villages, such as IJzendijk, all have their 'holy trinity' of the Dutch country skyline: a church steeple, a stadhuis tower and a windmill.

No part of Zeeuws-Vlaanderen is joined to the rest of the Netherlands by land. Instead, two ferry routes provide connections. The Vlissingen-Breskens ferry (see the Vlissingen section for details) provides a useful link for people using the Belgian channel ferry ports.

It is also useful for foot passengers, who can travel from Brugge in Belgium by bus No 2 to Breskens (75 minutes, every hour). From the ferry port in Vlissingen, catch a bus or ferry to points beyond.

The other ferry route, Perkpolder to Kruiningen on Zuid Beveland, is primarily useful to local motorists. The ferry runs every 30 minutes in both directions and costs f13 per car.

Sluis
☎ 0117 • pop 6477
This small town 1km from the Belgian border is on the busy N58 route to Oostende. It has a nice little canal and a handsome **Stadhuis**. However, you'll be lucky to see either as it serves as a major retail outlet for Belgians who like its extended shopping hours and good prices on items more expensive at home.

Judging by what's for sale in the dozens of gaudy shops, the Belgians are primarily interested in bargains on cosmetics, porn and underwear.

However, should you stop here (parking f3 in the huge lots), *Brasserie de Molen van Sluis (☎ 46 12 50, Nieuwstraat 26)* is in the base of a restored windmill at the far end of town from the parking lots. It serves mid-priced Dutch dishes and has a large range of beers.

The Brugge-Breskens bus (No 3) stops near the parking lots.

ZUID HOLLAND & ZEELAND

Friesland

At first Friesland seems typically Dutch: it's flat, it's green and there's plenty of cows (the namesake Frisian black and white jobbies here). But explore a bit and you'll find differences. Around the aquatic sports town of Sneek, you'll wonder what's this *Snit* all about? Well, Snit is Frisian for Sneek. The province has its own language, and while you won't encounter it widely, you will find it on road signs and other signage.

Language is just one thing that sets Frisians apart. Even by Dutch standards, they're a very self-reliant bunch. They didn't just have to build dikes to protect their land, they had to build the land as well. North Friesland segues into the Waddenzee in such a subtle way that in the old days you could never be sure whether you were on watery mud or muddy water. To provide a place to live over a thousand years ago, they laboriously built *terpen*, which are huge piles of mud. North of Leeuwarden you can still see these piles, most notably in Hogebeintum.

Self-reliant and stoic, the Frisians were integrated further into Dutch society in 1932 when the Afsluitdijk opened, closing the Zuiderzee. This provided better transport links to Amsterdam and the south but it also proved devastating for small fishing villages who found themselves now sitting on a lake. Only now are places like Hindeloopen and Makkum finding sure footing as popular destinations.

North of the mainland, but still very much a part of the muddy ooze, the Frisian Islands can disappoint or delight, depending on whether you get caught in the summer mobs of the developed areas or you are bale to set off over the vast and unpopulated natural tracts.

Getting There & Around
The capital of Friesland, Leeuwarden, is easily reached by train and the entire province is accessible by car from the south; the quickest route from Amsterdam

HIGHLIGHTS

- Sailing from Sneek
- Skating through the skating museum in Hindeloopen
- Climbing the terp at Hogebeintum
- Exploring the wilds of car-free Vlieland
- Biking around Ameland

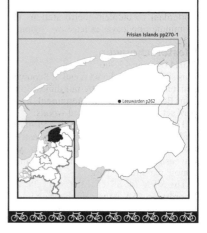

is over the Afsluitdijk. Alternatively, you can take the car ferry from Enkhuizen to Stavoren. See the Enkhuizen section of the Noord Holland chapter for details.

By bus, the Interliner No 350 line runs between Alkmaar in Noord Holland and Leeuwarden via Harlingen. The journey takes two hours and buses run hourly through the day.

Getting around the province requires more patience. Netherlands Railways has hived off most of the local lines to an outfit called NoordNed and standards have fallen. With patience, however, you can reach all points of Friesland by bus, train, or better yet, bike.

Ferry information for the Frisian Islands is included in each island's listing.

260

LEEUWARDEN
☎ 058 • pop 90,200

Leeuwarden is a pleasant place that reflects the serenity of the farmland around it. Not as vivacious as Groningen to the east, the town has many quiet old streets that are good for wandering. There's just enough action to provide interest.

The town has a tradition of trade and agriculture dating back to the 15th century, when it was a centre of power struggles between its wealthy dukes and those of Holland. Earlier than that, it was formed from three terpen, the piles of mud used as home sites by the first Frisians. Its most famous daughter is WWI spy Mata Hari.

Orientation
The old town is compact and easily traversed by foot from the train station. Much of the commercial life is on or near the network of canals which wind through the centre.

Information
Tourist Offices The VVV (☎ 0900-202 40 60, f0.50 per minute, fax 215 35 93, @ vvvleeuwarden@chello.nl), Stationsplein 1, is in the train station building. It's

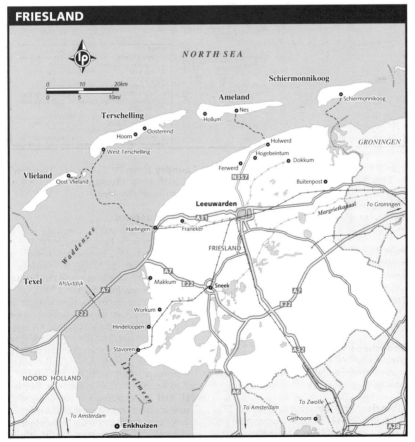

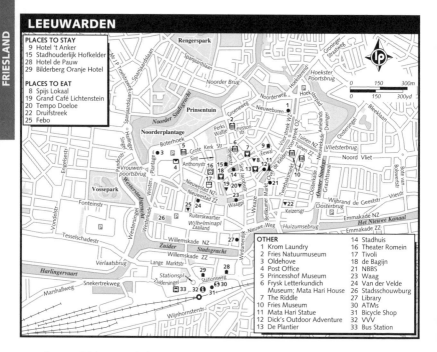

LEEUWARDEN

PLACES TO STAY
9 Hotel 't Anker
15 Stadhouderlijk Hofkelder
28 Hotel de Pauw
29 Bilderberg Oranje Hotel

PLACES TO EAT
8 Spijs Lokaal
19 Grand Café Lichtenstein
20 Tempo Doeloe
22 Druifstreek
25 Febo

OTHER
1 Krom Laundry
2 Fries Natuurmuseum
3 Oldehove
4 Post Office
5 Princesshof Museum
6 Frysk Letterkundich Museum; Mata Hari House
7 The Riddle
10 Fries Museum
11 Mata Hari Statue
12 Dick's Outdoor Adventure
13 De Plantier
14 Stadhuis
16 Theater Romein
17 Tivoli
18 de Bagijn
21 NBBS
23 Waag
24 Van der Velde
26 Stadsschouwburg
27 Library
30 ATMs
31 Bicycle Shop
32 VVV
33 Bus Station

open 9 am to 5.30 pm weekdays and 10 am to 2 pm Saturday.

Money There is no GWK exchange in the station. However, there are ATMs to the right as you exit as well as throughout the town.

Post The post office (☎ 213 09 98), Oldehoofster Kerkhof 4, is open 7.30 am to 6 pm weekdays and until 1.30 pm Saturday.

Travel Agencies NBBS (☎ 212 54 32), Over de Kelders 20, specialises in discount tickets.

Bookshops Van der Velde (☎ 213 23 60), Nieuwestad 90, has a smallish but decent selection of English-language and travel books.

Libraries The library (☎ 234 77 77), Wirdumerdijk 34, is open 10 am to 5.30 pm weekdays and until 1 pm Saturday.

Laundry Krom (☎ 213 08 45), Voorstreek 102, will do your laundry for you from 9 am to 5 pm weekdays only.

Fries Museum

The main sight worth checking out in Leeuwarden is the Fries Museum (☎ 212 30 01), Turfmarkt 11, a large institution spread over two historic buildings, the **Kanselarij**, a 16th-century courthouse, and the **Eysinghaus**, a mansion from the late 1700s.

The museum traces the development of Frisian culture from the mud-stacking era of the terp-builders onwards. There's everyday items like old drinking cups made from cow horns as well as artworks from the 12th century to the present. A huge collection of silver items – long a Frisian speciality – is not to be missed. The museum is laid out well and the explanations are thoughtful. There is also a section on the efforts by locals to resist the Nazis and a both delightful and sorrowful examination of the life of

Mata Hari. It's open 11 am to 5 pm (closed Monday) and admission is f7.50/5 for adults/children.

Princessehof Museum

Pottery lovers will flip over – and possibly never leave – this 17th-century palace housing the Princessehof Museum (☎ 212 74 38) at Grote Kerkstraat 11. It is the official museum for ceramics in the Netherlands and as such holds an unparalleled selection of glazed tiles. It also has works from around the world, and the Japanese, Chinese and Vietnamese sections are world-class. The museum's downfall is that you have to be a bit of a fan as everything is presented in a rather staid manner. However, recent changes, such as the addition of a room for contemporary works by young artists, bode well and there is a fair amount of commentary in English. It's open 11 am to 5 pm (closed Monday) and admission is f7.50/5.

Mata Hari

Had she been born a few decades later, Leeuwarden's own Margaretha Geertruida Zelle probably would have been given a TV chat show. Instead, the irrepressible Margaretha changed her name to Mata Hari, moved to Paris and ended up a martyr to salacious legend.

Born in 1876, Margaretha was a bright child who friends said 'had an active imagination'; always a recipe for trouble. Her wealthy family fell apart in her teens and she married a stodgy military man 20 years her senior. While they were living in what is now Indonesia, on a military posting, one of their two children died in a bizarre poisoning incident.

Back in Leeuwarden in 1902, the marriage collapsed. Margaretha left her other child with the ex-husband and moved to Paris, where the rest really is history. She began a career as a dancer and achieved wide fame, no doubt helped by the fact that she danced naked. She also changed her name to Mata Hari, which she said was Malaysian for 'sun'.

Mata Hari's love affairs and dalliances were legendary in her own time. She favoured rich men in uniform and when WWI broke out in 1914, she had lovers in the high ranks of the military on both sides. This soon got her in trouble, as her numerous partners asked her to spy on her other partners. This web of intrigue was not helped by her keen imagination, and soon she was mistrusted by all sides.

In 1917, at age 40, she was arrested by the French for spying. There was a dubious trial, during which none of her former 'pals' offered any assistance – probably out of embarrassment – and later that year she was sentenced to death and shot.

In Leeuwarden today you can trace a good part of Mata Hari's early life as Margaretha. Her birthplace is at Kelders 33, a building next to a decent sporting goods shop named Dick's Outdoor Adventure (☎ 215 87 46). The Mata Hari Flower Shop is just a few doors away. On the nearby bridge over the canal, there is a statue of Mata Hari as a (clothed) dancer.

Much of Margaretha's childhood was spent at Grote Kerkstraat 212, which now houses the Frysk Letterkundich Museum (☎ 212 08 34), a small institution devoted to Frisian literature.

The Fries Museum has a large and detailed exhibit on the life of both Margaretha and Mata Hari.

Mata Hari

Other Attractions

The streets around Bagijnestraat and Hofplein mix the genteel with the shabby and are the best places to wander. The **Stadhuis** on Hofplein is dignified and dates from 1715.

Just past the west end of Bagijnestraat, the **Oldehove** dominates its unfortunate spot on the Oldehoofsterkerkhof parking lot. The tower was started in 1529 and was to be part of a grand cathedral planned for the site. But like so many Dutch cathedral projects, things went wrong and the tower started to lean severely when it was only 40m high. The tower is open 9.30 am to 4.30 pm from May to September (closed Monday) and admission costs f2.50/1.

The ornamental **Waag** dominates Waagplein, which is now surrounded by stores. It was the weigh house for butter and goods from 1598 to 1884.

On the north side of the old town in one of the parks which replaced the old fortifications, the **Fries Natuurmuseum** (☎ 212 90 58), Schoenmakersperk 2, does a good job of showing that there's far more alive in the canals and mud flats of Friesland than you'd expect. It's open 10 am to 5 pm (from 1 pm Sunday) and is closed Monday. Admission costs f6/4.

Places to Stay

De Kleine Wielen (☎ 0511-43 16 60, fax 43 25 84, De Groene Ster 14) is about 6km east of the city off the N355. A tent site for two people costs f36. Bus Nos 10, 13, 50, 51 and 62 all pass close by. Tell the driver you want to get off at De Skieppepoel, from where it's a five-minute walk south.

Hotel 't Anker (☎ 212 52 16, fax 212 82 93, Eewal 73) is in a fun and pretty part of town. The decent rooms cost f47/86 for a single/double without bath and f104/118 with bath.

Hotel de Pauw (☎ 212 36 51, fax 216 07 93, Stationsweg 10) is quiet, comfy and close to the station. The simple rooms cost f50/90 without bath and f63/110 with bath.

The **Stadhouderlijk Hofkelder** (☎ 216 21 80, fax 216 38 90, Hofplein 29) is a monument in itself. Once the residence of local royalty, it has lavish appointments.

The elegant rooms start at f175 and rapidly escalate from there.

Bilderberg Oranje Hotel (☎ 212 62 41, fax 212 14 41, Stationsweg 10) is charmless and modern on the outside, but the rooms are well appointed and the staff friendly. It's across from the station, has its own parking and costs from f203/260.

Places to Eat

There's a ubiquitous **Febo** (☎ 212 54 88, Ruiterskwartier 105) near the Wilhelminaplein ready to satisfy your urges for machine-bought chow until late.

Grand Café Lichtenstein (☎ 213 15 14, Weerd 18) has a large garden and is in a truly grand building. The menu is cafe standard, and it's open until after midnight most nights.

Het Leven (☎ 212 12 33, Druifstreek 57/A) is a classic eetcafe with a diverse menu of dishes from Holland and the rest of Europe. Most are under f26. It's open until 11 pm.

Spijs Lokaal (☎ 216 22 14, Eewal 54) has a kitchen visible from the street. The chefs are busy preparing modern European fare which blends tastes from all over. Most of the mains are under f30. It's open daily until 10 pm.

Tempo Doeloe (☎ 215 33 33, St Jacobsstraat 21) is a gem of a place run by a charming Dutchman who has worked all over the world. The evocative decor from Indonesia matches the food; *rijsttafels* start at f30 per person.

Entertainment

De Bagijn (☎ 212 77 38, Bagijnestraat 63) is a cool and funky place with good beer. It's open most days past midnight.

The Riddle (☎ 215 79 76, Kleine Kerkstraat 2) has tables out front and an excellent CD collection inside. The music leans toward funk and soul and it's lively until late.

De Plantier (☎ 213 91 18, Grote Hoogstraat 32) is one of several nightspots on this street. It's like a big house party, with a small bar up front, dancing in the middle room and folks chilling out in the back room with whatever mellows them out.

Theater Romein (☎ *215 57 83, Bagijne-straat 59*) is a performance venue built in 1846 with a distinctly Spanish look. It's the scene of all manner of musical and theatrical performances.

Stadsschouwburg Leeuwarden De Harmonie (☎ *233 02 33, Ruiterskwartier 4*) is a real mouthful of a name for a striking modern performance hall for classical music and big name visitors.

Tivoli (☎ *212 38 87, Nieuwestad 85*) unspools an interesting line-up of films.

Getting There & Around

Train Leeuwarden is at the end of the main train line from the south. It is also the hub for local services in Friesland. The large station has numerous services including a barber and a large newsstand. The lockers are by track No 8. Fares and schedules include:

destination	price (f)	duration (mins)	frequency (per hr)
Amsterdam	48	150	1
Groningen	15.25	50	2
Utrecht	42	120	1

Bus For once the buses are to the left as you exit the station.

Taxi Leeuwarden is part of the treintaxi scheme (☎ 213 25 25).

Bicycle The bicycle shop (☎ 213 98 00) is to the right as you exit the station. It is open 6 am to 12.30 am (from 7 am Sunday).

AROUND LEEUWARDEN

North of Leeuwarden there are several good routes for driving or riding. The N357, which connects Leeuwarden with the Ameland ferry port at Holwerd, 23km away, passes some of the oldest settled parts of Friesland.

At Ferwerd, 6km west of Holwerd, watch for a road south to **Hogebeintum**, which is 3km off the N357. You'll soon see the highest terp in Friesland with a lovely old church perched on top. There are some good displays explaining the ongoing archaeological digs. It's a peaceful place and as the wind

whips past you think of what must have been the cold and lonely lives of those who first toiled to build the place, one bucketful of mud at a time.

From Hogebeintum, it's 9km east to **Dokkum**, a pretty little canal town with a couple of well-placed windmills. Look for the small road, **Trekweg**, that follows the Dokkumer south-west for 12km to Buitenpost. This is one of the prettiest canal roads in Friesland.

SNEEK
☎ 0515 • pop 29,800

Sneek is the gateway to the myriad of water activities on the surrounding Frisian Lakes, the IJsselmeer and the many canals and rivers of the region. It is a tidy town with a distinctly nautical air and makes a good base if you are heading out over the waters. When you see *Snit* on signs, you're seeing Frisian for Sneek.

Information

The VVV (☎ 41 40 96, fax 42 37 03, **ⓔ** vvv sneek@ tref.nl), Marktstraat 18, is a nexus for all information on the region. It has long lists of boat rental and charter firms, sailing schools and more. It's open 9 am to 5 pm weekdays and until 2 pm Saturday.

The SNS Bank (☎ 41 27 96) Marktstraat 1, is near the VVV. There are ATMs throughout town. The post office (☎ 43 02 80), Martiniplein 15A, is open 9 am to 6 pm weekdays and until 1.30 pm Saturday.

The library (☎ 42 30 23), Wijde Noorderhorne 1, has Internet access and is open 1.30 to 7.30 pm weekdays and 10.30 to 1.30 on Saturday.

Things to See

The **Waterpoort** dates from 1613 and is the former gateway to the old port. Its twin towers are local landmarks. Across from the VVV, the **Stadhuis**, Marktstraat 15, is an excellent example of the breed. The **Fries Scheepvaart Museum** (☎ 41 40 57), Kleinzand 14, has pretty interesting exhibits on the local seafaring life. It's open 10 am to 5 pm (from noon Sunday) and costs f4/2 for adults/children.

Activities

Anything you can do on the water is big in Sneek. For a list of some local **boat rental** companies, of which there are many, see the Boating section of the Facts about the Netherlands chapter.

During the summer months, there are many opportunities for **boat cruises** on the local waters. These are run by numerous operators and the schedules change by whim, weather and mood. Most leave from the Oosterkade, at the end of Kleinzand. You can either wander over there to see what's up or inquire at the VVV.

There are several **sailing and windsurfing schools** where you can learn from scratch or add skills to those you already have. One of the largest is Zeilschool te Friese Meren (☎ 41 21 41, fax 43 54 36), Eeltjebaasweg 7, which has a range of courses. Web site: www.zfm.nl.

Places to Stay & Eat

De Domp 1 Camping (☎ 41 25 59, Domp 4) is a 20-minute walk through town. Follow the signs for the *zwembad* (public swimming pool). Sites cost f26 and there are some away from the vehicles for hikers.

NJHC-herberg Wigledam (☎ 41 21 32, fax 41 21 88, Oude Oppenhuizerweg 20) is a relaxed hostel with a nice garden. From the train station, take a treintaxi, or walk 30 minutes through town and then south-west via Oppenhuizerweg and Kamerling Onnestraat. Beds cost f27.

The VVV has lists of local rooms which cost from f35 to f45 per person.

De Wijnberg (☎ 41 24 21, fax 41 33 69, Marktstraat 23) is a comfortable place with a good restaurant. The rooms with TV and bath cost f85/130 for a single/double.

Landlubbers rub elbows with seamen at *Café De draai (☎ 42 28 66, Wijde Noorderhorne 13)*, a cheery place behind the library. It has a good beer selection and cheap specials for f15.

Getting There & Around

Since NoordNed took over running the local trains, the station has been stripped of all services, including lockers. The remaining employees will watch your bags, however, during office hours, 7 am to 7 pm. From the station, the centre is a five-minute walk along Stationstraat. Trains to/from Leeuwarden cost f7.50 (20 minutes, two per hour).

Buses leave from the area to the right of the station.

Sneek is part of the treintaxi scheme (☎ 41 50 00).

Given the dearth of life at the station, you have to rent your bike in town. Rijwielhandel Twa Tsjillen (☎ 41 38 78), Wijde Noorderhorne 8, rents a range of bikes from f10 per day.

HARLINGEN
☎ 0517 • pop 15,100

Of all the old Frisian ports, only Harlingen has kept its link to the sea. It's an important port and the base for ferries to Terschelling and Vlieland.

As ferry ports go, it's an attractive one, worth a stop even if you're not heading out to the islands. Much of the centre near the port is a preserved zone of 16th- and 18th-century buildings. Voorstraat is the main commercial street.

Information

The VVV (☎ 0900-919 19 99, fax 41 51 76, ✉ info@vvv-harlingen.nl), Voorstraat 34, is open 10 am to 4 pm weekdays and until 2 pm Saturday. The hours are extended until 6 pm weekdays and 5 pm Saturday from mid-April to September.

Several banks can be found on Voorstraat. The post office (☎ 41 99 21), Grote Bredeplaats 6, is 200m from the front of the ferry terminal and is open 9 am to 6 pm weekdays and 10 am to 1.30 pm Saturday.

Things to See

Harlingen is best enjoyed on foot. Stroll along the canals, especially **Noorderhaven**, with its many yachts, and **Zuiderhaven**. The **Gemeentemuseum Het Hannemahuis** (☎ 41 36 58), Voorstraat 56, is housed in a solid 18th-century building and has the municipal collections that include a lot of material on Harlingen's past as a whaling town. It's open 1.30 to 5 pm weekdays from

April to October and also on weekends in July and August. Admission is f2.50/1.50.

Places to Stay & Eat

De Zeehoeve Camping (☎ 41 34 65, fax 41 69 71, Westerzeedijk 45) is about a 1km walk south from the ferry terminal along the dike. It has a variety of sites and facilities, including cabins. Simple sites cost f27 for two people and a tent.

Pension Arends (☎/fax 41 50 88, Noorderhaven 63) has a fine location near the many moored yachts. Simple rooms cost f60/85 (single/double).

Nearby, the *Hotel Anna Casparii (☎ 41 20 65, fax 41 45 40, Noorderhaven 67–71)* is a bit more upmarket. The rooms have baths and TV and cost f80/100.

You might be inspired to sing *You Light Up My Life* at *Vuurtoren van Harlingen (☎ 41 59 11, fax 41 51 76; office: Voorstraat 34)* because the establishment's one room is located near the top of Harlingen's lighthouse. The suite comes with all manner of luxuries and mighty fine views. It costs f495 per night.

Restaurant Noorderpoort (☎ 41 50 43, Noorderhaven 17) has a casual menu of Dutch food with French touches. The dining room has views to the canal and the ferry port. Expect to pay at least f40 per person. The adjoining cafe has sandwiches and a good selection of beers and is open until at least midnight daily.

Getting There & Around

See the Frisian Islands section for details on the ferry service to the ports at Vlieland and Terschelling.

The ferry terminal is modern, with large waiting areas. Nearby there is a modern train station, Harlingen Haven. However, Noord-Ned runs only a few trains there, and those don't operate every day. All the rest of the services from Leeuwarden terminate at Harlingen station, which is 1km from the centre. In another NoordNed cost-cutting move, this once proud station building has been closed. While the one train to/from Leeuwarden each hour (f8.50, 24 minutes) stops here, there are infrequent bus connections to the centre

which means you have to either walk or take a treintaxi (☎ 42 00 00). It's a deplorable situation when the Harlingen Haven station is so well suited for both the ferries and the centre of town.

You don't need a bike in Harlingen (although one would be handy for getting from the train station to the ferry port), and if you are planning to use one on the islands, you can wait and rent one there.

FRANEKER
☎ 0517 • pop 14,600

You'll have to forgive any resident of Franeker, 6km east of Harlingen, if they cry out, 'We could have been Groningen!'. Indeed they could have been if Napoleon hadn't closed the university in 1810. What's left is a once prosperous town that was the centre of northern culture. It's spent the last two centuries dozing and licking its intellectual wounds. Of course, this means that it's quite well preserved and makes for a fine hour of strolling.

The highlight of the town is the **Eise Eisinga Planetarium** (☎ 39 30 70), Eise Eisingastraat 3, which is the world's oldest working planetarium. The namesake owner was a carpenter who clearly could have been somebody in the astronomical world. Beginning in 1774, he built the planetarium himself to show how the heavens worked to a populace who thought that the wrong alignment of the stars could mean death. It's an amazing accomplishment by one person. The planetarium is open 10 am to 5 pm Tuesday to Saturday (also 1.30 to 5 pm Sunday and Monday from May to September) and admission costs f5/4.

The Harlingen-Leeuwarden train stops in Franeker 500m from the centre.

COASTAL TOWNS

Friesland has a string of coastal towns that made their living from the sea until the Zuiderzee was dammed and became the freshwater IJsselmeer. After a few decades in limbo the islanders are aggressively courting tourists to their old streets and many charms. Each town has a permanent population of under 1000 that swells in summer.

The route south from Makkum to Hinde-loopen passes many traditional Frisian dairy farms. Moo.

Makkum
☎ 0515 • pop 7600

The town's inherent prettiness is offset by the busy shipping channel near the docks. The VVV (☎ 23 14 22, fax 23 29 20), Pruik-makershoek 2, is conveniently located in the same 1698 building as the local **museum**, where you can see examples of the local ceramics. Both are open 10 am to 4 pm weekdays (also weekends from May to September).

Watching the various boats pass on the waterfront is the most popular local activity. If you decide to stay, **Hotel De Waag** (☎ 23 14 47, fax 23 27 37, Markt 13) has pleasant single/double rooms with bath for f75/126. It also has a good bistro. There are several other restaurants and cafes nearby.

Bus No 96 connects Makkum with Harlingen train station (40 minutes) and the Bolsward train station (20 minutes) every one or two hours.

Workum
☎ 0515 • pop 4300

This was a working port until the 1800s when the shoreline moved 3km west. The town is strung like a string bean along one long street (that changes names a few times). Interest is centred on **Merk**, the very cute main square. All manner of shops, banks and sights are within a five-minute walk from here.

The VVV (☎ 54 13 00, fax 54 36 05), Noard 5, is open 10 am to 5 pm Tuesday to Saturday (and 1 to 5 pm Sunday and Monday from May to September). Staff can find private rooms and advise on nearby boat rentals.

The **Warkums Erfskip** (☎ 54 31 55), Merk 4, is a museum of local life located in the 17th-century Waag. It has the same hours as the VVV, but is closed entirely from December to March. Admission is f4/2.50. Nearby is the massive **St Gertrudeskerk** which dates from 1515. The **Jopie Huisman Museum** (☎ 54 31 31),

Noard 6, is a tasteful place devoted to the contemporary work of the namesake Frisian artist. It has the same hours as the other museum and charges f5/2.50.

Workum's train station is 3km east of Merk on the line from Leeuwarden to Sta-voren via Sneek. There is an hourly service.

Hindeloopen
☎ 0514 • pop 985

Huddled up against the water, Hindeloopen has been set apart from Friesland for centuries. Until recently, the local women still wore characteristic green and red costumes that were similar to the also characteristic hand-carved furniture.

With its narrow streets, tiny canals, little bridges and long waterfront, Hindeloopen is very appealing. In winter it is one of the key towns on the route of the Elfstedentocht (Eleven Cities Race) and has a skating museum devoted to the race (see the boxed text 'A Day at the Races' for details).

Information The VVV (☎ 52 25 50), Nieuwstad 26, is open 1 to 5 pm from April to October (closed Monday) and is open from 10 am in July and August. Staff can help with accommodation and other services. For most services, you'll have to go 4km north to Workum. Unless noted below, most everything in Hindeloopen is closed from November to March.

Things to See Hindeloppen is definitely a place to just hang out and take in the scene. However, the **Het Eerste Friese Schaatsmu-seum** (☎ 52 16 83), Kleine Weide 1–3, is a fascinating diversion with its many displays on the Elfstedentocht.

Note the section on two-time winner Evert Van Benthem (1985 and 1986) who had both a cheese and wine named after him. This skating museum is open 10 am to 5 pm (Sunday from 1.30 pm) and costs f3.50/1.75.

The other museum in town, **Hidde Nij-land Stichting** (☎ 52 14 20), Dijkweg 1, is devoted to the unusual local folk art and costumes. It's open 10 am to 5 pm (Sunday from 1.30 pm) and costs f3.50/1.75.

Places to Stay & Eat *Camping Hinde-loopen (☎ 52 14 52, fax 52 32 21, Wester-dijk 9)* has tent sites for f26.

SkipsMaritiem (☎ 52 45 50, fax 52 45 51, Oosterstrand 22) is a bit of an empire on the marina. Besides servicing boats, it rents out simple rooms for two without bath for f55 per night. Fully equipped rooms with a kitchenette go for f130. Bikes are also available for rent.

De Stadsboerderij (☎ 52 12 78, fax 52 30 16, Nieuwe Weide 9) is away from the main crowds and charges from f100 for comfort-able rooms. There is also a casual restaurant.

There are more than 20 places to eat that range from cheap fried-fish wagons to fine restaurants.

Getting There & Away The train stop is a pleasant 2.5km walk from town. There is an hourly service to Sneek (f6.50, 15 min-utes) and Leeuwarden (f13.25, 40 minutes).

FRISIAN ISLANDS
The four Frisian Islands, which with Texel to the south form the Wadden Island chain, have always been little more than raised banks of sand and mud, which have nonetheless played a vital role in protecting the Netherlands' north coast. In the 1800s the government began aggressively plant-ing vegetation to help stabilise them. The resulting pine forests, while attractive, are definitely not native.

The islands' primary appeal is to city-bound Dutch people looking to get away to the beach. They have all been developed for tourism and the number of pensions, hotels and rooms and cottages for rent is enormous. Even so, in summer the islands are very crowded so don't just show up and expect to find a room. Populations rou-tinely multiply by a factor of 10 on warm weekends.

Despite the development, all have large open spaces where you can get close to the sea grasses. Any of the four islands would make an interesting day trip and there are copious supplies of rental bicycles near the ferry ports. Paths suitable for hiking and biking circle each of the islands and if you

A Day at the Races

Skating and the Dutch culture are interwoven and no event better symbolises this than the Elfstedentocht (Eleven Cities Race). Begun of-ficially in 1909, although it had been held for hundreds of years before that, the race is 200km long, starts and finishes in Leeuwar-den and passes through 11 Frisian towns: Sneek, IJlst, Sloten, Stavoren, Hindeloopen, Workum, Bolsward, Harlingen, Franeker and Dokkum. The record time for completing the race is six hours, 47 minutes, set in 1985.

Marathon that it is, what really makes the race a truly special event is that it can only be held in years when it is cold enough for all the canals to freeze, and this has only happened 15 times since 1909, the last time in 1997. So how do you schedule such an event? You don't.

Instead, there is a huge Elfstedentocht committee which waits for the weather to get real cold. When it looks like the canals will be properly frozen, a 48-hour notice is given for the race. At this point all work effectively ends throughout the province as armies of volun-teers make all the preparations for the race and the thousands of competitors get ready.

On the third day, the race begins at 5.30 am. The next few hours are a holiday for the rest of the Netherlands as well, as the population gathers around TVs watching the live coverage.

There is a good Elfstedentocht museum in Hindeloopen that covers all the winners of this amazing event.

get away from the built-up areas, you will be rewarded with long sandy beaches on the seaward sides. Remember, however, that this is the Netherlands, so don't expect the weather to be tropical.

This said, if you only have time for one Dutch island, it should probably be Texel in Noord Holland (see that chapter for details). Otherwise, read on to see which of the Frisian islands might suit you. And if you want some windblown solitude, try going in the off-season. Note too that of the four, Vlieland and Schiermonnikoog are the wildest and both ban nonresidents' cars.

FRISIAN ISLANDS

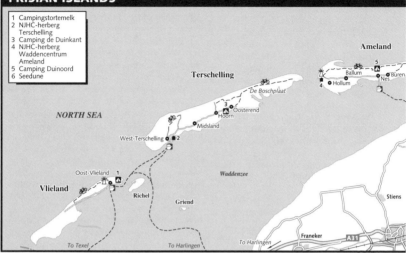

1 Campingstortemelk
2 NJHC-herberg
  Terschelling
3 Camping de Duinkant
4 NJHC-herberg
  Waddencentrum
  Ameland
5 Camping Duinoord
6 Seedune

Given the myriad of accommodation choices on all four islands – and the demand – your best bet is to either request a copy of the accommodation guide from the relevant VVV far in advance, or place yourself in the hands of the tourist office's highly efficient reservation services. The VVV offices on the islands are also the places to go for information on the many, many activities such as windsurfing, bird-watching, fishing etc. The offices also sell excellent hiking maps for the islands.

All of the islands have banks, groceries, stores and other services in their main towns. But don't expect any extras like Internet access. As for the ferries, if you're bringing a car – really, don't – be sure to reserve a spot in advance.

Terschelling
☎ 0562 • pop 4700

The island has a long and rich nautical past and the islanders once earned a living repairing ships and boats. Many more ships were wrecked on the uncertain waters around the island.

This is the largest, most visited and most commercial Frisian island. The main town

is West Terschelling, where the ferry from Harlingen docks at the busy port. You can find just about any service and amusement you'd want here.

The smaller towns of Hoorn and Oosterend are east of West Terschelling and much less commercial, but much closer to the natural parts of the island. There is one main road, from the ferry dock east to Oosterend.

Information The VVV (☎ 44 30 00, fax 44 28 75, @ vvvter@euronet.nl), Willem Barentszkade 19A, is open 9.30 am to 5.30 pm Monday to Saturday.

Things to See The Terschelling Museum 't Behouden Huys (☎ 44 23 89), Commandeurstraat 30–32, is a good museum covering the island's maritime past. It's open 10 am to 5 pm weekdays from April to October and Saturdays from June to September. It costs f6/4 for adults/children.

Elsewhere, **De Boschplaat** at the eastern end of the island is a huge car-free natural reserve. It is the only European Natural Monument in the Netherlands, designated as such by the EU.

Places to Stay & Eat

Among the many places to camp, *Camping de Duinkant* (☎ 44 89 17), at the end of the road in Oosterend, is the most remote. It charges f17 for two people and a tent.

The *NJHC-herberg Terschelling* (☎ 44 23 38, fax 44 33 12, Burg. van Heusdenweg 39) is a simple and sandy hostel with room for 148. Reserve well in advance in summer when beds cost f30.

Hotel-Restaurant Lutine (☎ 44 21 94, fax 44 34 46, Boomstraat 1) is a simple place in West Terschelling with single/double rooms from f45/90. The cafe is casual and typical of the scores that dot the island's towns.

Getting There & Around

Ferries leave from Harlingen for Terschelling and are operated by Rederij Doeksen (☎ 44 21 41). The large car ferries take two hours in either direction and depart once a day in the dead of winter and up to six times or more in the summer. Call ☎ 0517-49 15 00 for the latest schedule information. Return fares with taxes cost f42.25/21.15 for adults/children. Bikes cost f18.15. Cars are best left ashore.

There is also a passenger-only hydrofoil that operates several times a day from mid-April to September. The journey takes 50 minutes and costs the same as the ferries plus a f8 surcharge each way.

On the island there are frequent buses running the length of the main road.

Vlieland

☎ 0562 • pop 1100

Historically the most isolated of the islands, Vlieland had one of its two towns washed away by a storm in the 18th century. Even today it is one of the least-visited islands. Nonresidents are not allowed to bring cars, which means that, away from the sole town of Oost-Vlieland, it's a wild and natural place.

Information The VVV (☎ 45 11 11, fax 45 13 61, @ info@vlieland.net), Havenweg 10, is open 9 am to 5 pm weekdays as well as for one hour after each ferry arrival on weekends.

Things to See & Do There's not much in the way of man-made attractions on Vlieland and that's the point: nature is the attraction. There are a few roads around Oost Vlieland and that is it. The rest of the island is waiting to be explored by bike or foot. The VVV organises **nature hikes** and **bird-watching walks**. There is also a small boat that runs from the southern tip to Texel in summer. It is linked to town by a tractor pulling a cart. Ask at the VVV about this.

Places to Stay *Campingstortemelk* (☎ 45 12 25, fax 45 12 59, @ info@stortemelk.nl, Kampweg 1) is an enormous place set back from the beach west of town. Two people and a tent can camp for f26 per night. It has numerous services.

Pension Hotelletje de Veerman (☎ 45 13 78, Dorpsstraat 173) is a homy place with simple rooms for f50 per person.

Getting There & Around Many of the details for the ferries from Harlingen to Vlieland are the same as for Terschelling. The cost is a bit lower – return fares with

FRIESLAND

Frisian Island Facts

Island	Size	Length of beach
Terschelling		
	11,000 hectares	30km
Vlieland	4022 hectares	12km
Ameland	8500 hectares	27km
Schiermonnikoog		
	7200 hectares	18km
Texel	16,000 hectares	30km

taxes are f38/19.90 for adults/children – and so is the journey time at 105 minutes. The fast ferry goes via Terschelling and takes 80 minutes. The schedule is also much less frequent; sometime there is only one ferry a day even in high season, so it's worth checking in advance.

There is a little bus that wanders the few paved roads of Oost Vlieland.

Ameland
☎ 0519 • pop 3400
Second only to Terschelling in popularity, Ameland has two distinct population centres: Nes, which is near the ferry dock, and Hollum, which is at the west end.

Of the villages, Nes is the prettiest as it has been carefully preserved and dates back to the 18th century when it was a whaling port. The streets are lined with tidy little brick houses.

Information The VVV (☎ 54 65 46, fax 54 29 32, @ vvv@ameland.nl), Rixt van Doniastraat, is open 9 am to 12.30 pm and 1.30 to 6 pm weekdays and 10 am to 3 pm Saturday. If nothing else, buy its excellent map (f5).

Things to See & Do All four towns on Ameland are interesting for a brief stroll. The Ballum **cemetery** has some eerie tombstones for dead sailors. Hollum has a famous red and white **lighthouse**. The eastern end of the island is the place to head to lose sight of humans.

The VVV organises all manner of tours, hikes and even boats out to view some sea lions offshore.

Places to Stay & Eat *Camping Duinoord* (☎ 54 20 70, fax 54 21 46, Jan van Eijckweg 4) is 2km from Nes, by the beach. It has tent sites for two from f25.

NJHC-herberg Waddencentrum Ameland (☎ 55 53 53, fax 55 53 55, Oranjeweg 59) is right near the base of the lighthouse in Hollum. It is a simple place with beds in mostly four-person rooms costing f30.

Hotel Restaurant de Jong (☎ 54 20 16, fax 54 20 24, Reeweg 29) is a comfortable lodge in Nes. It has decent rooms from f100/150 for singles/doubles and a cafe.

All four villages have numerous cafes. In Hollum, *Herberg De Zwaan* (☎ 55 40 02, Zwaneplein 6) is popular with locals in the off-season. Its building dates from 1772.

Getting There & Around Wagenborg (☎ 54 61 11) operates ferries between Nes and the large ferry port at Holwerd on the mainland. The latter has a large parking area, for people who forgo the hassle of taking cars to the island. The ferries run about every two hours through the year and take 45 minutes. At busy times the ferries run as often as every hour; call to confirm. The return fare is f17.25/9.20. Bikes cost f8.10. All the prices are slightly higher in summer.

To reach the Holwerd ferry terminal from Leeuwarden, take bus No 60 or 66 (40 minutes, hourly). From Groningen, take bus No 34 (80 minutes, four or five times daily).

Taxis and a small network of public buses that serve all four towns meet the ferries. Nes is a 20-minute walk from the ferry port or a two-minute bus ride.

Schiermonnikoog
☎ 0519 • pop 1000
The smallest of the Frisian Islands, Schiermonnikoog's name means 'grey monk island', a reference to the holy men who once lived here in the 15th century. All traces of these folk are gone and much of the island is wild. The Dutch government made Schiermonnikoog a national park in 1989 so the wilderness should remain untamed.

The sole town, Schiermonnikoog, is quiet, even when crowded. Nonresidents are not allowed to bring cars onto the island.

FRIESLAND

Information The VVV (☎ 53 12 33, fax 53 13 25) is in the middle of town and is open 9 am to 1 pm and 2 to 5.30 pm weekdays. It closes at 4.30 pm Saturday.

Things to See & Do Enjoy nature. That's about it, but if you're looking for a natural experience then what more do you want? Get a map from the VVV and start exploring.

The national park has a **visitors centre** (☎ 53 16 41) in an old power station in town. It highlights the natural features of the island and is open 10.30 am to 5.30 pm (closed Sunday) from April to October and 1.30 to 5.30 pm Saturday only the rest of the year.

The island is the most popular destination for mud-walkers from the mainland. See the boxed text 'Pounding Mud' in the Groningen & Drenthe chapter for details.

Places to Stay & Eat *Seedune (☎ 53 13 98, Seeduneweg 1)* is just north of town and has room for 800 tents. A site costs f24.

Pension Lulu (☎ 53 13 06, ✆ *pension .lulu@planet.nl, Langestreek 70)* has simple rooms for f55 per person.

There are many *cafes* lining the few streets of downtown Schiermonnikoog.

Getting There & Away Wagenborg (☎ 54 61 11) runs ferries between Schiermonnikoog and the port of Lauwersoog in Groningen province at the border with Friesland. Three to five ferries make the 45-minute voyage daily depending on the season. Return fares are f18.45/10.40 for adults/children and bicycles cost f8.10. Prices are slightly higher from April to September.

Bus No 63 makes the one-hour run between Lauwersoog and Groningen five times daily. Bus No 50 makes the 45-minute run between Lauwersoog and Leeuwarden five times daily.

A bus meets all ferries which arrive at the island's port for the 3km run into the town of Schiermonnikoog.

Groningen & Drenthe

The two north-eastern provinces of Groningen and Drenthe are primarily agricultural, with an emphasis on growing pigs. One sniff of the air in the countryside will confirm this. However, amid all the future bacon is a real gem; the town of Groningen itself is one of the most delightful in the Netherlands. It has a rich history, good museums and a vibrant nightlife.

The city of Groningen is reason enough to venture to this part of the Netherlands. A few day trips and the chance to engage in the unusual sport of *wadlopen* (mudwalking) are the only other attractions.

Groningen

Like Utrecht, Groningen is another small province named after its primary city. Beyond the city itself, the province has few notable attributes. Much of the land is given over to farming, while the north coast is mostly a muddy mire that sort of segues between land and sea in an indecisive manner. The scenery is best near the German border where the restored old fortified town of Bourtange is worth a trip.

Getting There & Away
Groningen, the city, is well served by frequent trains. For the other sights in this section plan on car, bus or bike.

GRONINGEN CITY
☎ 050 ● pop 173,000
At any given time, up to 20,000 of Groningen's population are students at the university or institutions such as the medical school. This ensures that there's plenty to do at night, you can enjoy the latest trends and prices are within the budget of scholars.

Groningen was founded around 1000. It was an early member of the Hanseatic League and from 1251 it had a regional monopoly on the grain trade that brought it prosperity for six centuries. The university

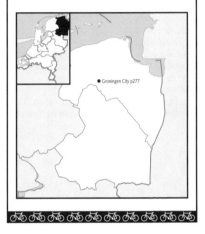

HIGHLIGHTS

- Cafe-hopping in Groningen
- Sailing through Groningen's Noordelijk Scheepvaartmuseum
- Walking the walls at Bourtange
- Contemplating Drenthe's *hunebedden*

● Groningen City p277

opened in 1614 and has had an excellent reputation in Europe for studies such as theology ever since.

Orientation
The old centre is entirely ringed by canals and you can walk from one end to the other in 15 minutes. The train station is just across from the controversial Groninger Museum, a less than 10-minute walk from Grote Markt, the main town square. Virulent anti-car policies dating from the 1970s mean that the centre is delightfully free of traffic, although drivers will find plenty of parking around the periphery.

Information
Tourist Offices The local VVV office in Groningen (☎ 0900-202 30 50, fax 050-311

GRONINGEN & DRENTHE

NORTH SEA

Schiermonnikoog

GERMANY

Ameland

Uithuizen

Bierum

Hogebeintum

GRONINGEN

N46

Dokkum

N360

Bedum

Ten Boer

Garmerwolde

Eemskanaal

N355

Groningen

Margrietkanaal

Leeuwarden

A7

Winschoterdiep

E22

FRIESLAND

To Emden &
Oldenburg

Midlaren

Annen

Bourtange

0   10   20km
0   5   10mi

Assen

E232

N34

Borger

A28

Westerbork

Odoorn   Klijndijk

A32

Orvelte

N381

Emmen

DRENTHE

A6

Giethoorn

A37

E233

To Oldenburg

E232   A28

To Zwolle

GERMANY

02 58, ℮ info@vvvgroningen.nl), Gedempte Kattendiep 6, offers advice on a wide range of topics and sells tickets, tours and more. Its own map (f2.50) is excellent.

Money At the time of research, the GWK exchange was outside the train station in a trailer, although this will change when the ongoing renovations are complete. It's open 8 am to 7 pm daily. ATMs can be found throughout town.

Post There is a post office (☎ 313 63 75), at Munnekeholm 1, which is open 10 am to 6 pm weekdays and until 1.30 pm Saturday. Another branch (☎ 318 96 42) at Gedempte Zuiderdiep 19 is open the same hours.

Travel Agencies NBBS (☎ 312 63 33), at Brugstraat 15, is popular with students.

Bookshops Scholtens Wristers (☎ 313 97 88), Guldenstraat 20, is huge and has a strong selection of academic titles.

Libraries The main city library (☎ 368 36 83), Oude Boteringestraat 18, has loads of computers for Internet access.

It is open 10 am to 6 pm weekdays (from 1 pm Monday and until 9 pm Thursday) and 11 am to 4 pm on Saturday and 1 to 4 pm on Sunday.

Laundry Handy Wash (☎ 318 75 87), Schuitendiep 58, is open 7.30 am to 8 pm daily.

Medical Services The Academisch Ziekenhuis Groningen (☎ 361 61 61), Hanzeplein 1, is a huge teaching hospital. Try not to end up as an exhibit in its in-house anatomy museum.

Dangers & Annoyances Groningen is a very safe place, although the red-light district on Hoekstraat can get fairly raucous.

Groninger Museum

Arriving by train it's impossible to miss the Groninger Museum, which is built on islands in the middle of the canal in front of the station. If its disharmonious parts make it look like it was designed by a committee, that's because it was. Chief architect Alessandro Mendini invited three 'guest architects' to each design a major component of the building. The results are invigorating, stupid, inspired, aggressive or any number of other adjectives, depending on who you ask.

The polychromatic tile work surrounding the entrance and continuing on the inside is the work of Mendini, who first used the pattern on a Swatch he designed in 1991. The tall bronze-coloured tower is where the museum has its storage, and at the moment it's very full as you'll learn in a minute.

As originally designed, the museum was meant to combine a permanent exhibit on Groningen's rich history with an area for modern applied arts and other regional artworks. Much of the permanent collection was placed in galleries below the water line, while the areas above were for temporary exhibitions. Locals who wondered about the wisdom of having so much space below water level were told essentially to 'shut up' by the architects who proclaimed the museum would stay dry 'for 200 years'. In 1998 the waters rose far over the 200-year mark and all of the lower museum was

flooded. Some precious works were rushed out on the heads of swimming curators. The architects were nowhere to be found.

Pending an expensive reconstruction of the lower levels, the permanent collection remains in the bronze tower. The rest of the cavernous space is used for temporary exhibitions which, given the museum's hefty budget, can be quite good. It's open 10 am to 5 pm (closed Monday) and admission is f12/6 for adults/children. The tables outside the cafe are definitely great places for people-watching.

Noordelijk Scheepvaartmuseum & Niemeyer Tabaksmuseum

Dedicated to the history of the local maritime industry, the Noordelijk Scheepvaartmuseum (Northern Shipping Museum; ☎ 312 22 02), Brugstraat 24–26, is well funded, well organised and well worth an hour or two. The museum is laid out over several floors of a complex of buildings that was once a 16th-century distillery. Just getting through the labyrinth of 18 rooms is an adventure in itself and guarantees an excellent work-out.

Highlights of the museum include: an intricately carved church in a bottle (room 3) that shows just how much time sailors had to kill on long voyages; exhibits explaining how peat was harvested and transported (room 6) and cool models demonstrating just how the many local shipyards operated through the centuries (room 8).

After room 8, there are three rooms devoted to what's called the Niemeyer Tabaksmuseum. It's dedicated to how Dutch people have smoked tobacco through the ages. The expressions on the faces of the dummies in the first room will make you wonder what's in their pipes.

The courtyard of the buildings has some nice old boats and is open to Schuitemakersstraat as well as Brugstraat. The museum is open 10 am to 5 pm (from noon Sunday, closed Monday) and admission is f6/3.

Canals

On the western side of town, the canalside streets of **Hoge Der A** and **Lage Der A** are

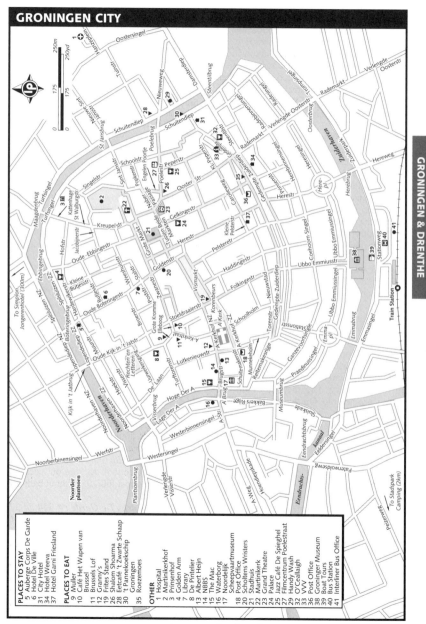

GRONINGEN CITY

PLACES TO STAY
5 Auberge Corps De Garde
6 Hotel De Ville
31 City Hotel
34 Hotel Weeva
37 Hotel Garni Friesland

PLACES TO EAT
10 Muller
13 Café Het Wapen van
   Brussel
11 Brussel's Lof
12 Granny's
19 Frites Stand
26 Shalom Shoarma
28 Eetcafé 't Zwarte Schaap
30 't Pannekoekchip
   Groningen
35 Roezemoes

OTHER
1 Hospital
2 Martinikerkhof
3 Prinsenhof
4 Golden Arm
7 Library
8 De Pintelier
9 NBBS
14 Albert Heijn
15 The Mac
16 Waterborg
17 Noordelijk
18 Scheepvaartmuseum
20 Post Office
21 Scholtens Wristers
22 Stadhuis
23 Martinikerk
24 Grand Theatre
   Palace
25 Jazz Café De Spieghel
27 Filmcentrum Poelestraat
29 Handy Wash
32 O'Ceallaigh
33 VVV
36 Post Office
38 Groninger Museum
39 Boat Tours
40 Bus Station
41 Interliner Bus Office

lined with old buildings once used as breweries. Water was drawn from the canals and the yeast and resulting alcohol were counted on to take care of any 'impurities'. The facades of the houses display a great variety that's best appreciated at night when they are starkly lit. A barrel hanging on the building at the corner of Visserstraat is a reminder of the neighbourhood's past.

Churches & Squares

The **Grote Markt** is big, cafe-ringed and fairly charmless because of its size. It also suffered bomb damage during WWII and the rebuilding was less than sensitive. The **Stadhuis** dates from 1810.

At the northern corner of the Grote Markt, the **Martinikerk** (☎ 311 12 77) was built in the 16th century. Its tower, the **Martinitoren**, is 96m tall and is considered to have one of the most finely balanced profiles in the country. A climb to the top yields the expected stellar views. In the choir of the church, there are some fine 16th-century paintings portraying the life of Jesus. It is open noon to 5 pm Tuesday to Saturday from June to September. The rest of the year it's open only on Saturday. Admission is f1 and a climb up the tower costs f2.50.

To the north of Martinikerk is **Martinikerkhof**, a large open area on the site of an old cemetery. The facades of the old houses are notable. On the northern side is the **Prinsenhof**, a former 16th-century bishop's residence.

Just south-west of the Grote Markt, **Vismarkt** is a more intimate and attractive square.

Organised Tours

Canal tours (☎ 312 83 79) leave from in front of the train station. The trips take 75 minutes and don't operate if the canals freeze (duh!). Otherwise there's a 1.45 pm departure daily through the year with additional departures by demand. The fare is f13/8.

The VVV operates guided **city walks** every Monday in July and August. The cost is f7.50 and the tours – which are in English and Dutch – last 90 minutes.

Special Events

Noorderslag January – a series of concerts by up and coming (they hope) bands

Good Friday – a huge flower market held on Vismarkt

Bommen Berend August 28 – is a city celebration of the day the invading troops of the Bishop of Munster were repulsed

Student Cabaret Festival October – draws performers from around Europe

November 11 – locally grown sugar beets are distributed to children who carve them into lanterns, not unlike pumpkins at Halloween

Places to Stay

Camping *Stadspark Camping* (☎ 525 16 24, *Campinglaan 4*) has a shop, restaurant, laundry, playground and more. It charges f21 for two people and a tent and is open mid-March to mid-October. From the train station, take bus No 4 (direction: Hoogkerk) about 3km west to the Stadspark stop. From there follow the signs for about a 10-minute walk.

Hostels *Simplon Jongerenhotel* (☎ 313 52 21, fax 313 30 27, Boterdiep 73–2) is 300m north of Noorderhaven. Beds in the large dorms cost f21.50. After 11 pm there is a club with live bands and dancing. Take bus Nos 1 or 11 from the station to the Boteringestraat stop.

Hotels *Hotel Garni Friesland* (☎/fax 312 13 07, Kleine Pelsterstraat) is bare bones but it has a good location on a street with several cafes and the prices are unbeatable: f45/80 single/double.

Hotel Weeva (☎ 312 99 19, fax 312 79 04, Gedempte Zuiderdiep 8) is a decent and unaffected place with parking out back – a rarity. Rooms cost f60/105 without bath and f98/145 with.

Auberge Corps De Garde (☎ 314 54 37, fax 313 63 20, 74, Oude Boteringestraat 74) is simple yet comfortable and the rooms have TVs. Without bath, tariffs are f105/154 and with bath, f165/194.

City Hotel (☎ 588 65 65, fax 311 51 00, Gedempte Kattendiep 25) is architecturally distinctive, except for the fact that the architect thought that the oddball-sized windows were cool. But it scores everywhere else; there's a rooftop deck with good views and free coffee and tea on every floor around the clock. Rooms have baths and TVs and cost from fl73/190.

The stylish and luxurious *Hotel De Ville* (☎ *318 12 22, fax 318 17 77,* ❷ *hotel@ devill.nl, Oude Boteringestraat 43)* harbours a quiet back garden and a good bistro off the lobby. Prices start from fl195/210.

Places to Eat
Gedempte Zuiderdiep is lined with cheap fast-food places and cafes of all stripes. Unless otherwise noted, the following places are open daily.

Restaurants *Shalom Shoarma* (☎ *313 51 55, Poelestraat 3)* is a small place in a great location with tables inside and out. The falafel special platter is fl7.50.

Brussels Lof (☎ *312 76 03, A-Kerkstraat 24)* has fish and vegetarian creations on a creative dinner menu. Polenta with asparagus costs f32.50 and a three-course special is f59.

Muller (☎ *318 32 08, Grote Kromme Elleboog 13)* has a window in the kitchen facing the street from where you can watch the chefs at work. Only the freshest local ingredients are used in the changing menus that start at f77. Directly across the street, it has a smart brown cafe where you can order many of the same items off the menu in a much more casual atmosphere.

Cafes *Roezemoes* (☎ *314 03 82, Gedempte Zuiderdiep 15)* has been around some time. So long in fact that this typical brown cafe still has bullet holes from the 1672 invasion attempt. Sandwiches start at f6 and pasta dishes are f15. It's open until well after midnight and on many nights there's live blues.

Café Het Wapen van Brussel (☎ *312 23 85, Grote Kromme Elleboog 4)* is a classic brown cafe run by a delightful gentleman from Belgium who really knows his beer. He regularly returns to his homeland for kegs of unusual brews. The dinner specials for f20 are simple but tasty. It's open from 4 pm until midnight.

Eetcafé 't Zwarte Schaap (☎ *311 06 91, Schuitendiep 52)* is one of a string of casual eetcafes on this side of the canal. Look for black sheep over the door to find this one where dinners average under f30.

Other *Frites* is an especially good stand selling just that most days from the western end of Vismarkt.

Granny's (☎ *318 91 17, A-Kerkhof NZ 43)* is a bakery/cafe devoted to all things apple. It has good pies, juice and coffee and is open during shopping hours.

't Pannekoekschip Groningen (☎ *312 00 45, Schuitendiep opposite No 45)* is in an old boat. It markets itself directly at kids and has a vast array of the doughy delights from f7. Its open noon to 9 pm.

The *Albert Heijn Supermarket* (☎ *313 18 00, Brugstraat 14)* is across the street from a cheap fruit and vegetable market.

Entertainment
At night Poelestraat and the adjoining streets team with energy from people cruising, scoping, loving, drinking etc.

To find out what's going on around town, check out some of the posters that appear everywhere. The free and widely available *UitLoper* is a simple listing of each week's music and films.

Bars *O'Ceallaigh* (☎ *314 76 94, Gedempte Kattendiep 13)* is a spot-on Irish bar that's as authentic as they come. No faux chain bar this. There's frequent live music and it's open until at least 2 am.

De Pintelier (☎ *318 51 00, Kleine Kromme Elleboog 9)* buzzes with gossip from midday until late. Unchanged since 1920, it has a long wooden bar and thicket of tables.

Jazz Café De Spieghel (☎ *312 63 00, Peperstraat 11)* is a lively brown cafe with regular live jazz.

Clubs Clubs open and close all the time in Groningen. Try the following and ask around for the latest hot spots.

Palace (☎ *313 62 62, Gelkingestraat 1)* is a huge club just off Grote Markt on a street with numerous coffeeshops and cafes. It's a venue for all types of music, including house, techno, rock, blues and more. The cover varies with the act or the theme of the evening.

The Golden Arm *(☎ 313 16 76, Hardewikerstraat 7)* is a gay club and bar in a huge old storehouse. It's open after 11.30 pm Wednesday to Sunday.

The Mac *(☎ 312 71 88, Hoge Der A 3)* is located next to the canal and has a bar area open most nights. The music varies each night.

Other *Grand Theatre (☎ 314 46 44, Grote Markt 35)* has a constantly changing bill of live theatre.

Filmcentrum Poelestraat *(☎ 312 04 33, Poelestraat 30)* shows a good mix of off-beat films.

Shopping

Folkingestraat has a funky and fun collection of off-beat shops.

Regular markets are held most days on either Grote Markt, Vismarkt or both. On Tuesday there is an organic food market on Vismarkt.

Waterborg (☎ 312 07 02), Lage der A2, has a huge range of outdoor, sporting and travel gear.

Getting There & Away

Train The train station, built in 1896, is a sight in itself. A multi-year restoration due to conclude in 2001 will have returned the station to its original glories. There is stained glass everywhere; look upwards in the main entrance hall as the ceiling alone is stunning.

Pounding Mud

You have to give the Dutch credit. Many would see the north coast of Groningen as an ill-defined muddy mess. But for the locals, it is a land of golden – er, brown – opportunity. When the tide is out they enjoy a good few hours of *wadlopen* (mud-walking).

The mud stretches all the way to the Frisian Islands offshore and treks of up to 12km are possible, although the 7km walk to Schiermonnikoog is the most popular. Once on the island, you can watch the brown waters of the Waddenzee return with the rising tide and then take a ferry back to the mainland.

Those who enjoy wadlopen say that it is strenuous and in its own way a bit exhilarating, given that if you lag too much the rising tide washes you away. They also say that there is a certain intoxicating quality to being out in an absolutely flat place where the wet, brown mud reflects the often grey skies above and frames of reference evaporate.

The important point for anyone considering a stint on the mud to remember is not to head out without a skilled guide. It's all too easy to get lost on the mud flats and without a good knowledge of the tides, you can end up under water, permanently.

The centre for wadlopen is the tiny village of Pieterburen, 22km north of Groningen. There are several groups of trained guides based here. They include:

Wadloopcentrum (☎ 0595-52 83 00) Hoofdstraat 105
Dijkstra's Wadlooptochten (☎ 0595-52 83 45) Hoofdstraat 118

The usual cost of a trip is f15, with additional costs such as the ferry ride back and possible pick-up in Groningen extra. It's essential to book in advance, as times vary with the tides. You will be told what clothes to bring depending on the time of year.

If you are taking public transport to Pieterburen, you can either take bus No 168 all the way from Groningen (one hour, four daily), or catch a train to Warffum (25 minutes, hourly) and then connect with one of several buses to Pieterburen. The best thing to do is work out in advance which routing is best by calling ☎ 0900-92 92 (f0.75 per minute).

Lockers are in the station, but they keep moving around during the construction. Other services are available; you just have to look. Some fares and schedules include:

destination	price (f)	duration (mins)	frequency (per hr)
Amsterdam	51	140	1
Leeuwarden	15.25	50	2
Rotterdam	56	160	1
Utrecht	45	120	1

There are additional frequencies on all of these routes if you change trains, usually at Amersfoort.

A rather feeble service runs three times per day to Leer, across the border in Germany (50 minutes). From here you can catch trains to Bremen and beyond.

Bus The bus station is in front of the train station. An Interliner Bus Office sells tickets and gives useful information on regional buses. It's just to the right of the train station as you exit. Hours are 7.15 am to 6.30 pm weekdays and 8 am to 5 pm Saturday.

Car & Motorcycle Car rental firms in Groningen include the following, which will often deliver the car from their inconvenient suburban locations:

Avis (☎ 527 15 03) Van Ketwich Verschuurin 106
Europcar (☎ 309 16 86) Machlaan 10A
Hertz (☎ 525 45 36) Laan Van De Vrijheid 280A

Getting Around
Public Transport You won't really need public transport to get around Groningen unless you're going to the hostel or the camping ground. The buses leave from in front of the train station and bus Nos 1 to 6 pass near Grote Markt.

Car & Motorcycle As mentioned before, cars are discouraged from entering the centre of Groningen, but there are many parking areas nearby.

Taxi Groningen is part of the treintaxi scheme (☎ 311 46 28).

Bicycle The bicycle shop (☎ 312 41 74) is to the left of the train station entrance as you exit. It is open 5.30 am to 1 am (from 7 am Sunday). For information on a 40km bicycle route, the Paterwoldsemeer Route, which begins and ends at Groningen, see the special section 'Cycling in the Netherlands'.

NORTH-EAST GRONINGEN
Churches
There are several towns as you go north-east from Groningen towards the coast with ancient churches worth seeing. Reaching these can be difficult on the bus, as once you get off one, another won't be along for some time. But they make for good stops on bike or by car. In each case, the towns are tiny and finding the church is never a problem: look for the tower. You are unlikely to be able to get inside any of these churches because their hours – if any – are very short.

Garmerwolde is 6km from Groningen on the N360. Its church sits serenely among a grove of mature trees. Dating from the 12th century, it has a solid and detached brick tower. The cemetery nearby is also old and, given that there's seldom anyone around, the entire place can be quite moody.

Ten Boer is a further 5km north-east from Garmerwolde. The church is small and simple, set on a little knoll among modern houses. Built in the 13th century, it was once the chapel for a nunnery that stood nearby.

Bedum has a 12th-century church with a leaning tower. The town is 10km north of Groningen, off the N46.

Out by the coast, tiny **Bierum** solved the problem of its 12th-century church's leaning tower by building a huge flying buttress in the 1800s. To reach the town, travel 24km from Groningen along the N360, then turn north for 6km on the N33 and watch for the signs.

Uithuizen
☎ 0595 • pop 8750
This small farm town would otherwise not be worth a visit except for **Menkemaborg** (☎ 43 19 70), the moated estate just east of town on Menkemaweg 2. Originally a fortified castle, it received its present gentrified appearance in

the 17th century. Since then it has barely been altered, making it one of the most authentic manor houses in the Netherlands.

The formal gardens date from the 17th century. Inside, the furnishings have been collected from other houses and, while not original to Menkemaborg, give a fair indication of what things would have looked like in their prime. It's open 10 am to 5 pm daily from mid-April to September. The rest of the year it closes at 4 pm and all day Monday. It also takes a holiday for the whole of January. Admission is f7.50/5.

Across from Menkemaborg, the **Museum 1939–1945 Cold War Historical Center** (☎ 43 41 00), Dingeweg 1, manages to cover a fair amount of history, not just with its name but with its eclectic collection of military gear. There are planes, tanks, weapons and just about any other type of military item once financed by hard-pressed taxpayers the world over. It's open 9 am to 6 pm daily, April to October, and costs f10/5.

Hourly trains run between Uithuizen and Groningen (f9.50, 34 minutes). There's no bike rental, so bring one from Groningen. The train station (it's really a stop) is 10 minutes' walk west of Menkemaborg.

BOURTANGE
☎ 0599 • pop 1200

Huddled near the German border, Bourtange was built in the late 1500s and represented the pinnacle of the arms race at the time. Behind its multiple walls and moats it could withstand months of siege by an invading army. Hopefully the attackers would weary of the fight before the residents.

It's common to find evidence of the fortification building that was all the rage 500 years ago throughout the Netherlands. The canals of Middelburg, for instance, follow the angled lines of the old walls. But in most towns the walls are long gone, replaced by parks and development. Only by looking at a map is it possible to see evidence of the old defences. Bourtange was no different, by the early 1960s many of the walls had been breached or levelled and the moats were largely filled in. A regional road ran through the centre.

This changed in 1964 when the regional government decided on a multi-year plan to restore the town's fortifications and the town itself to its exact appearance in 1742, when the fortifications around the defensive citadel had reached their maximum size.

It took three decades, during which time roads were moved, buildings demolished, others reconstructed and archaeologists generally had a field day. The results today are impressive. The star-shaped rings of walls and canals have been completely rebuilt. The village itself has been re-created in its 18th-century incarnation. It's an overused cliche, but a visit to Bourtange is truly a step into the past, a time when rogue armies wandered the lands and villagers hid behind defences designed to keep them at bay.

The region around Bourtange is off the beaten path and consists of pretty countryside and tree-shaded canals that is ideal for exploring by bike.

Information
The VVV (☎ 35 46 00) and visitor centre are outside the main entrance to the old town at William Lodewijkstraat 33. This is a good place for a brief visit as there are good displays showing what was entailed in the reconstruction and restoration. Aerial photographs show the remarkable changes between 1965 and the late 1990s. There are also toilets and the staff can help find accommodation. The English-language booklet (f3) is a good guide to the town and its buildings. The centre is open 10 am to 5 pm weekdays and from 12.30 pm weekends.

The Town
From the parking area and visitor centre, you pass through two gates and across three drawbridges over the moats, before you reach the old town proper. The entire course is over 500m long and was designed to be as circuitous as possible so that if you were an unwelcome visitor the townsfolk could take plenty of pot-shots at you. Although once designed to frustrate invaders, the course now delights all but the laziest of visitors.

Inside the walls at the core, Bourtange's old town consists of a few dozen restored buildings along little streets radiating off a tree-shaded central square, the **Marktplein**. Among the old buildings are several that were used by the militia, including **officers' quarters** and large **stone barracks**. A **synagogue** built in 1842 has a plaque on the side listing the 42 local people taken away to their deaths by the Nazis, an amazing number given the town's small size.

The town is surprisingly low-key in its efforts to milk the tourist trade. Perhaps there's a minimum of gift shops because real people continue to live within the walls year-round.

The best way to explore Bourtange is along the old walls, which afford views over the town and countryside. You can imagine what it was like when a lookout would spot some motley crew of invaders heading towards the town. On one corner there is a little hut built high over the inner moat. Closer inspection reveals that it not only provided relief for the militia, but ensured that the waters were as unpalatable as possible to unwanted visitors.

Places to Stay & Eat

There's no place to stay inside the walls, but just outside, *Albertha Hof (☎ 35 47 37, Vlagtwedderstraat 57)* is one of several small family-run places that has rooms and fields for camping. Camp sites will cost you f19, a double room with bath and breakfast is f75.

A little more upmarket than Albertha Hof, the *Hotel Restaurant De Staakenborgh (☎/fax 35 42 16, Vlagtwedderstraat 33)* has rooms without bath for f45/90 (single/double). The restaurant serves the usual Dutch standards in heaping portions.

In the old town, there are two places to eat on the Marktplein, *'t Oal Kroegie (☎ 35 45 80)* is open from 10 am to 10 pm and has snacks, sandwiches and pancakes. It has a few good beers on tap as well. *'s Lands Huys (☎ 35 45 14)* offers a longer menu with many lunch and dinner specials for under f25. Both places have tables outside in fine weather.

Getting There & Away

Reaching Bourtange takes a little effort. It is 50km south-east of Groningen and not any closer to other notable population centres.

By public transport from Groningen, take the train east to Winschoten (f10.50, 33 minutes, two per hour). Then take bus No 14 south to Vlagtwedde (25 minutes, at least one per hour) and transfer to bus No 272 for Bourtange (10 minutes, at least one per hour). With waiting time and transfers, count on the trip taking about two hours.

By car, you'll need a good road map as there are several minor roads involved in the journey.

If touring by bike, combine Bourtange with visits over a few days to the *hunebedden* in Drenthe, some 30km to the west. See the following Drenthe section for details.

Drenthe

The agricultural province of Drenthe is the least densely populated in the Netherlands. And spread as thinly as people are the sights and attractions of interest to visitors. It is a quiet place; Vincent van Gogh wrote of Drenthe in 1833: 'Here is peace'. Of course, he later went mad.

People were enjoying the quiet as early as 3000 BC, when prehistoric tribes lived amid the bogs and peat fields. In fact it's these early residents who are responsible for the most interesting aspect of Drenthe today, the hunebedden. These large grey stones were used as burial chambers and many survive today in a line of towns between Emmen and Groningen. There are also some interesting open-air museums that highlight Drenthe's history of hard work as well as one that covers a much darker chapter in Dutch history.

There's certainly no other reason to spend the night in Drenthe. Groningen and Zwolle are much more attractive places to use as bases for exploration.

While travelling through the province, you'll notice many traditional farmhouses with thatched roofs. These are huge affairs as they accommodate not just the family but also the barnyard animals.

GRONINGEN & DRENTHE

The farms themselves are large and prosperous, as evidenced by the huge tracts of land under cultivation around the town of Norg.

EMMEN
☎ 0591 • pop 93,500

A modern city of industry, Emmen is a useful transportation centre for Drenthe and the hunebedden. The VVV (☎ 061 30 00, fax 64 41 06), Marktplein 9, is open 10 am to 5 pm weekdays and 10 am to 1 pm (until 4 pm June to August) on Saturday. It can help with finding accommodation if you are stuck here. There's also a good range of bike maps for exploring the hunebedden.

The town's **zoo**, the Noorder Dierenpark (☎ 61 88 00), Hoofdstraat 18, is a short walk from the train station. It is noted for its ape collection and African animals displayed in a 'natural' setting – although few areas of the savannas ever had weather like this. To the zoo's credit, a recent exhibit explores the life of that constant companion, the sewer rat. It's open 9 am to 5 pm daily and costs f26/23.

If you end up with a little time to kill in Emmen, do so at ***Brasserie (☎ 61 66 75, Hoofdstraat 53)*** between the station and Marktplein. It's large and lively and has a fine selection of beers and cheap sandwiches.

Emmen is at the end of the train line from Zwolle (f21.25, 51 minutes, two per hour). The station has lockers and is 600m from the VVV office. Buses leave from in front of the station. The station bicycle shop (☎ 61 37 31) is open 7 am to 9 pm daily (from 8 am weekends).

Around Emmen

Much of Drenthe was first developed by the Dutch as a source of peat; the rich fuel extends several metres under the boggy surface. However, harvesting the gunk before mechanical aids was back-breaking and those who made their livelihoods in this manner lived little better than serfs well into the 20th century. Many of the old peat fields are now either farms or lakes, you can always tell when the latter was once a peat field by its angular shape.

Veenpark (☎ 32 44 44), Berkenrode 4 in the village of Barger-Compascuum 20km south-east of Emmen, recalls the tough lives of the peat harvesters and shows how the industry operated. The open-air museum has a re-created village and there are demonstrations of how the peat was dug from the ground. It's open 10 am to 5 pm daily from April to October and costs f17.75/16.75. Bus No 45 runs from Emmen to the park (24 minutes, hourly weekdays, five on Saturday, two on Sunday).

HUNEBEDDEN

Borger, a little town 17km north-west of Emmen, is the centre for the prehistoric hunebedden. Here and along the N34 road are most of the 53 known examples in the Netherlands of these groupings of sombre grey stones.

Little is known about the builders of the hunebedden, except that they took burying their dead very seriously. The arrangements of the huge stones – some weighing 20 metric tonnes – were each used to bury many people, along with their everyday items and tools.

The **Nationaal Hunebedden Infocentrum** (☎ 0599-52 60 92), Kamstraat 4 in Borger, is the logical place to start a tour. Here there are many displays relating to the stones as well as quite a few of the excavated artefacts. There are also good maps for finding the many nearby sites. It's open 10 am to 5 pm (from 1 pm weekends) and is closed all January. Admission is f5.50/4.

Away from Broger, the villages of **Klijndijk**, **Odoorn**, **Annen** and **Midlaren**, running north from Emmen to Groningen along the N34, are among those villages that have hunebedden.

Getting There & Around

Bus No 59 operates between Emmen and Groningen and stops at Borger and the other four hunebedden towns. It runs every hour and you may want to limit your visit to Borger and one other town, as getting on and off a bus to view what is essentially a pile of big grey rocks may get tiresome after a bit.

Watch for the large brown signs showing a pile of rocks while driving or biking, which are the best ways to quickly view a smattering of hunebedden.

ASSEN
☎ 0592 • pop 54,000

This farming centre is not worth the stop except as a means of getting to the sights nearby. The VVV (☎ 31 43 24, fax 31 73 06), Marktstraat 8, is open 9 am to 6 pm weekdays (from noon Monday) and until 5 pm Saturday. It has the usual maps and information.

The town's one attraction, the **Drents Museum** (☎ 31 27 41), Brink 1, has hunebedden artefacts and various artworks and furnishings from Drenthe's history. It is housed in a collection of 19th-century buildings. Opening hours are 11 am to 5 pm (closed Monday) and admission costs f10/5.

The VVV and museum are 500m from the station by way of Stationsstraat. The station itself is on the main train line between Zwolle (f21.25, 41 minutes, three per hour) and Groningen (f8.50, 17 minutes, three per hour).

Buses depart from the area to the left as you exit the station. Assen is part of the treintaxi scheme (☎ 37 31 11). The bicycle shop (☎ 31 04 24) is open 7 am to 8 pm daily (from 7.30 am Sunday).

Near Assen
A foundation governs the tiny village of **Orvelte**, 17km south of Assen. Its goal is to preserve the look and feel of a 19th-century Drenthe farming community. To this end, no cars are permitted and owners can't alter the old buildings in uncharacteristic ways.

The residents mainly engage in traditional activities. There's the baker, butcher, candle-stick… you get the idea. During the summer, there are lovely vegetable gardens growing near every house.

As people live in Orvelte, it's not an attraction as such, but you're welcome to visit and wander around. On any given day, some locals might be demonstrating traditional skills or crafts. For more information, call ☎ 0593-32 23 35. Orvelte is on the No 22 bus route from Assen.

About 10km north of the nice little farming community of Westerbork is a site that has given that name a place in the annals of the Holocaust. **Kamp Westerbork** was first built by the Dutch government on isolated land in 1939 to house German Jews fleeing the Nazis. When the Germans invaded in May 1940, they found the camp ideal for their horrible deeds. At first Camp Westerbork remained a relatively benign place, but beginning in 1942 it was used as a transit point for those being sent east to the death camps. Over 104,000 Dutch Jews and over 250 Roma were shipped through Westerbork and a smaller camp, Vaught, close to Den Bosch. The vast majority never returned.

Today the camp is a memorial to those killed and a museum of the Holocaust. Most of the old wooden buildings are gone, but the exhibits and monuments are sobering and moving. The camp is open 10 am to 5 pm daily (weekends from 1 pm) and is closed January. Admission is f7.50/3.50. Bus No 22 from Assen stops in Hooghalen, 2km west of the camp (12 minutes, every 30 minutes weekdays, much less often weekends). Better yet, get a treintaxi from Assen.

GRONINGEN & DRENTHE

Overijssel & Gelderland

The two provinces of Overijssel and Gelderland don't have a blockbuster attraction like an Amsterdam or a Maastricht – although De Hoge Veluwe National Park comes close. On the other hand, the two have lots of small pleasures that when taken together add up to a compelling draw.

Deventer is a jewel of a town from the time of the Hanseatic League. De Weerribben is a tortured but beautiful area that almost feels alien. Nijmegen has plenty of fun cafes and an energetic student population. And, of course, there's possibly the finest Van Gogh collection in the world at the Kröller-Müller Museum.

Together the two provinces are an interesting place to explore and are a definite change of pace from the Randstad.

Overijssel

The name Overijssel means 'beyond the IJssel' and when you see which river forms much of the province's western border, you'll see where the name comes from. That the name is not more descriptive is possibly because the province is hilly in the east near Germany and flat as a board and soggy in the west, along what was once its coast, but which is now jammed up against Noordoostpolder.

Deventer makes a good base for exploration of Overijssel, although you may want to try out Giethoorn in the north as well (just beware of July and August crowds).

DEVENTER
☎ 0570 • pop 68,800
This old Hanseatic League town is something of an undiscovered gem. Within its compact circle of canals, there's not a single gift shop. Nowhere to buy wooden shoes? Whatever will you do?

Deventer was a busy port as far back as AD 800. It maintained its prosperous trading

Deventer p288

De Hoge Veluwe p299

Nijmegen p294

ties for centuries, evidence of which you'll see in its many richly detailed old buildings.

Today Deventer has largely escaped the mass tourism that has inundated other parts of the Randstad. But it is every bit as interesting as cities to the west and walking its ancient and beautifully preserved streets is a step back in time.

It's five minutes by foot from the train station to the heart of the old town. The focus is the elongated square, the Brink, and the streets running north-west from there.

Information
Tourist Offices The VVV (☎ 61 31 00, fax 64 33 38), Keizerstraat 22, shares a large space with the ANWB. There are vast amounts of guides and maps for sale as well

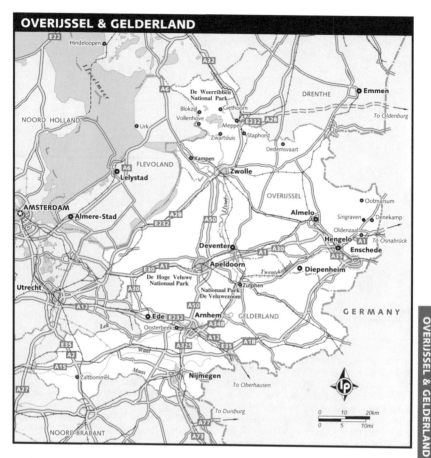

OVERIJSSEL & GELDERLAND

as all manner of travel gear. It's open 9.30 am to 6 pm weekdays and until 5 pm Saturday.

Money There are ATMs around the Brink.

Post The post office (☎ 64 16 42), Nieuwstraat 100, is open 9 am to 6 pm weekdays.

Travel Agencies NBBS (☎ 64 58 58), Nieuwstraat 3, is a popular travel agency.

Libraries The library (☎ 67 57 00), Brink 70, is open 10 am to 6 pm weekdays (until 8 pm Thursday) and 10 am to 2 pm Saturday.

Things to See

The **Brink** is the main square, and thus also the most commercial part of Deventer You'll find most sights from here, but don't miss the **Waag**, the 1528 weigh house in the middle of the square, before leaving. Look for the cauldron on the north side of the Waag. Legend has it (and it's fairly well documented) that this cauldron was used to boil alive an assistant money clerk who was accused of substituting cheap metals for precious ones in the local money supply. Ouch.

The **Grotekerk** (☎ 61 25 48), on Grote Kerkhof, is the city's main church. It stands

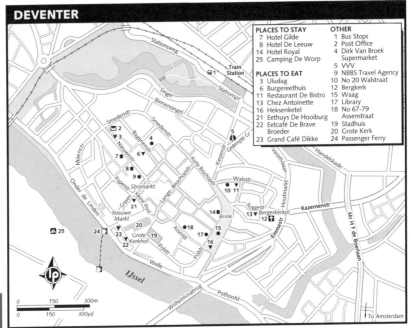

DEVENTER

PLACES TO STAY	OTHER
7 Hotel Gilde	1 Bus Stops
8 Hotel De Leeuw	2 Post Office
14 Hotel Royal	4 Dirk Van Broek
25 Camping De Worp	Supermarket
	5 VVV
PLACES TO EAT	9 NBBS Travel Agency
3 Uludag	10 No 20 Walstraat
6 Burgereethuis	12 Bergkerk
11 Restaurant De Bistro	15 Waag
13 Chez Antoinette	17 Library
16 Heksenketel	18 No 67-79
21 Eethuys De Hooiburg	Assenstraat
22 Eetcafé De Brave	19 Stadhuis
Broeder	20 Grote Kerk
23 Grand Café Dikke	24 Passenger Ferry

on the site of various churches that burned down innumerable times before the present Gothic number was built between 1450 and 1530. It's huge and draughty, but there are some fine murals inside. It's open 10 am to 5 pm (closed Sunday). Tacked onto the south end is the little 14th-century **Mariakerk**.

The other important church, **Bergkerk**, has a commanding position on a small hill at the east end of town. It's mostly from the 15th century with a few bits at the base of the two towers from the 13th century. It's now used for special exhibitions, so if something is on, you can go inside.

The best activity in Deventer is to simply stroll the streets admiring the buildings. The town is so well preserved that there really aren't any uninteresting streets to walk. A couple of highlights include **Walstraat**, where No 20 shows a woman climbing down the wall while hanging by a sheet. On **Assenstraat** there are wall-carvings and window decorations created over several centuries. No 67–79 is contemporary and has an antipollution message, the focus of which shows the French blowing up the *Rainbow Warrior*. Other good areas include the streets around Bergkerk, as this was the heart of Deventer during the Hanseatic time, and **Papenstraat**.

Cycling

The banks of the IJssel River are an especially good and scenic place for biking. There are large natural areas and many old picturesque farms.

Riding 36km north to Zwolle, another attractive Hanseatic town, is a fine option. You can either make the trip one-way and stay there, or return by train. A good 32km round trip follows the river north to Olst, where you take a ferry across and then return along the other side to the Deventer ferry. You can basically do the same thing going south from Deventer to Zutphen, for a trip of 47km.

OVERIJSSEL & GELDERLAND

Abstract art is on the nose in Scheveningen

The Kurhaus Hotel is a landmark on the beach at Scheveningen

The Groninger Museum's disharmonious design continues to cause controversy in Groningen

LEANNE LOGAN

LIZ BARRY

LEANNE LOGAN

RICK GERHARTER

LEANNE LOGAN

CHRIS MELLOR

LEANNE LOGAN

The Dutch love to 'say it with flowers'.

Places to Stay

Camping De Worp (☎ 61 36 01, Worp 12) is right across the IJssel from the centre of town and about two minutes north of the passenger ferry. It's open May to September and sites cost f24.

Hotel Royal (☎ 61 18 80, fax 64 48 80, Brink 94) is looking a bit tired but the prices and location are tops. The basic rooms have TVs and bath and cost f75/100 (single/double).

Hotel De Leeuw (☎ 61 02 90, fax 61 31 83, Nieuwstraat 25) is a recent addition and it has well-designed, yet simple, rooms from f90/95.

Hotel Gilde (☎ 64 18 46, fax 64 18 19, ⊜ gilde@hsij.nl, Nieuwstraat 41) is in a restored 17th-century convent. It's the best place in Deventer and the rooms cost f145/165.

Places to Eat & Drink

Uludag (☎ 61 82 65, Nieuwstraat 96) is a spotless Turkish fast-food place with pita sandwiches for f8. It's open noon to 1 am.

Eetcafé De Brave Broeder (☎ 64 58 94, Grote Kerkhof 25/26) has tasty lunch specials that locals love. The name refers to the massive wall painting of monks risking their superior's wrath by enjoying a tasty mug of ale.

Heksenketel (☎ 61 34 12, Brink 62) is inspired by the cauldron on the nearby Waag. However, here the idea is to boil witches. It has its own stuffed witch mounted on the ceiling. There's a long list of beers and some decent snacks.

Grand Café Dikke (☎ 61 44 44, Nieuwe Markt) is a big place with books on the walls and large windows for watching the world go by. The menu is inviting; two-course dinners cost f30. The bar has good beer and is open until at least 1 pm.

Burgereethuis (☎ 61 91 98, Bagijnenstraat 9) is a mellow cafe with a cool courtyard and occasional live music.

Chez Antoinette (☎ 61 66 30, Roggestraat 10–12) has popular Portuguese dinners that average f30, but you can go all out and spend f59 for six courses. It's closed Monday.

Eethuys De Hooiburg (☎ 61 82 03, Stromarkt 29/30) is dark and candlelit. The menu of steaks and seafood is popular, so reserve. With drinks, dinner will run to about f40 each.

Restaurant De Bistro (☎ 61 95 08, Golstraat 6) is an excellent restaurant set in a refurbished 16th-century horse barn. The interior brims with eclectic antiques and the menu brims with gourmet preparations of fresh fish. Expect to pay at least f55 each with wine.

Dirk Van Den Broek Supermarket (☎ 61 42 48, Broederenplein 5) is about five minutes from the station.

Shopping

The local speciality is Deventer Koek, a spicy gingerbread made with honey. It is widely available and, for once with a 'local speciality', it is made by local people for local people who actually enjoy it.

Getting There & Around

Train Deventer sits at the junction of two important train lines and service is good in all directions, making the town a good hub for exploring. Services at the train station are not great. However, there are lockers in the diminutive main concourse. Some fares and schedules are:

destination	price (f)	duration (mins)	frequency (per hr)
Amsterdam	27	75	1
Apeldoorn	5.50	12	2
Arnhem	13.25	36	2
Enschede	17.25	43	2
Nijmegen	17.25	51	2
Zwolle	9.50	24	2

Bus The bus area is located to the right as you leave the station.

Car & Motorcycle There is parking around the town's periphery. But the best place to park is the free lot on the other side of the IJssel. You take the passenger ferry across.

Taxi Deventer is part of the treintaxi scheme (☎ 62 23 23).

OVERIJSSEL & GELDERLAND

The Hanseatic League

Although primarily composed of northern German cities such as Lübeck and Hamburg, the Hanseatic League also included several Dutch towns. The powerful trading community was organised in the mid-13th century and its member towns quickly grew rich off the importing and exporting of goods that included grain, ore, honey, textiles, timbers and flax. The league was not a government as such, but it did defend its ships from attack and it entered into monopolistic trading agreements with other groups, such as the Swedes. That it achieved its powerful trading position through bribery, boycotts and other methods shouldn't sound too unusual to business students today. The Hanseatic League members did work hard to prevent war among their partners for the simple reason that conflict was bad for business.

Seven Dutch cities along the IJssel River were prosperous members of the league: Hasselt, Zwolle, Kampen, Hattem, Deventer, Zutphen and Doesburg. It's ironic that the Hanseatic League's demise is mostly attributable to the Dutch. The traders of Amsterdam recognised a good thing and during the 15th century essentially beat the league at its own game, out-muscling it in market after market.

In recent years, the seven Dutch towns have banded together to form what could be called a Hanseatic League of tourism. All publish walking-tour brochures highlighting their (usually beautiful) surviving buildings from the era. There is even a scheme where some restaurants are serving 'Hanseatic Menus'. Gotta love those eels!

Bicycle The bicycle shop (☎ 61 38 32) in the train station is open 6 am to midnight (from 7.30 am weekends).

Boat A free passenger ferry connects Deventer with the parking area and camping ground on the west bank of the IJssel. The voyage takes less than five minutes and the ferry operates most of the day and night. The pier on the town side is near Vispoort.

ZWOLLE
☎ 038 • pop 102,300

Zwolle gained wealth as the main trading port for the Hanseatic League cities of the IJssel and those in Germany. It's a compact town that can occupy an afternoon or a night.

Information

The VVV (☎ 0900-112 23 75, fax 422 26 79), Grote Kerkplein 14, is open 9 am to 5.30 pm weekdays and until 4 pm Saturday. The GWK exchange in the station is open 8 am to 8 pm (from 10 pm Sunday). The post office (☎ 421 78 21), Nieuwe Markt 1/A, is open 9 am to 6 pm weekdays and until 2 pm Saturday.

Things to See & Do

The **Stedelijk Museum Zwolle** (☎ 421 46 50), Melkmarkt 41, has a fine collection of items from the city's history, including a fair amount of Hanseatic material. It's open 10 am to 5 pm (from 1 pm Sunday, closed Monday) and costs f7.50/5.

Standing on the Oude Vismarkt, you have a good view of the other two main sights. The **Grotekerk** is grand but was much grander before the usual series of disasters knocked down the tower etc. Much of what's left is from the 15th century. Next door, the **Stahuis** has a typically Dutch old part (15th century) and a typically oddball new part. Somebody thought the two styles would fit together.

The best way to appreciate the canals, which follow the line of the old defensive walls, is on a **boat tour** (☎ 444 54 28). The boats depart from near the Luttekestenbrug Monday to Saturday from mid-June to September. The 2 pm boat always sails and there are also other sailings if demand warrants. Tickets cost f7.50/4.

Places to Stay & Eat

City Hotel (*☎ 421 81 82, fax 422 08 29, Rode Torenplein 10–11*) is well located and has good rooms from f110/140 (single/double).

The ***Bilderberg Grand Hotel Wientjes*** (*☎ 425 42 54, fax 425 42 60, Stationsweg 7*) is a truly grand place with rooms from f157/260.

Eethuis De Klok (☎ 423 02 67) is at the corner of Steenstraat and Nieuwestraat. It is a superb place with a delightful atmosphere and a wide-ranging menu of items from f5 to f20.

Grand Cru Café Public (☎ 422 66 00, Blijmarkt 23) is across from the museum and is very popular with locals. It has nice tables outside and a good menu of items under f20. It's open until 1 am but closed Monday.

Getting There & Around

Zwolle is a transfer point for trains and has very good connections. The lockers are below the tracks. Some fares and schedules are:

destination	price (f)	duration (mins)	frequency (per hr)
Deventer	9.50	24	2
Groningen	29	60	2
Leeuwarden	25	60	2

Buses leave from the right as you exit the station. Zwolle is part of the treintaxi scheme (☎ 460 04 66).

The bicycle shop (☎ 421 45 98) is open 5.30 am to midnight (from 7.30 am Sunday).

KAMPEN
☎ 038 • pop 32,100
Another Hanseatic city just 15km west of Zwolle, Kampen is a perfect afternoon trip from Zwolle.

Information

The VVV (☎ 331 35 00, 332 89 00), Oudestraat 151, is open 9.30 am to 5.30 pm weekdays and until 4 pm Saturday. Staff can help organise a private room for about f40 per person if you decide to stay the night. Otherwise, be sure to get its walking-tour booklet (f1), which points out a myriad sights.

Things to See

The best **view** of Kampen comes from the far bank of the IJssel, where the train station is located. Note the many old boats tied up along the waterfront.

Most of the major sights are along Oudestraat. The **Nieuwe Toren** is immediately obvious as it's the 17th-century tower with the incredible lean. They might want to remove some of the thicket of bells at the top.

At the south end of Oudestraat, **Bovenkerk** is a serene 14th-century church on a large square. The lack of cheesy cafes and other geegaws is testament to the fact that, like Deventer, Kampen has yet to be overrun by tourists. Two lovely 15th-century **city gates** survive along the park on Kampen's west side.

Places to Stay & Eat

Camping Seveningen (☎ 331 48 91, Frieseweg 7) is on a pretty spot on the water. It's open April to October and charges f22 per site. From the station walk north-west along the river for 20 minutes.

Hotel Van Dijk (☎ 331 49 25, fax 331 65 08, IJsselkade 30–31) has a delightful owner and rooms from f112/133 (single/double).

There are numerous *cafes* along Oudestraat.

Getting There & Around

Trains make the 11-minute run between Kampen and Zwolle (f5.50) every 30 minutes. This is excellent biking country. The bicycle shop is open 7 am to 11 pm daily.

NORTHERN OVERIJSSEL

Before the Noordoostpolder was created in the 1940s, this part of Overijssel was on the Zuiderzee. Today the many former coastal villages are landlocked, but retain their charm and maintain their links to the water through the spiderweb of canals that crisscross this marshy area. It's a difficult place to get around, without a bike and energetic legs or a car, as the buses are infrequent and often involve inconvenient connections. But it's worth the effort to explore as you'll take in great scenery and feel a bit detached from the rest of the Netherlands.

Nationaal Park De Weerribben

A bizarre landscape of watery striations, the National Park De Weerribben (☎ 0561-47

72 72) covers 3500 hectares and preserves a marshy land that more than anything is a monument to human toil. This entire area was worked by peat and reed harvesters; jobs that are among the hardest imaginable. The long water-filled lines across the soggy landscape are the result of peat removal. The workers would start at one end and dig their way along to the other end. It was muddy, cold, backbreaking work. The stripes occurred because, as one line of peat was dug, it was laid on the adjoining land to dry.

Generations of peat harvesters lived out here with almost no outside contact. Even now, their descendants live on some of the isolated farms that dot the countryside.

Reed harvesting was no easier. It again left the workers exposed to the elements while engaging in very hard work cutting and bundling the long reeds. Even today some of the families out here survive by cutting reeds.

De Weerribben is also an amazing natural landscape and is one of the most important migratory bird stops in Europe. Riding along one of the isolated bike paths or rowing along one of the channels is an otherworldly experience.

The park **visitors centre** is in Ossenzijl, an isolated village on the northern edge of the park. It has a full range of information on the park and its natural and manmade features, and can also advise on boat and canoe rental. It's open 10 am to 5 pm Tuesday to Friday and from noon weekends.

To reach Ossenzijl, take bus No 81 from Steenwijk, a stop on the train line from Leeuwarden to Zwolle. The bus takes 25 minutes and runs every two hours on weekdays and just a few times on weekends. You can also rent bikes at the bicycle shop (☎ 0521-51 39 91), which is open 7 am to 8 pm daily. Ossenzijl is about 18km from Steenwijk.

Giethoorn
☎ 0521 • pop 3500

Cute as a button, Giethoorn has a special place in the hearts of most Dutch people. It was the setting for a popular postwar film called *Fanfare*, which followed the amusing lives of the local folk. Although actually fairly funny, the film also holds a fair amount of truth. Giethoorn is absolutely surrounded by water. In fact, where the typical Dutch town is built on land crossed by a few canals, Giethoorn feels like water crossed by a few bits of land. Farmers once moved their cows from plot to plot in rowboats filled with hay.

Now Giethoorn has been discovered in a big way and it can get crowded in July and August. But at other times it's well worth a visit, when the scores of little bridges among the buildings take on a charm of their own. At any time there are countless chances to go for a boat ride, although joining a cow will be tough these days.

Information The VVV (☎ 36 12 48, fax 36 22 81, ✉ vvv.giethoorn@wxs.nl), Beulakerweg 114A, is on the main road and is open 9 am to 6 pm from mid-May to mid-September (until 5 pm Sunday). The rest of the year it is open 9 am to 5 pm weekdays. This is a good place to get your accommodation options sorted as there are scores of camping grounds, rooms and cabins for rent. The town itself, five minutes up the road from the VVV, has banks and other services.

Places to Stay *Camping Brederwiede (☎ 36 15 05, Binnenpad 1)* is typical of the scores of camping grounds. It is 10 minutes from the main bus stop and has sites from f25.

Huize Beulaekewyck (☎ 06-22 82 36 33, Beulakerweg 128) has splendid views of a nature preserve. It's one of literally hundreds of options and charges f40 per person.

Getting There & Away Bus No 70 passes through Giethoorn on its route between Steenwijk (18 minutes) and Zwolle (one hour). Service is hourly on weekdays and greatly reduced on weekends.

Coastal Towns
The following former coastal villages are worth a car or bike tour, but don't even bother with the bus, as it could take days.

Blokzijl looks like a tiny Amsterdam with the familiar gabled architecture. Its port, an important Hanseatic League stop, now overlooks a polder. In 20 minutes you'll have covered every street.

Vollenhove sits on a small knoll. Sint Nicolaaskerk dates from the 15th century and is a little Gothic charmer.

Zwartsluis has a tiny Jewish cemetery with a heartbreaking memorial to the entire town's Jewish population who were taken away during the war. The town has a nice little waterfront on a canal.

EASTERN OVERIJSSEL

The gently rolling hills of the Twenthe region are filled with holiday retreats for city-bound Dutch ready to trade their concrete high-rise for a few trees come July. For travellers, there's not a whole lot to see or do. The land is pleasant and the people delightful as always, but nothing worth a trip in and of itself.

Enschede

☎ 053 • pop 146,300

This industrial town was in the headlines in 2000 after a horrific explosion at a fireworks factory destroyed a neighbourhood killing many and injuring hundreds. It was a tragic repeat of history as a fire had destroyed most of the town in 1862.

The VVV (☎ 432 32 00, fax 430 41 62), Oude Markt 31, is open 9 am to 5.30 pm weekdays and until 2 pm Saturday (until 4 pm June to August). Staff try hard and can find you a room if you decide to stay, and also have many, many touring maps into the Twenthe countryside.

Enschede's main interest for visitors is the **Rijksmuseum Twenthe** (☎ 435 86 75). In an architecturally significant building originally from 1930 (the stunning addition is from 1996), the museum covers Dutch art from the 13th century onwards. However, its speciality is 19th-century European art and the star of this collection is Monet's *Cliffs at Pourville*. The museum, 800m north of the station, is open 11 am to 5 pm (closed Monday).

The train station is at the end of a major route and there are good connections. Some fares and schedules are:

destination	price (f)	duration (mins)	frequency (per hr)
Amsterdam	39	150	1
Deventer	17.25	50	2

Villages

If you're travelling by car or bike, the following are small villages out in the Twenthe countryside that are worth a stop.

Popular with weekend day-trippers from the region, **Ootmarsum** has a few nice old buildings from the 18th century. Even more attractive, however, are the scores of tiny roads leading away from the town atop dikes. This is very good cycling country.

Not on many maps, **Singraven** is 2km west of Denekamp; watch carefully for signs. The entire area was once part of a manor and there a lot of interesting little tree-lined trails, tiny canals and the like.

Gelderland

Gelderland is like a Rorschach test: each person will see it differently.

Nijmegen's college students look forward to the future, while Arnhem looks forward in order to escape its infamous WWII past. Zutphen has a few echoes of the Hanseatic League while De Hoge Veluwe National Park echoes with just a few calls of the wild. The latter, with its natural setting and superb museum is, of course, the star of the province.

NIJMEGEN

☎ 024 • pop 146,400

There's a minor rivalry between Nijmegen and Maastricht to claim the title of the oldest city in the Netherlands. Unfortunately the Romans, who would know the answer, are long dead. However, it is known that the Romans conquered Nijmegen in AD 70 and promptly burnt it down. A sad taste of things to come.

Nijmegen built itself up as a trading and manufacturing town. It rolled with the many invasions through the centuries right up until WWII. A marshalling point for German forces, it was bombed heavily by

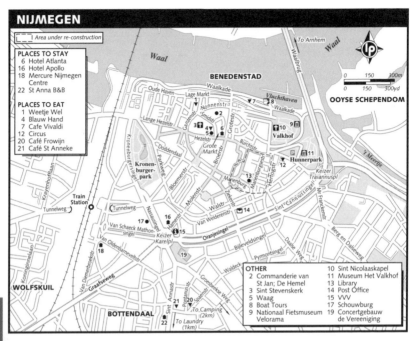

NIJMEGEN

Area under re-construction

PLACES TO STAY
6 Hotel Atlanta
16 Hotel Apollo
18 Mercure Nijmegen Centre
22 St Anna B&B

PLACES TO EAT
1 Weetje Wel
4 Blauw Hand
7 Cafe Vivaldi
12 Circus
20 Café Frowijn
21 Café St Anneke

OTHER
2 Commanderie van St Jan; De Hemel
3 Sint Stevenskerk
5 Waag
8 Boat Tours
9 Nationaal Fietsmuseum Velorama
10 Sint Nicolaaskapel
11 Museum Het Valkhof
13 Library
14 Post Office
15 VVV
17 Schouwburg
19 Concertgebouw de Vereeniging

the Americans in February 1944. Later that year, the town was left devastated by the Operation Market Garden fiasco (see the boxed text 'Operation Market Garden' later in the chapter).

The postwar years have seen several rebuilding schemes, some better than others. A huge one is changing the face of several streets around Mariënburg and is due for completion in 2001.

Nijmegen is home to many delightful cafes and it has a fun nightlife, helped along by the 13,000 students at the Netherlands' only Catholic university. It is a good base for exploring Gelderland and the centre is only 10 minutes from the train station. The waterfront along the Waal River is lined with cafes which have an interesting feature: slots in the front windows where boards can be inserted to keep out the water during the frequent floods. Patrons use back doors for entrance and can sit with the windows open while the waters flow past.

Information

Tourist Offices The VVV (☎ 0900-112 23 44, f1 per minute, fax 329 78 79), Keizer Karelplein 2, is open 9.30 am to 5.30 pm weekdays and until 5 pm Saturday.

Money The GWK exchange in the train station is open 8 am to 9 pm daily. ATMs are scattered through the centre of town.

Post The post office (☎ 323 90 92), Van Schevichavenstraat 1, is open 8 am to 6 pm weekdays and until 1 pm Saturday.

Bookshops Dekker vb Vegt (☎ 322 10 10), Nijmegen's main bookshop, will be moving to the new Mariënburg shopping district.

Libraries Not yet open at the time of research, the new library (☎ 327 49 11), Mariënburg 29, will also be in the new shopping complex. It will have Internet access when it opens.

Laundry Karreman Wasserettes (☎ 355 10 76), St Jacobslaan 430, is 15 minutes from the centre by bus Nos 5 and 8 (direction: Hatert).

Things to See & Do
The site of an old castle belonging to Charlemagne, the **Valkhof** has been turned into a grassy knoll, which still holds a few ruins of the palace and good views of the Waal. Also on the hill, **Sint Nicolasskapel** dates from the old 11th-century castle.

The **Museum Het Valkhof** (☎ 360 88 05), Kelfkensbos 59, is housed in a striking building. The collections cover regional history and art and there is a first-rate section of Roman artefacts. It's open 10 am to 5 pm (closed Monday) and costs f7.50/5 for adults/children.

Nearby is a small but must-see museum given that this is the Netherlands; the **National Fietsmuseum Velorama** (☎ 322 58 51), Waalkade 107, is the national bicycle museum. It has over 250 models and is open 10 am to 5 pm daily (f10/6).

A few important bits of the old town either survived the war or have been reconstructed. The **Waag** on Grote Markt was built in 1612 in handsome Renaissance style. It stands in the shadow of **Sint Stevenskerk** (☎ 360 47 10), the large 14th-century church, which is open 1 to 4 pm weekends. Entry costs f1 and you can climb the tower for good views.

Not far from Grote Markt, the **Commanderie van St Jan** on Franseplaats was a 12th-century hospital for the Knights of St John. It has a more healthy use today: it's a brewery. See the listing for De Hemel in the Places to Eat & Drink section.

Cruises (☎ 323 32 85) on the Waal depart from the waterfront along Waalkade from April to October. The cost starts at f10, depending on the cruise's length. Some last an entire day and go to Rotterdam (f50).

Special Events
Nijmegen's big event is the **Internationale Wandelvierdaagse**, a four-day 200km walking marathon through the surrounding countryside held in mid-July every year. Thousands walk – often getting debilitating blisters as 200km is a *long* way – while thousands more party.

Places to Stay
Camping Maikenshof (☎ 684 16 51, fax 684 28 83, Oude Kleefsbaan 134) has sites from f20. Take bus No 6 east for 6km (direction: Beek) to the last stop in Berg en Dal.

Hotel Apollo (☎ 322 35 94, fax 322 35 94, Bisschop Hamerstraat 14) is a basic place with rooms with TVs and baths from f98/145 (single/double).

A short stroll from the Apollo, **Hotel Atlanta** (☎ 360 30 00, fax 360 32 10, Grote Markt 38–40) is almost the same. The prices are f98/145.

The most charming place is **St Anna Bed & Breakfast** (☎ 350 18 08, fax 350 18 18, *ⓔ* lankhpr@euronet.nl, St Annastraat 208) which has owners who also run a travel agency specialising in New Zealand, which explains the sheep motif. There are numerous comforts and rooms start at f110/150. It's a 10-minute walk south of Keizer Karelplein.

Mercure Nijmegen Centre (☎ 323 88 88, fax 324 20 90, Stationsplein 29) is a large hotel aimed at business travellers. Rooms start at f160.

Places to Eat & Drink
Nijmegen has some wonderful cafes.

Weetje Wel (☎ 322 82 02, Priemstraat 11) has great apple pie and coffee. Its name is a play on words meaning 'you know it', thus ensuring confusion when someone asks 'where shall we meet?'

Cafe Vivaldi (☎ 322 28 90, Waalkade 65) is a modern cafe on the waterfront with good food for under f20.

Blauw Hand (☎ 360 61 67, Achter de Hoofdwacht 3) is an old survivor whose name derives from its 17th-century customers who worked at a nearby indigo dye shop. It's friendly and atmospheric and the banner over the ancient bar, when translated, reads: 'A frosty mug of rich beer gives you warmth, joy and sweet pleasure'.

De Hemel (☎ 360 61 67), on Franseplaats, is the brewery in the ancient Commanderie

OVERIJSSEL & GELDERLAND

van St Jan. The beer is excellent and the snacks are good. It's open noon to 8 pm (closed Monday).

Café St Anneke (☎ 322 82 28, St Anna-straat 55) is a classic brown cafe popular with students.

Near the St Anneke, *Café Frowijn (☎ 324 16 13, Pontanusstraat)* is a brown cafe with some flair and great music.

Circus (☎ 360 66 56, Kelfkensbos 21) is a stylish restaurant whose theme you shouldn't have to guess. Dinners such as fondue start at f23.

Entertainment

Nijmegen boasts two large regional performance venues right across from each other: the *Schouwburg (Keizer Karelplein 32)* and the *Concertgebauw de Vereeniging (Oran-jesingel 11A)*. Call ☎ 322 11 00 for schedule and ticket information for both venues.

Getting There & Around

Train The train station is large and modern with many services. Lockers are near the ticket windows. Fares and schedules from Nijmegen include:

destination	price (f)	duration (mins)	frequency (per hr)
Amsterdam	30.50	90	2
Arnhem	6.50	12	5
Den Bosch	13.25	30	4

Bus Regional and local buses depart from the area in front of the station.

Taxi Nijmegen is part of the treintaxi scheme (☎ 378 84 85).

Bicycle The bicycle shop (☎ 322 96 18) is underground in front of the station and is open 6 am to 1.30 am (from 8 am Sunday).

ARNHEM

☎ 026 • pop 134,500

All but levelled during WWII (see the boxed text 'Operation Market Garden'), Arnhem is a bland and prosperous town that is not a compelling place to stay. However, there are several nearby museums worthy of

attention and the city is a good place to set off from for De Hoge Veluwe National Park to the north.

Information

The VVV (☎ 370 02 26, fax 442 26 44, ✉ info@vvvarnhem.nl) is just east of the train station at Willemsplein 8. It's open 9 am to 6 pm weekdays and until 1 pm Saturday. It's a good place to get maps for cycling in the region.

The GWK exchange in the station is open 7.30 am to 9 pm (from 9 am Sunday). There are several ATMs nearby.

The Centre

Near the Markt, close to the station, the **Grote Kerk** originally dated from the 15th century but has been heavily reconstructed. Twenty minutes' walk west, the **Museum voor Moderne Kunst** (☎ 351 24 31), Utrechtseweg 87, has a commanding spot overlooking the Rhine River. Its modern art collection represents Arnhem's determination to look forward. Most of the collection is by Dutch artists and the policy is that at least half of the works on display at any time will be by women. It's open 10 am to 5 pm (weekends from 11 am, closed Monday) and costs f7.50. Children under 18 are free.

Burger's Zoo

Arnhem's large 'People's Zoo' (☎ 442 45 34), Schelmseweg 85, tries to recreate the natural environment of animals from around the world. Whether the critters have fallen for this ruse is debatable, especially given the climate. It's open 9 am until sundown or 7 pm year-round, whichever comes first, and costs a lion-sized f27.50/22.50. Trolleybus No 3 goes right to the gate from the train station.

Oosterbeek

An old suburb 5km west of Arnhem, Oosterbeek was the scene of heavy combat during Operation Market Garden. The **Airborne Museum Hartenstein** (☎ 333 77 10), Utrechtsweg 232, is located in a mansion that the British used as headquarters during the battle. It has an audiovisual show that

Operation Market Garden

Before leaving on an enormous military invasion of the Netherlands in September 1944, a British general told his troops, 'This is a tale you will tell your grandchildren and mightily bored they'll be.' Unfortunately, thousands didn't survive the mission to bore their grandchildren.

The battle was called Operation Market Garden and it was a scheme by British General Bernard Montgomery to end WWII in Europe by Christmas. Despite advisers warning that the entire operation was likely to be a fiasco (many of whom were hurriedly transferred away), Montgomery pushed on with it. He had often groused that the Americans under General George Patton were getting all the headlines in their charge across France. The plan was for British forces in Belgium to make a huge push along a narrow corridor to Arnhem in the Netherlands where they would cut off large numbers of German troops from being able to return to Germany and allow the British army to dash east to Berlin and end the war.

However, the entire plan was dubious from the start. About 10,000 British troops were to be parachuted into Arnhem where they would hold the operation's key bridge for two days while another force of British and American troops fought their way north from Belgium to relieve them. The odds were long from the start. The British paratroops were only given two days rations and the forces from the south had to cross 14 bridges, all of which had to be intact and lightly defended for the timetable to work.

Everything went wrong. The southern forces encountered some of the best troops of the German army and the bridges weren't all intact. This, in effect, stranded the Arnhem paratroops. They held out in Arnhem and neighbouring Oosterbeek for eight days without rations or reinforcement. The survivors, a mere 2163, retreated under darkness. Over 17,000 other British troops were killed.

The results of the debacle were devastating for the Dutch. Arnhem and other towns were levelled and hundreds of civilians were killed. The Dutch resistance, thinking that liberation was at hand, had gone into the open to fight the Germans. But without Allied forces to support them, hundreds were rounded up and killed.

Finally Montgomery abandoned the Netherlands. The winter of 1944–45 came to be known as 'the Winter of Hunger' with hundreds starving as no food could be imported from Allied-held Belgium and the Germans had enough problems without trying to feed the Dutch. Most of the country was still occupied when the war ended in Europe in May 1945.

does an excellent job of explaining the battle. It's open 11 am to 5 pm (from noon Sunday) and costs f6/5 (adults/children). The museum is 800m south of the Oosterbeek train stop (to/from Arnhem f3, five minutes, hourly). It is, however, best reached by the No 1 trolleybus which serves both the Oosterbeek and Arnhem stations.

The **Oosterbeek War Cemetery** is in a grove of trees about 200m east and north of the Oosterbeek station (follow the signs). Over 1700 Allied (mostly British and Free Polish) troops are buried here. It's strangely eerie with the wind rustling the trees and crows cawing. The day we were there, an old Dutch gentleman was sitting on a bench waiting for visitors. He was giving out literature

he'd prepared himself on the battle. This is but one example of the esteem in which the British forces are held locally. Even though the abortive battle resulted in much suffering, the Dutch are reverent when it comes to the Allied armies. The main bridge over the Rhine in Arnhem is named for John Frost, commander of the lone battalion of British troops to reach Arnhem.

Nederlands Openluchtmuseum

The national open-air museum of Dutch heritage, the Nederlands Openluchtmuseum (☎ 357 61 11), Schelmseweg 89, is a collection of old buildings and artefacts assembled from every province. There's everything here from ancient farmhouses and old trams to working windmills. Volunteers in authentic costume demonstrate traditional skills such as weaving, smithing and farming. It's a good spot to get a full dose of Dutch social-economic history. A new attraction, HollandRama, opened in 2000 conveying the same information in a 'spectacular multimedia show'. It will no doubt be a hit with the couch potato generation. The museum is open 10 am to 5 pm from late-April to October and costs f22.50/15.

Places to Stay & Eat
For *camping* information see the following De Hoge Veluwe National Park section.

NJHC-herberg Alteveer (☎ 442 01 14, fax 351 48 92, Diepenbrocklaan 27) is 2km north of town. It charges f30 per bed. Take bus No 3 (direction: Alteveer) and get off at Rijnstate Ziekenhuis (hospital).

Pension Parkzicht (☎ 442 06 98, 443 62 02, Apeldoornsestraat 16) is 10 minutes downhill from the station and has basic singles/ doubles for f53/95.

Hotel Blanc (☎ 442 80 72, fax 443 47 49, Coehoornstraat 4) is just east of the station and has well-equipped rooms for f145/190.

Terrace *cafes* rim the Korenmarkt and all seem rather similar. A bit east, *Cafe Verheyden (☎ 443 70 35, Wezenstraat 6)* has sandwiches, soups, salads and fresh seafood at moderate prices in a stylish 19th-century building.

Getting There & Around
Arnhem's train station, hurriedly constructed after the war, is due for a massive replacement program beginning in 2001. The lockers are by track No 4. Fares and schedules include:

destination	price (f)	duration (mins)	frequency (per hr)
Amsterdam	25	70	2
Deventer	13.25	36	2
Nijmegen	6.50	12	5

Buses and public transport leave from in front of the station, although the reconstruction will change all this.

Arnhem is part of the treintaxi scheme (☎ 442 66 68).

The bicycle shop (☎ 442 17 82) is open 5.15 am to 1 am weekdays and from 7 am weekends.

DE HOGE VELUWE NATIONAL PARK
The largest national park in the Netherlands would be a nice enough place to visit owing to its interesting mixture of marshlands, forests and sand dunes, but the addition of its world-class museum means it should not be missed.

The park was purchased by Anton and Helene Kröller-Müller, a wealthy German-Dutch couple, in 1914. He wanted land for hunting and she wanted a place to build a museum. They got both.

It was given to the state in 1930 and in 1938 a museum opened for Helene's remarkable collection of art. A visit to the park can fill an entire day, and even if you don't have a bicycle, you can borrow one of the hundreds of famous and free 'white bicycles'.

Information
The ticket booths at each of the three *ingang* (entrances) at Hoenderloo, Otterlo and Rijzenburg have basic information and the highly useful park maps (f5). In the heart of the park, the main visitors centre (☎ 0318-59 16 27) is an attraction itself. It has numerous displays on the flora and fauna found in the diverse environment, including one showing the gruesome results when a deer has a bad day and a crow has a good day.

Admission & Hours An entrance ticket good for just the park costs f8/4 (adults/ children). A ticket good for the park and the Kröller-Müller Museum costs f16/8. Cars cost an additional f8.50.

The park is open 9 am to 5.30 pm November to March, 8 am to 8 pm April, 8 am to 9 pm May, 8 am to 10 pm June and July, 8 am to 9 pm August, 9 am to 8 pm September and 9 am to 7 pm October. Cars are never allowed in after 8 pm.

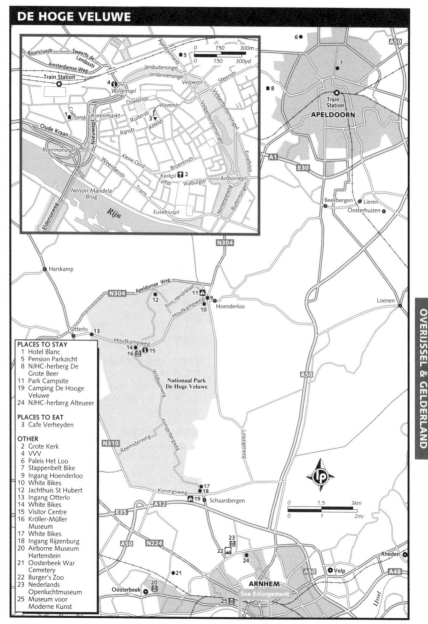

DE HOGE VELUWE

OVERIJSSEL & GELDERLAND

PLACES TO STAY
1 Hotel Blanc
5 Pension Parkzicht
8 NJHC-herberg De
   Grote Beer
11 Park Campsite
19 Camping De Hooge
   Veluwe
24 NJHC-herberg Alteueer

PLACES TO EAT
3 Cafe Verheyden

OTHER
2 Grote Kerk
4 VVV
6 Paleis Het Loo
7 Stappenbelt Bike
9 Ingang Hoenderloo
10 White Bikes
12 Jachthuis St Hubert
13 Ingang Otterlo
14 White Bikes
15 Visitor Centre
16 Kröller-Müller
   Museum
17 White Bikes
18 Ingang Rijzenburg
20 Airborne Museum
   Hartenstein
21 Oosterbeek War
   Cemetery
22 Burger's Zoo
23 Nederlands
   Openluchtmuseum
25 Museum voor
   Moderne Kunst

euro currency converter f1 = €0.45

The Park

Roads through the park are fortunately limited. There are many more bike paths and hiking trails, 42km in fact, with three routes signposted. The most interesting area is the **Wildbaan** south of the Kröller-Müller Museum. At the north edge, **Jachthuis St Hubert** is the baronial hunting lodge Anton had built. Named after the patron saint of hunting (but not the hunted), you can tour its woodsy interior.

Kröller-Müller Museum

One of the best museums in the Netherlands, the Kröller-Müller (☎ 591 16 27) has works by **Picasso**, **Renoir**, **Sisley** and **Manet**, but it's the **Van Gogh collection** that makes it world-class. In a series of chronological rooms you can trace Vincent van Gogh's (1853–90) development as an artist. Starting in the first room and following the counterclockwise course, the highlights include:

1885 – Van Gogh's early studies appear conventional but hint at things to come.
1887 – In *Zonne Bloemen* his dramatic use of colour emerges.
1888 – The heavens explode with colour in *Place du Forum*, a study of cafe life.
1890 – The heartbroken subject of *Old Man is Sorrow* is a metaphor for Van Gogh's life.

An evocative **sculpture garden** behind the museum is worth an hour to just stroll. The museum is a 1km stroll from the visitors centre.

Places to Stay & Eat

The park *camp site* (☎ 055-378 22 32) is near the northern Hoenderloo entrance. It's open April to October and sites cost f7 per person. You cannot reserve in advance.

Right by the southern Schaarsbergen entrance, *Camping De Hooge Veluwe* (☎ 026-443 22 72, fax 443 68 09, ✆ hooge.veluwe@vvc.nl, Koningsweg 14) is open April to October and has sites from f25. Bus No 12 passes close.

There are *hostels* in Arnhem and Apeldoorn; see those listings for details. For *hotels*, the delightful towns of Deventer and

Nijmegen make good and easily reached bases.

There are decent *cafes* at the visitors centre and at the museum.

Getting There & Around

There is a bus service from the train stations in Arnhem and Apeldoorn. From the former, bus No 12 runs to the Schaarsbergen entrance and on to the Kröller-Müller Museum. The first bus leaves at 10.10 am from April to October and there are three more through the day (hourly in July and August). From Apeldoorn, bus No 110 leaves the station every hour from 8.42 am to 4.42 pm. Confirm both services in advance by calling ☎ 0900-92 92 (f0.75 per minute).

By car there is parking at the visitors centre, museum and lodge. Or you can park at the entrances and use a 'white bicycle'.

By bike, the park is easily reached from any direction. However, if you are renting, it's easier to do so at the Arnhem train station rather than in Apeldoorn. You can also wait and use one of the free white bicycles at the entrances, but sometimes they run out.

NATIONAL PARK DE VELUWE ZOOM

This 4800-hectare wooded park 5km east of De Hoge Veluwe is a good place to extend your biking or hiking.

APELDOORN

☎ 055 • pop 152,800

There's little to lure you here except the sight of a big house, or a bus connection to De Hoge Veluwe. The city is staid and not particularly scenic.

The one important sight is **Paleis Het Loo** (☎ 577 24 00), the official home of the Dutch royal family from the time of William the III and Mary in 1685 until 1975. It's magnificent, filled with marble, gilt, tapestries and all the trapping of power and wealth, but you can't help but wish that the House of Orange wasn't so darn boring. A few beheadings, back-stabbings, illicit affairs and the like would really add interest.

It's a must-see if you're into sumptuous palaces; otherwise you can skip it. The **gardens** are nice, if you're into sumptuous gardens... It's open 10 am to 5 pm (closed Monday) and costs f15. Several buses run north past Het Loo from the station.

The *NJHC-herberg De Grote Beer* (☎ *355 31 18, fax 355 38 11, Asselstraat 330)* costs f30 per person. It's 3km west of the station; take bus No 4 or 7 to the Chamavenlaan stop.

Getting There & Around
Apeldoorn is on the line between Deventer (f5.50, 12 minutes) and Amersfoort (f13.25, 26 minutes); trains run every 30 minutes in both directions. The major fault with the station is that it doesn't have a bicycle shop. The closest place to rent a bike, a 15-minute walk, is Stappenbelt Bike (☎ 387 17 46) at Kanaal Noord 152. Buses leave from in front of the station.

ZUTPHEN
☎ 0575 • pop 33,700
Zutphen is an old Hanseatic city on the IJssel with a very compact old town that can make for a pleasant stroll for an hour or

more. It makes a good cycling destination from Deventer.

The VVV (☎ 0900-269 28 88, fax 0575-51 79 28), Stationsplein 39, can help with accommodation and will sell you even more bike routes.

There's no outstanding sight here, but 13th-century **Sint Walburgskerk** and the 15th-century **Stadhuis**, both on 's Gravenhof, help to set the scene of a town with a rich history.

Should you decide to stay the night, *Berkhotel* (☎ *51 11 35, fax 54 19 50, Marshpoortstraat 19)* has rooms from f60 per person. It also has a fine vegetarian restaurant. Houtmarkt has several attractive *cafes*.

The train station is five minutes from the Stadhuis. Trains to Deventer (f5.50) take 13 minutes and run every 30 minutes.

ZALTBOMMEL
An old walled city, Zaltbommel is well preserved and has a number of attractive buildings that date as far back as the 12th century. It's 15km north of Den Bosch, in lower west Gelderland, but you'll need a car or a bike to visit as it has woeful transport connections.

Noord Brabant & Limburg

The bottom of the Netherlands belies most cliches about the country. Tulips, windmills and dikes are in limited supply. What you do find are some hills, and even more interestingly, Catholics. Neither Noord Brabant (North Brabant) or Limburg has its roots in the asceticism of the north, a fact that is abundantly clear during *carnaval* when the streets are filled with fireworks, bands and impromptu parties.

The one outstanding attraction in these two provinces is Maastricht, which is as diametrically different from Amsterdam as its geographic position, except in one key area: its people are just as irreverent and just as interested in fun.

Getting There & Away
Most important places in Noord Brabant and Limburg are well served by trains.

Noord Brabant

The Netherlands' largest province, Noord Brabant, spans the bottom of the country, from the waterlogged lands of the west to the somewhat hilly lands of the east. Den Bosch is its main city and an interesting place to spend the day. Breda is also worth a look. However, despite its size, Noord Brabant won't fill your schedule. It's primarily a land of agriculture and industry.

DEN BOSCH
☎ 073 • pop 127,200

The full name of Den Bosch is 's-Hertogenbosch, which is understandably not used often. The capital of Noord Brabant has a remarkable church and a good museum. It has some fine cafes and makes a good place to spend a night.

The city's full name means 'the count's forest' which was true in the 12th century when there was a castle and large forest here. Both are long gone. It was hotly contested during the Eighty Years' War and the shape

• Den Bosch p305

• Maastricht p308

of today's canals show where the lines of fortifications once were. Today, Den Bosch is a regional shopping and industrial town.

The town's pedestrianised centre is based around the Markt, a 10-minute walk east of the train station.

Information
Tourist Offices The VVV (☎ 0900-112 23 34, fax 612 89 30), Markt 77, is open 11 am to 5.30 pm Monday, 9 am to 5.30 pm Tuesday to Friday and until 4 pm Saturday.

Money The GWK exchange in the train station is open 8 am to 8 pm (until 5 pm Sunday). There are ATMs on Markt.

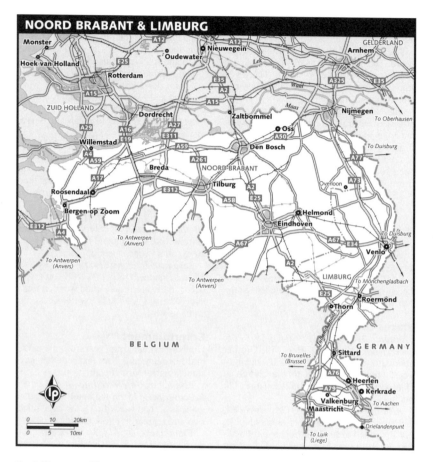

NOORD BRABANT & LIMBURG

Post The post office (☎ 613 43 63), Kerkstraat 67, is open 9 am to 6 pm weekdays (until 2 pm Saturday).

Travel Agencies The Travel Store (☎ 613 13 20), Eerste Korenstraatje 14, is a combination travel agency and travel book shop.

Bookshops Adr Heinen (☎ 613 00 12), Kerkstraat 27, has a decent selection of books.

Libraries The library (☎ 612 30 33), Hinthamerstraat 72, is open 11 am to 8 pm (until 4 pm weekends, closed Monday).

Medical Services Bosch Medicentrum (☎ 616 20 00), Nieuwstraat 34, is the regional hospital.

Things to See & Do

The main attraction is **St Janskathedraal**, which is the finest Gothic church in the Netherlands. It took from 1336 to 1550 to complete its construction. There's an interesting contrast between the red brick tower and the ornate stone buttresses. The interior is fairly barren because the Protestants, who controlled the church from 1629 to 1810, stripped its decor away. It's open 10 am to

4.30 pm daily. At night the cathedral is dramatically lit.

The **Markt** is a good example of the genre. The **Stadhuis** was given its classical baroque appearance in 1670. There's a statue of local artist-made-good Hieronymus Bosch in front.

The **Noordbrabants Museum** (☎ 687 78 00), Verwersstraat 41, in the former governor's residence, features exhibits about Brabant life and art from earlier times. It has drawings and other work by Bosch. It's open 10 am to 5 pm Tuesday to Friday and from noon weekends. Admission is f12.50/6.50 for adults/children.

The **Bosch Architectuur Initiatief**, (☎ 612 17 38), Nieuwstraat 28, is a small gallery with changing shows that explore the often unhappy marriage of architecture and the environment. It's open 1 to 6 pm Wednesday to Friday and until 5 pm Saturday.

Boat tours leave from the canal by Sint Janssingel from April to October. Check the pier for times.

Places to Stay

Camping De Wildhorst (☎ 0413-29 14 66, Meerstraat 30) is in Heeswijk-Dinther about 12km to the south-east. It's open all year; take bus No 158 to the church at Heeswijk and then it's 2km. It charges f24 per site.

All Inn (☎/fax 613 40 57, Gasselstraat 1) has rooms for f45/75 for a single/double, but it's rough around the edges and breakfast is f10 extra. Note the gold elephant gable across the street.

Hotel Terminus (☎ 613 06 66, fax 613 07 26, Boschveldweg 15) is near to the station and has decent rooms starting at f50/95. It also has a great bar; see the listing in the Entertainment section.

Hotel Euro (☎ 613 77 77, fax 612 87 95, Hinthamerstraat 63) has standard rooms that will suit business travellers. It costs f100/150.

Places to Eat

Snackcafé Sint Janneke is a tiny place near the cathedral on Torenstraat. It has *frites* and other treats until 10 pm but is closed Monday.

Cafe Cordes (☎ 612 42 42, Parade 4) stands out from the other uninspired cafes near the cathedral. It's a see-and-be-seen place and it has specials for under f20.

Cafe September (☎ 613 03 08, Verwersstraat 55–57) is in a sober little white building and has a couple of tables outside. Inside there are eight beers on tap and 80 more in bottles. Simple meals are served as well.

Tapperij Het Veulen (☎ 612 30 38, Korenbrugstraat 9A) has peanuts on the floor and simple wooden tables. It has unusual cheeses to go with the many beers and there are many good dishes like lasagne for f12.50.

Cafe De Keulse Kar (☎ 613 61 29, Hinthamerstraat 101) caters to older, richer patrons with a fine menu for about f30 and an excellent wine selection.

Javaanse Jongens Eetcafe (☎ 613 41 07, Korte Putstraat 27) has truly inspired decor; there are little carved wooden tigers everywhere. The food is excellent and fine value as well.

Entertainment

Hinthamerstraat going east from the cathedral has numerous bars that together have something for virtually any taste.

Elsewhere, *Café Terminus (☎ 613 06 66, Boschveldweg 15)* in the hotel of the same name is a great bar with a good beer selection and regular live folk music.

Flamineeke (☎ 614 36 46, Eerste Korenstraatje 16) is a gay bar that opens after 10 pm.

De Muzerije (☎ 614 10 84, Hinthamerstraat) is one of those big multicultural places with ongoing programs of theatre, dance, film and the like.

Theater Aan De Parade (☎ 612 51 25, Parade 23) is a mainstream venue with classic films, theatre, music etc.

Shopping

Farfallino (☎ 614 04 81, Lange Putstraat 10) is a housewares shop filled with whimsical, trendy and even practical items. It's one of many interesting places on this street.

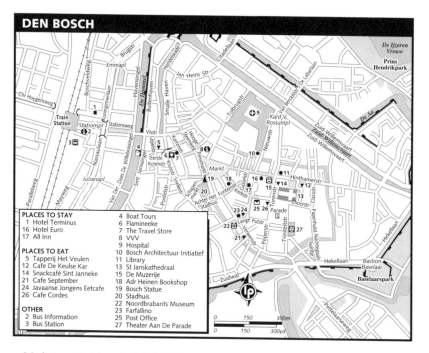

DEN BOSCH

PLACES TO STAY	
1 Hotel Terminus	4 Boat Tours
16 Hotel Euro	6 Flamineeke
17 All Inn	7 The Travel Store
	8 VVV
PLACES TO EAT	9 Hospital
5 Tapperij Het Veulen	10 Bosch Architectuur Initiatief
12 Cafe De Keulse Kar	11 Library
14 Snackcafé Sint Janneke	13 St Janskathedraal
21 Cafe September	15 De Muzerije
24 Javaanse Jongens Eetcafe	18 Adr Heinen Bookshop
26 Cafe Cordes	19 Bosch Statue
	20 Stadhuis
OTHER	22 Noordbrabants Museum
2 Bus Information	23 Farfallino
3 Bus Station	25 Post Office
	27 Theater Aan De Parade

Markets are held on the Markt Wednesday and Saturday.

Getting There & Around

Train The train station is new and brimming with services, including a good grocery store aimed at travellers. Lockers are on the concourse over the tracks. Some fares and schedules are:

destination	price (f)	duration (mins)	frequency (per hr)
Amsterdam	23.25	60	2
Maastricht	33	90	1
Nijmegen	13.25	30	4
Utrecht	13.25	30	4

Bus Buses leave from the area to the right as you exit the station. There is a very helpful bus information office that's open 8 am to 7 pm weekdays and 10 am to 5.30 pm Saturday.

Taxi Den Bosch is part of the treintaxi scheme (☎ 614 14 10).

Bicycle The bicycle shop (☎ 613 47 37) is below the station and is open 5 am to 1 am weekdays and from 7 am weekends.

EINDHOVEN
☎ 040 • pop 198,000

During the 1990s, Dutch electronics giant Philips found it was having trouble recruiting employees to work in its hometown of Eindhoven. Eventually it solved the problem by moving to Amsterdam. This story sums up the woes of this huge industrial town which is just not a pleasant place.

It was a mere village in 1900, but thanks to Philips grew to its present size. Even with its corporate offices gone, Philips' research and engineering arms remain. Eindhoven is best known for its winning football team PSV, but don't even think about tickets; the games are always sold out.

euro currency converter f1 = €0.45

If you must visit Eindhoven, the charming VVV (☎ 246-3005), Stationsplein 1, in front of the train station, can provide information. It's open 7.30 am to 7 pm weekdays and until noon Saturday.

The city's one attraction of note, the **Stedelijk Van Abbemuseum** (☎ 275 52 75), Vonderweg 1, seems to be under interminable renovation (contrary to the popular joke, it hasn't moved to Amsterdam). When open, it has a first-rate collection of 20th-century paintings.

The Eindhoven Airport, 6km west of the centre, is aimed at business travellers. KLM exel (☎ 020-474 77 47) flies to London, Hamburg, Paris and makes connections at Schiphol. British Airways (☎ 020-346 95 59) flies tiny commuter planes to points in the UK. The train station is at a junction of lines to Amsterdam, Maastricht, Rotterdam and Venlo.

TILBURG
☎ 013 • pop 191,000

A former textile town, Tilburg is today still determining its future now that the mills have closed due to foreign competition. Its centre bears the scars of some unfortunate urban renewal schemes of the 1960s. Think East Berlin and you have the right idea.

Should you decide to hop off the train – it's on the lines from Breda to Den Bosch and Maastricht – then the main sight worth checking out is the **Nederlands Textielmuseum** (☎ 549 45 64), Goirkestraat 96. It's a 10-minute walk from behind the station. Housed in an old mill, it shows how the fine work once produced in Tilburg was made. The museum is open 10 am to 5 pm (from noon weekends, closed Monday) and costs f7.50/2.50 for adults/children.

On the way to the textile museum, you'll pass the **De Pont** (☎ 543 83 00), Wilhelminapark 1, where there are exhibitions of modern art. You might want to see what's on at the museum.

BREDA
☎ 076 • pop 155,700

Breda is a very pleasant place to spend an afternoon. The streets are lined with interesting shops and cafes, it has some flower-filled parks and its main church is a stunner.

Breda's present peace belies its unpeaceful past. It's been overrun by invading armies scores of times. The town centre is a 10-minute walk south from the station through the large park, the Valkenberg.

Information

The VVV (☎ 522 24 44, 521 85 30, ✉ vvvbreda@tref.nl), Willemstraat 17, is near the train station. It is open 9 am to 6 pm weekdays and until 5 pm Saturday.

The GWK exchange in the train station is open 8 am to 8 pm daily. The post office (☎ 522 55 20), Willemstraat 30, is open 9 am to 6 pm weekdays and 10 am to 1.30 pm Saturday.

Things to See

The **Valkenberg** is the huge park between the station and the centre. It was where hunting falcons were once trained by the royalty, which explains the park's name. The paths wander through the grounds, which come alive with flowers in the spring. On the south side is the 12th-century **Begijnhof**. Breda is a wonderfully preserved example of these homes, which once sheltered unmarried women and were found throughout the Netherlands.

In the centre, the **Grote Kerk** has recently emerged from years of restoration that removed the grime from its gleaming ivory stones. It was built from the 15th to the 17th century and is a classic example of Brabant Gothic architecture. Crane your neck to see the golden cock weather vane atop the copper cupola. Inside, there are grand tombs and monuments to various Breda rulers. It's open 10 am to 5 pm (from 1 pm Sunday).

Places to Stay & Eat

Camping Liesbos (☎ 514 35 14, fax 514 65 55, Liesdreef 40) has sites for f27. It's open April to October. Take bus No 10 or 111 (direction: Etten-Leur) to the Buswachterij Liesbos stop.

Pension Singel (☎ 521 62 71, fax 521 40 67, ✉ grapost@hetnet.nl, Delpratsingel 14) has simple rooms from f48/95 for

NOORD BRABANT & LIMBURG

singles/doubles. It's a five-minute walk from the station.

Hotel De Fabriek (☎ 581 00 08, fax 581 13 35, Speelhuislaan 150) has comfortable rooms from f95/125. It's right behind the station.

Den Boerenstamppot (☎ 514 01 62, Schoolstraat 3) is like an old-time cafeteria and it has old-time prices: f11.75 for a three-course meal with choice of dessert. It's open 1.30 am to 7.30 pm (closed Sunday).

Café De Beyerd (☎ 521 42 65, Boschstraat 26) has a great beer selection and nice tables outside. It has a typical Dutch menu and specials under f15.

Getting There & Around

The train station has all the usual services. Some fares and schedules are:

destination	price (f)	duration (mins)	frequency (per hr)
Amsterdam	33	120	1
Den Bosch	13.25	33	2
Roosendaal	7.50	18	2
Rotterdam	15.25	42	4

Buses leave from the area to the right as you exit the station. Breda is part of the treintaxi scheme (☎ 571 06 99).

The bicycle shop is open 5.30 am to 11.30 pm (from 7 am weekends). For information on a 52km bicycle route, the Baronie Route, which begins and ends at Breda, see the special section 'Cycling in the Netherlands'.

WEST NOORD BRABANT

Near the border with Zeeland, Noord Brabant more closely resembles its soggy neighbour. Canals and rivers crisscross the land and everything is absolutely flat. There's not much reason to spend a lot of time trying to make sense of the region, but you might want to check out three of its towns.

Willemstad is a well-preserved little fortified old harbour that overlooks the Haringvliet, a large channel that's a direct result of the St Elizabeth's Day flood all the way

back in 1421. There are a few cafes and if it's a Sunday you'll be joined by plenty of Dutch out for a drive. In fact, without a car it's difficult to reach Willemstad.

Roosendaal is a major junction between the train lines north to Rotterdam, south to Belgium, east to Breda and west to Zeeland. Fortunately, the connections are good, and you won't need to linger in the town, which has a grimly efficient shopping district.

Except for one week a year, **Bergen Op Zoom** is not all that noteworthy. Like many Dutch towns, it was plundered at various times by the Spanish, French and even, in 1814, the British. The results look like the aftermath of a big party; it's a hodgepodge of buildings and styles. But if you really want to see the aftermath of a big party, show up in Bergen Op Zoom on the Wednesday after Shrove Tuesday. Its carnaval is the most raucous west of Maastricht, drawing revellers from throughout Europe who basically go on a multiday bender. Thus you can become still another invader: arriving, plundering and departing on the frequent trains to Roosendaal.

Limburg

This long and narrow province at times barely seems like part of the rest of the Netherlands, especially in the south where it's actually hilly. In fact, there are all sorts of dire notices on the A2 motorway into Maastricht warning drivers of impending steep grades that in other countries would be considered minor hills.

Maastricht is the star – almost the supernova – of Limburg. Little else is worth a fraction of the time Maastricht demands.

MAASTRICHT

☎ 043 • pop 113,400

Just like that other great afterthought, the appendix, Maastricht hangs down from the rest of the Netherlands hemmed in on all sides by Belgium and Germany. It was this very precarious position that saved the town from war damage in the 20th century; the Dutch government didn't bother mounting a defence.

NOORD BRABANT & LIMBURG

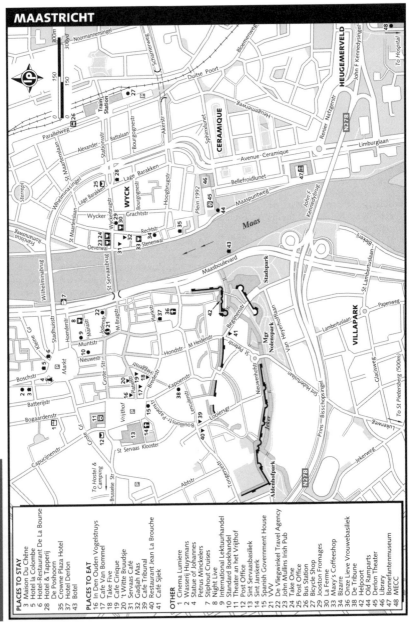

MAASTRICHT

PLACES TO STAY
3 Maison Du Chêne
5 Hotel la Colombe
6 Hotel-Restaurant De La Bourse
28 Hotel & Tapperij
   De Poshoorn
35 Crowne Plaza Hotel
37 Hotel Derlon
43 Botel

PLACES TO EAT
16 In Den Ouden Vogelstruys
17 Cafe Van Bommel
18 Take Five
19 Cafe Cinique
20 't Witte Bruudsje
31 Servaas Café
32 Gadjah Mas
39 Cafe Tribunal
40 Restaurant Jean La Brouche
41 Café Sjiek

OTHER
1 Cinema Lumiere
2 Wasserij Huysmans
4 Statue of Johannes
   Petrus Minckelers
7 Stiphout Cruises
8 Night Live
9 International Lektuurhandel
10 Standard Boekhandel
11 Theater an het Vrijhof
12 Post Office
13 Sint Servaasbasiliek
14 Sint Janskerk
15 Spanish Government House
21 VVV
22 De Vliegwinkel Travel Agency
23 John Mullins Irish Pub
24 Take One
25 Post Office
26 Bus Station
27 Bicycle Shop
29 Jooston Fromages
30 La Ferme
33 Maxy's Coffeeshop
34 Bizarre
36 Onze Lieve Vrouwebasiliek
38 De Tribune
42 Helpoort
44 Old Ramparts
45 Derlon Theater
46 Library
47 Bonnefantenmuseum
48 MECC

In the centuries before, however, Maastricht was captured at various times by most of Europe's powers. This legacy as a crossroads for invading armies has helped give Maastricht its pan-European flavour. The average Maastricht citizen bounces with ease between Dutch, English, French, German, Flemish and more. This makes it all the more fitting that the city was the site of two seminal moments in the history of the European Union: the signature on 10 December 1991 by the 12 members of the then European Community of the treaty for economic, monetary and political union, and the following February, the nations gathered again to sign the treaty which created the EU.

Maastricht has a liveliness and energy out of proportion to its size. The people are irreverent, there's hordes of university students and the streets are steeped in history. No visit to the Netherlands is complete without a visit to Maastricht.

Orientation

The centre of Maastricht is quite compact, bisected by the River Maas. The area on the east side is known as Wyck, and to the south of here is the new area of Céramique. The walk from the train station to the Vrijthof, the cultural centre of the city, takes 15 minutes. The other major square, the Markt, is slated for a massive reconstruction beginning in 2001 that is meant to undo the damage caused by previous massive reconstructions.

Information

Tourist Offices In a land of efficient tourist offices, the Maastricht VVV (☎ 325 21 21, fax 321 37 46, ✉ info@vvvmaastricht.nl), Kleine Staat 1, is possibly the most efficient. It has reams of English-language information on the city and surroundings. It's open 9 am to 6 pm weekdays and until 5 pm Saturday (until 6 pm May to October, when it is also open 11 am to 3 pm Sunday).

Money The GWK Exchange in the train station is open 8 am to 9 pm (until 6 pm Sunday). ATMs abound along Brugstraat and the Markt.

Post There is a post office (☎ 329 91 99) at Statenstraat 4. It's open 9 am to 6 pm weekdays and until 1.30 pm Saturday. Penetrating the succession of powered doors at the entry is like something out of the opening credits to *Get Smart*. There's another post office (☎ 321 45 11), Stationstraat 60, that's near the train station and open similar hours.

Travel Agencies De Vliegwinkel (☎ 326 11 00), Kesselskade 59, sells budget tickets.

Bookshops Standard Boekhandel (☎ 321-0825), Nieuwstraat 9, has a good selection of travel and English-language books.

Internationale Lektuurhandel Palero (☎ 321 14 10), Muntstraat 17, has a huge selection of magazines and newspapers.

De Tribune (☎ 325 19 78), Kapoenstraat 8–10, is a serious and academic bookstore.

Libraries Maastricht's new library (☎ 350 56 00), at Ave Céramique 50, is a sight in itself. It's huge, bright and inviting and has free Internet access. It's open 10 am to 5 pm (until 8 pm Tuesday and Thursday, closed Sunday).

Laundry Wasserij Huysmans (☎ 325 09 59), 82 Boschstraat, seems to have erratic hours, but it's the most convenient.

Medical Services Academisch Ziekenhuis Maastricht (☎ 387 65 43), P Debyelaan 25, is a huge academic hospital just east of the MECC exposition centre.

Bonnefantenmuseum

A controversial erection on the Maas, the Bonnefantenmuseum (☎ 329 01 90), Ave Céramique 250, features a 28m tower that has become a local landmark. Designed by Aldo Rossi, the museum opened in 1995. It is well laid-out and the collections are divided into departments, each with its own floor: Old Masters and medieval sculpture on the 1st floor and contemporary art by Limburg artists on the 2nd. A dramatic sweep of stairs beckons visitors to both floors.

The star attraction of the museum is the **Neutelings Collection** of late medieval

NOORD BRABANT & LIMBURG

religious sculpture and artefacts. Much of the space is devoted to special exhibitions and shows. The museum, which has a fine cafe, is open 11 am to 5 pm (closed Monday except on holidays). Admission costs f12.50 and is free for children under 13.

The Vrijthof

A large square dominated by **Sint Servaasbasiliek**, the Vrijthof is surrounded by lively cafes and cultural institutions.

A pastiche of architecture dating to 1000, Sint Servaasbasiliek is a huge barn of a place that makes for a good wander. Look for individual features within the overall whole to best appreciate it. A good example is the **Royal Portal** on the south side which is from the 13th century and has some lovely colours. The **Treasury** holds much gold and silver, including the St Servatius' Shrine, a good example of the work of Maastricht artisans in the 12th century. The church and treasury are open 10 am to 5 pm daily (Sunday only November to March). Admission is f4/1 for adults/children.

Almost hidden behind Sint Servaasbasiliek, **Sint Janskerk** is a small 17th-century red Gothic church.

The south side of the Vrijthof is dominated by the 16th-century **Spanish Government House**, so named because this is where Philip II outlawed his former lieutenant William the Silent at the start of the Eighty Years' War. There's a small museum (☎ 321 13 27) with items from the building's later years. It's open 1 to 5 pm Wednesday to Sunday and costs f5.

Streets, Squares & Bridges

The best way to see Maastricht is to stroll aimlessly. Streets not to miss include those south and east of the Vrijthof; you'll be rewarded with a medieval labyrinth punctuated by interesting shops and cafes.

Onze Lieve Vrouweplein is an intimate cafe-filled square named after its church, the **Onze Lieve Vrouwebasiliek**, which has parts dating before 1000 and may well be built on the foundations of a Roman cathedral. The entire area was the centre of the Roman town and the church has many Romanesque

architectural features. Inside, the choir is a splendid study of proportion. The church is 10 am to 5 pm daily, except during services. The **treasury** with an array of artworks and relics costs f3.50/1.

At the north end of the **Markt** look for the statue of **Johannes Petrus Minckelers**, who holds a flaming rod, which is fitting as he invented the gas light.

The busy pedestrian **Sint Servaasbrug** dates from the 13th century and links Maastricht's centre with the Wyck district.

Fortifications

At the end of St Bernardusstraat, the **Helpoort** is the oldest surviving town gate in the Netherlands (1229). It is linked to the surviving fortifications that run north and west of here. The entire area can be explored and there are many good views.

Across the Maas in the new Céramique district, you can see the remains of the 13th-century **old ramparts** and fortifications.

Much of Maastricht is riddled with defensive tunnels dug into the soft sandstone over the centuries. Thirteen species of bats have been found living below the surface. The best place to see some of these tunnels is **Sint Pietersberg**, 2km south of Helpoort. The large fort has tunnels throughout the hill. The VVV tourist office leads **cave tours** (☎ 321 78 78) at 3.30 pm daily in July and August and during school holidays. The cost is f6/3.75. Bus No 29 goes past the fort from the Vrijthof.

Organised Tours

Stiphout Cruises (☎ 351 53 00), Maaspromenade 27, runs **boat cruises** on the Maas daily April to October and weekends November and December. The cruises last 50 minutes and cost f11/7. There are also day-long round-trip cruises to Liege in Belgium on certain days that cost f34/12.50, although you can get a single ticket if you want to use the boat instead of the train.

The VVV runs English-language **walking tours** at 12.30 pm daily July and August. The talks leave from the VVV office, take 90 minutes and cost f6/3.75.

NOORD BRABANT & LIMBURG

Special Events

Two events stand out from the busy Maastricht calendar:

Carnaval Celebrated in February/March with greater vigour in Maastricht than almost anywhere else in Europe. The orgy of partying and carousing begins the Friday before Shrove Tuesday and lasts until the last person collapses sometime early in the morning on Wednesday.

TEFAF The ungainly name given to Europe's largest art show held in late March at the cavernous MECC exposition hall just south of Céramique. Over 200 exhibitors converge on Maastricht offering masterpieces for sale to those with a few million euros spare. The event is open to the public, so go browse.

Places to Stay

Maastricht is a popular weekend destination through the year, so reservations are a must. The VVV has a list of private rooms it can book.

Camping Just west of the centre, *Camping De Dousberg* (☎ 343 21 71, fax 343 05 56, *Dousbergweg 102)* is a posh place to pitch a tent, with access to indoor and outdoor pools and more. Sites cost f26 for two people. Local bus No 11 from the train station finishes its run at the camping site during the opening months from April to October. On weekends take bus No 8 or 18.

Hostels *NJHC-herberg De Dousberg* (☎ 346 67 77, fax 346 67 55, *Dousbergweg 4)* is just down the hill from the camping site. Beds in the simple but modern building cost f32.50 to f37 and it is open all year. The same buses serving the camping site serve the hostel.

Hotels *Botel* (☎ 321 90 23, fax 325 79 98, *Maasboulevard 95)* is just that, a hotel on an old boat on the Maas. The small but comfy rooms cost f57/90 (single/double).

Maison Du Chêne (☎ 321 35 23, fax 325 80 82, *Boschstraat 104–106)* is a fine budget option in an elegant 1855 building. The rooms have baths and cost from f85/110. There is a good brasserie on the ground

floor, where you can have breakfast in the mornings.

Hotel-Restaurant De La Bourse (☎ 321 81 12, fax 321 77 06, *Markt 37)* is unassuming but has a good location and a decent cafe for catching up on postcards. Rooms with bath and TV cost from f110/120.

Hotel la Colombe (☎ 321 57 74, fax 325 80 77, *Markt 30)* is in a simple, white building on the Markt. The rooms are equally unadorned but have TV and bath and cost f100/145.

Hotel & Tapperij De Poshoorn (☎ 321 73 34, fax 321 07 47, *Stationsstraat 47)* is a solid place with a great cafe (see the listing in Places to Eat). The rooms have baths and TVs and cost f110/135.

Crowne Plaza Hotel (☎ 350 91 91, fax 350 91 92, ✉ hicpmaastricht@bilderberg .nl, Ruiterij 1) is a large, modern hotel in Wyck favoured by conventioneers. It costs from f305/475.

Hotel Derlon (☎ 321 67 70, fax 325 19 33, ✉ derlon@hospitality.nl, Onze Lieve Vrouweplein 6) is the best place to stay in town, with lovely rooms and enthusiastic staff. The breakfast room in the basement is built around old Roman ruins. Rooms cost from f420.

Places to Eat

Maastricht's streets are lined with restaurants and cafes. Unless otherwise noted, all of the following are open at least for dinner daily.

Restaurants *Gadjah Mas* (☎ 321 15 68, Rechtstraat 42)* has Indonesian food that is as carefully thought out as the artistic interior. Dinner specials start at f24.

Take Five (☎ 321 09 71, Bredestraat 14)* combines the fusion cooking of chef Takashi Asai with a stark, black interior. Dinners cost about f30. On many nights there is live jazz.

Restaurant Jean La Brouche (☎ 321 46 09, Tongersestraat 9)* is a family French restaurant with three courses of the classic cuisine for f59. It is closed Sunday.

Cafes *Cafe Van Bommel* (☎ 321 44 00, Platielstraat 15)* is in a 17th-century building and is the best of the scores of Vrijthof cafes.

NOORD BRABANT & LIMBURG

There is a classic U-shaped bar and on weekends staff will watch your kids while you shop. Some of the cheap lunch specials carry over to dinner.

In Den Ouden Vogelstruys (☎ 321 48 88, Vrijthof 15) has a great terrace of tables.

Cafe Tribunal (☎ 321 03 90, Tongersestraat 1) is popular with students and profs. There's sand on the floors, big windows for people-watching and cheap lunch-time sandwiches.

Cavernous *Cafe Clinique (☎ 350 04 99, Platielstraat 15)* serves Greek and Italian dinner specials from f17. Late at night there's live music and dancing.

Tapperij De Poshoorn (☎ 321 73 34, Stationsstraat 47) in the hotel of the same name is a classic brown cafe with a sensational beer list and specials for under f20.

Servaas Café (☎ 321 76 69, Corvesplein 10) is an excellent river-front cafe in Wyck. The young owners cook simple yet wonderful Belgian specials for under f30 and among their good beer selection they have Celis White on tap, which is one of the best beers in the US.

Café Sjiek (☎ 321 01 58, Sint Pieterstraat 13) is always crowded with locals who know they've found possibly the best place for a meal in town. Give your name to wise-cracking bartenders and settle back with some of the fine beers and wines while you wait for a spot to open up. The *zoervleis* (f19.50) is an addictive local stew.

Fast Food & Self-Catering *'t Witte Bruudsje (☎ 321 00 57, Platielstraat 12)* has fresh salads and various gourmet hot snacks, It's open 10 am to 2 am daily.

Joosten Fromages (☎ 321 44 64, Wyckerbrugstraat 43) has a superb selection of local cheeses and other produce that can make for a great picnic.

Entertainment
Bars & Clubs *Take One (☎ 321 64 23, Rechtstraat 28)* is a long and narrow tavern that feels little changed since the 1930s. It has an excellent beer selection.

Nearby, *John Mullins Irish Pub (☎ 350 01 41, Wyckerbrugstraat 50)* is an Irish pub popular with students. Every St Patrick's Day they cover the floor with actual, live sod. It's quite remarkable.

La Ferme (☎ 321 89 28, Rechtstraat 29) is a mellow gay bar, open nightly from 8 pm.

Maxy's Coffeeshop (Rechtstraat 49) is open 10 am to midnight.

Night Live (☎ 0900-202 01 58, Kesselskade 43) is a disco in an old church that opens after midnight at weekends. Cover charge is usually f7.

Theatre & Cinema *Derlon Theater (☎ 350 71 71, Plein 1992)* is near the new library and has drama and music. The cafe has fine river views from the terrace.

Theater an het Vrijthof (☎ 350 55 55, Vrijthof 47) is a grand theatre that was built in 1805 and now is the home to several theatre and dance groups.

Cinema Lumiere (☎ 321 40 80, Bogaardenstraat 40B) shows off-beat and classic films.

Shopping
Rechtstraat in Wyck has a fun variety of stores, including Bizarre (☎ 627 68 44) at No 63 which has a selection that speaks for itself. Kapoenstraat off Vrijthof is another good street for interesting shops.

Getting There & Away
Air Maastricht Airport is a small facility served by KLM exel (☎ 020-474 77 47) which has flights to London and connecting flights to Schiphol. It has one pay phone and one ATM.

Train Maastricht has a grand old train station with numerous services. Some fares and schedules are:

destination	price (f)	duration (mins)	frequency (per hr)
Amsterdam	51	150	1
Rotterdam	48	135	1
Utrecht	42	120	1

There is an hourly international service to Liege (f14.50, 30 minutes) where you can catch trains to Brussels, Paris and Cologne.

Bus The bus station is to the right as you exit the station. Eurolines has one bus a day to/from Brussels (f30, two hours). Interliner has hourly buses to/from Aachen (f5.50, one hour).

Car & Motorcycle The major car-rental firms have desks at the airport and offices in the suburbs. When reserving, make arrangements to get picked up.

Avis (☎ 325 23 77)
Budget (☎ 364 00 46)
Europcar (☎ 364 54 30)
Hertz (☎ 325 19 71)

Getting Around
To/From the Airport Maastricht Airport is 10km north from the centre. Bus Nos 51 and 61 link the two every two hours (25 minutes).

Bus Lijnnet operates the local buses, which you may not ever need.

Car & Motorcycle There is parking in massive underground lots by the river.

Taxi Maastricht is part of the treintaxi scheme (☎ 363 81 00). For a regular taxi call ☎ 343 00 00.

Bicycle The bicycle shop (☎ 321 11 00) is in a separate building to the left as you exit the station. It is open 6 am to midnight daily.

AROUND MAASTRICHT
The hills and forests of south Limburg make for excellent hiking and biking. The hill at the convergence of the Netherlands, Belgium and Germany, **Drielandenpunt**, is an excellent driving or biking destination. It's 26km south-east of Maastricht.

Valkenburg
☎ 043 • pop 18,200
This small, once charming town in the hills east of Maastricht has possibly the most overcommercialised centre in the Netherlands. The town attracts gobs of tour buses filled with folks who appreciate such a

scene. But away from the town are excellent trails and paths through the forests, so there's no reason to stay.

The VVV (☎ 0900-97 98, fax 609 8608), Dorrenplein 5, has a huge selection of maps of the area and is good at making recommendations. You might start at the over-restored **castle** above town (open 10 am to 4 pm daily, f5) from where trails radiate out through the countryside.

Cycle Center (☎ 601 53 38), Oosterweg 26, rents everything from simple bikes to mopeds. Prices start at f15 per day for simple models, while mountain bikes cost f40. It's open 9 am to 6 pm (until 5 pm weekends) and is closed Sunday and Monday from October to March. It's five minutes north of the station.

ASP Adventure (☎ 604 06 75, @ asp@cuci.nl) gives guided tours of the networks of caves that riddle the soft sandstone of the hills. A basic 90-minute tour costs f40 and there are many options, including riding bikes underground. Call in advance (from 9 am to noon) for reservations and pick-up.

Valkenburg is easily reached from Maastricht by train (f4.25, 12 minutes, every 30 minutes).

Sittard
If you need a break from your journey by road or train, Sittard has a compact downtown with an old quarter featuring the 14th-century **Sint Petruskerk** and the 17th-century baroque **Sint Michielskerk**.

NORTH LIMBURG
Clinging to the Maas River and barely 30km across at its widest point, the northern half of Limburg is a no-nonsense place of industry and agriculture. Venlo, the major town, has a small historic quarter near the train station. It's worth a quick look if you are changing trains for the hourly service to Cologne (90 minutes).

Roermond & Thorn
☎ 0475
Roermond is another place where you can have a pleasant ramble if you are changing

NOORD BRABANT & LIMBURG

trains. The compact centre sits on an inlet from the Maas River. The 13th-century **Munster** dominates the skyline and there are several pleasant cafes near its base.

Buses leave from in front of Roermond's train station. Train services include those on the main line to Maastricht (f13.25, 30 minutes, two per hour) as well as the local line that runs north along the Maas to Nijmegen. The bicycle shop (☎ 35 00 85) is open 6 am to midnight (from 8 am Sunday).

Thorn is well worth a visit. It is across the Maas and 10km from Roermond and can be reached by small pretty roads, well suited for bikes. The village dates back to at least the 10th century and is very scenic, with all of the buildings whitewashed and huddled along tiny canals and cafe-lined streets.

The VVV (☎ 56 27 61), Wijngaard 14, is helpful and can find local accommodation. It has a small **museum** and is open 10 am to 5 pm daily April to October (until 4 pm and closed Monday the rest of the year).

About 300m south of the centre, *Camping Vijerbrock (☎ 56 19 14, Kessenicherweg 20)* is in a peaceful spot and is open April to October. It charges f20 per site.

If not visiting Thorn by bike or car, bus No 73 runs hourly from Roermond (every two hours Sunday).

Nationaal Oorlogs-en Verzetmuseum

Overloon, a tiny and unremarkable town on the border with Noord Brabant, was the scene of fierce battles between the Americans, British and the Germans as part of Operation Market Garden in 1944. The heart of the battlefield is now the site of the National War & Resistance Museum (☎ 0478-64 18 20), Museumpark 1, a sober and thoughtful place that examines the role of the Netherlands in WWII.

The heart of the complex is a detailed chronological examination of the war. The privations suffered by the Dutch people are documented, but so is the complicity of many Dutch, who worked with the Nazis and helped persecute the Jews. A memorial building recalls the Holocaust. Outside there are numerous war relics left from the battles.

The museum is open 10 am to 5 pm daily and costs f12.50/8.50 for adults/children. To reach the museum ride the hourly local trains to Venray from either Roermond (f13.25, 40 minutes) or Nijmegen (f11.50, 25 minutes). Then call a treintaxi (0478-51 10 00) and buy your ticket (f7.50) from the ticket machine. The museum is 7km from the station. Make arrangements with the driver for your return.

Language

Most English speakers use the term 'Dutch' to describe the language spoken in the Netherlands and 'Flemish' for that spoken in the northern half of Belgium. Both are in fact the same language, called Netherlandic *(Nederlands)*. The differences between Dutch and Flemish *(Vlaams)* are similar to those between British and North American English.

Dutch nouns come in one of three genders: masculine, feminine (both with *de* for 'the') and neuter (with *het*). Where English uses 'a' or 'an', Netherlandic uses *een*, regardless of gender.

There's also a polite and an informal version of the English 'you'. The polite is *u* (pronounced like the German 'ü'), the informal is *je*. As a general rule, people who are older than you should be addressed as *u*.

Pronunciation
Vowels

a	short, as the 'u' in 'cut'
a, aa	long, as the 'a' in 'father'
au, ou	pronounced somewhere between the 'ow' in 'how' and the 'ow' in 'glow'
e	short, as in 'bet', or as the 'er' in 'fern' (without pronouncing the 'r')
e, ee	long, as the 'ay' in 'day'
ei	as the 'ey' in 'they'
eu	a tricky one; try saying 'eh' with rounded lips and the tongue forward, then slide the tongue back and down to make an 'oo' sound; it's similar to the 'eu' in French *couleur*
i	short, as in 'it'
i, ie	long, as the 'ee' in 'meet'
ij	as the 'ey' in 'they'
o	short, as in 'pot'
o, oo	long, as in 'note'
oe	as the 'oo' in 'zoo'
u	short, similar to the 'u' in 'urn'
u, uu	long, as the 'u' in 'flute'
ui	a very tricky one; pronounced somewhere between **au/ou** and **eu**; it's similar to the 'eui' in French *fauteuil*, without the slide to the 'i'

What's in a Name?

Dutch, like German, strings words together, which can baffle a foreigner trying to decipher (let alone remember) street names. *Eerste Goudsbloemdwarsstraat* (First Marigold Transverse Street) is a good example! Chopping a seemingly endless name into its separate components might help a bit. The following terms appear frequently in street names and on signs:

baan – path, way
binnen – inside, inner
bloem – flower
brug – bridge
buiten – outside, outer
dijk – dyke
dwars – transverse
eiland – island
gracht – canal
groot – great, large
haven – harbour
hoek – corner
huis – house
kade – quay
kapel – chapel
kerk – church
klein – minor, small
laan – avenue
markt – market
molen – (wind)mill
nieuw – new
noord – north
oost – east
oud – old
plein – square
poort – city gate
sloot – ditch
sluis – sluice, lock
steeg – alley
straat – street
toren – tower
veld – field
(burg)wal – (fortified) embankment
weg – road
west – west
wijk – district
zuid – south

Consonants

ch, g   a strong guttural 'kh' sound as in Scottish *loch*

j   as the 'y' in 'yes'; sometimes as the 'j' in 'jam' or the 's' in 'pleasure'

r   a trilled sound made with the tip of the tongue

s   as the 's' in 'save'; sometimes as the 'z' in 'zoo'

v   similar to English 'f'

w   at the beginning of a word, a clipped sound almost like a 'v'; at the end of a word, like English 'w'

Greetings & Civilities

Hello.	*Dag/Hallo.*
Goodbye.	*Dag.*
See you soon.	*Tot ziens.*
Yes/No.	*Ja/Nee.*
Please.	*Alstublieft/Alsjeblieft.*
Thank you.	*Dank u/je (wel)* or *Bedankt.*
Excuse me.	*Pardon.*
How are you?	*Hoe gaat het met u/jou?*
I'm fine, thanks.	*Goed, bedankt.*
What's your name?	*Hoe heet u/je?*
My name is ...	*Ik heet ...*
Where are you from?	*Waar komt u/kom je vandaan?*
I'm from ...	*Ik kom uit ...*

Language Difficulties

Do you speak English?	*Spreekt u/Spreek je Engels?*
I don't understand.	*Ik begrijp het niet.*
Please write it down.	*Schrijf het alstublieft/alsjeblieft op.*

Getting Around

What time does the ... leave/arrive?	*Hoe laat vertrekt/arriveert de ...?*
bus	*bus*
train	*trein*
tram	*tram*

Where is the ... ?	*Waar is de/het ... ?*
bus stop	*de bushalte*
metro station	*het metrostation*
train station	*het (trein) station*
tram stop	*de tramhalte*

Signs

INGANG	ENTRANCE
UITGANG	EXIT
VOL	FULL, NO VACANCIES
INFORMATIE, INLICHTINGEN	INFORMATION
OPEN/GESLOTEN	OPEN/CLOSED
POLITIEBUREAU	POLICE STATION
VERBODEN	PROHIBITED
KAMERS VRIJ	ROOMS AVAILABLE
WC'S/TOILETTEN	TOILETS
HEREN/DAMES	MEN/WOMEN

I'd like a one-way/return ticket.	*Ik wil graag een enkele reis/een retour.*
I'd like to hire a car/bicycle.	*Ik wil graag een auto/fiets huren.*

Directions

What street/road is this?	*Welke straat/weg is dit?*
How do I get to ...?	*Hoe kom ik bij ...?*
(Go) straight ahead.	*(Ga) rechtdoor.*
(Turn) left.	*(Ga naar) links.*
(Turn) right.	*(Ga naar) rechts.*
at the traffic lights	*bij het stoplicht*
at the next corner	*bij de volgende hoek*

Around Town

Where is the ...?	*Waar is de/het ...?*
bank	*de bank*
embassy	*de ambassade*
exchange office	*het wisselkantoor*
post office	*het postkantoor*
public toilet	*het openbaar toilet*
telephone centre	*het telefoonkantoor*
tourist office	*de VVV*

What time does it open/close?	*Hoe laat opent/sluit het?*

Accommodation

Do you have a room?	*Heeft u een kamer?*
How much is it per night/per person?	*Hoeveel is het per nacht/per persoon?*
Is breakfast included?	*Is ontbijt inbegrepen?*

May I see the room?	*Mag ik de kamer zien?*
camping ground	*camping*
guesthouse	*pension*
hotel	*hotel*
youth hostel	*jeugdherberg*

Food

I'm vegetarian.	*Ik ben vegetarisch.*
breakfast	*ontbijt*
lunch	*lunch/middageten*
dinner	*diner/avondeten*
restaurant	*restaurant*

Shopping

How much is it?	*Hoeveel is het?*
Can I look at it?	*Kan ik het zien?*
It's too expensive for me.	*Het is mij te duur.*
bookshop	*boekwinkel*
chemist/pharmacy	*drogist/apotheek*
clothing store	*kledingzaak*
laundry	*wasserette*
market	*markt*
supermarket	*supermarkt*
newsagency	*krantenwinkel*
stationers	*kantoorboekhandel*

Health

I need a doctor.	*Ik heb een dokter nodig.*
Where is the hospital?	*Waar is het ziekenhuis?*
I'm ...	*Ik ben ...*
asthmatic	*astmatisch*
diabetic	*suikerziek*
epileptic	*epileptisch*
antiseptic	*ontsmettingsmiddel*
aspirin	*aspirine*
condoms	*condooms*
constipation	*verstopping*
diarrhoea	*diarree*
nausea	*misselijkheid*

Emergencies

Call the police!	*Haal de politie!*
Call an ambulance!	*Haal een ziekenauto!*
Help!	*Help!*
I'm lost.	*Ik ben de weg kwijt.*

sunblock cream	*zonnebrandolie*
tampons	*tampons*

Time, Dates & Numbers

What time is it?	*Hoe laat is het?*
When?	*Wanneer?*
today	*vandaag*
tonight	*vanavond*
tomorrow	*morgen*
yesterday	*gisteren*
Monday	*maandag*
Tuesday	*dinsdag*
Wednesday	*woensdag*
Thursday	*donderdag*
Friday	*vrijdag*
Saturday	*zaterdag*
Sunday	*zondag*

1	*één*
2	*twee*
3	*drie*
4	*vier*
5	*vijf*
6	*zes*
7	*zeven*
8	*acht*
9	*negen*
10	*tien*
100	*honderd*
1000	*duizend*
10,000	*tienduizend*
one million	*een miljoen*
1st	*eerste*
2nd	*tweede*
3rd	*derde*
4th	*vierde*
5th	*vijfde*

Glossary

(See also the Language chapter for a list of terms commonly encountered in street names and sights.)

abdij – abbey
apotheek – chemist/pharmacy

bezoeker – visitor
borrel(tje) – slang for an alcoholic drink
bos – woods or forest
botter – type of 19th-century fishing boat
bruin cafe – brown cafe; traditional drinking establishment

cafe – pub, bar; also known as *kroeg*
coffeeshop – cafe, usually authorised to sell cannabis
CS – Centraal Station

dagschotel – dish of the day in Dutch restaurants

eetcafe – cafes serving meals

fietsenstalling – secure bicycle storage
fietspad – bicycle path

gasthuis – hospital or hospice
gemeente – municipal
genever – Dutch gin
gezellig – convivial
GG&GD – Municipal Medical & Health Service
GVB – Gemeentevervoerbedrijf; the Municipal Transport Company in Amsterdam
GWK – Grenswisselkantoren; official money exchange offices

haven – port
herberg – hostel
hof – courtyard
hofje – almshouse or series of buildings around a small courtyard, also known as Begijnhof
hoofd – main

jacht – yacht

kerk – church
koninkijk – royal

markt – town square
meer – lake
molen – windmill

NS – Nederlandse Spoorwegen; national railway company

plein – square
polder – area of drained land
poort – gate
Postbus – post office box

Randstad – literally 'rim-town'; the urban agglomeration including Amsterdam, Utrecht, Rotterdam and Den Haag
rijks – state

scheepvaart – shipping
sluis – lock (for boats/ships)
spoor – platform
stadhuis – city hall
stedelijk – civic
strand – beach
strippenkaart – ticket used on all public transport

treintaxi – special taxi for train passengers

veerboot – ferry
Vlaams – Flemish
voorlichting – information
VVV – tourist information office

waag – old weigh house
wasserette/wassalon – laundrette
werf – wharf, shipyard
wielklem – wheel clamp attached to illegally parked vehicles
windmolen – windmill
winkel – shop

zaal – hall
zee – sea
ziekenhuis – hospital

LONELY PLANET

You already know that Lonely Planet produces more than this one guidebook, but you might not be aware of the other products we have on this region. Here is a selection of titles that you may want to check out as well:

Western Europe
ISBN 1 86450 163 4
US$27.99 • UK£15.99

Europe phrasebook
ISBN 1 86450 224 X
US$8.99 • UK£4.99

Read this First: Europe
ISBN 1 86450 136 7
US$14.99 • UK£8.99

Europe on a shoestring
ISBN 1 86450 150 2
US$24.99 • UK£14.99

Amsterdam City Map
ISBN 1 86450 081 6
US$5.95 • UK£3.99

Amsterdam Condensed
ISBN 1 86450 133 2
US$9.99 • UK£5.99

Amsterdam
ISBN 0 86442 789 1
US$14.99 • UK£8.99

Available wherever books are sold

LONELY PLANET

ON THE ROAD

Travel Guides explore cities, regions and countries, and supply information on transport, restaurants and accommodation, covering all budgets. They come with reliable, easy-to-use maps, practical advice, cultural and historical facts and a rundown on attractions both on and off the beaten track. There are over 200 titles in this classic series, covering nearly every country in the world.

 Lonely Planet Upgrades extend the shelf life of existing travel guides by detailing any changes that may affect travel in a region since a book has been published. Upgrades can be downloaded for free from **www.lonelyplanet.com/upgrades**

For travellers with more time than money, **Shoestring** guides offer dependable, first-hand information with hundreds of detailed maps, plus insider tips for stretching money as far as possible. Covering entire continents in most cases, the six-volume shoestring guides are known around the world as 'backpackers bibles'.

For the discerning short-term visitor, **Condensed** guides highlight the best a destination has to offer in a full-colour, pocket-sized format designed for quick access. They include everything from top sights and walking tours to opinionated reviews of where to eat, stay, shop and have fun.

CitySync lets travellers use their Palm™ or Visor™ hand-held computers to guide them through a city with handy tips on transport, history, cultural life, major sights, and shopping and entertainment options. It can also quickly search and sort hundreds of reviews of hotels, restaurants and attractions, and pinpoint their location on scrollable street maps. CitySync can be downloaded from **www.citysync.com**

MAPS & ATLASES

Lonely Planet's **City Maps** feature downtown and metropolitan maps, as well as transit routes and walking tours. The maps come complete with an index of streets, a listing of sights and a plastic coat for extra durability.

Road Atlases are an essential navigation tool for serious travellers. Cross-referenced with the guidebooks, they also feature distance and climate charts and a complete site index.

LONELY PLANET

ESSENTIALS

Read This First books help new travellers to hit the road with confidence. These invaluable predeparture guides give step-by-step advice on preparing for a trip, budgeting, arranging a visa, planning an itinerary and staying safe while still getting off the beaten track.

Healthy Travel pocket guides offer a regional rundown on disease hot spots and practical advice on predeparture health measures, staying well on the road and what to do in emergencies. The guides come with a user-friendly design and helpful diagrams and tables.

Lonely Planet's **Phrasebooks** cover the essential words and phrases travellers need when they're strangers in a strange land. They come in a pocket-sized format with colour tabs for quick reference, extensive vocabulary lists, easy-to-follow pronunciation keys and two-way dictionaries.

Miffed by blurry photos of the Taj Mahal? Tired of the classic 'top of the head cut off' shot? **Travel Photography: A Guide to Taking Better Pictures** will help you turn ordinary holiday snaps into striking images and give you the know-how to capture every scene, from frenetic festivals to peaceful beach sunrises.

Lonely Planet's **Travel Journal** is a lightweight but sturdy travel diary for jotting down all those on-the-road observations and significant travel moments. It comes with a handy time-zone wheel, world maps and useful travel information.

Lonely Planet's eKno is an all-in-one communication service developed especially for travellers. It offers low-cost international calls and free email and voicemail so that you can keep in touch while on the road. Check it out on **www.ekno.lonelyplanet.com**

FOOD & RESTAURANT GUIDES

Lonely Planet's **Out to Eat** guides recommend the brightest and best places to eat and drink in top international cities. These gourmet companions are arranged by neighbourhood, packed with dependable maps, garnished with scene-setting photos and served with quirky features.

For people who live to eat, drink and travel, **World Food** guides explore the culinary culture of each country. Entertaining and adventurous, each guide is packed with detail on staples and specialities, regional cuisine and local markets, as well as sumptuous recipes, comprehensive culinary dictionaries and lavish photos good enough to eat.

LONELY PLANET

OUTDOOR GUIDES

For those who believe the best way to see the world is on foot, Lonely Planet's **Walking Guides** detail everything from family strolls to difficult treks, with 'when to go and how to do it' advice supplemented by reliable maps and essential travel information.

Cycling Guides map a destination's best bike tours, long and short, in day-by-day detail. They contain all the information a cyclist needs, including advice on bike maintenance, places to eat and stay, innovative maps with detailed cues to the rides, and elevation charts.

The **Watching Wildlife** series is perfect for travellers who want authoritative information but don't want to tote a heavy field guide. Packed with advice on where, when and how to view a region's wildlife, each title features photos of over 300 species and contains engaging comments on the local flora and fauna.

With underwater colour photos throughout, **Pisces Books** explore the world's best diving and snorkelling areas. Each book contains listings of diving services and dive resorts, detailed information on depth, visibility and difficulty of dives, and a roundup of the marine life you're likely to see through your mask.

LONELY PLANET

OFF THE ROAD

Journeys, the travel literature series written by renowned travel authors, capture the spirit of a place or illuminate a culture with a journalist's attention to detail and a novelist's flair for words. These are tales to soak up while you're actually on the road or dip into as an at-home armchair indulgence.

The new range of lavishly illustrated **Pictorial** books is just the ticket for both travellers and dreamers. Off-beat tales and vivid photographs bring the adventure of travel to your doorstep long before the journey begins and long after it is over.

Lonely Planet **Videos** encourage the same independent, tough-minded approach as the guidebooks. Currently airing throughout the world, this award-winning series features innovative footage and an original soundtrack.

Yes, we know, work is tough, so do a little bit of deskside dreaming with the spiral-bound Lonely Planet **Diary**, the tearaway page-a-day **Day-to-Day Calendar** or a Lonely Planet **Wall Calendar**, filled with great photos from around the world.

TRAVELLERS NETWORK

Lonely Planet Online. Lonely Planet's award-winning Web site has insider information on hundreds of destinations, from Amsterdam to Zimbabwe, complete with interactive maps and relevant links. The site also offers the latest travel news, recent reports from travellers on the road, guidebook upgrades, a travel links site, an online book-buying option and a lively traveller's bulletin board. It can be viewed at **www.lonelyplanet.com** or AOL keyword: lp.

Planet Talk is a quarterly print newsletter, full of gossip, advice, anecdotes and author articles. It provides an antidote to the being-at-home blues and lets you plan and dream for the next trip. Contact the nearest Lonely Planet office for your free copy.

Comet, the free Lonely Planet newsletter, comes via email once a month. It's loaded with travel news, advice, dispatches from authors, travel competitions and letters from readers. To subscribe, click on the Comet subscription link on the front page of the Web site.

LONELY PLANET

Guides by Region

Lonely Planet is known worldwide for publishing practical, reliable and no-nonsense travel information in our guides and on our Web site. The Lonely Planet list covers just about every accessible part of the world. Currently there are sixteen series: Travel guides, Shoestring guides, Condensed guides, Phrasebooks, Read This First, Healthy Travel, Walking guides, Cycling guides, Watching Wildlife guides, Pisces Diving & Snorkelling guides, City Maps, Road Atlases, Out to Eat, World Food, Journeys travel literature, Traveller's Advice titles and Illustrated pictorials.

AFRICA Africa on a shoestring • Cairo • Cairo Map • Cape Town • Cape Town Map • East Africa • Egypt • Egyptian Arabic phrasebook • Ethiopia, Eritrea & Djibouti • Ethiopian (Amharic) phrasebook • The Gambia & Senegal • Healthy Travel Africa • Kenya • Malawi • Morocco • Moroccan Arabic phrasebook • Mozambique • Read This First: Africa • South Africa, Lesotho & Swaziland • Southern Africa • Southern Africa Road Atlas • Swahili phrasebook • Tanzania, Zanzibar & Pemba • Trekking in East Africa • Tunisia • Watching Wildlife East Africa • Watching Wildlife Southern Africa • West Africa • World Food Morocco • Zimbabwe, Botswana & Namibia
Travel Literature: Mali Blues: Traveling to an African Beat • The Rainbird: A Central African Journey • Songs to an African Sunset: A Zimbabwean Story

AUSTRALIA & THE PACIFIC Aboriginal Australia & Torres Strait Islands • Auckland • Australia • Australian phrasebook • Australia Road Atlas • Bushwalking in Australia • Cycling Australia • Cycling New Zealand • Fiji • Fijian phrasebook • Healthy Travel Australia, NZ and the Pacific • Islands of Australia's Great Barrier Reef • Melbourne • Melbourne Map • Micronesia • New Caledonia • New South Wales & the ACT • New Zealand • Northern Territory • Outback Australia • Out to Eat – Melbourne • Out to Eat – Sydney • Papua New Guinea • Papua New Guinea Phrasebook • Pidgin phrasebook • Queensland • Rarotonga & the Cook Islands • Samoa • Solomon Islands • South Australia • South Pacific • South Pacific phrasebook • Sydney • Sydney Map • Sydney Condensed • Tahiti & French Polynesia • Tasmania • Tonga • Tramping in New Zealand • Vanuatu • Victoria • Walking in Australia • Watching Wildlife Australia • Western Australia
Travel Literature: Islands in the Clouds: Travels in the Highlands of New Guinea • Kiwi Tracks: A New Zealand Journey • Sean & David's Long Drive

CENTRAL AMERICA & THE CARIBBEAN Bahamas, Turks & Caicos • Baja California • Bermuda • Central America on a shoestring • Costa Rica • Costa Rica Spanish phrasebook • Cuba • Dominican Republic & Haiti • Eastern Caribbean • Guatemala • Guatemala, Belize & Yucatán: La Ruta Maya • Havana • Healthy Travel Central & South America • San Diego & Tijuana • Jamaica • Mexico • Mexico City • Panama • Puerto Rico • Read This First: Central & South America • World Food Mexico • World Food Caribbean • Yucatán
Travel Literature: Green Dreams: Travels in Central America

EUROPE Amsterdam • Amsterdam Map • Amsterdam Condensed • Andalucía • Austria • Baltic States phrasebook • Barcelona • Barcelona Map • Belgium & Luxembourg • Berlin • Berlin Map • Britain • British phrasebook • Brussels, Bruges & Antwerp • Brussels Map • Budapest • Budapest Map • Canary Islands • Central Europe • Central Europe phrasebook • Copenhagen • Corfu & the Ionians • Corsica • Crete • Crete Condensed • Croatia • Cycling Britain • Cycling France • Cyprus • Czech & Slovak Republics • Denmark • Dublin • Dublin Map • Eastern Europe • Eastern Europe phrasebook • Edinburgh • England • Estonia, Latvia & Lithuania • Europe on a shoestring • Europe Phrasebook • Finland • Florence • France • Frankfurt Condensed • French phrasebook • Georgia, Armenia & Azerbaijan • Germany • German phrasebook • Greece • Greek Islands • Greek phrasebook • Hungary • Iceland, Greenland & the Faroe Islands • Ireland • Istanbul • Italian phrasebook • Italy • Krakow • Lisbon • The Loire • London • London Map • London Condensed • Madrid • Malta • Mediterranean Europe • Milan, Turin & Genoa • Moscow • Mozambique • Munich • The Netherlands • Normandy • Norway • Out to Eat – London • Paris • Paris Map • Paris Condensed • Poland • Polish Phrasebook • Portugal • Portuguese phrasebook • Prague • Prague Map • Provence & the Côte d'Azur • Read This First: Europe • Rhodes & the Dodecanese • Romania & Moldova • Rome • Rome Condensed • Rome Map • Russia, Ukraine & Belarus • Russian phrasebook • Scandinavian & Baltic Europe • Scandinavian phrasebook • Scotland • Sicily • Slovenia • South-West France • Spain • Spanish phrasebook • St Petersburg • St Petersburg Map • Sweden • Switzerland • Trekking in Spain • Tuscany • Ukrainian phrasebook • Venice • Vienna • Walking in Britain • Walking in France • Walking in Ireland • Walking in Italy • Walking in Spain • Walking in Switzerland • Western Europe • World Food France • World Food Ireland • World Food Italy • World Food Spain
Travel Literature: A Small Place in Italy • After Yugoslavia • Love and War in the Apennines • On the Shores of the Mediterranean The Olive Grove: Travels in Greece • Round Ireland in Low Gear

LONELY PLANET

Mail Order

Lonely Planet products are distributed worldwide. They are also available by mail order from Lonely Planet, so if you have difficulty finding a title please write to us. North and South American residents should write to 150 Linden St, Oakland, CA 94607, USA; European and African residents should write to 10a Spring Place, London NW5 3BH, UK; and residents of other countries to Locked Bag 1, Footscray, Victoria 3011, Australia.

INDIAN SUBCONTINENT Bangladesh • Bengali phrasebook • Bhutan • Delhi • Goa • Healthy Travel Asia & India • Hindi & Urdu phrasebook • India • Indian Himalaya • Karakoram Highway • Kerala • Mumbai (Bombay) • Nepal • Nepali phrasebook • Pakistan • Rajasthan • Read This First: Asia & India • South India • Sri Lanka • Sri Lanka phrasebook • Tibet • Tibetan phrasebook • Trekking in the Indian Himalaya • Trekking in the Karakoram & Hindukush • Trekking in the Nepal Himalaya
Travel Literature: The Age of Kali: Indian Travels and Encounters • Hello Goodnight: A Life of Goa • In Rajasthan • A Season in Heaven: True Tales from the Road to Kathmandu • Shopping for Buddhas • A Short Walk in the Hindu Kush • Slowly Down the Ganges

ISLANDS OF THE INDIAN OCEAN Madagascar & Comoros • Maldives • Mauritius, Réunion & Seychelles
Travel Literature: Maverick in Madagascar

MIDDLE EAST & CENTRAL ASIA Bahrain, Kuwait & Qatar • Central Asia • Central Asia phrasebook • Dubai • Farsi (Persian) phrasebook • Hebrew phrasebook • Iran • Israel & the Palestinian Territories • Istanbul • Istanbul Map • Istanbul to Cairo on a shoestring • Istanbul to Kathmandu • Jerusalem • Jerusalem Map • Jordan • Lebanon • Middle East • Oman and the United Arab Emirates • Syria • Turkey • Turkish phrasebook • World Food Turkey • Yemen
Travel Literature: Black on Black: Iran Revisited • The Gates of Damascus • Kingdom of the Film Stars: Journey into Jordan

NORTH AMERICA Alaska • Boston • Boston Map • Boston Condensed • British Colombia • California & Nevada • California Condensed • Canada • Chicago • Chicago Map • Deep South • Florida • Great Lakes • Hawaii • Hiking in Alaska • Hiking in the USA • Honolulu • Las Vegas • Los Angeles • Los Angeles Map • Louisiana & The Deep South • Miami • Miami Map • Montreal • New England • New Orleans • New York City • New York City Map • New York City Condensed • New York, New Jersey & Pennsylvania • Oahu • Out to Eat – San Francisco • Pacific Northwest • Puerto Rico • Rocky Mountains • San Francisco • San Francisco Map • San Diego & Tijuana • Seattle • Southwest • Texas • Toronto • USA • USA phrasebook • Vancouver • Virginia & the Capital Region • Washington DC • Washington DC Map • World Food Deep South, USA • World Food New Orleans
Travel Literature: Caught Inside: A Surfer's Year on the California Coast • Drive Thru America

NORTH-EAST ASIA Beijing • Beijing Map • Cantonese phrasebook • China • Hiking in Japan • Hong Kong • Hong Kong Map • Hong Kong Condensed • Hong Kong, Macau & Guangzhou • Japan • Japanese phrasebook • Korea • Korean phrasebook • Kyoto • Mandarin phrasebook • Mongolia • Mongolian phrasebook • Seoul • Shanghai • South-West China • Taiwan • Tokyo • World Food – Hong Kong
Travel Literature: In Xanadu: A Quest • Lost Japan

SOUTH AMERICA Argentina, Uruguay & Paraguay • Bolivia • Brazil • Brazilian phrasebook • Buenos Aires • Chile & Easter Island • Colombia • Ecuador & the Galapagos Islands • Healthy Travel Central & South America • Latin American Spanish phrasebook • Peru • Quechua phrasebook • Read This First: Central & South America • Rio de Janeiro • Rio de Janeiro Map • Santiago • South America on a shoestring • Santiago • Trekking in the Patagonian Andes • Venezuela
Travel Literature: Full Circle: A South American Journey

SOUTH-EAST ASIA Bali & Lombok • Bangkok • Bangkok Map • Burmese phrasebook • Cambodia • East Timor Phrasebook • Hanoi • Healthy Travel Asia & India • Hill Tribes phrasebook • Ho Chi Minh City • Indonesia • Indonesian phrasebook • Indonesia's Eastern Islands • Jakarta • Java • Lao phrasebook • Laos • Malay phrasebook • Malaysia, Singapore & Brunei • Myanmar (Burma) • Philippines • Pilipino (Tagalog) phrasebook • Read This First: Asia & India • Singapore • Singapore Map • South-East Asia on a shoestring • South-East Asia phrasebook • Thailand • Thailand's Islands & Beaches • Thailand, Vietnam, Laos & Cambodia Road Atlas • Thai phrasebook • Vietnam • Vietnamese phrasebook • World Food Thailand • World Food Vietnam

ALSO AVAILABLE: Antarctica • The Arctic • The Blue Man: Tales of Travel, Love and Coffee • Brief Encounters: Stories of Love, Sex & Travel • Chasing Rickshaws • The Last Grain Race • Lonely Planet Unpacked • Not the Only Planet: Science Fiction Travel Stories • Lonely Planet On the Edge • Sacred India • Travel with Children • Travel Photography: A Guide to Taking Better Pictures

Index

Text

A

Aalsmeer 190
Aalsmeer Flower Auction 190
accommodation 75-7
  camping 75
  hostels 76
  hotels 76-7
Afsluitdijk 166, 176, 194
air travel 84-91, 96
  airlines 84
  airports 84
  to/from the Netherlands 87-91
Alkmaar 176-9, **177**
Alphen 105
Ameland 272
Amerongen 205
Amersfoort 204-5
Amstelveen 106
Amsterdam 109-62, **336-352**
  accommodation 139-44
  attractions 116-37
  entertainment 149-54
  food 144-9
  shopping 155-7
  tourist offices 111
  travel to/from 157-9
  travel within 159-62
Annen 284
Apeldoorn 300-1
Appel, Karel 32
architecture 32-5, 128, 201, 239, 304
area codes 55
Arnhem 296-8
art galleries
  Centraal Museum 200
  Chabotmuseum 238
  Civic Guard Gallery 121
  De Hallen 186
  Frans Hals Museum 185-6
  Gemeentemuseum 223
  Kröller-Müller Museum 300
  Mauritshuis 220
  Mesdag Museum 221
  Museum Boijmans van Beuningen 238
  Museum Catharijneconvent 200

Museum voor Moderne Kunst 296
Prince William V Gallery 221
Rijksmuseum 133-4
Singer Museum 193
Stedelijk 134
Stedelijk Museum 178
Van Gogh Museum 134
Assen 285

B

Baarle-Nassau 105
Barger-Compascuum 284
Beatrix, Queen 20-5, 71, 224
Bedum 281
beer 81, 136, 178
Bergen Op Zoom 307
Beveland 257
Bierum 281
Biesbosch National Park 250-2
Binnenhof 220-1
Bloemenmarkt (Flower Market) 122
Blokzijl 292-3
boat travel 94, 102
  to/from the Netherlands 94
  within the Netherlands 102
boating 72-3, 166-7, 191, 195
Bolsward 269
Bonnefantenmuseum 309-10
books 56-8, see also literature
Borger 284
Bosch, Hieronymus 28, 238
Bourtange 282-4
Breda 105
Breukelen 203-4
brown cafes 68
Bruegel the Elder 28, 238
Buitenpost 265
Burger's Zoo 296
bus travel 92-3, 99
  to/from the Netherlands 92-3
  within the Netherlands 99
business hours 70

C

cafes 68-9
car travel 93, 99-101
  driving licence 47, 93
  rental 100-1

road distance chart 100
road rules 100
Carnaval 311
castles 105, 106, 175, 190-1, 205, 221, 281-2, 295, 310, 313
Centraal Station 116-18
Chaam 105
children, travel with 66
churches
  Amstelkerk 129
  Augustinerkerk 247
  Bergkerk 288
  Bovenkerk 291
  Domkerk 200
  Grotekerk (Alkmaar) 178
  Grotekerk (Arnhem) 296
  Grotekerk (Den Haag) 221
  Grotekerk (Deventer) 287-8
  Grotekerk (Dordrecht) 249
  Grotekerk (Edam) 170
  Grotekerk (Monnickendam) 166
  Grotekerk (Naarden) 192
  Grotekerk (Zwolle) 291
  Grotekerk van St Bavo (Haarlem) 185
  Krijtberg 122
  Martinikerk 278
  Nieuwekerk (Delft) 233
  Nieuwekerk (Amsterdam) 118
  Noorderkerk 125
  North-East Groningen 281
  Oudekerk aan de Amstel (Amsterdam) 107
  Oudekerk (Delft) 233
  Oudekerk (Rotterdam) 240
  Oudekerk (Amsterdam) 118-19
  Pieterskerk 200, 211
  Ronde Luthersekerk 121
  St Janskathedraal 303-4
  St Lodewijkerk 214
  St Nicolaaskerk 117
  Sint Janskerk 228-9
  Sint Joriskerk 204
  Sint Stevenskerk 295
  The Abbey 253-4
  Westerkerk (Amsterdam) 125
  Westerkerk (Enkhuizen) 173
  Zuiderkerk 130

Bold indicates maps.

cinema 38-9, 201
climate 22
CoBrA 32, 137, 186
CoBrA Museum 137
coffee 80, 83
coffeeshops 69
Concertgebouw 134-5
consulates 48-9
courses 74, 138-9
    language 74
cultural considerations 40-2,
    45, 67-70, 119
customs regulations 49
cycling 71, 93, 97, 101, 103-8
    Amsterdam 139, 161-2
    Bourtange 283
    Breda 307
    De Hoge Veluwe National
        Park 298-300
    Deventer 288
    Hilversum 193
    IJmuiden 190
    National Fietsmuseum
        Velorama 295
    rental 103
    road rules 104
    Scheveningen 223-4
    Texel Island 181-2
    Zutphen 301

D
dance 35
De Boschplaat 270-1
De Cocksdorp 180-3
De Hoge Veluwe National Park
    298-300, **299**
De Koog 180
De Stijl 31-2, 223
De Witt, Johann 15-6
Delfshaven 240
Delft 230-5, **231**
delftware 232
Delta Expo 257-8
Delta Project 250-2, 256
Den Bosch 302-5, **305**
Den Burg 180-3
Den Haag 218-27, **219**, **222**
Den Helder 179-80
Den Hoorn 180-3
Denekamp 293
Deventer 286-90, **288**
disabled travellers 65-6
documents 46-8

Doesburg 290
Dokkum 265, 269
Domburg 105, 256-7
Domtoren 199-200
Doorn 205
Dordrecht 245-50, **248**
Dordrechts Museum 249
Drenthe 283-5, **275**
Drielandenpunt 313
drinks 80-1
Dutch East India Company 14-
    16, 83, 171-2, 194
Dutch West India Company
    14-16

E
Ecomare 181
economy 24-5
Edam 168-71, **169**
education 25-7
Eindhoven 305-6
electricity 59
Elfstedentocht 268-70
embassies 48-9
emergencies 67
Emmen 284
Enkhuizen 172-5, 176
Enschede 293
entertainment 81-2
Erasmus, Desiderius 26
Euromast 238
Europoort 245

F
fauna 23
fax services 55
festivals 201, 214, 224, 241,
    246, 278, 295, 311
films 58, see also cinema
Flevoland 193-6, **164**
flora 23
    tulips 16-17, 216
food 77-80
fortress, see castles
Franeker 267, 269
Frank, Anne 18-19, 125
Friesland 260-73, **261**
Frisian Islands 269-73, **270**
Frisian Lakes 265-6

G
Galder 105
Garmerwolde 281
gay travellers 64-5, 154
Gelderland 293-301, **287**

Gemeentemuseum 223
geography 21-2
Giethoorn 292
Glimmen 107
Goes 257
Golden Age 14-16, 28-30
Gouda 227-30, **228**
Gouwzee Bay 167
government 24-5
grand cafes 68
Groningen 107, 274-83,
    275
Groningen City 274-81, **277**
Groninger Museum 276
Grotekerk (Arnhem) 296

H
Haarlem 183-9, **184**
Hals, Frans 29-30, 133, 185-6
Haren 107
Harlingen 266-7, 269
Hasselt 290
Hattem 290
Havelaar, Max 83
health 60-4
    AIDS 62-3
    infectious diseases 61-2
    insurance 60
Heineken Museum 136
Het Gooi 191-3
Hilversum 192-4
Hindeloopen 268-70
history 12-20
    Golden Age 14-16
    Hanseatic League 286, 290,
        291, 293
    Independence 13-14
    Roman era 12
    Spanish 13-14, 176, 191,
        208-9
    United Provinces 14
    WWII 18-19, 19-20, 71,
        223-4, 248, 282, 285,
        293-6, 314
hitching 93-4, 101-2
Hoek van Holland 245
Hogebeintum 265
holidays 70-1
Hollandsche Schouwburg 132
Hollum 272
Holwerd 265
Hooghalen 285
Hoorn 171-2, 176, 270-1
Hortus Botanicus 211
hunebedden 12, 283-4,
    284-5

Bold indicates maps.

I

IJlst 269
IJsselmeer 176, 265-6, 267-9
insurance
  health 60
  travel 47
Internet
  access 55-6
  resources 56

K

Kaasmarkt 169-70
Kamp Westerbork 285
Kampen 290, 291
Kasteel Radboud 175
Katwijk aan Zee 218
Kennemerduinen National Park
  189
Keukenhof 217-18
Kinderdijk 245, 246
Klijndijk 284
Kok, Wim 24-5, 103, 189
Kröller-Müller Museum 300

L

language 41-2
Laren 193
laundry 59
Leeuwarden 261-5, **262**
legal matters 67-70
Leiden 208-17, **212**
Leiden University 211
Lelystad 194-5
lesbian travellers 64-5, 154
Limburg 307-14, **303**
Lisse 217
literature 37-8
Loosdrechtse Plassen 204

M

Maastricht 307-13, **308**
Madurodam 223
magazines 58
Makkum 268
maps 44
Marken 167-8
markets
  Albert Cuypmarkt 135-6
  Alkmaar Cheese Market 177-8
  Gouda Cheese Market 229
  Kaasmarkt 169-70
Mastbos 105
Mata Hari 261, 263
Mauritshuis 220
Medemblik 175-6

Menkemaborg 281-2
Middelburg 252-6, **253**
Midlaren 284
Mondriaan, Piet 31-2, 105, 223
money 49-53
  ATMs 51
  bargaining 52
  costs 52
  credit cards 51
  currency 49-50
  exchange rates 50
  taxes 52-3
  tipping 52
  travellers cheques 51
Monnickendam 166-7
Monster 245
motorcycle travel 93, 99-101
  rental 101
  road rules 100
Muiderslot 190-1
Museum Catharijneconvent
  200
museums
  Airborne Museum Harten-
    stein 296-7
  Allard Pierson Museum 118
  Amsterdams Historisch
    Museum 121
  Anne Frankhuis 125
  Batavia Werf 194
  Bijbels Museum 124
  Bonnefantenmuseum 309-10
  Breda 306-7
  Comenius Museum 192
  Cruquius Museum 189
  De Dubbelde Palmboom 240
  Dordrechts Museum 249
  Drents Museum 285
  Edams Museum 170
  Eise Eisinga Planetarium 267
  Erotic Museum 119
  Fries Museum 262-3
  Fries Scheepvaart Museum
    265
  Frysk Letterkundich
    Museum 263
  Geels & Co 118
  Groninger Museum 276
  Hash & Marihuana Museum
    119
  Heineken 136
  Het Eerste Friese
    Schaatsmuseum 268-70
  Het Netherlands Spoorweg-
    museum 200-1
  Historisch Museum (Mon-
    nickendam) 166

Historisch Museum Het
  Schielandhuis 240
Holland Experience 130
Hollands Kaasmuseum 178
IJmuiden 189-190
Joods Historisch Museum 131
Legermuseum 233
Madurodam 223
Maritiem Museum Rotter-
  dam 238-240
Maritime and Beachcombers
  Museum 181
Maritime Museum 181
Multatuli Museum 121
Museum 1939–1945 Cold
  War Historical Center 282
Museum 1940–1945 248
Museum Amstelkring 119
Museum Beelden aan Zee 223
Museum de Zwarte Tulp 217
Museum Flehite 204
Museum Het Catharina
  Gasthuis 229
Museum Het Rembrandthuis
  130
Museum Het Valkhof 295
Museum Lambert van
  Meerten 232
Museum of the 20th Cen-
  tury 171
Nationaal Biermuseum 178
Nationaal Hunebedden
  Infocentrum 284
Nationaal Oorlogs- en
  Verzetmuseum 314
National Fietsmuseum
  Velorama 295
National War and Resistance
  Museum 18-19
Naturalis – Nationaal Natu-
  urhistorisch Museum 214
Nederlands Filmmuseum 135
Nederlands Omroepmuseum
  193
Nederlands Openluchtmu-
  seum 297-298
Nederlands Scheepvaartmu-
  seum 132
Nederlands Textielmuseum
  306
newMetropolis 133
Niemeyer Tabaksmuseum 276
Nieuw Land Poldermuseum
  194
Noordbrabants Museum 304
Noordelijk Scheepvaartmu-
  seum 276

museums *(cont)*
  Oosterbeek War Cemetery
    297
  Paleis Museum 221
  Paul Tétar van Elven
    Museum 233
  Pilgrim Fathers Center 210
  Princessehof Museum 263
  Prinsenhof 233
  Rijksmuseum Twenthe 293
  Rijksmuseum van Oudheden
    211
  Rijksmuseum voor
    Volkenkunde 214
  Seksmuseum Amsterdam 117
  Stedelijk Museum Zwolle 290
  Stedelijk Van Abbemuseum
    306
  Tattoo Museum 119
  Terschelling Museum 't
    Behouden Huys 270-1
  Teylers Museum 186
  Theatermuseum 124
  Universiteitmuseum 200
  Veenpark 284
  Vestingmuseum 191-2
  Volendams Museum 168
  Westfries Museum 171
  World Museum 240
  Zaanse Schans 165-6
  Zeeland Museum 254
  Zuiderzeemuseum 173-4
music 35-7, 152-3

N
Naarden 191-2
Nationaal Oorlogs- en
  Verzetmuseum 314
national parks 23-5
  Biesbosch 250-1
  De Hoge Veluwe 298-300
  De Veluwezoon 300
  De Weerribben 291-2
  Kennemerduinen 189
  Schiermonnikoog 272-3
National War and Resistance
  Museum 18-19
NBT 46
Nederlands Openluchtmuseum
  297-298
Nederlands Scheepvaartmu-
  seum 132
Nes 272

newspapers 58
Nijmegen 293-6, **294**
Noord Brabant 302-7, **303**
Noord Holland 163-96, **164**
Noordelijk Scheepvaartmuseum
  276
Noordoostpolder 194, 195-6,
  291
Noordwijk aan Zee 218
North Sea Jazz Festival 224

O
Odoorn 284
Olst 288
Onze Lieve Vrouwe Toren 204
Oosterbeek 296-7
Oosterbroek 107
Oosterend 180-3, 270-1
Oost-Vlieland 271-2
Ootmarsum 293
Operation Market Garden 19-20,
  297
Orvelte 285
Oudeschild 180-3
Oudewater 205-6
Overijssel 286-93, **287**
Overveen 189

P
painting 27-32
palaces
  Royal Palace 118
  Paleis Het Loo 300-1
  Paleis Museum 221
  Paleis Noordeinde 221
Panorama Mesdag 221
Peace Palace 221
philosophy 26-7
photography & video 59
Pieterburen 280
Pilgrims 210, 240
pillarisation 40
politics 24-5
postal services 53
Provos 20-3

R
radio 58-9
religion 41
Rembrandt 29, 130, 133, 209,
  238
Rietveld Schröder House 201
Rijksmuseum 133-4
Roermond 313-14
Roosendaal 307

Rotterdam 235-45, **237**
Royal Palace 118

S
safe travel 66-7
Scheveningen 223-4
Schiermonnikoog 272-3, 280
Schiermonnikoog National Park
  272-3
Schokland 196
science 25-6
Scouwen-Duiveland 258-9
senior tarvellers 66
shopping 82-3
Singraven 293
Sinterklaas 72
Sittard 313
skating 72, 138, 269
Sloten 269
Sluis 259
Sneek 265-6, 269
special events 70-1
spectator sports 82, 154
Spinoza, Baruch 26
Stavoren 269
Stedelijk Museum 134
Stevinsluizen 176

T
taxis 102
telephone services 53-5
Ten Boer 281
Terschelling 270-1
Texel Island 179-83, 269, **180**
The Hague, *see* Den Haag
theatre 39, 153
Thorn 313-14
Tilburg 306
time 59
toilets 59-60
tourist offices 45-6
tours 94-5, 102, 139
train travel 91-2, 96-9
  to/from the Netherlands 91-2
  train passes 98-9
  within the Netherlands 96-9
treintaxi 99
Trekweg 265
tulips 16-17, 190, 211, 216-
  17, 217-18
TV 58-9

U
Uden 302
Uithuizen 281-2

Bold indicates maps.

Ulvenhout 105
Urk 195-6
Utrecht City 197-203, **199**
Utrecht province 197-206,
    198

V

Valkenburg 313
Van Eyck, Jan 28
Van Gogh Museum 134
Van Gogh, Vincent 31, 105,
    134, 238, 283, 300
Veere 106, 256
Velsen 190
Vermeer, Jan 29-30, 133, 230,
    232-3
video, see photography &
    video
visas 46-8
Vlieland 271-2
Vlissingen 257
Volendam 167-8

Vollenhove 293
VVV 45-6

W

Wadden Islands 176
wadlopen 280
Walcheren Peninsula 252, 256-7
walking 71-2, 295
WaterLand 258
Waterpoort 265-6
weights 59
West Terschelling 270-1
Westerbork 285
Westerkerk (Enkhuizen) 173
Westerschouwen 259
wildlife, see fauna
Wilhelmina, Queen 19-20, 221
Willemstad 307
windmills 105, 107, 132, 165-6,
    245, 246, 256, 259, 213, 240
windsurfing 73, 166-7, 168, 195
women travellers 64

work 74-5
Workum 268, 269
WWII 296-8

Z

Zaandam 165-6
Zaandijk 165-6
Zaanse Schans 165-6, 246
Zaanstad 165-6
Zaltbommel 301
Zandvoort 189
Zeeland 251-9, **208**
Zeeuws-Vlaanderen 259
Zierikzee 258-9
zoo 115, 132
Zuid Holland 207-51, **208**
Zuiderzee 21-2, 166, 173-4,
    176, 194, 195, 267-9, 291
Zuiderzeemuseum 173-4
Zutphen 288, 290, 301
Zwartsluis 293
Zwolle 288, 290-1

Boxed Text

Afsluitdijk, The 176
Blowing in the Wind 246
Cafe Society 68-9
Coffee: from Yemen to You 80
Day at the Races, A 269
Delta Project, The 252
Dutch Jews 18-19
Frisian Island Facts 272
Gables & Hoists 128
Good to the Last Scrape – or
    Drop 40

Haarlemmer Hofjes 186
Hanseatic League, The 90
How-To Guide to Bike Theft 161
In a Tight Spot 120
Mad about Tulips 16-17
Making the Blue & White Gold
    232
Mata Hari 263
Moment in Time, A 71
Operation Market Garden 297
Pilgrims' Progress 210

Pounding Mud 280
Provos 21
Rotterdam Architecture 239
Roxy Burns 153
Seal of Fairness 83
Sinning in Safety 119
Sinterklaas, the Original Santa
    Claus 72
Tasty Brew, A 81
Tulips – The Beloved Bulb 216
What's in a Name? 315

MAP 1 - GREATER AMSTERDAM

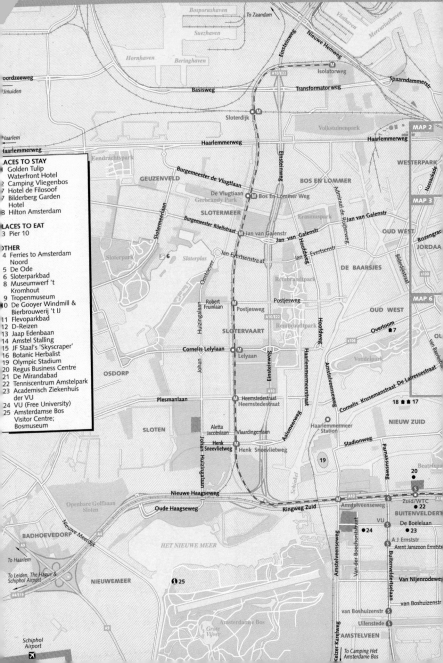

PLACES TO STAY
1 Golden Tulip
  Waterfront Hotel
2 Camping Vliegenbos
7 Hotel de Filosoof
7 Bilderberg Garden
  Hotel
8 Hilton Amsterdam

PLACES TO EAT
3 Pier 10

OTHER
4 Ferries to Amsterdam
  Noord
5 De Ode
6 Sloterparkbad
8 Museumwerf 't
  Kromhout
9 Tropenmuseum
10 De Gooyer Windmill &
   Bierbrouwerij 't IJ
11 Flevoparkbad
12 D-Reizen
13 Jaap Edenbaan
14 Amstel Stalling
15 JF Staal's 'Skyscraper'
16 Botanic Herbalist
19 Olympic Stadium
20 Regus Business Centre
21 De Mirandabad
22 Tenniscentrum Amstelpark
23 Academisch Ziekenhuis
   der VU
24 VU (Free University)
25 Amsterdamse Bos
   Visitor Centre;
   Bosmuseum

De Kaaskamer – best cheese in town

Clogs, clogs, everywhere

Get some flowers on the way home

Viscenter Volendam – fresh fish aplenty

Puccini Bomboni – best chocolate in town

Just in case the wheels fall off

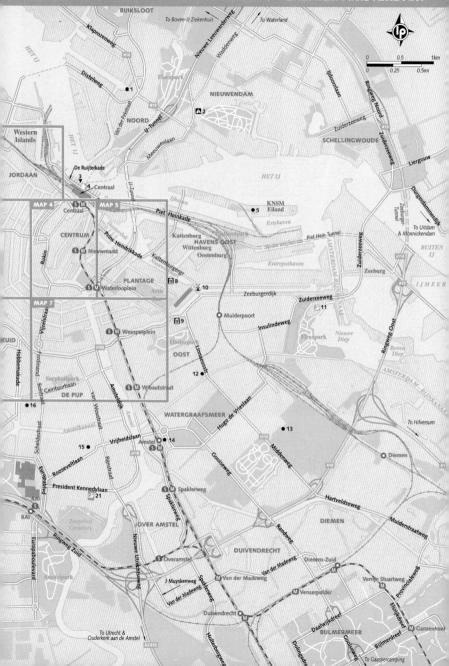

MAP 1 - GREATER AMSTERDAM

BUIKSLOOT

Klaprozenweg

To Boven-IJ Ziekenhuis

Nieuwe Leeuwarderweg

Waddenweg

To Waterland

Distelweg

Floraspark

■ 1

Van der Pekstraat

NOORD

NIEUWENDAM

▲ 2

HET IJ

IJ-Tunnel

Meeuwenlaan

SCHELLINGWOUDE

Ringweg Noord

Zuiderzeeweg

Zuiderzeeweg

Liergouw

To Uitdam & Monnickendam

Western Islands

De Ruijterkade

3 ▲

4 Centraal

JORDAAN

HET IJ

IJhaven

KNSM Eiland

■ 5

Ertshaven

Duigerdammerdijk

Zeeburger-Tunnel

BUITEN IJ

MAP 4

S M Centraal

MAP 5

Piet Heinkade

Oostenburg

CENTRUM

Prins Hendrikkade

Kattenburg Wittenburg Oostenburg

HAVENS OOST

Piet Hein Tunnel

AMSTERDAM-RIJNKANAAL

Zeeburg

IJMEER

Rokin

S M Nieuwmarkt

Kattenburgergr

Entrepothaven

Zuiderzeeweg

A10

PLANTAGE

S M Waterlooplein

Artis

■ 8

✈ 10

Zeeburgerdijk

Zuiderzeeweg

Nieuwe Diep

Boven Diep

Ringweg Oost

MAP 7

Vijzelstraat

■ 9

Muiderpoort

■ 11

Flevopark

AMSTERDAM M. RIJNKANAAL

ZUID

Hobbemakade

Ferdinand Bolstraat

S M Weesperplein

Oosterpark

Linnaeusstraat

OOST

Insulindeweg

Sarphatipark

Ceintuurbaan

DE PIJP

Amsteldijk

van Woustraat

S M Wibautstraat

■ 12

WATERGRAAFSMEER

Hugo de Vrieslaan

■ 13

To Hilversum

■ 16

Amstelkanaal

Scheldestraat

Rijnstraat

Vrijheidstraat

Amstel

S M 14

15 ■

Gooiseweg

Middenweg

A10

Roosevelttaan

President Kennedylaan

■ 21

Europaplein

Europaboulevard

RAI

RAI

Zorgvlied Cemetery

Ringweg Zuid

Nieuwe Utrechtseweg

S M Spaklerweg

OVER AMSTEL

Spaklerweg

Randweg

Hartveldseweg

Muiderstraatweg

DIEMEN

Diemen

A1

To Diemen

Amstelpark

S Overamstel

DUIVENDRECHT

Van der Madeweg

Dienen-Zuid

Verrijn Stuartweg

Provincialeweg

J Muyskenweg

M Van der Madeweg

Spaklerweg

Van der Madeweg

M Venserpolder

Daalwijkdreef

To Utrecht & Ouderkerk aan de Amstel

A2/E35

Duivendrecht

Hoftenbergweg

Dolingadreef

BIJLMERMEER

Gooiseweg

Bijlmerdreef

M Ganzenhoef

Elsrijkdreef

To Gaaspercamping

0   0.5   1km
0   0.25   0.5mi

Small cafe, big saxaphone

Cosy spot for a late night bite

Trance Buddha – trance temple

Le Pêcheur – renowned for its fantastic fish dishes

Cafe de Jaren – read a foreign newspaper and sip on a coffee overlooking the Amstel

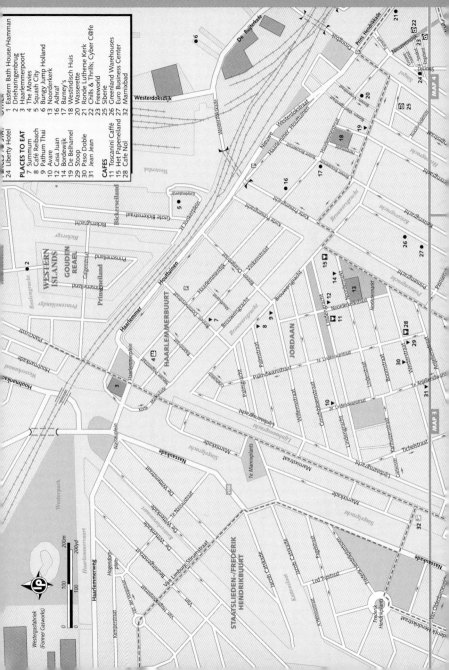

MAP 2 - AMSTERDAM

OTHER
1 Eastern Bath House/Hamman
2 Driehangenbrug
3 Haarlemmerpoort
4 The Movies
5 Squash City
6 Bungy Jump Holland
13 Noorderkerk
16 Ashraf
17 Barney's
18 Westindisch Huis
19 De Belhamel
21 Wasserette
22 Ronde Lutherse Kerk
23 Chills & Thrills; Cyber C@fe
25 Freeworld
26 Siberie
27 Greenland Warehouses
27 Euro Business Center
32 Marnixbad

24 Liberty Hotel

PLACES TO EAT
7 Summum
8 Café Reibach
9 Pathum Thai
10 Avare
12 Casa Juan
14 Bordewijk
19 De Belhamel
29 Stoop
30 Paso Doble
31 Jean Jean

CAFES
11 Toscanini Caffé
15 Het Papeneiland
28 Cafe Nol

MAP 3 - AMSTERDAM

MAP 2

1
Marnixplein

2 ▼

3 ☐
▼ 4
▼ 7
6
5
Herenstraat

8 ▼

Anjeliersstraat
Tuinstraat

9 ☐

JORDAAN

15 ■

16

Egelantiersgracht

10 ☐
11 ▼

▼ 14

Leliegracht

27 ▼
25 ☐
24 ●
Nieuwe Leliestraat

Leliegracht
12
13

18 17
Oude Tolbrug-Torensluis
Torensluis Bridge

26 ■
Bloemgracht

☐ 23
Westermarkt

Bloemgracht

🕯 22
21 ●
19 🏛

20

Bloemstraat

29 ●
30 ●

▼ 31

Raadhuisstraat

28 ■

32 ●

33

34

Rozenstraat
Laurierstraat

Reestraat
35 ●
Hartenstraat
36 ●
Gasthuismolenst

JORDAAN

Lauriergracht

☐ 37

Treeftst
Romeinsarmst

38 ●
Lauriergracht
42 ●
44 ●

45 ▼
Berenstraat
46 ●
47
48 ▼
Wolvenstraat
49 ●
Oude Spiegelstr

50
51 ■
52 ☐
Raam

39 ●
40 ●
41 ●
Elandsstraat

▼ 43
Elandsgracht

53 ▼
54 ☐
59
55 ■
Wijde Heist
60 ☐
61 ▼
62
63
64

71

Looiersgracht
Runstraat
Huidenstraat
56 ●
57 ▼
58 🏛

73 ●

72

Looiersgracht
Passeerdersgracht

65 ☐

66 ●
67

70

68 ●
69 ●
Koningsplein

Raamplein
74 ☐

76 ☐
75 ■
77 ▼

78

79
80 ●
81 ■
82 ●
83 ●
84

85 ■
86 ☆

MAP 6

MAP 3 - AMSTERDAM

PLACES TO STAY

15 Canal House Hotel
26 Hotel van Onna
28 Christian Youth Hostel Eben Haëzer
33 Pulitzer Hotel
50 Hotel Estheréa
55 Ambassade Hotel
67 Hotel Agora
75 International Budget Hotel
81 Aerohotel

PLACES TO EAT

1 Albatros
2 De Bolhoed
4 ! Zest
6 Dimitri's
7 Pancake Bakery
8 Burger's Patio
11 Rozen & Tortillas
14 Christophe
18 Foodism
27 De Vliegende Schotel
31 Koh-I-Noor
43 Rakang Thai
45 Hein
46 Nielsen
48 Turqoise
52 Grekas
53 d'Vijff Vlieghen Restaurant
57 Goodies
77 Pastini

CAFES

3 de Vergulde Gapper Cafe
9 t' Smalle Cafe
10 De 2 Zwaantjes
37 Van Puffelen
51 Gollem
54 Dante Cafe
60 Hoppe
62 Luxembourg
76 De Pieper

OTHER

5 Reina
12 Anne Frankhuis
13 Greenpeace Headquarters
16 House With the Heads
17 Grey Area
19 Theatermuseum
20 Bartolotti House
21 Let's Go
22 Homomonument
23 Westerkerk
24 Bike City
25 Mad Processor
29 Kitsch Kitchen
30 Galleria d'Arte Rinascimento
32 COC Amsterdam
34 Main Post Office; NBBS
35 Analik
36 Lady Day
38 Moped Rental Service
39 MacBike
40 Korsakoff
41 Maloe Melo
42 The English Bookshop
44 Xantippe Unlimited
47 Felix Meritis Building
49 Evenaar Literaire Reis-boekhandel
56 Van Ravenstein
58 Bijbels Museum
59 Athenaeum Bookshop & Newsagency
61 Pied á Terre
63 Kilroy Travels
64 Mini Office
65 Krijtberg
66 Odeon
68 Albert Heijn Supermarket
69 Scheltema Holkema Ver-meulen
70 Centrale Bibliotheek (Main Public Library)
71 Art Unlimited
72 Police Headquarters
73 Amber Travel Agency
74 De Koe
78 Metz & Co Department Store Cafe
79 PC Hooft Store
80 Antiques Market de Looier
82 The Clean Brothers
83 Cora Kemperman
84 Paleis van Justitie
85 Police Station
86 Boom Chicago

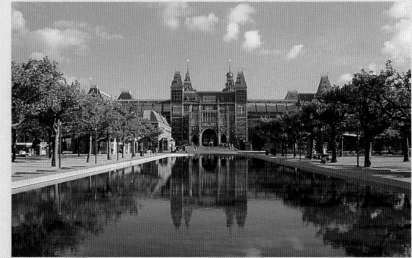

Rijksmuseum, the grand national museum of the Netherlands, is a must-see for art lovers

AMERENS HEDWICH

MAP 4 - AMSTERDAM

MAP 4 - AMSTERDAM

PLACES TO STAY
5 Hotel BA
(Budget Amsterdam)
13 Black Tulip Hotel
17 Flying Pig
Downtown Hostel
19 Hotel Brian
21 Bob's Youth Hostel
25 Frisco Inn
29 Hotel Kabul
31 Centrumhotel
32 Stablemaster Hotel
34 Hotel Crown
40 Hotel Winston
57 Grand Hotel Krasnapolsky
94 Grand Westin Demeure
112 Stadsdoelen Youth Hostel
137 Hotel De l'Europe
167 Golden Tulip Schiller Hostel

PLACES TO EAT
3 Keuken van 1870
4 Dorrius
37 Hemelse Modder
38 Hoi Tin
44 De Roode Leeuw
65 Café Bern
67 Zosa
72 Oriental City
77 Supper Club
81 Caprese
82 Haesje Claes
86 De Visscher
91 Beaufort
110 Tom Yam
114 Eetcafé de Staalmeesters
116 Atrium
121 Caffe Esprit
126 Vlaamse Friteshuis
144 Szmulewicz
152 MAOZ Falafel
155 Gauchos
156 Gary's Muffins
159 Rose's Cantina
160 Le Pêcheur
163 Memories of India

CAFES
47 De Drie Fleschjes
58 Proeflokaal Wijnand Fockinck
62 Maximiliaan
63 Lokaal 't Loosje
78 Bar Bep / Diep
85 Pilsener Club
(Engelse Reet)
115 Café de Jaren
123 De Schutter
143 Vivelavie
146 Mediacafé De Kroon
165 Heeren van Aemstel
166 Café Schiller

OTHER
1 Multatuli Museum
2 Poezenboot (Cat Boat)
6 Internet Café
7 Thomas Cook
8 GVB (Public Transport)
Information Office
9 Lovers Museum Boat
Terminal
10 VVV Office
11 Rijwielshop (Bicycle Rental)
12 Schreierstoren
(Wailing Tower)
14 St Nicholaaskerk
15 Seksmuseum De Venustempel
16 Lindbergh Travel
18 Yellow Bike Tours
20 Deco sauna
22 Hema Department Store
23 American Express
24 Holland Rent-a-Bike
26 Geels & Co
27 Himalaya
28 Warmoesstraat Police Station
30 Happy Inn Laundry
33 Museum Amstelkring
35 African Heritage
36 GVB Head Office
39 Erotic Museum
41 Effectenbeurs
42 Condomerie Het Gulden Vlies
43 Bijenkorf
45 Holland International
46 Fun Fashion
48 Homegrown Fantasy
49 Nieuwekerk
50 Albert Heijn
51 Vrolijk
52 Eurolines
53 Thomas Cook
54 Amsterdam Diamond Center
55 Key Tours
56 Nationaal Monument
59 Trance Buddha
60 Tattoo Museum
61 Bethaniënklooster
64 Waag
66 Jacob Hooy & co
68 Kleine Trippenhuis
69 Hash & Marihuana Museum
70 Wasserette Van den Broek
71 Greenhouse
73 Damstraat Rent-a-Bike
74 Options Exchange
75 Budget Air
76 De Slegte
79 Magic Mushroom Gallery
80 Intermale
83 Art Market
84 Begijnhof
87 Civic Guard Gallery

88 Amsterdams Historisch
Museum
89 NBBS
90 Berlitz Translation Services
92 Huis aan de Drie Grachten
(House on the Three Canals)
93 Universiteitsmuseum De
Agnietenkapel
95 Antiquariaat Kok
96 Narrow House
97 The Book Exchange
98 Oostindisch Huis
99 Trippenhuis
100 De Klompenboer
101 Zuiderkerk
102 Pintohuis
103 Bimhuis
104 Museum Het Rembrandthuis
105 Holland Experience
106 Albert Heijn
107 Garden Gym
108 MacBike
109 Mozes en Aäronkerk
111 GG&GD VD Clinic
113 Bookmarket
117 Allard Piersonmuseum
118 Hajenius
119 Joho
120 Arti et Amicitiae
122 Waterstone's
124 Maison de Bonneterie
125 American Book Center
127 Dansen bij Jansen
128 Maagdenhuis
129 Lutheran Church
130 University Library
131 Fair Trade Shop
132 Shoebaloo
133 Maranón Hangmatten
134 Havana
135 Kalvertoren Shopping Centre
136 Vroom & Dreesmann
138 Joods Historisch Museum
139 Soul Kitchen
140 iT
141 Sinners in Heaven
142 Stoeltie Diamonds
145 Monopole
147 Escape
148 Montmartre
149 Prestige Art Gallery
150 Tuschinskitheater
151 EasyEverything
153 Munttoren
154 VSB Bank
157 Exit
158 Soho
161 Lieve Hemel
162 Kattenkabinet
164 Art Market
168 Museum Willet-Holthuysen

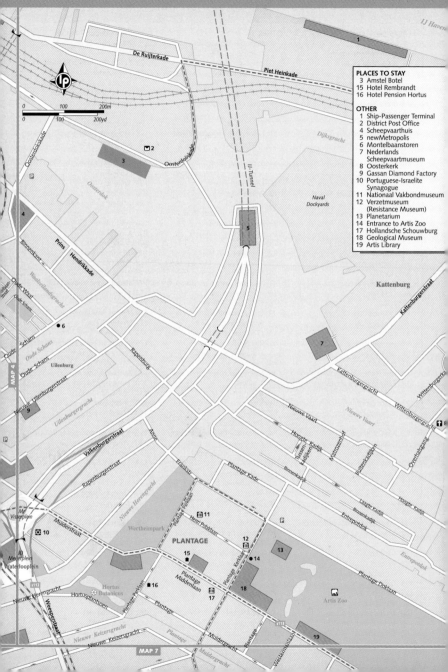

MAP 5 - AMSTERDAM

De Ruijterkade

Piet Heinkade

PLACES TO STAY
3 Amstel Botel
15 Hotel Rembrandt
16 Hotel Pension Hortus

OTHER
1 Ship-Passenger Terminal
2 District Post Office
4 Scheepvaarthuis
5 newMetropolis
6 Montelbaanstoren
7 Nederlands
  Scheepvaartmuseum
8 Oosterkerk
9 Gassan Diamond Factory
10 Portuguese-Israelite
  Synagogue
11 Nationaal Vakbondmuseum
12 Verzetsmuseum
  (Resistance Museum)
13 Planetarium
14 Entrance to Artis Zoo
17 Hollandsche Schouwburg
18 Geological Museum
19 Artis Library

Oosterdoksbade

Oosterdok

IJ-Tunnel

Dijksgracht

Naval
Dockyards

Kattenburg

Kattenburgerstraat

Prins Hendrikkade

Binnenkant

Oude Waal

Oude Schans

Oude Schans

Uilenburg

Rapenburg

Kattenburgergracht

Wittenburgerstraat

Wittenburgergracht

Nieuwe Uilenburgerstraat

Uilenburgergracht

Nieuwe Vaart

Nieuwe Vaart

Hoogte-Kadijk

Tussen-Kadijk

Middijksgang

Matrozenhof

Buitenkadijken

Overhaalsgang

Valkenburgerstraat

Rapenburgerstraat

Anne

Frankstr

Plantage Kade

Binnenkadijk

Laagte-Kadijk

Binnenkadijk

Hoogte-Kadijk

Entrepotdok

Nieuwe Herengracht

Plantage Parklaan

Henri Polaklaan

Plantage Kerklaan

Entrepotdok

Wertheimpark

PLANTAGE

Muiderstraat

Mr
Visserplein

Meijerplein
Waterlooplein

Plantage
Middenlaan

Hortus
Botanicus

Hortusplantsoen

Plantage Parklaan

Plantage

Plantage

Nieuwe Herengracht

Weesperstraat

Nieuwe Keizersgracht

Nieuwe Keizersgracht

Muidergracht

Plantage

Westerdoksgracht

Plantage Doklaan

Artis Zoo

IJ Haven

MAP 4

MAP 7

0   100   200m
0   100   200yd

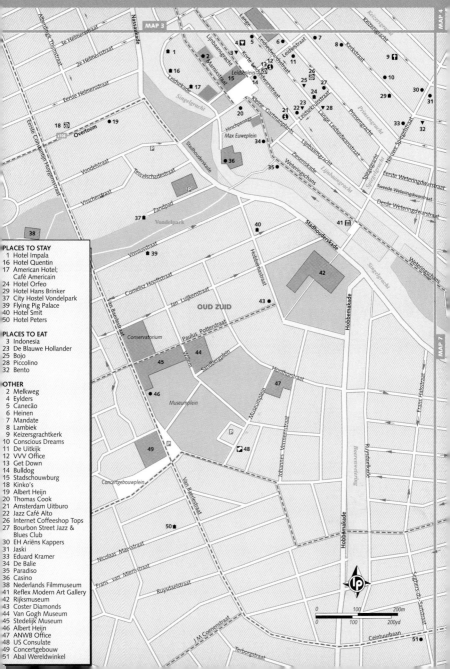

MAP 6 - AMSTERDAM

MAP 4

MAP 3

MAP 7

OUD ZUID

Vondelpark

Museumplein

Concertgebouwplein

PLACES TO STAY
1 Hotel Impala
16 Hotel Quentin
17 American Hotel;
   Café Americain
24 Hotel Orfeo
29 Hotel Hans Brinker
37 City Hostel Vondelpark
39 Flying Pig Palace
40 Hotel Smit
50 Hotel Peters

PLACES TO EAT
3 Indonesia
23 De Blauwe Hollander
25 Bojo
28 Piccolino
32 Bento

OTHER
2 Melkweg
4 Eylders
5 Canecão
6 Heinen
7 Mandate
8 Lambiek
9 Keizersgrachtkerk
10 Conscious Dreams
11 De Uitkijk
12 VVV Office
13 Get Down
14 Bulldog
15 Stadschouwburg
18 Kinko's
19 Albert Heijn
20 Thomas Cook
21 Amsterdam Uitburo
22 Jazz Café Alto
26 Internet Coffeeshop Tops
27 Bourbon Street Jazz &
   Blues Club
30 EH Ariëns Kappers
31 Jaski
33 Eduard Kramer
34 De Balie
35 Paradiso
36 Casino
38 Nederlands Filmmuseum
41 Reflex Modern Art Gallery
42 Rijksmuseum
43 Coster Diamonds
44 Van Gogh Museum
45 Stedelijk Museum
46 Albert Heijn
47 ANWB Office
48 US Consulate
49 Concertgebouw
51 Abal Wereldwinkel

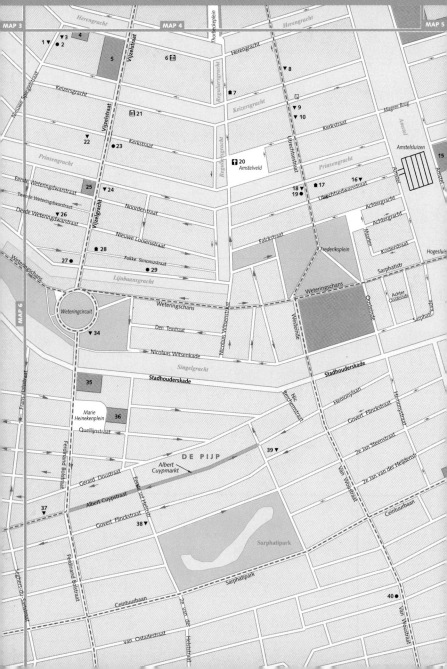

MAP 7 - AMSTERDAM

MAP 3

MAP 4

MAP 5

Thorbeckeplein

Herengracht

Herengracht

Herengracht

1 ▼
▼ 3
3
4

2

5

6

Vijzelstraat

Nieuwe Spiegelstraat

Keizersgracht

Herengracht

▼ 8

7

Keizersgracht

Magere Brug

9

Amstel

Kerkstraat

10

Reguliersgracht

21

Vijzelgracht

Kerkstraat

22

23

Prinsengracht

Utrechtsestraat

Prinsengracht

20
Amstelveld

Amstelsluizen

15

Amstel

Eerste Weteringdwarsstraat

25

24

18 ▼

17

16 ▼

Twee de Weteringdwarsstraat

Vijzelgracht

Noorderstraat

19

Utrechtsedwarsstraat

Achtergracht

Derde Weteringdwarsstraat

26

Nieuwe Looiersstraat

Achtergracht

Kosterstraat

Maanen

28

Falckstraat

Frederiksplein

27

Fokke Simonszstraat

Sarphatistr

Hogeslui

29

Lijnbaansgracht

Weteringschans

Weteringschans

Achter Oosteinde

Sarphati kade

MAP 6

Weteringcircuit

Weteringschans

Oosteinde

Weteringschans

Nicolaas Witsenkade

Den Texstraat

34

Weesterinde

Nicolaas Witsenkade

Singelgracht

Stadhouderskade

Stadhouderskade

35

Stadhouderskade

Nic Berchemstraat

Hemonylaan

Hemonystraat

Marie
Heinekenplein

36

Govert Flinckstraat

Quellijnstraat

2e Jan Steenstraat

Ferdinand Bolstraat

39 ▼

DE PIJP

2e Jan van der Heijdenstr

Gerard Doustraat

Albert
Cuypmarkt

Van Woustraat

Ceintuurbaan

37

Albert Cuypstraat

Eerste Jan Steenstraat

38 ▼

Govert Flinckstraat

Sarphatipark

Ferdinand Bolstraat

Sarphatipark

40

Ceintuurbaan

2e van der
Heijstraat

Van Woustraat

van Ostadestraat

MAP 7 - AMSTERDAM

MAP 4

MAP 5

🏛 11

Nieuwe Keizersgracht
Nieuwe Keizersgracht
Muidergracht
Westermanlaan
Plantage
Muidergracht
Plantage Lepellaan
12

Nieuwe Kerkstraat
Nieuwe Prinsengracht
Korte Lepelstr
Nieuwe Achtergracht
Nieuwe Achtergracht
Valkenierstr
Sarphatistraat
Plantage Badlaan
Plantage Muidergracht

Lepelstraat
Nieuwe Achtergracht
Nieuwe Achtergracht
Roeterstraat
Singelgracht

Onbekendegracht
Korte Amstelstraat
Weesperstraat
13 🏠
14 🏠

Weesperplein Ⓜ
Ⓢ
Weesperplein
Sarphatistraat
Spinozahof
Mauritskade
OOST
31

Voormalige Stadstimmertuin
Spinozastraat
Mauritskade

Huddestr
Prof Tulpstr
Huddekade
Rhijnspoorplein
Mauritskade
Muntendamstraat
M. Zeldenruststraat
's Gravesandestraat
Singelgracht

30
Prof Tulpl
Huddekade
Singelgracht
Mauritskade
Masschenbroeksstraat
Andreas Bonnstr
Sajetplein
2e Boerhaavestraat
Oosterpark

Torontobrug B100
Mauritsstraat
Wibautstraat
Boerhaaveplein
2e Boerhaavestraat
's Gravesandeplein
Oosterpark

Weesperzijde
Swammerdamstraat
Tilanusstraat
Camperstraat

33
Ruyschstraat
32 ✚

Blasiusstraat
OOSTERPARKBUURT
Wibautstraat
2e Oosterparkstraat

1e Oosterparkstraat
3e Oosterparkstraat

Vrolikstraat

Amsteldijk
Weesperzijde
Wibautstraat Ⓜ
Ⓢ

41 ●
Amstel

Rustenburgerstraat B110

Tolstraat

Ⓛⓟ

0   100   200m
0   100   200yd

PLACES TO STAY
7 Seven Bridges
14 Liliane's Home
17 Hotel Prinsenhof
28 Euphemia Budget Hotel
31 Hotel Arena
30 Amstel Inter-Continental Hotel

PLACES TO EAT
1 Pasta e Basta
3 Pygma-lion
8 Sluizer
9 Tujuh Maret
10 Tempo Doloe
16 Zuidlande

18 Pata Negra
22 Hollands Glorie
24 Panini
26 Dwars
34 Carrousel
37 Albert Cuyp 67; Albina
38 Euphraat
39 Harvest

OTHER
2 Decorativa
4 Goethe Institute
5 ABN-AMRO Bank
6 Geelvinck Hinlopen Huis
11 Artis Zoological Museum
12 Artis Aquarium
13 Kriterion Cinema

15 Koninklijk Theater Carré
19 á la Carte
20 Amstelkerk
21 Museum van Loon
23 Albert Heijn Supermarket
25 Maison Descartes (French Consulate & Restaurant)
27 Aldi Supermarket
29 Barry's Fitness Centre
32 Onze Lieve Vrouwe Gasthuis (Hospital)
33 Café De Ijsbreker; Muziekcentrum De Ijsbreker
35 Heineken Brewery
36 Dirk van den Broek
40 Albert Heijn Supermarket
41 Gemeentearchief

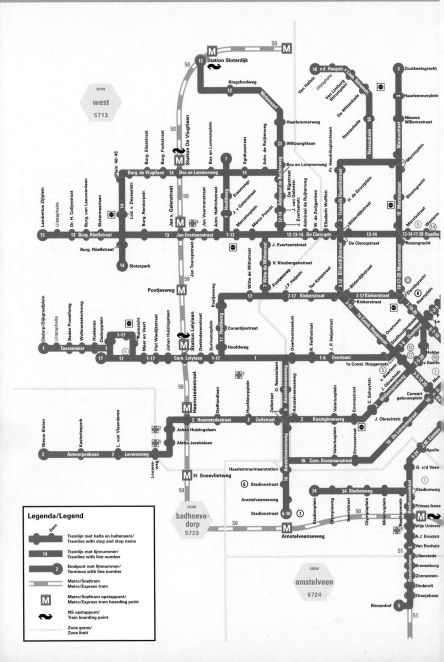

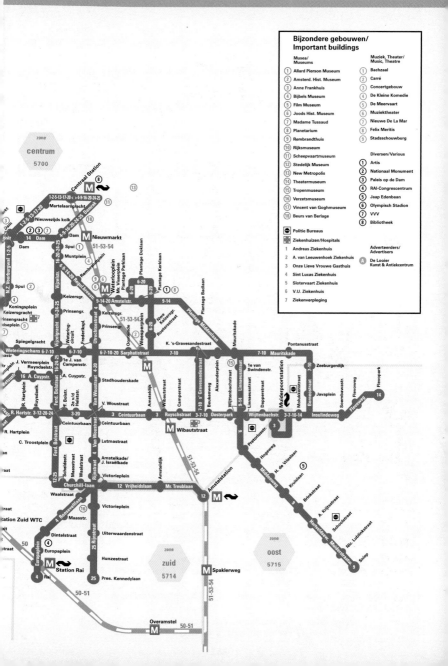

Bijzondere gebouwen/
Important buildings

Musea/
Museums

① Allard Pierson Museum
② Amsterd. Hist. Museum
③ Anne Frankhuis
④ Bijbels Museum
⑤ Film Museum
⑥ Joods Hist. Museum
⑦ Madame Tussaud
⑧ Planetarium
⑨ Rembrandthuis
⑩ Rijksmuseum
⑪ Scheepvaartmuseum
⑫ Stedelijk Museum
⑬ New Metropolis
⑭ Theatermuseum
⑮ Tropenmuseum
⑯ Verzetsmuseum
⑰ Vincent van Goghmuseum
⑱ Beurs van Berlage

Muziek, Theater/
Music, Theatre

① Bachzaal
② Carré
③ Concertgebouw
④ De Kleine Komedie
⑤ De Meervaart
⑥ Muziektheater
⑦ Nieuwe De La Mar
⑧ Felix Meritis
⑨ Stadsschouwburg

Diversen/Various

① Artis
② Nationaal Monument
③ Paleis op de Dam
④ RAI-Congrescentrum
⑤ Jaap Edenbaan
⑥ Olympisch Stadion
⑦ VVV
⑧ Bibliotheek

▣ Politie Bureaus

Ziekenhuizen/Hospitals
1 Andreas Ziekenhuis
2 A. van Leeuwenhoek Ziekenhuis
3 Onze Lieve Vrouwe Gasthuis
4 Sint Lucas Ziekenhuis
5 Slotervaart Ziekenhuis
6 V.U. Ziekenhuis
7 Ziekenverpleging

Adverteerders/
Advertisers

Ⓐ De Looier
Kunst & Antiekcentrum

MAP LEGEND

CITY ROUTES

Freeway .... Freeway
Highway .... Primary Road
Road .... Secondary Road
Street .... Street
Lane .... Lane
.... On/Off Ramp

======= .... Unsealed Road
------- .... One Way Street
.... Pedestrian Street
.... Stepped Street
)=== .... Tunnel
======= .... Footbridge

REGIONAL ROUTES

.... Tollway, Freeway
.... Primary Road
.... Secondary Road
.... Minor Road

BOUNDARIES

--- .... International
--- .... State
--- --- .... Disputed
.... Fortified Wall

HYDROGRAPHY

.... River, Creek
.... Canal
.... Lake

.... Dry Lake; Salt Lake
.... Spring; Rapids
.... Waterfalls

TRANSPORT ROUTES & STATIONS

---O--- .... Train
---S--- .... S-Bahn
---M--- .... Metro
+ + + + ... Underground Train
----- .... Tramway

----□ .... Ferry
.... Walking Trail
.... Walking Tour
.... Path
.... Pier or Jetty

AREA FEATURES

.... Building
.... Park, Gardens

.... Market
.... Sports Ground

.... Beach
.... Cemetery

.... Campus
.... Plaza

POPULATION SYMBOLS

◎ **CAPITAL** .... National Capital
◉ **CAPITAL** .... State Capital

● **CITY** .... City
● **Town** .... Town

● Village .... Village
.... Urban Area

MAP SYMBOLS

■ .... Place to Stay
▼ .... Place to Eat
● .... Point of Interest

✈	Airport	☜	Cycling	Ⓟ	Parking
↻	Bank	☑	Embassy, Consulate	✚	Police Station
⊟	Bus Terminal	✛	Hospital	☷	Post Office
⬛	Camping	☑	Internet Cafe	☐	Pub or Bar
⬛	Castle, Chateau	☒	Lighthouse	☒	Shopping Centre
⬛ ⬛	Cathedral, Church	▲	Monument	⬛	Swimming Pool
⊞	Cinema	⬓	Museum	⬛	Synagogue

☎ .... Telephone
☐ .... Theatre
♿ .... Toilet
❶ .... Tourist Information
☐ .... Transport
✗ .... Windmill
⬛ .... Zoo

Note: not all symbols displayed above appear in this book

LONELY PLANET OFFICES

Australia
Locked Bag 1, Footscray, Victoria 3011
☎ 03 8379 8000 fax 03 8379 8111
email: talk2us@lonelyplanet.com.au

UK
10a Spring Place, London NW5 3BH
☎ 020 7428 4800 fax 020 7428 4828
email: go@lonelyplanet.co.uk

USA
150 Linden St, Oakland, CA 94607
☎ 510 893 8555 TOLL FREE: 800 275 8555
fax 510 893 8572
email: info@lonelyplanet.com

France
1 rue du Dahomey, 75011 Paris
☎ 01 55 25 33 00 fax 01 55 25 33 01
email: bip@lonelyplanet.fr
www.lonelyplanet.fr

World Wide Web: www.lonelyplanet.com *or* AOL keyword: lp
Lonely Planet Images: lpi@lonelyplanet.com.au

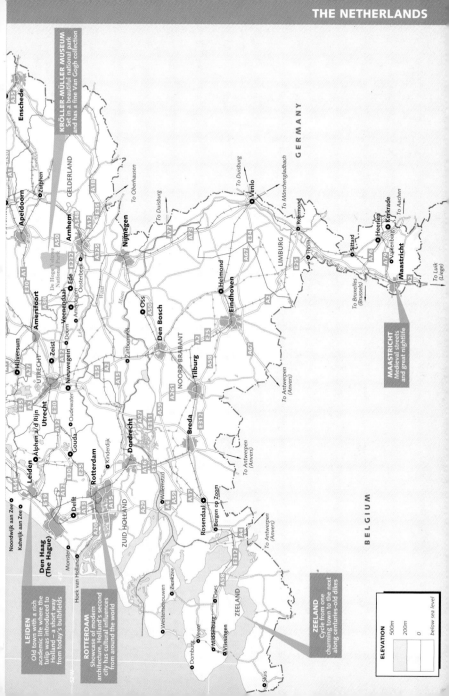

KRÖLLER-MÜLLER MUSEUM
Set in a beautiful national park and has a fine Van Gogh collection

MAASTRICHT
Medieval streets and great nightlife

LEIDEN
Old town with a rich academic life where the tulip was introduced to Holland – a short way from today's bulbfields

ROTTERDAM
Showcase of modern architecture, Holland's second city has cultural influences from around the world

ZEELAND
Cycle from one charming town to the next along centuries-old dikes

GERMANY

BELGIUM

GELDERLAND

UTRECHT

ZUID HOLLAND

NOORD-BRABANT

LIMBURG

ZEELAND

Enschede
Apeldoorn
Zutphen
Arnhem
Nijmegen
Venlo
Roermond
Sittard
Heerlen
Kerkrade
Valkenburg
Maastricht
Hilversum
Amersfoort
Zeist
Nieuwegein
Doorn
Ede
Meerveldhoven
Oosterbeek
Oss
Den Bosch
Helmond
Eindhoven
Tilburg
Leiden
Alphen a/d Rijn
Gouda
Oudewater
Rotterdam
Delft
Den Haag (The Hague)
Monster
Hoek van Holland
Dordrecht
Breda
Kinderdijk
Willemstad
Rosendaal
Bergen op Zoom
Noordwijk aan Zee
Katwijk aan Zee
Westenschouwen
Zierikzee
Goes
Domburg
Veere
Middelburg
Vlissingen
Sluis

To Oberhausen
To Duisburg
To Mönchengladbach
To Aachen
To Luik (Liège)
To Antwerpen (Anvers)
To Bruxelles (Brussel)

ELEVATION
500m
200m
0
below sea level

Netherlands
1st edition – January 2001

Published by
Lonely Planet Publications Pty Ltd ABN 36 005 607 983
90 Maribyrnong St, Footscray, Victoria 3011, Australia

Lonely Planet Offices
Australia Locked Bag 1, Footscray, Victoria 3011
USA 150 Linden St, Oakland, CA 94607
UK 10a Spring Place, London NW5 3BH
France 1 rue du Dahomey, 75011 Paris

Photographs
Many of the images in this guide are available for licensing from
Lonely Planet Images.
email: lpi@lonelyplanet.com.au

Front cover photograph
Tulips in the rain. (F Lemmens, The Image Bank)

ISBN 0 86442 705 0

text & maps © Lonely Planet 2001
photos © photographers as indicated 2001

Printed by Colorcraft Ltd, Hong Kong

**Although the authors
and Lonely Planet try
to make the information as accurate as
possible, we accept
no responsibility for
any loss, injury or
inconvenience sustained by anyone
using this book.**

Contents – Text

THE AUTHORS   5

THIS BOOK   7

FOREWORD   8

INTRODUCTION   11

FACTS ABOUT THE NETHERLANDS   12

History 12   Ecology & Environment 22   Society & Conduct 39
Geography 21   Education 25   Religion 41
Climate 22   Arts 27   Language 41

FACTS FOR THE VISITOR   43

Suggested Itineraries 43   Radio & TV 58   Emergencies 67
Planning 43   Photography & Video 59   Legal Matters 67
When to Go 43   Time 59   Business Hours 70
Responsible Tourism 45   Electricity 59   Public Holidays & Special
Tourist Offices 45   Weights & Measures 59   Events 70
Visas & Documents 46   Laundry 59   Activities 71
Embassies & Consulates 48   Toilets 59   Courses 74
Customs 49   Health 60   Work 74
Money 49   Women Travellers 64   Accommodation 75
Post & Communications 53   Gay & Lesbian Travellers 64   Food 77
Internet Resources 56   Disabled Travellers 65   Drinks 80
Books 56   Senior Travellers 66   Entertainment 81
Films 58   The Netherlands for Children 66   Spectator Sports 82
Newspapers & Magazines 58   Dangers & Annoyances 66   Shopping 82

GETTING THERE & AWAY   84

Air 84   Land 91   Sea 94

GETTING AROUND   96

Air 96   Car & Motorcycle 99   Boat 102
Train 96   Bicycle 101   Local Transport 102
Bus 99   Hitching 101   Organised Tours 102

CYCLING IN THE NETHERLANDS   103

AMSTERDAM   109

History 110   Activities 137   Entertainment 149
Orientation 111   Language Courses 138   Spectator Sports 154
Information 111   Organised Tours 139   Shopping 155
Things to See & Do 116   Places to Stay 139   Getting There & Away 157
Walking Tours 137   Places to Eat 144   Getting Around 159

NOORD HOLLAND   163

North of Amsterdam 165   Monnickendam 166   Edam 168
Zaanstad & Zaanse Schans 165   Volendam & Marken 167   Hoorn 171

Enkhuizen 172
Medemblik 175
Alkmaar 176
Texel Island 179
West of Amsterdam 183
Haarlem 183

Around Haarlem 189
Ijmuiden 189
Aalsmeer Flower Auction ..190
East of Amsterdam 190
Muiden 190
Het Gooi 191

Naarden 191
Hilversum 192
Flevoland 193
Lelystad 194
Urk 195
Schokland 196

UTRECHT   197

Utrecht City 197
Around Utrecht 203

Amersfoort 204
South-East Utrecht 205

Oudewater 205

ZUID HOLLAND & ZEELAND   207

Zuid Holland 207
Leiden 208
Around Leiden 217
Den Haag (The Hague) 218
Gouda 227
Delft 230

Rotterdam 235
Near Rotterdam 245
Kinderdijk 245
Dordrecht 245
Biesbosch National Park 250
Zeeland 251

Middelburg 252
Around Middelburg 256
Beveland 257
Delta Expo 257
Schouwen-Duiveland 258
Zeeuws-Vlaanderen 259

FRIESLAND   260

Leeuwarden 261
Around Leeuwarden 265
Sneek 265

Harlingen 266
Franeker 267
Coastal Towns 267

Frisian Islands 269

GRONINGEN & DRENTHE   274

Groningen 274
Groningen City 274
North-East Groningen 281

Bourtange 282
Drenthe 283
Emmen 284

Hunebedden 284
Assen 285

OVERIJSSEL & GELDERLAND   286

Overijssel 286
Deventer 286
Zwolle 290
Kampen 291
Northern Overijssel 291

Eastern Overijssel 293
Gelderland 293
Nijmegen 293
Arnhem 296
De Hoge Veluwe NP 298

National Park De
Veluwezoom 300
Apeldoorn 300
Zutphen 301
Zaltbommel 301

NOORD BRABANT & LIMBURG   302

Noord Brabant 302
Den Bosch 302
Eindhoven 305

Tilburg 306
Breda 306
West Noord Brabant 307

Limburg 307
Maastricht 307
North Limburg 313

LANGUAGE   315

GLOSSARY   318

INDEX   319

Text 319

Boxed Text 323

MAP LEGEND   back page

METRIC CONVERSION   inside back cover